SUFISM AND TAOISM

SUFISM AND TAOISM

A Comparative Study of
Key Philosophical Concepts

Toshihiko Izutsu

UNIVERSITY OF CALIFORNIA PRESS
Berkeley — Los Angeles — London

SUFISM AND TAOISM:
A Comparative Study of Key Philosophical Concepts
by Toshihiko Izutsu

University of California Press
Berkeley and Los Angeles, California
University of California Press, Ltd.
London, England

Copyright © 1983 by Toshihiko Izutsu
First published 1983 by Iwanami Shoten, Publishers, Tokyo
This edition is published by The University of California Press, 1984,
by arrangement with Iwanami Shoten, Publishers

Library of Congress Cataloging in Publication Data

Izutsu, Toshihiko, 1914–
    Sufism and Taoism.

    Rev. ed. of: A comparative study of the key philo-
sophical concepts in Sufism and Taoism. 1966–67.
    1. Sufism.   2. Taoism.   3. Ibn al- Arabī, 1165–1240.
4. Lao-tzu.   5. Chuang-tzu.   I. Title.
BP189.I96   1984   181'.074   84-78
ISBN 0-520-05264-1

Printed in the United States of America
        4   5   6   7   8   9

The paper used in this publication meets the minimum
requirements of American National Standard for Information
Sciences—Permanence of Paper for Printed Library
Materials, ANSI Z39.48-1984. ⊚

Contents

Preface

This is originally a book which I wrote more than fifteen years ago, when I was teaching Islamic philosophy at the Institute of Islamic Studies, McGill University, Montreal, Canada.

At that time I was becoming conscious of myself gradually getting into a new phase of my intellectual life, groping my way towards a new type of Oriental philosophy based on a series of rigorously philological, comparative studies of the key terms of various philosophical traditions in the Near, Middle, and Far East. The present work was the very first product of my endeavour in this direction.

The book was subsequently published in Japan in two separate volumes in 1966–1967, under the title *A Comparative Study of Key Philosophical Concepts in Sufism and Taoism* (with the subtitle 'Ibn 'Arabī and Lao-tzŭ – Chuang-tzŭ') as a publication of the Institute of Cultural and Linguistic Studies, Keio University, Tokyo, under the directorship of the late Professor Nobuhiro Matsumoto.

A growing demand for a new, revised edition made me decide to republish the book while I was in Iran. Printed in England, it had been scheduled to come out in Tehran towards the end of the year 1978, when the sudden outbreak of the Khomeini 'revolution' rendered its publication impossible. Thus it was that, by a strange working of fate, the book – completely revised, but still in the form of galley proofs – came back with its author once again to Japan, the place where it had first seen the light of day.

In the process of revising the book in its entirety, I did my best to eliminate all the defects and imperfections that had come to my notice in the meantime. But, of course, there are natural limits to such work of correction and amendment.

I only hope that this old book of mine in a new form, despite many mistakes and shortcomings that must still be there, might at least make a modest contribution towards the development of 'meta-historical dialogues' among representatives of the various philosophical traditions in the East and West, a special kind of philosophical dialogue of which the world today seems to be in urgent need.

It is my pleasant duty to express my deep gratitude to the Iwanami Shoten, Publishers, for having undertaken the publication of this book. My thanks go in particular to Mr Atsushi Aiba (of the same publishing house) who has spared no effort in smoothing the way for the realization of this project. I take this occasion to thank also the authorities of my alma mater, Keio University, from whom, as I recall now, I derived inestimable encouragement while I was engaged in writing this book in its original form.

T.Izutsu
October 4, 1981
Kamakura, Japan

Introduction

As indicated by the title and the subtitle, the main purpose of the
present work in its entirety is to attempt a structural comparison
between the world-view of Sufism as represented by Ibn 'Arabī and
the world-view of Taoism as represented by Lao-tzŭ and Chuang-
tzŭ. I am aware of the fact that this kind of study has a number of
pitfalls. A comparison made in a casual way between two thought-
systems which have no historical connection may become superficial observations of resemblances and differences lacking in
scientific rigor. In order to avoid falling into this error, an effort will
be made to lay bare the fundamental structure of each of the two
world-views independently and as rigorously as possible before
proceeding to any comparative considerations.

With this in view, the First Part will be entirely devoted to an
attempt at isolating and analyzing the major ontological concepts
which underlie the philosophical world-view of Ibn 'Arabī, while in
the second part exactly the same kind of analytic study will be made
concerning the world-view of Lao-tzŭ and Chuang-tzŭ, in such a way
that both parts may constitute two entirely independent studies, one
of Ibn 'Arabī and the other of ancient Taoism. Only in the third part
will an attempt be made to compare, and co-ordinate, the key-
concepts of these two world-views which have been previously
analyzed without any regard to similarities and differences between
them.

However this may be, the dominant motive running through the
entire work is the desire to open a new vista in the domain of
comparative philosophy and mysticism. A good starting point for
such a comparison is provided by the fact that both world-views are
based on two pivots, the Absolute and the Perfect Man,[1] a whole
system of ontological thought being developed in each case between
these two poles.

It is to be noted that as an ontological structure this is nothing
peculiar to Sufism and Taoism. The opposition of the Absolute and
the Perfect Man in various forms as the two pivots of a world-view is
a basic pattern common to many types of mysticism that have

developed in the world in widely different places and ages. And a comparative consideration of a number of systems sharing the same broad pattern and differing from each other in details both of origin and historical circumstance would seem to prove very fruitful in preparing the ground for that which Professor Henry Corbin has aptly called 'un dialogue dans la métahistoire', meta-historical or transhistorical dialogue, and which is so urgently needed in the present situation of the world.

Referring to the fact that Ibn 'Arabī has evoked so much discussion and controversy, unprecedented in the history of Islamic thought, and attributing this fact to the nature of Islam itself which combines two Truths: *ḥaqīqah* 'the truth based on Intellection' and *sharī'ah* 'the truth based on Revelation', Dr Osman Yahya makes the following interesting remark[2]: le cas d'Ibn 'Arabi ne se poserait pas avec autant d'acuité dans une tradition de pure métaphysique comme le taoism ou le védanta où la personalité du Maître . . . eut pu s'épanouir librement, ni non plus dans une tradition de pure loi positive où son cas n'eut même pas pu être posé puisqu'il eut été refusé par la communauté tout entière, irrémédiablement. Mais le destin a voulu placer Ibn 'Arabī à la croisée des chemins pour dégager, en sa personne, la véritable vocation de l'Islam.

There can be no denying that Lao-tzǔ's metaphysics of Tao presents in its abysmal depth of thought a number of striking similarities to Ibn 'Arabī's conception of Being. This is the more interesting because, as I shall indicate in the Second Part, Lao-tzǔ and Chuang-tzǔ represent a culmination point of a spiritual tradition which is historically quite different from Sufism.

We must, as I have remarked above, guard ourselves against making too easy comparisons, but we must also admit, I believe, that a comparative study of this kind, if conducted carefully, will at least furnish us with a common ground upon which an intercultural dialogue may fruitfully be opened.

In accordance with the general plan above outlined, the first half of the present book will be concerned exclusively with an analytic study of the key-concepts which constitute the ontological basis of Ibn 'Arabī's world-view. This world-view, as I have said, turns round two pivots, the Absolute and the Perfect Man, in the form of an ontological Descent and Ascent. In describing this cosmic process Ibn 'Arabī develops at every stage a number of concepts of decisive importance. It is these concepts that the present work intends to analyze. It purports to analyze methodically the ontological aspect of Ibn 'Arabī's mystical philosophy regarding it as a system of key-concepts that relate to 'being' and existence'.

Ontology, we must admit, is but one aspect of the thought of this extraordinary man. It has other no less important aspects such as psychology, epistemology, symbolism, etc., which, together, constitute an original and profound world-view. But the concept of Being, as we shall see, is the very basis of his philosophical thinking, and his theory of Being is doubtless of such originality and of such a far-reaching historical importance that it calls for separate treatment.

At the very outset I would like to make it clear that this is not a philologically exhaustive study of Ibn 'Arabī. On the contrary, the present study is based, as far as concerns Ibn 'Arabī himself, almost exclusively on only one of his works: 'The Bezels of Wisdom' or *Fuṣūṣ al-Ḥikam*. It is essentially an analysis of the major ontological concepts which Ibn 'Arabī develops in this celebrated book that has often been described as his *opus magnum*, and has been studied and commented upon by so many people throughout the centuries.[3] So on the material side, the present work does not claim to offer anything new.

From the beginning it was not my intention to be exhaustive. My intention was rather to penetrate the 'life-breath' itself, the vivifying spirit and the very existential source of the philosophizing drive of this great thinker, and to pursue from that depth the formation of the whole ontological system step by step as he himself develops it. In order to understand the thought of a man like Ibn 'Arabī, one must grasp the very spirit which pervades and vivifies the whole structure; otherwise everything will be lost. All considerations from outside are sure to go wide of the mark. Even on an intellectual and philosophical level, one must try to understand the thought from inside and reconstruct it in one's self by what might be called an existential empathy. For such a purpose, to be exhaustive, though of course desirable, is not the first requirement.

Ibn 'Arabī was not merely a profound thinker; he was an unusually prolific writer, too. The authorities differ among themselves on the exact number. Al-Sha'rānī, to give an example, notes that the Master wrote about 400 works.[4] The *répertoire général* of the above-mentioned bibliographical work by Dr Osman Yahya lists as many as 856 works, although the number includes doubtful works and those that are evidently spurious.

In a situation like this, and for purposes like ours, it is not only irrelevant but, even more, positively dangerous to try to note everything the author has said and written on each subject over a period of many years, For one might easily drown oneself in the vast ocean of concepts, images and symbols that are scattered about in utter disorder throughout the hundreds of his works, and lose sight of the main line or lines of thought and the guiding spirit that underlies the whole structure. For the purpose of isolating the latter from the disorderly (as it looks at first sight) mass of symbols and images, it will be more wise and perhaps, more profitable to concentrate on a work in which he presents his thought in its maturest form.[5] In any case, the present work consists exclusively of an analysis of the 'Bezels of Wisdom' except in a few places where I shall refer to one of his smaller works for elucidation of some of the important points.[6] As remarked above, *Fuṣūṣ al-Ḥikam* has been studied in the past by many people in many different forms. And yet I hope that my own analysis of the same book has something to contribute toward a better understanding of the great Master who has been considered by many people one of the profoundest, but at the same time, obscurest thinkers Islam has ever produced.

Notes

1. In Ibn 'Arabī's system, the Absolute is called *ḥaqq* (Truth or Reality) and the Perfect Man is called *insān kāmil* meaning literally 'perfect man'. In Taoism, the Absolute is *tao* and the Perfect Man is *shêng jên* (Sacred Man or Saint), *chên jên* (True Man), etc. I have dealt with the relationship between the Absolute and the Perfect Man in Taoism in particular in my Eranos lecture for 1967: 'The Absolute and the Perfect Man in Taoism', *Eranos-Jahrbuch*, XXXVI, Zürich, 1968.

2. *Histoire et classification de l'œuvre d'Ibn 'Arabī*, 2 vols. 1964, Damas, *avant-propos*, pp. 18–19.

3. Dr Osman Yahya lists more than 100 commentaries on *Fuṣūṣ al-Ḥikam*, cf. *op. cit.*, I, p. 17, pp. 241–257.

4. al-Sha'rānī, *al-Yawāqīt wa-al-Jawāhir*, Cairo, 1305 A.H., vol. I., p. 10.

5. Ibn 'Arabī (born in Spain in 1165 A.D.) died in Damascus in 1240. *Fuṣūṣ al-Ḥikam* was written in 1229, ten years before his death. As regards his life and his works the best introduction, to my knowledge, is found in Seyyed Hossein Nasr's *Three Muslim Sages*, Cambridge, Mass., 1964, pp. 84–121.

6. As a concrete illustration of the oft-repeated attempt at bringing philosophical coherence and order into the world-view of the Master, I shall in most cases give al-Qāshānī's comments side by side with Ibn 'Arabī's words. 'Abd al-Razzāq al-Qāshānī (d. 1330) is one of the greatest figures in the school of Ibn 'Arabī. The edition used in the present book is *Sharḥ al-Qāshānī 'alà Fuṣūṣ al-Ḥikam*, Cairo, 1321 A.H. For the interpretation of difficult passages of the text I have also used Qayṣarī and Jāmī.

Part I
Ibn 'Arabī

I Dream and Reality

So-called 'reality', the sensible world which surrounds us and which we are accustomed to regard as 'reality', is, for Ibn 'Arabī, but a dream. We perceive by the senses a large number of things, distinguish them one from another, put them in order by our reason, and thus end up by establishing something solid around us. We call that construct 'reality' and do not doubt that it is real.

According to Ibn 'Arabī, however, that kind of 'reality' is not reality in the true sense of the word. In other terms, such a thing is not Being (wujūd) as it really is. Living as we do in this phenomenal world, Being in its metaphysical reality is no less imperceptible to us than phenomenal things are in their phenomenal reality to a man who is asleep and dreaming of them.

Quoting the famous Tradition, 'All men are asleep (in this world); only when they die, do they wake up,' he remarks:

> The world is an illusion; it has no real existence. And this is what is meant by 'imagination' (khayāl). For you just imagine that it (i.e., the world) is an autonomous reality quite different from and independent of the absolute Reality, while in truth it is nothing of the sort[1]. . . . Know that you yourself are an imagination. And everything that you perceive and say to yourself, 'this is not me', is also an imagination. So that the whole world of existence is imagination within imagination.[2]

What, then, should we do, if what we have taken for 'reality' is but a dream, not the real form of Being, but something illusory? Should we abandon once for all this illusory world and go out of it in search of an entirely different world, a really real world? Ibn 'Arabī does not take such a position, because, in his view, 'dream', 'illusion' or 'imagination' does not mean something valueless or false; it simply means 'being a symbolic reflection of something truly real'.

The so-called 'reality' certainly is not the true Reality, but this must not be taken to mean that it is merely a vain and groundless thing. The so-called 'reality', though it is not the Reality itself, vaguely and indistinctively reflects the latter on the level of imagination. It is, in other words, a symbolic representation of the Reality.

All it needs is that we should interpret it in a proper way just as we usually interpret our dreams in order to get to the real state of affairs beyond the dream-symbols.

Referring to the above-quoted Tradition, 'All men are asleep; only when they die, do they wake up', Ibn 'Arabī says that 'the Prophet called attention by these words to the fact that whatever man perceives in this present world is to him as a dream is to a man who dreams, and that it must be interpreted'.[3]

What is seen in a dream is an 'imaginal' form of the Reality, not the Reality itself. All we have to do is take it back to its original and true status. This is what is meant by 'interpretation' (*ta'wīl*). The expression: 'to die and wake up' appearing in the Tradition is for Ibn 'Arabī nothing other than a metaphorical reference to the act of interpretation understood in this sense. Thus 'death' does not mean here death as a biological event. It means a spiritual event consisting in a man's throwing off the shackles of the sense and reason, stepping over the confines of the phenomenal, and seeing through the web of phenomenal things what lies beyond. It means, in short, the mystical experience of 'self-annihilation' (*fanā'*).

What does a man see when he wakes up from his phenomenal sleep, opens his real eyes, and looks around? What kind of world does he observe then – that is, in the self-illuminating state of 'subsistence' (*baqā'*)? To describe that extraordinary world and elucidate its metaphysical-ontological make-up, that is the main task of Ibn 'Arabī. The description of the world as he observes it in the light of his mystical experiences constitutes his philosophical world-view.

What, then, is that Something which hides itself behind the veil of the phenomenal, making the so-called 'reality' a grand-scale network of symbols vaguely and obscurely pointing to that which lies beyond them? The answer is given immediately. It is the Absolute, the real or absolute Reality which Ibn 'Arabī calls *al-ḥaqq*. Thus the so-called 'reality' is but a dream, but it is not a sheer illusion. It is a particular appearance of the absolute Reality, a particular form of its self-manifestation (*tajallī*). It is a dream having a metaphysical basis. 'The world of being and becoming (*kawn*) is an imagination', he says, 'but it is, in truth, Reality itself'.[4]

Thus the world of being and becoming, the so-called 'reality', consisting of various forms, properties and states, is in itself a colorful fabric of fantasy and imagination, but it indicates at the same time nothing other than Reality – if only one knows how to take these forms and properties, not in themselves, but as so many manifestations of the Reality. One who can do this is a man who has attained the deepest mysteries of the Way (*ṭarīqah*).

Prophets are visionaries. By nature they tend to see strange visions which do not fall within the capacity of an ordinary man. These extraordinary visions are known as 'veridical dreams' (*ru'yā ṣādiqah*) and we readily recognize their symbolic nature. We ordinarily admit without hesitation that a prophet perceives through and beyond his visions something ineffable, something of the true figure of the Absolute. In truth, however, not only such uncommon visions are symbolic 'dreams' for a prophet. To his mind everything he sees, everything with which he is in contact even in daily life is liable to assume a symbolic character. 'Everything he perceives in the state of wakefulness is of such a nature, though there is, certainly, a difference in the states'.[5] The formal difference between the state of sleep (in which he sees things by his faculty of imagination) and the state of wakefulness (in which he perceives things by his senses) is kept intact, yet in both states the things perceived are equally symbols.[6]

Thus, a prophet who lives his life in such an unusual spiritual state may be said to be in a dream within a dream all through his life. 'The whole of his life is nothing but a dream within a dream'.[7] What Ibn 'Arabī means by this proposition is this: since the phenomenal world itself is in truth a 'dream'[8] (although ordinary people are not aware of its being a 'dream'), the prophet who perceives unusual symbols in the midst of that general 'dream'-context may be compared to a man who is dreaming in a dream.

This, however, is the deepest understanding of the situation, to which most people have no access, for they are ordinarily convinced that the phenomenal world is something materially solid; they do not notice its symbolic nature. Not even prophets themselves – not all of them – have a clear understanding of this matter. It is a deep mystery of Being accessible only to a perfect prophet like Muḥammad. Ibn 'Arabī explains this point taking as an illustration the contrast between the prophet Yūsuf (Joseph) and the Prophet Muḥammad regarding their respective depth of understanding.

It is related in the Qoran (XII, 4) that Joseph as a small boy once saw in a dream eleven stars, and the sun and the moon bowing down before him. This, Ibn 'Arabī observes, was an event which occurred only in Joseph's imagination (*khayāl*). Joseph saw in his imagination his brothers in the form of stars, his father in the form of the sun, and his mother in the form of the moon. Many years later, before Joseph, who was now a 'mighty prince' in Egypt, his brothers fell down prostrate At that moment Joseph said to himself, 'This is the interpreted meaning (*ta'wīl*) of my dream of long ago. My Lord has made it true!' (XII, 99).

The pivotal point, according to Ibn 'Arabī, lies in the last phrase:

'has made it true'.[9] It means: 'God has made to appear in the sensible world what was in the past in the form of imagination'.[10] This implies that the realization or materialization in a sensible form of what he had seen in a dream was, in the understanding of Joseph, the final and ultimate realization. He thought that the things left the domain of 'dream' and came out to the level of 'reality'.

Against this Ibn 'Arabī remarks that, as regards being sensible, there is fundamentally no difference at all between 'dream' and 'reality'; what Joseph saw in his dream was from the beginning sensible, for 'it is the function of imagination to produce sensible things (*maḥsūsāt*), nothing else'.[11]

The position of Muḥammad goes deeper than this. Viewed from the standpoint of the prophet Muḥammad, the following is the right interpretation of what happened to Joseph concerning his dream. One has to start from the recognition that life itself is a dream. In this big dream which is his life and of which Joseph himself is not conscious, he sees a particular dream (the eleven stars, etc.). From this particular dream he wakes up. That is to say, he dreams in his big dream that he wakes up. Then he interprets his own (particular) dream (the stars = his brothers, etc.). In truth, this is still a continuation of his big dream. He dreams himself interpreting his own dream. Then the event which he thus interprets comes true as a sensible fact. Thereupon Joseph thinks that his interpretation has materialized and that his dream has definitely come to an end. He thinks that he stands now completely outside of his dream, while, in reality, he is still dreaming. He is not aware of the fact that he is dreaming.[12]

The contrast between Muḥammad and Joseph is conclusively summed up by al-Qāshānī in the following way:

> The difference between Muḥammad and Joseph in regard to the depth of understanding consists in this. Joseph regarded the sensible forms existing in the outer world as 'reality' whereas, in truth, all forms that exist in imagination are (also) sensible without exception, for imagination (*khayāl*) is a treasury of the sensible things. Everything that exists in imagination is a sensible form although it actually is not perceived by the senses. As for Muḥammad, he regarded the sensible forms existing in the outer world also as products of imagination (*khayālīyah*), nay even as imagination within imagination. This because he regarded the present world of ours as a dream while the only 'reality' (in the true sense of the word) was, in his view, the Absolute revealing itself as it really is in the sensible forms which are nothing but so many different loci of its self-manifestation. This point is understood only when one wakes up from the present life – which is a sleep of forgetfulness – after one dies to this world through self-annihilation in God.

The basic idea which, as we have just observed, constitutes the very starting-point of Ibn 'Arabī's ontological thinking, namely, that so-called 'reality' is but a dream, suggests on the one hand that the world as we experience it under normal conditions is not in itself Reality, that it is an illusion, an appearance, an unreality. But neither does it mean, on the other hand, that the world of sensible things and events is nothing but sheer fantasy, a purely subjective projection of the mind. In Ibn 'Arabī's view, if 'reality' is an illusion, it is not a subjective illusion, but an 'objective' illusion; that is, an unreality standing on a firm ontological basis. And this is tantamount to saying that it is not an illusion at all, at least in the sense in which the word is commonly taken.

In order that this point become clear, reference must be made to the ontological conception peculiar to Ibn 'Arabī and his school of the 'five planes of Being'. The structure of these 'planes' (*ḥaḍarāt*)[13] is succinctly explained by Al-Qāshānī as follows.[14] In the Sufi world-view, five 'worlds' (*'awālim*) or five basic planes of Being are distinguished, each one of them representing a Presence or an ontological mode of the absolute Reality in its self-manifestation.

(1) The plane of the Essence (*dhāt*), the world of the absolute non-manifestation (*al-ghayb al-muṭlaq*) or the Mystery of Mysteries.[15]

(2) The plane of the Attributes and the Names, the Presence of Divinity (*ulūhīyah*).[16]

(3) The plane of the Actions, the Presence of Lordship (*rubūbīyah*).

(4) The plane of Images (*amthāl*) and Imagination (*khayāl*).[17]

(5) The plane of the senses and sensible experience (*mushāhadah*).

These five planes constitute among themselves an organic whole, the things of a lower plane serving as symbols or images for the things of the higher planes. Thus, according to al-Qāshānī, whatever exists in the plane of ordinary reality (which is the lowest of all Divine Presences) is a symbol-exemplification (*mithāl*) for a thing existing in the plane of Images, and everything that exists in the world of Images is a form reflecting a state of affairs in the plane of the Divine Names and Divine Attributes, while every Attribute is an aspect of the Divine Essence in the act of self-manifestation.

Details about the five planes will be given in the following chapters. Suffice it here to note that the whole world of Being, in Ibn 'Arabī's view, consists basically of these five levels of Divine self-manifestation, and that there exists between the higher and lower levels such an organic relation as has just been mentioned. With this in mind, let us return to the problem of our immediate concern.

Anything that is found at the lowest level of Being, i.e., the sensible world, or any event that occurs there, is a 'phenomenon' in the etymological meaning of the term; it is a form (*ṣūrah*) in which a state of affairs in the higher plane of Images directly reveals itself, and indirectly and ultimately, the absolute Mystery itself. To look at things in the sensible world and not to stop there, but to see beyond them the ultimate ground of all Being, that precisely is what is called by Ibn 'Arabī 'unveiling' (*kashf*) or mystical intuition.[18] 'Unveiling' means, in short, taking each of the sensible things as a locus in which Reality discloses itself to us. And a man who does so encounters everywhere a 'phenomenon' of Reality, whatever he sees and hears in this world. Whatever he experiences is for him a form manifesting an aspect of Divine Existence, a symbol for an aspect of Divine Reality. And in this particular respect, his sensory experiences are of the same symbolic nature as visions he experiences in his sleep.[19]

In the eyes of a man possessed of this kind of spiritual capacity, the whole world of 'reality' ceases to be something solidly self-sufficient and turns into a deep mysterious *forêt de symboles*, a system of ontological correspondences. And dreams which arise in the 'imaginal' plane of Being turn out to be the same as the things and events of the world of sensory experience. Both the world of sensible things and the world of dreams are, in this view, the same domain of symbols. As al-Qāshānī says, 'Everything which comes manifesting itself from the world of the Unseen into the world of sensible experience – whether it manifests itself in the senses or imagination, or again in an image-similitude – is a revelation, an instruction or communication from God'.[20]

The symbolic structure of the world here depicted, however, is accessible only to the consciousness of an extremely limited number of persons. The majority of people live attached and confined to the lowest level of Being, that of sensible things. That is the sole world of existence for their opaque consciousness. This lowest level of Being only, being tangible and graspable through the senses, is real for them. And even on this level, it never occurs to them to 'interpret' the forms of the things around them. They are asleep.

But since, on the other hand, the common people, too, are possessed of the faculty of imagination, something unusual may – and does – occur in their minds on rare occasions. An invitation from above visits them and flashes across their consciousness like lightning when it is least expected. This happens when they have visions and dreams.

Ordinarily, imagination or fantasy means the faculty of producing in the mind a deceptive impression of the presence of a thing which is not actually there in the external world or which is totally non-existent. With Ibn 'Arabī, it has a different meaning. Of course in his theory, too, imagination is the faculty of evoking in the mind those things that are not externally present, i.e., things that are not immediately present in the plane of sensible experience. But it is not a wild fantasy or hallucination which induces the mind to see things that are nowhere existent. What it produces is not a groundless reverie. It makes visible, albeit in an obscure and veiled way, a state of affairs in the higher planes of Being. It is a function of the mind directly connected with the 'world of Images'.

The 'world of Images' (*'ālam al-mithāl*) is ontologically an intermediate domain of contact between the purely sensible world and the purely spiritual, i.e., non-material world. It is, as Affifi defines it, 'a really existent world in which are found the forms of the things in a manner that stands between "fineness" and "coarseness", that is, between pure spirituality and pure materiality'.[21]

All things that exist on this level of Being have, on the one hand, something in common with things existing in the sensible world, and resemble, on the other, the abstract intelligibles existing in the world of pure intellect. They are special things half-sensible and half-intelligible. They *are* sensible, but of an extremely fine and rarefied sensible-ness. They *are* intelligible, too, but not of such a pure intelligibility as that of the Platonic Ideas.

What is commonly called imagination is nothing but this world as it is reflected in the human consciousness, not in its proper forms, but obliquely, dimly, and utterly deformed. Images obtained in such a way naturally lack an ontological basis and are rightly to be disposed of as hallucinations.

Sometimes, however, the 'world of Images' appears as it really is, without deformation, in the consciousness even of an ordinary man. The most conspicuous case of this is seen in the veridical dream. The 'world of Images' is eternally existent and it is at every moment acting upon human consciousness. But man, on his part, is not usually aware of it while he is awake, because his mind in that state is impeded and distracted by the material forces of the external world. Only when he is asleep, the physical faculties of his mind being in abeyance, can the faculty of imagination operate in the proper way. And veridical dreams are produced.

However, even if a man sees in his sleep a veridical dream, it is always presented in a series of sensible images. And it remains devoid of significance unless it be 'interpreted'. Ibn 'Arabī sees a typical example of this in the Biblical-Qoranic anecdote of Abraham sacrificing his son.

Abraham once saw in a dream a sacrificial ram appearing in the image of his son Isaac (Ishāq). In reality, this was a symbol. It was a symbol for the first institution of an important religious ritual;

namely, that of immolation of a sacrificial animal on the altar. And since this ritual itself was ultimately a symbol of man's offering up his own soul in sacrifice, Abraham's vision was to be interpreted as a sensible phenomenal form of this spiritual event. But Abraham did not 'interpret' it. And he was going to sacrifice his son. Here is the explanation of this event by Ibn 'Arabī.[22]

> Abraham, the Friend (of God), said to his son, 'Lo, I have seen myself in my dream sacrificing thee'. (Qoran XXXVII, 102). Dream, in truth, is a matter, pertaining to the plane of Imagination.[23] He, however, did not interpret (his dream). What he saw in the dream was a ram assuming the form of the son of Abraham. And Abraham supposed his vision to be literally true (and was about to sacrifice Isaac). But the Lord redeemed him from the illusion of Abraham with the Great Sacrifice (i.e. the sacrifice of a ram). This was God's 'interpretation' of the dream of Abraham, but the latter did not know it. He did not know it because all theophany in a sensible form in the plane of Imagination needs a different kind of knowledge which alone makes it possible for man to understand what is meant by God through that particular form. . . .
>
> Thus God said to Abraham, calling out to him, 'O Abraham, thou hast taken the vision for truth' (XXXVII, 104–105). Mark that God did not say, 'Thou has grasped the truth in imagining that it is thy son'. (The mistake pointed out here) arose from the fact that Abraham did not 'interpret' the dream but took what he had seen as literally true, when all dreams must of necessity be 'interpreted' . . . If what he imagined had been true, he would have sacrificed his son.[24] He merely took his vision for truth and thought that (Isaac, whom he had seen in the dream) was literally his own son. In reality, God meant by the form of his son nothing more than the Great Sacrifice.
>
> Thus He 'redeemed' him (i.e., Isaac) simply because of what occurred in Abraham's mind, whereas in itself and in the eye of God it was not at all a question of redeeming.[25]
>
> Thus (when Isaac was 'redeemed') his visual sense perceived a sacrificial animal (i.e., a ram) while his imagination evoked in his mind the image of his son. (Because of this symbolic correspondence) he would have interpreted his vision as signifying his son or some other thing if he had seen a ram in imagination (i.e., in his dream, instead of seeing his son as he actually did). Then says God, 'Verily this is a manifest trial' (XXXVII, 106), meaning thereby the trial (of Abraham by God) concerning his knowledge; namely, whether or not he knows that the very nature of a vision properly requires an 'interpretation'. Of course Abraham did know that things of Imagination properly require 'interpretation'. But (in this particular case) he carelessly neglected to do that. Thus he did not fulfil what was properly required of him and simply assumed that his vision was a literal truth.

Abraham was a prophet. And a man who stands in the high spiritual position of prophethood must know (theoretically) that a veridical dream is a symbol for an event belonging to the plane of higher realities. And yet Abraham actually forgot to 'interpret' his dream. If prophets are like that, how could it be expected that ordinary men 'interpret' rightly their dreams and visions? It is but natural, then, that an ordinary man cannot see that an event occurring in so-called 'reality' is a symbol for an event corresponding to it in the higher plane of the Images.

How can man cultivate such an ability for seeing things symbolically? What should he do in order that the material veil covering things be removed to reveal the realities that lie beyond?

Regarding this question, Ibn 'Arabī in a passage of the *Fuṣūṣ* points to a very interesting method. It is a way of discipline, a way of practice for cultivating what he calls the 'spiritual eyesight' (*'ayn al-baṣīrah*). It is a way that renders possible the inner transformation of man.

This inner transformation of man is explained by Ibn 'Arabī in terms of transition from the 'worldly state of being (*al-nash'ah al-dunyawīyah*) to the 'otherworldly state of being' (*al-nash'ah al-ukhrawīyah*).[26] The 'worldly state of being' is the way the majority of men naturally are. It is characterized by the fact that man, in his natural state, is completely under the sway of his body, and the activity of his mind impeded by the physical constitution of the bodily organs. Under such conditions, even if he tries to understand something and grasp its reality, the object cannot appear to his mind except in utter deformation. It is a state in which man stands completely veiled from the essential realities of things.

In order to escape from this state, Ibn 'Arabī says, man must personally re-live the experiences of Elias-Enoch and re-enact in himself the spiritual drama of the inner transformation symbolized by these two names.

Elias (*Ilyās*) and Enoch (*Idrīs*) were two names assumed by one and the same person. They were two names given to one person in two different states. Enoch was a prophet before the time of Noah. He was raised high by God and was placed in the sphere of the sun. His name was Enoch in that supreme position. Later he was sent down as an apostle to the Syrian town of Baalbek. In that second state he was named Elias.[27]

Elias who was sent down in this manner to the earth from the high sphere of heaven did not stop halfway but became totally 'earthly'. He pushed the 'elemental (*'unṣurī*) state of being' on the earth to its extreme limit. This symbolizes a man who, instead of exercising his human reason in a lukewarm way as most people do, abandons himself thoroughly and completely to the elemental life of nature to the degree of being less than human.

While he was in that state, he had once a strange vision, in which he saw a mountain called Lubnān split up and a horse of fire coming out of it with a harness made entirely of fire. When the prophet noticed it, he immediately rode the horse, bodily desires fell from him and he turned into a pure intellect without desire. He was now completely free from all that was connected with the physical self.[28] And only in this purified state could Elias see Reality as it really is.

However, Ibn 'Arabī observes, even this supreme 'knowledge of God' (*ma'rifah bi-Allāh*) attained by Elias was not a perfect one. 'For in this (knowledge), Reality was in pure transcendence (*munazzah*), and it was merely half of the (perfect) knowledge of God'.[29] This means that the pure intellect that has freed itself completely from everything physical and material cannot by nature see God except in His transcendence (*tanzīh*). But transcendence is only one of the two basic aspects of the Absolute. Its other half is immanence (*tashbīh*). All knowledge of God is necessarily one-sided if it does not unite transcendence and immanence, because God *is* transcendent and immanent at the same time. Who, how-ever, can actually unite these two aspects in this knowledge of God? It is, as we shall see in Chapter III, the prophet Muḥammad, no one else, not even Elias.

Keeping what has just been said in mind, let us try to follow the footsteps of Enoch-Elias in more concrete, i.e., less mythopoeic, terms.

As a necessary first step, one has to go down to the most elemen-tal level of existence in imitation of the heavenly Enoch who went down to the earth and began by living at the lowest level of earthly life. As suggested above, one must not stop halfway. Then abandon-ing all activity of Reason and not exercising any longer the thinking faculty, one fully realizes the 'animality' (*ḥayawānīyah*) which lies hidden at the bottom of every human being. One is, at this stage, a pure animal with no mixture of shallow humanity. Such a man 'is freed from the sway of Reason and abandons himself to his natural desires. He is an animal pure and simple'.[30]

In this state of unmixed animality, the man is given a certain kind of mystical intuition, a particular sort of 'unveiling' (*kashf*). This 'unveiling' is the kind of 'unveiling' which is naturally possessed by wild animals. They experience this kind of 'unveiling' because, by nature, they do not exercise, and are therefore not bothered by, the faculty of Reason.

In any case, the man who seriously intends to re-experience what was once experienced by Enoch-Elias must, as a first step, thoroughly actualize his animality; so thoroughly, indeed, that 'in the end is "unveiled" to him what is (naturally) "unveiled" to all animals except mankind and jinn. Only then can he be sure that he has completely actualized his animality'.[31]

Whether a man has attained to this degree of animality may be known from outside by two symptoms: one is that he is actually experiencing the animal 'unveiling', and the other is that he is unable to speak. The explanation by Ibn 'Arabī of these two symptoms, particularly of the first one, is quite unusual and bizarre, at least to our common sense. But it is difficult to deny the extraordinary weight of reality it evokes in our minds. It strikes as real because it is a description of his own personal experience as an unusual visionary.

The first symptom, he says, of a man actually experiencing the animal *kashf*, is that 'he sees those who are being chastised (by the angels) in the graves, and those who are enjoying a heavenly felicity, that he sees the dead living, the dumb speaking, and the crippled walking'. To the eye of such a man there appear strange scenes which our 'sane and healthy' Reason would unhesitatingly consider sheer insanity. Whether such a vision is rightly to be regarded as 'animal' experience is a question about which the ordinary mind is not in a position to pass any judgment. For here Ibn 'Arabī is talking out of his personal experience.[32] But we can easily see at least that, in the mind of a man who has completely liberated himself from the domination of natural Reason, all those petty distinctions and differentiations that have been established by the latter crumble away in utter confusion, and things and events take on entirely different and new forms. What Ibn 'Arabī wants to say by all this is that all the seemingly watertight compartments into which Reality is divided by human Reason lose their ontological validity in such an 'animal' experience.

The second symptom is that such a man becomes dumb and is unable to express himself 'even if he wants and tries to describe in words what he sees. And this is a decisive sign that he has actualized his animality'[33] Here he gives an interesting description of his own experience concerning this point:

> Once I had a disciple who attained to this kind of 'unveiling'. However, he did not keep silent about his (experience). This shows that he did not realize his animality (in perfect manner.) When God made me stand at that stage, I realized my animality completely. I had visions and wanted to talk about what I witnessed, but I could not do so. There was no actual difference between me and those who were by nature speechless.

A man who has thus gone all the way to the furthest limit of animality, if he still continues his spiritual exercise, may rise to the state of pure Intellect.[34] The Reason (*'aql*) which has been abandoned before in order to go down to the lowest level of animality is an *'aql* attached to and fettered by his body. And now at this second stage, he acquires a new *'aql*, or rather recovers possession of his once-abandoned *'aql* in a totally different form. The new *'aql*, which Ibn 'Arabī calls 'pure Intellect' (*'aql mujarrad*),[35] functions on a level where its activity cannot be impeded by anything bodily and physical. The pure Intellect has nothing at all to do with the body. And when a man acquires this kind of Intellect and sees things with the eye of the pure Intellect itself, even ordinary things around him begin to disclose to him their true ontological structure.

This last statement means, in terms of Ibn 'Arabī's world-view, that the things around us lose their independence in the eye of such a man and reveal their true nature as so many 'phenomena' of things belonging to the ontological stage above them.

> (Such a man) has transformed himself into a pure Intellect away from all natural material elements. He witnesses things that are the very sources of what appears in the natural forms. And he comes to know by a sort of intuitive knowledge why and how the things of nature are just as they are.[36]

In still more concrete terms, such a man is already in the ontological stage above that of the things of nature. He is in the stage of the Divine Names and Attributes. In the language of ontology peculiar to Ibn 'Arabī, he is in the stage of the 'permanent archetypes' (*a'yān thābitah*),[37] and is looking down from that height on the infinitely variegated things of the sensible world and understanding them in terms of the realities (*ḥaqā'iq*) that lie beyond them.

He who has attained to this spiritual height is an *'ārif* or 'one who knows (the transcendental truth)', and his cognition is rightly to be regarded as an authentic case of *dhawq* or 'immediate tasting'. Such a man is already 'complete' (*tāmm*).

As we have remarked before, however, the cognition of Enoch was only 'half' of the cognition of the Absolute reality. A man of this kind is certainly *tāmm*, but not yet 'perfect' (*kāmil*). In order that he might be *kāmil*, he has to go a step further and raise himself to a point where he sees that all, whether the 'permanent archetypes' or the things of nature or again he himself who is actually perceiving them, are after all, nothing but so many phenomenal forms of the Divine Essence on different levels of being; that through all the ontological planes, there runs an incessant and infinite flcw of the Divine Being.[38] Only when a man is in such a position is he a 'Perfect Man' (*insān kāmil*).

The above must be taken as an introduction to the major problems of Ibn 'Arabī and a summary exposition of the experiential basis on which he develops his philosophical thinking. It has, I think, made clear that Ibn 'Arabī's philosophy is, in brief, a theoretic description of the entire world of Being as it is reflected in the eye of the Perfect Man. It is, indeed, an extraordinary world-view because it is a product of the extraordinary experience of an extraordinary man. How, then, does the Perfect Man, that is, a man who has been completely awakened, see the world? That will be the main theme of the following chapters.

Before we close this chapter, however, it will not be out of place to look back and re-examine the major concepts that have been touched upon, and consider the relations that are recognizable among them. In so doing we have to keep in mind that we are still at a preliminary stage of our research, and that all we have done is simply to adumbrate the structure of the whole system.

First and foremost, I would like to draw attention to a fact of capital importance which has been suggested in the course of the present chapter but not explicitly stated; namely, that the philosophical thought of Ibn 'Arabī, with all its perplexing complexity and profundity, is dominated by the concept of Being. In this sense, his thought is, in essence, through and through ontological.

The concept of Being in the double meaning of *ens* and *esse* is the highest key-concept that dominates his entire thought. His philosophy is theological, but it is more ontological than theological. That is why even the concept of God (*Allāh*) itself which in Islam generally maintains its uncontested position is given here only a secondary place.[39] As we shall see presently, God is a 'phenomenal', i.e., self-manifesting, form assumed by Something still more primordial, the Absolute Being. Indeed, the concept of Being is the very foundation of this world-view.

However, it is by no means a common-sense notion of Being. Unlike Aristotle for whom also Being had an overwhelming fascination, Ibn 'Arabī does not start his philosophizing from the concept of Being on the concrete level of ordinary reality. For him, the things of the physical world are but a dream. His ontology begins – and ends – with an existential grasp of Being at its abysmal depth, the *absolute* Being which infinitely transcends the level of common sense and which is an insoluble enigma to the minds of ordinary men. It is, in short, an ontology based on mysticism, motivated by what is disclosed only by the mystical experience of 'unveiling' (*kashf*).

The absolute Being intuitively grasped in such an extraordinary experience reveals itself in an infinite number of degrees. These degrees or stages of Being are classified into five major ones which were introduced in this chapter as 'five planes of Being'. Ibn 'Arabī himself designates each of these planes of Being *ḥaḍrah* or 'presence'. Each *ḥaḍrah* is a particular ontological dimension in which the absolute Being (*al-wujūd al-muṭlaq*) manifests itself. And the absolute Being in all the forms of self-manifestation is referred to by the term *ḥaqq*

The first of these five planes of Being, which is going to be our topic in the next chapter, is Reality in its first and primordial absoluteness or the absolute Being itself. It is the Absolute *before*[40] it begins to manifest itself, i.e., the Absolute in a state in which it does not yet show even the slightest foreboding of self-manifestation. The four remaining stages are the essential forms in which the Absolute 'descends' from its absoluteness and manifests itself on levels that are to us more real and concrete. This self-manifesting activity of the Absolute is called by Ibn 'Arabī *tajallī*, a word which literally means disclosing something hidden behind a veil.

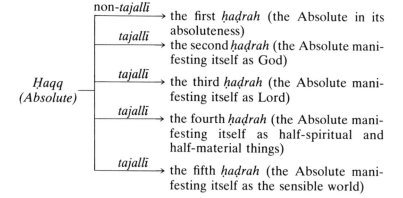

non-*tajallī* → the first *ḥaḍrah* (the Absolute in its absoluteness)

tajallī → the second *ḥaḍrah* (the Absolute manifesting itself as God)

Ḥaqq (Absolute) — *tajallī* → the third *ḥaḍrah* (the Absolute manifesting itself as Lord)

tajallī → the fourth *ḥaḍrah* (the Absolute manifesting itself as half-spiritual and half-material things)

tajallī → the fifth *ḥaḍrah* (the Absolute manifesting itself as the sensible world)

As this diagram shows, everything in Ibn 'Arabī's world-view, whether spiritual of material, invisible or visible, is a *tajallī* of the Absolute except the Absolute in its absoluteness, which is, needless to say, not a *tajallī* but the very source of all *tajallīyāt*.

Another point to note is that these five planes constitute an organic system of correspondences. Thus anything found in the second *ḥaḍrah*, for example, besides being itself a 'phenomenon' of some aspect of the first *ḥaḍrah*, finds its ontological repercussions in all the three remaining *ḥaḍarāt* each in a form peculiar to each *ḥaḍrah*.

It is also important to remember that the first three planes are purely spiritual in contrast with the fifth which is material, while the fourth represents a border-line between the two.

With these preliminary notions in mind we shall turn immediately to the first *ḥaḍrah*.

Notes

1. *Fuṣūṣ al-Ḥikam*, p. 117/103. In quoting from the *Fuṣūṣ al-Ḥikam (Fuṣ.)*, I shall always give two paginations: (1) that of the Cairo edition of 1321 A.H., containing al-Qāshānī's commentary, and (2) that of Affifi's critical edition, Cairo, 1946 (1365 A.H.).

2. *Fuṣ.*, p. 199/104. 'Imagination within imagination' here means that the world as we perceive it is a product of our personal faculty of imagination which is active within the larger domain of the 'objective' Imagination. For a lucid and most illuminating exposition of the concept of Imagination in this latter sense, see Henry Corbin *L'imagination créatrice dans le soufisme d'Ibn 'Arabī*, Paris, 1958.

3. *Fuṣ.*, p. 200/159.

4. *Fuṣ.*, p. 200/159

5. *Fuṣ.*, p. 110/99.

6. *Fuṣ.*, p. 111/99.

7. *ibid.*

8. i.e., a system of symbols pointing to the Absolute.

9. *ja'ala-hā ḥaqqā.*

10. *Fuṣ.*, p. 112/101.

11. *Fuṣ.*, p. 113/101.

12. *Fuṣ.*, pp. 112–113/101. The following words of al-Qāshānī are found in his commentary, p. 113.

13. literally, (Divine) Presences. They are the five fundamental modes or dimensions of the self-manifestation of the Absolute.

14. p. 110. It is to be remembered that this is not the only form in which the 'planes of Being' are presented. Al-Qāshānī himself gives in another place a slightly different explanation (see later, Chapter XI).

15. to be explained in the following chapter.

16. to be discussed in Chapter VII together with the next plane, the plane of the Actions.

17. This is an intermediary plane which lies between the properly Divine domain of Being (1, 2, 3) and the material world of senses, the so-called 'reality' (5). It is a world *sui generis* of eternal Archetypes or Images, in which the originally formless Ideas assume 'imaginal' forms and in which the material things of our empirical world appear as 'subtle (*laṭīf*) bodies' having been divested of their grossly material forms.

18. p. 111/99.

19. *ibid.*

20. p. 110.

21. Commentary on the *Fuṣūṣ*, p. 74. This commentary is found in the above-mentioned Cairo edition by Affifi. Throughout the present work, this commentary will be referred to as Affifi, *Fuṣ.*, Com.

22. *Fuṣ.*, pp. 84–86/85–86.

23. i.e., it is a symbol, and needs 'interpretation'.

24. i.e., God would not have stopped him.

25. The last sentence means: God redeemed Isaac with a sacrificial ram. But the truth is that the whole matter merely looked to Abraham as 'redeeming'. There was, in fact, no 'redeeming' because from the beginning it was not God's intention to make Abraham sacrifice his son. Since, however, Abraham had misunderstood God's intention, what God did to his son was in his eyes an act of redemption.

26. *Fuṣ.*, pp. 234–235/186.

27. *Fuṣ.*, p. 227/181.

28. *Fuṣ.*, p. 228/181.

29. *ibid.*

30. *Fuṣ.*, p. 235/186.

31. *ibid.*

32. Besides, all his statements are, in general, based on his personal experience, whether he explicitly says so or not. And this is one of the reasons why his description (of anything) is so powerful and persuasive.

33. These words, together with the following quotation, are from *Fuṣ.*, p. 235/186–187.

34. i.e., a spiritual state in which the intellect (*'aql*) is free from all physical fetters (al-Qāshānī).

35. The Arabic here is a bit confusing because the same word *'aql* is used for both forms: the 'physical' or 'natural' *'aql* which a mystic must abandon and the 'pure' 'spiritual' *'aql* which he acquires afterwards.

36. *Fuṣ.*, p. 236/187.

37. About the 'permanent archetypes' details will be given later.

38. *Fuṣ.*, p. 236/187.

39. unless, of course, we use, as Ibn 'Arabī himself often does, the word *Allāh* in a non-technical sense as a synonym of the Absolute (*ḥaqq*).

40. Strictly speaking, the word 'before' is improper here because the 'absoluteness' is beyond all temporal relations: there can be neither 'before' nor 'after' in the temporal sense.

II The Absolute in its Absoluteness

In religious non-philosophical discourse the Absolute is normally indicated by the word God or *Allāh*. But in the technical terminology of Ibn 'Arabī, the word *Allāh* designates the Absolute not in its absoluteness but in a state of determination. The truly Absolute is Something which cannot be called even God. Since, however, one cannot talk about anything at all without linguistic designation, Ibn 'Arabī uses the word *ḥaqq* (which literally means Truth or Reality) in referring to the Absolute.

The Absolute in such an absoluteness or, to use a peculiarly monotheistic expression, God *per se* is absolutely inconceivable and inapproachable. The Absolute in this sense is unknowable to us because it transcends all qualifications and relations that are humanly conceivable. Man can neither think of anything nor talk about anything without first giving it some qualification and thereby limiting it in some form or another. Therefore, the Absolute in its unconditional transcendence and essential isolation cannot be an object of human knowledge and cognition. In other words, as far as it remains in its absoluteness it is Something unknown and unknowable. It is forever a mystery, the Mystery of mysteries.

The Absolute in this sense is said to be *ankar al-nakirāt*, i.e., 'the most indeterminate of all indeterminates',[1] because it has no qualities and bears no relation to anything beside itself. Since it is absolutely indeterminate and undetermined it is totally unknowable. Thus the phrase *ankar-nakirāt* means 'the most unknown of all the unknown'.

From the particular viewpoint of the Divine self-manifestation (*tajallī*) which will be one of our major topics in what follows, the Absolute in the state of unconditional transcendence is said to be at the level of 'unity' (*aḥadīyah*). There is as yet no *tajallī*. *Tajallī* is only expected of it in the sense that it is to be the very source of *tajallī* which has not yet begun. And since there is actually no occurrence of *tajallī*, there is absolutely nothing recognizable here. In this respect the Absolute at this stage is the One (*al-aḥad*). The word 'one' in this particular context is not the 'one' which is a whole of 'many'. Nor is it even 'one' in opposition to 'many'. It means the essential, primordial and absolutely unconditional simplicity of Being where the concept of opposition is meaningless.

The stage of Unity is an eternal stillness. Not the slightest movement is there observable. The self-manifestation of the Absolute does not yet occur. Properly speaking we cannot speak even negatively of any self-manifestation of the Absolute except when we look back at this stage from the later stages of Being. The *tajalli* of the Absolute begins to occur only at the next stage, that of the 'oneness' (*wāḥidīyah*) which means the Unity of the Many.

It is impossible that the Absolute manifest itself in its absoluteness. 'Those who know God in the true sense assert that there can never be self-manifestation in the state of Unity',[2] because, not only in the normal forms of cognitive experience in the phenomenal world but also even in the highest state of mystical experience, there is, according to Ibn 'Arabī, kept intact the distinction between the one who sees (*nāẓir*) and the object seen (*manẓūr*). Mystics often speak of 'becoming one with God', which is the so-called *unio mystica*. In the view of Ibn 'Arabī, however, a complete unification is but a fallacy on their part or on the part of those who misconstrue their expressions. If a mystic, for example, describes his experience of *unio mystica* by saying, 'I have seen God through Him' (*Naẓartu-hu bi-hi*) meaning 'I have transcended my own existence into God Himself and have seen Him there with his own eyes', and supposing that the expression is true to what he has really experienced, yet there remains here a distinction between himself who sees and himself who is seen as an object.

If, instead of saying 'I have seen Him through Him', he said, 'I have seen Him through myself', (*Naẓartu-hu bī*), does the expression describe the experience of the Unity? No, by the very fact that there intervenes 'I' (*ana*) the absolute Unity is lost. What about, then, if he said 'I have seen Him through Him and myself' (*Naẓartu-hu bi-hi wa-bī*)? Even in that case – supposing again that the expression is a faithful description of the mystic's experience – the pronominal suffix *-tu* (in *naẓartu*) meaning 'I (did such-and-such a thing)' suggests a split. That is to say, the original Unity is no longer there. Thus in every case 'there is necessarily a certain relation which requires two elements: the subject and object of seeing. And this cannot but eliminate the Unity, even if (the mystic in such an experience) only sees himself through himself'.[3]

Thus even in the highest degree of mystical experience, that of *unio*, the prime Unity must of necessity break up and turn into duality. The Absolute on the level of Unity, in other words, remains for ever unknowable. It is the inescapable destiny of the human act of cognition that, whenever man tries to know something, there comes in a particular relation, a particular condition which impedes an immediate grasp of the object. Man is unable to know anything without taking up some position, without looking at it from some definite point. The Absolute, in its absoluteness, however, is precisely Something which transcends all such relations and aspects.

Is it impossible, then, for man to say even a word about the Absolute? Can we not predicate anything at all of the absolute Absolute? As is clear from what has just been said, strictly speaking no predication is possible. Philosophically, however, there is one single thing which we predicate of the Absolute on this level. It is 'being'. As long as it is a word with a meaning, it also delimits and specifies the Absolute. But within the boundaries of philosophical thinking, 'being' is the most colorless – and therefore the least specifying predication thinkable. It describes the Absolute with the highest degree of unconditionality.

The Absolute viewed from this standpoint is called by Ibn 'Arabī *dhāt*[4] or 'essence'. The world *dhāt* in this context means absolute Being (*wujūd muṭlaq*), Being *qua* Being, or absolute Existence, that is, Existence viewed in its unconditional simplicity. As the epithet 'absolute' indicates, it should not be taken in the sense of a limited and determined existent or existence; it means Something beyond all existents that exist in a limited way, Something lying at the very source of all such existents existentiating them. It is Existence as the ultimate ground of everything.

The ontological conception of the Absolute is a basic thesis that runs through the whole of the *Fuṣūṣ*. But Ibn 'Arabī in this book does not deal with it as a specifically philosophic subject. On behalf of the Master, al-Qāshānī explains the concept of *dhāt* scholastically. He considers it one of the three major ideas that concern the very foundation of Ibn 'Arabī's thought. The whole passage which is reproduced here is entitled 'an elucidation of the true nature of the Essence at the level of Unity'.[5]

> The Reality called the 'Essence at the level of Unity' (*al-dhāt al-aḥadīyah*) in its true nature is nothing other than Being (*wujūd*) pure and simple in so far as it is Being. It is conditioned neither by non-determination nor by determination, for in itself it is too sacred (*muqaddas*) to be qualified by any property and any name. It has no quality, no delimitation; there is not even a shadow of multiplicity in it.
>
> It is neither a substance nor an accident, for a substance must have a quiddity other than existence, a quiddity by which it is a substance as differentiated from all other existents, and so does an accident which, furthermore, needs a place (i.e., substratum) which exists and in which it inheres.

And since everything other than the Necessary Being (*wājib*) is either
a substance or an accident, the Being *qua* Being cannot be anything
other than the Necessary Being. Every determined (i.e., non-
necessary) being is existentiated by the Necessary Being. Nay, it is
essentially [no other than the Necessary Being]⁶; it is entitled to be
regarded as 'other' than the Necessary Being only in respect of its
determination. (Properly speaking) nothing can be 'other' than it in
respect to its essence.

Such being the case (it must be admitted that in the Necessary Being)
existence is identical with essence itself, for anything which is not
Being *qua* Being is sheer non-Being (*'adam*). And since non-Being is
'nothing' pure and simple, we do not have to have recourse, in order
to distinguish Being *qua* Being from non-Being, to a particular act of
negation, namely, the negation of the possibility of both being comprehended under a third term.⁷ Nor does Being ever accept non-
Being; otherwise it would, after accepting non-Being, be existence
which is non-existent. Likewise, pure non-Being, on its part, does not
accept Being. Besides, if either one of them (e.g., Being) accepted its
contradictory (e.g., non-Being) it would turn into its own contradictory (i.e., non-Being) while being still actually itself (i.e., Being). But
this is absurd.

Moreover, in order that anything may 'accept' something else there
must necessarily be multiplicity in it. Being *qua* Being, however, does
not include any multiplicity at all. That which does accept Being and
non-Being is (not Being *qua* Being but) the 'archetypes' (*a'yān*) and
their permanent states in the intelligible world, becoming visible with
Being and disappearing with non-Being.

Now everything (in the concrete world of 'reality') is existent through
Being. So in itself such an existent is not Being. Otherwise when it
comes into existence, we would have to admit that its existence had
already existence even before its own (factual) existence. But Being
qua Being is from the beginning existent, and its existence is its own
essence. Otherwise, its quiddity would be something different from
existence, and it would not be Being. If it were not so, then (we would
have to admit that) when it came into existence, its existence had an
existence (i.e., as its own quiddity) even before its own existence.
This is absurd.

Thus Being itself must necessarily exist by its own essence, and not
through existence of some other thing. Nay, it is that which makes
every other existent exist. This because all other things exist only
through Being, without which they would simply be nothing at all.

It is important to notice that al-Qāshānī in this passage refers to
three categories of Being: (1) Being *qua* Being, that is, absolute
Being, (2) the archetypes, and (3) the concrete beings or existents of
the sensible world. This triple division is a faithful reflection of the
main conception of Ibn 'Arabī himself. In the *Fuṣūṣ*, he does not
present a well-organized ontological discussion of this problem
from this particular point of view. It is nonetheless one of the

cardinal points of his philosophy. A concise systematic presentation is found in his short treatise, *Kitāb Inshā' al-Dawā'ir*.[8] There he mentions the three categories, or, as he calls them, three 'degrees' or 'strata' (*marātib*), of Being, and asserts that there can be no other ontological category. These three are: (1) the absolute Being (2) the limited and determined Being, and (3) something of which neither Being nor non-Being can be predicated. The second of the three is the world of the sensible things while the third, which he says can neither be said to exist nor not to exist, is the world of the archetypes.

As for the ontological nature of the archetypes and the sensible things we shall have occasions to discuss it in detail later on. The first degree of Being alone is what interests us in the present context.

> Know that the things that exist constitute three degrees, there being no other degree of Being. Only these three can be the objects of our knowledge, for anything other than these is sheer non-Being which can neither be known nor be unknown and which has nothing at all to do with anything whatsoever.
>
> With this understanding I would assert that of these three (categories) of things the first is that which possesses existence by itself, i.e., that which is existent *per se* in its very essence. The existence of this thing cannot come from non-Being; on the contrary, it is the absolute Being having no other source than itself. Otherwise, that thing (i.e., the source) would have preceded it in existence. Indeed, it is the very source of Being to all the things that exist; it is their Creator who determines them, divides them and disposes them. It is, in brief, the absolute Being with no limitations and conditions. Praise be to Him! He is Allah, the Living, the Everlasting, the Omniscient, the One, who wills whatever He likes, the Omnipotent.[9]

It is remarkable that Ibn 'Arabī, in the concluding sentence of the passage just quoted, explicitly identifies the absolute Being with Allah, the Living, Omniscient, Ominpotent God of the Qoran. It indicates that he has moved from the ontological level of discourse with which he began to the religious level of discourse peculiar to the living faith of the believer.

As we have remarked before, the Reality in its absoluteness is, in Ibn 'Arabī's metaphysical-ontological system, an absolutely unknowable Mystery that lies far beyond the reach of human cognition. Properly speaking, in the name of *Allāh* we should see the self-manifestation (*tajallī*) of this Mystery already at work, although, to be sure, it is the very first beginning of the process and is, in comparison with the remaining levels of *tajallī*, the highest and the most perfect form assumed by the Mystery as it steps out of its abysmal darkness. However, from the viewpoint of a believer who talks about it on the level of discourse directly connected with his living faith, the absolute Being cannot but take the form of Allah. Existence *per se* cannot in itself be an object of religious belief.

This fact makes it also clear that whatever we want to say about the absolute Being and however hard we try to describe it as it really is, we are willy-nilly forced to talk about it in one aspect or another of its self-manifestation, for the Absolute in the state of non-manifestation never comes into human language. The absolute Reality *in itself* remains for ever a 'hidden treasure', hidden in its own divine isolation.

It will be natural, then, that, from whatever point of view we may approach the problem, we see ourselves ultimately brought back to the very simple proposition from which we started; namely, that the Absolute in its absoluteness is essentially unknown and unknowable. In other words, the inward aspect of the Absolute defies every attempt at definition. One cannot, therefore, ask, 'What is the Absolute?' And this is tantamount to saying that the Absolute has no 'quiddity' (*māhīyah*).[10]

This, however, does not exclude the possibility of a believer justifiably asking what is the *māhīyah* of God. But the right answer to this question can take only one form. And that sole answer is, according to Ibn 'Arabī, represented by the answer given by Moses in the Qoran.

The reference is to XXVI (23–24) where Moses, asked by Pharaoh, 'And what is the Lord of the worlds?' (*Mā rabbu al-'ālamīna?*), answers, 'The Lord of the heavens and earth and what is between them'. Ibn 'Arabī considers the question hurled at Moses by Pharaoh ('What is . . . ?') as a philosophical one asking about the *māhīyah* of God, asking for a definition of God. And he gives the situation of this dialogue quite an original interpretation.[11]

He argues: this question was asked by Pharaoh not because he was ignorant, but simply because he wanted to try Moses. Knowing as he did to what degree a true apostle of God must know about God, Pharaoh wanted to try Moses as to whether the latter was truly an apostle as he claimed to be. Moreover, he was sly enough to attempt cheating those who were present, that is, he designed the question in such a way that, even if Moses were a genuine apostle, those present would get the impression of Moses being far inferior to Pharaoh, for it was to be expected from the very beginning that Moses – or anybody else for that matter – could not in any case give a satisfactory answer to the question. However, Ibn 'Arabī does not clarify the point. On his behalf, al-Qāshānī gives the following explanation.[12]

By asking, 'What is God?', Pharaoh gave those who were there the impression that God had somehow a *māhīyah* in addition to His existence. The onlookers were thereby led to the idea that, since God had a *māhīyah*, a true apostle must know it and must, therefore, be able to give a satisfactory answer to the question. Since, however, there can be no 'definition' (*ḥadd*) of God in the logical sense, a true apostle – if he *is* a true apostle, and not a fraud – can never give a 'satisfactory' answer in the form of a definition. But in the eyes of those who are not conversant with the real nature of the problem, a vague non-definitive answer is a sign indicating that the man who gives such an answer is not a real 'knower'.

Now the actual answer given by Moses runs: 'the Lord of the heavens and earth and what is between them''. This is just the right answer and the only possible and the most perfect answer in this case. It is, as Ibn 'Arabī puts it, 'the answer of those who truly know the matter'. Thus Moses in his answer said what there was really to be said. And Pharaoh, too, knew perfectly well that the right answer could not be anything other than this. Superficially, however, the answer looks as if it were not a real answer. So Pharaoh achieved his aim of producing the impression in the minds of the onlookers that Moses was ignorant of God, while he, Pharaoh, knew the truth about God.

Is it wrong, then, philosophically to ask, 'What is God?' as Pharaoh did? No, Ibn 'Arabī says,[13] the question in this form is not at all wrong in itself. To ask about the *māhīyah* of something is nothing other than asking about its reality or real essence. And God does possess reality. Strictly speaking, asking about the *māhīyah* of something is not exactly the same as asking for its logical definition. To ask about the *māhīyah* of a thing, as understood by Ibn 'Arabī, is to ask about the reality (*ḥaqīqah*) of that object, which is unique and not shared by anything else.[14] 'Definition' in the logical sense is different from this. It consists of a combination of a genus and a specific difference, and such a combination is thinkable only in regard to things (i.e., universals) that allow of common participation.

Anything, therefore, that has no logical genus in which to belong cannot be 'defined', but this does not in any way prevent such a thing having its own unique reality which is not common to other things. More generally speaking, 'there is nothing', as al-Qāshānī observes,[15] 'that has not its own reality (*ḥaqīqah*) by which it is just as it is to the exclusion of all other things. Thus the question (what is God?) is a perfectly justifiable one in the view of those who know the truth. Only those who do not possess real knowledge assert that anything that does not admit of definition cannot be asked as to ''what'' (*mā*) it is'.

Moses, in reply to the question: 'What is God?', says that He is 'the Lord of the heavens and earth and what is between them, if you have a firm faith'. Ibn 'Arabī sees here 'a great secret' (*sirr kabīr*) that is to say, a profound and precious truth hidden under a seemingly commonplace phrase.

> Here is a great secret. Observe that Moses, when asked to give an essential definition (*ḥadd dhātī*), answered by mentioning the 'act' (*fiʿl*)[16] of God.
> Moses, in other words, identified[17] the essential definition (of God) with the (essential) relation of God to the forms of the things by which He manifests Himself in the world or the forms of the things which make their appearance in Him. Thus it is as though he said, in reply to the question: 'What is the Lord of the worlds?', 'It is He in whom appear all the forms of the worlds ranging from the highest – which is the heaven – to the lowest – which is the earth, or rather the forms in which He appears'.[18]

Pharaoh, as the Qoran relates, sets out to show that such an answer can come only from a man who is ignorant of God or who has but a superficial knowledge of God. He tries thereby to prove in the presence of his subjects his superiority over Moses. The latter, against this, emphasizes that God is 'the Lord of the East and West and what is between them, if you but have understanding' (XXVI, 28).

This second statement of Moses is interpreted by Ibn 'Arabī in such a way that it turns out to be a symbolic expression of his own ontology. The East, he says, is the place from which the sun makes its appearance. It symbolizes the visible and material aspect of theophany. The West is the place into which the sun goes down to conceal itself from our eyes. It symbolizes the invisible aspect (i.e., *ghayb*) of the self-manifestation of the Absolute. And these two forms of theophany, visible and invisible, correspond to the two great Names of God: the Outward (*al-ẓāhir*) and the Inward (*al-bāṭin*). The visible theopany constitutes the world of concrete material things (*ʿālam al-ajsām*), while the invisible theophany results in the rise of the non-material spiritual world (*ʿālam al-arwāḥ*). Naturally 'what lies between the East and West' would refer to those forms that are neither purely material nor purely spiritual, that is, what Ibn 'Arabī calls *amthāl* or Images on the level of Imagination.[19]

Here Ibn 'Arabī draws attention to a fact which seems to him to be of decisive importance; namely that, of the two answers given by Moses, the first is qualified by a conditional clause: 'if you have a firm faith'.[20] This indicates that the answer is addressed to those who have *yaqīn*, i.e., the 'people of unveiling' (*kashf*) and immediate unitative knowledge (*wujūd*).[21] Thus in the first answer Moses simply confirms what the true 'knowers' have *yaqīn* about. What, then, is the content of this *yaqīn* which Moses is said simply to be confirming here? The answer is given by al-Qāshānī in the following way.[22]

> The truth of the matter is that it is an impossibility to give a direct answer to the question about the reality of God without any reference to any relation. Thus Moses, instead of anwering directly to the question asked concerning the *māhīyah* (of God), mentions the act (of theophany). He thereby indicates that the Absolute is above all limitation and definition, and that it does not come under any genus nor can it be distinguished by any specific difference because it comprehends the whole in itself.
>
> So (instead of trying to define the Absolute) Moses has recourse to an explication of the reality of the Lordship (*rubūbīyah*). In this way (instead of explaining God) he is content with explaining what is attributed to Him, namely with stating that He is the One to whom belongs the Lordship of the world of the higher spirits, the world of the lower objects and all the determinations, relations and attributions that lie between the two worlds. He states that God is the Outward by his Lordship over all and the Inward by his inmost nature (*huwīyah*, lit. 'He-ness') which resides in all, because He is the very essence of everything that is perceived in any form of experience.
>
> Moses makes it clear that the definition of God is impossible except in this way, that is, except by putting Him in relation to all without limitation or to some (particular things). This latter case occurs when he says (for example): '(He is) *your* Lord and the Lord of *your* ancient ancestors'.

In contrast to the first answer which is of such a nature, the second one is qualified by a different conditional clause: 'if you have understanding', or more precisely 'if you know how to exercise your reason'.[23] This clause indicates that the second answer is addressed to those who understand everything by Reason (*'aql*), those, in other words, who 'bind and delimit' things[24] in their understanding. These people are those whom Ibn 'Arabī calls 'the people of binding, limiting and restricting' (*ahl 'aql wa-taqyīd wa-ḥasr*). These are the people who grasp any truth only through arguments created by their own reason, i.e., the faculty of setting formal limitations.

The gist of both the first and the second answer consists in identifying the object asked about (i.e., the Absolute) with the very essence of the world of Being. Moses, to put it in another way, tried to explain the Absolute in its self-revealing aspect, instead of making the futile effort to explain it in its absoluteness. Pharaoh who asked that question – apart from his bad intention – and Moses who replied as he did, were right each in his own way. When Pharaoh asked him 'What is God?' Moses knew that what Pharaoh was asking for was not a 'definition' of God in the philosophical or logical sense. Therefore he did give the above-mentioned answers.

If he had thought that Pharaoh's intention was to ask for a definition, he would not have answered at all to the question, but would have pointed out to Pharaoh the absurdity of such a question.[25]

All this has, I think, made it clear that for Ibn 'Arabī the Absolute in its absoluteness is an 'absolute mystery' (*ghayb muṭlaq*), and that the only way to approach the Absolute is to look at it in its self-revealing aspect. Is it then possible for us to see the Absolute itself at least in this latter aspect? Will the Unknown-Unknowable transform itself into Something known and knowable? The answer, it would seem, must be in the affirmative. Since, according to a Tradition, the 'hidden treasure' unveils itself because it 'desires to be known', self-manifestation must mean nothing other than the Absolute becoming knowable and known.

But, on the other hand, the Absolute in this aspect is no longer the Absolute in itself, for it is the Absolute in so far as it reveals itself. In Ibn 'Arabī's world-view, the world of Being consists of material objects (*ajsām,* sg. *jism*) and non-material or spiritual beings (*arwāḥ,* sg. *rūḥ*). Both these categories are the forms of self-manifestation assumed by the Absolute. In this sense everything, whether material or spiritual, reveals and discloses the Absolute in its own way. However, there is a certain respect in which these things cover up the Absolute as thick impenetrable veils in such a way that the Absolute hides itself behind them and is invisible in itself. As a famous Tradition says: 'God hides Himself behind seventy thousand veils of light and darkness. If He took away these veils, the fulgurating lights of His face would at once destroy the sight of any creature who dared to look at it.'

In referring to this Tradition, Ibn 'Arabī makes the following remark:[26]

Here God describes Himself (as being concealed) by veils of darkness, which are the physical things, and by (veils) of light, which are fine spiritual things, for the world consists of 'coarse' things and 'fine' things, so that the world in itself constitutes a veil over itself. Thus the world does not see the Absolute as directly as it sees its own self.[27]
The world, in this way, is forever covered by a veil which is never removed. Besides (it is covered by) its knowledge (or consciousness) that it is something different and distinct from its Creator by the fact that it stands in need of the latter.[28] But (in spite of this inner need) it cannot participate in the essential necessity which is peculiar to the existence of the Absolute and can never attain it.
Thus the Absolute remains for this reason forever unknowable by an intimate knowledge, because no contingent being has access to it (i.e., the essential necessity of the Absolute).

Here again we come across the eternal paradox: the things of the world, both material and non-material, are, on the one hand, so many forms of the Divine self-manifestation, but on the other, they act exactly as veils hindering a (complete) self-manifestation of God. They cover up God and do not allow man to see Him directly.

In this latter sense, the created world in relation to the absolute Absolute is referred to in the Qoran by the pronoun 'they' (*hum*). *Hum* is grammatically a 'pronoun of absence'. It is a word designating something which is not actually present. The creatures, in other words, are not there in the presence of the Absolute. And this 'absence' precisely is the 'curtain'.

The recurring Qoranic phrase *hum alladhīna kafarū* 'they are those who cover up' means, according to the interpretation of Ibn 'Arabī, nothing other than this situation of 'absence'. The verb *kafara* in the Qoran stands in opposition to *āmana* 'to believe in', and signifies 'infidelity' or 'disbelief'. But etymologically the verb means 'to cover up'. And for Ibn 'Arabī, who takes the word in this etymological meaning, *alladhīna kafarū* does not mean 'those who disbelieve (in God)' but 'those who cover and veil'. Thus it is an expression referring to people who, by their 'absence', conceal the Absolute behind the curtain of their own selves.[29]

The whole world, in this view, turns out to be a 'veil' (*ḥijāb*) concealing the Absolute behind it. So those who attribute Being to the world enclose the Absolute within the bounds of a number of determinate forms and thereby place it beyond a thick veil. When, for example, the Christians assert that 'God is Messiah, Son of Mary' (V, 72), they confine the Absolute in an individual form and lose sight of the absoluteness of the Absolute. This makes them absent from the Absolute, and they veil it by the personal form of Messiah. It is in the sense that such people are Kāfirs, i.e., 'those who cover up (→those who disbelieve)'.[30]

The same thing is also explained by Ibn 'Arabī in another interesting way. The key-concept here is the Divine self-manifestation (*tajallī*). And the key-symbol he uses is that of a mirror, which incidentally, is one of his most favorite images.

The Absolute, 'in order that it be known', discloses itself in the world. But it discloses itself strictly in accordance with the requirement of each individual thing, in the form appropriate to and required by the nature of 'preparedness' (*istiʿdād*) of each individual existent. There can absolutely be no other form of self-manifestation. And when the locus, i.e., the individual thing in which the Absolute discloses itself happens to be a human being endowed with consciousness, he sees by intuition the self-revealing

Absolute in himself. Yet, since it is after all the Absolute in a
particular form determined by his own 'preparedness', what he sees
in himself is nothing other than his own image or form (*ṣūrah*) as
mirrored in the Absolute. He never sees the Absolute itself. His
Reason may tell him that his own image is visible there reflected in
the Divine mirror, but, in spite of this consciousness based on
reasoning, he cannot actually see the mirror itself; he sees only
himself.

> The Divine Essence (*dhāt*) discloses itself only in a form required by
> the very 'preparedness' of the locus in which occurs the self-
> manifestation. There can be no other way.
> Thus the locus of the Divine self-manifestation does not see any-
> thing, other than its own form as reflected in the mirror of the
> Absolute. It does not see the Absolute itself. Nor is it at all possible
> for it to do so, although it is fully aware of the fact that it sees its own
> form only in the Absolute.
> This is similar to what happens to a man looking into a mirror in the
> empirical world. When you are looking at forms or your own form in
> a mirror you do not see the mirror itself, although you know well that
> you see these forms or your own form only in the mirror.

Thus we are faced with a curious fact that the forms or images of
things in a mirror, precisely because *they* are visible, intervene
between our eyesight and the mirror and act as a veil concealing the
mirror from our eyes.

> This symbol (of mirror) has been put forward by God as a particularly
> appropriate one for His essential self-manifestation so that the per-
> son who happens to be the locus of this Divine self-manifestation
> might know what exactly is the thing he is seeing. Nor can there be a
> symbol closer than this to (the relation between) contemplation (on
> the part of man) and self-manifestation (on the part of God).
> (If you have some doubt of this) try to see the body of the mirror
> while looking at an image in it. You will not be able to do so, never!
> So much so that some people who have experienced this with regard
> to images reflected in the mirror maintain that the form seen in the
> mirror stands between the eyesight of the person who is looking and
> the mirror itself. This is the furthest limit which (an ordinary intel-
> lect) can reach.[31]

Thus the view that the image in the mirror behaves as a 'veil'
concealing the mirror itself is the highest knowledge attainable by
ordinary people; that is, by those who understand things through
their intellect. But Ibn 'Arabī does not forget to suggest in the same
breath that for those who are above the common level of understanding there is a view which goes one step further than this. The
deepest truth of the matter, he says, is represented by a view which
he already expounded in his *al-Futūḥāt al-Makkīyah*.

The 'deepest truth' here referred to is explained by al-Qāshānī as follows:[32]

> That which is seen in the mirror of the Absolute is the form of the man who is looking; it is not the form of the Absolute. To be sure, it is no other than the very Essence of the Absolute that discloses itself to his eye, but this self-manifestation is done in his (i.e., the man's) form, not in its (i.e., the Essence's) form.
> However, the form seen in (the mirror of) His Essence is far from constituting a veil between Him and the man who is looking. On the contrary, it is the Essence at the level of Unity (*aḥadīyah*) disclosing itself to the man in his form. And shallow indeed is the view of those who assert in connection with the (symbol of the) mirror that the form (seen) works as a veil between it and the man who sees (the form therein).

And al-Qāshānī adds that a deep understanding of this nature is only obtainable in the experience of immediate vision and 'unveiling'. This may be explained somewhat more theoretically and briefly in the following manner.

The image reflected in the mirror of the Absolute has two different aspects. It is, in the first place, a self-manifestation of the Absolute in a particular form in accordance with the demand of the 'preparedness' of the locus. But in the second place, it *is* the Form of the Divine self-manifestation, however much it may be particularized by the demand of the locus. The reflected image behaves as a concealing veil because the spiritual eye of an ordinary man is riveted to the first of these aspects. And as the second aspect looms in the consciousness of the man through the profound experience of 'unveiling' the reflected image ceases to be a veil, and the man begins to see not only his own image but the Form of the Absolute assuming the form of his own.

This, Ibn 'Arabī asserts, *is* the highest limit beyond which the human mind is never allowed to go.[33]

> Once you have tasted this, you have tasted the utmost limit beyond which there is no further stage as far as concerns the creatures. So do not covet more than this. Do not make yourself weary by trying to go up further than this stage, for there is no higher stage than this. Beyond this there is sheer nothing.

We may remark that the 'highest limit' here spoken of is the stage peculiar to the Perfect Man. Even for the Perfect Man there can be no spiritual stage realizable at which he is able to know the Absolute as it really is, i.e., in its absoluteness. Yet, such a man is in a position to intuit the Absolute as it reveals itself in himself and in all other things. This is the final answer given to the question: To what extent and in what form can man know the Absolute?

And this will be the only and necessary conclusion to be reached concerning the metaphysical capability of the Perfect Man if we are to start from the basic assumption that Divine Essence (*dhāt*) and Unity (*ahadīyah*) are completely identical with each other in indicating one and the same thing, namely, the Absolute in its absoluteness as the highest metaphysical stage of Reality. There is, however, another theoretical possibility. If, following some of the outstanding philosophers of the school of Ibn 'Arabī, we are to divide the highest level of Reality into two metaphysical strata and distinguish between them as (1) *dhāt*, the absolute Absolute and (2) *ahadīyah* which, although it is still the same absolute Absolute, is a stage lower than *dhāt* in the sense that it represents the Absolute as it is turning toward self-manifestation – then, we should say that the Perfect Man in his ecstatic experience is capable of knowing the Absolute *qua* Absolute just before it reveals itself in eidetic and sensible forms, that is, the Absolute at the stage of *ahadīyah*, though to be sure the Absolute at the stage of *dhāt* still remains unknown and unknowable.

Notes

1. *Fuṣ.*, p. 238/188. We may remark in this connection that in another passage (p. 188) Ibn 'Arabī uses the same phrase, *ankar al-nakirāt*, in reference to the word *shay'* 'thing'. He means thereby that the concept of 'thing' is so indeterminate that it is comprehensive of anything whatsoever.

2. *Fuṣ.*, p. 95/91.

3. *ibid.*

4. Here and elsewhere in this book in the conceptual analysis of the Absolute at the stage of absoluteness I follow the tradition of those who completely identify the metaphysical stage of *dhāt* with that of *ahadīyah*, like Qāshānī and Qayṣarī. It is to be remarked that there are others (like Jīlī) who distinguish between *dhāt* and *ahadīyah*. For them, *dhāt* is the absolute Absolute while *ahadīyah* is the next metaphysical stage at which the Absolute discloses itself as the ultimate source of *tajallī*.

5. *Fuṣ.*, Com., p. 3.

6. The printed text is here obviously defective. I read: *bal huwa bi-i'tibār al-haqīqah* [*'aynu-hu, wa-ghayru-hu*] *bi-i'tibār al-ta'ayyun*.

7. because there cannot be a wider concept that would comprehend within itself both Being and non-Being.

8. *K.S.*, H.S. Nyberg, ed., Leiden, 1919, p. 15 *et. sqq.*

9. *ibid.*

10. *Māhīyah* from *Mā hiya?* meaning 'what is it?' corresponding to the Greek expression *to ti ēn einai.*

11. *Fuṣ.*, p. 259/207–208.

12. p. 259.

13. *Fuṣ.*, pp. 259–260/208.

14. It is to be noted that in Islamic philosophy in general the *māhīyah* 'what-is-it-ness' is of two kinds: (1) *māhīyah* 'in the particular sense' and (2) *māhīyah* 'in a general sense'. The former means 'quiddity' to be designated by the definition, while the latter means ontological 'reality', that which makes a thing what it is.

15. p. 260.

16. i.e., the act of 'Lordship' which in the philosophy of Ibn 'Arabī means the act of self-manifestation in the concrete phenomena of the world.

17. i.e., replaced the definition of God by the mentioning of the relation of God to His phenomenal forms.

18. *Fuṣ.*, pp. 260/208.

19. *Fuṣ.*, p. 260/208–209. Concerning 'what lies between the East and West', however, Ibn 'Arabī in this passage simply says that it is intended to mean that God is Omniscient (*bi kull shay' 'alīm*).

20. *in kuntum mūqinīn*, the last word being a derivative of the same root *YQN* from which is derived the word *yaqīn*. *Yaqīn* means a firm conviction in its final form.

21. *ahl al-kashf wa-al-wujūd.* The word *wujūd* here does not mean 'existence', but a particular stage in myscal experience which follows that of *wajd*. In *wajd*, the mystic is in the spiritual state of 'self-annihilation' (*fanā'*), a state in which he has lost his individual consciousness of the self, while in *wujūd* he is in the state of 'subsistence' (*baqā'*) in the Absolute. Only in this latter state does the mystic 'finds' (*wajada*) God in the true sense, cf. Affīfī, *Fuṣ.*, Com., p. 310.

22. p. 260.

23. *in kuntum ta'qilūn*; the last word comes from the root from which is derived the word *'aql* 'reason'.

24. The verb *'aqala* meaning 'to understand by reason or intellect' etymologically means 'to bind the folded legs of a camel to his thighs (in order to prevent him from moving freely)'.

25. *Fuṣ.*, p. 260/208–209.

26. *Fuṣ.*, p. 22/54–55.

27. i.e., the only possible way in which we can see the Absolute is through the 'things', yet, on the other hand, since what we actually and directly see are the 'things', they intervene between our sight and the Absolute. Thus *indirectly* we see the Absolute, but *directly* we see only the things which prevent our direct vision of the Absolute.

28. We feel at every moment that we are in need of our Creator for our existence. This very feeling produces in us the consciousness of separation or distinction between us and the Absolute.

29. *Fuṣ.*, p. 188/148–149.

30. Cf. Qāshānī, p. 189.

31. *Fuṣ.*, p. 33/61–62.

32. p. 33.

33. *Fuṣ.*, p. 33/62.

III The Self-knowledge of Man

It has been made clear by the preceding that the Absolute *per se* is unknowable and that it remains a dark mystery even in the mystical experience of 'unveiling' (*kashf*) and 'immediate tasting' (*dhawq*). Under normal conditions the Absolute is knowable solely in its forms of self-manifestation. The same thing may be expressed somewhat differently by saying that man is allowed to know the Absolute only when the latter descends to the stage of 'God'. In what follows the structure of this cognition will be analyzed. The central question will be: How and where does the absolutely unknowable appear as 'God'?

Answering this question Ibn 'Arabī emphatically asserts that the only right way of knowing the Absolute is for us to know ourselves. And he bases this view on the very famous Tradition which runs: 'He who knows himself knows his Lord'.[1] What is suggested is, for Ibn 'Arabī, that we should abandon the futile effort to know the Absolute *per se* in its absolute non-manifestation, that we must go back into the depth of ourselves, and perceive the Absolute as it manifests itself in particular forms.

In Ibn 'Arabī's world-view, everything, not only ourselves but all the things that surround us, are so many forms of the Divine self-manifestation. And in that capacity, there is objectively no essential difference between them. Subjectively, however, there is a remarkable difference. All the exterior things surrounding us are for us 'things' which we look at only from outside. We cannot penetrate into their interior and experience from inside the Divine life pulsating within them. Only into the interior of ourselves are we able to penetrate by our self-consciousness and experience from inside the Divine activity of self-manifestation which is going on there. It is in this sense that to 'know ourselves' can be the first step toward our 'knowing the Lord'. Only he who had become conscious of himself as a form of the Divine self-manifestation is in a position to go further and delve deep into the very secret of the Divine life as it pulsates in every part of the universe.

However, not all self-knowledge of man leads to the utmost limit of knowledge of the Absolute. Ibn 'Arabī in this respect roughly divides into two types the way of knowing the Absolute through man's self-knowledge. The first is 'knowledge of the Absolute (obtainable) in so far as ("thou" art) "thou" ' (*ma'rifah bi-hi min hayth anta*), while the second is 'knowledge of the Absolute (obtainable) through "thee" in so far as ("thou" art) "He", and not in so far as ("thou" art) "thou" ' (*ma'rifah bi-hi min hayth huwa lā min hayth anta*).

The first type is the way of reasoning by which one infers God from 'thee', i.e., the creature. More concretely it consists in one's becoming first conscious of the properties peculiar to the creatural nature of 'thou', and then attaining to knowledge of the Absolute by the reasoning process of casting away all these imperfections[2] from the image of the Absolute and attributing to it all the opposite properties. One sees, for example, ontological possibility in oneself, and attributes to the Absolute ontological necessity which is its opposite; one sees in oneself 'poverty' (*iftiqār*), i.e., the basic need in which one stands of things other than oneself, and attributes to the Absolute its opposite, that is, 'richness' (*ghinà*) or absolute self-sufficiency; one sees in oneself incessant 'change', and attributes to the Absolute eternal constancy, etc. This type of knowledge, Ibn 'Arabī says, is characteristic of philosophers and theologians, and represents but an extremely low level of the knowledge of God, though, to be sure, it *is* a kind of 'knowing one's Lord by knowing oneself'.

The second type, too, is knowledge of 'Him' through 'thee'. But in this case the emphasis is not on 'thee' but definitely on 'Him'. It consists in one's knowing the Absolute – albeit in a particularized form – by knowing the 'self' as a form of the direct self-manifestation of the Absolute. It is the cognitive process by which one comes to know God by becoming conscious of oneself as God manifesting Himself in that particular form. Let us analyze this process in accordance with Ibn 'Arabī's own description. Three basic stages are distinguished here.

The first is the stage at which man becomes conscious of the Absolute as his God.

> If from the Divine Essence were abstracted all the relations (i.e., the Names and Attributes), it would not be a God (*ilāh*). But what actualizes these (possible) relations (which are recognizable in the Essence) are ourselves. In this sense it is we who, with our own inner dependence upon the Absolute as God, turn it into a 'God'. So the Absolute cannot be known until we ourselves become known. To this refer the words of the Prophet: 'He who knows himself knows his Lord'. This is a saying of one who of all men knows best about God.[3]

What is meant by this passage is as follows. The nature of the
Absolute *per se* being as it is, the Absolute would remain for ever an
unknown and unknowable Something if there were no possibility of
its manifesting itself in infinitely variegated forms. What are generally known as 'Names' and 'Attributes' are nothing but theological
expressions for this infinite variety of the possible forms of self-
manifestation of the Absolute. The Names and Attributes are, in
other words, a classification of the unlimited number of relations in
which the Absolute stands to the world.

These relations, as long as they stay in the Absolute itself, remain
in potentia; they are not *in actu*. Only when they are realized as
concrete forms in us, creatures, do they become 'actual'. The
Names, however, do not become realized immediately in individual
material things, but first within the Divine Consciousness itself in
the form of permanent archetypes. Viewed from the reverse side, it
would mean that it is our individual essences (i.e., archetypes) that
actualize the Absolute. And the Absolute actualized in this way is
God. So 'we (i.e., our permanent archetypes), turn the Absolute
into God' by becoming the primal objects or loci of the Divine
self-manifestation. This is the philosophical meaning of the dictum:
'Unless we know ourselves, God never becomes known.'

> Some of the sages – Abu Ḥāmid[4] is one of them – claim that God can
> be known without any reference to the world. But this is a mistake.
> Surely, the eternal and everlasting Essence can (conceptually) be
> known (without reference to the world), but the same Essence can
> never be known *as God* unless the object to which it is God (i.e., the
> world) is known, for the latter is the indicator of the former.[5]

The commentary of al-Qāshānī makes this point quite explicit. He
says:[6]

> What is meant by Ibn 'Arabī is that the essence in so far as it is
> qualified by the attribute of 'divinity' (*ulūhīyah*) cannot be known
> except when there is the object to which it appears as God . . . Surely,
> our Reason can know (by inference) from the very idea of Being itself
> the existence of the Necessary Being which is an Essence eternal and
> everlasting, for God in His essence is absolutely self-sufficient. But
> not so when it is considered as the subject of the Names. In the latter
> case the object to which He is God is the only indicator of His being
> God.

The knowledge that the whole created world is no other than a
self-manifestation of the Absolute belongs to the second stage,
which is described by Ibn 'Arabī in the following terms:[7]

> After the first stage comes the second in which the experience of
> 'unveiling' makes you realize that it is the Absolute itself (and not the

world) that is the indicator of itself and of its being God (to the world). (You realize also at this stage) that the world is nothing but a self-manifestation of the Absolute in the forms of the permanent archetypes of the things of the world. The existence of the archetypes would be impossible if it were not for the (constant) self-manifestation of the Absolute, while the Absolute, on its part, goes on assuming various forms in accordance with the realities of the archetypes and their states.

This comes after (the first stage at which) we know that the Absolute is God.

Already at the first stage the Absolute was no longer Something unknown and unknowable, but it was 'our God'. Yet, there was an essential breach between the Absolute as God and the world as the object to which it appeared as God. The only real tie between the two was the consciousness that we, the world, are not self-subsistent but essentially dependent upon God and that we, as correlatives of the Absolute *qua* God, are indicators of the Names and Attributes and are thereby indirectly indicators of the Absolute.

At the second stage, such an essential breach between God and the world disappears. We are now aware of ourselves as self-manifestations of the Absolute itself. And looking back from this point we find that what was (as the first stage) thought to be an indicator-indicated relation between God and the object to which the Absolute appeared as God is nothing but an indicator-indicated relation between the Absolute in its self-manifesting aspect and the Absolute in its hidden aspect. Here I give a more philosophical formulation of this situation by al-Qāshānī.[8]

When by Divine guidance Reason is led to the conclusion that there must exist the Necessary Being existing by itself away from all others, it may, if aided by good chance, attain the intuition that it is nothing but this real Necessary Being that is manifesting itself in the form of the essence of the world itself. Then it realizes that the very first appearance of this Necessary Being is its self-manifestation in the One Substance or the One Entity[9] in which are prefigured all the forms of the permanent archetypes in the Divine Consciousness, and that they (i.e., the archetypes) have no existence independently of the Necessary Being,[10] but have an eternal, everlasting existence in the latter. And to these archetypes are attributed all the Attributes of the Necessary Being as so many Names of the latter, or rather as so many particularizing determinations of it. Thus only through the archetypes do the Names become (actually) distinguishable and through their appearance does Divinity (i.e., the Necessary Being's being God) make its appearance. And all this occurs in the forms of the world. The Absolute in this way is the Outward (appearing explicitly) in the form of the world and the Inward (appearing invisibly) in the forms of the individual essences of the world. But it is always the same Entity making its appearance (in diverse forms). The Absolute here behaves as its own indicator. Thus after having known (at the first stage) that the Absolute is our God, we now know (at the second stage) that it diversifies into many kinds and takes on various forms according to the realities of the archetypes and their various states, for, after all, all these things are nothing else than the Absolute itself (in its diverse forms.)

In this interesting passage al-Qāshānī uses the phrase 'the first appearance' (*al-ẓuhūr al-awwal*), i.e., the first self-manifestation of the Absolute, and says that it means the Absolute being manifested in the 'One Substance'. This, in fact, refers to a very important point in Ibn 'Arabī's metaphysics, namely, the basic distinction between two kinds of self-manifestation (*tajalliyyān*): (1) self-manifestation in the invisible (*tajallī ghayb*) and (2) self-manifestation in the visible (*tajallī shahādah*).[11]

The first of these two is the self-manifestation of the Essence within itself. Here the Absolute reveals itself to itself. It is, in other words, the first appearance of the self-consciousness of the Absolute. And the content of this consciousness is constituted by the permanent archetypes of things before they are actualized in the outward world, the eternal forms of things as they exist in the Divine Consciousness. As we shall see later in detail, Ibn 'Arabī calls this type of the self-manifestation of the Absolute 'the most holy emanation' (*al-fayḍ al-aqdas*), the term 'emanation' (*fayḍ*) being for Ibn 'Arabī always synonymous with 'self-manifestation' (*tajallī*).[14]

> This is a (direct) self-manifestation of the Essence (*tajallī dhātiy*) of which invisibility is the reality. And through this self-manifestation the 'He-ness' is actualized.[13] One is justified in attributing 'He-ness' to it on the ground that (in the Qoran) the Absolute designates itself by the pronoun 'He'. The Absolute (at this stage) is eternally and everlastingly 'He' for itself.[14]

It is to be remarked that the word 'He' is, as Ibn 'Arabī observes, a pronoun of 'absence'. This naturally implies that, although there has already been self-manifestation, the subject of this act still remains 'absent', i.e., invisible to others. It also implies that, since it is 'He', the third person, the Absolute here has already split itself into two and has established the second 'itself' as something *other* than the first 'itself'. However, all this is occurring only within the Consciousness of the Absolute itself. It is, at this stage, 'He' only to itself; it is not 'He' to anybody or anything else. The Consciousness of the Absolute is still the world of the invisible (*'ālam al-ghayb*). The second type of self-manifestation, the *tajallī shahādah*, is

different from this. It refers to the phenomenon of the permanent
archetypes which form the content of the Divine Consciousness
coming out of the stage of potentiality into the outward world of
'reality'. It means the actualization of the archetypes in concrete
forms. In distinction from the first type, this second type of self-
manifestation is called by Ibn 'Arabī 'the holy emanation' (*al-fayḍ
al-muqaddas*). And the world of Being thus realized constitutes the
world of sensible experience (*'ālam al-shahādah*).

So much for the second stage of man's 'knowing his Lord by
knowing himself'. Now we turn to the third and the last of the three
stages distinguished above.

Let us begin by quoting a short description of the third stage by Ibn
'Arabī himself.[15]

> Following these two stages there comes the final 'unveiling'. There
> our own forms will be seen in it (i.e., the Absolute) in such a way that
> all of us are disclosed to each other in the Absolute. All of us will
> recognize each other and at the same time be distinguished from one
> another.

The meaning of this somewhat enigmatic statement may be
rendered perfectly understandable in the following way. To the eye
of a man who has attained this spiritual stage there arises a scene of
extraordinary beauty. He sees all the existent things as they appear
in the mirror of the Absolute and as they appear one in the other.
All these things interflow and interpenetrate in such a way that they
become transparent to one another while keeping at the same time
each its own individuality. This is the experience of 'unveiling'
(*kashf*).

We may remark in this connection that al-Qāshānī divides the
'unveiling' into two stages.[16]

> The first 'unveiling' occurs in the state of 'self-annihilation' (*fanā'*) in
> the Absolute. In this state, the man who sees and the object seen are
> nothing other than the Absolute alone. This is called unification'
> (*jam'*). The second 'unveiling' is 'subsistence' (*baqā'*) after 'self-
> annihilation'. In this spiritual state, the forms of the created world
> make their appearance; they make their appearance one to the other
> in the Absolute itself. Thus the Reality here plays the role of a mirror
> for the creatures. And the One Being diversifies itself into many
> through the innumerable forms of the things. The reality (of the
> mirror) is the Absolute and the forms (appearing in it) are creatures.
> The creatures in this experience know one another and yet each is
> distinguished from others.

Al-Qāshānī goes on to say that of those whose eyes have been
opened by the second-'unveiling', some attain the state of 'perfec-

tion' (*kamāl*). These are men 'who are not veiled by the sight of the creatures from the Absolute and who recognize the creaturely Many in the very bosom of the real Unity of the Absolute'. These are the 'people of perfection' (*ahl al-kamāl*) whose eyes are not veiled by the Divine Majesty (i.e., the aspect of the phenomenal Many) from the Divine Beauty (i.e., the aspect of the metaphysical One), nor by the Divine Beauty from the Divine Majesty. The last point is mentioned with particular emphasis in view of the fact that, according to al-Qāshānī's interpretation, the first 'unveiling' consists exclusively in an experience of Beauty (*jamāl*), while the second is mainly an experience of Majesty (*jalāl*), so that in either case there is a certain danger of mystics emphasizing exclusively either the one or the other.

> The first 'unveiling' brings out Beauty alone. The subject who experiences it does not witness except Beauty . . . Thus he is naturally veiled by Beauty and cannot see Majesty.
> But among those who experience the second 'unveiling' there are some who are veiled by Majesty and cannot see Beauty. They tend to imagine and represent the (state of affairs) on this level in terms of the creatures as distinguished from the Absolute, and thus they are veiled by the sight of the creatures from seeing the Absolute.

The same situation is described in a different way by Ibn 'Arabī himself by a terse expression as follows:[17]

> Some of us (i.e., the 'people of perfection') are aware that this (supreme) knowledge about us[18] (i.e., about the phenomenal Many) occurs in no other than the Absolute. But some of us (i.e., mystics who are not so perfect) are unaware of the (true nature of this) Presence (i.e., the ontological level which is disclosed in the *baqā'*-experience) in which this knowledge about us (i.e., the phenomenal Many) occurs to us.[19] I take refuge in God from being one of the ignorant!

By way of conclusion let us summarize at this point the interpretation given by Ibn 'Arabī to the Tradition: 'He who knows himself knows his Lord'.

He begins by emphasizing that the self-knowledge of man is the absolutely necessary premise for his knowing his Lord, that man's knowledge of the Lord can only result from his knowledge of himself.

What is important here is that the word 'Lord' (*rabb*) in Ibn 'Arabī's terminology means the Absolute as it manifests itself through some definite Name. It does not refer to the Essence which surpasses all determinations and transcends all relations. Thus the dictum: 'He who knows himself knows his Lord' does not in any way suggest that the self-knowledge of man will allow man to know the

Absolute in its pure Essence. Whatever one may do, and however deep one's experience of 'unveiling' may be, one is forced to stop at the stage of the 'Lord'. Herein lies the limitation set to human cognition. In the opposite direction, however, the same human cognition is able to cover an amazingly wide field in its endeavor to know the Absolute. For, after all, the self-revealing Absolute is, at the last and ultimate stage of its activity, nothing but the world in which we live. And 'every part of the world' is a pointer to its own ontological ground, which is its Lord.'[20] Moreover, man is the most perfect of all the parts of the world. If this most perfect part of the world comes to know itself through self-knowledge or self-consciousness, it will naturally be able to know the Absolute to the utmost limit of possibility, in so far as the latter manifests itself in the world.[21]

There still seems to remain a vital question: Is man really capable of knowing himself with such profundity? This, however, is a relative question. If one takes the phrase 'know himself' in the most rigorous sense, the answer will be in the negative, but if one takes it in a loose sense, one should answer in the affirmative. As Ibn 'Arabī says, 'You are right if you say Yes, and you are right if you say No.'

Notes

1. *Man 'arafa nafsa-hu 'arafa rabba-hu.*

2. i.e., all the attributes peculiar to the created things as 'possible' and 'contingent' existents.

3. *Fuṣ.*, p. 73/81.

4. al-Ghazālī.

5. *Fuṣ.*, p. 74/81.

6. p. 74.

7. *Fuṣ.*, p. 74/81–82.

8. p. 74.

9. This does not mean the *absolute* One at the level of primordial Unity which has already been explained above. The 'One' referred to here is the One containing in a unified form all the Names before they become actually differentiated. It is, in brief, the unity of Divine Consciousness in which exist all the archetypes of the things of the world in the form of the objects of Divine Knowledge.

10. Since the archetypes are no other than the very content of the Divine Consciousness as prefigurations of the things of the world, they cannot exist outside the Divine Consciousness.

11. *Fuṣ.*, pp. 145–146/120–121.

12. That is to say, the term 'emanation' should not be taken in the usual neo-Platonic sense.

13. As a result of the 'most holy emanation' the Absolute establishes itself as 'He'. And as the Divine 'He' is established, the permanent archetypes of all things are also established as the invisible content of the 'He'-consciousness of God.

14. *Fuṣ.*, p. 146/120.

15. *Fuṣ.*, p. 74/82.

16. pp. 74–75.

17. *Fuṣ.*, p. 74/82.

18. The '(supreme) knowledge about us' refers back to what has been mentioned above; namely, the extraordinary scene of all the existent things penetrating each other while each keeping its unique individuality.

19. This means that the phenomenal Many, being as it is Divine Majesty, is no less an aspect of the Absolute than the metaphysical One appearing as Divine Beauty. The knowledge of the phenomal Many through *baqā'* is no less a knowledge of the Absolute than the knowledge of the metaphysical One through *fanā'*.

20. *Fuṣ.*, p. 267/215.

21. Cf. Affifi, *Fuṣ.*, Com., p. 325.

IV Metaphysical Unification and Phenomenal Dispersion

What the preceding chapters have made clear may briefly be summarized by saying (1) that the Absolute has two aspects opposed to each other: the hidden and the self-revealing aspect; (2) that the Absolute in the former sense remains for ever a Mystery and Darkness whose secret cannot be unveiled even by the highest degree of *kashf*-experience; (3) that the Absolute comes fully into the sphere of ordinary human cognition only in its self-revealing aspect in the form of 'God' and 'Lord'; and (4) that between these two is situated a particular region in which things 'may rightly be said to exist and not to exist', i.e., the world of the permanent archetypes, which is totally inaccessible to the mind of an ordinary man but perfectly accessible to the ecstatic mind of a mystic. This summary gives the most basic structure of Ibn 'Arabī's world-view from the ontological standpoint.

Since the hidden aspect of the Absolute can neither be known nor described, the whole of the rest of the book will naturally be concerned with the self-revealing aspect and the intermediate region. But before we proceed to explore these two domains which are more or less accessible to human understanding, we must consider the radical opposition between the hidden and the self-revealing aspect of the Absolute from a new perspective. The analysis will disclose an important phase of Ibn 'Arabī's thought.

From this new perspective Ibn 'Arabī calls the hidden and the self-revealing aspect *tanzīh* and *tazhbīh*, respectively. These are two key-terms taken from the terminology of the traditional Islamic theology. Both terms played an exceedingly important role in theology from the earliest times of its historical formulation. *Tanzīh* (from the verb *nazzaha* meaning literally 'to keep something away from anything contaminating, anything impure') is used in theology in the sense of 'declaring or considering God absolutely free from all imperfections'. And by 'imperfections' is meant in this context all qualities that resemble those of creatures even in the slightest degree.

Tanzīh in this sense is an assertion of God's essential and absolute incomparability with any created thing, His being above all creaturely attributes. It is, in short, an assertion of Divine transcendence. And since the Absolute *per se*, as we have seen, is an Unknowable which rejects all human effort to approach it and frustrates all human understanding in any form whatsoever, the sound reason naturally inclines toward *tanzīh*. It is a natural attitude of the Reason in the presence of the unknown and unknowable Absolute.

In contrast to this, *tashbīh* (from the verb *shabbaha* meaning 'to make or consider something similar to some other thing') means in theology 'to liken God to created things'. More concretely, it is a theological assertion posited by those who, on the basis of the Qoranic expressions suggesting that 'God has hands, feet, etc.', attribute corporeal and human properties to God. Quite naturally it tends to turn toward crude anthropomorphism.

In traditional theology, these two positions are, in their radical forms, diametrically opposed and cannot exist together in harmony. One is either a 'transcendentalist' (*munazzih*, i.e., one who exercises *tanzīh*) or an 'anthropomorphist' (*mushabbih*, i.e., one who chooses the position of *tashbīh,* and holds that God 'sees with His eyes', for example, and 'hears with His ears', 'speaks with His tongue' etc.).

Ibn 'Arabī understands these terms in quite an original manner, though of course there still remains a reminiscence of the meanings they have in theological contexts. Briefly, *tanzīh* in his terminology indicates the aspect of 'absoluteness' (*iṭlāq*) in the Absolute, while *tashbīh* refers to its aspect of 'determination' (*taqayyud*).[1] Both are in this sense compatible with each other and complementary, and the only right attitude is for us to assert both at the same time and with equal emphasis.

Of all the prophets who preceded Muḥammad in time, Ibn 'Arabī mentions Noah as representative of the attitude of *tanzīh*. Quite significantly, Ibn 'Arabī entitles the chapter in his *Fuṣūṣ*, in which he deals with Noah, 'the transcendentalist wisdom (*ḥikmah subbūḥiyyah*) as embodied in the prophet Noah'.[2])

According to the Qoran, Noah in the midst of an age in which obstinate and unbridled idol-worship was in full sway, denied the value of the idols, openly exhorted the worship of the One God, and advocated monotheism. In other words, he emphasized throughout his life the principle of *tanzīh*. This attitude of Noah, in the view of Ibn 'Arabī, was an historical necessity and was therefore quite justifiable. For in his age, among his people, polytheism was so rampant that only a relentless exhortation to a pure and extreme *tanzih* could have any chance of bringing the people back to the right form of religious belief.

Apart from these historical considerations, however, *tanzih* as a human attitude toward God is definitely one-sided. Any religious belief based exclusively on *tanzih* is essentially imperfect and incomplete. For to 'purify' God to such an extent and to reduce Him to something having nothing at all to do with the creatures is another way of delimiting Divine Existence which is actually infinitely vast and infinitely profound. '*Tanzih*', as Ibn 'Arabi says,[3] 'in the opinion of the people who know the truth, is nothing less than delimiting and restricting God'. This sentence is explained by al-Qāshānī as follows:[4]

> *Tanzih* is distinguishing the Absolute from all contingent and physical things, that is, from all material things that do not allow of *tanzih*. But everything that is distinguished from some other thing can only be distinguished from it through an attribute which is incompatible with the attribute of the latter. Thus such a thing (i.e., anything that is distinguished from others) must necessarily be determined by an attribute and delimited by a limitation. All *tanzih* is in this sense delimitation.
>
> The gist of what is asserted here is the following. He who 'purifies' God purifies Him from all bodily attributes, but by that very act he is (unconsciously) 'assimilating' (*tashbīh*) Him with non-material, spiritual beings. What about, then, if one 'purifies' Him from 'limiting' (*taqyīd*) itself? Even in that case he will be 'limiting' Him with 'non-limitation' (*iṭlāq*), while in truth God is 'purified' from (i.e., transcends) the fetters of both 'limitation' and 'non-limitation'. He is absolutely absolute; He is not delimited by either of them, nor does He even exclude either of them.

Ibn 'Arabi makes a challenging statement that 'anybody who exercises and upholds *tanzih* in its extreme form is either an ignorant man or one who does not know how to behave properly toward God'.

As regards the 'ignorant', Ibn 'Arabi gives no concrete example. Some of the commentators, e.g., Bālī Efendi,[5] are of the opinion that the word refers to the Muslim Philosophers and their blind followers. These are people, Bālī Effendi says, who 'do not believe in the Divine Law, and who dare to 'purify' God, in accordance with what is required by their theory, from all the attributes which God Himself has attributed to Himself'.

As to 'those who do not know how to behave properly', we have Ibn 'Arabi's own remark. They are 'those of the people who believe in the Divine Law (i.e., Muslims) who "purify" God and do not go beyond *tanzih*'. They are said to be behaving improperly because 'they give the lie to God and the apostles without being conscious of it'. Most probably this refers to the Mu'tazilite theologians[6] who are notorious for denying the existence of Attributes in the Essence of God. They are believers, but they recklessly go to this extreme driven by the force of their own reasoning, and end by completely ignoring the aspect of *tashbīh* which is so explicit in the Qoran and Traditions.

Now to go back to the story of Noah which has been interrupted. The kind of *tanzīh* symbolized by Noah is an attitude peculiar to, and characteristic of, Reason. Al-Qāshānī calls it '*tanzīh* by Reason' (*al-tanzīh al-'aqliy*). Reason, by nature, refuses to admit that the Absolute appears in a sensible form. But by doing so it overlooks a very important point, namely, that 'purifying' the Absolute from all sensible forms is, as we have seen a few lines back, not only tantamount to delimiting it but is liable to fall into a kind of *tashbīh* which it detests so violently.

Commenting upon a verse by Ibn 'Arabī which runs: 'Every time (the Absolute) appears to the eye (in a sensible form), Reason expels (the image) by logical reasoning in applying which it is always so assiduous', al-Qāshānī makes the following remark:[7]

The meaning of the verse is this: Whenever (the Absolute) manifests itself (*tajallī*) in a sensible form, Reason rejects it by logical reasoning, although in truth it (i.e., the sensible phenomenon) *is* a reality (in its own way) on the level of the sensible world as well as in itself (i.e., not merely *qua* a sensible phenomenon but in its reality as an authentic form of the self-manifestation of the Absolute). Reason 'purifies' it from being a sensible object because otherwise (the Absolute) would be in a certain definite place and a certain definite direction. Reason judges (the Absolute) to be above such (determinations). And yet, the Absolute transcends what (Reason) 'purifies' it from, as it transcends such a 'purifying' itself. For to 'purify' it in this way is to assimilate it to spiritual beings and thereby delimit its absoluteness. It makes the Absolute something determinate.

The truth of the matter is that the Absolute transcends both being in a direction and not being in a direction, having a position and not having a position; it transcends also all determinations originating from the senses, reason, imagination, representation and thinking.

Besides this kind of *tanzīh* symbolized by Noah, which is '*tanzīh* by Reason', Ibn 'Arabī recognizes another type of *tanzīh*. This latter is '*tanzīh* of immediate tasting' (*al-tanzīh al-dhawqiy*), and is symbolized by the above-mentioned prophet Enoch.

The two types of *tanzīh* correspond to two Names: the one is *subbūḥ* which has been mentioned at the beginning of this chapter, and the other is *quddūs*, the 'Most Holy'.[8] Both are *tanzīh*, but the one symbolized by Noah is 'purifying' the Absolute from any partners and from all attributes implying imperfection, while the second, in addition to this kind of *tanzīh*, removes from the Absolute all properties of the 'possible' beings (including even the highest perfections attained by 'possible' things) and all connections with materiality as well as any definite quality that may be imaginable and thinkable about the Absolute.[9]

The second type of *tanzīh* represents the furthest limit of 'subtraction' (*tajrīd*) which attributes to the Absolute the highest degree of transcendence. According to Ibn 'Arabī, the prophet Enoch was literally an embodiment of such *tanzīh*. Depicting the mythological figure of Enoch as a symbol of this kind of *tanzīh*, al-Qāshānī says:[10]

> Enoch went to the extreme of 'subtracting' himself (i.e., not only did he 'subtract' everything possible and material from the Absolute, but he 'subtracted' all such elements from himself) and 'spiritualization' (*tarawwuḥ*), so much so that in the end he himself was turned into a pure spirit. Thus he cast off his body, mixed with the angels, became united with the spiritual beings of the heavenly spheres, and ascended to the world of Sanctity. Thereby he completely went beyond the ordinary course of nature.

In contrast to this, al-Qāshānī goes on to say, Noah lived on the earth as a simple ordinary man with ordinary human desires, got married and had children. But Enoch became himself a pure spirit.

> All the desires fell off from him, his nature became spiritualized, the natural bodily properties were replaced by spiritual properties. The assiduous spiritual discipline completely changed his nature, and he was transformed into a pure unmixed Intellect (*'aql mujarrad*). And thus he was raised to a high place in the fourth Heaven.

In less mythological terminology this would seem to imply that the *tanzīh* of Noah is that exercised by the Reason of an ordinary man living with all his bodily limitations, while that of Enoch is a *tanzīh* exercised by the pure Intellect or mystical Awareness existing apart from bodily conditions.

Intellect, being completely released from the bondage of body, works, not as the natural human faculty of logical thinking, but as a kind of mystical intuition. This is why its activity is called '*tanzīh* of immediate tasting'. In either of the two forms, however, *tanzīh*, in Ibn Arabī's view, is one-sided and imperfect. Only when combined with *tashbīh* does it become the right attitude of man toward the Absolute. The reason for this is, as has often been remarked above, that the Absolute itself is not only an absolute Transcendent but also Self-revealer to the world in the world.

> The Absolute has an aspect in which it appears in each creature. Thus it is the Outward making itself manifest in everything intelligible,

while being, at the same time, an Inward concealing itself from every
intelligence except in the mind of those who hold that the world is its
Form and its He-ness as (a concrete manifestation of) the Name 'the
Outward'.[11]

This passage is reproduced by al-Qāshānī in a more explicitly articu-
late form as follows:[12]

> The Absolute appears in every creature in accordance with the
> 'preparedness' (i.e., natural capacity) of that particular creature. It is
> in this sense the Outward appearing in everything intelligible in
> accordance with the 'preparedness' of the individual intelligence.
> And that (i.e., the particular 'preparedness') is the limit of each
> intelligence. . . .
> But (the Absolute) is also the Inward, (and in that capacity it is) never
> accessible to the intelligence beyond the limit set by the latter's own
> 'preparedness'. If the intelligence attempts to go beyond its natural
> limit through thinking, that is, (if it tries to understand) what is
> naturally concealed from its understanding, the heart goes off the
> track, except in the case of the real sages whose understanding has no
> limit. Those are they who understand the matter of God from God,
> not by means of thinking. Nothing is 'inward' (i.e., concealed) from
> their understanding. And they know that the world is the Form or
> He-ness of the Absolute, that is, its inward reality, manifesting itself
> outwardly under the Name 'the Outward'. For the Divine Reality
> (*ḥaqīqah*) in its absoluteness can never be 'He-ness' except in view of
> a determination (or limitation), be it the determination of 'absolute-
> ness' itself, as is exemplified by the Qoranic words: 'He is God, the
> One.'
> As to the Divine Reality *qua* Divine Reality, it is completely free
> from any determination, though (potentially) it is limited by all the
> determinations of the Divine Names.

Not only does the Absolute manifest itself in everything in the world
in accordance with the 'preparedness' of each, but it *is* the 'spirit'
(*rūḥ*) of everything, its 'inward' (*bāṭin*). This is the meaning of the
Name 'the Inward'. And in the ontological system of Ibn 'Arabī, the
Absolute's constituting the 'spirit' or 'inward' of anything means
nothing other than that the Absolute manifests itself in the
archetype (or the essence) of that thing. It is a kind of self-
manifestation (*tajallī*) in no less a degree than the outward *tajallī*.
Thus the Absolute, in this view, manifests itself both internally and
externally.

> (The Absolute) is inwardly the 'spirit' of whatever appears outwardly
> (in the phenomenal world). In this sense, it is the Inward. For the
> relation it bears to the phenomenal forms of the world is like that of
> the soul (of man) to his body which it governs.[13]

The Absolute in this aspect does manifest itself in all things, and the

latter in this sense are but so many 'determined (or limited)' forms
of the Absolute. But if we, dazzled by this, exclusively emphasize
'assimilation' (*tashbīh*), we would commit exactly the same mistake
of being one-sided as we would if we should resort to *tanzīh* only.
'He who "assimilates" the Absolute delimits and determines the
Absolute in no less a degree than he who "purifies" it, and is
ignorant of the Absolute'.[14] As al-Qāshānī says:[15]

> He who 'assimilates' the Absolute confines it in a determined form,
> and anything that is confined within a fixing limit is in that very
> respect a creature. From this we see that the whole of these fixing
> limits (i.e., concrete things), though it is nothing other than the
> Absolute, is not the Absolute itself. This because the One Reality
> that manifests itself in all the individual determinations is something
> different from these determinations put together.

Only when one combines *tanzīh* and *tashbīh* in one's attitude, can
one be regarded as a 'true knower' (*'ārif*) of the Absolute. Ibn
'Arabī, however, attaches to this statement a condition, namely,
that one must not try to make this combination except in a general,
unspecified way, because it is impossible to do otherwise. Thus
even the 'true knower' knows the Absolute only in a general
way, the concrete details of it being totally unknown to him. This
may be easily understood if one reflects upon the way man knows
himself. Even when he does have self-knowledge, he knows himself
only in a general way; he cannot possibly have a comprehensive
knowledge of himself in such a way that it would cover *all* the details
of himself without leaving anything at all. Likewise no one can
have a truly comprehensive knowledge of all the concrete details of
the world, but it is precisely in all these forms that the self-
manifestation of the Absolute is actualized. Thus *tashbīh* must of
necessity take on a broad general form; it can never occur in a
concretely specified way.[16]

As to the fact that the Absolute manifests itself in all, i.e., all that
exists outside us and inside us, Ibn 'Arabī adduces a Qoranic verse
and adds the following remark:[17]

> God says (in the Qoran): 'We will show them Our signs[18] in the
> horizon as well as within themselves so that it be made clear to them
> that it is Reality' (XLI, 53). Here the expression 'signs in the horizon'
> refers to all that exists outside yourself,[19] while 'within themselves'
> refers to your inner essence.[20] And the phrase: 'that it is Reality'
> means that it is Reality in that you are its eternal form and it is your
> inner spirit. Thus you are to the Absolute as your bodily form is to
> yourself.

The upshot of all this is the view mentioned above, namely, that the
only right course for one to follow in this matter is to couple *tanzīh*

and *tashbīh*. To have recourse exclusively to *tashbīh* in one's conception of the Absolute is to fall into polytheism; to assert *tanzīh* to the exclusion of *tashbīh* is to sever the divine from the whole created world. The right attitude is to admit that, 'thou art not He (i.e., the phenomenal world is different from the Absolute), nay thou art He, and thou seest Him in concretely existent things absolutely undetermined and yet determined'.[21] And once you have attained this supreme intuitive knowledge, you have a complete freedom of taking up the position either of 'unification' (*jam'*, lit, 'gathering') or of 'dispersion' (*farq*, lit. 'separating'),[22] Concerning these two terms, *jam'*, and *farq*, al-Qāshānī remarks:[23]

> Taking up the position of 'unification' means that you turn your attention exclusively to the Absolute without taking into consideration the creatures. This attitude is justified because Being belongs to the Absolute alone, and any being *is* the Absolute itself.
>
> (The position of 'dispersion' means that) you observe the creatures in the Absolute in the sense that you observe how the essentially One is diversified into the Many through its own Names and determinations. The position of 'dispersion' is justified in view of the creaturely determinations (of the Absolute) and the involvement of the 'Heness' of the Absolute in the 'This-ness' (i.e., concrete determinations) of the created world.

The distinction between 'unification' and 'dispersion', thus explained by al-Qāshānī, is an important one touching upon a cardinal point of Ibn 'Arabī's ontology. As we already know, the distinction is more usually expressed by *tanzīh* and *tashbīh*. We shall now examine the distinction and relation between the two in more detail and from a somewhat different angle.

Ibn 'Arabī starts from a well-known and oft-quoted Qoranic verse: *Laysa ka-mithli-hi shay'un, wa-huwa al-samī'u al-baṣīr* meaning 'there is nothing like unto Him, and He is All-hearing, All-seeing' (XLII, 11), which he interprets in an original way. The interpretation makes it clear from every aspect that *tanzīh* and *tashbīh* should be combined if we are to take the right attitude toward God.

Let us start by observing that the verse grammatically allows of two different interpretations, the pivotal point being the second term *ka-mithli-hi*, which literally is a complex of three words: *ka* 'like' *mithli* 'similar to', and *hi* 'Him'.

The first of these three words, *ka* 'like', can syntactically be interpreted as either (1) expletive, i.e., having no particular meaning of its own in the combination with *mithli* which itself connotes similarity or equality, or (2) non-expletive, i.e., keeping its own independent meaning even in such a combination.

If we choose (1), the first half of the verse would mean, 'there is nothing like Him' with an additional emphasis on the non-existence of anything similar to Him. It is, in other words, the most emphatic declaration of *tanzīh*. And in this case, the second half of the verse: 'and He is All-hearing, All-seeing' is to be understood as a statement of *tashbīh*, because 'hearing' and 'seeing' are pre-eminently human properties. Thus the whole verse would amount to a combination of *tanzīh* and *tashbīh*.

If we choose the second alternative, the first half of the verse would mean the same thing as *laysa mithla-mithli-hi shay'* meaning 'there is nothing like anything similar to Him'. Here something 'similar to Him' is first mentally posited, then the existence of anything 'similar' to that (which is similar to Him) is categorically denied. Since something similar to Him is established at the outset, it is a declaration of *tashbīh*. And in this case, the second half of the verse must be interpreted as a declaration of *tanzīh*. This interpretation is based on the observation that the sentence structure – with the pronominal subject, *huwa* 'He, put at the head of the sentence, and the following epithets, *samī'* (hearing) and *baṣīr* (seeing) being determined by the article, *al-* (the) – implies that He is the only *samī'* and the only *baṣīr* in the whole world of Being.[24] Thus, here again we get a combination of *tanzīh* and *tashbīh*.

The following elliptic expression of Ibn 'Arabī will be quite easily understood if we approach it with the preceding explanation in mind.[25]

> God Himself 'purifies' (i.e., *tanzīh*) by saying: *laysa ka-mithli-hi shay*, and 'assimilates' (i.e., *tashbīh*) by saying: *wa-huwa al-samī' al-baṣīr*. God 'assimilates' or 'declares Himself to be dual' by saying: *laysa ka-mithli-hi shay*, while he 'purifies' or 'declares Himself to be unique' by saying: *wa-huwa al-samī' al-baṣīr*.

What is very important to remember in this connection is that, in Ibn 'Arabī's conception, *tanzīh* and *tashbīh* are each a kind of 'delimitation' (*taḥdīd*). In both the Qoran and Tradition, he observes,[26] we often find God describing Himself with 'delimitation', whether the expression aims at *tanzīh* or *tashbīh*. Even God cannot describe himself in words without delimiting Himself. He describes Himself for example, as, 'sitting firm on the throne', 'descending to the lowest heaven', 'being in heaven', 'being on the earth', 'being with men wherever they may be', etc.; none of these expressions is free from delimiting and determining God. Even when He says of Himself that 'there is nothing like unto Him' in the sense of *tanzīh*,[27] He is setting a limit to Himself, because that which is distinguished from everything determined is, by this very act of distinction, itself determined, i.e., as something totally different from everything determined. For 'a complete non-determination is a kind of determination'.

Thus *tanzīh* is a 'delimitation' no less than *tashbīh*. It is evident that neither of them alone can ever constitute a perfect description of the Absolute. Strictly speaking, however, even the combination of the two cannot be perfect in these respects, for delimitations will remain delimitations in whatever way one combines them. But by combining these two delimitations which of all the delimitations are the most fundamental and most comprehensive in regard to the Absolute, one approaches the latter to the utmost extent that is humanly possible.

Of these two basic attitudes of man toward the Absolute, Noah, as remarked above, represents *tanzīh*. In order to fight idolatry which was the prevalent tendency of the age, he exclusively emphasized *tanzīh*. Naturally this did nothing but arouse discontent and anger among the idol-worshippers, and his appeal fell only upon unheeding ears. 'If, however, Noah had combined the two attitudes in dealing with his people, they would have listened to his words'.[28] On this point al-Qāshānī makes the following observation:

> In view of the fact that his people were indulging in an excessive *tashbīh*, paying attention only to the diversity of the Names and being veiled by the Many from the One, Noah stressed *tanzīh* exclusively. If, instead of brandishing to them the stringent unification and unmitigated *tanzīh*, he had affirmed also the diversity of the Names and invited them to accept the Many that are One and the Multiplicity that is Unity, clothed the Unity with the form of Multiplicity, and combined between the attitude of *tashbīh* and that of *tanzīh* as did (our prophet) Muḥammad, they would readily have responded to him in so far as their outward familiarity with idolatry was agreeable to *tashbīh* and in so far as their inner nature was agreeable to *tanzīh*.

As is clearly suggested by this passage, the idols that were worshipped by the people of Noah were, in Ibn 'Arabī's conception, properly 'the diversity of the Names'; that is, so many concrete forms assumed by the Divine Names. The idols in this sense are sacred in themselves. The sin of idolatry committed by the people of Noah consisted merely in the fact that they were not aware of the idols being concrete forms of the self-manifestation of the One, and that they worshipped them as independent divinities.

The kind of absolute *tanzīh* which was advocated by Noah is called by Ibn 'Arabī *furqān*, a Qoranic term, to which he ascribes an original meaning,[29] and which is to play the role of a key-term in his system.

The word *furqān*, in Ibn 'Arabī's interpretation derives from the root *FRQ* meaning 'separating'. One might expect him to use it to designate the aspect of 'dispersion' (*farq*) referred to a few paragraphs back, which is also derived from exactly the same root. Actually, however, he means by *furqān* the contrary of 'dispersion'. 'Separating' here means 'separating' in a radical manner the aspect of Unity from that of the diversified self-manifestation of the Absolute. *Furqān* thus means an absolute and radical *tanzīh*, an intransigent attitude of *tanzīh* which does not allow even of a touch of *tashbīh*.

Noah exhorted his people to a radical *tanzīh*, but they did not listen to him. Thereupon Noah, according to the Qoran, laid a bitter complaint before God against these faithless people saying, 'I have called upon my people day and night, but my admonition has done nothing but increase their aversion' (LXXI, 5-6).

This verse, on the face of it, depicts Noah complaining of the stubborn faithlessness of his people and seriously accusing them of this sinful attitude. However much he exhorts them to pure monotheism, he says, they only turn a deaf ear to his words. Such is the normal understanding of the verse.

Ibn 'Arabī, however, gives it an extremely original interpretation, so original, indeed, that it will surely shock or even scandalize common sense. The following passage shows how he understands this verse.[30]

> What Noah means to say is that his people turned a deaf ear to him because they knew what would necessarily follow if they were to respond favorably to his exhortation. (Superficially Noah's words might look like a bitter accusation) but the true 'knowers of God' are well aware that Noah here is simply giving high praise to his people in a language of accusation. As they (i.e. the true 'knowers' of God) understand, the people of Noah did not listen to him because his exhortation was ultimately an exhortation to *furqān*.

More simply stated, this would amount to saying that (1) Noah reproaches his people outwardly but (2) in truth he is merely praising them. And their attitude is worthy of high praise because they know (by instinct) that that to which Noah was calling them was no other than a pure and radical *tanzīh*, and that such a *tanzīh* was not the right attitude of man toward God. *Tanzīh* in its radical form and at its extreme limit would inevitably lead man to the Absolute *per se*, which is an absolutely Unknowable. How could man worship something which is absolutely unknown and unknowable?

If Noah had been more practical and really wished to guide his people to the right form of religious faith, he should have combined *tanzīh* and *tashbīh*. A harmonious combination of *tanzīh* and *tashbīh* is called by Ibn 'Arabī *qur'ān*.[31] The *qur'ān* is the only right attitude of man toward God.

The right (religious) way is *qur'ān* not *furqān*. And (it is but natural) that he who stands in the position of *qur'ān* should never listen to (an exhortation to) *furqān*, even though the latter itself is contained in the former. *Qur'ān* implies *furqān*, but *furqān* does not imply *qur'ān*.[32]

Thus we see that the relation of Noah with his people, as Ibn 'Arabī understands it, has a complex inner structure. On the one hand, Noah, as we have just observed, outwardly reproaches his people for their faithlessness, but inwardly he praises them because of the right attitude they have taken on this crucial question. On the other hand, the people, on their part, know, if not consciously, that pure monotheism in its true and deep sense is not to reduce God to one of his aspects such as is implied by the kind of *tanzīh* advocated by Noah, but to worship the One God in all the concrete forms of the world as so many manifestations of God. Outwardly, however, they give the impression of committing an outrageous mistake by refusing to accept Noah's admonition and exhorting each other to stick to the traditional form of idol-worship.

Ibn 'Arabī terms this relation between Noah and his people '(reciprocal) *makr*', a word meaning 'stratagem', 'artifice' or 'cunning deceit'. This is based on a Qoranic verse: 'And they tried to deceive by a big artifice' (LXXI, 22). This situation is explained by Affifi in a very lucid way. He writes:[33]

> When Noah called upon his people to worship God by way of *tanzīh*, he did try to deceive them. More generally speaking, whoever calls upon others to worship God in such a way, does nothing other than trying to exercise *makr* upon them to deceive them. This is a *makr* because those who are admonished, whatever their religion and whatever the object they worship, are in reality worshipping nothing other than God. (Even an idolater) is worshipping the Absolute in some of its forms of self-manifestation in the external world.
>
> To call upon the idolaters who are actually worshipping God in this form and tell them not to worship the idols but worship God alone, is liable to produce a false impression as if the idolaters were worshipping (in the idols) something other than God, while in truth there is no 'other' thing than God in the whole world.
>
> The people of Noah, on their part, exercised *makr* when they, to fight against Noah's admonition, called upon one another saying, 'Do not abandon your gods!' This is also a clear case of *makr*, because if they had abandoned the worship of their idols, their worship of God would have diminished by that amount. And this because the idols are nothing other than so many self-manifestations of God.

Affifi in this connection rightly calls attention to the fact that, for Ibn 'Arabī, the Qoranic verse: 'And thy Lord hath decreed that you should worship none other than Him' (XVII, 23) does not mean, as it does normally, 'that you should not worship anything other than God', but rather 'that whatever you worship, you are thereby not (actually) worshipping anything other than God'.[34]

In explaining why Noah's call to the worship of God is to be understood as a *makr*, Ibn 'Arabī uses the terms the 'beginning' (*bidāyah*) and the 'end' (*ghāyah*).[35] That is to say, he distinguishes between the 'beginning' stage and the 'end' stage in idol-worship, and asserts that these two stages are in this case exactly one and the same thing. The 'beginning' is the stage at which the people of Noah were indulging in idol-worship, and at which they were reproached by Noah for faithlessness. They were strongly urged by him to leave this stage and go over to the other end, i.e., the 'end' stage where they would be worshipping God as they should. However, already at the 'beginning' stage Noah's people were worshipping none other than God albeit only through their idols. So, properly speaking, there was no meaning at all in Noah's exhorting them to leave the first stage and go over to the last stage. Indeed, it was even more positively an act of *makr* on the part of Noah that he distinguished between the 'beginning' and the 'end' when there was nothing at all to be distinguished.

As al-Qāshānī puts it, 'how can a man be advised to go to God when he is already with God?' To tell the idolaters to stop worshipping God and to worship God alone amounts exactly to the same thing as telling those who are actually worshipping God to abandon the worship of God and to resort to the worship of God! It is absurd, or rather it is worse than absurd, because such an admonition is liable to make people blind to the self-revealing aspect of the Absolute.

The secret of idol-worship which we have just seen may be understood in more theoretical terms as a problem of the compatibility of the One and the Many in regard to the Absolute. There is no contradiction in the Absolute being the One and the Many at the same time. Al-Qāshānī offers a good explanation of this fact, comparing it to the essential unity of a human being.[36]

(Since there is nothing existent in the real sense of the word except the Absolute itself, a true 'knower of God') does not see in the form of the Many anything other than God's face, for he knows that it is He that manifests Himself in all these forms. Thus (whatever he may worship) he worships only God.

This may be understood in the following way. The divergent forms of the Many within the One are either spiritual, i.e., non-sensible, such as angels, or outwardly visible and sensible such as the heavens and earth and all the material things that exist between the two. The former are comparable to the spiritual faculties in the bodily frame of a man, while the latter are comparable to his bodily members. The existence of multiplicity in man in no way prevents him from having a unity. (Likewise, the existence of the Many in God does not deprive Him of His essential Unity.)

The conclusion to be reached from all this is that there is nothing wrong with idolatry, for whatever one worships one is worshipping through it God Himself. Are all idol-worshippers, then, right in indulging in idolatry? That is another question. Idolatry, though in itself it has nothing blamable, is exposed to grave danger. Idolatry is right in so far as the worshipper is aware that the object of his worship is a manifested form of God and that, therefore, by worshipping the idol he is worshipping God. Once, however, he forgets this fundamental fact, he is liable to be deceived by his own imagination and ascribe real divinity to the idol (a piece of wood or a stone, for example) and begin to worship it as a god existing independently of, and side by side with, God. If he reaches this point, his attitude is a pure *tashbīh* which completely excludes *tanzīh*.

Thus in Ibn 'Arabī's view, there are two basic attitudes toward idolatry that are opposed to each other: the one is an attitude peculiar to the 'higher' (*a'lā*) people, while the other is characteristic of the 'lower' (*adnà*). He says:[37]

> The 'knower' knows who (really) is the object of his worship; he knows also the particular form in which the object of his worship appears (to him). He is aware that the 'dispersion' and 'multiplicity' are comparable to the corporeal members in the sensible form (of man's body) and the non-corporeal faculties in the spiritual form (of man), so that in every object of worship what is worshipped is no other than God Himself.
>
> In contrast to this, the 'lower' people are those who imagine a divine nature in every object of their worship. If it were not for this (wrong) imagination, nobody would worship stones and other similar things. This is why (God) said to men of this kind, 'Name them (i.e., designate each object of your worship by its name)!' (XIII, 23). If they were really to name these objects they would have called them a stone, a tree, or a star, (because their idols were in fact stones, trees and stars). But if they had been asked, 'Whom are you worshipping?', they would have replied, 'a god!' They would never have said, 'God' or even 'the god'.[38]
>
> The 'higher' people, on the contrary, are not victims of this kind of deceitful imagination. (In the presence of each idol) they tell themselves, 'This is a concrete form of theophany, and, as such, it deserves veneration'. Thus they do not confine (theophany) to this single instance (i.e., they look upon everything as a particular form of theophany).

If we are to judge the attitude of Noah's people who refused to respond to his advice, we must say that it was right in one respect and it was wrong in another. They were right in that they upheld (though unconsciously) the truly divine nature of the outward forms of theophany. This they did by resolutely refusing to throw away their idols. But they were wrong in that they, deceived by their own imagination, regarded each idol as an independently existing god, and thus opposed in their minds 'small goods'[39] to God as the 'great God'.

According to Ibn 'Arabī, the ideal combination of *tanzīh* and *tashbīh* was achieved only in Islam. The real *qur'ān* came into being for the first time in history in the belief of Muḥammad and his community. On this point Ibn 'Arabī says:[40]

> The principle of *qur'ān* was upheld in its purity only by Muḥammad and his community 'which was the best of all communities that had ever appeared among mankind'.[41] (Only he and his community realized the two aspects of) the verse: *laysa ka-mithli-hi shay* 'There is nothing like unto Him', for (their position) gathered everything into a unity.[42]

As we have seen above, the Qoran relates that Noah called upon his people 'by night and day'. Over against this, Muḥammad, Ibn 'Arabī says, 'called upon his people, not "by night and day" but "by night in the day and by day in the night" '.[43]

Evidently, 'day' symbolizes *tashbīh* and 'night' *tanzīh*, because the daylight brings out the distinctive features of the individual things while the nocturnal darkness conceals these distinctions. The position of Muḥammad, in this interpretation, would seem to suggest a complete fusion of *tashbīh* and *tanzīh*.

Was Noah, then, completely wrong in his attitude? Ibn 'Arabī answers to this question in both the affirmative and the negative. Certainly, Noah preached outwardly *tanzīh* alone. Such a pure *tanzīh*, if taken on the level of Reason, is, as we have already seen, liable to lead ultimately to assimilating the Absolute with pure spirits. And *tanzīh* in this sense is a '*tanzīh* by Reason', and is something to be rejected. With Noah himself, however, *tanzīh* was not of this nature. Far from being a result of logical thinking, it was a *tanzīh* based on a deep prophetic experience.[44] Only, the people of Noah failed to notice that; for them the *tanzīh* advocated by Noah was nothing but a *tanzīh* to be reached by the ordinary process of reasoning.

Real *tanzīh* is something quite different from this kind of logical *tanzīh*. And according to Ibn 'Arabī, the right kind of *tanzīh* was first advocated consciously by Islam. It does not consist in recognizing the absolute Unknowable alone with a total rejection and denial of the phenomenal world of things. The real *tanzīh* is established on the basis of the experience by which man becomes conscious of the unification of all the Divine Attributes, each Attribute being actualized in a concrete thing or event in the world. In more plain terms, the real *tanzīh* consists in man's peeping through the things and events of this world into the grand figure of the One God beyond them. It is 'purifying' (*tanzīh*), no doubt, because it stands on the consciousness of the essential 'oneness' of God, but it is not a purely logical or intellectual 'purifying'. It is a *tanzīh* which comprises in itself *tashbīh*.

In Ibn 'Arabī's view, the *tanzīh* practised by Muḥammad was inviting men not to the absolute Absolute which bears no relation at all to the world, but to Allah the Merciful, that is, the Absolute as the ultimate ground of the world, the creative source of all Being. It is worthy of notice also that of all the Divine Names the 'Merciful' (*al-Raḥmān*) has been specially chosen in this context. The name 'Merciful' is for Ibn 'Arabī the most comprehensive Name which comprises and unifies all the Divine Names. In this capacity the 'Merciful' is synonymous with *Allāh*. Al-Qāshānī is quite explicit on this point.[45]

> It is remarkable that the 'Merciful' is a Name which comprises all the Divine Names, so that the whole world is comprised therein, there being no difference between this Name and the Name *Allāh*. This is evidenced by the Qoranic verse: 'Say: Call upon (Him by the Name) Allah or call upon (Him by the Name) Merciful. By whichever Name you call upon Him (it will be the same) for all the most beautiful Names are His' (XVII, 110).
>
> Now each group of people in the world stands under the Lordship of one of His Names. And he who stands under the Lordship of a particular Name is a servant of that Name. Thus the apostle of God (Muḥammad) called mankind from this state of divergence of the Names unto the unifying plane of the Name Merciful or the Name Allah.

To this Bālī Efendi[46] adds the remark that, unlike in the case of Noah, there is no relation of reciprocal 'deceit' (*makr*) between Muḥammad and his people, for there is no motive, neither on the part of Muḥammad nor on the part of the community, for having recourse to *makr*. Muḥammad, he goes on to say, certainly invited men to the worship of the One God,[47] but he did not thereby call men to the Absolute in its aspect of He-ness. In other words, he did not unconditionally reject the idols which men had been worshipping; he simply taught men to worship the idols (or, indeed, any other thing in the world) in the right way, that is, to worship them as so many self-manifestations of God. In the Islamic *tanzīh* there is included the right form of *tashbīh*.

If a man wants to know the Absolute by the power of his Reason alone, he is inevitably led to the kind of *tanzīh* which has no place for *tashbīh*. If, on the contrary, he exercises his Imagination (i.e., the faculty of thinking through concrete imagery) alone, he falls into pure *tashbīh*. Both *tanzīh* and *tashbīh* of this sort are by themselves imperfect and positively harmful. Only when man sees by the experience of 'unveiling' the true reality of the matter, can *tanzīh* and *tashbīh* assume a form of perfection.

> If Reason functions by itself quite independently of anything else so that it acquires knowledge by its own cognitive power, the knowledge it obtains of God will surely be of the nature of *tanzīh*, not *tashbīh*. But if God furnishes Reason with a (true) knowledge of the Divine self-manifestation (pertaining to the *tashbīh* aspect of the Absolute), its knowledge of God attains perfection, and it will exercise *tanzīh* where it should, and exercise *tashbīh* where it should. Reason in such a state will witness the Absolute itself pervading all cognizable forms, natural and elemental. And there will remain no form but that Reason identifies its essence with the Absolute itself.
> Such is the perfect and complete knowledge (of God) that has been brought by the revealed religions. And the faculty of Imagination exercises its own judgment (upon every thing) in the light of this knowledge (i.e., Imagination collaborates with Reason by modifying the *tanzīh*-view of Reason with its own *tashbīh*-view).[48]

The gist of what Ibn 'Arabī says in this passage may be summarized as follows. Under normal conditions, *tanzīh* is the product of Reason, and *tashbīh* is the product of Imagination (*wahm*). But when the experience of 'unveiling' produces in the mind a perfect knowledge, Reason and Imagination are brought into complete harmony, and *tanzīh* and *tashbīh* become united in the perfect knowledge of God. Of Reason and Imagination in such a state, however, it is invariably the latter that holds regal sway (*sulṭān*).

Concerning the proper activity of Reason in this process and the controlling function exercised by Imagination over Reason in such a way that a perfect combination of *tanzīh* and *tashbīh* may be obtained, Bālī Efendi makes the following illuminating remark:[49]

> In just the same place where Reason passes the judgment of *tanzīh*, Imagination passes the judgment of *tashbīh*. Imagination does this because it witnesses how the Absolute pervades and permeates all the forms, whether mental or physical. Imagination in this state observes the Absolute in the (completely purified) form peculiar to *tanzīh* as established in Reason, and it realizes that to affirm *tanzīh* (exclusively, as is done by Reason) is nothing but delimiting the Absolute, and that the delimitation of the Absolute is nothing but (a kind of) *tashbīh* (i.e., the completely purified Absolute is also a particular 'form' assumed by the Absolute). But Reason is not aware that the *tanzīh* which it is exercising is precisely one of those forms which it thinks must be rejected from the Absolute by *tanzīh*.

These words of Bālī Efendi makes the following argument of Ibn 'Arabī easy to understand:[50]

> It is due to this situation that Imagination[51] has a greater sway in man than Reason for man, even when his Reason has reached the utmost limit of development, is not free from the control exercised over him by Imagination and cannot do without relying upon representation regarding what he has grasped by Reason.
>
> Thus Imagination is the supreme authority (*sulṭān*) in the most perfect form (of Being), namely, man. And this has been confirmed by all the revealed religions, which have exercised *tanzīh* and *tashbīh* at the same time; they have exercised *tashbīh* by Imagination where (Reason has established) *tanzīh*, and exercised *tanzīh* by Reason where (Imagination has established) *tashbīh*. Everything has in this way, been brought into a close organic whole, where *tanzīh* cannot be separated from *tashbīh* nor *tashbīh* from *tanzīh*. It is this situation that is referred to in the Qoranic verse: 'There is nothing like unto Him, and He is All-hearing All-seeing', in which God Himself describes Him with *tanzīh* and *tashbīh* . . .
>
> Then there is another verse in which He says, 'exalted is thy Lord, the Lord of majestic power standing far above that with which they describe Him (XXXVII, 180). This is said because men tend to describe Him with what is given by their Reason. So He 'purifies' Himself here from their very *tanzīh*, because they are doing nothing but delimit Him by their *tanzīh*. All this is due to the fact that Reason is by nature deficient in understanding this kind of thing.

Notes

1. Cf. Affifi, *Fuṣ.*, Com., p. 33.

2. The epithet *subbūḥiyyah* is a derivative of *subbūḥ* or *sabbūḥ* which is one of the Divine Names meaning roughly 'One who is glorified' 'the All-Glorious'. The verb *sabbaḥa* (*Allāh*) means to 'glorify' God by crying out *Subḥāna Allāh!* ('Far above stands God beyond all imperfections and impurities!')

3. *Fuṣ.*, p. 45/68.

4. p. 45.

5. *Fuṣ.*, Com., p. 47. (The commentary of Bālī Efendi is given in the same Cairo edition of the *Fuṣūṣ* which we are using in the present work.)

6. Cf. Affifi, *Fuṣ.*, Com., p. 12.

7. p. 88.

8. Ibn 'Arabī calls the wisdom embodied by Noah 'wisdom of a *subbūḥ* nature', and calls the wisdom symbolized by Enoch 'wisdom of a *quddūs* nature' (*ḥikmah quddūsīyah*), *Fuṣ.*, p. 6 /75.

9. Cf. Qāshānī, p. 60.

10. ibid.

11. Fuṣ., p. 46/68.

12. pp. 46–47.

13. Fuṣ., p. 47/68. Ibn 'Arabī takes this occasion to point out that the Absolute does not allow of definition not only in its absoluteness but also in its self-revealing aspect. The impossibility of defining the Absolute per se has already been fully explained in Chapter II. But even in its aspect of self-manifestation, the Absolute cannot be defined because, as we have just seen, the Absolute in this aspect is everything, external or internal, and if we are to define it, the definition must be formulated in such a way that it covers all the definitions of all the things in the world. But since the things are infinite in number, such a definition is never to be attained.

14. Fuṣ., p. 47/69.

15. p. 47.

16. Fuṣ., p. 47/69.

17. Fuṣ., p. 48/69.

18. 'Our signs', that is, 'Our Attributes' – al-Qāshānī.

19. 'in so far as their determinations (ta'ayyunāt, i.e., properties conceived as 'determinations' of the Absolute) are different from your determination' – al-Qāshānī. This means that, although essentially it is not necessary to distinguish the things of the outer world and yourself, there is a certain respect in which 'all that exist outside of yourself', i.e., the modes of determination peculiar to the things of the outer world, are different from the mode of determination which is peculiar to 'yourself', i.e., the inner world.

20. 'i.e., what is manifested in yourself by His Attributes. If it were not for this manifestation, you would not exist in the world'. – al-Qāshānī.

21. Fuṣ., p. 49/70.

22. Fuṣ., p. 98–99/93.

23. p. 99.

24. that is to say, whenever anybody sees or hears something, it is not the man who really sees or hears, but God Himself who sees or hears in the form of that man.

25. Fuṣ., p. 49/70.

26. Fuṣ., p. 131/111.

27. taking ka as expletive.

28. Fuṣ., p. 50/70.

29. The word *furqān*, whatever its etymology, denotes in the Qoran the Qoran itself. For Ibn 'Arabī, its meaning is totally different from this.

30. *Fuṣ.*, p. 51/70.

31. *Qur'ān* as a technical term of Ibn 'Arabī's philosophy is not the name of the Sacred Book *Qur'ān* (or Qoran). He derives this word from the root *QR'* meaning 'to gather together'.

32. *Fuṣ.*, p. 51/70.

33. *Fuṣ.*, Com., p. 39.

34. *ibid.* Cf. also *Fuṣ.*, p. 55/72.

35. *Fuṣ.*, p. 54/71–72.

36. p. 55. The problem of the One and the Many will form the specific topic of Chapter VII.

37. *Fuṣ.*, p. 55/72.

38. This implies that for these people each idol is 'a god', i.e., an independent divinity; they are not aware that in the forms of the idols they are ultimately worshipping the One God.

39. Cf. Qāshānī, p. 55.

40. *Fuṣ.*, p. 51/71.

41. Reference to III, 110 of the Qoran.

42. i.e., it affirmed 'separating' (*farq*) in 'gathering' (*jam'*), and affirmed 'gathering' in 'separating', asserting thereby that the One is Many from a relative point of view and that the Many are One in their reality – al-Qāshānī, p. 51.

43. *Fuṣ.*, p. 52/71.

44. *Fuṣ.*, p. 53/71.

45. p. 54.

46. *ibid.*, footnote.

47. Outwardly this might be considered a pure *tanzīh*.

48. *Fuṣ.*, p. 228/181.

49. p. 229, footnote.

50. *Fuṣ.*, p. 229/181–182.

51. The word Imagination (*wahm*) must be taken in this context in the sense of the mental faculty of thinking through concrete imagery based on representation (*taṣawwur*).

V Metaphysical Perplexity

As the preceding chapter will have made clear, in Ibn 'Arabī's conception, the only right attitude of man toward God is a harmonious unity composed of *tanzīh* and *tashbīh*, which is realizable solely on the basis of the mystical intuition of 'unveiling'.

If man follows the direction of Imagination which is not yet illumined by the experience of 'unveiling', he is sure to fall into the wrong type of idolatry in which each individual idol is worshipped as a really independent and self-sufficient god. Such a god is nothing but a groundless image produced in the mind of man. And the result is a crude type of *tashbīh* which can never rise to the level of *tanzīh*. If, on the other hand, man tries to approach God by following the direction of Reason unaided by Imagination, man will inevitably rush toward an exclusive *tanzīh*, and lose sight of the Divine life pulsating in all the phenomena of the world including himself.

The right attitude which combines in itself *tanzīh* and *tashbīh* is, in short, to see the One in the Many and the Many in the One, or rather to see the Many as One and the One as Many. The realization of this kind of *coincidentia oppositorum* is called by Ibn 'Arabī 'perplexity' (*ḥayrah*). As such, this is a metaphysical perplexity because here man is impeded by the very nature of what he sees in the world from definitely deciding as to whether Being is One or Many.

Ibn 'Arabī explains the conception of 'perplexity' by an original interpretation of a Qoranic verse. The verse in question is: 'And they (i.e., the idols) have caused many people to go astray' (LXXI, 24). This is interpreted by Ibn 'Arabī to mean that the existence of many idols has put men into perplexity at the strange sight of the absolute One being actually diversified into Many through its own activity.[1]

The idols in this context represent the multiplicity of forms that are observable in the world. And, as al-Qāshānī remarks, anybody who looks at them 'with the eye of unification (*tawḥīd*)', i.e., with the preconception of *tanzīh*, is sure to become embarrassed and perplexed at the sight of the One being diversified according to the relations it bears to its loci of self-manifestation.

The Qoranic verse just quoted ends with another sentence: 'and (o God) increase Thou not the people of injustice (*zālimīn*) except in going astray', and the whole verse is put in the mouth of Noah. This second sentence, too, is interpreted by Ibn 'Arabī in quite an original way. The interpretation is, in fact, more than original, for it squeezes out of the verse a conception of *zālim* which is exactly the opposite of what is meant by the Qoran. He begins by saying that the word *zālim* or 'a man of injustice' here is equivalent to a phrase which occurs repeatedly in the Qoran, *zālim li-nafsi-hi*, meaning 'he who does injustice or wrong to himself'. Now according to the actual usage of the Qoran, 'he who wrongs himself' designates a stubborn unbeliever who disobeys God's commands and by sticking obstinately to polytheism, drives himself on to perdition. But, as interpreted by Ibn 'Arabī *zālim li-nafsi-hi* refers to a man who 'does wrong to himself' by refusing himself all the pleasures of the present world and devotes himself to seeking 'self-annihilation' (*fanā'*) in God.[2]

This interpretation is based on another Qoranic verse, namely XXXV, 32, which reads: 'Some of them are doing injustice to themselves and some of them are moderate, while some others vie one with another in doing good works with the permission of God'. And quite opposite to the usual ranking, Ibn 'Arabī considers 'those who do injustice to themselves' the highest and best of all the three classes of men. They are, he says, 'the best of all people, the specially chosen of God'.[3]

Al-Qāshānī quotes, in this connection, a Tradition from al-Tirmidhī's *Ṣaḥīḥ* which reads: 'These men are all in one and the same grade; all of them will be in the Garden'. He says that this Tradition refers to the three classes of men mentioned in the verse just quoted. These three classes are, as the Tradition explicitly states, in the same grade in the sense that they all are destined to go to the Garden, but al-Qāshānī thinks that this does not prevent them from forming a hierarchy, the highest being 'those who do injustice to themselves', the middle the 'moderate', and the lowest 'those who vie with one another in the performance of good works'. The theoretical explanation he gives of this hierarchy, however, does not seem to be convincing at all. It would seem to be better for us to take, as Affifi does, 'the man who does injustice to himself' as meaning a mystic who has had the experience of 'unveiling' in self-annihilation, and 'the moderate man' as meaning 'a man who keeps to the middle course'. Then most naturally, 'those who vie one another' would mean those who are still in the earlier stage of the mystical training.

However this may be, what is important for Ibn 'Arabī is the conception that the 'man who does injustice to himself' occupies the

highest rank precisely by being in metaphysical perplexity. As is
easy to see, this has a weighty bearing on the interpretation of the
latter half of the Qoranic verse, in which Noah implores God to
increase more and more the 'going astray' of the 'people of injustice'.
Noah, according to this understanding, implores God to increase
even more the metaphysical 'perplexity' of the highest class of men,
while the standard, i.e., common-sense, interpretation of the verse
sees Noah calling down Divine curses upon the worst class of men,
the stubborn idol-worshippers.

In exactly the same spirit, Ibn 'Arabī finds a very picturesque
description of this 'perplexity' in a Qoranic verse (II, 20) which
depicts how God trifles with wicked people who are trying in vain to
beguile and delude Him and those who sincerely believe in Him. A
dead darkness settles down upon these people. From time to time
roars frightful thunder, and a flash of lightning 'almost snatches
away their sight'. And 'as often as they are illuminated they walk in
the light, but when it darkens again they stand still'.

This verse in Ibn 'Arabī's interpretation, yields a new meaning
which is totally different from what we ordinarily understand.
Although he merely quotes the verse without any comment, what
he wants to convey thereby is evident from the very fact that he
adduces it in support of his theory of 'perplexity'. On behalf of his
Master, al-Qāshānī makes it explicit in the following way:[4]

> This verse describes the 'perplexity' of these people. Thus, when the
> light of the Unity (*aḥadīyah*) is manifested they 'walk', that is, they
> move ahead with the very movement of God, while when it darkens
> against them as God becomes hidden behind the veil and the Multi-
> plicity appears instead (of Unity) obstructing their view, they just
> stand still in 'perplexity'.

This 'perplexity' necessarily assumes the form of a circular movement. 'The man in "perplexity" draws a circle', as Ibn 'Arabī says.[5]
This is necessarily so, because the 'walking' of such a man reflects
the very circle of the Divine self-manifestation. The Absolute itself
draws a circle in the sense that it starts from the primordial state of
Unity, 'descends' to the plane of concrete beings and diversifies
itself in myriads of things and events, and finally 'ascends' back into
the original non-differentiation. The man in 'perplexity' draws the
same circle, for he 'walks with God, from God, to God, his onward
movement being identical with the movement of God Himself'.[6]

This circular movement, Ibn 'Arabī observes, turns round a pivot
(*quṭb*) or center (*markaz*), which is God. And since the man is
merely going round and round the center, his distance from God
remains exactly the same whether he happens to be in the state of
Unity or in that of Multiplicity. Whether, in other words, he is

looking at the Absolute in its primordial Unity or as it is diversified in an infinite number of concrete things, he stands at the same distance from the Absolute *per se*.

On the contrary, a man who, his vision being veiled, is unable to see the truth, is a 'man who walks along a straight road'. He imagines God to be far away from him, and looks for God afar off. He is deceived by his own imagination and strives in vain to reach his imagined God. In the case of such a man, there is a definite distinction between the 'from' (*min*, i.e., the starting-point) and the 'to' (*ilà*, i.e., the ultimate goal), and there is naturally an infinite distance between the two points. The starting-point is himself imagined to be far away from himself, and the distance between is an imaginary distance which he thinks separates him from God. Such a man, in spite of his desire to approach Him, goes even farther from God as he walks along the straight road stretching infinitely ahead.

The thought itself, thus formulated and expressed with the image of a man walking in a circle and another going ahead along a straight line, is indeed of remarkable profundity. As an interpretation of the above-cited Qoranic verse, however, it certainly does not do justice to the meaning given directly by the actual context. The extraordinary freedom in the interpretation of the Qoran comes out even more conspicuously when Ibn 'Arabī applies his exegesis to other verses which he quotes as a conclusive evidence for his thesis.[7] The first is LXXI, 25, which immediately follows the one relating to the 'people who do injustice to themselves'. It reads: 'Because of their mistakes (*khatī'āt*) they (i.e., the people of injustice), were drowned, and then put into fire. And they found nobody to help them in place of God'.

The word *khatī'āt* meaning 'mistakes' or 'sins' comes from the root *KH-Ṭ*' which means 'to err' 'to commit a mistake'. It is a commonly used word with a definite meaning. Ibn 'Arabī, however, completely disregards this etymology, and derives it from the root *KH-ṬṬ* meaning 'to draw lines' 'to mark out'. The phrase *min khatī'āti-him* 'from their mistakes' is thus made to mean something like: 'because of that which has been marked out for them as their personal possessions'. And this, for Ibn 'Arabī, means nothing other than 'their own individual determinations (*ta'ayyunāt*)', that is, 'the ego of each person'.

'Because of their egos', i.e., since they had their own egos already established, they had to be 'drowned' once in the ocean before they could be raised into the spiritual state of 'self-annihilation' (*fanā'*).

This ocean in which they were drowned, he says, symbolizes 'knowledge of God', and that is no other than the 'perplexity'. And al-Qāshānī:[8]

('This 'ocean'-'perplexity') is the Unity pervading all and manifesting itself in multiple forms. It is 'perplexing' because of the Unity appearing in a determined form in every single thing and yet remaining non-determined in the whole. (It is 'perplexing') because of its (simultaneous) non-limitation and limitation.

As regards the sentence in the verse: 'then (they) were put into fire', Ibn 'Arabī remarks simply that this holocaust occurred in the very water, that is, while they were in the ocean. The meaning is again explicated by al-Qāshānī:[9]

> This 'fire' is the fire of love (*'ishq*) for the light of the splendor of His Face, which consumes all the determined forms and individual essences in the very midst of the ocean of 'knowledge of God' and true Life. And this true Life is of such a nature that everything comes to life with it and yet is destroyed by it at the same time. There can be no perplexity greater than the 'perplexity' caused by the sight of 'drowning' and 'burning' with Life and Knowledge, that is, simultaneous self-annihilation and self-subsistence.

Thus 'they found nobody to help them in place of God', because when God manifested Himself to these sages in His Essence, they were all burned down, and there remained for them nothing else than God who was the sole 'helper' for them, i.e., the sole vivifier of them. God alone was there to 'help' them, and 'they were destroyed (i.e., annihilated) in Him for ever'. Their annihilation in God was the very vivification of them in Him. And this is the meaning of 'self-subsistence' (*baqā'*), of which *fanā'*, 'self-annihilation', is but the reverse side.

If God, instead of destroying them in the ocean, had rescued them from drowning and brought them back to the shore of Nature (i.e., brought them back to the world of limitations and determinations) they would not have attained to such a high grade (i.e., they would have lived in the natural world of 'reality' and would have remained veiled from God by their very individualities).

Ibn 'Arabī adds that all this is true from a certain point of view,[10] 'although, to be more strict (there is no 'drowning', no 'burning', and no 'helping' because) everything belongs (from beginning to end) to God, and is with God; or rather, everything *is* God.

In a Qoranic verse following the one which has just been discussed, Noah goes on to say to God: 'Verily, if Thou shouldst leave them as they are, they would surely lead Thy slaves astray and would beget none but sinful disbelievers'.

The words: 'they would surely lead Thy slaves astray' mean, according to Ibn 'Arabī,[11] 'they would put Thy slaves into perplexity and lead them out of the state of being slaves and bring them to their inner reality which is now hidden from their eyes, namely, the state of being the Lord. (If this happens,) then those who think themselves to be slaves will regard themselves as Lords'. The 'perplexity' here spoken of is considered by al-Qāshānī not the true metaphysical perplexity but a 'Satanic perplexity' (*ḥayrah shayṭānīyah*). But this is evidently an overstatement. Ibn 'Arabī is still speaking of the same kind of metaphysical 'perplexity' as before. The point he makes here is that, if one permits those who know the Mystery of Being to lead and teach the people, the latter will in the end realize the paradoxical fact that they are not only slaves, as they have thought themselves to be, but at the same time Lords.

The interpretation which Ibn 'Arabī puts on the ending part of the verse: 'and would beget none but sinful disbelievers', is even more shocking to common sense than the preceding one. We must remember, however, that this interpretation is something quite natural and obvious to Ibn 'Arabī's mind.

The Arabic word which I have translated as 'sinful' is *fājir*, a well-established Qoranic term which is derived from the root *FJR* meaning 'to commit unlawful, i.e., sinful, acts'. Ibn 'Arabī derives it from another *FJR* meaning 'to open and give an outlet for water'. And in this paticular context it is taken in the sense of 'making manifest' (*iẓhār*). Thus the word *fājir*, instead of meaning 'a man who commits sinful acts', means 'a man who manifests or unveils what is veiled'. In a terminology which is more typical of Ibn 'Arabī, a *fājir* is a man who manifests the Absolute in the sense that he is a locus of the Absolute's self-manifestation.

As for the second term translated here as 'disbeliever', the Arabic is *kaffār*, an emphatic form of *kāfir* meaning 'one who is ungrateful to, i.e., disbelieves in, God'. But, as we have observed before, Ibn 'Arabī takes this word in its etymological sense; namely, that of 'covering up'. So *kaffār* in this context is not an 'ingrate' or 'disbeliever', but a man who 'covers up' or hides the Absolute behind the veil of his own concrete, determined form.

Moreover, it is important to remember, the *fājir* and *kāfir* are not two different persons but one and the same person. So that the meaning of this part of the verse amounts to: 'these people would do nothing but unveil what is veiled and veil what is manifest at the same time'. As a result, those who see this extraordinary view naturally fall into 'perplexity'.

But precisely the act of falling into this kind of 'perplexity' is the very first step to attaining ultimately the real 'knowledge'. And the 'perplexity' here in question has a metaphysical basis. We shall consider in what follows this point in more theoretical terms, remaining faithful to Ibn 'Arabī's own description.

*　　　*　　　*

What we must emphasize before everything else is that, in Ibn 'Arabī's world-view, the whole world is the locus of theophany or the self-manifestation of the Absolute, and that, consequently, all the things and events of the world are self-determinations of the Absolute. Therefore, the world of Being cannot be grasped in its true form except as a synthesis of contraditions. Only by a simultaneous affirmation of contradictories can we understand the real nature of the world. And the 'perplexity' is nothing other than the impression produced on our minds by the observation of the simultaneous existence of contradictories.

Ibn 'Arabī describes in detail some of the basic forms of the ontological contradiction. And the explanation he gives of the *coincidentia oppositorum* is of great value and importance in that it clarifies several cardinal points of his world-view. Here we shall consider two most fundamental forms of contradiction.

The first[12] is the contradictory nature of the things of the world as manifested in the relation between the 'inward' (*bāṭin*) and the 'outward' (*ẓāhir*). When one wants to define 'man', for example, one must combine the 'inward' and the 'outward' of man in his definition. The commonly accepted definition – 'man is a rational animal – is the result of the combination, for 'animal' represents the 'outward' of man, while 'rational' represents his 'inward', the former being body and the latter the spirit governing the body. Take away from a man his spirit, and he will no longer be a 'man'; he will merely be a figure resembling a man, something like a stone or a piece of wood. Such a figure does not deserve the name 'man' except in a metaphorical sense.

Just as man is man only in so far as there is spirit within the body, so also the 'world' is 'world' only in so far as there is the Reality or Absolute within the exterior form of the world.

> It is utterly impossible that the various forms of the world (i.e., the things in the empirical world) should subsist apart from the Absolute. Thus the basic attribute of divinity (*ulūhīyah*) must necessarily pertain to the world in the real sense of the word, not metaphorically, just as it (i.e., the complex of spirit, the 'inward', and body, the 'outward') constitutes the definition of man, so long as we understand by 'man' a real, living man.

Furthermore, not only is the 'inward' of the world the Reality itself but its 'outward' also is the Reality, because the 'outward' of the world is, as we have seen, essentially the forms of theophany. In this sense, both the 'inward' and 'outward' of the world must be defined in terms of divinity.

Having established this point, Ibn 'Arabī goes on to describe the strange nature of the praising (*thanā'*) of the 'inward' by the 'out-

ward'. 'Just as', he says, 'the outward form of man constantly praises
with its own tongue the spirit within, so the various forms of the
world praise, by a special disposal of God, the inward spirit of the
world'. How does the bodily form of man 'praise with its own
tongue' the spirit within? This is explained by al-Qāshānī in the
following way:[13]

> The bodily form of man praises the spirit, i.e., the soul, by means of its
> movements and by manifestation of its peculiar properties and per-
> fections. (The reason why this is 'praise' is as follows.) The bodily
> members of man are in themselves but (lifeless) objects which, were
> it not for the spirit, would neither move nor perceive anything;
> besides, the bodily members as such have no virtue at all such as
> generosity, liberal giving, magnanimity, the sense of shame, courage,
> truthfulness, honesty, etc. And since 'to praise' means nothing other
> than mentioning the good points (of somebody or something), the
> bodily members (praise the spirit) by expressing (through actions)
> the virtues of the spirit.
> Exactly in the same way, the various forms of the world 'praise' the
> inner spirit of the universe (i.e., the Reality residing within the
> universe) through their own properties, perfections, indeed, through
> everything that comes out of them. Thus the world is praising its own
> 'inward' by its 'outward'.

We, however, usually do not notice this fact, because we do not have
a comprehensive knowledge of all the forms of the world. The
language of this universal 'praise' remains incomprehensible to us
'just as a Turk cannot understand the language of a Hindu'.[14] The
contradictory nature of this phenomenon lies in the fact that if the
'outward' of the world praises its 'inward', properly speaking both
the 'outward' and 'inward' are absolutely nothing other than the
Absolute itself. Hence we reach the conclusion that the one who
praises and the one who is praised are in this case ultimately the
same.

The phenomenon just described, of the Absolute praising itself in
two forms opposed to each other, is merely a concrete case illustrating the more profound and more general fact that the Absolute,
from the point of view of man, cannot be grasped except in the form
of *coincidentia oppositorum*. Ibn 'Arabī quotes in support of his
view a famous saying of Abū Saʿīd al-Kharrāz, a great mystic of
Bagdad of the ninth century: 'God cannot be known except as a
synthesis of opposites'.[15]

> Al-Kharrāz, who was himself one of the many faces of the Absolute
> and one of its many tongues, said that God cannot be known except
> by attributing opposites to Him simultaneously. Thus the Absolute is
> the First and the Last, the Outward and the Inward. It is nothing

other than what comes out outwardly (in concealing itself inwardly), whereas in the very moment of coming out outwardly it is what conceals itself inwardly.

There is no one who sees the Absolute except the Absolute itself, and yet there is no one to whom the Absolute remains hidden. It is the Outward (i.e., self-manifesting) to itself, and yet it is the Inward (i.e., self-concealing) to itself. The absolute is the one who is called by the name of Abū Sa'īd al-Kharrāz and by other names of other contingent beings.

The Inward belies the Outward when the latter says 'I', and the Outward belies the Inward when the latter says 'I'. And this applies to every other pair of opposites. (In every case) the one who says something is one, and yet he is the very same one who hears. This is based on the phrase said by the prophet (Muḥammad): 'and what their own souls tell them', indicating clearly that the soul is the speaker and the hearer of what it says at the same time, the knower of what itself has said. In all this (phenomenon), the essence itself is one though it takes on different aspects. Nobody can ignore this, because everybody is aware of this in himself in so far as he is a form of the Absolute.

Al-Qāshānī reminds us concerning this fundamental thesis of his Master that everything, in regard to its ontological source and ground, is the Absolute, and that all the things of the world are but different forms assumed by the same essence. The fact that the phenomenal world is so variegated is simply due to the diversity of the Divine Names, i.e., the basic or archetypal forms of the Divine self-manifestation.

Nothing exists except the Absolute. Only it takes on divergent forms and different aspects according to whether the Names appear outwardly or lie hidden inwardly as well as in accordance with the relative preponderance of the properties of Necessity (*wujūb*) over those of Possibility (*imkān*) or conversely: the preponderance of spirituality, for instance, in some and the preponderance of materiality in others.[16]

As regards Ibn 'Arabī's words: 'The Inward belies the Outward when the latter says "I", etc.', al-Qāshānī gives the following explication:

Each one of the Divine Names affirms its own meaning, but what it affirms is immediately negated by an opposite Name which affirms its own. Thus each single part of the world affirms its own I-ness by the very act of manifesting its property, but the opposite of that part immediately denies what the former has affirmed and brings to naught its self-assertion by manifesting in its turn a property which is the opposite of the one manifested by the first.

Each of the two, in this way, declares what it has in its own nature, and the other responds (negatively) to it. But (in essence) the one which declares and the one which responds are one and the same thing. As an illustration of this, Ibn 'Arabī refers to a (famous) saying of the prophet (Muḥammad) describing how God pardons the sins committed by the people of this community, namely, 'both what their bodily members have done and what their souls have told them (to do) even if they do not actually do it.' This is right because it often happens that the soul tells a man to do something (evil) and he intends to do it, but is detained from it by another motive. In such a case, the man himself is the hearer of what his own soul tells him, and he becomes conscious of the conflicting properties at work in himself when he hesitates to do the act.

The man at such a moment is the speaker and the hearer at the same time, the commander and the forbidder at the same time. Morover, he is the knower of all this. And (he manifests and gathers in himself all these contradictory properties), notwithstanding his inner essence being one and the same, by dint of the diversity of his faculties and governing principles of his actions such as reason, imagination, repulsion, desire etc. Such a man is an image of the Absolute (which is essentially one) in its divergent aspects and the properties coming from the Names.

Close to the relation between the 'inward' and 'outward' is the contradictory relation between the One and the Many. The two kinds of contradictory relations are, at bottom, one and the same thing. For the dictum that the Absolute (or the world) is One and yet Many, Many and yet One, arises precisely from the fact that the infinitely various and divergent things of the world are but so many phenomenal forms of one unique Being which is the Absolute. The (apparent) difference is due to our taking a slightly different viewpoint in each case.

Regarding the second relation which we will now consider, Ibn 'Arabī offers two explanations, one mathematical and the other ontological. We begin with the 'mathematical' aspect of the problem.

The structure of the metaphysical fact that the One appears in the multiplicity of things, and the things that are many are ultimately reducible to the One or the Absolute, is identical with the structure of the reciprocal relation between the mathematical 'one', which is the very source of all numbers, and the numbers.

The numbers are produced in a serial form by the (repetition of) 'one'. Thus the 'one' brings into existence the numbers, while the numbers divide the 'one', (the only essential difference between them being that) a 'number' subsists as a number by virtue of something which is counted.[17]

Ontologically, as we have seen, the diversification of the unique Essence by concrete delimitations and various degrees is the cause of things and events being observable related to one another in an infinitely complicated manner. The basic structure of this phenomenon, however, is quite simple. It is, Ibn 'Arabī says, the same as the proceeding of the infinite series of numbers out of 'one'. In his view, the mathematical 'one' is the ultimate source of all numbers, and the numbers are nothing but various forms in which 'one' manifests itself.

'One' itself is not a number; it is the source or ground of all numbers. Every number is a phenomenal form of 'one' brought into being by the repetition of the latter (just as all the things in the world are products of the one Essence 'repeating itself', *mutakarrir*, in various forms of self-determination).[18] The important point is that a number thus constituted by repetition of 'one', is not a mere conglomeration of the units, but an independent reality (*ḥaqīqah*). For example, the number 'two' is explained by al-Qāshānī in the following way:[19]

> When 'one' manifests itself (*tajallā*)[20] in a different form it is called 'two'. But 'two' is nothing other than 'one' and 'one' put together, while 'one' itself is not a number. It is to be remarked that the structure of this putting together (of two 'one's) is one, and the product of this putting together, which is called 'two', is also *one* number. So that the essential form here is one, the matter is one, and the two 'one's put together is also one, i.e., 'one' manifesting itself in a form of the Many. Thus 'one' produces the number ('two') by manifesting itself in two different forms. The same is true of 'three', for example, which is 'one' and 'one' and 'one', and the nature and structure of its one-ness is exactly the same as in the case of 'two'.

Thus, all the numbers are each a particular form in which 'one' manifests itself according to its peculiar determination and the rank it occupies in the numerical series.

It is very important to note that the numbers brought into being in this way are all intelligibles (*ḥaqā'iq ma'qūlah*, lit. 'realities grasped by Reason'), and have no existence in the external world; they exist only in our mind. They exist in the external world merely in so far as they are recognizable in the objects that are countable. This must be what is meant by Ibn 'Arabī when he says (in the above-quote passage) that a 'number' is actualized only by something which is counted. And this situation corresponds exactly to the ontological structure of the world of Being.

'Something which is counted' (*ma'dūd*), in al-Qāshānī's interpretation, refers to the One Reality which manifests itself and diversifies itself in the Many. But this is clearly a misinterpretation. The *ma'dūd* in this context must denote a concrete object which exists in the external world and which manifests the transcendental 'one' in a concrete form. In terms of the correspondence between the mathematical and the ontological order of being, 'one' corresponds to the One Reality, i.e., the Absolute, and the numbers that are intelligibles correspond to permanent archetypes, and finally the 'countable things' correspond to the things of the empirical world. Bālī Efendi brings out this system of correspondences with an admirable lucidity:[21]

> You must notice that 'one' corresponds symbolically to the one inner essence (*'ayn*) which is the reality itself of the Absolute, while the numbers correspond to the multiplicity of the Names arising from the self-manifestation of that reality (i.e., of the Absolute) in various forms in accordance with the requirement of its own aspects and relations. (The multiplicity of the Names here spoken of) is the multiplicity of the permanent archetypes in the Knowledge (i.e., within the Divine Consciousness). Finally, the 'things counted' correspond to the concrete things of this world, that is, creaturely forms of theophany, without which neither the properties of the Names nor the states of the permanent archetypes can become manifest (in the external world in a concrete way).

Only when we understand the word 'things counted' in this sense, are we in a position to see correctly what is meant by the following words of Ibn 'Arabī:[22]

> The 'thing counted' partakes of both non-existence and existence, for one and the same thing can be non-existent on the level of the senses while being existent on the level of the intellect.[23] So there must be both the 'number' and the 'thing counted'.
> But there must be, in addition, also 'one' which causes all this and is caused by it.[24] (And the relation between 'one' and the numbers is to be conceived as follows.) Every degree in the numerical series (i.e., every number) is in itself *one* reality. (Thus each number is a self-subsistent unity and) not a mere conglomeration, and yet, on the other hand, there certainly is a respect in which it must be regarded as 'one's put together. Thus 'two' is *one* reality (though it is a 'gathering' of 'one' and 'one'), 'three' is also *one* reality (though it is a 'gathering' of 'one' and 'one' and 'one'), and so on, however far we go up the numerical series. Since each number is in this way *one* (i.e., an independent reality), the essence of each number cannot be the same as the essences of other numbers. And yet, the fact of 'gathering' (of 'one's) is common to all of them (i.e., as a genus, as it were, which comprises all the species). Thus we admit the (existence of) various degrees (i.e., different numbers, each being unique as an independent number) in terms of the very essence of each one of them, recognizing at the same time that they are all one.[25] Thus we inevitably affirm the very thing which we think is to be negated in itself.[26]
> He who has understood what I have established regarding the nature of the numbers, namely, that the negation of them is at the same time the affirmation of them, must have thereby understood how the Absolute in *tanzīh* is at the same time the creatures in *tashbīh*,

although there *is* a distinction between the Creator and the creatures. The truth of the matter is that we see here the Creator who is the creatures and the creatures who are the Creator. Moreover, all this arises from one unique Essence; nay, there is nothing but one unique Essence, and it is at the same time many essences.

In the eye of a man who has understood by experience the ontological depth of this paradox the world appears in an extraordinary form which an ordinary mind can never believe to be true. Such an experience consists in penetrating into the 'real situation' (*amr*) beyond the veils of normal perception and thought. In illustration, Ibn 'Arabī gives two concrete examples from the Qoran.[27] The first is the event of Abraham going to sacrifice his own son Isaac, and the second is the marriage of Adam with Eve.

> (Isaac said to his father Abraham): 'My father, do what you have been commanded to do!' (XXXVII, 102). The child (Isaac) is essentially the same as his father. So the father saw (when he saw himself in his vision sacrificing his son) nothing other than himself sacrificing himself. 'And We ransomed him (i.e., Isaac) with a big sacrifice' (XXXVII, 107). At that moment, the very thing which (earlier) had appeared in the form of a human being (i.e., Isaac) appeared in the form of a ram. And the very thing which was 'father' appeared in the form of 'son', or more exactly in the capacity of 'son'.
> (As for Adam and Eve, it is said in the Qoran): 'And (your Lord) created from it (i.e., the first soul which is Adam) its mate' (IV, 1). This shows that Adam married no other than himself. Thus from him issued both his wife and his child. The reality is one but assumes many forms.

Of this passage, al-Qāshānī gives an important philosophical explanation.[28] It is to be remarked in particular that, regarding the self-determination of the Absolute, he distinguishes between the 'universal self-determination' (*al-ta'ayyun al-kulliy*), i.e., self-determination on the level of species, and the particular or 'individual self-determination' (*al-ta'ayyun al-juz'iy*). These two self-determinations correspond to the ontological plane of the archetypes and that of the concrete things.

> 'The reality is one but assumes many forms' means that what is in reality the one unique Essence multiplies itself into many essences through the multiplicity of self-determinations.
> These self-determinations are of two kinds: one is 'universal' by which the Reality in the state of Unity becomes 'man', for example, and the other is 'individual' by which 'man' becomes Abraham. Thus, in this case, (the one unique Essence) becomes 'man' through the universal self-determination: and then, through an individual self-determination, it becomes Abraham, and through another (individual self-determination) becomes Ishmael.[29]

In the light of this, (Abraham, not as an individual named Abraham, but on the level of) 'man' before individuation, did not sacrifice anything other than himself by executing the 'big sacrifice' (i.e., by sacrificing the ram in place of his son). For (the ram he sacrificed) was himself in reality (i.e., if we consider it on the level of the Absolute before any self-determination). (It appeared in the form of the ram because) the Absolute determined itself by a different universal self-determination[30] (into 'ram') and then by an individual self-determination (into the particular ram which Abraham sacrificed.) Thus the same one Reality which had appeared in the form of a man appeared in the form of a ram by going through two different self-determinations, once on the level of species, then on the level of individuals.

Since 'man' remains preserved both in father and child on the level of the specific unity, (Ibn 'Arabī) avoids affirming the difference of essence in father and child and affirms only the difference of 'capacity' (*ḥukm*) saying 'or more exactly, in the capacity of son'. This he does because there is no difference at all between the two in essence, that is, in so far as they are 'man'; the difference arises only in regard to their 'being father' and 'being son' respectively.

The same is true of Adam and Eve. Both of them and their children are one with respect to their 'being man'.

Thus the Absolute is one in itself, but it is multiple because of its various self-determinations, specific and individual. These self-determinations do not contradict the real Unity. In conclusion we say: (The Absolute) is One in the form of Many.

It is remarkable that here al-Qāshānī presents the contradictory relation between the One and the Many in terms of the Aristotelian conception of genus-species-individual. There is no denying that the world-view of Ibn 'Arabī has in fact a conspicuously philosophical aspect which admits of this kind of interpretation. However, the problem of the One and the Many is for Ibn 'Arabī primarily a matter of experience. No philosophical explanation can do justice to his thought unless it is backed by a personal experience of the Unity of Being (*waḥdah al-wujūd*). The proposition: 'Adam married himself', for example, will never cease to be perplexing and perturbing to our Reason until it is transformed into a matter of experience.

Philosophical interpretation is after all an afterthought applied to the naked content of mystical intuition. The naked content itself cannot be conveyed by philosophical language. Nor is there any linguistic means by which to convey immediately the content of mystical intuition. If, in spite of this basic fact, one forces oneself to express and describe it, one has to have recourse to a metaphorical or analogical language. And in fact, Ibn 'Arabī introduces for this purpose a number of comparisons. Here I give two comparisons which particularly illumine the relation of the One and the Many.

The first is the organic unity of the body and the diversity of the bodily members.[31]

> These forms (i.e., the infinite forms of the phenomenal world) are comparable to the bodily members of Zayd. A man, Zayd, is admittedly one personal reality, but his hand is neither his foot nor his head nor his eye nor his eyebrow. So he is Many which are One. He is Many in the forms and One in his person.
>
> In the same way, 'man' is essentially One no doubt, and yet it is also clear that 'Umar is not the same as Zayd, nor Khālid, nor Ja'far. In spite of the essential one-ness of 'man', the individual exemplars of it are infinitely many. Thus man is One in essence, while he is Many both in regard to the forms (i.e., the bodily members of a particular man) and in regard to the individual exemplars.

The second is a comparison of the luxuriant growth of grass after a rainfall. It is based on the Qoran, XXII, 5, which reads: 'Thou seest the earth devoid of life. But when We send down upon it water, it thrills, swells up, and puts forth all magnificent pairs of vegetation'. He says:[32]

> Water[33], is the source of life and movement for the earth, as is indicated by the expression: 'it thrills'. 'It swells up' refers to the fact that the earth becomes pregnant through the activity of water. And 'it puts forth all magnificent pairs of vegetation', that is, the earth gives birth only to things that resemble it, namely, 'natural' things like the earth.[34] And the earth obtains in this way the property of 'doubleness' by what is born out of it.[35]
>
> Likewise, the Absolute in its Being obtains the property of multiplicity and a variety of particular names by the world which appears from it. The world, because of its ontological nature, requires that the Divine Names be actualized. And as a result, the Divine Names become duplicated by the world (which has arisen in this way), and the unity of the Many (i.e., the essential unity of the Divine Names) comes to stand opposed to the world.[36] Thus (in the comparison of the earth and vegetation, the earth) is a unique substance which is one essence like (the Aristotelian) 'matter' (*hayūlà*). And this unique substance which is one in essence is many in its forms which appear in it and which it contains within itself.
>
> The same is true of the Absolute with all the forms of its self-manifestation that appear from it. So the Absolute plays the role of the locus in which the forms of the world are manifested, but even then it maintains intact the intelligible unity. See how wonderful is this Divine teaching, the secret of which God discloses to some only of His servants as He likes.

The general ontological thesis that the Many of the phenomenal world are all particular forms of the absolute One in its self-manifestation is of extreme importance in Ibn 'Arabī's world-view not only because of the central and basic position it occupies in his thought but also because of the far-reaching influence it exercises on a number of problems in more particular fields. As an interesting example of the application of this idea to a special problem, I shall here discuss the view entertained by Ibn 'Arabī concerning the historical religions and beliefs that have arisen among mankind.

The starting-point is furnished by the factual observation that various peoples in the world have always worshipped and are worshipping various gods. If, however, all the things and events in the world are but so many self-manifestations of the Absolute, the different gods also must necessarily be considered various special forms in which the Absolute manifests itself.

All gods are ultimately one and the same God, but each nation or each community believes in, and worships, Him in a special form. Ibn 'Arabī names it 'God as created in various religious beliefs'. And pushing this argument to its extreme, he holds that each man has his *own* god, and worships his *own* god, and naturally denies the gods of other people. God whom each man thus worships as *his* god is the Lord (*rabb*) of that particular man.

In truth, everybody worships the same one God through different forms. Whatever a man worships, he is worshipping indirectly God Himself. This is the true meaning of polytheism or idolatry. And in this sense, idol-worship is, as we have seen above, nothing blamable.

In order to bring home this point, Ibn 'Arabī refers to an article of belief which every Muslim is supposed to acknowledge; namely, that God on the day of Resurrection will appear in the presence of the believers in diverse forms.[37]

> You must know for sure, if you are a real believer, that God will appear on the day of Resurrection (in various forms successively): first in a certain form in which He will be recognized, next in a different form in which He will be denied, then He will transform Himself into another form in which He will be again recognized. Throughout this whole process, He will remain He; in whatever form He appears it is He and no one else. Yet, on the other hand, it is also certain that *this* particular form is not the same as *that* particular form.
>
> Thus, the situation may be described as the one unique Essence playing the role of a mirror. A man looks into it, and if he sees there the particular image of God peculiar to his religion he recognizes it and accepts it without question. If, however, he happens to see an image of God peculiar to some other religion than his, he denies it. This is comparable to the case in which a man sees in a mirror his own image, then the image of some one else. In either case, the mirror is one substance while the images reflected upon it are many in the eye of the man who looks at it. He cannot see in the mirror one unique image comprising the whole.[38]

Thus the truth itself is quite simple: in whatever form God appears
in the mirror, it is always a particular phenomenal form of God, and
in this sense every image (i.e., every object worshipped as a god) is
ultimately no other than God Himself. This simple fact, however, is
beyond the reach of Reason. Reason is utterly powerless in a matter
of this nature, and the reasoning which is the activity of Reason is
unable to grasp the real meaning of this phenomenon.[39] The only
one who is able to do so is the real 'knower' (*'ārif*). Ibn 'Arabī calls
such a true 'knower' who, in this particular case, penetrates into the
mystery of the paradoxical relation between the One and the Many,
a 'worshipper of the Instant' (*'ābid al-waqt*),[40] meaning thereby a
man who worships every self-manifestation of God at every
moment as a particular form of the One.

> Those who know the truth of the matter show a seemingly negative
> attitude toward the various forms which ordinary people worship as
> gods. (But this attitude of denial is merely a make-believe. In reality
> they do not deny such a form of worship for themselves) for the high
> degree of spiritual knowledge makes them behave according to the
> dictates of the Instant. In this sense they are 'worshippers of the
> Instant.'[41]

In the consciousness of such men of high spirituality, each Instant is
a glorious 'time' of theophany. The Absolute manifests itself at
every moment with this or that of its Attributes. The Absolute,
viewed from this angle, never ceases to make a new self-
manifestation, and goes on changing its form from moment to
moment.[42] And the true 'knowers', on their part, go on responding
with flexibility to this ever changing process of Divine self-
manifestation. Of course, in so doing they are not worshipping the
changing forms themselves that come out outwardly on the surface;
they are worshipping through the ever changing forms the One that
remains eternally unchanging and unchangeable.

These men know, further, that not only themselves but even the
idol-worshippers are also (unconsciously) worshipping God beyond
the idols. This they know because they discern in the idol-
worshippers the majestic power of Divine self-manifestation (*sulṭān
al-tajallī*) working actively quite independently of the conscious
minds of the worshippers.[43]

If, in spite of this knowledge, the 'knowers' hold outwardly an
attitude of denial toward idolatry, it is because they want to follow
the footsteps of the prophet Muḥammad. The prophet forbad
idol-worship because he knew that the understanding of the mass of
people being shallow and superficial, they would surely begin to
worship the 'forms' without going beyond them. He urged them,
instead, to worship One God alone whom the people could know

only in a broad general way but never witness (in any concrete form). The attitude of the 'knowers' toward idol-worship is pious imitation of this attitude of Muḥammad.

Let us go back to the point from which we started. We opened this chapter with a discussion of the problem of 'perplexity' (*ḥayrah*). We are now in a better position to understand the true nature of the 'perplexity' and to see to what extent the ontological structure of Being is really 'perplexing'. A brief consideration of the problem at this stage will make a suitable conclusion to the present chapter.

An infinity of things which are clearly different from each other and some of which stand in marked opposition to one another are, with all the divergencies, one and the same thing. The moment man becomes aware of this fact, it cannot but throw his mind into bewildering confusion. This 'perplexity' is quite a natural state for those who have opened their eyes to the metaphysical depth of Being.

But on reflection it will be realized that the human mind falls into this 'perplexity' because it has not yet penetrated deeply below the level of superficial understanding. In the mind of a sage who has experienced the Unity of Being in its real depth there can no longer be any place for any 'perplexity'. Here follows what Ibn 'Arabī says on this point.[44]

> The 'perplexity' arises because the mind of man becomes polarized (i.e., toward two contradictory directions, one toward the One and the other toward the Many). But he who knows (by the experience of 'unveiling') what I have just explained is no longer in 'perplexity', no matter how many divergent things he may come to know. For (he knows that) the divergence is simply due to the nature of the locus, and that the locus in each case is the eternal archetype itself of the thing. The Absolute goes on assuming different forms in accordance with different eternal archetypes, i.e., different loci of self-manifestation, and the determinate aspects which man perceives of it go on changing correspondingly. In fact, the Absolute accepts every one of these aspects that are attributed to it. Nothing, however, is attributed to it except that in which it manifests itself (i.e., the particular forms of its self-manifestation). And there is nothing at all (in the whole world of Being) except this.[45]

On the basis of this observation al-Qāshānī gives a final judgment concerning the metaphysical 'perplexity'. It is, he says, merely a phenomenon observable in the earliest stage of spiritual development.[46]

> The 'perplexity' is a state which occurs only in the beginning when there still lingers the activity of Reason and the veil of thinking still

remains. But when the 'unveiling' is completed and the immediate intuitive cognition becomes purified, the 'perplexity' is removed with a sudden increase of knowledge coming from the direct witnessing of the One manifesting itself in diverse forms of the archetypes in accordance with the essential requirement of the Name 'All-knowing' (*'alīm*).[47]

Notes

1. *Fuṣ.*, p. 55/72.

2. Cf. Affifi, *Fuṣ.*, Com., p. 40; *Fuṣ.*, p. 56/72–73.

3. Reference to Qoran, XXXVIII, 47.

4. p. 56.

5. *Fuṣ.*, p. 56/73.

6. Qāshānī, p. 56.

7. *Fuṣ.*, p. 57/73.

8. p. 57.

9. *ibid.*

10. i.e., from the point of view of the Names, in whose plane alone there come into existence all these differences in degrees.

11. *Fuṣ.*, p. 58/74.

12. *Fuṣ.*, p. 48/69.

13. p. 48.

14. Qāshānī, *ibid.*

15. *Fuṣ.*, p. 64/77.

16. p. 64.

17. *Fuṣ.*, p. 64/77.

18. The words in parentheses belong to al-Qāshānī, p. 65.

19. *ibid.*

20. It is to be remarked that the multiplication of the mathematical 'one' is described in terms of 'self-manifestation' (*tajallī*) just in the same way as the Absolute is described as 'manifesting itself' in the Many.

21. p. 65, footnote.

22. *Fuṣ.*, p. 65/77–78.

23. i.e., one and the same thing *qua* 'number' is non-existent on the level of the senses, existing only on the level of intellect, but it is, *qua* 'a thing counted', existent on the level of the senses. In other words, it is the 'thing counted' that makes a 'number' exist in a concrete, sensible form. The same applies to the relation between an archetype and a thing which actualizes it in a sensible form.

24. i.e., besides the 'number' and the 'thing counted', there must necessarily be also 'one' which is the ultimate source of all numbers and things counted. But 'one' which thus causes and establishes the numbers is also caused and established by the latter in concrete forms.

25. That is to say: we admit the one-ness (i.e., uniqueness) of each number, while recognizing at the same time the one-ness (i.e., sameness) of all numbers.

26. You affirm of every number that which you negate of it when you consider it in itself. This may be explained in more concrete terms in the following way. You admit the inherence of 'one' in every number; 'one' is the common element of all the numbers and is, in this respect, a sort of genus. But, on the other hand, you know that 'one' is not inherent in every number in its original form but only in a particularized form in each case; 'one' may be considered a sort of species as distinguished from genus. Thus 'one', although it does exist in every number, is no longer the 'one' *per se* in its absoluteness. And this precisely corresponds to the ontological situation in which the Absolute is manifested in everything, but not as the absolute Absolute.

27. *Fuṣ.*, p. 67/78.

28. p. 67.

29.

30. i.e., by a specific self-determination different from the self-determination by which the Absolute became 'man'.

31. *Fuṣ.*, pp. 231–232/183–184.

32. *Fuṣ.*, p. 253/200.

33. 'Water' for Ibn 'Arabī is a symbol of cosmic Life.

34. The idea is that the earth produces only 'earth-like' things, i.e., its own 'duplicates', the symbolic meaning of which is that the things of the world are ultimately of the same nature as the Absolute which is their ontological ground.

35. i.e., the luxuriant vegetation which grows forth from the earth, being of the same nature as the latter, 'doubles' so to speak the earth.

36. This is a difficult passage, and there is a remarkable divergence between the Cairo edition and that of Affifi. The Affifi text reads: *fa-thabata bi-hi wa-khāliqi-hi aḥadīyah al-kathrah* 'thus the unity of the Many becomes established by the world and its Creator'. The Cairo edition, which I follow here, reads: *fa-thunniyat bi-hi wa-yukhālifu-hu aḥadīyah al-kathrah.*

37. *Fuṣ.*, p. 232/184.

38. i.e., what he actually sees in the mirror is always the particular image of a particular object which happens to be there in front of the mirror; he can never see a universal image comprising all the particular images in unity.

39. *Fuṣ.*, p. 233/185.

40. The word *waqt* 'Time' in this context means, as al-Qāshānī remarks, the present moment, or each successive moment as it is actualized (p. 247).

41. *Fuṣ.*, p. 247/196.

42. a view comparable with the atomistic metaphysics of Islamic theology.

43. *Fuṣ.*, p. 247/196.

44. *Fuṣ.*, p. 68/78.

45. All the divergent aspects (*aḥkām*) that are recognizable in the world of Being are so many actualizations of the eternal archetypes. And the eternal archetypes, in their turn, are nothing but so many self-manifestations of the Absolute. In this sense everything *is* ultimately the Absolute. And there is no place for 'perplexity'.

46. p. 68.

47. The archetypes are, as we shall see later in more detail, the eternal essential forms of the things of the world as they exist in the Divine Consciousness. They are born in accordance with the requirement of the Attribute of Omniscience.

VI   The Shadow of the Absolute

In the preceding chapter the special relation between the Absolute and the world has been discussed. We have seen how the Absolute and the world are *contradictorily* identical with one another. The two are ultimately the same; but this statement does not mean that the relation between them is one of simple identification: it means that the Absolute and the world are the same while being at the same time diametrically opposed to each other. The creatures are in essence nothing other than God, but in their determined forms they are far from being the same as God. Rather, they are infinitely distant from God.

Ibn 'Arabī, as we have observed, tries to describe this contradictory situation by various images. 'Shadow' (*ẓill*) is one of them. Using this metaphor he presents his view in a basic proposition: 'The world is the shadow of the Absolute'. The world, as the shadow of the Absolute, is the latter's form, but it is a degree lower than the latter.

> Know that what is generally said to be 'other than the Absolute' or the so-called 'world', is in relation to the Absolute comparable to shadow in relation to the person. The world in this sense is the 'shadow' of God.[1]

It is to be remarked concerning the passage just quoted that in Ibn 'Arabī's thought, there is, strictly speaking, nothing 'other than the Absolute'. This last phrase is merely a popular expression.[2] But the popular expression is not entirely groundless, because philosophically or theologically the world is a concrete phenomenal form of the Divine Names, and the Divine Names are in a certain sense opposed to the Divine Essence. In this respect the world is surely 'other than the Absolute'. The argument of Ibn 'Arabī continues:

> (To say that the world is the shadow of the Absolute) is the same as attributing existence (i.e., concrete, sensible existence) to the world. For shadow surely exists sensibly, except that it does so only when there is something[3] in which it makes its appearance. If there is nothing in which to appear, the shadow would remain merely

intelligible without existing in a sensible form. In such a case, the shadow rather remains *in potentia* in the person to whom it is attributed.

The structure of this phenomenon is made more explicit by al-Qāshānī in the following remark:[4]

> In order that there be shadow there must necessarily be three things: (1) a tall object which casts the shadow, (2) the place where it falls, and (3) light by which alone shadow becomes distinctively existent. The 'object' corresponds to the real Being or the Absolute. The 'place' in which shadow appears corresponds to the archetypal essences of the possible things. If there were no 'place', shadow would never be sensible, but would remain something intelligible like a tree in a seed. It would remain in the state of potentiality in the 'object' which would cast the shadow.
> The 'light' corresponds to the Divine Name the 'Outward'.
> If the world had not come into contact with the Being of the Absolute, the 'shadow' would have never come to exist. It would have remained for ever in the primordial non-existence which is characteristic of the possible things considered in themselves without any relation to their Originator (who brings them into the state of real existence). For 'shadow', in order to exist, needs the 'place' as well as an actual contact with the thing that projects it. God, however, 'existed when there was nothing beside Him', and in that state He was completely self-sufficient having no need of the whole world.

This interpretation by al-Qāshānī makes it clear that the 'shadow' is cast not on what we call the 'world' directly, but on the archetypes of the things. In other words, the 'world' begins to exist on a higher level than the one on which our common sense usually thinks it to exist. The moment the shadow of the Absolute is cast on the archetypes, the world is born, although, strictly speaking, the archetypes themselves are not the 'world' but rather the 'locus of the appearance of the world'.

Shadow, however, does not appear except by the activity of light. This is the reason why we have the Divine Name 'Light' (*nūr*).

> The locus of the appearance of this Divine 'shadow' called the 'world' is the archetypal essences of the possible things.[5] It is on these archetypes that the shadow (first) spreads. And the shadow becomes perceivable in accordance with the amount actually spread of the Being of the One who projects it upon them. The perception of it, however, can take place only in virtue of the Name 'Light'.[6]

It is remarkable that the shadows of things projected on the earth are said to take on a dark, blackish color. This has a symbolic meaning. It symbolizes in the first place that, in the particular case which is our immediate concern, the source of the 'shadow' is a Mystery, an absolutely Unknown-Unknowable. The blackness of shadow indicates, in the second place, that there is a distance between it and its source. Here is what Ibn 'Arabī says on this problem:[7]

> The 'shadow' spreading over the archetypal essences of the possible things, (becomes visible in the primal) manifestation-form of the unknown Mystery (*ghayb*).[8]
> Do you not see how all shadows appear blackish? This fact indicates the inherence of obscurity in the shadows due to an intervening distance in the relation between them and the objects which project them. Thus, even if the object be white, the shadow it casts takes on a blackish color.

As usual al-Qāshānī reformulates what is implied by this passage in more ontological terms:[9]

> The archetypes are dark because of their distance from the light of Being. And when the light which is of a totally different nature from their own darkness spreads over them, their proper darkness of non-Being (*zulmah 'adamīyah*) affects the luminosity of Being, and the light-nature turns toward darkness. In other words, the light of Being turns in this way toward obscurity, just as the shadow does in relation to the thing which casts it. The relation of the relative Being to the absolute Being is exactly like that, so that, if it were not for its being determined by the archetypal essences of the possible things, the absolute Being would shine forth with extreme incandescence and no one would be able to perceive it because of the intensity of the light.
> Thus it comes about that those who are veiled by the darkness of determination see the world but do not see the Absolute, for 'being in utter darkness they do not see' (Qoran, II, 17). But those who have come out of the veils of determinations witness the Absolute, for they have torn asunder the veil of darkness and veiled themselves with light against darkness, i.e., veiled themselves with the Essence against the 'shadow'. Those, however, who are not veiled by either of the two against the other can witness the light of the Absolute in the midst of the blackness and darkness of the creaturely world.

In the following passage Ibn 'Arabī emphasizes the effect of the distance that separates the archetypes from the Absolute in producing the darkish color of the former.[10]

> Do you not see how the mountains, if they happen to be far away from the sight of the man who looks at them, appear black, when in reality they may be quite different in color from what the sense perceives. And the distance is the only cause for this phenomenon. The same is true of the blue of the sky. In fact, anything which is not luminous produces the same kind of effect on the sense when there is a long distance between the object and sight.
> Exactly the same situation is found with regard to the archetypal

essences of the possible things, for they, too, are not luminous by
themselves. (They are not luminous) because they are non-existent
(*ma'dūm*). True, they do possess an ontological status intermediary
between sheer non-existence and pure existence but they do not
possess Being by themselves, because Being is Light.

Another important effect produced by distance on the sense of sight
is that it makes every object look far smaller that it really is. For Ibn
'Arabī this also has a deep symbolic meaning.

> Even the luminous objects, however, appear small to the sense by
> dint of distance. And this is another effect of distance on sense
> perception. Thus the sense does not perceive (distant luminous
> objects) except as very small things, while in reality they are far
> bigger and of greater quantities than they look. For example, it is a
> scientifically demonstrated fact that the sun is one hundred and sixty
> times bigger than the earth. Actually, however, it appears to the
> sense as small as a shield, for instance. This, again, is the effect
> produced by distance.
>
> The world is known just to the same degree as shadow is perceived,
> and the Absolute remains unknown to the same degree as the object
> which casts the shadow remains unknown.
>
> Thus, as long as the 'shadow' (which can be perceived and known) *is*
> the 'shadow' (of the Absolute), the Absolute also is known. But as
> long as we do not know the essential form of the object contained
> within the 'shadow', the Absolute remains unknown.
>
> This is why we assert that the Absolute is known to us in one sense,
> but is unknown to us in another.[11]

The Absolute in this comparison is the source of the 'shadow'. And
the former is known to us to the very extent that 'shadow', i.e., the
world, is known. This amounts to saying, if we continue to use the
same metaphor, that the Absolute is known to us only as something
'small and black'. And this 'something small and black' is what is
generally understood as our God or our Lord. The real Something
which projects this 'shadow' is never to be known. Ibn 'Arabī bases
his argument on a few Qoranic verses which he interprets as he
always does, in his own way.[12]

> 'Hast thou not seen how thy Lord spreads shadow? But if He so
> desired He could make them stand still' (XXV, 45). The phrase
> 'stand still' means 'remain within God in the state of potentiality.'
> God means to say (in this verse): It is not in the nature of the
> Absolute to manifest itself to the possible things (i.e., the archetypes)
> unless there appears first (upon them) its 'shadow'. Yet the 'shadow'
> (in this state and in itself) is no different from those of the possible
> things which have not yet been (actualized) by the appearance of the
> corresponding concrete things in the (phenomenal) world.

When the Absolute 'desires' to manifest itself in the archetypes (and through them in the concrete things), there appears first a dark 'shadow' upon them. The Divine self-manifestation never occurs unless preceded by the appearance of the 'shadow'. But if God so wishes at this stage, the 'shadow' would be made to 'stand still', i.e., it would remain forever in that state of potentiality and would not proceed further toward the level of concrete things. In such a case, the 'shadow' would simply be another possible thing just as the archetypes themselves which have no corresponding realities in the outer world. Ibn 'Arabī goes on:[13]

> 'Then We have made the sun its indicator' (XXV, 45). The sun (which is thus made to be the indicator of the 'shadow') is the Divine Name 'Light' to which reference has already been made. And the sense bears witness to it (i.e., to the fact that the indicator of the 'shadow' is no other than the Light) because shadows have no real existence where there is no light.
> 'Then We withdraw it toward us with an easy withdrawal' (XXV, 46). God withdraws to Himself the 'shadow', because it is His 'shadow' which He Himself has projected. Thus everything appears from Him and goes back to Him, for it is He, no one else.
> Everything you perceive is the Being of the Absolute as it appears through the archetypal essences of the possible things. The same thing, as the He-ness of the Absolute, is its Being, and, as the divergence of forms, is the archetypal essences of the possible things.
> Just as the name 'shadow' does not cease to subsist in it with the divergence of forms, the name 'world' does not cease to subsist in it with the divergence of forms. Likewise the name 'other than the Absolute'.
> In regard to its essential unity in being 'shadow', it is the Absolute, for the latter is the Unique, the One. But in regard to the multiplicity of forms it is the world.

Briefly, this means that the 'shadow', as it spreads over the archetypes, can be observed in two opposed aspects: the aspect of fundamental unity and the aspect of diversity. In fact, the 'shadow', as any physical shadow in this world is one; and in this aspect it turns toward its source. Or rather, it is nothing else than the Absolute itself, because it is a direct projection of the Divine Unity (*aḥad-iyah*). But in its second aspect, the same 'shadow' is already diversified, and is faced toward the world of concrete things; or rather, it is the world itself.

Thus considered, the world in the sense in which we ordinarily understand it has no reality; it is but a product of imagination.[14]

> If the truth is what I have just pointed out to you, the world is an illusion having no real existence in itself. And this is the meaning of imagination. The world, in other words, looks as if it were something independent and subsisting by itself outside the Absolute.

This, however, is not true. Do you not see how in your ordinary sensible experience shadow is so closely tied up with the thing which projects it that it is absolutely impossible for it to liberate itself from this tie?
This is impossible because it is impossible for anything to be detached from itself.

Since the world is in this way the 'shadow' of the Absolute, it is connected with the latter with an immediate tie which is never to be loosened. Every single part of the world is a particular aspect of the Absolute, and is the Absolute in a state of determination. Man, being himself a part of the world, and a very special part at that, because of his consciousness, is in a position to know intimately, within himself, the relation of the 'shadow' to the Absolute. The extent to which a man becomes conscious of this ontological relation determines his degree of 'knowledge'. There naturally result from this several degrees of 'knowledge'.

Know your own essence (*'ayn*, i.e., your archetypal essence). Know who you are (in your concrete existence) and what your He-ness is. Know how you are related with the Absolute; know in what respect you are the Absolute and in what respect you are the 'world', 'other' and something 'different' from the Absolute.
This gives rise to a number of degrees among the 'knowers'. Thus some are simply 'knowers', and some others are 'knowers' in a higher degree.[15]

These degrees of the 'knower' are described in a more concrete form by al-Qāshānī in his Commentary.[16] The lowest is represented by those who witness only the aspect of determination and diversification. They see the created world, and nothing beyond. The second rank is that of those who witness the Unity of Being which is manifested in these forms. They witness the Absolute (but forget about the created world). The third rank witness both aspects. They witness both the creatures and the Absolute as two aspects of one Reality. The fourth in degree are those who witness the whole as one Reality diversifying itself according to various aspects and relations, 'one' in Essence, 'all' with the Names. Those are the people of God who have the real knowledge of God. In terms of 'self-annihilation' (*fanā'*) and 'self-subsistence' (*baqā'*), al-Qāshānī says that those who witness only the Absolute, losing sight of the creatures, are people who are dominated by 'self-annihilation' and 'unification', while those who witness the Absolute in the creatures and the creatures in the Absolute are described as people who have obtained a perfect vision in the state of 'self-subsistence'-after-'self-annihilation' and the view of 'dispersion'-after-'unification'.

Ibn 'Arabī himself compares these spiritual degrees to a naturally colorless light being tinged with various colours as it passes through coloured pieces of glass.[17]

> The relation of the Absolute to a particular 'shadow', small, large, or pure in different degrees, may be compared to the relation of light to a piece of glass intervening between it and the eye of a man who looks at it. The light in such a case assumes the color of the glass, while in itself it is colorless. (The colorless light) appears to the sense of sight as colored – an appropriate comparison for the relation of your own reality with your Lord.
> If you say that the light has become green because of the green color of the glass, you are right. This is evidenced by your sense perception. But if you say that the light is not green nor, indeed, of any color at all, you are also right. You are, in this case, following what is given by your logical reasoning. And your judgment is based on the right activity of Reason.
> See how the light passes through a 'shadow' which is no other than the glass. The glass (is a 'shadow', but it is) a 'shadow' which is of the nature of light because of its transparency.[18]
> In just the same way, when one of us has realized in himself the Absolute, the Form of the latter appears in him more than it does in others. (He who has realized in himself the Absolute is of two different degrees): the first degree is represented by a man whose hearing, sight, and all other faculties and bodily members are the Absolute itself in accordance with the teaching of the Revelation concerning the Absolute.[19] Even in such a case, however, the 'shadow' itself is still there (in the form of his enlightened 'self') because the personal pronoun in '*his* hearing', '*his* sight' etc. refers to the man. He who represents the second (i.e., higher) degree is different from this. A man of this second degree is close to the Being of the Absolute than all others.

As we see, Ibn 'Arabī does not give any detailed description of those of the second degree. He is content with stating that they are closer to the Absolute than others. Al-Qāshānī makes this point more explicit and precise.[20]

> The first is he who has 'annihilated himself' from his own attributes in the Attributes of the Absolute so that the Absolute has taken the place of his attributes. The second is he (who has 'annihilated himself') from his own essence in the Essence of the Absolute so that the Absolute has taken the place of his essence.
> The first is the kind of man who is referred to when we say, 'the Absolute is his hearing, his sight, etc.' . . . Such a man is closer to the Absolute than other (ordinary) believers who act with their own attributes and who remain with their (natural) veils (i.e., the veils of human attributes). His attitude (toward God) is described as the 'closeness of supererogatory works' (*qurb al-nawāfil*). And yet, his 'shadow' itself, i.e., his relative existence, which is no other than his

ego, still subsists in him. And the self-manifestation of the Absolute in such a man occurs and is witnessed in accordance with his own attributes, for the personal pronoun in '*his* hearing' etc. refers to the particularized existence which is the 'shadow'.

Closer still than this closeness is the 'closeness of the obligatory works' (*qurb al-farā'iḍ*) which is represented by the second degree. A man of this second category is one who has 'annihilated himself' totally with his essence and is 'subsistent' in the Absolute. This is the kind of man by whom the Absolute hears and sees. Thus such a man is the hearing of the Absolute itself and the sight of the Absolute. Nay, he is the Form of the Absolute. To him refer God's words: '(when thou threwest,) thou wert not the one who threw, but God it was who really threw' (VIII, 17).

Thus it is clear that, although both categories are men who have realized themselves in the Absolute, the first is inferior to the second in that the 'shadow', that is, man's existence, still remains in the first, and in the view of such men the Absolute and the world stand opposed to each other. This is the standpoint of the 'exterior' (*ẓāhir*), while the second represents the standpoint of the 'interior' (*bāṭin*).

And this makes it also clear that the world, though it is a 'perfect form' in which the Absolute manifests itself with all its perfections, is necessarily a degree lower than the Absolute.

Just as woman is a degree lower than man according to the Divine words: 'men have a degree of superiority over them (i.e., women)' (II, 228), that which has been created in the image (of God) is lower than He who has brought it out to existence in His image. Its being in the image of God (does not prevent it from being lower than its Originator). And by that very superiority by which He is distinguished from the creatures He is completely independent of the whole world and is the Prime Agent. For the 'image' is only a secondary agent and does not possess the priority which belongs to the Absolute alone.[21]

Notes

1. *Fuṣ.*, p. 113/101.

2. *fī al-'urf al-'āmm* as al-Qāshānī says, p. 113.

3. Ibn 'Arabī actually uses a personal form, 'somebody', instead of 'something'.

4. pp. 113–114.

5. The expression *a'yān al-mumkināt* is explained by Jāmī as *a'yān al-mumkināt al-thābitah fī al-ḥaḍrah al-'ilmīyah* (*Sharḥ al-Fuṣūṣ*).

6. *Fuṣ.*, p. 114/102.

7. *Fuṣ.*, p. 114/102.

8. 'The primal manifestation-form of the Mystery' is nothing other than the metaphysical level of Divine Consciousness which is in fact the first visible form assumed by the Mystery (Jāmī).

9. p. 114.

10. *Fuṣ.*, p. 114/102.

11. *Fuṣ.*, p. 115/102.

12. *ibid.*

13. *Fuṣ.*, p. 116/103. Many of the leading commentators give quite a different interpretation to the latter part of the passage just quoted. The difference comes from the fact that they take the particle *ḥattà* in the sense of *kay* or *li-kay* 'in order that', while I take it to mean 'until.' The passage, according to their interpretation, would read: 'It is impossible, in view of the very nature of the Absolute, that it should manifest itself to possible things (i.e., archetypes) in order to produce its own "shadow" in such a way that the "shadow" (once produced) would remain the same as the rest of the possible things to which no reality has yet been actualized in the empirical world.' Thus interpreted, the passage would mean that those archetypes upon which the 'shadow' has been projected immediately obtain an ontological status differentiating them from the other archetypes that have not yet attained any degree of reality. This meaning, however, does not seem to fit in the present context.

14. *Fuṣ.*, p. 117/103.

15. *ibid.*

16. p. 117.

17. *Fuṣ.*, p. 118/103–104.

18. Al-Qāshānī says (p. 103): When the Absolute manifests itself in the world of Command (i.e., in the spiritual world) to pure Spirits and non-corporeal Intellects, the self-manifestation is of the nature of light, because the forms in which the Absolute appears in this domain of pure spirituality are a 'shadow' made of light; it is transparent and has no darkness within. But the light passing through a colored glass is a symbol of the Absolute appearing in the form of a soul tinged with the coloring of the bodily constitution. The intellectual soul (*al-nafs al-nāṭiqah*, i.e., the soul of man), although it is not bodily in itself, becomes turbid and colored by bodily elements.

19. The reference to a famous Tradition in which God Himself speaks in the first person (*ḥadith qudsiy*): 'The servant (i.e. believer) never ceases to strive for super-reogatory works until I love him. And when I do love him, I am his hearing with which he hears and I am his sight with which he sees, etc.'

20. p. 118.

21. p. 273/219.

VII   The Divine Names

The philosophical world-view of Ibn 'Arabī is, concisely stated, a world-view of Divine self-manifestation (*tajallī*), for, as we have seen, as long as the Absolute remains in its absoluteness there can be nothing in existence that may be called the 'world', and the word 'world-view' itself would lose all meaning in the absence of the world.

The principle of *tajallī*, on the world's side, is the 'preparedness' (or ontological aptitude), and the same principle of *tajallī* from the standpoint of the Absolute is constituted by the Divine Names. The present chapter will deal thematically with the problem of *tajallī* in so far as it directly bears upon the Divine Names.

Islamic theology discusses as one of the basic themes the question whether a Name (*ism*) is or is not the same as the 'object named' (*musammà*). Ibn 'Arabī gives his answer to this theological question by saying that a Name and its 'object named' are the same in one sense and different from each other in another sense.

The reason why they are one and the same thing is that all the Divine Names, in so far as they invariably refer to the Absolute, are nothing but the 'object named' (i.e., the Essence [*dhāt*] of the Absolute) itself. Each name is a special aspect, or special form, of the Absolute in its self-manifestation. And in this sense, each Name is identical with the Essence. All the Divine Names, in other words, are 'the realities of the relations' (*ḥaqā'iq al-nisab*),[1] i.e., the relations which the One Reality bears to the world, and in this respect they are all the Divine Essence itself viewed from the standpoint of the various special relations which are caused by the phenomenon of Divine self-manifestation.

The relations which the Absolute can possibly bear to the world are infinite, that is, to use Ibn 'Arabī's peculiar terminology, the forms of the Divine self-manifestation are infinite in number. Consequently, the Divine Names are infinite. However, they can be classified and reduced to a certain number of basic Names. For example, it is generally recognized that the Qoran gives ninety-nine Names of God.

These Names, whether infinite or finite in number, can also be considered by themselves independently of the Essence to which they refer. In other words, they can be regarded as so many independent Attributes. Considered in this way, each Name has its own 'reality' (*ḥaqīqah*) by which it is distinguished from the rest of the Names. And in this respect, a Name is different from the 'object named'.

Ibn 'Arabī explains this point by making reference to the famous Sufi of the West, Abū al-Qāsim b. Qasī (d. 1151).[2]

This is what is meant by Abū al-Qāsim b. Qasī when he says in his book *Taking Off The Sandals* that every Divine Name carries in itself all the Divine Names and all their properties; this because every Name indicates both the Essence and the particular meaning of which it is the Name and which is especially required by the latter. Thus every single Name, in so far as it points to the Essence, contains all the Names, but in so far as it points to its own proper meaning, is different from all the rest, like 'Lord', 'Creator' or 'Giver of the forms' etc. The Name, in short, is the same as the 'object named' in regard to the Essence, but it is not the same as the 'object named' in regard to its own particular meaning.

Thus the most conspicuous feature of the Divine Names is their double structure, that is, their having each two designations. Each Name designates, and points to, the unique Essence, while pointing to a meaning or reality which is not shared by any other Name.

In the first aspect, every Name is one and the same as all other Names, because they all are indicative of the same Essence. In this respect, even such Names as appear to contradict each other (e.g., 'All-Forgiving' and 'Revenger', 'Outward' and 'Inward', 'First' and 'Last') are identical with each other.

In the second aspect, on the contrary, each Name is something independent, something having its own peculiar reality. It definitely distinguishes itself from all others. The 'Outward' is not the same as the 'Inward'. And what a distance between the 'First' and the 'Last'!

It will have been made clear to you (by what precedes) in what sense each Name is the same as another and in what sense it is different from another. Each Name, in being the same as others, is the Absolute, and in being 'other' than others, is the 'Absolute as it appears as a particular image' (*al-ḥaqq al-mutakhayyal*). Glory be to Him who is not indicated by anything other than Himself and whose existence is established by nothing other than Himself and whose existence is established by nothing other than His own self![3]

The 'Absolute as it appears in particular images', i.e., the world, is nothing but the whole sum of the Divine Names as concretely actualized. And since it is the sole indicator of the absolute Absolute, the latter, after all, is not indicated by anything other than itself. The Absolute indicates itself by itself, and its concrete existence is established by itself. Ibn 'Arabī cannot withold his profound admiration for the beauty and the grandeur of this structure.

We discussed in Chapter V the relation between the One and the Many. In terms of the main topic of the present chapter, the Many are the forms of the Absolute actualized in accordance with the requirements of the Names. The Many are the 'Absolute as it appears in particular images', i.e., the Absolute 'imagined' under the particular forms of the Names. And from this point of view, the One is the Essence (*dhāt*) which is indicated by the Names and to which return all the Names. At this juncture Ibn 'Arabī uses an interesting expression, 'the names of the world' (*asmā' al-'ālam*), as a counterpart to the Divine Names (*al-asmā' al-ilāhīyah*).[4]

> Whatever really exists in the world of Being is solely what is indicated by (the word) 'unity' (*aḥadīyah*), whereas whatever exists only in imagination is what is indicated by 'multiplicity' *(kathrah)*. Therefore he who sticks to the multiplicity stands on the side of the world, the Divine Names and the names of the world, while he who takes the position of the Unity stands on the side of the Absolute. The Absolute here is the Absolute considered in the Essence which is completely independent of the whole world, not in its aspect of Divinity (i.e., being God) and its phenomenal forms.

In this passage Ibn 'Arabī states that the Absolute in its Essence is completely 'independent', i.e., has absolutely no need of the world. It is to be remarked that having no need of the world is the same as having no need of the Divine Names. The Names are, as we have observed above, the relations in which the Absolute stands to the creatures. They are there because of, and in the interests of, the creatures. The Essence in itself is not something which cannot subsist apart from such centrifugal relations. What needs the Names is not the Absolute, but the created world. He says:[5]

> If the Essence is completely independent of the whole world, this independence must be the same independence by which the Essence transcends the Names to be attributed to it. For the Names indicate not only the Essence but particular 'objects named'[6] which are different from the Essence. This is evidenced by the very effect of the Names.[7]

Thus, the Divine Names, in their centrifugal side turning toward multiplicity-diversity, are definitely 'other' than the Absolute, and the Absolute maintains its 'independence' in regard to them. But in their centripetal side turning toward the Essence, all the Divine Names are ultimately one because they are reducible to the

Absolute. And in this second aspect, the Absolute at the level of the Names is One as it is at the level of its absoluteness. The Absolute is in this way. One in two different senses.[8]

The Unity of God on the level of the Divine Names which require (the existence of) us (i.e., the phenomenal world) is the Unity of multiplicity (*aḥadīyah al-kathrah*). And the Unity of God in the sense of being completely 'independent' of us and even of the Names is the Unity of essence (*aḥadīyah al-'ayn*). Both aspects are called by the same name: 'One'.

The Unity of multiplicity here spoken of is also called the Unity of 'unification' (*aḥadīyah al-jam'*). It plays an exceedingly important role in the world-view of Ibn 'Arabī, as we have already seen in what precedes and as we shall see in more detail in what follows. In brief, it is a position which recognizes multiplicity existing *in potentia* in the Absolute which is essentially One.[9]

We have observed above that the Absolute, in so far as it is the Absolute, does not need the Names, and that it is the creatures that need them. The latter half of this statement, namely, that the world needs the Divine Names, may be formulated in more philosophical terms by saying that the Names have the property of causality (*'illīyah* or *sababīyah*). From this point of view, the Divine Names are the 'cause' (*'illah* or *sabab*) for the existence of the world. The world needs the Divine Names in the sense that nothing in the world can exist without them.

There can be no doubt that the world stands in essential need of many causes. And the greatest of all the causes which it needs is the Absolute. But the Absolute can act as the cause needed by the world only through the Divine Names as its cause.
By 'Divine Names' here is meant every Name that is needed by the world (as its cause), whether it be part of the world itself or the very Absolute. In either case it is God, nothing else.[10]

This passage makes it clear that, in Ibn 'Arabī's view, if the world essentially needs as its cause the Absolute, it does not need the Absolute in its absoluteness but in its various aspects, such as 'creativity', 'Lordship', etc. In other words, the Absolute on the level of the Names is the 'cause' of the world's existence. Regarding the latter half of the passage, nothing, I think, could make its meaning more lucid than the following explanation by al-Qāshānī.[11]

The Divine Names are the very things which are needed by the world (as its causes). (Two cases are distinguished). The first is when the Name needed is something similar to the thing which needs it: e.g., 'son' needs 'father' in his existence, sustenance and maintenance. In such a case the things needed are nothing but concrete forms taken by the Names of the Absolute, i.e., their concrete manifestations. The second case occurs when the thing needed is (directly) the Absolute itself: e.g., the 'son' is in need of the Absolute, the Former, the Creator, in having his own form, figure and character. This is different from (the first case in which) he needs something similar to himself (e.g., 'father').

In either case, however, the Name needed is no other than the Name 'Allah'. (This may not be clear) in the first case, (but that it is so will be known from the following consideration). The causality of 'father' does not lie in the permanent archetype of 'father', for the latter is (actually) non-existent. The causality of 'father' comes from 'father' in its real existence, his action, and his power. But the existence (of 'father') is essentially nothing but the Absolute as manifested in a locus of self-manifestation; and the action, the form, the ability, the power, the sustenance, and the maintenance – all these are but what naturally follows from existence: they are but Attributes of the Absolute and its Actions (in concrete forms). What properly pertains to 'father' is only being-receptive and being-a-locus-of-Divine-self-manifestation. As you already know, however, the one who merely receives has no positive activity; the positive activity belongs only to the One which manifests itself in (the receiver as) its locus of self-manifestation. (The causality of the Absolute) in the second case is too obvious to need explanation.

The gist of the argument may conveniently be given in the following way: in the second case in which the world directly needs God, God is the 'cause' of the world; but in the first case, too, in which the things in the world need each other in the form of a cause-caused relation, it is again God who is the ultimate 'cause' of everything. When, for example, 'son' needs 'father', it is the causality of God that is working through the medium of 'father'.

We see in this way that everything in this world, every event which occurs in this world, is an actualization of a Divine Name, that is to say, a self-manifestation of the Absolute through a definite relative aspect called Divine Name. The conclusion to be drawn from this is that there are as many Divine Names as there are things and events in the world. The Divine Names in this sense are infinite in number.

The Names of God are limitless because they become known by what comes out of them and what comes out of them is limitless.[12] However, they are reducible to a limited number of basic Names (*uṣūl*, lit. 'roots') which are the 'Mothers' of Names or, we might say, the 'Presences' (i.e., basic dimensions) of all the Names.

The truth of the matter is that there is only one Reality (*ḥaqīqah*) that receives all these relations and relative aspects which are called the Divine Names. And this same Reality requires that each of these Names that come into appearance limitlessly should have its own reality which distinguishes it from all other Names. The Name is this reality which distinguishes each individual Name, not that thing (i.e., the Reality) which is common to all. This situation is comparable to the fact that the Divine gifts are distinguished from each other by their individual natures, though they are all from one source.

It is evident that *this* is different from *that*, and the reason for this difference lies in the individual distinction of each Name. Thus in the Divine world, however wide it is, nothing repeats itself. This is a truly fundamental fact.[13]

Here again, as we see, we are brought back to the basic dictum: the One is the Many and the Many are the One. Only the dictum is here interpreted topically in terms of the Divine Names. The Many, i.e. the Divine Names, determine a point of view from which there is not even one thing that is the same as some other thing, because 'nothing repeats itself' in the world. Even 'one and the same thing' is not in reality the same in two successive moments.[14] In general, any two things that are normally considered the same are not in reality the 'same'; they are merely 'similar to each other' (*shab-īhān*). And of course, 'similar to each other' means 'different from each other' (*ghayrān*).[15] However, from the point of view of the Essence, not only similar things but things that are widely different from each other, are one and the same thing.

> The sage who knows the truth sees multiplicity in 'one'; likewise, he knows that the Divine Names, even though their (individual) realities are different and many, all point to one single Entity. This (difference among the Names) is but a multiplicity of an intelligible nature (i.e., existent only in *potentia*) in the reality of the One. And this (intelligible multiplicity) turns into sensible multiplicity to be witnessed in one single Reality, when (the One) manifests itself (in the world). The situation may be best understood by what happens to Prime Matter (*hayūlā*) as it enters the inner structure of every 'form'. In spite of their multiplicity and diversity, all the 'forms' ultimately are reducible to one single substance which is their 'matter'. And 'he who knows himself' in this way 'knows his Lord', because (the Lord) has created him in His own image, nay, He is the very He-ness of the man and his true reality.[16]

All the Divine Names point to one single Reality, and in this sense they are, as we have just seen, all one. This, however, does not mean that all the Names stand on an equal level. On the contrary, a difference of degrees or ranks is observable among them. This difference of ranks corresponds to the difference of ranks among the things of the world. And this is natural because, in Ibn 'Arabī's view, the Divine Names owe their very existence to the ontological requirements of the things. Ibn 'Arabī explains this difference of ranks among the Names in the following terms:[17]

There is absolutely nothing except it (i.e., the Absolute).[18] However, there must also be a certain respect in which we are obliged to use language of discrimination in order to account for the (observable) existence of 'higher' and 'lower' in the world, so that we might be able to talk about (for example) *this* man being 'more' learned than *that*, notwithstanding the essential unity (of 'knowledge') itself.[19] This implies (that there is a similar difference in rank between Attributes; that, for example,) the Will, in respect to the number of its objects, is inferior to Knowledge.

Although Will and Knowledge are both Attributes of God and are one in this aspect, Will is lower than Knowledge. But that same Will is higher than Power. This because, generally speaking, 'will' begins to work only after one 'knows' something, and 'will' not only precedes 'power' but covers a wider field than the latter. Exactly the same kind of superior-inferior relation obtains among all the Divine Names. The thing to which they all point, that is, the Essence, stands on a transcendental height above all comparisons and relations, but the things other than the Divine Essence are different in ranks, some being 'higher' and others 'lower'. Concerning the transcendental height of the Essence Ibn 'Arabī says:[20]

The Transcendent (*al-'aliy*) in itself is that which possesses the (absolute) perfection (*kamāl*) in which are engulfed all existent things as well as non-existent relations[21] in such a way that there can absolutely be no property that is not found therein, whether it be something which is considered 'good' according to convention, Reason, and the Divine Law, or something to be judged 'bad' by the same standards. And this is a state of affairs which is observable exclusively in what is designated by the Name *Allāh*.

This passage is explicated by al-Qāshānī as follows:[22]

The Transcendent with a real and essential – not a relative – height, possesses an absolute perfection which comprises all the perfections pertaining to all things. The perfections comprised are (exhaustive), covering as they do both those that are positively existent and those that are in the nature of non-existence; some of them are 'good' in every possible aspect, and some of them are 'bad' in a certain respect. This last point may be understood if one remembers that some of the perfections are essentially of a relative nature and are 'bad' in relation to some of the things; e.g., the valor of a lion in relation to his prey. But the *absolute* perfection must not lack even one property or ethical qualification or action. Otherwise, it would be imperfect in that particular aspect.

Ibn 'Arabī asserts that such an essential height and an absolute perfection can only belong to the One as determined by the primary self-determination on the level of the Oneness (*wāḥidīyah*) which gathers together all the Names. And this is the Greatest Name (*al-ism al-a'ẓam*) which is the very thing designated by the Name *Allāh* or the Name Merciful (*al-raḥmān*).[23] In this state, all the Divine Names which have a positive effect (on the things of the world) are considered together as a unity; they are not considered in their aspect of multiplicity.

Such is 'God' as the comprehensive whole unifying all the Names. As to 'what is *not* the thing designated by the Name *Allāh*', i.e., all things that are not God, Ibn 'Arabī distinguishes two kinds: (1) that which is a locus of theophany (*majlà*, i.e. the place of *tajallī*), and (2) that which is a form (*ṣūrah*) in God, the word 'form' in this context meaning a particular Name by which the Divine Essence becomes determined.

> 'What is not the thing designated by the Name *Allāh*' is either a locus of the self-manifestation of it or a form subsisting in it. In the former case, it is quite natural that there should occur a difference of ranks between individual loci. In the second case, the 'form' in question is the very essential perfection (belonging, as we have seen, to the Transcendent) for the form is nothing other than what is manifested in it (i.e., the Transcendent itself), so that what belongs to that which is designated by the Name *Allāh* must also belong to the form.[24]

The meaning of this seemingly obscure passage may be made explicit in the following way. In case 'other than God' signifies a locus of theophany, the One Absolute is witnessed in the concrete things of the world as so many loci of theophany. In this case the Absolute assumes various different aspects in accordance with the natures of the individual things. And there naturally arise various ranks and degrees according to the more-or-less of the self-manifestation.[25] But in case 'other than God' signifies a 'form' in God, various forms are witnessed in the Absolute itself. And in this case, each one of the forms will possess the very same essential perfection which is possessed by the whole, i.e., God. If God possesses perfection, the same perfection must necessarily be possessed by each 'form' because the latter appears in nothing other than God.

The existents thus differ ontologically from each other in rank, but taken as a whole, they constitute among themselves a well-organized order. And this ontological order corresponds to the order formed by the Divine Names.

Two things are worth remarking concerning this theologico-ontological hierarchy. (1) A higher Name implicitly contains all the Names that are lower than itself. And, correspondingly, a higher existent, as a locus of the self-manifestation of a higher Name, contains in itself all the lower existents. (2) Every single Name, regardless of its rank in the hierarchy, contains in a certain sense all the other Names. And, correspondingly, every single part of the world contains all the other parts of the world. Ibn 'Arabī says:[26]

When you assign a higher rank to a Divine Name, you are thereby calling it (implicitly) by all the Names (that stand lower than it) and attributing to it all the properties (that belong to the Names of lower ranks). The same is true of the things of the world; every higher being possesses the capacity of comprehending all that is lower than itself.

However, every particle of the world is (virtually) the whole of the world, that is, every single particle is capable of receiving into itself all the realities of all single particles of the world. So the observed fact, for instance, that Zayd is inferior to 'Amr in knowledge does not in any way prevent the same He-ness of the Absolute being the very essence of Zayd and 'Amr; nor does it prevent the He-ness being more perfect, more conspicuous in 'Amr than in Zayd.

This situation corresponds to the fact that the Divine Names differ from each other in rank while being all no other than the Absolute. Thus, for example, God as 'Knower' is more comprehensive, regarding the domain covered, than God as 'Willer' or 'Powerful', and yet God is God in every case.

Of the numerous Divine Names, the greatest and most comprehensive, and the most powerful one is the 'Merciful' (*raḥmān*). It is a 'comprehensive' (*shāmil*) Name in that it gathers all the Names together into a unity. And the Absolute on this level of unity is called *Allāh*. In the following two chapters these two Names will be discussed in detail.

Notes

1. *Fuṣ.*, p. 193/153.

2. *Fuṣ.*, p. 70/79–80.

3. *Fuṣ.*, p. 119/104.

4. *Fuṣ.*, p. 120/104–105.

5. *ibid.*

6. i.e., particular Attributes which are, more concretely, various particular aspects of the world.

7. i.e., the fact that the Names indicate besides the Essence the special aspects of the world as something different from the Essence is clearly shown by the created world itself which is the very effect of the Names.

8. *Fuṣ.*, p. 121/105.

9. Ibn 'Arabī here distinguishes between two types of *aḥadīyah* or 'Unity'. In his technical terminology, the first kind of Unity, i.e., the Unity of multiplicity at the ontological stage of Divine Names and Attributes, is specifically called *wāḥidīyah* 'Oneness (of Many)' and is thereby strictly distinguished from the absolute, pure Unity (aḥadīyah), the Unity of Divine Essence. It will be well to remember that there is in his system one more basic type of *aḥadīyah*. It is the Unity of 'actions and effects' (*aḥadīyah al-afʿāl wa-al-āthār*) and is symbolized by the name of the prophet Hūd. Al-Qāshānī (p. 123) refers to these three types of Unity as follows: 'There are three degrees in the Unity. The first is the Unity of the Essence. (God is called at this stage *aḥad* "One" or "Unique" in a non-numerical sense). The second is the Unity of the Names. This is the stage of Divinity, and God is called at this stage *wāḥid* "One" in a numerical sense). The third is the Unity of Lordship (*rubūbīyah*) or the Unity of actions and effects'. This last kind of Unity means that whatever we may do in this world, whatever may happen in this world, everything is 'walking along the straight road'. Everything, every event, occurs in strict accordance with the law of Being (which is nothing other than the Absolute). All are 'one' in this sense.

10. *Fuṣ.*, p. 122/105–106.

11. p. 122.

12. 'The Essence as the Unity is, in relation to each single thing that comes out of it, a particular Name. Thus whenever a determination comes into being there is a Name therein. And the relations (of the Essence with the things of the world) are limitless because the receptacles (i.e., the things that receive the self-manifestation of the Absolute) and their natural dispositions are limitless. Thus it comes about that the Names of God are limitless' – al-Qāshānī, p. 38.

13. *Fuṣ.*, pp. 38–39/65.

14. This is the concept of the 'ever new creation' (*khalq jadīd*), which will be discussed in detail later.

15. *Fuṣ.*, p. 152/124–125.

16. *ibid.*

17. *Fuṣ.*, p. 193/153.

18. He means to say: since everything is a self-manifestation of the Absolute through a particular Name, all that exist in the world are nothing but the Absolute.

19. This example properly concerns only the existence of degrees in one single attribute called 'knowledge'. But the real intention of Ibn 'Arabī is to maintain that there is also a difference of degrees between 'knowledge' itself and other attributes.

20. *Fuṣ.*, p. 69/79.

21. As we have observed before, the relations (*nisab*) are in themselves essentially non-existent.

22. p. 69.

23. On *Allāh* = the Merciful see the next two chapters which will be devoted specifically to this question.

24. *Fuṣ.*, p. 69/79.

25. If, for example, all the Divine Names are actualized in a thing, it will be the Perfect Man, while if the most of the Names are manifested, it will be an ordinary (non-perfect) man, and if the number of the Names manifested happens to be far less than that, it will be an inanimate thing – al-Qāshānī, p. 69.

26. *Fuṣ.*, pp. 193–194/153.

VIII   Allah and the Lord

One of the cardinal elements of Ibn 'Arabī's thought on God is the theologico-ontological difference between *Allāh* and the Lord (*rabb*). In the Chapter of Noah (Qoran, LXXI) to which reference was made before, Noah addressing himself to God uses the expression 'O my lord (*rabb-i*)',[1] he does not say 'O my God (*ilāh-i*)'. In this Ibn 'Arabī find a special meaning.

> Noah said 'O my Lord', he did not say 'O my God'. This because the 'Lord' has a rigid fixity (*thubūt*), while 'God' (*ilāh*) is variable with the Names in such a way that 'He is every day in a new state'.[2]

This short passage contains the gist of Ibn 'Arabī's thought on the difference and relation between *Allāh* and the Lord. It may be explicated as follows.

The Lord is the Absolute as manifested through a particular concrete Name, while *Allāh* is the Absolute who never ceases to change and transform Himself from moment to moment according to the Names. The Lord has a rigid 'fixity' in the sense that it is the Absolute in one particular aspect being bound and determined by one particular Name or Attribute suitable for the occasion. Hence a very particular relation between the Lord and man; namely, that man, whenever he prays to God and makes petition or supplication to Him, he must necessarily address himself to *his* Lord. An ailing man prays to God not vaguely and generally but in the 'fixed' form of the 'Healer' (*shāfī*). Likewise, a sinner asking for Divine forgiveness supplicated the 'All-forgiving' (*ghafūr*). And he who wants something prays to the 'Giver' (*muʿṭī*),[3] etc.

God under each of these and other similar Names is the Lord of the particular man who prays from a particular motive. Hence al-Qāshānī's definition[4] of the Lord: the Lord is the Essence taken with a particular Attribute through which (the man who prays) obtains what he needs; thus it is, of all the Divine Names, the most suitable one for the occasion which motivates the man when he addresses himself to God. This is the reason why Noah, in the Qoranic verse in questions, says 'my Lord'. Lordship (*rubūbīyah*) in this sense means the truly personal relationship of each individual man with God. It is to be remarked that this individual relationship is also of an ontological nature. In the Qoran (XIX, 55) it is related that Ismāʻīl (Ishmael) 'was approved by his Lord', that is, his Lord was satisfied with Ishmael. But if we understand the phrase 'his Lord' in the particular sense in which Ibn ʻArabī understands it, we must admit that not only Ishmael but every being is approved by *his* Lord. As Ibn ʻArabī says:[5]

> Indeed, every being is approved by his Lord. From the fact, however, that every being is approved by his Lord it does not follow necessarily that every being is approved by the Lord of another creature. This is because every being has chosen a particular form of Lordship from among all (the possible types of Lordship contained in the absolute Lordship) and not from one single Lordship (commonly shared by all). Every being has been given out of the (infinitely variable) whole only what particularly fits it, and that precisely is *its* Lord.

As al-Qāshānī says,[6] 'the Lord (i.e., its Lord) demands of every being only that which (naturally) appears in it, while the being, in its turn, because of its 'preparedness', does not demand of its Lord except those attributes and actions that its Lord causes to appear in it (naturally)'. In other words, when the Absolute manifests itself in each individual being, it is able to do so only through one particular Name because of the natural limitation set by the 'preparedness' of that particular being. But this is exactly what is willed by the Absolute and what is desired by the recipient, there being no discordance between the two parties. And this is what is meant by everything being approved by its own Lord.

It must be noticed that Ibn ʻArabī is no longer speaking of the personal relationship between a man and his Lord established by the act of prayer and supplication, but has clearly shifted his interest to the ontological aspect of the problem. And in fact, there *is* an ontological aspect to the personal relation between each individual being and his Lord.

In the phenomenon of 'prayer', from which Ibn ʻArabī has started, each single Name has been regarded as representing a particular aspect of the Absolute. But a Divine Name, in order to actualize, necessarily requires a particular being. A particular being in that capacity is a locus of the self-manifestation of that Name. And in this context, each individual being, as a locus in which a particular Name is manifested, maintains with the Absolute the same individual relationship as in the 'prayer' context. Only it maintains the same individual relationship, this time, on the ontological level.

It follows from this that each individual being or thing, at each particular moment, picks up only one out of many Names, and the Name chosen behaves as his or its Lord. Looking at the situation from the reverse side, we can express the same thing by saying that it never happens that the Absolute should manifest itself as it is in its original Oneness, i.e., the comprehensive unity of the Names, in any being. Ibn 'Arabī goes on to say:[7]

> No being can establish a particular Lord-servant relationship with the Absolute on the level of Unity. This is why the true sages have denied the possibility of Divine self-manifestation (*tajallī*) on the level of Unity. . . .[8]

The Absolute on the level of Oneness is a synthesis of all Names, and as such, no one single being is able to contain it. Only the world as an integral whole can actualize the Oneness of the Names and offer an ontological counterpart to it. However, Ibn 'Arabī seems to admit one exceptional case. As al-Qāshānī says, the exception arises in the case of the Perfect Man. Unlike ordinary men, the Perfect Man actualizes and manifests not one single particular Name but all the Names in their synthesis. An ordinary man is approved by his particular Lord. The latter is *his* Lord; not the Lord of other people. So that no ordinary man is in direct relation with the absolute Lord (*al-rabb al-muṭlaq*). The Perfect Man, on the contrary, actualizes in himself all the attributes and actions of the One who approves of him not as *his* Lord alone but as the absolute Lord.

The expression, 'the absolute Lord', used by al-Qāshānī corresponds to the Qoranic expression, 'the Lord of the worlds' (*rabb al-'alamīn*, and is equivalent to 'the Lord of all Lords' (*rabb al-arbāb*) or *Allāh*. Thus the statement that, in normal cases, the Names in their original synthesis can never be actualized in any single being, amounts to the same thing as saying that *Allāh* as such cannot be the Lord of any particular individual.

> Know that the object designated by the Name *Allāh* is unitary (*aḥadiy*) in regard to the Essence, and a synthesis (*kull*) in regard to the Names. Every being is related to *Allāh* only in the form of his particular Lord; it is impossible for any being to be related to *Allāh* directly in the original form of synthesis. . . .
> And blessed indeed is he who is approved by his Lord! But, properly speaking, there is no one who is not approved by his Lord, because he (i.e., every individual) is just the thing by which the Lordship of the Lord subsists. Thus every individual being is approved by his Lord, and every individual being is happy and blessed.[9]

In the latter half of this passage an intimate reciprocal relationship is affirmed between each individual being and his Lord. It goes without saying that every being depends essentially on his Lord for his existence. But the Lord also depends, in a certain sense, upon the receptive ability (*qābilīyah*)[10] of the individual being of whom He is the Lord. The Lord can never be a Lord without there being someone to be 'lorded over' (*marbūb*). Ibn 'Arabī refers at this point to the following dictum left by Sahl al-Tustarī, a famous Sufi-theologian of the ninth century.[11]

> 'The Lordship has a secret, and that (secret) is thyself' – here (by saying *thyself*) Sahl is addressing himself to every individual being that exists in concrete reality – 'if it were nullified,[12] the Lordship itself would come to naught'. Remark well that Sahl says *if*, which implies an impossibility of the actual occurrence of the event in question. In other words, this (secret) will never be nullified, and, consequently, the Lordship will never come to naught. For there can be no existence for any being except by virtue of its Lord, but as a matter of fact every individual being is forever existent (if not in the physical world, at least in some of the non-physical dimensions of reality). Thus the Lordship will forever be existent.

As has been suggested in the preceding more than once, the 'Lord', in Ibn 'Arabī's thought, is considered on two different levels: (1) 'absolute' (*muṭlaq*) and (2) 'relative' (*iḍāfiy*). The Lord on the 'absolute' level is *Allāh*, while on the second level the Lord is the Lord of one particular being and is an actualized form of one particular Name. From the viewpoint of the concept itself of 'Lord' (*rabb*), the 'relative' is the proper case, the Lord in the 'absolute' sense being only an extremely exceptional case. This fact is explained by al-Qāshānī in the following way:[13]

> *Rabb* is properly a relative term and necessarily requires its object (*marbūb*, lit. 'the one who is lorded over'). The word *rabb* in Arabic is used in three senses: (1) 'possessor', e.g. *rabb al-dār* (the possessor of the house), *rabb al-ghanam* (the possessor of the cattle) etc., (2) 'master', e.g., *rabb al-qawm* (the master of the people), *rabb al-'abīd* (the master of the slaves) etc., (3) 'one who brings up', e.g., *rabb al-ṣabī* (the one who brings up the boy), *rabb al-ṭifl* (one who brings up the infant) etc.
>
> The word *rabb* is not applicable in the non-relative sense except to the Lord of the whole universe. In this case we say *al-rabb* with a definite article (without mentioning the 'object' of Lordship). Thereby is meant *Allāh* alone. And to Him belongs in an essential way the Lordship in the three meanings distinguished above, while to anybody other than *Allāh* the lordship belongs only accidentally. For 'other than *Allāh*' is but a locus in which it (i.e., the Lordship belonging properly to *Allāh*) is manifested.
>
> Thus Lordship is an attribute properly belonging to one single thing (i.e., *Allāh*) but appearing in many forms (as 'relative' lordships). Everybody in whom it is manifested possesses an accidental lordship

in accordance with the degree to which he is given the power of free disposal which he may exercise over his possessions, slaves or children.

Since the attribute of Lordship differs from locus to locus in its self-manifestation, there necessarily arise a number of degrees. Thus he who has been given a stronger control (over his possessions) than others has naturally a higher lordship.

Thus we see that the 'Lord', whether 'absolute' or 'relative', essentially requires an object over which to exercise the Lordship. The *rabb*, in short, cannot subsist without *marbūb*. And this holds true even when the Lord in question happens to be no other than God. The only one who does not need anything other than himself is, as we know, the Absolute in its absoluteness, i.e., the Divine Essence.

The Divine Names are essentially the same as the Named. And the Named is (ultimately) no other than God. (But a difference comes into being because) the Names (unlike the Essence) do not cease to require the realities which they themselves produce. And the realities which the Names require are nothing other than the world. Thus Divinity (*ulūhiyah*, i.e., the Absolute's being God) requires the object to which it appears as God (*ma'lūh*, lit. an object which is 'god-ed'), as Lordship requires its own object (*marbub* 'lord-ed'). Otherwise, i.e., apart from the world, it (i.e., Divinity or Lordship) has no reality of its own.

What is absolutely free from any need of the world is solely the Absolute *qua* Essence. The Lordship has no such property.

Thus Reality is reducible to two aspects: what is required by the Lordship on the one hand, and, on the other, the complete independence from the world which is rightly claimed by the Essence. But (we may go a step further and reduce these two aspects to one, because) in reality and in truth the Lordship is nothing other than the Essence itself.[14]

We come to know in this way that the 'Lord' is no other than the Essence (*dhāt*) considered as carrying various relations (*nisab*). We must not forget, however, that these relations are no real entities subsisting in the Divine Essence. They are simply so many subjective points of view peculiar to the human mind which cannot by nature approach the Divine Essence except through them.

Incidentally, we have seen, in the above-quoted passage, Ibn 'Arabī making a distinction between Divinity (*ulūhiyah*) and Lordship (*rubūbiyah*). The Divinity represents, as al-Qāshānī says,[15] the 'Presence' or ontological plane of the Names, that is, of those Names that belong to the Absolute considered as God. In this plane, the Absolute (*qua* God) is the object of veneration, praise, awe, fear, prayer, and obedience on the part of the creatures. The Lordship is the 'Presence of actions (af'āl)', i.e., the plane of those Names that are specifically concerned with Divine actions in administering, sustaining, and controlling the affairs of the creatures.

Notes

1. LXXI, 5, 21, 26.

2. *Fuṣ.*, p. 57/73.

3. Cf. Affifi, *Fuṣ.*, Com., p. 42.

4. p. 57.

5. *Fuṣ.*, p. 95/91.

6. p. 95.

7. *Fuṣ.*, p. 95/91–92.

8. In this passage Ibn 'Arabī uses the term 'Unity' (*aḥadīyah*) in the sense of *wāḥidīyah*. It goes without saying that there can be no exterior *tajallī* on the level of *aḥadīyah*, because, as we have seen in the earlier contexts, *aḥadīyah* is the absolute state of Essence (*dhāt*) before it begins to split itself into the Names. The real intention of Ibn 'Arabī in this passage, however, is to assert that even on the level of the Oneness (*wāḥidīyah*) where the Absolute is 'God comprising and unifying all the Names into one' no individual being is able to be a locus of the self-manifestation of the Oneness in its integrity.

9. *Fuṣ.*, pp. 93–94/90–91.

10. Qāshānī, p. 94.

11. *Fuṣ.*, p. 94/90–91.

12. As Affifi (Com., p. 87) says, the word *ẓahara* 'appear', 'be disclosed' here has a meaning diametrically opposed to the usual one; namely, that it must be understood in the meaning of *zāla* 'disappear' or 'cease to exist'. Many examples of this usage of the word can be adduced from ancient poetry.

13. pp. 262–263.

14. *Fuṣ.*, p. 143/119.

15. pp. 143–144.

IX Ontological Mercy

The two preceding chapters will have made it clear that there is a difference of ranks among the Divine Names, and that a higher Name virtually contains in itself all the Names of lower ranks. If such is the case, then it is natural for us to suppose that there must be in this hierarchy the highest, i.e., the most comprehensive, Name that contains all the rest of the Names. And in fact, according to Ibn 'Arabī, there actually is such a Name: 'Merciful' (*Raḥmān*). The present chapter will be devoted to a detailed consideration of Ibn 'Arabī's thought concerning this highest Name, its nature and its activity.

From the very beginning, the concept of Divine Mercy was a dominant theme in Islamic thought. The Qoran emphasizes constantly and everywhere the boundless Mercy of God shown toward the creatures. The Mercy of God is indeed 'wide'; it covers everything. Ibn 'Arabī, too, greatly emphasizes the boundless width of Divine Mercy. 'Know that the Mercy of God extends to everything, both in actual reality and possibility'.[1]

However, there is one important point at which his understanding of 'mercy' (*raḥmah*) differs totally from the ordinary common-sense understanding of the term. In the ordinary understanding, *raḥmah* denotes an essentially emotive attitude, the attitude of compassion, kindly forbearance, pity, benevolence, etc. But, for Ibn 'Arabī, *raḥmah* is rather an ontological fact. For him, *raḥmah* is primarily the act of making things exist, giving existence to them. It is bestowal of existence, with, of course, an overtone of a subjective, emotive attitude on the part of the one who does so.

God is by essence 'overflowing with bounteousness' (*fayyāḍ bi-al-jūd*), that is, God is giving out existence limitlessly and endlessly to everything. As al-Qāshānī says, 'existence (*wujūd*) is the first overflowing of the Mercy which is said to extend to everything'.[2]

Such an understanding of *raḥmah* gives a very particular coloring to the interpretation of the ethical nature of God which plays an important role in the Qoran and in Islam in general. This is best illustrated by Ibn 'Arabī's interpretation of the concept of Divine 'wrath'.

As is well known, the Qoran, while emphasizing that God is the Merciful, stresses at the same time that He is also a God of Wrath, a God of Vengeance. The God of the Qoran is God of justice. He shows unlimited love and compassion toward the good and pious, but that does not prevent Him from inflicting relentless punishment and chastisement upon those who do wrong, those who refuse to believe in Him and obey Him.

Ibn 'Arabī, too, admits God's wrath' (*ghaḍab*). For him, however, *ghaḍab* is not an ordinary emotion of anger. It is, like its counterpart, *raḥmah*, something of an ontological nature. Moreover, it is put in a subordinate position in relation to *raḥmah*, for *ghaḍab* itself is but an object of the boundless *raḥmah* of God.

> The very existence of Wrath originates from the Mercy of God for the Wrath. Thus His Mercy precedes His Wrath.[3]

This statement would seem to need an explication. Here is what al-Qāshānī says about it:[4]

> Mercy pertains essentially to the Absolute because the latter is by essence 'Bounteous' (*jawād*) ... Wrath, however, is not of the essence of the Absolute. On the contrary, it is simply a negative property that arises from the absence of receptivity on the part of some of the things for a perfect manifestation of the effects of existence and the various properties of existence.
> The absence of receptivity in some of the things for Mercy entails the non-appearance of Mercy (in those things), whether in this world or the Hereafter. And the fact that Divine Mercy is prevented from overflowing into a thing of this kind because of its non-receptivity is called Wrath in relation to that particular thing. . . .
> Thus it is patent that Mercy has precedence over Wrath with regard to the Absolute, for Wrath is nothing but the actual non-receptivity of the locus which is (supposed to receive) Mercy in a perfect form.

We ordinarily imagine that what we call 'evil' (*sharr*) is something positive, something positively existent. But 'evil' is in itself a pure non-existence (*'adam*). It exists only in the purely negative sense that a certain thing, when Divine Mercy works upon it, cannot by nature receive and accept it as it should. In other words, 'evil' is the negative situation of those things which cannot receive Mercy (= existence) in its full and perfect form, and which, therefore, cannot fully realize existence.

Apart from these things which constitute the objects of Divine Wrath, or, more philosophically speaking, the things that properly cannot have existence, all the remaining things which naturally have

the proper receptivity for existence, demand of God existence. And
the Divine activity which arises in response to this demand is Mercy.
It is natural, then, that Mercy should cover all things that can
possibly exist.

> Every essence (*'ayn*, i.e., everything in its archetypal state) asks for
> existence from God. Accordingly God's Mercy extends to, and cov-
> ers, every essence. For God, by the very Mercy which He exercises
> upon it, accepts (i.e., recognizes approvingly) the thing's (latent)
> desire to exist (even before the desire actually arises) and brings it
> (i.e., the desire) out to existence. This is why we assert that the Mercy
> of God extends to everything both in actual reality and possibility.[5]

Everything, already in its archetypal state, cherishes latently a
desire (*raghbah*) for actual existence. God's Mercy extends even to
this ontological desire while it is still in the state of mere possibility,
and brings it out into existence. The desire thus actualized constitutes the 'preparedness' (*isti'dād*) of the thing. The explication of
the above passage by al-Qāshānī is philosophically of great
importance.[6]

> The permanent archetypes in their state of latency have only an
> intelligible existence (as objects of God's Knowledge); by themselves
> they have no actual existence. They are desirous of actual existence,
> and are asking for it from God. When the archetypes are in such a
> state, God's essential Mercy extends to every archetype by giving it a
> capacity to receive an ontological Divine self-manifestation. This
> receptivity, or the essential 'preparedness' for receiving existence, is
> exactly the archetype's desire for actual existence.
> Thus the very first effect of the essential Mercy upon an archetype
> appears in the form of its natural aptitude for receiving existence.
> This aptitude is called 'preparedness'. God exercises Mercy upon an
> archetype, even before it has the 'preparedness' for existence, by
> existentiating the 'preparedness' itself through the 'most holy emana-
> tion' (*al-fayḍ al-aqdas*), i.e., the essential self-manifestation occur-
> ring in the Unseen. Thus the 'preparedness' of an archetype is itself (a
> result of) Divine Mercy upon it (i.e., the archetype), for previous to
> that, the archetype properly speaking has no existence if only to ask
> for its own 'preparedness'.

These words make it clear that the exercise of Divine Mercy is
nothing other than the process of the self-manifestation of the
Absolute, which has often been referred to in the preceding pages.
For Mercy is bestowal of existence, and, in Ibn 'Arabī's conception,
the Absolute's bestowing existence upon the things of the world is
exactly the same as the Absolute's manifesting itself in these things.

In the passage just quoted, al-Qāshānī states that the first stage in
the appearance of Mercy is the giving of 'preparedness' for existence to things not yet actually existent. And he says this stage

corresponds to the 'most holy emanation' in the theory of Divine self-manifestation. But this is somewhat misleading because it presents the whole matter in an extremely simplified form. We shall have to reconsider in detail the process by which Divine Mercy is manifested, following closely what Ibn 'Arabī himself says about it. Unfortunately, though, this is one of the most obscure parts of the *Fuṣūṣ*. Let us first quote the whole passage, and then split it into three parts representing, as I think, the three major stages in the gradual appearance of Mercy.[7]

> The Divine Names are 'things', and they all are ultimately reducible to one single Essence (1). The first object to which the Mercy is extended is the very thing-ness (i.e., the primary ontological reality by dint of which anything becomes cognizable as 'something') of that Essence (*'ayn*) which produces the Mercy itself out of Mercy. Thus the first thing to which the Mercy is extended is the Mercy itself (2). Then (in the second stage, the object of the Mercy is) the thing-ness of (the Names) that has just been mentioned (3). Then (in the third stage, it is) the thing-ness of all existents that come into being without end, both of this world and of the Hereafter, whether substances or accidents, composite or simple (4).

The first stage in the appearance of Divine Mercy is referred to in the second sentence (2) in this passage. The situation will be more understandable if we describe it analytically in the following terms.

In the bosom of the absolute Absolute, or the abysmal Darkness, there appears first a faint foreboding, a presentment, so to speak, of the Mercy. Since, however, the Mercy, before it begins positively to manifest itself, is a non-existent (*'adam*), it needs something which would bestow upon it 'existence', that is, another Mercy preceding it. But there can be no Mercy preceding the Divine Mercy. The only possibility then, is that the Divine Mercy is exercised upon itself. The self-Mercy of the Mercy constitutes the very first stage in the appearance of Mercy.

Looking at the same situation from the point of view of the ontological Divine self-manifestation (*tajallī*) we might describe it as the first appearance of a foreboding of 'existence'. And the appearance of a foreboding (or possibility) of 'existence' in the absolute Absolute means nothing else than the Absolute becoming conscious of itself as 'existence'. It is the self-manifestation of the Absolute to itself. And in terms of 'emanation' to which reference has been made, this stage represents the beginning of the 'most holy emanation' of the Absolute.

The sentence (2) in the above passage is intended to be a theoretical formulation of this phenomenon. It means that 'the first object of the Mercy is the thing-ness (*shay'īyah*) of that Essence (i.e., the absolute Divine Essence) which, with its own Mercy, brings Mercy into existence'. It implies that by the very first manifestation of its own Mercy, the absolutely Unknown-Unknowable turns into a 'thing' (*shay'*). And to say that the Absolute obtains 'thing-ness', i.e., an ontological status by which it presents itself as a 'thing' – which is the most general, the most undetermined of all determinations – is to say that a process of 'self-objectification' has already begun to take place within the Absolute itself. This is the appearance of self-consciousness on the part of the Absolute, and is, for the world, the appearance of a faint light just preceding the advent of the dawn of existence. In this state there exists as yet nothing at all except the Absolute, but the bestowal of existence which is, theologically, the 'creation', is already steadily operating.

The second stage in the appearance of Mercy is the establishment of the thing-ness of the Names or the permanent archetypes, referred to by sentences (1) and (3) in the above-quoted passage. At this stage, the Mercy, which has turned the absolutely Unknown-Unknowable into a 'thing', now extends to all the Names and bestows upon them existence. The Names are thereby given 'thing-ness', and become 'things'.

On the side of *tajallī*, the second stage represents the completion of the 'most holy emanation'. Unlike the first stage, the second stage brings us closer to the external world of sensible experience, but even at this stage the *tajallī* is not an external *tajallī*; it is still an event occurring inside the Unseen. Only the Unseen (*ghayb*) here is no longer a primordial state of total indiscrimination, for the essential forms of the things are already clearly discernible. These forms of the things (*ṣuwar al-mawjūddāt*) in the darkness of the Unseen are the Divine Names. And the Absolute, as we have seen earlier, reveals itself to itself by being manifested in these essences. This is the final form in which Divine Consciousness makes its appearance, and thus is completed the 'most holy emanation'.

These essential forms constituting the content of Divine Consciousness are the first 'determinations' (*ta'ayyunāt*) that appear in the Essence in its relation with the creaturely world. And the 'thing-ness' that arises at this stage is nothing other than the being of the permanent archetypes, and is, therefore, different from the thing-ness of the first stage. For all the existents at this stage, although they still maintain the essential unity peculiar to the first stage, have, at the same time, the meaning of being the totality of the essences which are *in potentia* divisible. And the Mercy which is at work at this stage is the Mercy of the Divine Names (*raḥmah asmā'iyah*), and is to be distinguished from the Mercy operating at the first stage, which is the Mercy of the Essence (*raḥmah dhātiyah*).

The third stage in the appearance of the Mercy is described in sentence (4) of the above passage. After having brought into existence the Divine Names (the second stage), the Mercy causes the individual things to arise as concrete actualizations of the Names. The ontological activity of the Mercy becomes thereby completed, and the *tajallī*, on its part, reaches its final stage. This is what Ibn 'Arabī calls the 'holy emanation' (*al-fayḍ al-muqaddas*) to be technically distinguished from the above-mentioned 'most holy emanation' (*al-fayḍ al-aqdas*). Thus, the Mercy, starting from the Divine Essence itself, ends by being extended over all the possible beings of phenomenal reality, and comes to cover the whole world.

It is to be remarked that the activity of the Mercy covering the whole world of Being is absolutely impartial and indiscriminating. It extends literally over everything. In understanding the nature of its activity, we should not associate with it anything human with which the word 'mercy' (*raḥmah*) is usually associated.

There does not come into its activity any consideration of attaining an aim, or of a thing's being or not being suitable for a purpose. Whether suitable or unsuitable, the Divine Mercy covers everything and anything with existence.[8]

Such an indiscriminating and gratuitous Mercy is called by Ibn 'Arabī the 'Mercy of gratuitous gift' (*raḥmah al-imtinān*).[9] It is totally gratuitous; freely bestowed without any particular justification. The gift is given not in reward for something good done. As al-Qāshānī defines it,[10] the 'Mercy of gratuitous gift' is an essential Mercy which extends to all things without exception. It is extended to anything whatsoever because it is not a reward for some act. Thus anything that acquires thing-ness obtains this Mercy.

The Mercy in this sense is synonymous with 'existence'. And to exercise 'mercy' means to bestow 'existence' by way of a gratuitous gift. This is, for Ibn 'Arabī, the meaning of the Qoranic verse: 'My Mercy covers everything' (VII, 156). It means that the Absolute bestows existence upon everything without any discrimination.

In contrast, there is a kind of 'mercy' which is more human in nature, that is, the kind of 'mercy' which is exercised in reward for some act done. Ibn 'Arabī calls this second type the 'Mercy of obligation' (*raḥmah al-wujūb*). The conception is based on another Qoranic verse: 'Your Lord has written upon Himself Mercy' (VI, 12). This is the kind of Mercy exercised with discrimination, i.e., in accordance with what each person actually has done. Ontologically speaking, it is Mercy exercised in accordance with the 'preparedness' of each individual being.

There are, therefore, two different kinds of Mercy (*raḥmatān*);

and the 'Merciful' is, accordingly, given two meanings. These two senses are differentiated in Arabic by two different Names: the first is *al-Raḥmān* and the second is *al-Raḥīm*. The *Raḥmān* is the Merciful in the sense of the One who exercises the 'Mercy of gratuitous gift', while the *Raḥīm* is the Merciful in the sense of the One who exercises the 'Mercy of obligation'.[11]

Since, however, the act of Mercy of the second category is but a special case of the first (which consists in bestowing existence on all beings), the Name *Raḥīm* is included in the Name *Raḥmān*. This point is explained by Ibn 'Arabī in the following way:[12]

> (The Mercy is of two kinds:) the 'Mercy of gratuitous gift' and the 'Mercy of obligation' corresponding to (the Names) the *Raḥmān* and *Raḥīm* respectively. (God) exercises Mercy as a gratuitous act under the Name of the *Raḥmān*, while He obligates Himself to (requite with Mercy) under the Name of *Raḥīm*.
>
> This kind of 'obligation', however, is part of 'gratuitous gift', and so the *Raḥīm* is contained within the *Raḥmān*. God 'has written upon Himself Mercy' in such a way that Mercy of this kind may be extended to His servants in reward for the good acts done by them individually – those good works which are mentioned in the Qoran. This kind of Mercy is an obligation upon God with which He has bound Himself toward those servants, and the latter rightfully merit this kind of Mercy by their good works.

Thus the 'Mercy of obligation' would seem to indicate that each person merits this kind of Mercy by whatever good work he has done. For Ibn 'Arabī, this is merely a superficial understanding of the matter. In the eyes of those who know the truth, he who really does a good work is not man; the real agent is God Himself.

> He who is in this state (i.e., whoever is *fully* entitled to the 'Mercy of obligation') knows within himself *who* is the real agent (of the good works which he does). Good works are distributed among the eight bodily members of man. And God has definitely declared that He is the He-ness (i.e., the inmost reality) of each of these bodily members. From this point of view, the real agent cannot be other than God; what belongs to man is only the outward form. (When we say that) the Divine He-ness itself is inherent in man, (what is meant thereby is that) it inheres in nothing other than one of His Names (i.e., man as a concrete form of one of the Divine Names, not in man as a physical being.)[13]

As regards the 'Mercy of gratuitous gift', the most important point to remember is that it covers all without exception. Quite naturally, then, the Divine Names themselves are objects of this kind of Mercy.

> God has put the 'Mercy of gratuitous gift' above all restrictions when He has declared: 'My Mercy covers everything' (VII, 156). So it

covers even the Divine Names, i.e., the realities of all relative determinations (of the Divine Essence). God has shown 'Mercy of gratuitous gift' to the Names by (the very act of bestowing existence to) us (i.e., the world). Thus we (the world) are the result of the 'Mercy of gratuitous gift' exercised upon the Divine Names, i.e., the relations pertaining to the Lordship (i.e., the various relations which arise because of the Absolute being the 'Lord').[14]

This universal, unconditional, and indiscriminating nature of the 'Mercy of gratuitous gift' cannot but affect gravely that part of Ibn 'Arabī's ontology which concerns the value of things. His position on this problem may succinctly be described by the phrase 'Beyond Good and Evil'.

As we have seen, the Mercy in this sense is nothing but bestowing upon everything existence *qua* existence. And this is done by the Absolute's manifesting itself in the creaturely forms. This ontological act has in itself nothing to do with moral judgments. In other words, it does not matter essentially whether a thing as an object of the Mercy be good (*khayr*) or bad (*sharr*). Things assume these and other evaluational properties only after having been given existence by the act of the universal Mercy. The actual appearance of goodness, badness, etc., is the result of the activity of the 'Mercy of obligation', for a thing's assuming properties of this kind is due to the nature of the thing itself.

The 'Mercy of gratuitous gift' is bestowal of existence. It concerns existence *qua* existence; it does not concern existence being good or bad. This is one of the major theses of Ibn 'Arabī. Briefly stated, everything is a self-manifestation of the Absolute; the Mercy extends in this sense to all, and all are on the 'straight way' (*sirāṭ mustaqīm*); and there is no distinction at this stage between good and evil.

Verily God's is the straight Way; the Way is there, exposed to sight everywhere. Its reality is inherent in great things and small, in those who are ignorant of the truth as well as in those who know it well. This is why it is said that His Mercy covers everything, whether it be vile and contemptible or grand and stately.
Thus (it is said in the Qoran:) 'There is not even one single animal on earth but that He seizes its forelock. Verily my Lord is on the straight Way'. (XI, 56). It is clear, then, that everybody walking on the earth is on the straight Way of the Lord. From this point of view nobody is of 'those upon whom is God's wrath' (I, 7) nor of 'those who go astray' (*ibid.*). Both 'wrath' and 'going astray' come into being only secondarily. Everything goes ultimately back to the Mercy which is universal and which precedes (the appearance of all secondary distinctions).[15]

God himself seizes the forelock of every animal and leads it along the straight Way. This means that everything *qua* being is good as it is, and is, as we have seen earlier, actually approved by God.

As all things go in this manner along the straight Way of God under His own guidance, each shows its own characteristic feature, i.e., each goes on doing individually various acts which are peculiar to it. These acts are each a concrete manifestation of the particular Name which acts as the personal Lord of each being. In other words, everything, after having been put on the straight Way by the ontological activity of the Mercy, begins to show secondarily its own characteristic traits in accordance with the individual peculiarity (*khuṣūṣīyah*) of the Name of which it happens to be an embodiment.

> Everything except the Absolute is (what is described by the Qoran as) an animal walking on the earth. It is called 'animal' because it is possessed of a spirit (*rūḥ*).[16]
> But there is nothing that 'walks around' by itself. Everything that 'walks around' does so only secondarily, following the movement of (its own Lord) who is the one who really walks along the straight Way. But the Way, on its part, cannot be a way unless there be people who walk upon it.[17]

Thus the statement is fundamentally right that everything is primarily, i.e., *qua* being, neither good nor bad. However, since existence is a direct manifestation of the essential Mercy of the Absolute, everything in that sense must be said to be essentially 'good' (*ṭayyib*). Anything whatsoever is good in its existence. Only when man, from his subjective and relative point of view, begins to like and dislike things, does the distinction between good and bad come into being. For Ibn 'Arabī, 'good' and 'bad' are a sheer matter of relative viewpoints. He explains this in the following way:[18]

> Concerning the 'badness' of garlic, the Prophet once observed: 'It is a plant whose scent I dislike'. He did not say, 'I dislike garlic', because the thing itself is not to be disliked; what is liable to be disliked is only what appears from the thing.
> Thus displeasure arises either because of a habit, namely, because a thing does not suit one's nature or purpose, or because of some regulation in the Law, or because of the thing falling short of the desired perfection. There can be no other cause than those which I have just enumerated.
> And as the things of the world are divided into categories: good (i.e., agreeable) and bad (i.e., disagreeable), the Prophet (Muḥammad) was made to be of such a nature that he liked the good and disliked the bad.
> The Prophet also says in describing the angels that they are annoyed by the offensive odors, (which the human beings exhale) because of the natural putrefaction peculiar to the elemental constitution of

man. Man has been 'created of clay of black mud wrought into shape' (XV, 26), so he emits a repulsive odor. The angels dislike it by nature. The dung-beetle finds repulsive the scent of rose, which, in reality, is a sweet fragrance. For the dung-beetle, rose does not emit a sweet smell. Likewise, a man who is like a dung-beetle in his nature and inner constitution, finds truth repulsive and is pleased with falsehood. To this refer God's words: 'And those who believe in falsehood and disbelieve in God' (XXIX, 52). And God describes them as people at a loss when He says: 'they it is who are the losers' (*ibid.*), meaning thereby that these are the people who lose themselves. For they do not discern good from bad and, therefore, totally lack discernment. As to the Apostle of God (Muḥammad), love was inspired into his heart for the good concerning everything. And, properly speaking, everything without exception is (essentially) good.

However, is it at all imaginable that there be in the world (a man of) such an inner constitution that he would find in everything only the good and nothing bad? I should say, 'No, that is impossible.' Because we find the (opposition between good and bad) even in the very Ground from which the world arises, I mean, the Absolute. We know that the Absolute (as God) likes and dislikes. And the bad is nothing other than what one dislikes, while the good is nothing other than what one likes. And the world has been created in the image of the Absolute (i.e., having likes and dislikes), and man has been created in the image of these two (i.e., the Absolute and the world).

Thus it is natural that no man should be (of such a) constitution that he would perceive exclusively one aspect (i.e., either the good or bad aspect) of everything. But there does not exist a (man of such a) constitution that he discerns a good element in anything bad, being well aware that what is bad is bad simply because of (the subjective impression caused by) the taste, and that it is (essentially) good if considered apart from the (subjective impression caused by the) taste. In the case of such a man, the perception of the good may be so overwhelming as to make him forget completely the perception of the bad. This is quite possible. But it is impossible to make the bad disappear completely from the world, i.e., from the realm of Being. The Mercy of God covers both good and bad. Anything bad considers itself good, and what is good (for others) looks bad to it. There is nothing good in the world but that it turns into something bad from a certain point of view and for a certain constitution, and likewise, conversely.

Viewed from such a height, even the good and bad in the religious sense, i.e., 'obedience' (*ṭā'ah*) and 'disobedience' (*ma'ṣiyah*), turn out ultimately to be two aspects of one and the same thing. Ibn 'Arabī explains this by the symbolic meaning contained in the story of Moses throwing down his staff in the presence of Pharaoh.[19]

'Then he threw down his staff' (XXVI, 32). The staff (*'aṣā*) symbolizes something (i.e., the spirit or nature of Pharaoh) with which

Pharaoh disobeyed (*'aṣà*) Moses in his haughtiness and refused to respond to the call of Moses. 'And, lo, it turned into a serpent manifest' (*ibid.*), that is, the staff was changed into an apparent snake (*ḥayyah*). Thus (the Qoranic verse here quoted means that) the disobedience, which was a bad thing, transformed itself into obedience, which was a good thing.

In competing with the magicians of the Egyptian court in the presence of Pharaoh, Moses throws down on the floor the staff in his hand. The staff – in Arabic, *'aṣà* – is immediately associated in the mind of Ibn 'Arabī with the verb *'aṣà* (meaning 'to rebel' 'to disobey') by phonetic association, and the staff becomes a symbol of 'disobedience'. The staff becomes the symbol of the fact that Pharaoh disobeyed Moses, and did not respond to the latter's call.

The staff, thrown down, changes at once into a serpent. The Arabic word for 'serpent' or 'snake', *ḥayyah*, arouses in Ibn 'Arabī's mind, again by phonetic association, the word *ḥayāh*, i.e., 'life'. 'Life' in this particular context, is the spiritual life resulting from man's getting into immediate touch with the depth structure of Reality. And, for Ibn 'Arabī, it means 'obedience' to God.

Thus the feat enacted by Moses depicts symbolically the naturally disobedient soul of Pharaoh being transformed into an obedient, docile soul. Not that there are two different souls: one obedient, another disobedient. As al-Qāshānī remarks,[20] soul itself is 'one and single reality', except that it becomes good or bad according to contexts. One and the same reality shows two different aspects, and appears in two different modes.

The staff of Moses *per se* remains the same, but it appears sometimes as a staff, sometimes as a serpent according to particular situations, i.e., according to the point of view from which one looks at it. Likewise, whatever Pharaoh may do, the act itself is neither good nor bad. The only thing that changes are its properties. The same act of Pharaoh becomes sometimes obedience, sometimes disobedience.

All this happens in accordance with God's words: 'God will change their evil deeds into good deeds' (XXV, 70), that is to say, in so far as concerns their qualifications (and not the essences themselves of their deeds). Thus, in this case, different qualifications appeared as distinctive realities within one single substance. That is to say, one single substance appeared as a staff and as a snake or, (as the Qoran says) 'a serpent manifest.' As a snake, it swallowed up all the other snakes, while as a staff, it swallowed up all the staffs.[21]

Ibn 'Arabī develops the same thought from a properly theological point of view, as the problem of Divine Will (*mashī'ah*).

All events that occur in this world, all actions that are done, are, without even a single exception, due to Divine Will. In this sense, there can be no distinction between good and bad, or right and wrong. Every phenomenon, as it actually is, is a direct effect of the Will of God. Every event occurs as it actually does because it is so willed by God.

This standpoint is totally different from that of the Sacred Law which approves of this and disapproves of that. When a 'bad' man does something 'evil', his act obviously goes against the Sacred Law, but, according to Ibn 'Arabī it never goes against Divine Will. For it is absolutely impossible that something should occur against the Will of God. Here is what Ibn 'Arabī, says about this problem:[22]

> Every decree which is carried out now in the world (i.e., anything that actually occurs in the world as a concrete phenomenon) *is* a decree of God, even if it violates the particular kind of decree which has been established under the name of a Sacred Law. For in reality only when a decree is truly God's decree, is it actually carried out. Everything that occurs in the world occurs solely in accordance with what is decreed by the Will of God, not in accordance with the decree of an established Sacred Law, although, to be sure, the very establishment of a Sacred Law is itself due to Divine Will. Besides, precisely because it is willed by God, establishment of the Sacred Law is actualized. However, Divine Will in this case concerns only the establishment of the Law; it does not concern the practice of what is enjoined by the Law.
>
> Thus the Will has a supreme authority. And this is why Abū Ṭālib (al-Makkī) regarded it as the 'Throne of the Divine Essence', because the Will demands for itself that the decrees should be carried out.
>
> Such being the case, nothing occurs in this world apart from the Will, nor is anything removed from the sphere of Being except by the Will. And whenever the Divine Command[23] is violated in this world by what is called 'disobedience' (or 'sin'), it is the matter of the 'mediate' Command, not the 'creational' Command. Nobody, whatever he may do, can ever act against God in so far as the Command of the Will (i.e., the creational Command) is concerned. Disobedience occurs only in regard to the 'mediate' Command.

The Will of God concerns only *takwīn*, i.e., 'bringing into existence', or 'creation'. Within the sphere of human acts, for instance, the Will concerns the coming into existence of a certain act. The Will is not directly concerned with the question as to who happens to be the individual person through whom the act occurs. All acts occur necessarily through individual persons. Every individual, in this sense, is a 'responsible' (*mukallaf*) person, that is, a person who bears a number of moral responsibilities within the boundaries of the system of a Sacred Law. And every human act becomes 'good' or 'bad' through this very process of personal 'mediation'.

In reality the Command of the Will is directed exclusively toward the bringing into existence of an act itself; it is not a matter of concern to the Will 'who' actually manifests the act. So it is absolutely impossible that the act should not occur. But in regard to the particular locus (in which it actually occurs), the (same) act is called sometimes 'disobedience' to the Divine Command (namely, when the particular person who does it happens to be prohibited to do it by the Sacred Law of his community), and sometimes 'obedience' (namely, when the person happens to belong to a community whose Sacred Law enjoins the act). And (the same act) is followed by blame or praise accordingly.

The situation being just as we have shown, all creatures are destined ultimately to reach happiness in spite of the difference in kind that exists among them. God Himself expresses this fact when He states that His Mercy covers everything and that the Mercy forestalls Divine Wrath. 'Forestall' means to get ahead of something. Thus, as soon as a particular person who has already been given a (negative) judgment by that which (essentially) comes afterward (i.e., Wrath) overtakes that which goes ahead of it (i.e., Mercy), the latter pronounces a (new) judgment upon him, so that Mercy gets hold of him. Such a (miraculous) thing can actually occur because there is absolutely nothing that can ever forestall it (i.e., Mercy).

This is what is meant by the dictum: 'God's Mercy forestalls His Wrath', because of the decisive influence Mercy exercises upon whatever reaches it, for it stands at the ultimate goal (awaiting everything), and everything is running toward the goal. Everything necessarily attains to the ultimate goal. So everything necessarily obtains Mercy and leaves Wrath.[24]

The preceding description of the Mercy clearly suggests that Ibn 'Arabī is considering the phenomenon of the universal Mercy from two different points of view at one time. The basic dictum: 'the Mercy of God runs through all beings',[25] means ontologically that everything existent is existent by the Divine act of the bestowal of existence. The dictum also means that everything is under Divine Mercy, and that everything, therefore, is essentially blessed and is in felicity.

Everything which is remembered by Mercy is happy and blessed. But there is nothing that has not been remembered by Mercy. And Mercy's remembering things is exactly the same as its bringing them into existence. Thus everything existent is affected by Mercy.

Do not, o my friend, lose sight of what I have told you under the influence of your vision of the people of misery and your belief in the torments of the Hereafter which are never to be slackened once men are put into them. Know before everything else that Mercy is primarily exercised in bringing everything into existence, so that even the torments of Hell themselves have been brought into existence by Mercy that has been directed toward them.[26]

Then, in the passage which immediately follows what we have just quoted, Ibn 'Arabī distinguishes two different kinds of effect produced by the Mercy: (1) an ontological effect produced directly by its Essence, and (2) an effect produced in accordance with man's asking. This distinction corresponds to what we have already discussed in terms of the distinction between the 'Mercy of gratuitous gift' and the 'Mercy of obligation'. Only he considers it this time from a somewhat different perspective.

> Mercy in its effect has two different aspects. The first concerns an effect it produces in accordance with essential requirement of itself. It consists in that Mercy brings into existence every individual essence (*'ayn,* i.e., archetype). In doing this, it does not pay any attention to purpose or non-purpose, suitability or non-suitability, for the object of Mercy is the essence of every existent thing before the latter actually exists, that is, while it is still in the state of a permanent archetype.
>
> So (for instance,) Mercy discerns the Absolute as 'created' in the various religions, (even before its actual existence) as one of the permanent archetypes (i.e., as a potential existent), and spontaneously shows Mercy upon it by bringing it into actual existence. This is the reason why I assert that the Absolute as 'created' in the various religions constitutes the first object of Mercy immediately after the Mercy has exercised Mercy upon itself by concerning itself with the existentiation of all existents.
>
> The second kind of effect is that induced by 'asking' (on the part of creatures). But (there are two kinds of 'asking'). Those who are veiled (from the truth) ask the Absolute to show Mercy upon them, each representing the Absolute in (the particular form provided by) his own religion. The people of 'unveiling', on the contrary, ask the Mercy of God to reside in them. They ask for Mercy in the Name *Allāh,* saying, 'O *Allāh,* show Mercy upon us!' And (the Absolute, in response) shows Mercy upon them only by making Mercy reside in them. And Mercy (thus residing in these sages) produces its positive effect in them (i.e., they themselves become the possessors of the Mercy and begin to act as 'merciful' ones).[27]

We must try to grasp exactly what is meant by Ibn 'Arabī in this important but obscure passage. The first of the two aspects of the effect of Mercy here described is not difficult to understand, because it concerns the ontological activity of Mercy which we have already discussed earlier in terms of the Mercy of the *raḥmān* type. It refers to one of the most fundamental theses of Ibn 'Arabī, that beings obtain their existence by the Essence of the Absolute manifesting itself in the particular form of each one of them in accordance with the capacity determined in eternity for each thing.

Ibn 'Arabī here leaves the plane of general theoretical considerations and narrows down his observation to a very particular case;

namely, the problem of the relation between the believer and the object of his belief within the boundaries of the traditional religion of his community. The effect of Mercy, he argues, appears first in Mercy exercising an ontological (i.e., existentiating) Mercy upon its own self. Following this, Mercy bestows existence upon the Absolute as 'created' in various religions.

It goes without saying that the believers themselves, in so far as they are 'beings', are originally permanent archetypes, and as such must necessarily be objects of the ontological Mercy. But the objects of belief of these believers, i.e., their gods, are also originally permanent archetypes which are included within the archetypes of the believers. So it is natural that they, too, should be affected by the ontological Mercy. In other words, the very same activity of the Mercy, which brings into existence the believers as so many objects of Mercy, brings into existence also the 'created' Absolute within the believers themselves.

In contrast to this activity of the ontological Mercy, the second aspect concerns the effect of the Mercy which is produced in accordance with what an individual person asks from his Lord, each being motivated by a personal purpose. This aspect of Mercy varies in accordance with the nature of what is asked by individual 'seekers'.

Ibn 'Arabī divides the 'seekers' (*ṭālibūn*) of Mercy into two classes: (1) the 'veiled' people, and (2) the people of 'unveiling'. Each one of the first class implores *his* Lord saying, 'Have mercy upon me!' 'Give me this, or give me that!' This, in Ibn 'Arabī's view, is nothing but a silly act which arises from the ignorance of the truth. The Mercy of God does not produce any effect except on the basis of what has been eternally determined in the form of permanent archetypes. However much they may implore God, the permanent archetypes of himself and of others can never be altered.

The people of the second class, on the contrary, ask for something extraordinary. First of all, they do not direct their supplication to any individual Lord. They address themselves to *Allāh* as the point of comprehensive unification of all the Names. They cry out, 'O *Allāh*, have mercy upon us!' This should not be taken literally as if they implored God to show mercy to them in the manner in which a 'merciful' man shows mercy to other human beings. What they are asking for is that God should make them subjectively conscious of the universal Mercy which is implied in the Name *Allāh*. Their wish is to go beyond the passive state of being objects of the Mercy (*marḥūm*) and to put themselves in the position of the *rāḥim*, i.e., one who shows mercy, and thereby have the consciousness of all the Names being, so to speak, their own attributes.

When this wish is really fulfilled, Mercy begins to show its positive effect within these people as their own personal attributes. And each one of them turns from the state of *marḥūm* to that of *rāḥim*. Mercy works in this way according to Ibn 'Arabī because the real effect of a property begins to appear positively only when the non-material content (*ma'nà*) of it comes to reside in a particular locus.

> Thus it (i.e., the non-material essence of Mercy residing in a particular locus) functions as the *rāḥim* in the real sense of the word. God shows Mercy to His servants about whom He is concerned only through Mercy, and when this Mercy becomes established in them (as their subjective state), they experience by 'immediate tasting' the positive effect of Mercy as their own property. For he whom Mercy remembers (in this sense) is himself a subject of Mercy. His state then (will be more properly expressed by) a name descriptive of an agent (rather than a name descriptive of the passive state, *marḥūm*), that is, the 'merciful' or *rāḥim*.[28]

Such a man, Ibn 'Arabī says, is conscious within himself of Mercy being active as his own subjective state. He is no longer an 'object' of Mercy, one to whom Mercy is shown; he is rather a 'subject' of Mercy, one who exercises it toward other beings. He is now a man worthy to be called 'merciful'. The grave consequence of this personal transformation through the appropriation of Mercy will be studied later when we deal with the problem of the Perfect Man.

In what precedes, we have been following Ibn 'Arabī as he develops his thought on the Divine Name 'Merciful' (*raḥmān*), and we have tried to clarify the structure of Mercy (*raḥmah*) which is the conceptual core of this Name.

The next problem to consider is: How does Mercy issue forth from the Absolute? Ibn 'Arabī explains his view on this problem using a very bold and colorful image of 'breathing out'.

It is a matter of common experience that, when we hold our breath for some time, the air compressed in the chest makes us feel unbearable pain. And when the utmost limit is reached, and we cannot hold it any longer, the air that has been held inside bursts out all at once. It is a natural phenomenon that the breath compressed in the breast seeks forcibly for an outlet, and finally explodes and gushes forth with a violent outburst. Just as air bursts forth from the chest of man, the compressed existence within the depths of the Absolute, taking the form of Mercy, gushes forth from the Absolute. This he calls the 'breath of the Merciful' (*al-nafas al-raḥmāniy*).[29]

The state preceding the bursting forth of the breath of Mercy is described by Ibn 'Arabī by an equally expressive word *karb*. The word is derived from a root meaning 'to overload' or 'to fill up', and is used to designate the state in which the stomach, for instance, is surfeited. It is a state of extreme tension, just short of explosion, caused by an excessive amount of things accumulated inside.

> Because of this surfeit (i.e., in order to relieve itself from the excess of inner tension) the Absolute breathes out. The breath is attributed to the Merciful (and called the 'breath of the Merciful') because the (Absolute under the Name of) Merciful shows Mercy by means of this breath toward the Divine Relations (i.e., the Names) and responds to their demand that the forms of the world be brought into existence.[30]

The Mercy, as we have seen above, means bestowal of existence. So the 'breathing out' of the breath of the Merciful is a symbolic expression for the manifestation of Being, or the Divine act of bringing into existence the things of the world. In the imagery peculiar to Ibn 'Arabī, this phenomenon may also be described as the Divine Names bursting out into the real world of existence. The Divine Names, in this imagery, are originally in the state of intense compression within the Absolute. And at the extreme limit of interior compression, the Names 'burst out' from the bosom of the Absolute. Ibn 'Arabī depicts in this vividly pictorial way the ontological process by which the Divine Names become actualized in the forms of the world. This is the birth of the world as the whole of outwardly existent beings. The process itself is explained in more plain terms by Bālī Efendi in the following manner.[31]

> The Names, previous to their existence in the outer world, exist hidden in the Essence of the Absolute, all of them seeking an outlet toward the world of external existence. The state is comparable to the case in which a man holds his breath within himself. The breath, held within, seeks an outlet toward the outside, and this causes in the man a painful sensation of extreme compression. Only when he breathes out does this compression cease . . . Just as the man is tormented by the compression if he does not breathe out, so the Absolute would feel the pain of compression if it did not bring into existence the world in response to the demand of the Names.

To this Bālī Efendi adds the remark that this phenomenon of Divine 'breathing' (*tanaffus*) is the same as God's uttering the word 'Be!' (*kun*) to the world. 'He breathed out' means 'He sent out what was in His Interior to the Exterior by means of the word Be. Thus He Himself, after having been in the Interior, has come to exist in the Exterior'.

What is important to observe is that, in Ibn 'Arabī's world-view, this 'breathing out' of Mercy is not something that took place, once for all, sometime in the past. On the contrary, the process of the 'compressed breath', i.e., the Names contained in the Absolute, bursting out in virtue of its own pressure toward the outside, is going on continuously without intermission. And it is this continuous process that maintains the present world in subsistence. To use the Aristotelian terminology, things are constantly turning from the state of potentiality to that of actuality. It is a constant and everlasting process of a universal overflow of the Being of the Absolute into Being of the creatures. Thus the real and absolute Being (*al-wujūd al-ḥaqīqiy*) goes on transforming itself without a moment's rest into the relative Being (*al-wujūd al-iḍāfiy*). And this ontological transformation, which Ibn 'Arabī sometimes calls 'emanation' (*fayḍ*), is, in his view, a natural and necessary movement of Being caused by the inner pressure of the ontological potentiality kept within the Absolute. Without this constant transformation, i.e., 'breathing out', the Being would be compressed within beyond its extreme limit, and the Essence of the Absolute would be in structurally the same situation as when we suffer an unbearable pain by holding our breath.

The phenomenon of the 'breath of the Merciful' has been interpreted in the preceding pages in terms of the Divine Names. It may also be understood in terms of the Lordship (*rubūbīyah*), for, as we have seen, 'Lord' is a particularized form of the Absolute on the level of the Divine Names. The Absolute in its absoluteness is completely 'independent'; it does not need anything, it does not seek anything outside itself. But the Absolute *qua* Lord needs objects of its Lordship; it does not subsist without *marbūb*.

But *marbūb* ('one who is lorded over') is nothing other than the world in existence. Thus the Lord must bring into existence the things of the world. The same thing can be expressed in religious terms by saying that to the Absolute *qua* Lord essentially belongs solicitude for his servants.

> In the plane of Being where it is split into various relations opposed to each other,[32] God describes Himself in a (famous) Tradition as having 'solicitude (*shafaqah*) for His servants'.
> The very first thing which (the Absolute) breathed out by its 'breath of Mercy' was Lordship. And this was actualized by the bringing into existence of the world, because the world was what was essentially required by Lordship and all (the other) Divine Names. From this point of view it is evident that Mercy covers everything.[33]

Thus the 'breath of the Merciful' is the principle of Being or the ground of Being extending over both the world of material things and the world of spiritual beings. In this ontological capacity, the 'breath of the Merciful' is regarded by Ibn 'Arabī as Nature (*ṭabī'ah*).

Viewed from this perspective, the 'breath' is a Substance (*jawhar*, in the Aristotelian sense of Prime Matter) in which all the forms of

Being, both material and spiritual, are manifested. In this sense,
Nature necessarily precedes any form which becomes manifest in it.

Nature precedes all that are born out of it with definite forms. But in
reality, Nature is no other than the 'breath of the Merciful'. All the
forms of the world become manifest in the latter, ranging from the
highest forms to the lowest, in virtue of the spreading of the 'breath'
through the material substance in the world of physical bodies in
particular. The 'breath' spreads also through the Being of the spirits
of a luminous nature and the attributes. But that is another kind of
the spreading of the 'breath'.[34]

According to this passage, the Divine 'breath' pervades the material
substance, i.e., the Prime Matter (*hayūlà*), which is receptive of the
physical forms, and it brings into existence the physical bodies in
the material world. The 'breath' pervades, at the same time, the
spiritual substances bringing into existence the spirits of the Light-
nature, i.e., immaterial things by spreading through the spiritual
Nature which is another kind of Prime Matter. It also spreads
through the accidental Nature and thereby brings into being various
accidents which exist as inherent attributes of substances.

To consider bestowal of existence by the Absolute as the 'breath'
of the Merciful is, for Ibn 'Arabī, by no means a mere metaphor
which has come to his mind haphazardly. It is an *essential* metaphor.
The ontological phenomenon, in his view, coincides in every important respect with the physiological phenomenon of breathing.
All the basic attributes which characterize the human act of breathing apply analogically to the 'breath' of God. We shall in what
follows consider this point, basing ourselves on Ibn 'Arabī's own
description.[35]

The Absolute attributes to itself the 'breath of the Merciful'. Now
whenever anything is qualified by an attribute, all the qualities that
naturally follow that attribute must necessarily be attributed to that
thing. (In our particular case), you know well what qualities naturally
follow the attribute of breathing in an animal that breathes.[36] This is
why the Divine breath receives the forms of the world. Thus the
Divine breath acts as the Prime Matter in relation to the forms of the
world. And (the Divine breath in this capacity) is precisely what we
call Nature.

Accordingly, the four elements, everything that has been generated
from the elements, the higher spiritual beings, and the spirits of
seven Heavens, all these are found to be 'forms' of Nature.[37]

Thus the four elements are forms (i.e., specific determinations) of
Nature. And those beings above the elements, namely, the 'higher
spirits' that are (ranged in a hierarchical order down to a level just)
above the seven Heavens – they are forms of Nature. And those

being born of the elements are also forms of Nature. (By 'those that are born of the elements') I mean the spheres of the seven Heavens and the spirits (governing their movements); they are of an elemental nature, because they are made of, and born of, the vapor[38] of the elements. Each one of the angels born in any of the seven Heavens is likewise of the elements. Thus all the heavenly angels are elemental. Those (angels) above the heavenly spheres (are not elemental, but they nonetheless) belong to Nature. And this is the reason why God described the angels as mutually rivaling. This may be explained by the fact that Nature itself tends by essence to be split into opposed poles. And the essential opposition among the Divine Names, i.e., the Divine Relations, has been caused only by the 'breath of the Merciful'. Do you not see how even in the Divine Essence which is in itself completely free from such a property (i.e., polarization) there appears (at the level of the Divine Names) the definite property of essential independence?[39] Thus the world has been produced in the image of its creator which is (not the Essence but) the 'breath of the Merciful'[40] . . . He[41] who wants to know (the nature of) the Divine breath must try to know the world, for (as the Prophet said) 'he who knows himself knows his Lord' who manifests Himself in him. That is to say, the world makes its appearance in the 'breath of the Merciful' by which God breathes out from the Divine Names the inner compression that has been caused by the non-manifestation of their effects. (God relieves the Names of the pain of their inner compression by letting them manifest their effects.) At the same time, God thereby shows Mercy toward Himself, that is, by what He brings into existence in the 'breath'.[42] Thus the first effect shown by the Divine 'breath' appears in God Himself (by the manifestation of His Names). Then, following that stage, the process goes on stage by stage by the 'breathing out' of all the Divine Names until it reaches the last stage of Being (i.e., the world).

Ibn 'Arabī concludes with a short poem, the first verse of which runs: 'Thus everything is contained in the bosom of the Breath, just as the bright light of day is in the very darkness before dawn'. The whole world is still completely shrouded in darkness. But it is not the darkness of midnight, for the light of dawn is already potentially there, ready to appear at any moment. Commenting on this verse, Affifi writes:[43] The 'breath' symbolizes the material substance (*al-jawhar al-hayūlānī*) in which the forms of all beings become manifested. In itself, it is utter darkness, i.e., utterly unknowable, but seen from the viewpoint of manifestation, all the forms of the universe are faintly observable in the midst of the darkness.

Mercy (*raḥmah*) is unquestionably one of the key-concepts which characterize in a definite way the structure of Ibn 'Arabī's thought. Probably a little less important than Mercy, but very close to it in content is another key-concept, Love (*maḥabbah*). The Divine Love is, after all, the same thing as Mercy, but looked at from a somewhat different angle. It is, theologically speaking, the fundamental motive of the creation of the world by God, and in terms of the ontology peculiar to Ibn 'Arabī, it is the driving force of the self-manifestation of the Absolute. Before we close the present chapter, we shall analyze this concept and discuss the place it occupies in the philosophical system of Ibn 'Arabī.

There is a particular reason why the concept of Love plays such an important role in Ibn 'Arabī's thought. Its importance is due to the existence of an explicit statement put in the mouth of God Himself in a famous Tradition which may be considered the starting-point, the basis, and the very gist of his philosophy: 'I was a hidden treasure, and I desired (*aḥbabtu*, 'loved') to be known. Accordingly I created the creatures and thereby made Myself known to them. Any they did come to know Me'.

As this Tradition tells us with utmost clarity, Love (*ḥubb*) is the principle which moved the Absolute toward the creation of the world. It is, in this sense, the 'secret of creation' (*sirr al-khalq*) or 'cause of creation' (*'illah al-khalq*). If we are to express the thought in terms more characteristic of Ibn 'Arabī, we might say that Love is something because of which the Absolute steps out of the state of abysmal Darkness and begins to manifest itself in the forms of all beings.

For Ibn 'Arabī, speaking more generally, 'love' is the principle of all movement (*ḥarakah*). All movements that actually occur in the world (e.g., when a man does something) are due to the driving force of 'love'. In explaining events that take place in and around ourselves, our attention tends to be drawn toward various causes[44] other than 'love'. We usually say, for example, that the 'cause' of such-and-such an action we do is such-and-such a thing (e.g., fear, anger, joy, etc.). In doing so, we are overlooking the real cause, i.e., the most basic cause of all causes. In the eyes of those who know the truth, all phenomena of movement, on all levels of Being, are caused by 'love'. If it were not for the activity of 'love', everything would remain in the state of eternal rest, i.e., non-movement. And non-movement (*sukūn*) means nothing other than non-existence (*'adam*).[45]

From this point of view, the fact that the world has come out of the state of non-existence into the state of existence is a grand-scale ontological 'movement', and this movement has been caused by the Divine Love. Ibn 'Arabī expresses this conception in the following way:[46]

> The most basic and primary movement was the movement of the world from the state of non-existence (i.e., the archetypal state), in

which it had been reposing, into the state of existence. This is the reason why it is said that the reality of existence is a movement from the state of repose. And the movement which is coming into existence of the world is a movement of Love. This is clearly indicated by the Apostle when he says (conveying God's own words): 'I was a hidden treasure, and I *loved* to be known'. If it were not for this love, the world would never have appeared in this concrete existence. In this sense, the movement of the world toward existence was a movement of Love which brought it into existence. . . .

And the world, on its part, *loves* to witness itself in the existence as it used to witness itself in the state of archetypal repose. Thus, from whichever side one considers it, the movement of the world from the state of the archetypal non-existence toward concrete existence was a movement of Love, both from the side of the Absolute and from the side of the world itself.

And all this is ultimately due to the Love of the Absolute for being 'perfect' in both its Knowledge and Existence. If the Absolute remained in isolation in its own original absoluteness, neither its Knowledge nor its Existence would have attained perfection. Ibn 'Arabī goes on to say:[47]

Perfection (*kamāl*) is loved for its own sake. But as for God's Knowledge of Himself, in so far as He was completely independent of the whole world (i.e., in so far as He remained in isolation before the creation of the world), it was there (from the beginning in absolute perfection). The degree of the Knowledge was to be made perfect only by a temporal Knowledge ('*ilm ḥādith*)[48] which would concern the concrete individual objects of the world once these would be brought into existence. Thus the form of Perfection is realized (in God) by the two kinds of Knowledge, temporal and eternal, and the degree of His Knowledge is brought to perfection through these two aspects. Correspondingly, the degrees of Being are also perfected (by the creation of the world). For Being is of two kinds: eternal (*a parte ante*) and non-eternal, that is temporal. The 'eternal' (*azaliy*) Existence is the Existence of the Absolute for itself, while the 'non-eternal' is the Existence of the Absolute in the forms of the archetypal world. This latter kind of Being is called 'becoming' (*ḥudūth*) because the Absolute in it (splits itself into multiplicity and) appears to one another. The Absolute in this way appears to itself in the forms of the world. And this brings Being to perfection.

And so Ibn 'Arabī comes to a conclusion in which he connects the concept of Love with that of the breath of Mercy.

Thus you should understand that the movement of the world is born of Love for perfection.
Do you not see how the Absolute breathed out and relieved the Divine Names of (the pain of compression) which they had been feeling because of the non-appearance of their effects, in an entity

called the world? This happened because the Absolute loves relaxation (*rāḥah*). And relaxation was only to be obtained through the existence of the forms high and low. Thus it is patent that movement is caused by Love, and that there can be no movement in the world but that it is motivated by Love.

Notes

1. *Fuṣ.*, p. 222/177.

2. p. 222.

3. *Fuṣ.*, p. 222/177.

4. p. 222.

5. *Fuṣ.*, pp. 222–223/177.

6. p. 223.

7. *Fuṣ.*, p. 223/177.

8. *Fuṣ.*, p. 224/177

9. *Fuṣ.*, p. 227/180.

10. p. 227

11. Accordingly, *raḥmah al-imtinān* is sometimes called *al-raḥmah al-raḥmāniyah*, and *raḥmah al-wujūb* is called *al-raḥmah al-raḥīmīyah*.

12. *Fuṣ.*, p. 191/151.

13. *Fuṣ.*, p. 192/152.

14. *Fuṣ.*, p. 193/153.

15. *Fuṣ.*, pp. 123–124/106.

16. Why does Ibn 'Arabi specifically emphasize that everything other than the Absolute is 'possessed of a spirit' (*dhū rūḥ*)? Bālī Efendi thinks (p. 124) that it is because, according to the Qoran, everything is 'praising God', and the act of 'praising' comes only from a spirit. We may, I think, also understand the phrase 'possessed of a spirit' in the sense of 'possessed of life'. As we shall see in the next chapter, everything, in Ibn 'Arabī's world-view, is 'alive'.

17. *Fuṣ.*, p. 124/106.

18. *Fuṣ.*, pp. 276–278/221.

19. *Fuṣ.*, pp. 261–262/210.

20. p. 261.

21. *Fuṣ.*, p. 262/210.

22. *Fuṣ.*, pp. 206–207/165.

23. 'Command' (*amr*) is different from the Will (*mashī'ah*). The latter, as we have seen, is absolute, and its decree irrevocable. Disobedience is out of question here. The Command is of two kinds: (1) mediate (*bi-al-wāsiṭah*) and (2) creational (*takwīniy*). The second concerns the coming into existence of anything, and is identical with the Will. The first, however, is identical with the Sacred Law (*shar'*), and may be disobeyed.

24. *Fuṣ.*, pp. 207–208/165–166.

25. *Raḥmah Allāh fī al-akwān sāriyah, Fuṣ.*, p. 225/177.

26. *Fuṣ.*, p. 225/178.

27. *ibid.*

28. *Fuṣ.*, p. 226/178.

29. *Fuṣ.*, p. 273/219.

30. *Fuṣ.*, p. 133/112.

31. p. 133.

32. The Divine Names, as we already know, are the relations which the Absolute bears toward the things of the world. And on this level, there occur in the Absolute oppositions in accordance with the Names, such as 'Inward' – 'Outward', 'First' – 'Last', etc.

33. *Fuṣ.*, p. 144/119.

34. *Fuṣ.*, p. 273/219. In the case of 'spirits' or non-material beings, the 'breath' spreads through 'spiritual matter' (*hayūlà rūḥānīyah*), and in the case of 'accidents' through 'accidental matter'.

35. *Fuṣ.*, p. 182/143–144.

36. Man breathes, for example, and his breath 'receives' sounds and words, which are linguistic 'forms' – al-Qāshānī, p. 182.

37. *Fuṣ.*, pp. 182–183/mrmf

38. 'Vapor' (*dukhān*), or 'steam', to be compared with the *ch'i* of the ancient Chinese. Of the 'vapor' of the elements, that which is 'subtle' becomes the governing spirits of the seven Heavens, whereas that which is 'coarse' becomes the seven Heavens themselves.

39. The Essence itself has nothing to do with the appearance of the world. But as soon as it comes down to the level of Names it becomes 'independent'. And as soon as it becomes 'independent' it becomes opposed to 'dependent', thus causing a primary polarization within the Absolute itself.

40. The world, thus produced, necessarily reflects the nature of its immediate creator, the 'breath of the Merciful'. And since the 'breath of the Merciful' requires polarizations because of the self-polarizing nature of the Divine Names, the world also is split into oppositions.

41. *Fuṣ.*, p. 185/145.

42. 'God shows Mercy toward Himself' because the Divine Names are ultimately no other than God Himself.

43. *Fuṣ.*, Com., pp. 197–198.

44. i.e., the so-called 'proximate causes' (*asbāb qarībah*).

45. *Fuṣ.*, pp. 255–256/203.

46. *Fuṣ.*, p. 256/203.

47. *Fuṣ.*, p. 256/204.

48. Note that Ibn ʿArabī recognizes in God the temporally produced Knowledge in addition to the 'eternal' (*qadīm*) Knowledge. He thereby stands definitely against the majority of the theologians.

X   The Water of Life

In the preceding chapter we have seen that the Mercy of God pervades all beings on all levels of Being. We know also that this is another way of saying that the Being of the Absolute pervades all beings which are at all entitled to be described as 'existent', and that the Form of the Absolute runs through the entire world of Being. This thesis, in this general form, is the same as that which was discussed in Chapter IV under the key-word *tashbīh*. In the present chapter the same general problem will be reconsidered from a particular point of view.

The key-word to be considered as the starting-point of discussion in this particular context is *laṭīf*, meaning roughly 'subtle', 'thin' and 'delicate'. *Laṭīf* stands opposite to *kathīf*. This latter word connotes the quality of things 'thick', 'dense' and 'coarse', that is, those things that are characterized by dense materiality. As the semantic opposite of this, *laṭīf* means the quality of things, the materiality of which is in the extreme degree of rarefaction, and which, therefore, are capable of permeating the substances of other things, diffusing themselves in the latter and freely mixing with them. The fact that this word, *laṭīf*, is one of the Divine Names is, for Ibn 'Arabī, extremely significant.

The Name *laṭīf* or 'Subtle' with this particular connotation represents the Absolute as a Substance (*jawhar*) which, immaterial and invisible, permeates and pervades the entire world of Being just as a color permeates substances. This Substance which is infinitely variable runs through everything and constitutes its reality. All individual things are called by their own particular names and are thereby distinguished one from the other as something 'different', but these differences are merely accidental. Seen from the viewpoint of the invisible Substance running through the whole world, all things are ultimately one and the same. Let us listen to Ibn 'Arabī himself as he explains this point in his peculiar way.[1]

(God) says of Himself: 'Verily God is *laṭīf* ' (XXXI, 16). It is indeed the effect of His *laṭāfah* (i.e., His being *laṭīf*, in the above explained sense of non-material flexibility) and His *luṭf* (i.e., His being *laṭīf* in the sense of graciousness)[2] that He is (immanent) in every particular thing which is determined as such-and-such by a particular name, as the inner reality of that particular thing. He is immanent in every particular thing in such a way that He is, in each case, referred to by the conventional and customary meaning of the particular name of that thing. Thus, we say (usually), 'This is Heaven', 'This is the earth', 'This is a tree', 'This is an animal', 'This is a king', 'This is food' etc. But the essence itself that exists in every one of these things is simply one.

The Ash'arites uphold a similar view when they assert that the world in its entirety is homogeneous in its Substance, because the world as a whole is one single Substance. This corresponds exactly to my thesis that the essence is one. The Ash'arites go on to say that the world (in spite of the homogeneousness) differentiates itself (into different things) through accidents. This also is identical with my thesis that (the one single Essence) differentiates itself and becomes multiple through forms and relations so that (the things) become distinguishable from one another. Thus in both of these theories, *this* is not *that* (i.e., the particular things are different from one another) in regard to the 'form' (*ṣūrah*), or 'accident' (*'araḍ*), or 'natural disposition' (*mizāj*) – you may call this (differentiating principle) by whatever name you like – but, on the other hand, *this* is the same as *that* in regard to their 'substance'. And this is why the 'substance' itself (as 'matter') must be explicitly mentioned in the definition of every thing (having a particular) 'form' or 'natural disposition'.

However (there is also a fundamental difference between my position and the Ash'arites; namely), I assert that (the Substance here in question) is nothing other than the 'Absolute', while the (Ash'arite) theologians imagine that what is called Substance, although it *is* a 'reality', is not the same absolute Reality as understood by the people who (uphold the theory of) 'unveiling' and 'self-manifestation'.

But this (i.e., what I teach) is the profound meaning of God's being *laṭīf*.

It is remarkable that in this passage Ibn 'Arabī recognizes to a certain degree an identity between his thesis and the Ash'arite ontology. The theologians of this school take the position that the world is essentially one single Substance and all the differences between individual things are due to accidental attributes. However, Ibn 'Arabī does not forget to emphasize the existence of a basic difference between the two schools. As al-Qāshānī says, 'the Ash'arites, although they assert the unity of the Substance in all the forms of the world, assert also the essential duality, namely, that the essence of the Substance pervading the world is different from the Absolute'.[3]

The Qoran, immediately after stating that 'God is *laṭīf*', declares that 'God is *khabīr*', that is, God has information about everything.

This, too, has a very special significance for Ibn 'Arabī. If the *laṭīf* is a reference to the relation of the Absolute with the external things existing in the world, the *khabīr* refers to the relation of the Absolute with the 'interior' i.e., consciousness, of all those beings that possess consciousness. The Absolute, in other words, not only pervades all things that exist outwardly in the world, but runs through the interior of all beings possessed of consciousness and constitutes the inner reality of the activity of consciousness. The Absolute is Omniscient, and His Knowledge is eternal. So, in this sense, all without exception are known to the Absolute from eternity. But in addition to this kind of eternal Knowledge, the Absolute also penetrates into the interior of each one of the beings endowed with consciousness and knows things through the organs of cognition peculiar to those things. If one looks at the matter from the opposite, i.e., human, side, one will find that all those things that man thinks he sees or hears are in reality things that the Absolute residing in his interior sees and hears through his sense organs.

This latter kind of Knowledge is called by Ibn 'Arabī – in contrast to the 'absolute' Knowledge (*'ilm muṭlaq*) – the 'experiential' Knowledge (*'ilm dhawqiy* or *'ilm 'an ikhtibār*). According to him, the Qoranic verse: 'Surely We will try you in order to know' (XLVII, 31) refers precisely to this kind of Knowledge. Otherwise, it would be completely meaningless for God to say 'in order to know', because God knows (by the 'absolute' Knowledge) everything from the beginning. The verse is meaningful because it concerns the 'experiential' Knowledge.

It is characteristic of the 'experiential' Knowledge, which is evidently a temporal phenomenon (*ḥādith*), that it necessarily requires an organ of cognition through which it is obtained. Since, however, God has no organs, the cognition is operated through the organs of individual beings,[4] although, as we know by the principle of *laṭāfah*, the things that outwardly appear as *human* organs are nothing other than various phenomenal forms assumed by the Absolute itself.

God (in the Qoran) qualifies Himself by the word *khabīr*, that is, one who knows something by personal experience. This applies to the Qoranic verse: 'Surely We will try these people in order to know'. The words 'to know' here refer to the kind of Knowledge obtainable through personal experience. Thus God, despite the fact that He (eternally) knows everything as it really is, describes Himself as 'obtaining Knowledge' (in an non-absolute way) . . . And he distinguishes thereby between 'experiential' Knowledge and 'absolute' Knowledge.
The 'experiential' Knowledge is conditioned by the faculties of cognition. God affirms this by saying of Himself that He is the very cognitive faculties of man. Thus He says (in a Tradition), 'I am his

hearing', hearing being one of the faculties of man, 'and his sight', sight, being another of man's faculties, 'and his tongue', tongue being a bodily member of man, 'and his feet and hands'. And we see, He mentions in this explanation not only faculties of man, but even goes to the length of mentioning bodily members (and identifies Himself with them). And since man is after all no other than these members and faculties, the inner reality itself of that which is called man is (according to this Tradition) the Absolute. This, however, is not to say that the 'servant' (i.e., man) *is* the 'master' (i.e., God).[5] All this is due to the fact that the relations in themselves are essentially distinguishable from each other, but the (Essence) to which they are attributed is not distinguishable (i.e., divisible). There is only one single Essence in all the relations. And that single Essence is possessed of various different relations and attributes.[6]

The Absolute, in this sense, pervades and runs through all. The Absolute is in all beings of the world, according to what is required by the reality (i.e., the eternal 'preparedness') of each thing. If it were not for this permeation of the Form of the Absolute through the things, the world would have no existence.[7] For, as al-Qāshānī says,[8] 'The fundamental ground of the possible things is nonexistence. And existence is the Form of God. So if He did not appear in His Form, which is existence *qua* existence, the whole world would remain in pure non-existence'.

All beings in the state of ontological possibility absolutely require the permeation of Existence in order to leave the original state of non-existence and to come into the state of existence. This state of affairs is considered by Ibn 'Arabī analogous to the notion that any attribute or quality shown by a concrete particular thing cannot exist *in actu* except as an individualization of a Universal.[9] Incidentally, there is in Ibn 'Arabī's thought-pattern a conspicuous tendency toward Platonizing, although we surely cannot call him offhand a Platonist. The present case is an example illustrating this phase of his thought. The following remark by al-Qāshānī makes this point very explicit.[10]

(Ibn 'Arabī here) compares the essential dependence of the existence of the world on the 'form' (i.e., the essential reality) of the Existence of God to the dependence of particular properties on universal realities, like 'life' in itself and 'knowledge' in itself.

The existence, for example, of 'knowledge' in a particular person, Zayd, is dependent on the universal 'knowledge' *per se*. If it were not for the latter, there would be no 'knower' in the world, and the property of 'being a knower' would rightly be attributed to nobody. In exactly the same manner, every determinate individual existent is dependent on the Existence of the Absolute, Existence being the Absolute's 'Face' or Form. Apart from the Existence of the Absolute, nothing would be existent, nor would existence be predicated of anything.

Since, in this way, nothing can be called an 'existent' (*mawjūd*), except when it is pervaded by the Form of the Absolute, all the existents essentially need the Absolute. This need resides deep in the very core of every existent. It is not one of those ordinary cases in which something needs externally something else. This inner essential dependence is called by Ibn 'Arabī *iftiqār*[11] (lit. 'poverty', i.e., 'essential need').

But the Absolute, on its part, cannot be actualized on the level of the Names and Attributes without the world. The Absolute, in this sense, needs the world. And thus the relation of *iftiqār* is reciprocal; the *iftiqār* of the world to the Absolute is in its existence, and the *iftiqār* of the Absolute to the world concerns the 'appearance' or self-manifestation of the former. This is expressed by Ibn 'Arabī in verse:[12]

> We (i.e., the world) give Him that by which He appears in us, while He gives us (the existence by which we come into outward appearance). Thus the whole matter (i.e., Being) is divided into two, namely, our (giving) Him (appearance) and His (giving us existence.)

Ibn 'Arabī describes this particular relation that obtains between the Absolute and the creaturely world by a bold and vividly evocative image of Food (*ghidhā'*) which he ascribes to Sahl al-Tustarī. As al-Qāshānī says:[13]

> The Absolute is the 'food' of the creatures in regard to existence, because the creatures exist, subsist, and are kept alive by the Absolute just in the same way as food keeps the man existent and alive who eats it and gets nourishment out of it. . . .
> The Absolute, on its part, eats, and is nourished by, the properties of the phenomenal world and the forms of the creatures . . . in the sense that by virtue of the latter alone do the Names, Attributes, Properties and Relations make their actual appearance in the Absolute.

The Names and attributes would not have existence if there were no world, no creatures. The creatures 'nourish' the Absolute as its 'food' by making manifest all the perfections of the Names and Attributes.

> You are God's food through (your) particular properties. But He is also your food through the existence (which He confers upon you). In this respect He fulfils exactly the same function (toward you) as you do (toward Him). Thus the Command comes from Him to you, but it also goes from you to Him.[14]
> Certainly, you are called *mukallaf* in the passive form (i.e., you are in this world a morally responsible person who is 'charged' with the responsibilities imposed upon you by the Sacred Law) and yet God has 'charged' you only with what you yourself asked Him, saying 'charge me (with such-and-such)!', through your own state (i.e., permanent archetype) and through what you really are.[15]

The thesis that the Absolute *qua* Existence is the food and nourishment of all the creatures is relatively easy to understand even for common-sense. But less easily acceptable is the reverse of this thesis; namely, that the creatures are the food of the Absolute.

> Nourishing things nourish those who assimilate them. As nourishment penetrates the body of the living being in such a way that finally there does not remain a single part that has not been pervaded by it, so does the food go into all the parts of one who has assimilated it. The Absolute, however, has no parts. So there is no other way than the 'food' penetrating all the ontological stations (*maqāmāt*) of God which are usually called the Names. And the Divine Essence becomes actually manifest by means of those stations (when the latter become penetrated by the 'food').[16]

Food cannot act as food, that is, cannot nourish the body unless it penetrates all the parts of the body and is completely assimilated by the bodily organism. So the condition is that the body has parts. But the Absolute has no part, if we understand the word 'part' in a material sense. However, in a spiritual sense, the Absolute does have 'parts'. The spiritual 'parts' of the Absolute are the Names. This conception has a grave implication, for it affirms that the Absolute on the level of the Names is thoroughly penetrated by the creatures, and that only by this penetration do all the possibilities contained in the Absolute come into concrete existence.

Thus we see that the *tajallī* or Divine self-manifestation is not at all a unilateral phenomenon of the Absolute permeating everything in the world and making itself manifest in the forms of the world. The *tajallī* involves, at the same time, the permeation of the Absolute by the things of the world. Since, however, it is absurd even to imagine the things of the world *qua* substances penetrating the Absolute in such a way that they be assimilated by the latter, we must necessarily understand the process as something purely non-substantial. And the same is true of the other side of the process, I mean, the penetration of the world by the Absolute and the self-manifestation of the Absolute in the things of the world. The interpenetration of the two which takes place in the process of *tajallī* is not something that occurs between the Absolute as an Entity and things as entities. It is a phenomenon of pure Act on both sides. This point, I think, is of paramount importance for a right understanding of Ibn 'Arabī's conception of *tajallī*, for, unless we understand it in this way, we fall into a most coarse kind of materialism.

We shall bring this section to an end by quoting with running commentary a few verses in which Ibn 'Arabī describes this process of reciprocal penetration:[17]

> 'Thus we are to Him, as we are to ourselves. This has been proved by our proofs'. (Thus we, the world, are 'food' for God because it is we

who sustain Him in concrete existence, as we are 'food' to ourselves, i.e., we sustain ourselves in existence by being ourselves).
'He has no Being except my Being. And we owe Him our existence as we subsist by ourself'. (I, the world, am the only thing by which He manifests Himself in the world of Being. We, the world, exist only in the capacity of a locus for His self-manifestation, but, on the other hand, we are independent beings existing by ourselves as determinate things).
'Thus I have two faces, *He* and *I*. But He does not have *I* through (my) *I'. (I, as a concrete individual being, am possessed of two faces opposed to each other. One of them is the Absolute *qua* my inmost essence, i.e., my He-ness. The other face is turned toward the world, and is my outer I-ness by which I am a creature different from the Absolute. Thus every creature obtains through the Absolute both He-ness and I-ness, while the Absolute does not obtain I-ness from the world, because the I-ness of any individual creature does not constitute by itself the *I* of the Absolute).
'But He finds in me a locus in which to manifest Himself, and we are to Him like a vessel'. (By manifesting Himself in my I-ness, He establishes His I-ness in Himself.)

With these preliminary remarks, we turn now to the proper subject of the present chapter, the permeation of the entire world by Divine Life.

As we have seen, 'existence' (*wujūd*), in the world-view of Ibn 'Arabī, is primarily and essentially the Absolute itself in its dynamic aspect, i.e., as *Actus*. 'Existence' here does not simply mean that things are just there. The concept of 'existence' as the Absolute *qua Actus* is given special emphasis by Ibn 'Arabī when he identifies it with Life.

To say that the Absolute pervades and permeates all beings is to say that Divine Life pervades and permeates the world of Being in its entirety. The whole universe is pulsating with an eternal cosmic Life. But this pulsation is not perceptible to the majority of men. For them, only a small portion of the world, is alive, i.e., only some of the beings are 'animals' or living beings. In the eyes of those who see the truth, on the contrary, everything in the world is an 'animal' (*ḥayawān*).

> There is nothing in the world but living beings, except that this fact is concealed in the present world from the perception of some men, while it becomes apparent to all men without exception in the Hereafter. This because the Hereafter is the abode of Life.[18]

Existence-Life pervades all and flows through all. The Existence-aspect of this fact is easy to see for everybody because everybody understands without any difficulty that all 'things' are existent. But the Life-aspect is not so easily perceivable. This is the reason why the majority of people do not see that everything in the world is alive. To see this, the special experience of 'unveiling' (*kashf*) is necessary.

The Absolute in its self-manifestation does not, as we have already observed, possess uniformity; on the contrary, the self-manifestation is infinitely variable and multiple according to the loci of manifestation. Thus, although it is true that Existence or Life pervades all, it does not pervade all uniformly and homogeneously. The modes of this pervasion vary from case to case according to the degree of purity (*ṣafā'*) and turbidity (*kudūrah*). The Philosophers understand the differences thus produced in terms of the degree of the right proportion (*i'tidāl*) in the mixture of the 'elements' (*'anāṣir*).[19] In those cases, they maintain, in which the elemental mixture is actualized in a well-proportioned form, the result is the birth of animals. And when the mixture occurs in such a way that the right proportion of the elements is no longer maintained, we get plants. And if the mixture is further away from the right proportion, we get minerals or 'inanimate' things.

From the viewpoint of Ibn 'Arabī such a theory is characteristic of those who are blind to the basic fact that Divine Life is manifested in the things of the world in various degrees of 'purity' and 'turbidity'. Ordinary people will see the real fact only in the Hereafter when the 'veil' over their sight will be removed. But the people of 'unveiling' know already in the present world that everything is alive with the all-pervading Life of the Absolute.

For Ibn 'Arabī, the most appropriate symbol of Life is afforded by 'water'. Water is the ground of all natural elements, and it flows and penetrates into even the narrowest corners of the world. 'The secret of Life has diffused into water'.[20] And everything in existence has a watery element in its very constitution, because water is the most basic of all elements. Everything is alive because of the 'water' it contains. And the 'watery' element contained in all things in varying degrees corresponds to the He-ness of the Absolute which, as *Actus*, runs through all.

It is significant that Ibn 'Arabī mentions 'water' in this sense at the outset of the chapter which deals with the 'wisdom of the Unseen' symbolized by Job. Affīfī points out quite appropriately in this connection that Job is, for Ibn 'Arabī, a symbol of a man who strives to obtain 'certainty' (*yaqīn*) about the world of the Unseen. The excruciating pain which Job undergoes is, therefore, not a physical pain, but the spiritual suffering of a man who strives for, but cannot attain to, 'certainty'. And when Job implores God to remove from him this pain, God commands him to wash himself in the running water beneath his feet. Here 'water' symbolizes Life that runs through all the existents, and 'washing oneself in water' means to immerse oneself in the 'water of existence' and to know thereby the reality of existence.[21]

Thus the Water of Life is eternally flowing through all. Each single thing is in itself a unique existent, and yet it is immersed in the limitless ocean of Life together with all the other existents. In the first aspect, everything is unique and single, but in the second aspect, everything loses its identity in the midst of the 'water' that flows through all.

Everything in the world has, in this way, two distinct aspects: (1) the aspect in which it is its own self, and (2) the aspect in which it is Divine Life. The first aspect, which is the creaturely aspect of each individual existent, is called by Ibn 'Arabī *nāsūt* or the 'human (or personal) aspect' and the second, which is the aspect of the Absolute in each individual existent, is called *lāhūt* or the 'divine aspect'.

According to Ibn 'Arabī, 'life' is of a spiritual nature. For it is of the very essential nature of 'spirit' that it vivifies everything which it touches. As Bālī Efendi remarks,[22] 'life' is the primary attribute of 'spirit', and 'spirit' strikes whatever it touches with this primary attribute.

> Know that all spirits have a peculiar property by which they bring to life everything that comes under their influence. As soon as a spirit touches a thing, there flows through it life.[23]

And in the view of Ibn 'Arabī, the whole world of Being is under the direct influence of the Universal Spirit. So all the things that exist are without a single exception in touch with it, and are, therefore, alive. Only the way they are influenced by it actually varies from one individual to another in accordance with the particular 'preparedness' of each. In other words, things differ one from the other in the intensity of Life they manifest, but all are the same in that they maintain their 'selves' in the midst of the all-pervading Life.

> The (universal) Life which flows through all things is called the 'divine aspect' (*lāhūt*) of Being, while each individual locus in which that Spirit (i.e., Life) resides is called the 'human aspect' (*nāsūt*). The 'human aspect', too, may be called 'spirit', but only in virtue of that which resides in it.[24]

The intimate relationship between *nāsūt* and *lāhūt* in man may be compared to the relationship that exists between 'dough' (*'ajīn*) and 'leaven' (*khamīr*).[25] Every man has in himself something of the Divine 'leaven'. If he succeeds in letting it grow in a perfect form, his 'dough' will come completely under its influence and will finally be transformed into something of the same nature as the 'leaven'. This is what is called in the terminology of mysticism 'self-annihilation' (*fanā'*).

Sufism and Taoism

Notes

1. *Fuṣ.*, p. 239/188–189.

2. *Laṭīf* has two meanings: (1) 'subtle' and (2) 'gracious'. The property of being (1) is called *laṭāfah* and the property of being (2) is called *luṭf.*

3. p. 239.

4. In truth, however, the things that are called the organs of cognition in man are nothing other than particular phenomenal forms assumed by the Absolute itself. We know this by the above-explained principle of *laṭāfah.*

5. i.e., the He-ness (inmost essence) of 'servant', considered independently of the relation of servant-ness, *is* the Absolute as considered independently of the relation of its being God and Master. But, of course, the essence of 'servant' *qua* 'servant', i.e., considered in his servant-ness, is not 'master' *qua* 'master'. – al-Qāshāni p. 240.

6. p. 240/189.

7. *Fuṣ.*, p. 24/55.

8. p. 24.

9. 'If it were not for those universal, intelligible realities (*ḥaqā'iq ma'qūlah kulliyah*, corresponding to the Ideas of Plato), there would never appear anything in the world of concrete individual existents (*mawjūdāt 'ayniyyah*)' – *Fuṣ.*, p. 24/55.

10. p. 24.

11. *Fuṣ.*, p. 24/55.

12. *Fuṣ.*, p. 181/143.

13. pp. 180–181.

14. The Command is issued to Him by you in the sense that, in bestowing existence upon man, He never deviates from the way which has been eternally determined by the archetypes.

15. *Fuṣ.*, pp. 76–77/83.

16. *Fuṣ.*, p. 79/84.

17. *ibid.*

18. *Fuṣ.*, p. 194/154.

19. See, for instance, the explanation given by al-Ghazāli in his *Maqāṣid al-Falāsifah*, pp. 274–275, Cairo (Sa'ādah), 1331 A.H.

20. *Fuṣ.*, 213/170.

21. Affifi, *Fuṣ.*, Com., p.245.

22. p. 172.

23. *Fuṣ.*, p. 172/138.

24. *Fuṣ.*, p. 173/138.

25. *Fuṣ.*, p. 189/149.

XI   The Self-manifestation of the Absolute

Reference has frequently been made in the preceding pages to the concept of 'self-manifestation' (*tajallī*). And in not a few places the concept has been discussed and analyzed in some detail. This is proper because *tajallī* is the pivotal point of Ibn 'Arabī's thought. Indeed, the concept of *tajallī* is the very basis of his world-view. All his thinking about the ontological structure of the world turns round this axis, and by so doing develops into a grand-scale cosmic system. No part of his world-view is understandable without reference to this central concept. His entire philosophy is, in short, a theory of *tajallī*. So by discussing various problems relating to his world-view we have been in fact doing nothing other than trying to elucidate some aspects of *tajallī*. In this sense, we know already quite a lot about the main topic of the present chapter.

Tajallī is the process by which the Absolute, which is absolutely unknowable in itself, goes on manifesting itself in ever more concrete forms. Since this self-manifestation of the Absolute cannot be actualized except through particular, determined forms, the self-manifestation is nothing other than a self-determination or self-delimination of the Absolute. Self-determination (-delimination) in this sense is called *ta'ayyun* (lit. 'making oneself a particular, individual entity'). *Ta'ayyun* (pl. *ta'ayyunāt*) is one of the key-terms of Ibn 'Arabī's ontology.

The self-determination, as it develops, forms a number of stages or levels. Properly and essentially, these stages are of a non-temporal structure, subsisting as they do beyond the boundaries of 'time'. But at the same time they come also into the temporal order of things and give a particular ontological structure to it.

At any rate, when we describe this process we are willy-nilly forced to follow the temporal order. And this is naturally what Ibn 'Arabī himself does in his description of the phenomenon of *tajallī*. But it would be a mistake if we thought that this is merely a matter of necessity caused by the structure of our language, as it would be equally wrong to suppose that the self-manifestation of the Absolute is an exclusively temporal process.

The self-manifestation of the Absolute is, in fact, possessed of a double structure. It is a trans-historical, trans-temporal phenomenon, but it is also a temporal event. One might even say that this is precisely the greatest *coincidentia oppositorum* observable in the structure of Being. It is a temporal event because from eternity the same process of *tajallī* (the Absolute→the world) has been repeated and will go on being repeated indefinitely. Since, however, exactly the same ontological pattern repeats itself infinitely, and since, moreover, it is done in such a way that as the first wave is set in motion, there already begins to rise the second wave, the process in its totality comes to the same thing: an eternal, static structure.

This dynamic-static self-manifestation of the Absolute is described in terms of the 'strata' (*marātib,*sg.*martabah*). Let us first observe how al-Qāshānī explains the 'strata'.[1]

He begins by saying that there is in Being nothing except one single Reality (*'ayn*) which is the Absolute, and its 'realization' (*ḥaqīqah*), which is Being in its phenomenal (*mashhūd*) aspect. But, he adds, this phenomenal aspect of Being is not a one-stratum structure, but it comprises six major strata.

The first stratum: Being at this stage is still completely free from any limitation. This stratum represents 'Reality' in its non-determination (*lā-ta'ayyun*) and non-delimitation (*'adam inḥiṣār*). In other words, there is as yet absolutely no self-manifestation occurring; Being is still the absolute Essence itself rather than a part of phenomenal reality. And yet it *is* capable of being considered a part of phenomenal reality in the sense that it forms the starting-point of all the subsequent ontological stages. It is no longer the Essence *per se* in its metaphysical darkness.

The second stratum: Being is here 'determined' in itself by a kind of all-comprehensive self-determination comprising all the active determinations pertaining to the Divine aspect of Being (i.e., the Divine Names) as well as all the passive determinations pertaining to the creaturely or phenomenal aspect of Being. The Absolute at this stage still remains One. The One is not yet actually split into multiplicity; yet there is observable a faint foreboding of self-articulation. The Absolute, in other words, is *potentially* articulated.

The third stratum: this is the stage of Divine Unity (*al-aḥadīyah al-ilāhīyah*) or that of *Allāh*, where all the active (*fā'iliy*) and effective (*mu'aththir*) self-determinations are realized as an integral whole.

The fourth stratum: this is the stage at which the Divine Unity (3rd stage) is split into independent self-determinations, i.e., the Divine Names.

The fifth stratum: this stage comprises in the form of unity all the self-determinations of a passive nature (*infi'āliy*). It represents the unity of the creaturely and possible things of the world of becoming. The sixth stratum: here the unity of the preceding stage is dissolved into actually existent things and properties. This is the stage of the 'world'. All the genera, species, individuals, parts, accidents, relations, etc., become actualized at this stage.

As we see, this description by al-Qāshānī of the Divine self-manifestation as a multi-strata structure presents the phenomenon of *tajallī* in its static, i.e., non-temporal, aspect. Ibn 'Arabī himself prefers to present the same thing in a much more dynamic way. He distinguishes two major types of *tajallī* to which we have often referred in the preceding; namely, the 'most holy emanation' (*al-fayḍ al-aqdas*) and the 'holy emanation' (*al-fayḍ al-muqaddas*).

It is to be remarked that Ibn 'Arabī uses the Plotinian term 'emanation' (*fayḍ*) as a synonym of *tajallī*. But 'emanation' here does not mean, as it does in the world-view of Plotinus, one thing overflowing from the absolute One, then another from that first thing, etc. in the form of a chain. 'Emanation', for Ibn 'Arabī, simply means that the Absolute itself appears in different, more or less concrete forms, with a different self-determination in each case. It means that one and the same Reality variously articulates and determines itself and appears immediately in the forms of different things.

The first type of 'emanation', the 'most holy emanation', corresponds, as we have seen, to what is described by a famous Tradition in which the Absolute *per se*, i.e., the absolutely Unknown-Unknowable, desires to leave the state of being a 'hidden treasure' and desires to be known. Thus we see that the 'most holy emanation' is for the Absolute a natural and essential movement.

The 'most holy emanation' represents the first decisive stage in the self-manifestation of the Absolute. It is the stage at which the Absolute manifests itself not to others but to itself. It is, in modern terminology, the rise of self-consciousness in the Absolute. It is important to remark, further, that this kind of self-manifestation has occurred from eternity. It is, as Nicholson says, 'the eternal manifestation of the Essence to itself'.[2]

The self-manifestation of the Absolute to itself consists in the forms of all the possible existents making their appearance *in potentia* in the Consciousness of the Absolute. Another way of expressing the same idea is to say that the Absolute becomes conscious of itself as potentially articulated into an infinity of existents. The important point here lies in the word 'potentially' or *in potentia*. It indicates that the Consciousness of the Absolute being split into plurality is an event occurring only in the state of possibility; that the Absolute is not yet actually split into many, and, therefore, still maintains its original Unity. It is, in other words, a state in which the potential

Many are still actually One. In contradistinction to the real Unity in which there is not even a shadow of the Many, i.e., the Unity of *aḥadīyah*, this Unity which is potentially plurality is called *wāḥidīyah* or Oneness.

Since the Many in the plane of Oneness are Many as the content of the Consciousness of the Absolute (Divine 'Knowledge' as the theologians call it), they are, philosophically, pure intelligibles, and not real concrete existents. They are nothing more than 'recipients' (*qawābil*) for existence. They are those that would be real existents if they receive existence. In this sense the Many in this plane are 'possible existents' (*mawjūdāt mumkinah*) or 'existents *in potentia*' (*mawjūdāt bi-al-quwwah*).[3]

On this level, there is as yet nothing existent in actuality. The world itself is not existent. Yet there are dimly discernible the figures of the would-be things. I say 'dimly discernible'; this is merely an imaginary picture of this ontological situation supposedly seen from outside. In reality and in themselves, these figures are the content of the Consciousness of the Absolute, and as such, nothing can possibly be more solidly definite and distinct. They are 'realities' (*ḥaqā'iq*) in the full sense of the word. They are in themselves far more real than what we regard as 'real' in this world. They look dim and hazy from *our* point of view, because they belong to the world of the Unseen (*ghayb*). These realities as *intelligibilia* are called by Ibn 'Arabī 'permanent archetypes' (*a'yān thābitah*) of which details will be given in the next chapter.

The word 'emanation' (*fayḍ*) is, as remarked above, completely synonymous for Ibn 'Arabī with 'self-manifestation' (*tajallī*). And he calls the 'most holy emanation' also 'essential self-manifestation' (*tajallī dhātiy*). This latter term is defined by al-Qāshānī as follows:[4]

> The essential self-manifestation is the appearance of the Absolute under the form of the permanent archetypes which are ready to receive existence and whose domain is the Presence (i.e., ontological level) of Knowledge and Names, i.e., the Presence of Oneness (*wāḥidīyah*). By this appearance the Absolute descends from the presence of Unity (*aḥadīyah*) to the Presence of Oneness. And this is the 'most holy emanation' of the Absolute, which consists in that the pure Essence not yet accompanied by any Names manifests itself (in the plane of the Names). So there can be no plurality at all (in actuality) in this self-manifestation. It is called 'most holy' because it is holier than the self-manifestation which occurs in the visible world as actualization of the Names, which therefore occurs in accordance with the 'preparedness' of each locus.

The second stage of the self-manifestation, the 'holy emanation – also called 'sensuous self-manifestation' (*tajallī shuhūdiy*) – means that the Absolute manifests itself in the infinitely various forms of the Many in the world of concrete Being. In common-sense language we might say that the 'holy emanation' refers to the coming into being of what we call 'things', including not only substances, but attributes, actions, and events.

From the particular point of view in Ibn 'Arabī, the 'holy emanation' means that the permanent archetypes, which have been brought into being by the 'most holy emanation' leave the state of being intelligibles, diffuse themselves in sensible things, and thus cause the sensible world to exist in actuality. In plain Aristotelian terminology, it means the ontological process of the transformation of things in *potentia* into corresponding things *in actu*. This is clearly a deterministic ontology, because, in this world-view, the actual form in which everything exists in the world is an ultimate result of what has been determined from eternity. As al-Qāshānī says:[5]

> The sensuous self-manifestation which occurs through the Names follows the 'preparedness' of the locus in each case. This kind of self-manifestation is dependent upon the 'recipients' which are no other than the loci in which the Names become manifested. In this respect it is completely different from the essential self-manifestation, because the latter is not dependent upon anything whatsoever.

The relation between these two forms of self-manifestation is discussed by Ibn 'Arabī in an important passage of the *Fuṣūṣ*. In this passage he happens to be talking about the coming into being of the 'heart' (*qalb*). But we are entitled to replace it by anything else and thus to understand it as a general theoretical explanation of the two forms of self-manifestation.[6]

> God has two forms of self-manifestation: one is self-manifestation in the Unseen and the other in the visible world.
> By the self-manifestation in the Unseen He gives the 'preparedness' which will determine the nature of the heart (in the visible world). This is the essential self-manifestation whose reality is the Unseen. And this self-manifestation in the Unseen is (that which constitutes) the He-ness which rightly belongs to Him (as the objectifying projection of Himself toward the outside), as is witnessed by the fact that He designates Himself by (the pronoun of the third person) 'He'.[7] Thus God is 'He' eternally, everlastingly.
> Now when the 'preparedness' is actualized for the heart, there occurs correspondingly in the visible world the sensuous self-manifestation. The heart, on its part, perceives it, and assumes the form of that which has manifested itself to it.

We may summarize all this in a general theoretical form as follows. The first self-manifestation of the Absolute brings into being the permanent archetypes which are the self-manifesting forms of the

Divine Names, i.e., the ontological possibilities contained in the Absolute. These archetypes are 'recipients' waiting for concrete existentiation. They provide loci for the second type of self-manifestation. And each locus (*maḥall*) has a definite 'preparedness' which, as an immediate effect of the first self-manifestation of the Absolute, is eternal and unalterable. Even the Absolute cannot alter or modify it, because it is a form in which the Absolute manifests itself. Thus the Absolute, in making each 'recipient' a locus of its second (sensuous) self-manifestation, determines itself in strict accordance with the eternal 'preparedness' of the 'recipient'. The Absolute in this way takes on indefinitely various forms in its sensuous self-manifestation. And the totality of all these forms constitute the phenomenal world.

Such a description is liable to suggest that there is an interval of time between the first and the second self-manifestation. In reality, however, there is no relation of priority and posteriority between the two. Everything occurs at one and the same time. For, in the very moment in which 'preparedness' arises on the part of a thing (in truth, however, every 'preparedness' is already in existence from eternity because the first type of self-manifestation has been going on from eternity,) the Divine Spirit flows into it and makes it appear as a concretely existent thing. As we have remarked at the outset, the relation between the two kinds of self-manifestation is a temporal phenomenon, being at the same time a non-temporal or trans-temporal structure. In this latter sense, the self-manifestation in the Unseen and the self-manifestation in the visible world are nothing but two basic constituent elements of Being.

> The Divine procedure (concerning the self-manifestation) is such that God never prepares any locus but that it (i.e., that locus) receives of necessity the working of the Divine Spirit, a process which God describes as 'breathing into' it. And this refers to nothing else than the actualization, or the part of the locus thus formed, a particular 'preparedness' for receiving the emanation, that is, the perpetual self-manifestation that has been going on from eternity and that will be going on to eternity.[8]

Notes

1. p. 239. Cf. Chapter I, where al-Qāshānī gives a slightly different explanation of the matter.

2. R.A. Nicholson, *Studies in Islamic Mysticism*, Cambridge, 1921, p. 155, N. 1.

3. *Fuṣ.*, p. 10/49.

4. p. 10.

5. pp. 10–11.

6. *Fuṣ.*, pp. 145–146/120.

7. In the Qoran God frequently speaks in the third person, referring to Himself as 'He' instead of 'I'.

8. *Fuṣ.*, p. 10/49.

XII Permanent Archetypes

The concept of 'permanent archetype' (*'ayn thābitah*, pl. *a'yān thābitah*) has a number of important facets. So, in order that we might fully elucidate its essential structure, it must be considered analytically from different points of view. Although most of these different aspects of the 'permanent archetype' have been referred to in the course of the preceding chapters, some of them having been discussed at considerable length and others more or less incidentally touched upon, we shall deal with them all in the present chapter in a more systematic way.

I The Intermediary Nature of the Archetypes

That which we know best about the archetypes is their ontologically intermediate status. Briefly stated, the plane of the archetypes occupies a middle position between the Absolute in its absoluteness and the world of sensible things.

As a result of this peculiar ontological position, the archetypes have the double nature of being active and passive, that is, passive in relation to what is higher and active in relation to things that stand lower than themselves. Their passivity is expressed by the word *qābil* (pl. *qawābil*) which Ibn 'Arabī often uses in his description of the archetypes. They are 'recipients', receptive and passive in so far as they are nothing but potentialities in the Divine Essence. Their nature is passively determined by the very inner structure of the Essence. But considered in themselves, they are of a self-determining nature and exercise a determining power over the possible things of the world. They are each the eidetic reality (*'ayn*) of a possible thing. And all the possible things become actualized in the phenomenal world each according to the requirement of its own permanent archetype.

As we have remarked earlier,[1] the Absolute must 'breathe out' because of the intense inner compression of Being. It is in the very nature of the Absolute that it should externalize itself. The

Absolute, in this respect, is not a static 'One', but a dynamic 'One' with a natural propensity for self-externalization and self-articulation. Outwardly and actually it is unquestionably 'One', but inwardly and potentially it is Many.

It is important to note that this self-externalization of the Absolute is done according to certain fixed patterns at both the first and the second stage of *tajallī*. The Absolute, at the first stage of *tajallī*, articulates itself not haphazardly but through certain definite channels. These channels have been fixed from eternity by the very inner structure of the Absolute. Theologically, they are the Divine Names. And the permanent archetypes are the essential forms (*ṣuwar*) of the Divine Names. Since, moreover, all this is an occurrence within the Divine consciousness, the archetypes are realities (*ḥaqā'iq*) eternally subsistent in the world of the Unseen.

And these realities definitely determine the form of the second stage of the self-manifestation, i.e., the self-manifestation of the Absolute in the concrete individual things in the external world. Here again the Absolute manifests itself in the phenomenal world not in haphazard forms; the forms in which it manifests itself are determined by the eternal realities that have been produced by the first *tajallī*. If we suppose, for example, that there were in the plane of the archetypes nothing but Horse and Man, there would be in our world only horses and men, nothing else.

The archetypes are, in this sense, double-faced. On the one hand, they are essentially determined by the Absolute, because they owe their particular existence to the latter. But, on the other, they positively determine the way in which the Absolute actualizes itself in the phenomenal world. As to this determining force of the archetypes, details will be given presently. Here it is sufficient to note that the intermediary nature of the archetypes is clearly observable in the peculiarity which has just been mentioned.

The second important point in which the intermediary nature of the archetypes stands out with utmost clarity is their 'being non-existent' (*ma'dūm*).

> The essences of the possible things (i.e., the permanent archetypes) are not luminous because they are non-existent. Certainly they do have permanent subsistence (*thubūt*), but they are not qualified by existence, because existence is Light.[2]

The fact that Ibn 'Arabī designates the archetypes by calling them 'the essences of the possible things', though in itself an important statement, is not relevant to our present concern.[3] Rather, we should note here his judgment that the archetypes are 'non-existent'. Similarly in another passage he says:[4]

The archetypes are essentially characterized by non-existence (*'adam*). Surely they are 'permanently subsistent' (*thābitah*), but they are permanently subsistent only in the state of non-existence. They have not even smelt the fragrance of existence. Thus they remain eternally in that state (i.e., non-existence) despite the multiplicity of the forms (which they manifest in the existent things).

Ibn 'Arabī judges the archetypes to be 'non-existent' because in this particular context he understands the word 'existence' (*wujūd*) in the sense of 'external existence'. Seen from the viewpoint of external or phenomenal existence, the archetypes are not existent, although they are 'permanently subsistent'. The 'permanent subsistence' (*thubūt*) is different from external existence. Symbolically, the archetypes are 'dark'. They are dark because they are not yet illumined by the bright daylight of existence. Existence as Light belongs only to the individual things that exist concretely and externally.

It is patent, then, that it is not Ibn 'Arabī's intention to assert that the archetypes are non-existent in an absolute sense. We have already observed that the archetypes are permanent 'realities' that subsist in the Divine Consciousness. They do exist in the same sense in which concepts are said to exist in the human mind. He only means to say that the archetypes do not possess a temporally and spatially determined existence. And in this very particular sense, the Divine Names, too, must be said to be non-existent. 'The Names in their multiplicity are but relations which are of a non-existent nature'.[5]

Thus we see that it is not strictly exact to regard the archetypes as non-existent. More exact it is to say they are neither existent nor non-existent. And, in fact, Ibn 'Arabī himself explicitly says so in a short, but exceedingly important article to which incidental reference was made in an earlier place.[6] It is to be noted that in this passage he takes up a more philosophical position than in his *Fuṣūṣ* in dealing with the problem of the archetypes.

> The third thing[7] is neither qualified by existence nor by non-existence, neither by temporality nor by eternity (*a parte ante*). But it has always been with the Eternal from eternity. . . .
> It is neither existent nor non-existent. . . . But it is the root (i.e., the ontological ground) of the world. . . . For from this third thing has the world come into being. Thus it is the very essential reality of all the realities of the world. It is a universal and intelligible reality subsisting in the Mind. It appears as eternal in the Eternal and as temporal in the temporal. So, if you say that this thing is the world, you are right. And if you say that it is the Absolute, the Eternal, you are equally right. But you are no less right if you say that it is neither the world nor the Absolute, but something different from both. All these statements are true of this thing.

Thus it is the most general Universal comprising both temporality (*ḥudūth*) and eternity (*qidam*). It multiplies itself with the multiplicity of the existent things. And yet it is not divided by the division of the existent things; it is divided by the division of the intelligibles. In short, it is neither existent nor non-existent. It is not the world, and yet it is the world. It is 'other', and yet it is not 'other'.

The main point of this argument is that this 'third thing' *is* the world in potentiality, but that, from the viewpoint of the world as a real and concrete existent, it is not the world, but rather non-Being and the Absolute.

Then Ibn 'Arabī proceeds to examine the problem from the standpoint of Aristotelian philosophy and identifies this third thing which can neither be said to exist nor not to exist with the *hayūlà* or Prime Matter,[8]

> The relation of this thing . . . with the world is comparable to the relation of wood with (various things fabricated out of wood, like) a chair, wooden case, pulpit, litter etc., or to the relation of silver with (silver) vessels and objects made of silver like collyrium-cases, earrings, and rings.
> The comparison makes the nature and essence of this (third) thing clear. Take, then, only the relation here suggested (between wood and pieces of furniture made of wood) without, however, picturing in your mind any diminishing in it (i.e., in the third thing) as you picture actual diminishing in the wood when a writing-desk is taken out of it. Know that wood itself is a particular form assumed by 'wood-ness'. (Do not picture in your mind a piece of wood, but) concentrate your attention upon the intelligible universal reality which is 'wood-ness'. Then you will see that 'wood-ness' itself neither diminishes nor is divided (by your actually fabricating real objects out of wood). On the contrary, 'wood-ness' always remains in its original perfection in all the chairs and desks without ever diminishing. Nor does it increase a bit in spite of the fact that in a wooden desk, for example, there are many realities gathered together besides the reality of 'wood-ness', like that of 'oblong-ness', that of 'square-ness', that of 'quantity' etc., all of them being therein in their respective perfection. The same is true of any chair or pulpit.
> And the 'third thing' is precisely all these 'realities' in their respective perfection. So call it, if you like, the reality of realities, or *hayūlà* (Greek *hyle*), or Prime Matter, or the genus of all genera. And call these realities that are comprised by this third thing the 'primary realities' or 'high genera'.

One special point is worthy of notice in this connection. Ibn 'Arabī here observes the intermediary nature of the archetypes not only in their being neither existent nor non-existent, but also in their being neither 'temporal' nor 'eternal'. So it is wrong, or at least an oversimplification, to say that Ibn 'Arabī takes up the position that 'the world is eternal (*qadīm*)'[9] because the archetypes are eternal.

Surely the archetypes *are* 'eternal' in a certain sense precisely because they represent the intermediary stage between the Absolute and the phenomenal world. But they are 'eternal' only secondarily and derivatively in the sense that they, as the content itself of the Divine Consciousness or Knowledge, have been connected (*muqārin*) with the Absolute from eternity. Their eternity is in this sense essentially different from the eternity of the Absolute.

Generally speaking, and particularly in cases of this kind, the true nature of anything intermediary is impossible to describe adequately by language. Thus one is forced to resort, as Ibn 'Arabī actually does, to a clumsy expression, like 'it is neither eternal nor temporal, but it is, on the other hand, both eternal and temporal'. If from the whole of this complex expression we pick up only the phrase, '(it is) eternal' and draw from it the conclusion that Ibn 'Arabī maintained the doctrine of the eternity of the world,[10] we would be doing him gross injustice.

In a passage of the *Fuṣūṣ*, in connection with the problem of the absolute inalterability of the cause-caused relationship in this world, Ibn 'Arabī discusses the 'eternity'-'temporality' of the archetypes in the following way.[11]

> There is absolutely no way of making the causes effectless because they are what is required by the permanent archetypes. And nothing is actualized except in the form established for it in the archetypal state. For 'there is no altering for the words of God' (X, 64). And the 'words of God' are nothing other than the archetypes of the things in existence. Thus 'eternity' is ascribed to the archetypes in regard to their permanent subsistence, and 'temporality' is ascribed to it in regard to their actual existence and appearance.

These words clarify the intermediary state peculiar to the archetypes between 'eternity' and 'temporality'.

II   The Archetypes as Universals

As we have noticed in the preceding section, the archetypes in Ibn 'Arabī's thought are, theologically, 'realities' in the Knowledge of God, i.e., intelligibles existing permanently and eternally in the Divine Consciousness alone. But from the point of view of scholastic philosophy, they are Universals standing over against Particulars. And the relation of the archetypes to the world is exactly the ontological relation of Universals to Particulars. The problem of how the Divine self-manifestation is actualized in the realm of external existence through the fixed channels of the archetypes is nothing other than the problem of the individuation of Universals.

We must note that this aspect on Ibn 'Arabī's philosophy is to a considerable extent Platonic. In any event, the permanent archetypes, *in this particular aspect*, remind us of the Ideas of Plato. There is, in his *Fuṣūṣ*, an important passage where he develops this problem scholastically.[12] There he deals with the philosophical aspect of Divine Attributes such as Knowledge, Life, etc.[13] It will be clear by what has preceded that his theory of Attributes is identical with the theory of archetypes.

> We assert that the universal things (*umūr kullīyah*, i.e., Universals corresponding to Platonic Ideas), although they have no actual existence in themselves, are unquestionably (existent as) intelligibles and objects of knowledge, in the mind (i.e., primarily in the Divine Consciousness, and secondarily in the human minds). They remain 'interior' (*bāṭinah*) and never leave the state of invisible existence[14] (i.e., the state of existence in the plane of the Unseen).

The passage is paraphrased by al-Qāshānī as follows:[15]

> The 'universal things', that is, those things that are essentially non-material (*muṭlaqah*) such as Life and Knowledge, have a concrete existence only in Reason, while in the outer world they have an invisible existence. This is because existence in the outer world is the very same non-material intelligibles as determined by concrete, individual conditions. But (even when it is actualized in the outer world) a non-material Universal still remains in the state of being an intelligible and still stands under the name 'Interior'. A Universal never exists in the outer world in its universality, but only in a concretely determined form. And in this latter capacity only does a Universal come under the name 'Exterior'.

Ibn 'Arabī goes on to argue:[16]

> But (i.e., although their existence is invisible) Universals have a powerful and positive effect on everything that has a concrete individual existence. Rather, the individualized existence – I mean, all individual existents *are* nothing other than Universals. And yet Universals in themselves never cease to be pure intelligibles. Thus they are 'exterior' in respect to their being concrete existents, but they are 'interior' in respect to their being intelligibles. So every concrete thing that exists has its origin in the (realm of) these 'universal matters' which have the above-mentioned peculiarity, namely, that they are inseparably connected with Reason and that they can never come to exist in the plane of concrete existence in such a way as to cease to be pure intelligibles. This basic situation does not change whether a particular individual existent (in which a Universal is actualized) happens to be something temporally conditioned (e.g., ordinary material objects) or something beyond the limitations of time (e.g., higher Spirits). For a Universal bears one and the same relation to both temporal and non-temporal things.

The relation between Universals and Particulars is not as one-sided as this passage might suggest; it has also an aspect in which Particulars do exercise a determining force upon Universals. A Universal, as we have just seen, remains eternally the same as it appears in individual particulars, say, *a b c d*. But since each one of these particulars has its own peculiar 'nature' (*ṭabī'ah*), the Universal must necessarily be affected by *a b c d* as it is actualized in them. The Universal, in other words, becomes tinged in each case with a particular coloring.

> The 'universal matters', on their part, are also positively affected by the concrete existents in accordance with what is required by the individual realities of the latter.
> Take for example the relation of 'knowledge' to 'knower', and 'life' to 'living being'. 'Life' is an intelligible reality, and 'knowledge' is an intelligible reality, both being different and distinguishable from one another. Now we say concerning God that He has Life and Knowledge, so He is Living and He is a Knower. Likewise, we say concerning an angel that he has 'life' and 'knowledge', so he is 'living' and he is a 'knower'. Lastly, we say concerning man that he has 'knowledge' and 'life', so he is 'living' and a 'knower'.
> (Throughout all these cases) the reality of 'knowledge' is one, and the reality of 'life' is one. The relation of 'knowledge' to 'knower' and of 'life' to 'living' is equally one. And yet we say concerning the Knowledge of God that it is eternal, while concerning the 'knowledge' of man we say that it is temporal. See what a positive effect has been produced upon the intelligible reality ('knowledge') by the particular attribution. See how the intelligibles are connected with the concrete individual existents. Just as 'knowledge' affects the substrate in which it inheres to make it deserve the appellation 'knower', the particular substrate to which 'knowledge' is attributed affects the 'knowledge' in such a way that it becomes temporal in a temporal being and eternal in the eternal being. Thus both sides affect each other and are affected by each other.[17]

As to the ontological status of Universals, Ibn 'Arabī says that they are 'non-existent', meaning thereby that they are not endowed with concrete individual existence in the material world. But, of course, as we know already, they are not sheer 'nothing'; they do have a particular kind of existence, i.e., non-material, intelligible existence.

A Universal becomes actualized in an individual thing and naturally becomes tinged with a special coloring peculiar to the locus. But since in such a case it is not individualized in itself, it does not become qualified by the properties of distinction and divisibility which are characteristic of individual things. While, therefore, the relation between a Particular and a Particular is a solid one, being based on the strong tie of concrete physical existence, the relation between a Universal and a Particular, although far more essential than the former relation, is weaker because it is an essentially 'non-existential', i.e., intelligible relation.

It is patent that these 'universal matters', although they are intelligibles, are non-existent in terms of concrete physical existence, but are only existent as an invisible (but real) force (affecting the concrete individual things.) When, however, they enter into actual relation with individual existents, they also are affected by the latter. They do accept the positive effect (exercised by the individual existents) except that they do not thereby become physically distinct and divided. For this is absolutely impossible to occur (to a Universal). For it remains as it is in all individuals which are qualified by it – like, for example, 'humanity' (*insānīyah* 'being-a-man') appearing in each single individual of the species of man – being itself never particularized, never becoming multiple despite the multiplicity of individuals, and never ceasing to be intelligible.

Thus it is clear that there is a close reciprocal tie between things possessed of a concrete existence (i.e., Particulars) and things that are deprived of a concrete existence (i.e., Universals). And yet the Universals are in the nature of 'non-existence'. So the reciprocal tie existing between concrete things and concrete things is more easily conceivable, because in this case there is always a third term which connects the both sides together: I mean, concrete existence. In the former case, on the contrary, there is no such connecting link, and the reciprocal tie subsists here without a connecting link. Naturally, the relation with such a link is stronger and more real.[18]

III Necessity and Possibility

As we have seen already, Ibn 'Arabī often refers to the permanent archetypes as 'essences of the possible things' (*a'yān al-mumkināt*) meaning thereby the essential realities of the possible things. The word *mumkināt* or 'possible things' points, on the face of it, to concrete individual existents in the world. This is justified in so far as the concrete existents of Particulars are essentially 'possible' because they do not have in themselves the principle of existence. On the other hand, however, they are not 'possible' but rather 'necessary' in so far as they exist in actuality in definitely fixed forms. From this point of view, what are essentially 'possible'' are the archetypes. For the archetypes, as has been made clear in the preceding section, remain in themselves 'intelligible' without being individualized.

There are some among the thinkers, says Ibn 'Arabī, who, 'because of the weakness of their intellect' deny the category of 'possibility' (*imkān*) and assert that there are only two ontological categories: 'necessity by itself' (*wujūb bi-al-dhāt*) and 'necessity by (something) other (than itself)' (*wujūb bi-al-ghayr*). However, he goes on to say, those who know the truth of the matter admit the category of 'possibility', and know that 'possibility', though it is after all a kind of 'necessity by other', does possess its own peculiar nature which makes it the third ontological category.[19]

Explicating this idea of his Master, al-Qāshānī analyzes the concept of 'possible' (*mumkin*) as follows.[20] All existents are divisible into two major categories according to the relation which the reality of a thing bears to existence: (1) the thing whose reality by itself requires existence, and (2) those whose reality by itself does not require existence.

The first is the 'necessary by itself' or the Necessary Existent. The second is further divided into two categories: (1) those whose very nature requires non-existence, and (2) those whose nature by itself requires neither existence nor non-existence. The first of these is the category of the 'impossible', while the second is the 'possible'. Then he says:

> Thus the 'possible' is an ontological dimension (*ḥaḍrah*, lit. 'Presence') peculiar to the plane of Reason, a state before external existence, considered in itself. Take, for example, 'black'. In itself it is only in the plane of Reason, requiring neither existence nor non-existence. But in the outer world it cannot but be accompanied either by the existence of a cause or by the absence of cause, there being no third case between these two.
>
> And when the cause is present in its complete form, the existence of the thing (the 'possible') becomes 'necessary'. Otherwise, its non-existence is 'necessary' due to non-existence of a complete cause. (In the first case, it is 'necessary by other', while in the second case) it is 'impossible by other'. Thus we see that the 'possible' in the state of real existence is a 'necessary by other'. But in itself and in its essence, i.e., apart from its actual state of existence, it is (still) a 'possible by itself'.

The definition of the 'possible' by al-Qāshānī, namely, that it is an ontological state in which a thing finds itself previous to external existence, makes it patent that a Universal is essentially and in itself a 'possible', for a Universal in itself is an 'existent in Reason', that is, a pure intelligible, before it goes into the state of external existence. His explanation also makes it clear that a Universal, when it becomes particularized and enters into the domain of external existence in the form of an individual, obtains two features. In its essence, it is still a 'possible' even in the state of external existence, but it is a 'necessary by other' in so far as it is now existent externally and has thereby what we might call an ontic necessity. Such is the real nature of everything that is called 'temporal' (*ḥādith* or *muḥdath*).[21] And that which causes this ontological transformation, i.e., that which brings out an 'essentially possible' into the sphere of external existence and changes it into an 'accidentally necessary' can be nothing other than the 'essentially necessary', the Absolute.

There can be no doubt that a temporally originated thing (*muḥdath*) is definitely something brough into existence (by an agent), so it has an ontological need (*iftiqār*, lit. 'poverty') towards an agent that has produced it. This is due to the fact that, such a thing being essentially 'possible', its existence must come from something other than itself. The tie which binds such a thing to its originator is a tie of ontological need.

That (agent) to which a 'possible' owes its existence in such an essential way can be nothing other than something whose existence is necessary in itself, and which does not owe its existence to anything else and has, therefore, no need of anything else. It must be this thing that – by itself – gives existence to all temporal things so that the latter are essentially dependent upon it.

Since, however, the coming into existence of the 'possible' is what is required essentially by the 'necessary', the former acquires (in this respect) a 'necessity' from the latter. And since, moreover, the dependence of the 'possible' on the ('necessary') from which it comes into existence is essential, the 'possible' must necessarily appear in the likeness of the 'necessary'. And this likeness extends to every name and attribute possessed by the 'possible', except one single thing: the essential necessity (*wujūb dhātiy*), for this last thing can never come to a temporally produced thing. Thus it comes about that a temporal thing, although it *is* a 'necessary' existent, its 'necessity' is not its own but is due to something other than itself.[22]

IV   The Absolute Power of the Archetypes

The archetypes are 'permanent' or 'permanently subsistent' (*thābitah*), i.e., they have been fixed once for all in the eternal past, and are, therefore, absolutely unalterable and immovable. 'There is no altering for the words of God' (X, 64). This absolute unalterableness of the archetypes restricts in a certain sense even the activity of the Absolute. This may sound blasphemous at first, but in reality it is not so. For, theologically speaking, it is the very Will of God that has given them this unalterableness, and in a terminology more characteristic of Ibn 'Arabī, they are no other than inner determinations of the Absolute itself.

It is not for the Divine Will to change what has been determined at the stage of the archetypes. And it is unthinkable that God should will such a thing. The Qoranic statement concerning the disbelievers: 'but if He so willed, He would have guided you aright all together' (XVI, 91) might seem to imply that it is quite possible that

God should will just the contrary of what has actually happened, i.e., the contrary of what has been determined on the level of the archetypes. This, however, is due, according to Ibn 'Arabī, to a very simple misunderstanding. The particle *law* meaning 'if' (in the clause 'if He so willed' *fa-law shā'a*) is a grammatical device for expressing a supposition of something which is actually impossible. Thus the Qoranic verse suggests rather the absolute impossibility of God's wishing to guide aright the disbelievers.[23]

We established in the preceding section that the archetypes are 'possibles'. But in the light of what we have just seen about the immovable fixity of the archetypes, we must admit also that their 'possibility' is of a very particular nature. A 'possible' is a thing which is capable of becoming either *a* or its contradictory, non-*a*. Thus, to take an example directly relevant to the Qoranic verse just mentioned, a man as a 'possible' is capable of becoming either a 'believer' or a 'disbeliever', that is, of receiving in actuality either the 'guidance' of God or 'going astray from the Way'. In reality, however, it is determined from the very beginning whether the thing will be actualized as *a* or as non-*a*. If it happens to be determined in the direction of *a*, for instance, even God cannot change its course and actualize it as non-*a*.

> A 'possible' is in itself capable of receiving either something or its contradictory, on the level of rational reasoning. But as soon as it is actualized as either of the two logically possible things, (we come to know that) *that* was the thing for which the 'possible' was destined when it was in the archetypal state. . . .
>
> Thus (it is clear in the case of those disbelievers referred to in the above-quoted Qoranic verse that) God actually did not 'will' that way, so that He did not guide aright all those people. Nor will He ever 'will' that way. 'If-He-wills' will be of no avail. For is it at all imaginable that He should do so? No, such a thing will never come to pass. For His Will goes straight to its objects (in accordance with what has been determined from eternity) because His Will is a relation which strictly follows His Knowledge, and His Knowledge strictly follows the object of Knowledge. And the object of Knowledge is you and your states (i.e., the individual thing and its properties as they have been immovably fixed in the state of archetypal permanence). It is not the Knowledge that influences its object, but rather it is the object of Knowledge that influences the Knowledge, for the object confers what it is in its essence upon the Knowledge.[24]

God knows each individual thing in its eternal essence, and exercises His Will on the basis of that Knowledge. But, as we already know, God's exercising His Will is the same as His bestowing existence. So, since God's bestowal of existence is done in this way on the basis of His Knowledge about the eternal essence of each

thing, the existence bestowed upon individual things must necessarily assume a different form in each case.
  But there is also another aspect to the matter. The existence itself which God bestows upon the things is, in so far as it is existence, always one and the same. Existence *qua* existence can never differ from one case to another. God bestows upon all things one and the same existence, but the individual 'recipients' receive it in different ways, each according to its own particular nature, and actualize it in different forms. Ibn 'Arabī describes this aspect of the matter by saying: God does nothing more than bestowing existence; it is men who determine and delimit it individually, and give it particular coloring, each according to his archetype.

> 'There is not even one among us but has his own determined position' (XXXVII, 164). This (i.e., the 'determined position') refers to what you were in the state of archetypal subsistence according to which you have come into being. You can look at the matter in this way when you affirm that you *do* have existence. But even if you affirm that existence belongs to the Absolute, not to you, still you have unquestionably a determining power upon the existence coming from the Absolute. Of course, once you are a real existent, your determining power has undoubtedly a part to play in it, though properly speaking the ultimate Determiner is the Absolute.
> In this respect, then, to the Absolute belongs only the act of directing existence toward you, while the actual determination of it belongs to you. So do not praise except yourself, do not blame except yourself. There remains for the Absolute only the praise for having given (you) existence. For that definitely is the act of the Absolute, not yours.[25]

This way of thinking cannot but raise a number of crucial problems within the framework of Islamic thought. Most noteworthy of them is the repercussion it produces in the field of moral ideas.
  All men are just as they are, according to Ibn 'Arabī, because they have been so determined by their own permanent archetypes from eternity. No one in the world, whether he be good or bad, a believer or a disbeliever, goes against the Will of God. Taking the example of one who disobeys the Apostle of God, 'contender' (*munāzi'*), Ibn 'Arabī argues:[26]

> He who contends against him (i.e., the Apostle of God) is not thereby deviating from his own reality in which he was in the archetypal state when he was still in the state of non-existence. For nothing comes into being except that which he had in the state of non-existence, i.e., archetypal subsistence. So (by struggling in opposition to the Apostle of God) he is not stepping over the boundaries set by his reality, nor does he commit any fault on his (predetermined) road.
> Thus calling his behavior 'contending' (*nizā'*) is merely an accidental matter which is a product of the veils covering the eyes of ordinary

people. As God says: 'But the majority of men do not know. They know only the apparent surface of the present world, while being completely neglectful of the Hereafter' (XXX, 6–7). Thus it is clear that it (i.e., regarding their behavior as 'contending') is nothing but an inversion (i.e., one of those things which the people whose eyes are veiled turn upside down).

This argument on the 'contender' applies to every phenomenon in the world. Everything, whether good or bad from the human point of view, is what it is in accordance with what has been definitely and immovably determined from eternity. Everything, in this sense, goes the way prepared beforehand by the Divine Will, and nothing can deviate from it.

If the distinction between good and bad is but an accidental matter, and if everything occurs as it has been determined by its own archetype, the doctrine of the reward for the good and the chastisement for the bad, which is one of the most basic articles of faith in Islam, must necessarily be gravely affected. Here follows the peculiar interpretation by Ibn 'Arabī of the problem of 'reward and punishment' (*thawāb-'iqāb*).[27]

The rise of the distinction between good and bad (from the religious point of view) is a phenomenon which occurs only at the level upon which human beings live a social life in a religious community. He who, at this level, is regarded as morally responsible is called by the Law a *mukallaf* meaning 'one who is *charged* with responsibilities'.

Now when a *mukallaf* acts in the light of the Law, either he 'obeys' its injunctions or 'disobeys' and 'rebels' against it. It is a truism or even a tautology to say that in the former case the man is *muṭī'*, i.e., one who is obedient to God. But the important point is that, in Ibn 'Arabī's view, in the second case he is no less obedient to God than in the first. For even in the second case, the man acts as he does simply according to the dictates of his permanent archetype, which, as we know, is a direct manifestation of the Divine Will.

Of course, when a man 'disobeys' God, there is no other way for Him than either forgiving him or punishing him. But the remarkable fact about this is that God, on His part, 'obeys' the man, and acts according to the dictates of his actions. The 'obedience' (*inqiyād*) occurs here, as Bālī Effendi remarks, on both sides. And this, Ibn 'Arabī says, is the meaning of 'religion' (*dīn*) in the sense of *islām* (= *inqiyād* 'obedience') as well as in the sense of *jazā'* 'requital'.

Religion, indeed, is 'requital', he says. When a man 'obeys' God, He requites him with 'what pleases' him, while when he 'disobeys', God requites him with 'what displeases' him. Requital with what is pleasing is called 'reward', and requital with what is displeasing or painful is called 'punishment'. Subjectively, there is naturally a serious difference between 'reward' and 'punishment', and the difference is keenly felt by the man who obtains 'reward' and 'punishment' respectively. Objectively, however, there is no fundamental difference between the two. For in both cases, God is just acting in 'obedience' to the requirement of the archetype. A certain archetype necessarily requires a certain action on the part of a man, and that action necessarily requires, on the part of God, either 'reward' or 'punishment'.

> Thus when a man obtains something good (i.e., 'reward'), he himself is the one who gives it to him. And when he obtains something bad (i.e., 'punishment'), it is no other than himself that gives it to him. Nay, he is the one who is bountiful (*mun'im*) to him, and he is the one who is his own chastiser (*mu'adhdhib*). So let him praise only himself, and let him blame only himself. 'And God possesses the irrefutable argument' (VI, 149) in His Knowledge about men, because Knowledge follows its objects.
> There is, however, a still deeper understanding of the problems of this kind, which is as follows. All the 'possible' things, in effect, have their root in non-existence. (What is usually regarded as their 'existence') is nothing but the existence of the Absolute appearing in various forms of the modes of being peculiar to the 'possible' things in themselves and in their very essences. And this will make you understand who is the one who really enjoys and who is the one who really suffers. (That is to say, he who is really pleased by the reward and really pained by the punishment is not the man, but the Absolute which manifests itself in the particular form of the man according to his archetype, which, again, is no other than a state of the Absolute itself.) You will also understand thereby what really is the consequence of every state (or action) of the man. (That is to say, the reward or punishment, as the consequence of every action of the man is in reality a self-manifestation of the Absolute in a particular form determined by that action.) Properly speaking, any consequence (of an action) is simply *'iqāb* which is to be understood in the (etymological) sense of 'what follows or results' (*'aqaba*). *'Iqāb* in this sense comprises both a good consequence and a bad consequence, except that in the conventional usage of Arabic, only a bad consequence is called *'iqāb* (in the sense of 'punishment'), while a good consequence is called *thawāb* 'reward'.

If the true meanings of 'good' and 'bad', 'reward' and 'punishment' are what we have just seen, what, then, is the significance of God's raising among men 'apostles' whose function is generally thought to be bidding people do good and avoid evil in order to attain happiness? It is to be expected that in the particular context of Ibn 'Arabī's theory, the conception of 'apostle' (*rasūl*) should turn out to be radically different from the ordinary one.

Comparing the apostles to physicians, Ibn 'Arabī explicates his idea about apostleship as follows:[28]

> Know that, just as a physician is said to be a 'servant of Nature' (*khādim al-ṭabī'ah*), so the apostles and their successors are commonly said to be the 'servants of the Divine Command'. (i.e., It is generally held that the apostles are physicians of the souls, whose function it is to keep the souls in good health and, in case the souls happen to be ill, to bring them back to their normal state.)
>
> In reality, however, the apostles are servants of the ontological modes of the possible things (i.e., their real function is to 'serve', that is, to try to bring out exactly what is required by the essences of the possible things in their archetypal states). But this service of theirs is itself part of their own ontological modes (*aḥwāl*) which are peculiar to them in their state of archetypal subsistence. See how marvellous this is.
>
> Note, however, that the 'servant' to be sought after here, (whether a servant of Nature or a servant of an ontological mode of a possible thing) must remain within the boundaries which the object of his service (i.e., either a sick person or an ontological mode) determines, either by the actual state or by language. (i.e., A physician cures his patient either according to the observed bodily state of the patient or according to what the patient verbally asks for).
>
> A physician would be entitled to be called (unconditionally) a 'servant of Nature' only if he consistently acted to help promote Nature, (but actually no physician is supposed to do such a thing, as will be evident from the following consideration). A physician (is usually called for in those cases in which) Nature has produced in the body of his patient a special state for which the patient is called 'ill'. Now if the physician in such a situation (unreservedly) 'served' Nature, the illness of the patient would thereby simply be increased. So (instead of helping it) he tries to repel and keep off Nature for the sake of health by producing in the patient another bodily state which is just the opposite of his present state, although, to be sure, 'health' itself belongs to Nature, too.
>
> Thus it is clear that the physician is not a 'servant of Nature' (i.e., he does not serve Nature consistently in all cases without distinction). He is only a 'servant of Nature' in the sense that he brings the body of his patient back to health by altering his present bodily state by means of Nature. He serves Nature in a very particular way, not in a general way.

The physician must not serve and promote Nature in all circumstances without discrimination. When, for example, Nature has produced an unhealthy state like diarrhea, he must try to restrain the activity of Nature, and to produce a healthy state. But, since the healthy state thus produced is also part of Nature, he is, by producing it, serving after all the same Nature. And this analogy elucidates the function of the apostle who is the physician of the souls.

Thus the physician serves Nature and does not serve Nature. Likewise, the apostles and their successors serve and do not serve the
Absolute (i.e., they serve the Divine Command not in all its aspects,
but only in its beneficial aspect).

This means that the apostle is a servant of the Divine Command
only, and not a servant of the Divine Will. The Divine Command
does not necessarily coincide with the Will. On the contrary, there
often occurs discrepancy between the two. For the Command is
issued regardless of whether it will be obeyed or not, that is, whether
what is commanded will actually occur or not, while the Will is
absolute, what is willed being of such a nature that it necessarily
occurs. In those cases in which there is discrepancy between the
Command and the Will, the apostle serves the Command, not the
Will. If he served the Will, the apostle, instead of trying to curb evil,
would rather positively promote the evil-doers, and he would not
advise them to stop doing evil. But strangely enough, if the occurrence of 'evil', when it does actually occur, is due to the Will, the
admonishing act of the apostle against it is also due to the Divine
Will.

In a similar way, the effect of a 'miracle' will also appear to be far
less powerful than is commonly imagined. For no matter how many
miracles may be performed, what is determined by the archetypes
can never be altered. The apostles are possessed of a special
spiritual power called *himmah*[29] which enables them to perform
miracles. But whether they do exercise this supernatural faculty or
not, the result will ultimately be the same, because the actual course
of events will never deviate from what has already been determined
by the archetypes.

> The apostles know very well that when a miracle is performed in the
> presence of the (disbelieving) people, some of them turn believers on
> the spot, while some others recognize it but do not show any assent to
> it, acting unjustly, haughtily, and out of envy. There are even some
> who class it as magic and hypnotism. All the apostles are aware of
> this, and know that no one becomes a believer except when God has
> illumined his heart by the Light of belief, and that, if the person does
> not look at (a miracle performed) with this light which is called
> 'belief', the miracle is of no avail to him. This knowledge prevents
> them from exercising their *himmah* in search of miracles, because
> miracles do not have an effect uniformly on all the spectators and
> their hearts.
> To this refers the saying of God concerning the most perfect of the
> apostles and the most knowledgeable of all men: 'Verily thou dost
> not guide aright whomever thou desirest to guide, but it is God who
> guides whomever He wishes.' (XXVIII, 56) . . . In addition to this He
> says in the same place: 'but He is best aware of those who are guided

aright' (XXVIII, 56), that is to say, of those who have imparted to God – through their own permanent archetypes, while still in the state of non-existence – the knowledge that they would be guided aright. All this because God has so decreed that the Knowledge should follow its object in every case, and a man who was a believer in the archetypal permanence and in the state of non-existence should come into existence exactly according to that fixed form: God knows of every man that he will come into existence in such-and-such a form. And this is why He says: 'but He is best aware of those who are guided aright',[30]

The gist of Ibn 'Arabī's argument is given by al-Qāshānī in a more logical form, as follows:[31]

> A perfect knowledge (possessed by the apostles) of the reality of the things necessarily requires that they should behave with humble modesty in the presence of God and that they should not display the power of disposing things at will nor exercise their *himmah* upon anything. For he who really knows the truth knows that nothing at all comes into being except that which has been in the Eternal Knowledge. Everything that has been known (by the Absolute) to occur cannot but occur, and anything that has been known not to occur can never occur.
>
> The whole matter is thus reduced ultimately to a relation between an Agent who knows what is in potentiality in the recipient, and a recipient which does not receive except that which is in its essential and natural 'preparedness'. And if such is the case, upon what is an apostle to exercise his *himmah*? What is the use of his exercising the *himmah*? For anything whose actual occurrence or non-occurrence is known from the very beginning can in no way be altered by his *himmah*. The *himmah* cannot even advance or retard the exact point of time which is assigned to the thing from eternity.
>
> Thus the recipient does not receive except that which the Agent knows from the beginning that it will receive, while the Agent, on His part, does nothing except that which the recipient essentially is to receive. This because the archetypes strictly require by themselves from eternity to eternity what will actually happen to them when they come out into existence, while the Agent-Knower knows only that (i.e., that which is determined by the archetypes).

V   The Mystery of Predestination

As we have repeatedly pointed out in the preceding, the way in which each thing receives existence from the Absolute is strictly determined by its own 'preparedness'. The determining power of the 'preparedness' (*istiʿdād*) is supreme and even the Absolute must follow what it requires.[32]

Now the thesis of the absoluteness of the determining power of

the 'preparedness' is naturally and essentially connected with the
problem of predestination. The problem of predestination was
raised and discussed as something of a vital importance from the
earliest period of Islam under the key-terms *qaḍā'* and *qadar*. Ibn
'Arabī takes up the same problem and discusses it from his particular viewpoint in terms of the theory of the archetypes.

> Know that the 'pre-determination' (*qaḍā'*) is a decisive judgment
> (*ḥukm*, or decree) of God concerning the things. God's decisive
> judgment concerning things is given in strict accordance with His
> Knowledge of the latter themselves and their properties. And God's
> Knowledge about the things is based on what is given by the very
> essences of the things.
> And the 'allotment' (*qadar*) is the specification of the appointed time
> at which each of the things should actually occur in accordance with
> its archetypal state without any alteration. But the *qaḍā'* itself, when
> it decides upon the destiny of each thing, does so only in accordance
> with its archetype. And this is the mystery of the *qadar*. . . .
> Thus, the Judge (*ḥākim*) who issues a decree turns out in reality to be
> acting in obedience to the demand of the very thing upon which He
> makes the decision in accordance with the requirement of its essence.
> In this sense, the thing upon which the decision is made according to
> its essence determines the Judge so that He should decide upon it in
> strict accordance with what it requires. And, in fact, every 'judge'
> who makes a decision upon something becomes determined (lit.:
> decided) by the object on which he makes a decision as well as by the
> ground on which he makes the decision, be the 'judge' who he may
> (i.e., whether he be the Absolute or a human being).[33]

Everything, as we already know, has its essential constitution
irrevocably determined in the archetypal state of non-existence.
God knows it from eternity as it essentially is. And on the basis of
the requirement of this perfect Knowledge God makes a decisive
judgment concerning the thing. And this judgment is the *qaḍā'*.[34]

The *qadar* specifies and determines further what has been
decided by the *qaḍā'*. The specification is done in terms of time. In
other words, every state to be actualized in a thing is determined by
the *qadar* concretely as to the definite time at which it is to occur.
The *qaḍā'* does not contain any time determinations. It is the *qadar*
that assigns to every event its peculiar time. And once determined in
this way, nothing can occur even a minute earlier or later than the
assigned time.

Al-Qāshānī makes an interesting remark on the relation between
the *qaḍā'* and the *qadar* in reference to the Tradition. It is related
that the Prophet once passed under a wall which was about to fall
down. Somebody gave him warning against it and asked, 'Do you
flee from the *qaḍā'* of God?' To this the Prophet replied, 'I flee from
the *qaḍā'* to the *qadar*!' The falling down of the wall may have been

a matter already decided upon, i.e., *qaḍā'*. But, even if the falling down of the wall was in itself an absolutely inescapable thing, the question as to when it would actually occur was not part of the *qaḍā'*. So there was at least room for the Prophet to escape being crushed by the falling wall by having recourse to the *qadar* of the wall.

The relation between the *qaḍā'* and the *qadar* has been described here in such a way that it will naturally suggest to our mind that the former precedes the latter. This description should not be regarded as final and ultimate, for there is a deeper aspect to the whole matter.

We have just said that the *qadar* is a 'further' specification of the *qaḍā'* in terms of time. In reality, however, God determines the *qaḍā'* of a thing in accordance with His Knowledge, which, in its turn, follows in every detail the essential structure of the object of the Knowledge. And the object of the Knowledge is, as we have seen above, the permanent archetype of the thing. And most naturally, the specification of time – or, for that matter, all the possible specifications of the thing – is part of the archetype.[35] In this sense, the *qadar* itself is determined by the archetype. Or we might even say that the *qadar* is the permanent archetype.[36]

There is, however, a subtle difference between the two. The permanent archetype in itself is a Universal transcending the level of time; it is an intelligible in the Divine Consciousness. When a Universal is about to go into the state of actual existence and is about to be particularized in the form of an individual thing, it becomes first connected with a particular point of time and thereby becomes temporally specialized. An archetype in such a state is called *qadar*. It is, in other words, an archetype in a state where all preparations have been completed for being actualized as a concrete existent. Since God, on His part, knows all the conditions of the archetypes, He knows also that such-and-such an archetype is in a fully prepared state for being actualized. And, based on this Knowledge, He judges that this archetype will be actualized as such-and-such a particular thing. This judgment or decree is the *qaḍā'*. Thus we see that there is a certain respect in which the *qadar*, instead of being preceded by the *qaḍā'*, does precede the *qaḍā'* and determines it.

However this may be, it is certain that *qadar* is an extremely delicate state in which an archetype is about to actualize itself in the form of a concretely existent thing. To know *qadar*, therefore, is to peep into the ineffable mystery of Being, for the whole secret of Being extending from God to the world is disclosed therein. Ibn 'Arabī remarks that 'the mystery of *qadar* is one of the highest knowledges, which God grants only to (a small number of) men who are privileged with a perfect mystical intuition'. If a man happens to obtain the true knowledge of *qadar*, the knowledge surely brings him a perfect peace of mind and an intolerable pain at the same time.[37] The unusual peace of mind arises from the consciousness that everything in the world occurs as it has been determined from eternity. And whatever may happen to himself or others, he will be perfectly content with it. Instead of struggling in vain for obtaining what is not in his capacity, he will be happy with anything that is given him. He must be tormented, on the other hand, by an intense pain at the sight of all the so-called 'injustices', 'evils', and 'sufferings' that reign rampant around him, being keenly conscious that it is not in his 'preparedness' to remove them from the world. Ibn 'Arabī ends this passage by expressing a deep admiration for the supreme dominion of the *qadar* over the entire world of Being.[38]

> The reality of the *qadar* extends its sway over the Absolute Being (in the sense that the Absolute is decisively influenced by the 'preparedness' of each thing when the Absolute decides its *qaḍā'*) as well as over the limited beings (in the sense that no being is given anything beyond what has been determined by its own archetype). Nothing can be more perfect than the *qadar*, nothing can be more powerful nor greater than it, because of the universality of its effect, sometimes extending to all things and sometimes limited to particular things.

There is another passage in the *Fuṣūṣ*, in which Ibn 'Arabī pursues further the problem of the knowledge of the *qadar*. This time he attempts a classification of men into several degrees based on the extent to which they know about the *qadar*.

As we have seen above, to know something about the *qadar* is nothing other than knowing something about the permanent archetypes. But how can man know the truth about the archetypes? The archetypes are a deep mystery, the true reality of which is known only to the Absolute, because it is the inner structure of the Divine Consciousness.

Thus it comes about that the majority of people are simply ignorant of the archetypes, and consequently, of the *qadar*. These people constitute the lowest degree on the scale. They know nothing about the determining force of the archetypes, i.e., about the significance of the *qaḍā'* and *qadar*. Because of their ignorance, they ask and implore God to do for them this and that; they naively believe that by the power of prayer they can change the eternally fixed course of events.

Higher than this degree is the degree of people who are aware of the unalterableness of the archetypal determinations. They do not ask for things against or beyond what they know is determined.

These people are restrained from asking (God) by their knowledge that God has already unalterably decided their *qaḍā'*. So they are content with having prepared their places for accepting whatever will come from Him. They have already abandoned their egos and all their selfish motives.[39]

Among people of this kind there are some who know more in detail that the determining power of the *qaḍā'* and *qadar* is the determining power of the 'preparedness' of their own permanent archetypes. They know, so to speak, the inner structure of the *qaḍā'* and *qadar*. These people constitute the third degree of men in terms of their knowledge about the mystery of Being.

This kind of man knows that God's Knowledge concerning everything about him completely coincides with what he was in the state of archetypal subsistence prior to his coming into existence. And he knows that God does not give him except the exact amount determined by the Knowledge about himself with which his archetypal essence has furnished Him. Thus he knows the very origin of God's Knowledge about him.

There is no higher class among the people of God. They are the most 'unveiled' of all men, because they know the mystery of the *qadar*.[40]

But Ibn 'Arabī divides this highest class further into two groups, higher and lower. The lower degree is represented by those who know the mystery of the *qadar* in a broad and general way. The higher degree is represented by those who know it in all its concrete details.

In another place,[41] Ibn 'Arabī explains the same distinction between the higher and the lower degree of the highest class of 'knowers' in terms of 'preparedness' and 'receiving' (*qabūl*). The higher people are those who come to know the 'receiving' by knowing first the 'preparedness' by the experience of 'unveiling'. Once you know your 'preparedness' itself in its integrity, you are in a position to look over from above the whole field of the 'receiving', and nothing of what you will be receiving (i.e., what will be happening to you) will be unknown to you any longer. You are, in other words, the master of your own destiny. In contrast to this, the lower people come to know their own 'preparedness' by experiencing first the 'receiving'. Only after taking cognizance of what actually has happened to them do they realize that they have such-and-such a 'preparedness'. So the knowledge they obtain of their destiny, being conditioned by what actually happens, is necessarily partial. Besides, as al-Qāshānī points out, the knowledge thus obtained is always liable to be mistaken because the process involves inference (*istidlāl*).

Concerning this distinction within the higher degree Ibn 'Arabī remarks:[42]

> He who knows his own *qadar* in concrete details is higher and more complete than the one who knows his *qadar* only in a broad and general way. For the former knows what is in the Knowledge of God concerning him. He obtains his knowledge in one of the two possible ways: either (1) by God's instructing him according to the very knowledge about him which his archetypal essence has first furnished Him with, or (2) by his permanent archetype being directly revealed to him together with all the infinite states that unfold themselves from it. This kind of man is higher because his position in regard to his knowledge about himself is the same as that of God's Knowledge about him, for both derive from one and the same source (i.e., his permanent archetype).

This important passage may be clarified if we interpret it as follows.

Everything in the world is eternally and permanently determined by its own archetype. The inner structure or content of that archetype, however, is an impenetrable mystery because it is part of the Divine Consciousness. But there is only one small aperture, so to speak, through which man can have a peep into this unfathomable mystery. That aperture is the self-consciousness of man. Very exceptionally, when the spiritual force of a man is unusually elevated in the experience of 'unveiling', he may be given a chance of witnessing directly the content of his own archetype. And in such a case, his knowledge about his own archetype is the same as God's Knowledge about him, in the sense that both derive from one and the same source. And by knowing his own archetype, not externally but internally, he takes a peep at the great mystery of the *qadar*.

However, this does not mean that the Knowledge of God and the knowledge of a highest 'knower' are exactly identical with each other in every respect. For the knowledge of a man about his own archetype is conditioned by the actual forms or states in which the archetype is manifested. Though he looks into the content of his archetype with an unusual penetration of insight through and beyond the actual forms it assumes, he has no access to the archetype as it was in the original state prior to existence.

> (It is true that there occurs in the experience of 'unveiling' identification of the human knowledge with God's Knowledge), but if we consider this phenomenon from the side of the man, the whole matter turns out to be a special favor on the part of God who has prepared all this for him from eternity. And (the greatest wonder consists in the fact that) this special favor which God bestows upon him is itself part of the very content of his archetype.
>
> The man who experiences the 'unveiling' comes to know the whole content of his archetype when God lets him have a peep into it. But 'God lets him have a peep into it' means only that God allows him to observe (with unusual clarity and penetration) the states of his

archetype (as actualized in existence). For it is not in the capacity of any creature at all – even in such a (privileged) state in which God allows him to have an insight into all the forms of his permanent archetype in the state in which it receives existence – to gain the same insight as God Himself into the archetypes in their state of non-existence, because the archetypes prior to existence are but essential relations having no definite form at all.[43]

From this we must conclude that although there is a certain respect in which a man's knowledge about his archetype becomes identical with God's Knowledge about it in that both derive from one and the same source, there is also a fundamental difference between the two in that the human knowledge about an archetype concerns it only in the state of existence while God's Knowledge concerns it both before and after its existence. Furthermore, even this partial identification of the human knowledge with the Divine Knowledge is due to a special 'concern' of God with the particular man in whom it realizes.

The only way possible by which man can hope to get this kind of insight into the archetypes is, according to Ibn 'Arabī, the experience of 'unveiling'. Apart from 'unveiling' nothing, not even Divine Revelation to prophets, can give a knowledge of the inner structure of the archetypes. But this does not mean that the experience of 'unveiling' reveals the whole secret of this problem. Ibn 'Arabī is very reserved concerning this point. He merely says that in extremely special cases, the people of 'unveiling' can come to know through their experience something of the mystery (*ba'ḍ al-umūr min dhālik*).[44] The true reality of the *qadar* in its entirety is the deepest of all secrets into which God alone can penetrate, because it concerns the very delicate ontological moments at which the Divine act of 'creation' comes into actual relation with its objects. And in this depth, 'There can be no "immediate tasting" (*dhawq*), no self-manifestation, no "unveiling" except for God alone'.

Compared with Ibn 'Arabī, al-Qāshānī is extremely daring in that he admits straightforwardly that in the case of the mystics of the highest degree there is even the possibility of knowing the reality of the *qadar* in an absolute way.

There is in these words of our Master a clear suggestion that it is not impossible nor forbidden for a man to try to have an insight (into the secret of the *qadar*) through the experience of 'unveiling' and 'illumination' (*tajallī*).[45] It is possible for God to let anybody He likes gain an insight into 'something' of the mystery in a partial way.
Is it possible for a man to gain an unconditional insight into it? No, he can never do that in so far as he is a man. However, when a man becomes annihilated (i.e., in the mystical experience of

'self-annihilation' *fanā*') and loses his name and his personal identity to such a degree that there remains in him no trace of his I-ness and his own essence, thus losing himself completely, then it is possible that he gains an insight into the Reality through the Reality in so far as he himself is the Reality. Of course such a thing never happens except to a man of the most perfect 'preparedness'.[46]

A man who is allowed to have an insight into the depth of the *qadar* through 'immediate tasting' and 'unveiling', whether the insight he gains be partial (as Ibn 'Arabī suggests) or total and absolute (as al-Qāshānī states), is not an ordinary man. We are in the presence of a Perfect Man, a problem with which we shall be occupied in Chapter XV of the present work.

VI   The Mutual 'Constraint' between God and the World

We have seen in the preceding that, in the world-view of Ibn 'Arabī, the power of the 'preparedness' belonging to each of the archetypes is absolutely supreme, so supreme that no force, not even God Himself, can reduce it. Indeed, it is impossible for God even to desire to change its fixed form.

Ibn 'Arabī describes this fact in terms of the concept of reciprocal *taskhīr* between the Absolute and the world. The word *taskhīr*, or its verbal form *sakhkhara*, means in ordinary Arabic, in the field of human relations, that a person endowed with a strong power humbles and overwhelms another and constrains the latter to do whatever he wants him to do. Thus here again Ibn 'Arabī uses an extremely daring expression which might look simply blasphemous to common sense, and states that as the Absolute 'constrains' the world, so the world, on its part, 'constrains' the Absolute.

The idea that God governs the world, things and men, with His absolute power and 'constrains' everything to do whatever He wants it to do is something natural in Semitic monotheism and does not raise any difficulties; but its reverse, i.e., the idea that the world 'constrains' God, is beyond the comprehension of common sense. This idea is understandable and acceptable only to those who know thoroughly the basic structure of Ibn 'Arabī's philosophy and who, therefore, are able to see what he really means by this apparently blasphemous expression. To put it in a nutshell, he means that each thing determines existence in a particular way as required by its own 'preparedness', or that the self-manifestation of the Absolute is actualized in each thing in a definite form in strict accordance with the requirement of the archetype. Thus formulated, the idea turns out to be one which is already quite familiar to us. But this does not mean that the idea of *taskhīr* discloses nothing new to our eyes. In fact the ontological core itself of Ibn 'Arabī's entire philosophizing is surprisingly simple and solidly immovable; it is the different angles from which he considers it that constantly move and change, revealing at every step a new aspect of the core. Every new angle discloses some unexpected aspect of it. As he goes on changing his perspective, his philosophy becomes molded into a definite form. This process itself is, in short, his philosophy. The concept of *taskhīr* is one of those crucial perspectives.

As we have already observed, there are, in Ibn 'Arabī's view, a number of degrees distinguishable among the beings of the world. And the general rule is that a higher order exercises *taskhīr* over a lower order. And this not only applies to the relation between genera and species, but the same phenomenon occurs even among members of one and the same species. A man, for example, subjugates and subordinates another.

This is made possible in the particular case of man by the fact that man has two different aspects: (1) 'humanity' (*insānīyah*) and (2) 'animality' (*ḥayawānīyah*). In the first aspect, man is 'perfect' (*kāmil*), and the Arabic word for man in this sense is *insān*. The second aspect represents the material and animal side of man, and the Arabic word for man in this sense is *bashar*.[47] And the attribute proper to this aspect of man is 'imperfect' or 'defective' (*nāqiṣ*).

In the first aspect, all men are equal to each other; there is no difference of orders or degrees among them, and, therefore, *taskhīr* cannot occur on this level. In the second aspect, on the contrary, there is actually the 'higher'-'lower' relation among men in terms of wealth, rank, dignity, intelligence, etc. Naturally, on this level, a 'higher' man subjugates a 'lower' man.[48] To this we must add that the 'animality' of man and the 'animality' of the animals, though both are the same *qua* 'animality', are different in rank, the former being superior to the latter. Thus the 'animality' of man subjugates and constrains the 'animality' of the animals.

> The animality of man maintains its control over the animality of the animals, because, for one thing, God has made the latter naturally subservient to the former, but mainly because animal in its ontological root (*aṣl*) is non-animal. This is why animal surpasses man in the amount of *taskhīr* it suffers. For a non-animal (i.e., inanimate, which happens to be the ontological root of animal) possesses no will; it is completely at the mercy of one who controls it at will.[49]

Thus Ibn 'Arabī shows at the outset the descending order of *taskhīr*: man → animal → non-animal. Animal vis-à-vis man discloses its ontological 'root' which is non-animal. Thus, although man himself is also an animal, his animality is superior to the animality of animal, because non-human animal in the presence of human animal stands naked, so to speak, in its non-animal root, and behaves toward the latter as a non-animal devoid of will-power. But an animal taken as a full-fledged animal, and not in its non-animal root, is quite different from this.

But animal (not in its root but as an actual being) has will and acts in pursuit of aims. So it comes about that an animal displays obstinate refusal to obey in some cases when one tries to subjugate it. If the animal in question happens to possess the power to manifest this refusal, it does manifest it in the form of restiveness. But if it happens to lack that power or if what a man wants it to do happens to coincide with what it wants to do, then the animal obeys with docility the will of the man.

Similarly a man standing in the same position (as animal vis-à-vis man) to another man acts in obedience to the will of the latter because of something – wealth, for instance – by which God has raised the rank of the latter over the former. He acts this way because he wishes to obtain (part of) the wealth, which in certain cases is called 'wages'. To this refers the Qoranic verse: 'And We have raised some of the people above others by degrees so that they might force one another to servitude' (XLIII, 32). If (of two men) one is subjugated and constrained by the other who is his equal (as a member of the same species 'man'), it is only because of his 'animality', not 'humanity', for two equals *qua* equals remain opposed to each other (and there can be no *taskhīr* between them). Thus the higher of the two in terms of wealth or social status subjugates the lower, acting thereby on the basis of his 'humanity', while the lower is subjugated by the former either from fear or covetousness, acting on the basis of his 'animality', not 'humanity'. For no one can subjugate anybody who is equal to him in every respect. Do you not see how the beasts (that are so docilely subjugated by men) show among themselves a fierce and determined opposition to each other because they are equal?

This is why God says: 'And We have raised some of the people above others by degrees', . . . and *taskhīr* occurs precisely because of these different degrees.[50]

Ibn 'Arabī distinguishes between two kinds of *taskhīr*. One of them is what has just been described. It is called 'constraining by will' (*taskhīr bi-al-irādah*). It refers to a descending order of *taskhīr*, in which a higher being constrains a lower, and which is quite a natural phenomenon observable everywhere in the world of Being.

In contrast to this, the second is an ascending order of *taskhīr*, in which a lower being subjugates and constrains a higher being. In this phenomenon, 'will' (*irādah*) has no part to play. A lower being does not and can not constrain a higher one by exercising his will. Rather the higher being is constrained by the very natural state in which the lower being is found. It is therefore called 'constraining by the state (or situation)' (*taskhīr bi-al-ḥāl*). Here the 'constraining' occurs by the mere fact that the lower and the higher happen to be in a certain relationship with each other. The difference between the two kinds of *taskhīr* is explained by Ibn 'Arabī in the following way:[51]

> The *taskhīr* is of two kinds. The first is a *taskhīr* which occurs by the will of the 'constrainer' (*musakhkhir*) who subdues by force the 'constrained' (*musakhkhar*). This is exemplified by the *taskhīr* exercised by a master over his slave, though both are equal in 'humanity'. Likewise the *taskhīr* exercised by a Sultan over his subjects in spite of the fact that the latter are equal to him as far as their 'humanity' is concerned. The Sultan constrains them by virtue of his rank.
>
> The second kind is the *taskhīr* by the 'state' or 'situation', like the *taskhīr* exercised by the subjects over their king who is charged with the task of taking care of them, e.g., defending and protecting them, fighting the enemies who attack them, and preserving their wealth and their lives, etc. In all these things, which are the *taskhīr* by the 'state', the subjects do constrain their sovereign.[52] In reality, however, this should be called *taskhīr* of the 'position' (*martabah*),[53] because it is the 'position' that compels the king to act in that way.
>
> Some kings (just ignore this and) act only for their own selfish purposes. But there are some who are aware that they are being constrained by their subjects because of their 'position'. The kings of this latter kind know rightly how to estimate their subjects. And God requites them for this with the reward worthy to be given only to those who really know the truth of the matter. The reward which such people obtain is for God alone to give because of His being involved personally in the affairs of His servants. Thus, in this sense, the whole world acts by its very 'state' as a 'constrainer' who constrains the One who is impossible (on the level of common sense) to be called 'constrained'. This is the meaning of God's saying: 'Every day He is in some affair' (LV, 29).

This makes clear that the proposition: 'the Absolute is "constrained" by the creatures' – a proposition which is unimaginable on the level of common sense – has no other meaning for Ibn 'Arabī than that the Absolute perpetually manifests itself in the affairs (*shu'ūn*, i.e., various states and acts) of the creatures and confers upon them all kinds of properties in accordance with the requirements of their 'preparedness'. According to his interpretation, the Qoranic verse: 'Every day He is in some affair' refers to this fact, meaning as it does, 'every day (i.e., perpetually) the Divine "He" (i.e., He-ness) is manifesting itself in this or that mode of being in the creatures, according to the requirement of the "preparedness" of each'.

Thus, from whatever angle he may start, Ibn 'Arabī ultimately comes back to the central concept of 'self-manifestation'. And the problem of *taskhīr* in this context is reduced to that of the self-manifestation of the Absolute being determined variously in accordance with the natural capacities of the individual existents. We may express the same thing, still within the framework of Ibn 'Arabī's world-view, by saying that the permanent archetypes, or the eternal potentialities, must obey the strictly necessary and unchangeable laws laid down by themselves, when they become actualized in individual things. *Taskhīr* is after all the supreme power exercised by the 'preparedness' of each thing.

> God's self-manifestation varies according to the 'preparedness' of each individual locus. Junayd[54] was asked once about the mystical knowledge (*ma'rifah*) of God and the 'knower' (*'ārif*). He replied. 'The color of water is the color of its vessel'. This is, indeed an answer which hits the mark, for it describes the matter as it really is.[55]

Water has no color of its own; it is rather colored by the color of the vessel which contains it. This metaphor implies that the Absolute has no particular form to which we might point as the Form of the Absolute. The truth of the matter is that the Absolute manifests itself in infinitely various forms according to the particularities of the recipients. And the receptive power of the latter plays a decisive role in 'coloring' the originally 'colorless' Absolute. The Divine Name, the 'Last' (*al-ākhir*) expresses this aspect of the Absolute. The 'Last', i.e., One whose place is behind all, refers to that particular aspect of the Absolute in which it 'follows' the inborn capacity (or 'preparedness') of everything. Taken in this sense, the *taskhīr* of God by the creatures is something quite natural, particularly in the philosophical system of Ibn 'Arabī. But it is not for everybody to understand the problem in this way.

A man who has but 'a feeble intellect', Ibn 'Arabī says, cannot tolerate the dictum that God is 'constrained'. Such a man misunderstands the concept of the Omnipotence of God, and sets against this dictum another dictum that God can do *everything*, even impossible things. And by this he imagines that he has 'purified' (*tanzīh*) God from weakness and disability.

> Some of the thinkers whose intellect is feeble, being misled by the conviction that God is able to do whatever He wants to do, have come to declare it possible for God to do even those things that flatly contradict Wisdom and the real state of things.[56]

VII Gifts of God

We know already that the self-manifestation of the Absolute means, among other things, bestowal of Being. Being or existence is in this sense a precious gift bestowed by God upon all beings. Ibn 'Arabī discusses the nature of the archetypes from this particular point of view and emphasizes here again the decisive part played by them. In fact, the theory of the Divine gifts occupies a considerably important place in his philosophy, and he develops in the *Fuṣūṣ* a very detailed analysis of this problem.

He begins by classifying the gifts of the Absolute.[57]

> Know that the Divine gifts and favors, which appear in this world of Becoming through the medium of men or without their medium, are of two kinds: (1) 'essential gifts' (*'aṭāyā dhātīyah*) and (2) 'gifts given through the Names (*'aṭāyā asmā'īyah*). The distinction between these two kinds is clearly discerned by the people of 'immediate tasting'.

> There is also (another way of classifying the Divine gifts, according to which three kinds of gifts are distinguished:) (1) gifts that are given in response to an act of asking (on the part of the creatures) concerning some particular thing. This occurs when, for example, a man says, 'O my Lord, give me such-and-such a thing!' The man specifies a particular thing which he desires; he does not think of anything else. (2) Gifts that are given in response to a non-specified asking. This occurs when a man says without any specification, '(My Lord,) give me what Thou knowest to be beneficial to any part of my being, whether spiritual or physical. (3) Gifts that are given independently of any act of asking (on the part of the creatures), whether the gifts in question be 'essential' or 'through the Names'.

The theory of the Divine gifts that underlies the first of these two classifications is nothing else than the theory of the self-manifestation of the Absolute considered from a somewhat new point of view. The Essence (*dhāt*) of the Absolute, as we saw above in dealing with the concept of ontological 'breathing', pervades and runs through all beings. From the specific point of view of the present chapter, this means that the Absolute gives its own Essence, as it were, as a gift to all beings. Likewise, the Attributes (or Names) of the Absolute are manifested in the attributes of all beings. This would mean that the Absolute has given its Attributes as gifts to the creaturely world. It is to be remarked that both these gifts correspond to the (3) of the second classification mentioned above.

These gratuitous gifts are given by God to all, regardless of whether they ask for them or not. In common-sense understanding, a gift is generally given by God when someone asks Him to give it to him. In the second classification given above, Ibn 'Arabī divides the 'asking' into specified and non-specified.

Whether in a specified form or in a non-specified form, however, when a man asks anything of God, he is completely under the sway of his own 'preparedness'. What he obtains as a result of his asking is determined by his 'preparedness'. Even the fact itself that he asks for anything is determined by his 'preparedness'.

If everything is predetermined in this way, and if nothing at all can ever happen except that which has been predetermined, why do people ask anything of God? In answering this question, Ibn 'Arabī divides 'those who ask' (*sā'ilūn*) into two categories, and says:[58]

The first catégory is formed by those who are urged to ask by their natural impatience, for man is by nature 'very impatient' (XVII, 11). The second are those who feel urged to ask because they know that there are in the hands of God certain things which are predetermined in such a way that they shall not be obtained unless asked for. A man of this sort thinks, 'It may be that the particular thing which we ask God to give happens to belong to this kind'. His asking, in this case, is a kind of precaution taken for any possibility in the matter. (He takes such an attitude) because he knows neither what is in the Knowledge of God nor what the 'preparedness' (i.e., his own 'preparedness' and that of the thing he is asking for) will cause him to receive. For it is extremely difficult to know concerning every single moment what the 'preparedness' of an individual will give him in that very fraction of time. Besides, if the asking itself were not given by the 'preparedness', he would not even ask for anything. Those, of the people of the (constant) 'presence' (with God),[59] who cannot attain to such a (comprehensive) knowledge of their own 'preparedness', can at least attain to the point at which they obtain a knowledge of their 'preparedness' at every present moment. For due to their (constant) 'presence', they know what the Absolute has just given them at that moment, being well aware at the same time that they have received precisely what they have received because of their 'preparedness'. These people are subdivided into two classes:[60] (1) those who obtain knowledge about their own 'preparedness' judging by what they have received, and (2) those who know on the basis of (their knowledge of) their own 'preparedness' what they are going to receive. And this last represents the most perfect knowledge conceivable of the 'preparedness' within this class of people.

To this class also belong those who ask, not because of their natural impatience (the first category) nor because of the possibility (of the thing they want being dependent upon their asking (the second category), but who ask simply in obedience to God's Command as expressed by His words: 'Call upon Me, and I shall respond to you' (XL, 60).

Such a man is a typical 'servant'. He who asks in this way has no personal intention toward anything, specified or non-specified. His sole concern is to act in obedience to whatever his Master commands him to do. So if the objective situation (coming from the archetype) demands asking, he does ask out of sheer piety, but if it demands him to leave everything to God's care and to keep silence, he does keep silence. Thus, Job and others (like him) were made to endure bitter trials, but they did not ask God to remove the sufferings with which He tried them. But later, when the situation demanded them to ask, (they asked God,) and God did remove their sufferings from them.

Thus there are recognizable three categories of 'those who ask', each category being characterized by a particular motive from which they ask and by a particular way of asking. But whatever the motive and whatever the way, there seems to be practically no open space for the act itself of asking to be effective. For as we observe at the outset, everything is determined from eternity and the act of asking cannot possibly produce even a slight change in the strictly predetermined course of events. Indeed, man's asking for some 'gift' from God and God's granting him his wish are also predetermined. As Ibn 'Arabi says:[61]

> Whether the request is immediately complied with or put off depends upon the *qadar* which God Himself has decided from eternity.[62] If the asking occurs exactly at its determined time, God responds to it immediately, but in case its determined time is to come later, whether in this world or in the Hereafter, God's compliance with the request is also deferred. Note that by compliance (or response) here I do not mean the verbal response consisting in God's saying, 'Here I am!'[63]

What we have just dealt with concerns the situation in which man positively asks of God something, in a specified or non-specified way. And we have noticed the supreme determining power exercised by the 'preparedness' and *qadar* in such cases.

We turn now to the problem of gifts that are given independently of any positive act of asking on the part of man. Since this represents the self-manifestation of the Absolute in its typical form, it will be clear even without any further explanation that the nature of the particular thing that receives a gift of this kind (i.e., the nature of the locus of the self-manifestation) exercises a decisive influence upon the whole process. Our main concern will be, therefore, with an analysis of the way Ibn 'Arabi deals with the problem on the level of theoretical thinking.

He begins by pointing out that the word 'asking' in this particular case means specifically *verbal* asking. Otherwise, everything is 'asking' in some form or another in a broad sense. So by the phrase: 'gifts that are not due to asking', he simply means, he says, those gifts that are given independently of verbal asking.

Non-verbal 'asking' is divided into two kinds: (1) 'asking by situation' (*su'āl bi-al-ḥāl*), and (2) 'asking by preparedness' (*su'āl bi-al-isti'dād*). Of these two kinds Affifi gives the following explanation.[64] The 'asking by situation' is reducible to the second type of non-verbal asking, because the objective situation of a thing or a person asking for something depends ultimately on the nature of the 'preparedness' of that thing or person. When a man is ill, for example, his situation or state 'asks for' something (e.g., being cured), but the illness itself is due to the 'preparedness' of that particular man. The 'asking by preparedness' concerns this or that attribute pertaining to existence, which the very nature of each existent asks for. This is the only kind of 'asking' to which the Absolute responds in the real sense of the word. Thus if something has been predetermined from eternity that it should be such-and-such, and if the nature of that thing actually demands it as it has been predetermined, the demand is immediately satisfied. Everything that happens in this world of Being happens only in this way.

To this Affifi adds the remark that this puts the determinist position of Ibn 'Arabi beyond all doubt. Only it is not a mechanical material determinism but is rather close, he says, to the Leibnizian concept of pre-established harmony.

However this may be, Ibn 'Arabi himself explains his position in his peculiar way. Here follows what he says about this problem.[65]

> As regards (gifts) that are not due to asking, it is to be remarked that I mean by 'asking' here only the verbal expression of a wish. For properly speaking, nothing can do without 'asking' in some form or other, whether by language or situation or 'preparedness'. (The 'asking by situation' may be understood by the following analogy.)[66] An unconditioned praise of God is not possible except in a verbal form. As to its inner meaning, (praise of God) is necessarily conditioned by the situation which urges you to praise Him. And (the situation) is that which conditions you (and determines your praise) through a Name denoting an action or a Name denoting 'purification'. As to the 'preparedness', man is not (ordinarily) aware of it, he is only aware of the situation, for he is always conscious of the motive (from which he praises God), and that motive is precisely (what I mean by) 'situation'. Thus 'preparedness' is the most concealed of all (grounds of) 'asking'.

Let us first elucidate what is exactly meant by the analogy of 'praising'. Man praises God (in Arabic) by saying verbally *al-ḥamd li-Allāh* (i.e., 'praise be to God!').[67] Everybody uses the same formula. The formula itself in its verbal form remains always unconditioned. But if we go into the psychology of those who cry out *al-ḥamd li-Allāh!* and analyze it in each particular case, the person A, for example, is thinking of his own bodily state of health and says *al-ḥamd li-Allāh* as an effusion of his thankfulness for his health,[68] while the person B praises God by the same formula because he is keenly conscious of the greatness and eternity of[69] God. Thus the motive, or the concrete situation, which drives man to use the same formula differs from case to case. This particular motivating situation is called *ḥāl*, 'situation', or 'state'.

Now if we transpose this relation between the varying motives and the use of the same formula to the context of Divine gifts, we can easily grasp the basic structure of the latter. Everything in the world is always 'asking' of the Absolute an ontological 'gift' according to the requirement of its own 'preparedness'. This general form or pattern is everywhere the same. However, if we take each single unit of time and analyze minutely its content, we find that the 'asking' assumes at every moment a unique form according to the concrete situation peculiar to that particular moment. This is the requirement of the 'situation'.

The requirements of the 'situations', therefore, are concrete details within the 'preparedness', and are ultimately reducible to the latter. Subjectively, however, i.e., from the standpoint of a particular man, he is clearly conscious of his own 'situation', while he is ordinarily unconscious of his 'preparedness'. A sick man, for instance, asks for health because he feels pain. He is conscious of the motive from which he is making urgent supplication for health. But he is not conscious of the 'preparedness' which concerns his very existence and which dominates everything about himself.

The 'preparedness' for ordinary men is after all an insoluble mystery. So the 'asking by preparedness', although it is the most powerful of the above-mentioned three kinds of 'asking', turns out to be the 'most concealed' of all.

Reference has been made to the close relation that exists between the theory of 'gifts' and the theory of self-manifestation. In fact both are, as we have observed above, but one thing considered from two different perspectives. I would like to bring the present section to a close by discussing a particular point which emerges when we put these two perspectives together in one place.

At the outset of this section we saw Ibn 'Arabī dividing the 'gifts' into two major classes: (1) essential gifts and (2) gifts given through the Names. As to the first of these two classes, the word 'essential' (*dhātīyah*) itself will be enough to suggest that it has something to do with the self-manifestation of the Essence (*dhāt*).

In effect, 'the essential gifts' are, from the viewpoint of *tajallī*, a self-manifestation of the Divine Essence. It is to be noticed, however, that it is a particular kind of essential self-manifestation which is designated by the term 'holy emanation'. It is not what is designated by the term 'the most holy emanation'.[70] Ibn 'Arabī is evidently thinking of this distinction when he says:[71]

> Self-manifestation does not occur from the Essence except in the particular form determined by the locus in which it (the Essence) is manifested. No other way of (essential self-manifestation) is possible. So the locus sees nothing else than its own form as reflected in

the mirror of the Absolute. It never sees the Absolute itself. It is utterly impossible for it to see the Absolute although it is conscious that it is perceiving its own form in no other (place) than (the mirror of) the Absolute.

The intended meaning of this passage is explicated by al-Qāshānī in the following way:[72]

> There can be no self-manifestation coming from the pure attribute-less Essence, because the Essence in its attributeless aspect does not manifest itself to anybody (or anything). Indeed, that which manifests itself is the Essence in its aspect of Mercifulness (*rahmānīyah*)[73] ..., while the Essence *qua* Essence does not make self-manifestation except to itself. Toward the creatures, the self-manifestation is done exclusively according to the 'preparedness' of the locus in each case.

And this kind of self-manifestation is, as Bālī Efendi rightly remarks, nothing other than the 'holy emanation'. It is the self-manifestation of the Absolute, the direct source of which is the Presence (i.e., ontological level) of the all-comprehensive Name (which comprises all the Names or Attributes gathered together into a unity).

Bālī Efendi, in the same place, explains with utmost lucidity the relation between this 'holy emanation' and the 'essential gifts' and 'the gifts given through the Names':

> The self-manifestation whose source is the Essence and which takes a particular form according to the form of its locus is the 'holy emanation'. (This latter is divided into two kinds).
>
> (1) When the locus is of such a nature that it receives the self-manifestation of the Essence from the Presence of the comprehensive Name, the Essence manifests itself (in that locus) directly from the Presence of the comprehensive unity of all Names. This kind of self-manifestation is called 'Divine[74] self-manifestation', and the result of it are the 'essential gifts'.
>
> (2) But when the (locus) is of such a nature that it receives the self-manifestation of the Essence from the particular Presence of one particular Name, the Essence manifests itself from that particular Presence. This is what is called the 'self-manifestation through an Attribute or a Name', and there result from it the 'gifts given through the Names'.

Notes

1. See Chapter IX on Divine Mercy.

2. *Fuṣ.*, p. 114/102.

3. The point will be discussed later under III of the present chapter.

4. *Fuṣ.*, p. 63/76.

5. *ibid*.

6. *Inshā' al-Dawā'ir*, ed. Nyberg, pp. 16–17.

7. The first thing is the Absolute, the second is the world, and the third in the order of description is the archetype.

8. *op. cit.,* p. 19.

9. The English word 'eternal' in this context must always be strictly understood in the sense of 'eternal *a parte ante*'. The dictum: 'the world is eternal' means, therefore, that 'the world has no temporal beginning', which would seem flatly to contradict the Qoranic teaching of the 'creation' of the world.

10. 'Ibn 'Arabī upheld the thesis of the eternity of the world (*qidam al-'ālam*) with no less definiteness than the Peripatetic Philosophers' – Affifi, *Fuṣ.*, Com., p. 314.

11. *Fuṣ.*, p. 263/211.

12. *Fuṣ.*, p. 16/51.

13. The Attributes dealt with here are only those that are analogically common to the Absolute and the creatures. The Attributes like Eternity (*a parte ante*) and Eternity (*a parte post*) are naturally excluded from consideration, because they are never actualized in the creaturely world.

14. I read: *fa-hiya bāṭinah lā tazūl 'an al-wujūd al-ghaybiy*. The last word in the Affifi edition is *al-'ayniy*, 'individual and concrete'. What Ibn 'Arabī means is clearly that the Universals, even when they are actualized in the concrete things, remain in their original state of being 'interior'.

15. p. 16.

16. pp. 16–17/51–52.

17. pp. 16–17/51–52.

18. *Fuṣ.*, pp. 17–18/52–53.

19. *Fuṣ.*, 43/67.

20. p. 43.

21. The first term *ḥādith*, grammatically an active form, represents the thing as something 'coming into temporal existence', while the second, *muḥdath*, which is a passive form, represents it as something 'which has been brought into temporal existence'.

22. *Fuṣ.*, p. 18/53.

23. *Fuṣ.*, p. 18/53.

24. *Fuṣ.*, pp. 75–76/82.

25. *Fuṣ.*, pp. 76–77/83.

26. *Fuṣ.*, pp. 157–158/128.

27. *Fuṣ.*, pp. 104–105/95–96.

28. *Fuṣ.*, pp. 107–108/97–98.

29. For details about *himmah* see Chapter XVII.

30. *Fuṣ.*, pp. 159–160/130–1.

31. p. 160.

32. This conception which might strike common sense as blasphemous will be found to be not at all blasphemous if one but reflects that the 'preparedness' of a thing which is said to exercise such a tremendous power is after all nothing but a particular ontological mode of the Absolute. One must remember that, in Ibn 'Arabī's thought, the whole thing is ultimately an inner drama which is eternally enacted within the Absolute itself. All the other seemingly 'blasphemous' expressions which we are going to encounter presently like 'God obeys the creatures', 'The world forces God to compulsory service' etc., must be understood in terms of this basic framework.

33. *Fuṣ.*, pp. 161–162/131–132.

34. So there is practically no positive part played by the Absolute in this process except that the archetypes themselves are the manifested forms of the ontological modes of the Absolute.

35. *Fuṣ.*, pp. 162–163/132.

36. In effect, al-Qāshānī in a passage of his commentary simply identifies the *qadar* with the archetype, cf. p. 163.

37. *Fuṣ.*, p. 163/132.

38. *Fuṣ.*, p. 163/132–133.

39. *Fuṣ.*, p. 30/60.

40. *Fuṣ.*, pp. 30–31/60.

41. p. 42/67.

42. *Fuṣ.*, p. 31–32/60–61.

43. *Fuṣ.*, p. 32/61.

44. *Fuṣ.*, pp. 165–166/133–134.

45. Here the word *tajallī*, which usually means the self-manifestation of the Absolute, is used to designate the reverse side of this phenomenon, i.e., the same *tajallī* as reflected in the individual consciousness of a mystic.

46. p. 167.

47. usually translated as 'mortal'.

48. For the explanation just given I am indebted to Affifi, *Fuṣ.*, Com., p. 286.

49. *Fuṣ.*, p. 243/192–193.

50. *Fuṣ.*, p. 244/193–194.

51. *ibid.*

52. In the same way, a child exercises *taskhīr* with his 'state' over his parents.

53. because, properly speaking, what 'constrains' the king is not so much the 'state' of his subjects as the 'position' of kingship.

54. Junayd (d. 910 A.D.), one of the greatest names in the early phase of the historical development of Sufism.

55. *Fuṣ.*, p. 280/225.

56. *Fuṣ.*, p. 42/67.

57. *Fuṣ.*, p. 27/58.

58. *Fuṣ.*, p. 28/59.

59. The people of the presence (*ahl al-ḥuḍūr*), al-Qāshānī says, are 'those who see whatever happens to them as coming from God, whether it (actually) occurs through others or through themselves, and who do not recognize anything other than God as the cause of any effect or anything existent.' – p. 29.

60. This problem has been dealt with earlier in (V) of the present chapter.

61. *Fuṣ.*, p. 29/60.

62. This corresponds to the Qoranic conception that everything has a 'clearly stated term' (*ajal musammà*).

63. Whenever a man calls upon God in supplication, God responds by saying, 'Here I am!' (*Labbayka*) This verbal response (*ijābah bi-al-qawl*) is always immediate. But not always so is His response by action (*ijābah bi-al-fi'l*) which is the actualization of what the man has asked for.

64. *Fuṣ.*, Com., p. 22.

65. *Fuṣ.*, p. 30/60.

66. The analogy which Ibn 'Arabī offers, however, is not easy to understand due to his peculiar way of expressing himself. The meaning of the passage will be explicated in the paragraph immediately after the quotation.

67. Strictly speaking, *al-ḥamd li-Allāh* is an exclamatory descriptive sentence meaning 'all praise belongs to God (and to God alone)'.

68. This is expressed by Ibn 'Arabi by saying that 'the praise is done through a Name denoting an action', e.g., Guardian (*ḥāfiz*), All-giving (*wahhāb*) etc.

69. This corresponds to the case in which a man praises God 'through a Name denoting purification (*tanzīh*)', Most Holy (*qaddūs*), Eternal-Everlasting (*alladhī lam yazal wa-lā yazāl*) etc.

70. On this basic distinction see Chapter XI.

71. *Fuṣ.*, p. 33/61.

72. pp. 32–33.

73. See Chapter IX.

74. *ilāhiy*, i.e., the self-manifestation that occurs on the level of 'God'. As we have seen earlier, 'God' or *Allāh* is the all-comprehensive Name.

XIII Creation

I The Meaning of Creation

'Creation' (*khalq*) is unquestionably one of the concepts upon which stands the Islamic world-view. It plays a prominent role in all aspects of the religious thought of Islam. In theology, for example, it constitutes the very starting-point of all discussions in the form of the opposition between the 'temporality' (*ḥudūth*) and 'eternity *a parte ante*' (*qidam*). The world is an 'originated' (or 'temporally produced') thing because it is the result of Divine creation. And this conception of the world's being 'originated' (*muḥdath*) forms the basis of the entire system of Islamic theology.

In the world-view of Ibn 'Arabī, too, 'creation' plays an important part as one of the key-concepts. The creative word of God, 'Be!' (*kun*) has a decisive meaning in the coming-into-being of all beings. As we have seen, however, the most basic concept of Ibn 'Arabī's ontology is self-manifestation, and the world of Being is after all nothing but the self-manifestation of the Absolute, and no event whatsoever occurs in the world except self-manifestation. In this sense, 'creation' which means the coming-into-being of the world is naturally identical with self-manifestation.

But we would make a gross mistake if we imagine that since the ontology of Ibn 'Arabī is based on self-manifestation and since there is nothing but self-manifestation, 'creation' is after all, for him, a metaphor. To think that Ibn 'Arabī used the term 'creation' making a concession to the established pattern of Islamic thought, and that he merely described self-manifestation in a more traditional terminology, is to overlook the multilateral nature of his thought.

One of the characteristic features of Ibn 'Arabī's thought is its manifoldness. In the presence of one important problem, he usually develops his thought in various directions and in various forms with the help of rich imagery. This, I think, is due largely to the unusual profundity and fecundity of his experience which always underlies his thinking. The depth and richness of mystical experience demands, in his case, multiplicity of expression.

The theory of 'creation' which we are going to examine is not to be considered as a mere religious metaphor, or some esoteric teaching disguised in traditional theological terminology. 'Creation' is to him as real as 'self-manifestation'. Or we might say that one and the same fundamental fact existing in his consciousness has two different aspects, one 'creation', and the other 'self-manifestation'.

The first thing which attracts our attention about his theory of 'creation' is the important part played by the concept of 'triad' or 'triplicity', *thalāthīyah*. This marks it off from the theory of 'self-manifestation'.

The starting-point is as usual the Absolute. The ontological ground of existence is, as we already know, the One-Absolute. But the One, if considered in its phenomenal aspect, presents three different aspects. They are: (1) the Essence not *qua* Essence in its absoluteness, but in its self-revealing aspect), (2) the Will or *irādah* (here the Absolute is a 'Willer', *murīd*), and (3) the Command or *amr*[1] (here the Absolute is a 'Commander', *āmir*).

These three aspects in the order given here represent the whole process of 'creation'. The process may be briefly described as follows. First, there arises in the One-Absolute self-consciousness – or Knowledge (*'ilm*) – and the permanent archetypes appear in the Divine Consciousness. This marks the birth of the possible Many. And thereby the Presence of the Essence (i.e., the ontological level of the Absolute *qua* Absolute) descends to the Presence of Divinity (*ilāhīyah*, 'being God').

Then, in the second place, there arises the Will based on this Knowledge to bring out the archetypes from the state of non-existence into the state of existence. Then, on the basis of this Will, the Command – 'Be!' (*kun*) – is issued, and thus the world is 'created'.

Having these preliminary remarks in mind, let us read the passage in which Ibn 'Arabī describes the process.[2]

> Know – may God assist you in doing so! – that the whole matter (i.e., 'creation') in itself has its basis in the 'singleness' (*fardīyah*). But this 'singleness' has a triple structure (*tathlīth*). For the 'singleness' starts to appear only from 'three'. In fact 'three' is the first single (i.e., odd) number.

What Ibn 'Arabī wants to convey through these laconic expressions may be made clear if we explain it in the following way. He begins by saying that the very root of 'creation' is the 'singleness' of the Absolute. It is important to remark that he refers here to the Absolute as 'single' (*fard*), not as 'One'. In other words, he is not speaking of the Absolute as Absolute in its essential absoluteness.

We are here at a lower stage at which the Absolute has self-consciousness or Knowledge.

According to Ibn 'Arabi, 'one' is not a number at all; it is the principle and 'birth-place' of all numbers from 'two' onwards, but it is not itself a number. 'One' is absolutely above all relations; it is naturally above the concept itself of number.

'Single' is not like that. Outwardly it is 'one', but in its inner structure it is not 'one', because the concept of singleness contains in itself the concept of 'other'. It is 'one' in so far as it is other than others. In this sense, 'single' is internally divisible and divided, because we cannot represent it without at the same time representing – negatively, to be sure – the idea of otherness. In this sense it is 'one' composed of more than one unit. And 'three' is the smallest, i.e., first, 'single' number in the infinitely extending series of numbers – which makes it particularly appropriate for functioning as the starting-point of the Divine act of creation.

> And from this Presence of Divinity (i.e., the ontological plane where the Absolute is no longer One but Single endowed with an inner triplicity) the world has come into existence. To this God refers when He says: 'Whenever We decide (lit. 'will' the existence of) something, We only say to it, 'Be!', and it comes into existence' (XVI, 40). Thus we see (the triplicity of) the Essence, the Will, and the Word.[3] Anything would not come into existence if it were not for (1) the Essence and (2) its Will – the Will which is the drive with which the Essence turns towards bringing something in particular into existence – and then (3) the Word 'Be!' uttered to that particular thing at the very moment when the Will turns the Essence in that direction.[4]

The passage just quoted describes the structure of the triplicity on the side of the Agent, i.e., the Absolute. But the triplicity on the part of the Creator alone does not produce any effect. In order that the creative activity of the Absolute be really effective, there must be a corresponding triplicity also on the part of the 'receiver' (*qābil*), i.e., the thing to be created. Creation is actualized only when the active triplicity perfectly coincided with the passive triplicity.

> (The moment the creative Word of God is uttered) there arises in the thing to be created, too, a singleness having a triplicity. And by this triplicity alone does the thing, on its part, become capable of being produced and being qualified with existence. The triplicity in the object consists of (1) its thing-ness (*shay'iyyah*), (2) its hearing (*samā'*), and (3) its obeying (*imtithāl*) the Command of the Creator concerning its creation. So that the (creaturely) triad corresponds with the (Divine) triad.
> The first (1) is the permanent archetypal essence of the thing in the state of non-existence, which corresponds to the Essence of its Creator. The second (2) is the hearing of the Command by the thing,

which corresponds to the Will of its Creator. And the third (3) is its obedient acceptance of what it has been commanded concerning its coming into existence, which corresponds to the (Creator's) Word 'Be!' Upon this, the thing actually comes into being.

Thus the 'bringing-into-being' (*takwīn*, or 'production') is to be attributed to the thing (created). For if the thing had not in itself the power of coming into being when the Word ('Be!') is uttered, it would never come into existence. In this sense it is the thing itself that brings it into existence from the state of non-existence.[5]

It is remarkable that a special emphasis is laid here in the process of creation on the 'power' (*quwwah*) of the thing to be created. A thing is not created in a purely passive way, that is, mechanically and powerlessly, but it participates positively in its own creation. This is another way of looking at the supreme power of the 'preparedness', which we have discussed in the preceding chapter.

When God decides to bring something into existence, He simply says to it 'Be!' And the thing, in response, comes into existence. In this process, the coming-into-being (*takawwun*) itself is an act of that thing, not an act of God. This conception is explained by al-Qāshānī in the following terms:[6]

> The coming-into-being, that is, the thing's obeying the Command, pertains to nothing else than the thing itself, for it (i.e., coming-into-being) is (as Ibn 'Arabī says) in the power of the thing; that is to say, it is contained potentially in the thing, concealed. This is why God (in the above-quoted Qoranic verse) ascribes it (i.e., coming-into-being) to the thing, by saying, 'and *it* comes into existence'.[7] This sentence means that the thing (upon hearing the Word) immediately obeys the order and comes into existence. And the thing is capable of doing so simply because it is already existent in the Unseen (i.e., potentially), for the archetypal subsistence is nothing other than a concealed inner mode of existence. Everything that is 'inward' has in itself the power to come out into 'outward' existence. This is due to the fact that the Essence (designated by the) Name 'Inward' (*bāṭin*) is the same Essence (designated by the) Name 'Outward' (*ẓāhir*), and because the 'receiver' (*qābil*) is (ultimately) the same as the 'Agent' (*fā'il*).

Such is the original theory of 'creation' put forward by Ibn 'Arabī. He affirms very emphatically that the 'production' (*takwīn*) is to be ascribed to the thing produced, not to be Absolute. Such a position will surely be criticized by ordinary believers as considering God powerless' (*'ājiz*). But, as I have repeatedly pointed out, this position is not at all blasphemous in the eyes of those who really know the structure of Ibn 'Arabī's world-view. Surely, in this world-view, the things (creatures) are described as being so positively powerful that they leave but a limited space for the direct activity of the Absolute. On a deeper level, however, those things that are provisionally considered as independently existent are nothing but so many particularized, delimited forms of the Absolute, and all are involved in an ontological drama within the Absolute itself; all are a magnificent Divina Commedia.

The idea of 'production' (the last stage of the 'creation') being ascribable to the things and not to the Absolute is further explained by Ibn 'Arabī in the following way:[8]

> God states categorically that the 'production' pertains to the (created) thing itself, and not to God. What pertains to God in this matter is only His Command. He makes His part (in the creative process) clear by saying: 'Whenever We decide (the existence of) something, We only say to it "Be!"', and it comes into existence' (XVI, 40). Thus the 'production' is ascribed to the thing though, to be sure, the latter acts only in obedience to the Command of God. And (we must accept this statement as it is because) God is truthful in whatever He says. Besides, this (i.e., the ascription of the 'production' to the thing) is something quite reasonable, objectively speaking.
> (This may be illustrated by an example.) Suppose a master who is feared by everybody and whom nobody dares to disobey commands his slave to stand up by saying to him, 'Stand up!' (*qum*); the slave will surely stand up in obedience to the command of the master. To the master pertains in the process of the slave's standing up only his commanding him to do so, while the act of standing up itself pertains to the slave; it is not an act of the master.
> Thus it is clear that the 'production' stands on the basis of triplicity; in other words, three elements are involved on both sides, on the part of the Absolute as well as on the part of the creatures.

It will be evident, then, that in Ibn 'Arabī's thought, the principle of *creatio ex nihilo* holds true. But what makes his thesis fundamentally different from the ordinary Islamic *creatio ex nihilo* is that the *nihil*, for Ibn 'Arabī, is not a total unconditional 'non-existence', but 'non-existence' in the particular sense of something being as yet non-existent as an empirical or phenomenal thing. What he regards as *nihil* is 'existence' on the level of the intelligibles, or – which comes to the same thing – in the Consciousness of God. Ontologically, his *nihil* is the 'possible' (*mumkin*), i.e., something that has the power (or possibility) to exist. The ordinary view which makes 'creation' a sort of Divine monodrama has its origin in the ignorance of the positive power to be attributed to the 'possibles'. All things, in Ibn 'Arabī's view, have enough power to come out from the concealment into the field of existence in response to the ontological Command of God.

Thus the creaturely world is possessed of 'efficiency' (*fā'iliyah*). And the things that constitute this would participate actively and positively in the creation of themselves.

Looking at an artisan who is engaged in molding things out of clay, one might make a superficial observation that the clay has no positive 'efficiency' of its own, and that it lets itself molded into whatever form the artisan likes. In the view of such a man, the clay in the hands of an artisan is sheer passivity, sheer non-action. He overlooks the important fact that, in reality, the clay, on its part, positively determines the activity of the artisan. Surely, the artisan can make quite a considerable variety of things out of clay, but whatever he may do, he can not go beyond the narrow limits set by the very nature of the clay. Otherwise expressed, the nature of the clay itself determines the possible forms in which it may be actualized. Somewhat similar to this is the positive nature of a thing in the process of 'creation'.

The same observation, however, clearly shows that, although the things do possess 'efficiency', the latter is after all secondary, not primary. Herein lies the fundamental difference between God and the world. 'As women are by nature a degree lower than men', the creatures are a degree lower than the Absolute. The things, with all their positive powers and capacities, have no essential priority.

> As women are a degree lower than men according to God's saying: 'and men are a degree above them (i.e., women)' (II, 228), the things that have been created in the image (of God) are naturally a degree lower than the One who has brought them into being in His image, in spite of the fact that their forms are God's Form itself.
> And by that very degree which separates God from the world, God is completely independent (i.e., has absolutely no need) of the whole world, and is the primary Agent. As for the 'form', it is but a secondary agent and has no essential priority which pertains only to the Absolute.[9]

II   The Feminine Element in the Creation of the World

In the last part of the preceding section reference has incidentally been made to the idea that women are by nature a degree lower than men. This, however, should not be taken to mean that Ibn 'Arabī considers the role played by the feminine in the process of world creation quite secondary, let alone unimportant. On the contrary, the entire creative process, in his view, is governed by the principle of femininity.

The starting-point of his thinking on this problem is furnished by a famous Tradition which runs: 'Of all the things of your world, three things have been made particularly dear to me, women, perfumes, and the ritual prayer, this last being the "cooling of my eye" (i.e., a source of my highest joy)'. In this Tradition, Ibn 'Arabī observes, the number 'three' – triplicity again! – is put in the feminine form (*thalāth*), in spite of the fact that one of the three things here enumerated (*ṭīb* 'perfume') is a masculine noun. Ordinarily, in Arabic grammar, the rule is that, if there happens to be even one masculine noun among the things enumerated, one treats the whole as grammatically masculine, and uses the numeral in the masculine form (*thalāthah*, for example, instead of *thalāth*, meaning 'three').

Now in this Tradition, the Prophet *intentionally* – so thinks Ibn 'Arabī – uses the feminine form, *thalāth*, and this, in his view, has a very deep symbolic meaning. It suggests that all the basic factors that participate in creation are feminine, and that the whole process of creation is governed by the principle of femininity (*ta'nīth*). Ibn 'Arabī draws attention to the process by which a man (male) comes into being:[10]

> The man finds himself situated between an essence (i.e., the Divine Essence) which is his (ontological) source and a woman (i.e., his own mother) who is his (physical) source. Thus he is placed between two feminine nouns, that is to say, between the femininity of essence and the real (i.e., physical) femininity.

The Essence (*dhāt*), which is the original ground of all Being, is a feminine noun. The immediate ontological ground of the forms of all beings, i.e., the Divine Attributes, *ṣifāt* (sg. *ṣifah*), is a feminine noun. The creative power of God, *qudrah* is a feminine noun. Thus, from whatever aspect one approaches the process of creation, one runs into a feminine noun. The Philosophers (*falāsifah*) who blindly follow Greek philosophy assert that God is the 'cause' (*'illah*) of the existence of the world. This is a mistaken view, and yet it is significant, Ibn 'Arabī adds, that even in this wrong opinion about creation, a feminine noun, *'illah*, is used to denote the ultimate ground of the creation of the world.

The whole problem is dealt with by al-Qāshānī in a far more scholastic way as follows:[11]

> The ultimate ground (or origin) of everything is called Mother (*umm*), because the mother is the (stem) from which all branches go out. Do you not see how God describes the matter when He says: 'And He created from it (i.e., the first soul, meaning Adam) its mate, and out of the two He spread innumerable men and women' (IV, 1). As you see, the 'wife' (of Adam) was feminine. Moreover, the first unique 'soul' from which she was created was itself feminine.[12]
> Just in the same way, the Origin of all origins over which there is nothing is designated by a (feminine noun), *ḥaqīqah* or 'Reality' . . .
> Likewise the words designating the Divine Essence, *'ayn* and *dhāt*, are feminine.

Thus his (i.e., Muḥammad's) intention in making (the femininity) overcome (the masculinity)[13] is to draw attention to the special importance of the femininity which is the very origin and source of everything that spreads out from it. And this is true not merely of the world of Nature but even of Reality itself.

In fact, Reality is the Father (*ab*) of everything in that it is the absolute Agent (i.e., the absolutely Active, *fā'il*). But Reality is also the Mother (because of its passivity). It gathers together in itself both 'activity' (*fi'l*) and 'passivity' (*infi'āl*), for Reality is 'passive' (*munfa'il*) in so far as it manifests itself in the form of a 'passive' thing, while in the form of the 'active' (Agent) it is 'active'. The very nature of Reality requires this unification of the 'determination' (*ta'ayyun*) and 'non-determination' (*lāta'ayyun*).[14] Thus Reality is 'determined' by all determinations, masculine and feminine, on the one hand. But on the other, it stands high above all determinations.

And Reality, when it becomes determined by the first determination,[15] is One Essence requiring a perfect balance and equilibrium between 'activity' and 'passivity', between the exterior self-manifestation (*ẓuhūr*) and the interior self-concealment (*buṭūn*).[16] And in so far as it is the 'Inward' (*bāṭin*) residing in every form, it is 'active', but in so far as it is the 'Outward' (*ẓāhir*), it is 'passive'. . . .

The first determination, which occurs by (the Absolute's) manifesting itself by itself, attests to the fact that the Essence is absolute and non-determined, for its self-determination (*ta'ayyun bi-dhāti-hi*) must necessarily be preceded by non-determination (*lā-ta'ayyun*). Likewise when Reality *qua* Reality is actualized in every determined (i.e., concretely delimited) existent, its determination (also) requires that it be preceded by non-determination. Nay, rather, every determined existent, considered in its reality apart from all consideration of its actual delimitations, is an absolute (i.e., every determined existent is in its ontological core an absolute – which is nothing but the Absolute itself). A determined existent, in this sense, depends upon the Absolute (which is inherent in it) and is sustained by it. So everything is 'passive' in relation to that absolute (ontological) ground, and is a locus of self-manifestation for it, while that ground is 'active' and remains concealed in the thing.

Thus everything is 'passive' considered from the point of view of its being determined, but 'active' in itself,[17] considered from the point of view of its being absolute. But the thing itself is essentially one. . . . So Reality, wherever it goes and in whatever way it appears, has (two different aspects; namely), 'activity' and 'passivity', or 'fatherhood' (*ubuwwah*) and 'motherhood' (*umūmah*). And this justifies the (Prophet's having used) the feminine form.

The Absolute, which is the ultimate and real origin of 'creation', has something feminine in it, as indicated by the feminine form of the word 'Essence' (*dhāt*). Furthermore, if we consider analytically the ontological structure of the creative process, we find, even at its first stage, the 'first determination', a feminine principle, the 'motherhood', co-operating with a masculine principle, the 'father-hood'. The Divine Essence, in brief, is the Mother of everything in the sense that it represents the 'passive' element which is inherent in all forms of Being.

III Perpetual Creation

We turn now to one of the most interesting features of the theory of creation peculiar to Ibn 'Arabī. This part of his theory is historically of primary importance because it is a critique of the atomistic philosophy of the Ash'arite theologians.[18]

We have already seen in connection with another problem that, in Ibn 'Arabī's world-view, the self-manifestation of the Absolute is a perpetual process whose major stages – (1) the 'most holy emana-tion', (2) the 'holy emanation', and then (3) the appearance of concrete individual things – go on being actualized one after another like successive, recurrent waves. This ontological process repeats itself indefinitely and endlessly. At every moment, and moment after moment, the same eternal process of annihilation and re-creation is repeated. At this very moment, an infinite number of things and properties come into being, and at the next moment they are annihilated to be replaced by another infinity of things and properties.

Thus we cannot experience the same world twice at two different moments. The world we actually experience is in perpetual flow. It changes from moment to moment. But this continual and perpetual change occurs in such an orderly way according to such definite patterns that we, superficial observers, imagine that the same one world is there around us.

Describing this perpetual flow of things in terms of the concept of 'creation' which is the central topic of the present chapter, Ibn 'Arabī says that the world goes on being created anew at every single moment. This he calls 'new creation' (*al-khalq al-jadīd*). The expression must not be taken in the sense of a 'new' creation to be contrasted with the 'old', i.e., the earlier, creation of the world. The word 'new' (*jadīd*) in this context means 'ever new' or 'which is renewed from moment to moment'. The 'new creation' means, in short, the process of everlasting and ever new act of creation.

Man, being endowed with self-consciousness, can have a real living feel of this 'new creation' both inside and outside himself, i.e., both in his mind and in his body, by becoming conscious of 'himself', which goes on changing from moment to moment without ever stopping as long as he lives. However, ordinary people are not aware of the process of 'new creation' even with regard to them-selves.

Ibn 'Arabī describes this process also as a 'perpetual ascent' (*taraqqī dā'im*). This is a very important point at which we can look into the very basis of his idea of the 'new creation'.

> The wonder of all wonders is that man (and consequently, every-thing) is in a perpetual process of ascending. And yet (ordinarily) he is not aware of this because of the extreme thinness and fineness of the veil[19] or because of the extreme similarity between (the success-ive forms).[20]

That everything is involved in the process of the ever new crea-tion means primarily that the Absolute is continually manifesting itself in the infinity of 'possible' things. This is done by the ontologi-cal 'descent' (*nuzūl*) of the Absolute towards the lower levels of Being, first to the archetypes and then to the 'possible'. But the same process of perpetual 'descent' is, when it is looked at from the side of the 'possible', turns out to be a perpetual process of ontologi-cal 'ascent'. Everything, in this sense, is perpetually 'ascending' towards the Absolute by the very same 'descending' of the latter.

The 'ascent' (*taraqqī*) of the things, in other words, is nothing but the reverse side of the 'descent' of the Absolute towards them. The things in the state of non-existence receiving the mercy of the Absolute and obtaining thereby existence, produces, from the standpoint of these things, the image of their 'ascending' toward the original source of existence. Al-Qāshānī paraphrases the above-quoted passage in the following way:[21]

> One of the most miraculous things about man is that he is in a perpetual state of ascent with regard to the modes of the 'prepared-ness' of his own archetypal essence. For all the modes of the archetypes are things that have been known to God (from eternity), permanently fixed in potentiality, and God brings them out to actual-ity incessantly and perpetually. And so He goes on transforming the possibilities (*istiʿdādāt*, lit. 'preparednesses') that have been there from the beginningless past and that are (therefore) essentially uncreated, into infinite possibilities that are actually created.
>
> Thus everything is in the state of ascending at this very moment because it is perpetually receiving the endlessly renewed ontological (*wujūdīyah*) Divine self-manifestations, and at every self-manifestation the thing goes on increasing in its receptivity for another (i.e., the next) self-manifestation.
>
> Man, however, may not be conscious of this because of his eyes being veiled, or rather because of the veil being extremely thin and fine. But he may also become conscious of it when the self-manifestations take on the forms of intellectual, intuitive, imaginative, or mystical experiences.

The concept of 'new creation', thus comprising the ontological 'descent' and 'ascent', is a point which discloses most clearly the dynamic nature of the world-view of Ibn 'Arabī. In this world-view, nothing remains static; the world in its entirety is in fervent movement. The world transforms itself kaleidoscopically from moment to moment, and yet all these movements of self-development are the 'ascending' movements of the things toward the Absolute-One, precisely because they are the 'descending' self-expressions of the Absolute-One. In one of the preceding chapters dealing with the *coincidentia oppositorum*, we have already considered the same phenomenon from a different point of view. There we saw how the One is the Manifold and the Manifold is the One. In fact the 'descent' and 'ascent' describe exactly the same thing.

> (As a result of the 'new creation', we are constantly faced with similar forms, but of any two similar forms) one is not the same thing as the other. For in the eyes of one who recognizes them to be two *similar* things, they are different from one another. Thus a truly perspicacious man discerns Many in the One, while knowing at the same time that the Divine Names, in spite of their essential diversity and multiplicity, point to one single Reality, for the Names are nothing but multiplicity posited by the reason in Something which is essentially and really one.
>
> Thus it comes about that in the process of self-manifestation the Many becomes discernible in one single Essence. This may be compared to the Prime Matter which is mentioned in the definition of every form. The forms are many and divergent, but they all go back in reality to one single substance which is their Prime Matter.[22]

In this passage, Ibn 'Arabī seems to be speaking of the horizontal similarity-relationship between the concrete beings. He emphasizes the particular aspect of the 'new creation' in which the concretely existent things in the phenomenal world are after all infinitely various forms of the Divine self-manifestation, and are ultimately reducible to the One. But the same applies also to the vertical, i.e., temporal, relation between the ever new creations. In what is seemingly one and the same thing, the 'new creation' is taking place at every moment, so that the 'one and the same thing', considered at two successive moments, is in reality not one and the same, but two 'similar' things. And yet, despite all this, the thing maintains and never loses its original unity and identity, because all the new and similar states that occur to it succesively are eternally determined by its own archetype.

These two aspects of the 'new creation', horizontal and vertical, are brought to light by al-Qāshānī in his commentary on the passage just quoted.[23]

A truly perspicacious man discerns a multiplicity of self-
determinations in the one single Essence which appears in an infinite
number of 'similar' forms. All the Divine Names like the Omnipo-
tent, the Omniscient, the Creator, the Sustainer, etc., point in reality
to one single Essence, God, despite the fact that each of them has a
different meaning from the rest. This shows that the divergence of the
meanings of the Names is merely an intelligible and mental multiplicity existing in what is called the 'essentially One', that they are not a
really and concretely existent multiplicity. Thus the self-
manifestation in the forms of all the Names is but a multiplicity
discernible within one single Essence. The same is true also of the
events that take place successively (in 'one and the same thing'). All
the successive self-manifestations that are similar to each other are
one in reality, but many if taken as individual self-determinations.
(The Master) illustrates this with the example of the Prime Matter
(*hayūlà*). You mention the Prime Matter in defining any substantial
Form. You say, for example, 'Body (*jism*) is a substance having
quantity', 'Plant (*nabāt*) is a body that grows up', 'Stone (*ḥajar*) is a
body, inorganic, heavy, and voiceless', 'animal (*ḥayawān*) is a body
that grows up, has sense perception, and moves with will', 'Man
(*insān*) is a rational animal'. In this way, you mention 'substance' as
the definition of 'body', and you mention 'body' – which is 'substance'
(by definition) – in the definitions of all the rest. Thus all are traced
back to the one single reality which is 'substance'.

This fact can be known only by mystical vision, and is never disclosed to those who understand everything through rational thinking. Thus it comes about that the majority of men, including the
Philosophers, are not aware of the phenomenon of the 'new creation'. They do not see the infinitely beautiful scene of this kaleidoscopic transformation of things.

How splendid are God's words concerning the world and its perpetual renewal with each Divine breath which constitutes an 'ever
new creation' in one single reality. (But this is not perceived except
by a few), as He says in reference to a certain group of people –
indeed, this applies to the majority of men – 'Nay, they are in utter
confusion with regard to the new creation.' (L, 15).[24] These people
(are in confusion with regard to it) because they do not know the
(perpetual) renewal of the things with each Divine breath.[25]

Al-Qāshānī describes the scene of this perpetual renewal of the
things as he sees it in his philosophico-mystical intuition in the
following terms:[26]

The world in its entirety is perpetually changing. And every thing (in
the world) is changing in itself from moment to moment. Thus every
thing becomes determined at every moment with a new determination which is different from that with which it was determined a
moment ago. And yet the one single reality which is attained by all

these successive changes remains forever unchanged. This is due to the fact that the 'one single reality' is nothing but the reality itself of the Absolute as it has taken on the 'first determination', and all the forms (i.e., the successive determinations) are accidents that occur to it successively, changing and being renewed at every moment. But (ordinary) people do not know the reality of this phenomenon and are therefore 'in utter confusion' regarding this perpetual process of transformation which is going on in the universe. Thus the Absolute reveals itself perpetually in these successive self-manifestations, while the world is perpetually being lost due to its annihilation at every moment and its renewed birth at the next moment.

Al-Qāshānī goes a step further and asserts that this perpetual 'new creation' not only governs the concrete existents of the world, but that even the permanent archetypes are under its sway. The archetypes in the Divine Consciousness appear and disappear and then appear again, repeating the same process endlessly as innumerable lamp-lights that go on being turned on and put out in every successive moment. He says:[27]

The ontological emanation (*al-fayḍ al-wujūdiy*) and the Breath of the Merciful are perpetually flowing through the beings of the world as water running in a river, forever being renewed continuously. In a similar way, the determinations of the Absolute-Existence in the form of the permanent archetypes in the eternal Knowledge (i.e., Divine Consciousness) never cease to be renewed from moment to moment. (And this happens in the following way). Thus, as soon as the first ontological determination leaves an archetype in a place, at the next moment the next determination is attached to it in a different place. This is nothing other than the appearance of an archetype belonging in the sphere of Divine Knowledge in the second place following its disappearance in the first place, while that archetype itself remains forever the same in the Knowledge and in the world of the Unseen.

It is as if you saw millions of lights flickering against the background of an unfathomable darkness. If you concentrate your sight on any one of these illumined spots, you will see its light disappearing in the very next moment and appearing again in a different spot in the following moment. And the Divine Consciousness is imagined as a complicated meshwork formed by all these spots in which light goes on being turned on and extinguished at every moment endlessly. This is indeed an exceedingly beautiful and impressive image. But Ibn 'Arabī himself in his *Fuṣūṣ* does not seem to describe the permanent archetypes in this way in terms of the 'new creation'. The 'new creation' he speaks of in this book concerns the concrete things of the sensible world.

Let us return to Ibn 'Arabī and analyze his concept of 'new creation' as he develops it in relation to his atomistic philosophy. He finds in the Qoranic account of the miracle of Bilqīs, Queen of Sheba, an admirable illustration of this incessant annihilation and re-creation which is going on in the world of Being. The account is found in the Qoran, XXVII, 38–40.

Once Solomon asked those who were there in his presence, jinn and human beings, whether any of them could bring him the throne of the Queen. Thereupon one of the jinn said 'I will bring it to thee before thou risest from thy place!' But a man 'who had knowledge of the Scripture'[28] said, 'I will bring it to thee before thy gaze returns to thee (i.e., in the twinkling of an eye)'. And he did bring the throne on the spot from the far-off country in South Arabia and set it in front of Solomon.

How could he accomplish this miracle? Ibn 'Arabī says that the man simply took advantage of the 'new creation'. The throne of the Queen was not transported locally from Sheba to the presence of Solomon. Nobody, in fact, can carry any material object from one place to a distant place in the twinkling of an eye. Nor did Solomon and his people see the throne in hallucination. Rather the throne which had been with Bilqīs was annihilated and, instead of been re-created in the same place, was made to appear in the presence of Solomon. This is, indeed, a miraculous event, in the sense that a thing disappeared and in the next moment appeared in a different place. From the viewpoint of the 'new creation', however, such an event is not at all an impossibility. For, after all, it is nothing but a new throne being created in an entirely different place.

> The superiority of the human sage over the sage of the jinn consists in the (deeper knowledge possessed by the former concerning) the secrets of the free disposal of anything at will and the particular natures of things. And this superiority can be known by the amount of time needed. For the 'return of the gaze' towards the man who looks is faster than the standing up of a man who stands up from his seat. . . . For the time in which the gaze moves to an object is exactly the amount of time in which the gaze gets hold of the object however great the distance may be between the man who looks and the object looked. At the very moment the eye is opened, its gaze reaches the sphere of the fixed stars. And at the very moment the perception stops, the gaze returns to the man. The standing up of a man from his seat cannot be done so quickly.
>
> Thus Āṣaf b. Barakhiyā was superior to the jinn in his action. For the moment Āṣaf spoke, he accomplished his work. And Solomon saw at the same moment the throne of Bilqīs. The throne was actually placed in his presence in order that no one should imagine that Solomon perceived (from afar) the throne in its original place without its being transferred.

In my opinion, however, there can be no local transference in one single moment. There occurred (in Solomon's case) simply a simultaneous annihilation and re-creation in such a manner that no one could perceive it, except those who had been given a true knowledge (of this kind of thing). This is what is meant by God's saying: 'Nay, they are in utter confusion with regard to the new creation'. And there never occurs even a moment in which they cease to see what they have seen (at the preceding moment).[29]

Now if the truth of the matter is as I have just described, the moment of the disappearance of the throne from its original place coincided with the moment of its appearance in the presence of Solomon as a result of the 'new creation' occurring with every Breath. Nobody, however, notices this discrepancy (between two moments of the 'new creation').

Nay, the ordinary man is not aware of it (i.e., the 'new creation') even with regard to himself. Man does not know that he ceases to exist and then comes to existence again with every single breath.[30]

As we see, Ibn 'Arabī here writes that man ceases to exist at every moment and then (*thumma*) comes to existence again. But he immediately adds the remark that the particle *thumma*, meaning 'then' or 'after that', should not be taken as implying a lapse of time.

You must not think that by the word *thumma* I mean a temporal interval. This is not correct. The Arabs use this word in certain particular contexts to express the priority in causal relationship.[31] ...

In the process of 'the new creation with each Breath', too, the time of the non-existence (i.e., annihilation) of a thing coincides with the time of the existence (i.e., re-creation) of a thing similar to it (i.e., the thing that has just been annihilated). This view resembles the Ash'arite thesis of the perpetual renewal of the accidents (*tajdīd al-a'rāẓ*).

In fact, the problem of the transportation of the throne of Bilqīs is of the most recondite problems understandable only to those who know what I have explained above about the story. In brief, the merit of Āṣaf consisted only in the fact that (thanks to him) the 're-creation' in question was actualized in the presence of Solomon. ...

When Bilqīs (thereafter came to visit Solomon and) saw her own throne there, she said: 'It is as though (*ka'anna-hu*) it were (my throne)' (XXVII, 42). (She said 'as though') because she knew the existence of a long distance (between the two places) and because she was convinced of the absolute impossibility of the throne's having been locally transported in such a (short) period of time. Her answer was quite correct in view of the above-mentioned idea of the 'renewal of creation' in similar forms. And in reality it was (i.e., it was the same throne of hers in terms of its permanent archetype, but not as a concrete individual thing). And all this is true, just as you remain what you were in the past moments through the process of the perpetual re-creation.[32]

Quite incidentally, Ibn 'Arabī mentions in the passage just quoted the atomistic thesis of the Ash'arite theologians and points out the existence of a certain resemblance between his and their atomism. But what is more important and more interesting for our purpose is rather the difference between them which Ibn 'Arabī does not state explicitly in this passage, but which he explains in considerable detail in another part of the Fuṣūṣ.

The most salient feature of Ash'arite atomism is the thesis of the perpetual renewal (tajdīd) of accidents. According to this theory, of all the accidents of the things there is not even one that continues to exist for two units of time. Every accident comes into being at this moment and is annihilated at the very next moment to be replaced by another accident which is 'similar' to it being created anew in the same locus. This is evidently the thesis of 'new creation'.

Now if we examine Ibn 'Arabī's thought in relation to this Ash'arite thesis, we find a striking similarity between them. Everything is, for Ibn 'Arabī, a phenomenal form of the Absolute, having no basis for independent subsistence (qiwām) in itself. All are, in short, 'accidents' which appear and disappear in the one eternal-everlasting Substance (jawhar). Otherwise expressed, the existence itself of the Absolute comes into appearance at every moment in milliards of new clothes. With every Breath of God, a new world is created.

From the point of view of Ibn 'Arabī, the atomism of the Ash'arites, though it is not a perfect description of the real structure of Being, does grasp at least an important part of the reality. Mentioning together with the Ash'arites a group of sophists known as Ḥisbāniyyah or Ḥusbāniyyah, he begins to criticize them in the following manner:[33]

> The Ash'arites have hit upon the truth concerning some of the existents, namely, accidents, while the Ḥisbānites have chanced to find the truth concerning the whole of the world. The Philosophers consider these people simply ignorant. But (they are not ignorant; the truth is rather that) they both (i.e., the Ash'arites and the Ḥisbā-nites) are mistaken.

First, he criticizes the sophists of the Ḥisbānite school. The Ḥisbā-nites maintain that nothing remains existent for two units of time, that everything in the world, whether it be substance or accident, is changing from moment to moment. From this they conclude that there is no Reality in the objective sense. Reality or Truth exists only subjectively, for it can be nothing other than the constant flux of things as you perceive it in a fixed form at this present moment.[34]

> Though the Ḥisbānites are right in maintaining that the world as a whole and in its entirety is in perpetual transformation, they are

mistaken in that they fail to see the real oneness of the Substance which underlies all these (changing) forms. (They thereby overlook the fact that) the Substance could not exist (in the external world) if it were not for them (i.e., these changing forms) nor would the forms be conceivable if it were not for the Substance. If the Ḥisbânites could see this point too (in addition to the first point), their theory would be perfect with regard to this problem.[35]

Thus, for Ibn ʿArabī, the merit and demerit of the Ḥisbânite thesis are quite clear. They have hit upon a part of the truth in that they have seen the constant change of the world. But they overlook the most important part of the matter in that they do not know the true nature of the Reality which is the very substrate in which all these changes are happening, and consider it merely a subjective construct of each individual mind.

Concerning the Ashʿarites, Ibn ʿArabī says:[36]

> As for the Ashʿarites, they fail to see that the world in its entirety (including even the so-called 'substances') is a sum of 'accidents', and that, consequently, the whole world is changing from moment to moment since no 'accident' (as they themselves hold) remains for two units of time.

And al-Qāshānī:[37]

> The Ashʿarites do not know the reality of the world; namely, that the world is nothing other than the whole of all these 'forms' which they call 'accidents'. Thus they only assert the existence of substances (i.e., atoms) which are in truth nothing, having no existence (in the real sense of the word). And they are not aware of the one Entity (*'ayn*) which manifests itself in these forms ('accidents' as they call them); nor do they know that this one Entity is the He-ness of the Absolute. This is why they assert (only) the (perpetual) change of the accidents.

According to the basic thesis of the Ashʿarite ontology, the world is reduced to an infinite number of 'indivisible parts', i.e., atoms. These atoms are, in themselves, unknowable. They are knowable only in terms of the 'accidents' that occur to them, one accident appearing in a locus at one moment and disappearing in the next to be replaced by another.

The point Ibn ʿArabī makes against this thesis is that these 'accidents' that go on being born and annihilated in infinitely variegated forms are nothing but so many self-manifestations of the Absolute. And thus behind the kaleidoscopic scene of the perpetual changes and transformations there is always a Reality which is eternally 'one'. And it is this one Reality itself that goes on manifesting itself perpetually in ever new forms. The Ashʿarites who overlook the existence of this one Reality that underlies all 'accidents' are, according to Ibn ʿArabī, driven into the self-contradictory thesis that a collection of a number of transitory 'accidents' that appear and disappear and never remain for two moments constitute 'things' that subsist by themselves and continue to exist for a long time.

> This (i.e., the mistake of the Ash'arites) comes out clearly in their definitions of things. In fact, when they define anything, their definition turns the thing into (a collection of) accidents. And it is clear that it is all these accidents enumerated in the definition that constitute the very 'substance' and its reality which (they consider to be) self-subsistent. However, even that substance (being a totality of the accidents) must ultimately be an accident, and as such it is not self-subsistent. Thus (in their theory) accidents which do not subsist by themselves, when put together, produce something that subsists by itself.[38]

The passage is explicated by al-Qāshānī as follows. The Ash'arites, whenever they define something, define it as a whole (*majmū'*) of accidents. Defining 'man', for example, they say: 'a rational animal'. The word 'rational' (*nāṭiq*) means 'possessed of reason' (*dhū nuṭq*). The concept of 'being possessed of' is a relation, and 'relation' is evidently an accident. 'Reason' (*nuṭq*), on the other hand, being something added to the essence of 'animal', is also an accident. Thus to say that man is 'a rational animal' is to say that man is 'an animal with two accidents'. Then the Ash'arites go on to define 'animal' by saying that it is a 'physical body that grows, perceives, and moves by will'. The 'animal' turns in this way into a whole of accidents. And the same procedure is applied to the definition of the '(physical) body' appearing in the definition of 'animal'. As a result, 'man' ultimately turns out to be a bundle of accidents which are by definition momentary and transitory. And yet this bundle itself is considered to be something subsistent by itself, a substance.

The Ash'arites, Ibn 'Arabī continues, are not aware of the fact that the very 'substance', which they consider a self-subsistent entity, is of exactly the same nature as 'man', 'animal', and other things; it is also a bundle of accidents.

> Thus, in their theory, something (i.e., a bundle of *accidents*) which does not remain for two units of time remains (i.e., as a *bundle* of accidents) for two units of time, nay, for many units of time! And something which does not subsist by itself (must be said to) subsist by itself, according to the Ash'arites! However, they do not know that they are contradicting themselves. So (I say that) these are people 'who are in utter confusion with regard to the new creation'.[39]

Ibn 'Arabī brings out the contrast between the 'wrong' view of the Ash'arites and the 'true' thesis upheld by the people of 'unveiling' by saying:[40]

As to the people of 'unveiling', they see God manifesting Himself with every Breath, no single self-manifestation being repeated twice. They see also by an immediate vision that every single self-manifestation gives rise to a new creation and annihilates a creation (i.e., the 'creation' that has preceded), and that the disappearance of the latter at every (new) self-manifestation is 'annihilation' whereas 'subsistence' is caused by what is furnished (immediately) by the following self-manifestation.

Thus in Ibn 'Arabī's thought, everything in the world (and therefore the world itself) is constantly changing, but underlying this universal flux of changing things there is Something eternally unchanging. Using scholastic terminology he calls this unchanging Something the 'Substance', the absolute substratum of all changes. In this particular perspective, all things – not only the 'accidents' so called but the 'substances' so called – are represented as 'accidents' appearing and disappearing at every moment. It is interesting to observe how the theory of Divine self-manifestation becomes transformed, when translated into the language of the scholastic philosophy of 'substance' and 'accident'.

Notes

1. It is also called Word (*qawl*).

2. *Fuṣ.*, pp. 139–140/115–116.

3. Reading: *hādhihi dhāt wa-irādah wa-qawl.*

4. *Fuṣ.*, pp. 139–140/115–116.

5. *Fuṣ.*, p. 140/115–116.

6. p. 140.

7. The point is that God does not say in this verse *fa-yukawwin* ('and He brings it into existence') but says *fa-yakūn* ('and it comes into existence'), the subject of the sentence being the thing itself.

8. *Fuṣ.*, p. 140/115–116.

9. *Fuṣ.*, p. 273/219.

10. *Fuṣ.*, p. 274/220.

11. pp. 274–275.

12. Although Adam is a man, he is, as a 'soul' (*nafs*), feminine.

13. The reference is to the above-quoted Tradition, in which the Prophet uses the

feminine numeral *thalāth* in spite of the presence of a masculine noun among the three things enumerated.

14. 'Determination' (or more strictly 'being determined') refers to the passive side of the Absolute, i.e., the Absolute as manifesting itself in a concrete (determined) thing. 'Non-determination' refers to the active side of the Absolute, i.e., the Absolute as the absolute Agent.

15. The 'first determination' (*al-ta'ayyun al-awwal*) means the self-manifestation of the Absolute to itself as a unifying point of all the Divine Names. The Absolute is here the 'one' (*wāḥid*), and the ontological stage the *wāḥidīyah*, 'Oneness'.

16. The Absolute *qua* One is potentially all beings but it is in actuality still one. So it is neither in the state of pure exterior self-manifestation nor in that of pure interior concealment, but it keeps, so to speak, a perfect balance between these two terms.

17. I read: [*wa-fā'il*] *min nafsi-hi*, etc.

18. The idea presents a very important and interesting problem from the viewpoint of comparative Oriental philosophy. See my 'The Concept of Perpetual Creation in Islamic Mysticism and Zen Buddhism' (in *Mélanges offerts à Henry Corbin*, ed. Seyyed Hossein Nasr Tehran, 1977, pp. 115–148.

19. When you look at something through an extremely fine and transparent fabric you do not become aware of the existence of the veil between you and the thing. The 'veil' here refers to the outward form shown by the act of 'ascending'.

20. *Fuṣ.*, p. 151–152/124.

21. p. 152.

22. *Fuṣ.*, p. 152/124–125.

23. p. 152–153.

24. Ibn 'Arabī, as he often does, is giving quite an arbitrary meaning to the Qoranic verse. The actual context makes it clear beyond any doubt that God is here speaking of Resurrection after death, which is conceived of as a 'new creation'. The 'new creation' does not certainly mean in this verse the ever new process of creation which is Ibn 'Arabī's thesis.

25. *Fuṣ.*, p. 153/125.

26. p. 153.

27. pp. 195–196.

28. The Qoran does not give his name. Commentators assert that the man was a sage whose name was Āṣaf b. Barakhiyā.

29. This annihilation/re-creation is done so quickly that man does not notice any discontinuum between the two units of time in his sense perception and imagines that everything continues to be as it has been.

30. *Fuṣ.*, pp. 195–196/155.

31. 'A *thumma* B' in certain contexts means that A, as the cause of B, logically precedes the latter. It does not imply that A necessarily precedes B in terms of time; A and B may very well occur simultaneously.

32. *Fuṣ.*, p. 197/156–157.

33. *Fuṣ.*, p. 153/125.

34. The Name *Ḥisbāniyyah* is derived from the root ḤSB (the verb *ḥasiba*) meaning 'to opine' 'to surmise', i.e., the subjective act of estimation. The appellation implies that Reality or Truth consists in the subjective estimation of this or that individual person, and that, consequently, there is no such thing as an objectively universal Truth (cf. Affifi, Com., p. 153).

35. *Fuṣ.*, p. 153/125.

36. *Fuṣ.*, pp. 153–154/125–126.

37. p. 154.

38. pp. 154–155/125–126.

39. *Fuṣ.*, p. 154/126.

40. *ibid.*

XIV Man as Microcosm

As I remarked earlier, the world-view of Ibn 'Arabī stands on two bases: one is the Absolute, and the other the Perfect Man. And all through the preceding pages, we have been analyzing his ontological world-view exclusively from the first angle. The remaining chapters will be concerned with the analysis of the same world-view looked at from the second point of view.

I Microcosm and Macrocosm

In setting out to discuss the concept of the Perfect Man (*al-insān al-kāmil*) it is, I think of special importance to observe that Ibn 'Arabī considers 'man' on two different levels. It is important to keep this basic distinction in mind, because if we neglect to do so, we shall easily be led into confusion.

The first is the cosmic level. Here 'man' is treated as a cosmic entity. In popular terminology we might say that what is at issue on this level is 'mankind'. In logical terminology, we might say that it is 'man' as a species. In any event, the question is not about 'man' as an individual person.

'Man' on this level is the most perfect of all beings of the world, for he is the *Imago Dei*. Here 'man' himself is perfect; 'man' *is* the Perfect Man. The Perfect Man in this sense is 'man' viewed as a perfect epitome of the universe, the very spirit of the whole world of Being, a being summing up and gathering together in himself all the elements that are manifested in the universe. 'Man' is, in short, the Microcosm.

At the second level, on the contrary, 'man' means an individual. On this level, not all men are equally perfect. There are, from this point of view, a number of degrees among men. And only few of them deserve the appellation of the Perfect Man. The majority of men are far from being 'perfect'.

The present chapter will be concerned with the Perfect Man as understood in the first sense.

As has just been remarked 'man' on the first of the two levels is an epitome of the whole universe. He is, in this sense, called the 'comprehensive being' (*al-kawn al-jāmi'*, lit. 'a being that gathers together'), that is, Microcosm.

Concerning the birth of 'man' as the 'comprehensive being', there is at the very outset of the *Fuṣūṣ*, a very famous passage. The passage is filled with technical terms peculiar to Ibn 'Arabī, all of which have already been analyzed in the preceding chapters. Here Ibn 'Arabī describes the mysterious process by which the self-manifestation of the Absolute is activated by the inner requirement of the Divine Names, leading toward the creation of the world, and in particular the creation of 'man' as the being who sums up in itself all the properties that are diffused in the whole universe. The passage begins with the following words:[1]

> When the Absolute God, at the level of his Beautiful Names that exceed enumeration, wished to see the (latent) realities of the Names – or if you like, say, His inner reality itself – as (actualized) in a 'comprehensive being' which, because of its being qualified by 'existence', contains in itself the whole universe, and (wished) to make manifest to Himself His own secret through it (i.e., the 'comprehensive being') . . .

These opening words of the passage constitute a brief summary of the ontology of Ibn 'Arabī which we have been studying in detail in the preceding. The argument may be explained as follows.

Ibn 'Arabī begins by stating that the Divine Wish (*mashī'ah*) for the creation of the world (and man in particular) did not arise from the Absolute *qua* Absolute. The creative Wish arose due to the essential inner drive of the Beautiful Names or Attributes. The Absolute *qua* Absolute characterized by an absolute 'independence' (*istighnā'*) does not require by itself and for itself any creative activity. It is the Divine Names that require the existence of the universe, the created world. It is in the very nature of the Divine Names to require the world, because they are actualized only by the concrete existents, and without the latter they lose positive significance.

Ibn 'Arabī expresses this situation by saying: 'The Absolute wished to see the realities (*a'yān*) of the Divine Names', or 'The Absolute wished to see its own inner reality (*'ayn*). The first formula corresponds to what we already know as 'the holy emanation', while the second corresponds to the 'most holy emanation'. The distinction does not make much difference in this particular context, because 'the holy emanation' necessarily presupposes the 'most holy emanation', and the latter necessarily entails the former. What Ibn 'Arabī wants to say is that God had the *mashī'ah* to see Himself as reflected in the mirror of the world, that He wished to see Himself in the very manifestation-forms of His own Attributes.

The phrase, 'because of its being qualified by existence', gives an answer to the question: How is it possible for the Absolute to see itself by the creation of the universe as epitomized by Man? The universe possesses 'existence'. This 'existence' is not the absolute Existence itself, but is a 'relative existence' (*wujūd iḍāfiy*), i.e., 'existence' as determined and delimited in various ways and forms. But, however determined and delimited, the relative existence is, after all, a direct reflection of the absolute Existence. It is the figure of the Absolute itself as the latter is manifested in 'possible' exist-ents, being determined and particularized by each of the loci of its self-manifestation. The relative existence is – to use a favorite metaphor of Ibn 'Arabī – the absolute Existence as reflected in the mirror of relative determinations.

An image in a mirror is not the object itself, but it does represent the object. In this sense, the universe discloses the 'secret' (*sirr*) of the Absolute. The word 'secret' in the above-quoted passage means the hidden (i.e., absolutely invisible) depths of Existence, and cor-responds to the phrase 'the hidden treasure' (*kanz makhfiy*) in the famous Tradition which we discussed earlier.

Ibn 'Arabī sets out to develop his thought in terms of the metaphor of the mirror. He begins by distinguishing between two kinds of vision:[2]

> The vision which a being obtains of itself is different from the vision of itself which it obtains in something else serving as a mirror for it.

The first of these two kinds of vision consists in a being seeing itself in itself. And it goes without saying that the Absolute has vision of itself in this sense. Here the Absolute needs no mirror. The Abso-lute is 'All-seeing by itself from eternity', and nothing of itself is concealed from its inner gaze.

But the Absolute has also an aspect in which it is an Essence qualified by Attributes. And since the Attributes become real only when they are externalized, it becomes necessary for the Absolute to see itself in the 'other'. Thus the 'other' is created in order that God might see Himself therein in externalized forms.

The first thing which God created in order to see Himself therein was the world or universe. Ibn 'Arabī calls the world in this particu-lar context the Big Man (*al-insān al-kabīr*), i.e., Macrocosm.[3] The most salient feature of the Big Man is that every single existent in it represents one particular aspect (Name) of God, and one only, so that the whole thing lacks a clear delineation and a definite articulation, being as it is a loose conglomeration of discrete points. It is, so to speak, a clouded mirror.

In contrast to this, the second thing which God created for the purpose of seeing Himself as reflected therein, namely, Man, is a well-polished spotless mirror reflecting any object as it really is. Rather, Man is the polishing itself of this mirror which is called the universe. Those discrete things and properties that have been diffused and scattered all over the immense universe become united and unified into a sharp focus in Man. The structure of the whole universe with all its complicated details is reflected in him in a clear and distinctly articulated miniature. This is the meaning of his being a Microcosm. Man is a Small Universe, while the universe is a Big Man, as al-Qāshānī says.[4]

The contrast between the universe and Man in the capacity of a 'mirror' which God holds up to Himself is described by Ibn 'Arabī in the following terms:[5]

> God makes Himself visible to Himself in a (particular) form that is provided by the locus (i.e., the mirror) in which He is seen. Something in this way becomes visible to Him which would never be visible if it were not for this particular locus and His self-manifestation therein.
> (Before the creation of Man) God had already brought into being the whole universe with an existence like that of a vague and obscure image having a form but no soul within. It was like a mirror that was left unpolished. . . .
> This situation naturally demanded the polishing up of the mirror of the universe. And Man (*ādam*, i.e., the reality of Man) was (created to be) the very polishing of that mirror and the very spirit of that form.

The ontological meaning of the metaphor of the 'unpolished mirror' is explained by al-Qāshānī as follows:[6]

> Before Man, the Microcosm, was created, the universe (the Macrocosm) had already been existent due to the requirement of the Divine Names, because it is in the nature of each Name to require singly the actualization of its content, i.e., the Essence accompanied by an Attribute, or an existence particularized by an Attribute, while another Name asks for an existence particularized by another Attribute. No single Name, however, requires an existence which would unify all the Attributes together, for no Name has an essential unity comprising all the Attributes in itself. Thus the universe has no property of being a comprehensive locus for manifesting all the aspects of existence in its unity.

This fact that the universe was an 'unpolished mirror' required the creation of Man who was meant to be the very polishing of the mirror.

This is a very important statement for determining the cosmic significance of Man. We might interpret it in terms of modern philosophic thinking and say that what is symbolized by the 'polishing' – or rather 'the state of having been polished' (*jalā'*) – of the mirror is the 'consciousness' of Man. All beings other than Man only reflect, each one of them, singly, one aspect of the Absolute. It is only when put together in the form of the universe that they constitute a big whole corresponding to the Consciousness itself of the Absolute. In this sense, the universe, certainly, is 'one', but, since the universe lacks consciousness, it does not constitute real unity. Man, on the contrary, not only synthesizes all the forms of the Divine self-manifestation which are scattered over the world of Being, but also is conscious of this whole. This is why a true comprehensive unity is established by Man, corresponding to the Unity of the Absolute. Man is in this sense the *Imago Dei*. And because of this peculiarity, Man can be, as we shall see presently, the 'vicegerent' of God on the earth.

On the correspondence just mentioned between the human unity and the Divine Unity, al-Qāshānī makes the following remark:[7]

> The Presence (i.e., the ontological level) of 'God' gathers together all the Names without there being anything mediatory between them and the Divine Essence. The ontological level of Man gathers them together in a similar way. This can be understood from the following consideration. Existence comes down first from the comprehensive Unity of the Essence to the Presence of Divinity, and thence it overflows into all the degrees of the 'possible' things spreading more and more in various forms until, when it reaches Man, it has already been tinged with all the colors of the (ontological) grades.
> Man becomes in this way an intermediate stage (*barzakh*) comprising the properties both of necessity and possibility, as the Presence of Divinity comprises both the Essence and all the Names.

The above quoted passage from the *Fuṣūṣ*, together with this explanatory remark by al-Qāshānī, makes it clear that the most important significance of Man lies in his 'comprehensiveness' (*jam'iyah*, lit. 'gathering-ness'). Before we proceed with this problem, we must analyze further in detail the metaphor of the mirror.

A mirror reflects objects. Sometimes it reflects them as they really are. But in many cases an object is reflected in a mirror more or less changed or transformed.

The image of a person appearing on the polished (surface of a) body is nothing other than the person himself, except that the locus or the Presence, in which he perceives the reflection of his own image, gives back the image to him with a certain transformation[8] according to the constitution of that Presence. In the same way, a big thing appears small in a small mirror, oblong in an oblong mirror, and moving in a moving mirror (i.e., running water).

Thus the mirror sometimes gives back the image of the person in inversion, the inversion being caused by the particular constitution of a particular Presence. But sometimes it gives back the very thing (i.e., the person who is looking) appearing in it, in such a way that the left side (for example) of the reflected image faces the left side of the person.[9] Sometimes, again, the right side (of the image in the mirror) faces the left side (of the person) as is typical of what customarily happens to (an image in) a mirror. Only by a 'break of custom' does the right side (for example) face the right side.[10]

On the transforming effect of mirrors, Ibn 'Arabī says as follows in another passage:[11]

A mirror affects the images in a certain sense, but it does not affect them in another sense. It does affect in that it gives back the image of an object in a changed form as regards smallness, bigness, length, and shortness. Thus it has a positive effect upon the quantities, and that effect is properly due to it. On the other hand, however, (it has no positive effect of its own in the sense that) all these changes caused by the mirror are in the last resort due to the different sizes of the objects reflected.

Even one and the same object is reflected in varying magnitudes in mirrors of various magnitudes. Here we see clearly suggested the idea that although each individual man, as a mirror of the Absolute, reflects the Absolute and nothing else, the reflected images vary from person to person according to the individual capacities of different men. There is, however, as Ibn 'Arabī adds, a certain respect in which a man, the mirror, must be said to exercise no positive, transforming effect upon the image of the Absolute, for all transformations of the reflected image ultimately come from the internal modifications of the Absolute itself

Man, unlike the rest of the creatures, actualizes in himself the whole of the Divine Names in miniature, and is, in this sense, a miraculous mirror which is able to reflect the original unity of the Names as it is. But, on the other hand, men considered individually, differ from each other in the 'polishing' of the cosmic mirror. Only in the case of the highest 'knowers' does the human consciousness reflect on its spotless surface the Absolute as it really is.

But by making these observations, we are already encroaching upon the realm of the next chapter. We must turn our steps back and continue our discussion of the nature of Man as Microcosm.

II Comprehensiveness of Man

The 'humanity' (*insānīyah*) of Man on the cosmic level lies, as we
have already seen, in his 'comprehensiveness' (*jam'iyah*). Man, as
Microcosm, contains in himself all the attributes that are found in
the universe. The Absolute, in this sense, manifests itself in Man in
the most perfect way. And Man is the Perfect Man because he is the
most perfect self-manifestation of the Absolute.

The following is a very important passage in which Ibn 'Arabī
explains to us his concept of the Perfect Man on the cosmic level.[12]
He takes the prophet Moses as an illustration. Moses, when he was
born, was put into a chest, and was thrown into the Nile. Ibn 'Arabī,
by explicating the symbolic meaning of this story, develops it into a
theory of the Perfect Man.

> As regards the wisdom of Moses' being put into a chest and thrown
> into the great river, we must notice that the chest (*tābūt*) symbolizes
> the 'human aspect (of man)' (*nāsūt*, i.e., the body) while the 'great
> river' (*yamm*) symbolizes the knowledge which he acquires by means
> of this body.[13] This Knowledge is acquired by him through the power
> of thinking, and representation. These and similar powers of the
> human soul can only function when the physical body is in existence.
>
> So, as soon as the soul is actualized in the body and is commanded (by
> God) to use and govern the body freely, God produces in the soul all
> the above-mentioned powers as so many instruments by which the
> soul might achieve the purpose – according to the Will of God – of
> governing this 'chest' containing the invisible Presence (*sakīnah*)[14] of
> the Lord.
>
> Thus (Moses) was thrown into the great river so that he might acquire
> by means of these powers all kinds of knowledge. (God) let him
> understand thereby the fact that although the spirit (*rūḥ*) governing
> (the body) is the 'king' (i.e., the supreme commander of the human
> body), yet it cannot govern it at will save by means of the body. This is
> why God furnished the body with all these powers existing in the
> 'human aspect' which He called symbolically and esoterically the
> 'chest'.
>
> The same holds true of the governing of the world by God. For He
> governs the world at will only by means of it (i.e., the world), or by
> means of its form.[15]
>
> God governs the world only by the world (by establishing certain
> necessary relations among the things of the world): for example, the
> child depends upon the generating act of the father, the generated
> depend upon their generators, the conditioned upon their con-
> ditions, the effects upon their causes, the conclusions upon their
> proofs, and the concrete existents upon their inner realities. All these
> belong to the world as a result of God's disposal of the thing. Thus it is
> clear that He governs the world only by the world.
>
> I have said above: 'or by means of its form', i.e., by means of the form

of the world. What I understand here under the word 'form' (*ṣūrah*) is the Most Beautiful Names by which He has named Himself and the highest Attributes by which He has qualified Himself.

In fact, of every Name of God, which we have come to know, we find the meaning actualized in the world and its spirit being active in the world. So in this respect, too, God does not govern the world except by the form of the world.

Thus Ibn 'Arabī divides the governing (*tadbīr*) of the world by the Absolute into two kinds: (1) 'by the world' and (2) 'by the form of the world'. The first has been illustrated by such necessary relations as exist between the child and the father, the caused and the causes, etc. Here God, so to speak, lets the world govern itself by putting the things of the world in certain necessary relations. The second kind is completely different from this. It consists in God's making His Names and Attributes, i.e., the eternal forms, govern and regulate from inside the ever changing phenomenal forms of the world.[16] This point is brought out with admirable clarity by al-Qāshānī in his following remark on the just quoted passage of the *Fuṣūṣ*.[17]

> What is meant by the 'form of the world' here is not its sensible individual form. If it were so, it (i.e., the second type of governing) would simply be reduced to the first type. . . .
> What is really meant by it is the intelligible, specific form of the world, which is nothing but the Most beautiful Names and its realities, i.e., the highest Attributes.
> The (phenomenal) forms of the world are simply outwardly manifested forms of the Names and Attributes. These latter are the real inner forms of the world. All sensible things are but outward, individualized forms; they are ever changing imprints and external shapes, while the (inner forms) are permanent and everlasting, never changing. The former are transitory forms, surface phenomena, while the latter are the inner meanings and spirits of the former.
> All the Names by which God has named Himself, such as Living, Knowing, Willing, Powerful, are there in the world. All the Attributes with which He has qualified Himself, such as Life, Knowledge, Will, Power, are there in the world. Thus God governs the outside of the world by its inside.
> (So there are two types in God's governing the world:) the first is the governing exercised by some of the phenomenal forms of the world over other phenomenal forms. The second is the governing of the phenomenal individual forms by the internal specific forms. Both types are the governing of the world by the world.

Ibn 'Arabī goes on to argue:

> This is why (the Prophet) said concerning the creation of Adam: 'Verily God created Adam in His Form', for Adam is an exemplar synthesizing all the constituent elements of the Presence of Divinity,

namely, the Essence, the Attributes, and the Actions. The expression 'His Form' means nothing but the Presence of Divinity itself.

Thus God has put into this noble epitome (*mukhtaṣar*), the Perfect Man (as symbolized by Adam), all the Divine Names and the realities of all things existing outside of him in the Macrocosm which (apparently) subsists independently of him.

This passage explains the meaning of the 'comprehensiveness' of Man. As we have seen above, the Perfect Man synthesizes in himself all the things that exist in the universe, ranging from the four natural elements to minerals, plants, and animals. But the important point is that all these things do not exist in Man in their concrete individual forms. They exist in him only as 'realities' (*ḥaqā'iq*), that is, in their universality. Man gathers together in himself all the things of the universe in the sense that he is a synthesis of the non-material realities of the individual things. The Perfect Man is an epitome of the Macrocosm only in this particular sense.

> God in this way has made Man the Spirit (*rūḥ*) of the universe, and made everything, high and low, subservient to him because of the perfection of his (inner) form.
> Thus it comes about that, as 'there is nothing' in the whole universe 'but gives praises unto God' (XVII, 44), so there is nothing in the universe but is subservient to Man due to the essential merit of his inner form. To this refers God's saying: 'thus He has made all that is in the heavens and in the earth subservient unto you all together, from Him' (XXII, 65).
> So everything in the universe is under the supreme dominion of Man. But this fact is known only to those who know it – such a man is the Perfect Man[18] – and those who do not know it do not know – such is the Animal Man.
> Outwardly considered, the fact that Moses was put into a chest, which was then thrown into the great river, meant death, but inwardly, it was for him deliverance from being killed. For, as a result, he gained life, just as the souls are enlivened by knowledge and are delivered from the death of ignorance.

The long passage which we have quoted explains the real nature of the perfection of Man on the cosmic level. In the view of Ibn 'Arabī, the perfection of Man and the high position assigned to him[19] are due to his microcosmic nature, that is, his 'comprehensiveness'. And his 'comprehensiveness' consists in his reflecting and realizing faithfully the Divine Comprehensiveness.

> All the Names that are contained in the Divine Form[20] have been manifested in the ontological dimension of Man. And the latter has obtained through this (kind of) existence the (highest) rank of integral comprehensiveness.[21]

As regards the Divine Comprehensiveness (*al-jam'īyah al-ilāhīyah*) Ibn 'Arabī gives the following explanation, dividing it into three constituents.[22]

> (We can distinguish) in the Divine Comprehensiveness: (1) that which must be attributed to God Himself (as represented by the supreme Name *Allāh* or God, comprehending within itself all the Divine Names), (2) that which is ascribable to the Reality of realities, and (3) that which – in this constitution (i.e. the bodily constitution of Man which comprehends all the recipients of the world ranging from the highest to the lowest – is ascribable to what is required by the universal Nature.

The first of these three elements is evidently the Divine aspect of Unity, i.e., the Divine Essence, not in its absoluteness but as qualified by the Divine Name 'God'. The second is the ontological plane in which the permanent archetypes come into being, i.e., God conceived as the highest creative Principle regulating and unifying the archetypes. It is called the Reality of realities because through this Reality all the realities of the world become actualized. The third, the universal Nature (*ṭabī'ah kullīyah*) is the ontological region of 'reality' occupying the intermediary position between the purely Divine and positively creative 'reality' of Divine Names and the purely creaturely and essentially passive 'reality' of the physical world, comprising within itself both these properties – positively creative on the one hand, and passively receptive on the other.

From all this Ibn 'Arabī comes to the following conclusion.[23]

> This being (i.e., the 'comprehensive being') is called Man and also a Vicegerent (*khalīfah*).[24] His being (named) Man is due to the comprehensiveness of his constitution, comprising as it does all the realities. Furthermore (he deserves to be named Man – *insān* because) he is to God as the pupil (*insān*) is to the eye as the instrument of vision, i.e., seeing. Thus he is called *insān* because God sees His creatures through man, and has Mercy upon them.

Man on the cosmic level, or the Perfect Man, is endowed with a perfect 'comprehensiveness'. And because of this 'comprehensiveness' by which he synthesizes in himself all the existents of the universe not individually but in their universality, the Perfect Man shows two characteristic properties which are not shared by anything else. One is that he is the only being who is really and fully entitled to be a perfect 'servant' (*'abd*) of God. All other beings do not fully reflect God, because each actualizes only a single Divine Name; they cannot, therefore, be *perfect* 'servants'. The second characteristic feature of the Perfect Man consists in his being *in a certain sense* the Absolute itself. In the case of beings other than human, we can say that the Absolute is the inner reality (*'ayn*) of them, but we cannot surely reverse the relation and say that they are the inner reality of the Absolute, for they are but partial actualizations of the Divine Self. The following two verses by Ibn 'Arabī put these two characteristics of Man in a concise form.[25]

> Verily, we are real servants; verily, God is our Master.
> Verily, we are His Self, and all this is implied when I say 'Man'.

> That is to say, we are 'servants' in the true sense of the word, because we serve Him with an essential service, i.e., with the most comprehensive Unity which is realized on the ontological level of 'God', while God with the whole of His Names is our Master, governing us, administering our affairs. We are different in this respect from the rest of beings, for they are His servants merely in certain aspects, and God is their Master with some of His Names.
> The Perfect Man is the inner reality of the Absolute because he appears in the Form of the latter with its comprehensive unity. The rest of the things, on the contrary, though the Absolute is the inner reality of each one of them, are not the inner reality of the Absolute because they are but loci of manifestation for some of the Names so that the Absolute does not manifest itself in them in its essential Form.
> But when I say 'Man', meaning thereby the Perfect Man, i.e., Man perfect in 'humanity', what is meant is the being in which the Absolute manifests itself in its essential Form. Man, in this sense, is the very reality of the Absolute.

Ibn 'Arabī considers, further, the 'comprehensiveness' of Man from the point of view of the Inward-Outward opposition. In exact correspondence to the distinction between the Divine Names Inward and Outward, there is in Man also a distinction between the 'inward' and the 'outward', and he covers thereby the whole of the universe.

> You must know, further, that God describes Himself as being the Inward and the Outward. He has correspondingly produced the world of the Unseen and the world of sensory experience so that we might perceive the Inward by our own 'unseen' element and the Outward by our 'sensible' element.[26]

Thus God has created two worlds, the inner and the outer, corresponding to His own Inward and Outward, and has given Man, and Man only, the 'inner' and the 'outer'. In this respect, Man alone is the true *Imago* of the Absolute.

> You must have understood by now the real nature of Adam, i.e., his outward 'form', as well as the real nature of his spirit (*rūḥ*), i.e., his inward 'form'. Adam is the Absolute (in view of his inward form) and a creature (in view of his outward form). You know also the real

nature of his (ontological) rank which, being a synthesis, makes him entitled to be the Vicegerent (of God).[27]

The position of Adam, i.e., the Perfect Man as understood in this chapter, is 'in the middle' between the Absolute and the creatures. He essentially reflects both, represents both, and is a 'synthesis' (*majmū'*) of the two 'forms'. His 'outward' discloses the form of the created world and its realities, while his 'inward' reveals the Form itself of the Absolute and its essential Names. And because of this 'synthesis' and perfect 'comprehensiveness', his rank is higher than that of angels.

Thus all the Names that are contained in the Divine Form are manifested in the ontological dimension of Man. The latter has obtained through this (kind of) existence the rank of integral comprehensiveness.

And this precisely was the ground on which God the Exalted refuted the argument of the angels[28] . . . The angels were not aware of what was implied by the constitution of this 'vicegerent' (of God on the earth). Nor did they know the 'essential service'[29] required by the Presence of the Absolute. For nobody can know concerning the Absolute except that which his own essence allows him to know, and the angels did not possess the 'comprehensiveness' of Adam. They were not even aware of (the limitedness of) the Divine Names that were (manifested) in themselves. So they were praising the Absolute and sanctifying it simply through the (limited Names that they happened to have in themselves). They were not aware of the fact that God has (other) Names about which no knowledge had been given them. Consequently the angels were not praising Him through these Names; nor were they sanctifying Him in the same way as Adam did. Thus they were completely under the sway of what I have just mentioned (i.e., their limited knowledge of the Names), and were dominated by this (deficient) state of theirs.

Because of this (deficiency in their) constitution, the angels said (to God when He was about to create Adam): 'Art Thou going to place on the earth one who will do harm therein?' (II, 30). But 'harm' can be nothing other than 'opening up an argument (against God, instead of accepting His words with docility and submission)'. It was exactly what they themselves did (when they dared to put the above-mentioned question to God). So what they said concerning Adam was what they themselves were actually doing toward God. It is evident, then, that, if their own nature had not been agreeable to this particular behavior, they would not have said about Adam what they said without being conscious (of the truth of the matter). Had they but known their own selves, (i.e., their own essential constitution), they would have known (the truth about Adam), and had they but known (the truth) they would never have committed such a mistake. In reality, however, they were not content with denigrating (Adam); they went even further and boastfully claimed that they were praising and sanctifying God.[30]

But Adam had in himself such Divine Names as were not represented
by the angels. The latter naturally could not praise God with those
Names, nor could they sanctify Him with them, as Adam did.[31]

In the Qoran (II, 31) we read that 'God taught Adam all the
Names'. This means, according to Ibn 'Arabī, that Man represents
and actualizes all Divine Names. The angels, on the contrary, manifest only some of the Names. But they are not aware of it.

The difference between the human and the angelic act of praising
God which is discussed here by Ibn 'Arabī is also based on the
Qoranic verse which reads: 'There is nothing (in the world) but
praises Him in adoration, but you do not understand their praise'
(XVII, 44).

The dictum that everything in the world is praising God has, for
Ibn 'Arabī, a very special meaning. God manifests Himself in all
things, according to their peculiar capacities and within the limits
determined by the latter. This fact, when considered from the side
of the created things, is capable of being interpreted as the created
things manifesting the Divine Perfection (*kamāl*) in variously
limited forms. This manifestation of the Divine Perfection by each
thing in its peculiar form is what is understood by Ibn 'Arabī under
the word 'praising' (*tasbīḥ*) or 'sanctifying' (*taqdīs*).

Otherwise expressed, all things 'praise and sanctify' God by the
very fact that they exist in the world. But since each thing exists in its
own peculiar way, each thing praises and sanctifies God in a different way from all the rest. And the higher the level of Being to which
a thing belongs, the greater and stronger is its 'praising and sanctifying', because a higher being actualizes a greater number of Names
than those which belong to lower levels. In this respect, Man
occupies the highest position among all the beings of the world,
because he is a locus in which all the Names, i.e., all the Perfections
(*kamālāt*) of God become manifested.

We must recall at this juncture what we have observed in an
earlier context about the essential indifference of Perfection
(*kamāl*) to the commonly accepted distinction between good and
evil. In Ibn 'Arabī's world-view, the distinction which is ordinarily
made in human societies between good and evil is of an entirely
conventional, relative, and secondary nature. Primarily, existence
itself is Perfection, and every ontological attribute is also a Perfection. Just as 'obedience' (to God) is a Perfection, 'disobedience' is a
Perfection, because the latter is in no less a degree than the former
an ontological attribute, i.e., a form of Being. The fact that 'obedience' is a Perfection has essentially nothing to do with its being
ethically 'good'; 'obedience' is a Perfection because it is a locus in
which such Divine Names as the Merciful and the Bountiful are

manifested. And 'disobedience' is a Perfection because it is a locus in which such Names as the Vindictive and the Chastiser are manifested.

If we lose sight of this basic ontological fact, we cannot understand why Ibn 'Arabī considers the position of Man higher than that of angels. From the standpoint of Ibn 'Arabī, the nature (*ṭabī'ah*) of angels is solely 'spiritual' (*rūḥiyah*), while the nature of Man is 'spiritual-bodily' (*rūḥiyah-badanīyah*) and thus comprises all the attributes of Being, ranging from the highest to the lowest. And because of this particularly, Man is superior to angels.[32]

Regarding the highest position of Man in the hierarchy of Being, Ibn 'Arabī discerns a deep symbolic meaning in the Qoranic statement that God created Adam 'with both His hands'.

> God jointed His two hands for (creating) Adam. This He did solely by way of conferring upon him a great honor. And this is why He said to Iblīs (Satan): 'What hinders thee from falling prostrate before that which I have created with both My hands?' (XXXVIII, 76). The (joining of His two hands) symbolizes nothing other than the fact that Adam joins in him two 'forms': the form of the world and the form of the Absolute. These two are the 'hands' of God.
>
> Iblīs, on the contrary, is but a part of the world, and this 'gathering' has not been given him.[33]

In a different passage of the *Fuṣūṣ*, Ibn 'Arabī returns to the idea of God having created Adam with both His hands, and says:[34]

> God kneaded the clay of Man with both His hands, which are opposed to each other, though, (in a certain sense), each one of His two hands is a right hand (i.e., both are exactly equal to each other in being powerful and merciful). In any case, there can be no doubt that there is a difference between the two if only for the reason that they are 'two', i.e., *two* hands.
>
> Nature is not affected except by what is proportional to it, and Nature itself is divided into pairs of opposition. That is why (it is said that God created Adam) with both His hands.
>
> And since He created Adam with both His hands, He named him *bashar*,[35] because of His 'touching' (*mubāsharah*) him directly with the two hands that are attributed to Him, the word 'touching' being taken here in a special sense which is applicable to the Divine Presence.[36] He did so as an expression of His special concern with this human species. And He said to (Iblīs) who refused to fall prostrate before Adam: 'What hinders thee from falling prostrate before that which I have created with both My hands? Dost thou scornfully look down' upon one who is equal to thee, i.e., in being made of natural elements, 'or art thou of a higher order' which, in reality, thou art not – than elemental (*'unṣurī*) beings?[37] God means by 'those of a higher order' (*'ālīn*) those (spiritual beings) who, due to their luminous

constitution, transcend, by their own essence, being 'elemental',
though they are 'natural',[38]
Man is superior to other beings of the 'elemental' species only by
being a *bashar* of clay (i.e., clay kneaded directly by the two hands of
God). Thus he is higher than all that have been created of elements
without having been touched by his hands.
So Man is in rank higher than all the angels, terrestrial and celestial,
although, according to the sacred texts, the archangels are superior to
the human species.

As a concrete example showing in the most perfect form possible
the 'comprehensiveness' of the Perfect Man, Ibn 'Arabī discusses
Abraham (Ibrāhim).

In Islam, Abraham is generally known as the 'intimate friend of
God' (*khalīl Allāh*). Ibn 'Arabī finds this phrase quite symbolic.
But we must remember also that he understands the word *khalīl* in a
very special sense which is typical of his way of thinking.

The word *khalīl* appearing in the phrase *khalīl Allāh* means in
ordinary understanding an 'intimate friend'.[39] Ibn 'Arabī explains
the word by a completely different etymology; he derives it from
takhallul which means 'penetration', 'permeation'. The Perfect
Man is the one whom the Absolute penetrates and whose faculties
and bodily members are all permeated by the Absolute in such a
way that he thereby manifests all the Perfections of the Divine
Attributes and Names.

We have already discussed in an earlier context the problem of
Being running through (*sarayān*) all beings. The important point,
for our immediate purpose, is that this *sarayān* or 'pervasion',
although it is universal, differs in intensity or density from one thing
to another. The *sarayān* of Being reaches its highest degree in the
Perfect Man. And Being, that is, all the Perfections of the Absolute,
permeate Man and become manifested in him both inwardly and
outwardly. The title of honor of Abraham, *khalīl*, symbolizes this
fact. Ibn 'Arabī himself gives the following explanation on this
point:[40]

> (Abraham) is called *khalīl* for no other reason than that he 'perme-
> ates', and comprises in himself, all (the qualities) by which the Divine
> Essence is qualified[41] . . . just as a color 'permeates' a colored object
> in such a way that the accident (i.e., the color) exists in all the parts of
> the substance. The relation is different from that between a place and
> an object occupying it. Or rather we should say that (Abraham is
> called *khalīl*) because the Absolute 'permeates' the existence of the
> form of Abraham.[42]

Here Ibn 'Arabī distinguishes between two forms of 'permeation'
(*takhallul*): (1) one in which Man (symbolized by Abraham) plays

the active role, Abraham appearing in the Form of the Absolute, and (2) the other in which the Absolute plays the active role, the Absolute appearing in the form of Abraham. The distinction was explained in an earlier context from a somewhat different point of view, when we discussed the idea of the bestowal of Being. What is of particular importance in the present context is that in the second type of 'permeation' the Absolute manifests itself in an individualized form, determined by the latter in its Existence, so that in this case creaturely attributes are ascribed to God, including even attributes denoting 'defects'.

> Both these statements are right according to what God Himself affirms, for each of these aspects has its own proper field in which it is valid and which it never oversteps.
> Do you not see that God appears assuming the attributes that are peculiar to the temporal beings?[43] He affirms this about Himself. Thus He assumes even attributes of defects and attributes of a blamable nature.
> Do you not see (on the other hand)[44] that the creatures appear assuming the Attributes of the Absolute from the first Attribute to the very last?
> Thus all of them (i.e., all the Attributes of the Absolute) are necessarily and rightly to be ascribed to the creatures just as the attributes of the temporal beings are necessarily and rightly to be ascribed to the Absolute.

All the Attributes of the Absolute are to be affirmed of the creatures because the essential reality (*ḥaqīqah*) of the latter is nothing other than the Absolute appearing with its own Reality in their forms, so that the Attributes of the Absolute are the attributes of the creatures. In the same way, all the attributes of the temporal beings are rightly to be affirmed of the Absolute, because these attributes are so many states and aspects of the Absolute. If the very existence of the temporal beings is the Existence of the Absolute as manifested in them, how much more should this be the case with the attributes of the temporal beings.[45]

Regarding the structure of the phenomenon of 'permeation', Ibn 'Arabī gives the following explanation:[46]

> Know that whenever something 'permeates' (*takhallala*) another, the first is necessarily contained in the second. The permeater becomes veiled by the permeated, so that the passive one (i.e., the permeated) is the 'outward' while the active one (i.e., the permeater) is the 'inward' which is invisible. Thus it (i.e., the permeater) is food for the other (i.e., the permeated), just as water permeates wool and makes the latter bigger and more voluminous.
> And when it is God that plays the part of the 'outward', the creatures are hidden within Him, and they become all the Names of God,

namely, His hearing, His sight, etc., and all His relations and all His modes of cognition. But when it is the creatures that play the rôle of the 'outward', God becomes hidden in them, being inside of them, and God (in this case) is the hearing of the creatures, their sight, their hands and feet, and all their faculties.

Thus the ontological 'permeation' is completely reciprocal between the Absolute and the world, and the Perfect Man represents this reciprocal 'permeation' in its most perfect form. Abraham is a typical example of this phenomenon.

III   The Vicegerency of God

The Perfect Man is the 'vicegerent' (*khalīfah*) of God on the earth, or in the world of Being. Reference has been made earlier to this concept in an incidental way. The present section will be devoted to a more detailed and concentrated discussion of this problem.

The Perfect Man is entitled to be the 'vicegerent' of God because of his 'comprehensiveness'. This idea, which has been mentioned more than once in what precedes, will furnish us with a good starting-point for an analysis of the concept of vicegerency.

After having stated that Man alone in the whole world possesses the unique property of 'being comprehensive' (*jam'īyah*), Ibn 'Arabī goes on to argue:[47]

> Iblīs (Satan) was but a part of the world, having no such 'comprehensiveness'. But Adam was a 'vicegerent' because of this 'comprehensiveness'. If he had not appeared in the Form of God who appointed him as His 'vicegerent' to take care of the things (i.e., the world and everything in the world) in His stead, he would not have been His 'vicegerent'.[48] If, on the other hand, he had not contained in himself all the things of the world and all that was demanded of him by those people over whom he had been commanded to exercise sovereign power, (he would not have been His 'vicegerent'). For the people depended upon him, and he was naturally expected to take care of all the needs of the people. Otherwise, he would not have been a 'vicegerent' governing them (in the place of the King).
>
> Thus no one was entitled to be the 'vicegerent' except the Perfect Man, for God created his 'outward' form out of all the realities and forms of the world,[49] and his 'inward' form on the model of His own Form.[50] This is why God says (in a Tradition): 'I am his hearing and his sight'. It is to be remarked that God does not say: 'I am his eye and his ear'. God distinguishes here between the two forms (i.e., the outward form and the inward form).
>
> The same holds true of everything existent in the world (i.e., just as God appears in Adam in his form, so He appears in everything in its peculiar form) in accordance with the requirement of the reality of

each thing. However, nothing in the world possesses the 'comprehensiveness' which is possessed by the 'vicegerent'. In fact he has obtained (his vicegerency) only because of his 'comprehensiveness'.

In another passage Ibn 'Arabī considers again the same problem of 'vicegerency' of Man based on the 'comprehensiveness' of his constitution. This time he approaches the problem from a somewhat different angle.[51]

(The Perfect Man) is Man, temporally produced (in his body), but eternal (i.e., having no temporal origin, with regard to his spirit), something that grows up forever, the Word that distinguishes (between possibility and necessity) and gathers (them) together. The universe reached completion when he came into existence. He is to the universe what the bezel is to the seal. He is (comparable to) the place (of the seal) where there is engraved the device with which the king seals his treasuries.

This is the reason why God has called him a 'vicegerent',[52] because he acts as the guardian of His creatures just as the treasuries (of the king) are guarded by a seal. For as long as the royal seal is upon them, no one dares to open them unless the king gives permission.

Thus God has appointed him as the 'vicegerent' in the guarding of the universe. The universe will remain guarded as long as there is in the universe the Perfect Man.

Do you not see that when he departs (from the present world) and the seal of the treasuries is broken, there will not remain in the world that which God has stored there, and all that are therein will come out and will become confused one with another and everything will be transported to the Hereafter? And there (in the next world) he (i.e., the Perfect Man) will again become a seal on the treasury of the Hereafter to remain there as the seal for ever and ever.

The whole world of Being, or the universe, is the 'treasury' of God, and of God alone. And Man is a custodian and curator (*wakīl*) whom God Himself has put in charge of the guardianship of the treasury. This idea, which is the only right one concerning the position of Man in the cosmic order, is according to Ibn 'Arabī, an idea peculiar to the 'people of Muḥammad'.

Unlike Noah who had called his people exclusively to *tanzīh*, Muḥammad called his people to both *tanzīh* and *tashbīh*.[53] He called them to *tanzīh* because the whole universe is a possession of God, and of God alone. He called them to *tashbīh*, emphasizing thereby the human element in the created world, because God Himself has put the administration of His own possession in the hands of Man as His 'vicegerent'. Man is not the real owner of the 'treasury', but he has the status of its 'curator'.[54] And Man owes this high status to the fact that he is the only existent in the whole world of Being in whom all the Attributes and Names of the Absolute are manifested.

IV   The Reality of Muḥammad

The 'Reality of Muḥammad' (*ḥaqīqah Muḥammad* or *al-ḥaqīqah al-muḥammadīyah*), is one of the most important concepts in the philosophy of Ibn 'Arabī. But since it has been dealt with in detail by Affifi, as Ibn 'Arabī's doctrine of the *logos*, in his *Philosophy*,[55] I shall be content here with discussing it only as an aspect of the problem of the Perfect Man.

All prophets, in Ibn 'Arabī's view, are embodiments of the idea of the Perfect Man. But the Islamic Prophet, Muḥammad, occupies among them a very special place. What is particularly important about Muḥammad is that he had been a cosmic being before he was raised as an individual prophet at a certain moment of human history in the capacity of God's Messenger to the Arabs. Ibn 'Arabī bases this conception on a well-known Tradition in which Muḥammad describes himself as a being of a cosmic nature by saying: 'I was a prophet even while Adam was between clay and water'.[56]

Ontologically, Muḥammad as a cosmic being who existed from eternity corresponds to, or represents, the level of the permanent archetypes; that is, the level of Being 'which is neither existent nor non-existent', the intermediary stage (*barzakh*) between the absolute Absolute and the world which is the outer self-manifestation of the Absolute. This intermediary stage is divine in so far as it is identified with the Divine Consciousness, but it is, at the same time, essentially creaturely or human in that it has significance only as it is related to the created world. The intermediary stage in this latter aspect, i.e., considered in its human aspect, is the Reality of Muḥammad. And it is also the Perfect Man on the cosmic level.

Thus understood, the Reality of Muḥammad is not exactly the permanent archetypes themselves. Rather, it is the unifying principle of all archetypes, the active principle on which depends the very existence of the archetypes. Considered from the side of the Absolute, the Reality of Muḥammad is the creative activity itself of the Absolute, or God 'conceived as the self-revealing Principle of the universe'.[57] It is the Absolute in the first stage of its eternal self-manifestation, i.e., the Absolute as the universal Consciousness.

It is also called ontologically, the 'Reality of realities' (*ḥaqīqah al-ḥaqā'iq*). The 'Reality of realities' is ultimately nothing but the Absolute, but it is not the Absolute in its primordial absoluteness; it is the very first form in which the Absolute begins to manifest itself. And this Divine Consciousness is reflected most faithfully by the self-consciousness of the Perfect Man. The Perfect Man, in this sense, is the outwardly manifested Consciousness of God. Thus the

Prophet Muḥammad on the cosmic level corresponds almost exactly to the Plotinian First Intellect. Muḥammad, as the Perfect Man on the cosmic level, is the first of all self-determinations (*ta'ayyunāt*) of the Absolute. Theologically, it is the first 'creature' of God.

Basing himself on a Tradition: 'the first thing which God created was my Light', Ibn 'Arabī calls the Reality of Muḥammad also the 'Light of Muḥammad' (*al-nūr al-muḥammadiy*). This Light had been existent even before all the creatures came into existence. It is, in this sense, 'eternal (*a parte ante*)' (*qadīm*), and 'non-temporal' (*ghayr ḥādith*). And this eternal Light went on being manifested in successive prophets: Adam, Noah, Abraham, Moses, Jesus etc., until it reached its final historical manifestation, the Prophet Muḥammad.

Since the Light was that which God created before anything else and that from which he created everything else, it was the very basis of the creation of the world. And it was 'Light' because it was nothing else than the First Intellect, i.e., the Divine Consciousness, by which God manifested Himself to Himself in the state of the Absolute Unity. And the Light is in its personal aspect the Reality of Muḥammad.

Regarding Muḥammad's being the first self-determination of the Absolute and his being, therefore, the most comprehensive and the highest, al-Qāshānī writes:[58]

(Muḥammad was) the first self-determination with which the Essence at the level of Unity determined itself before any other forms of self-determination. So all the infinite self-determinations became actualized through him. As we have seen above, all the self-determinations (of the Absolute) are arranged in a hierarchy of genera, species, kinds, and individuals, all being disposed in a vertical order. So (Muḥammad) comprises in himself all these self-determinations without leaving anything. He is, in this sense, unique in the whole world of Being; nothing can compete with him, because nothing is found equal to him in the hierarchy. In fact, there is above him only the Essence at the level of its absolute Unity, which transcends all self-determinations, whether that of an attribute, name, description, definition, or qualification.

Such being the case, it will be evident that Muḥammad, as the Logos, is the most perfect being within the species of man.

He was the most perfect being of the human species. This is why the whole process of creation was commenced and finished through him. 'He was a prophet even while Adam was between water and clay' (as the cosmic Logos), but later (i.e., in historical time) he was born compounded of elements (i.e., in a bodily form) and proved to be the final seal of the prophets . . . (As an individual), Muḥammad was the most powerful proof of his Lord, because he had been given all the 'words' (*kalim*) which were the very contents of the names[59] (of all the things of the world) which (the Lord taught) Adam.[60]

As has been touched upon earlier in this section, Muḥammad as the first creature of the Absolute clearly corresponds to the First Intellect of Plotinus, which is the 'first emanation' from the absolute One. And in this aspect Muḥammad is called by Ibn 'Arabī the 'Muḥammadan Spirit' (*al-rūḥ al-muḥammadiy*).

In the world-view of Plotinus, the *Nūs*, the first emanation from the One, has two aspects: (1) it is 'passive' in relation to that from which it has emanated, and (2) 'active' in relation to that which emanates from itself. It is 'passive' toward the higher level of Being and 'active' toward the lower level of Being.

In the particular context of Ibn 'Arabī's philosophy, this Plotinian 'passivity' (*infi'al*) changes into 'servant-ness' (*'ubūdīyah*) and the 'activity' (*fi'l*) becomes 'Lordship' (*rubūbīyah*). Thus the 'Muḥammadan Spirit' stands in the position of 'passivity', i.e., 'servant-ness', in relation to the Creator, i.e., the source of its own appearance and manifestation, while in relation to the world it shows a thoroughgoing 'activity', acting as it does as the first principle of creation. Ibn 'Arabī explains this as follows in a mythopoetic form:[61]

> Muḥammad (i.e., the 'Muḥammadan Spirit') was created basically as a 'servant'. So he never dared raise his head seeking to be a master. Nay, he kept humbly prostrating and never transgressing the state of being 'passive', until, when God had produced from him all that He produced, He conferred upon him the rank of 'activity' over the world of (Divine) breaths.

Muḥammad, in this respect, shows perfectly his 'intermediary nature' (*barzakhīyah*). He is a 'servant' and is 'passive' vis-à-vis the Absolute, but he is a 'lord' and is 'active' vis-à-vis the world.

V   The Perfect Man and God

The Absolute, in its self-revealing aspect, reaches perfection in the Perfect Man. In the latter the Absolute manifests itself in the most perfect form, and there can be no self-manifestation more perfect than this. The Perfect Man, in this respect, *is* the Absolute, while being at the same time a creature. We know already what Ibn 'Arabī means when he says that Man *is* the Absolute. Man is the Absolute because of his essential 'comprehensiveness', or because, as Ibn 'Arabī says, God put into Adam, the human species, all of its

Attributes, whether active of passive. After stating that God joined both His hands 'to knead the clay of Adam' and created him in this particular way, Ibn 'Arabī goes on to say:[62]

> Then (i.e:, after having created Adam) God made him behold all that He had put into him, and grasped the whole in His two hands: in the one, He held the universe, and in the other, Adam and his offspring.

This passage is explicated by al-Qāshānī in the following terms:[63]

> This means that God let the Real Man (*al-insān al-ḥaqīqiy*) observe all the Divine secrets (i.e., invisible realities which are actualized at the ontological level of the all-comprehensive Name *Allāh*) which He had placed in him, then put together the whole of what He had created and the whole of what He had placed in Adam, grasping them with his both hands. He placed in His right hand, which is His stronger hand, the reality of Adam and his descendants, i.e., all His active Attributes and His (active) Names belonging to the higher spiritual world, and in the left hand, which is the weaker hand, the forms of the world, i.e., His passive (lit. receiving) Attributes and His (passive) Names belonging properly to the physical world.
> (This distinction between the right and the left hand as the stronger and the weaker is not an essential one, for) each of the two hands of the Merciful is in truth a right hand. (And, consequently, there is no real distinction in terms of rank between the two kinds of the Attributes) because the 'receptivity' (*qābilīyah*) with regard to the power of 'receiving' is perfectly equal to the 'positive activity' (*fā'ilīyah*) with regard to the power of 'acting', the former being in no way inferior to the latter.

Since Man in whom God has thus placed everything is His perfect image, whatever can be predicated of Man can also be predicated, at least in a certain sense, of God, And this is what is meant by the dictum: Man is the Absolute.

Is there, then, no essential difference between Man as the Microcosm, i.e., the Perfect Man and the Absolute? Of course, there is, and a very essential one. The difference lies in the 'necessity' (*wujūb*) of existence.

> You must know that since, as we have said every temporal thing appears in His Form, clearly God has so arranged that we should, in trying to know Him, resort to studying carefully the temporal things. Thus He Himself tells us (in the Qoran, XLI, 53) that He shows us His signs in the temporal things,[64] so that we might infer from our own states the state of God. And by whatever quality we may describe Him, we ourselves *are* that very quality. The only exception from this is the 'essential necessity' (*wujūb dhātiy*) which is peculiar to God alone.
> Since we come to know God, in this way, by ourselves, it is natural that we should attribute to Him whatever we attribute to ourselves.

This is confirmed by that of which God Himself has informed through
the tongues of the interpreters (i.e., the prophets). In fact He has
described Himself to us through us. Thus, whenever we observe Him
(through some attribute) we are observing (through the same attribute) our own selves. And whenever He observes us, He is observing
Himself. No one will doubt that we are many as individuals and species.
Certainly, all of us have in common one and the same 'reality' (or
'essence') which unites us, but we know definitely that there is also a
distinction by which are distinguished all the individuals one from
another. If it were not for this distinction there would not be multiplicity within the unity. Likewise, though God describes us precisely
with what He describes Himself with, there must be a distinction
(between us and God). And that distinction can consist only in our
essential need (for Him) regarding our existence, and the dependence of our existence upon Him because of our 'possibility', and in
His being absolutely free from all such need.[65]

Thus the Absolute and the creatures are the same in a certain
respect, but a fundamental distinction separates the one from the
other: the 'necessity of existence' (*wujūb al-wujūd*) which is peculiar to the Absolute alone. And due to this 'necessity', the Absolute
has certain Attributes which are not shared by anything else, like
quidam ('eternity *a parte ante*' and 'eternity *a parte post*').

It is to be remarked that, though this is philosophically the only
real difference between God and the creatures, it is an essential and
fundamental difference. And being a fundamental difference, it
determines the position of Man in a decisive way vis-à-vis God. Man
is certainly the highest of all in the world of Being. To him is
ascribed an ontological 'height' (*'uluw*). The 'height', however,
is not the 'height' of the Absolute. Unlike the latter, Man's 'height' is
only 'consequential' (*bi-al-tab'iyah*) or 'secondary'; it is not an
'essential (*dhātiy*) height'.

In the Qoran (XLVII, 35) God says to the followers of Muḥammad: 'You are the highest and so is God, too, with you'.[66] This verse,
Ibn 'Arabī says, might suggest that God and Man share the same
'height'. But such an understanding is completely wrong. For God
definitely denies such an equality in 'height' between Himself and
Man.

Although Man is the 'highest' in a particular sense and participates with God in the 'height' in the general connotation of the
word, the real content of the 'height' is different when the word is
applied to God from when it is applied to Man. A Peripatetic
philosopher would simplify the matter by saying that the same word
a'lā ('highest') is here used *secundum prius et posterius*. This is
clearly what is meant by al-Qāshānī when he says:[67]

The participation (of Man) in 'being the highest', which God affirms of him is liable to produce the wrong view that Man does participate (with God) in the same height of rank. So He says: 'Praise the Name of thy Lord, the Highest' (LXXXVII, 1) in order to deny categorically the possibility of such participation. In fact, the absolute and essential 'height' belongs to God, and to God alone. He is the highest by His Essence, in an absolute sense, not in relation to anything other than Himself. Thus all 'height' belongs properly to Him alone, and everything to which His 'height' is attributed (i.e., everything that is said to be 'high') is 'high' according to the degree in which God manifests himself under the Name 'High' (*'aliy*).

Nothing really participates with Him in the very source of the 'height'. God has no 'height' in a relative sense, while all other things become 'high' through His Name 'High'.

Ibn 'Arabī further stresses the non-essential nature of the 'height' of Man by pointing out that although Man, i.e., the Perfect Man, is the highest of all beings, his 'height' does not properly belong to himself, but rather to the 'place'[68] that has been assigned to him. What is high is not so much Man himself as his 'place'. This is why God says: 'And We raised him to a high place' (XIX, 57). It is worthy of remark that the adjective (*'aliy*) in this verse qualifies 'place' (*makān*), not Man. Likewise, Man's being the 'vicegerent' of God on the earth is simply the 'height' of place or position; it is not his essential 'height'.

The preceding pages have clarified Ibn 'Arabī's thesis that the 'height' of man is not of an essential nature. But whatever the nature of his 'height', it is true that Man is 'high' or even the 'highest' of all beings. Here Ibn 'Arabī points out a very paradoxical fact about Man. Certainly, Man is the highest of all beings as long as we consider him ideally. But once we open our eyes to the real situation of human existence, we find the strange fact that, far from being 'high' or 'highest', Man is the 'lowest' of all in the whole world of Being. Of course, in doing so we are taking a very particular point of view. But at least from this particular point of view, the hierarchy of values becomes completely reversed. For in this new system, the inanimate beings occupy the highest rank, then the plants, then the animals, and the human beings are found in the lowest position.

Usually, Man is considered the highest of all beings because of his Reason (*'aql*). But, in truth, this very Reason which is peculiar to Man weaves around him an opaque veil which develops into an 'ego'. And the 'ego' thus produced hinders Man from knowing the Absolute as it really is. Precisely because of his Reason, Man cannot but be a 'mirror which reflects the Absolute only with inversion'.

> There is no creature higher than minerals; then come the plants with their various degree and ranks. The plants are followed by those possessed of the senses (i.e., animals). Each of these (three classes of beings) knows its own Creator through natural intuition or through an immediate evidential knowledge. But what is called Adam (i.e., Man) is shackled by Reason and thinking or is in the pillory of belief.[69]

The inanimate things, or 'minerals', have no ego. So they are obedient to God's commandments absolutely and unconditionally. Their 'servant-ness' (*'ubūdīyah*) is perfect in this sense. They are exposed naked to God's activity upon them, there being no veil at all between them. In this respect, they occupy the highest place in the hierarchy of Being.

The second position is given to the plants. They grow, assimilate nourishment, and generate. To that extent they act positively on their own accord. And to that extent they are farther removed from the Absolute than the minerals.

The third position is occupied by the animals. They are possessed of senses, and they show the activity of will. The sense perception and will disclose a certain amount of ego. But the animal ego is not as strong as that of Man.

These three, the minerals, plants, and animals, having no Reason, know God by a natural 'unveiling' or immediate evidential knowledge. Man, on the contrary, possesses Reason, and the Reason develops his ego to a full extent, and he becomes veiled by his own ego.

Thus from the viewpoint of the ideal state of 'servant-ness', Man is situated on the lowest level on the scale of Being. In order to climb the scale upward, he must first of all dispel from himself Reason – which is, paradoxically, exactly the thing that makes him a Man – and bring to naught all the properties that derive from Reason. Only when he succeeds in doing so, does he ascend to the rank of animals. He must then go on to ascend to the rank of plants, and thence finally to the rank of minerals. Then only does he find himself in the highest position on the whole scale of Being. There will no longer remain in him even a shadow of Reason, and the Light of the Absolute will illumine him undimmed, unhindered, in its original splendor.

These considerations make us aware of the fact that Man as an Idea is *per se* 'perfect' and occupies the highest position, but that in his actual situation he is far from being a perfect realization of his own ideal. We can maintain that Man is the highest being in the world only when we take the viewpoint of a philosophical anthropology standing on the supposition that the ideal of Man is perfectly realized in the actual Man. The actual Man, however, is a being in full possession of Reason, a being dependent upon his Reason and brandishing it everywhere in his understanding of everything. He who brandishes his Reason is not capable of penetrating the mystery of Being.

But while making this observation, we realize that we are already far removed from the sphere in which we began our discussion of Man. We started from the basic assumption that Man can be considered on two entirely different levels: cosmic and individual. And the purpose of the present chapter has been to elucidate the concept of Man on the cosmic level, as Microcosm. And on this level, Man is certainly the highest of all beings. However, in the last section of this chapter, we have been moving down to the concept of Man on the individual level. We have learnt that on this latter level, Man is, in a certain sense, even lower than animals, plants and minerals. On this level, not all men, but only a small number of special men are worthy to be called 'perfect men'. They are 'perfect' because, having already died to their own ego through the mystical experience of self-annihilation and subsistence, they are no longer veiled by Reason. The next chapter will be devoted to a more detailed consideration of the idea of the Perfect Man on the individual level.

Notes

1. *Fuṣ.*, p. 8/48.

2. *Fuṣ.*, p. 9/48.

3. *Fuṣ.*, p. 11/49; p. 132/115.

4. p. 11.

5. *Fuṣ.*, p. 9/48–49.

6. p. 10.

7. p. 11.

8. I read with Qayṣarī: *tulqī ilay-hi bi-taqallub min wajh.*

9. Al-Qāshānī says that this is the case when the Absolute manifests itself in the very form of a Perfect Man – p. 42.

10. *Fuṣ.*, pp. 41–42/66–67.

11. *Fuṣ.*, p. 232/184.

12. *Fuṣ.*, pp. 251–253/198–199.

13. The 'great river' Nile symbolizes an ocean of Knowledge into which Moses' body was thrown in order that he might acquire all the possible perfections by which Man is distinguished from all other beings – cf. Affifi, *Fuṣ.*, Com., p. 293.

14. *sakīnah* from the Hebrew *shekīna* meaning the Divine Presence. Here it means the 'Divine aspect' (*lāhūt*) of man to be correlated with the above-mentioned *nāsūt*.

15. 'its form (*ṣūrah*)', that is, the form of the world. The meaning of this expression will be clarified by al-Qāshānī's explanatory remark which will immediately follow the present passage.

16. This is tantamount to saying that God governs all the things in the world by means of their permanent archetypes.

17. p. 252.

18. Here, be it noticed, Ibn 'Arabī understands Man not on the cosmic, but on the individual level.

19. As we shall see presently, Man occupies a higher position than angels in the world-view of Ibn 'Arabī.

20. The 'Divine Form' (*al-ṣūrah al-ilāhīyah*) itself means nothing else than the whole of the Divine Names.

21. *Fuṣ.*, p. 14/50.

22. *Fuṣ.*, p. 12/49.

23. *Fuṣ.*, 13/49–50.

24. On this concept see later, III.

25. *Fuṣ.*, p. 180/143. The explanatory words that follow the verses are by al-Qāshānī.

26. *Fuṣ.*, p. 21/54.

27. *Fuṣ.*, pp. 25–26/56.

28. Reference to the Qoran, II, 30–33.

29. *'ibādah dhātīyah* 'essential service' means, as we have seen above, the perfect and complete adoration of God which consists in that an existent actualizes in itself all the Names.

30. 'Art Thou going to place on the earth one who will do harm therein and shed blood, when *we* are praising and sanctifying Thee?' (II, 30).

31. *Fuṣ.*, pp. 14–15/50–51.

32. Although, to be sure, he is not superior to *all* the angels, as we shall see.

33. *Fuṣ.*, pp. 22–23/55.

34. *Fuṣ.*, p. 184/144–145.

35. Reference to the Qoran, XV, 28: *innī khāliqun basharan*, etc. *Bashar* means 'man' considered from the point of view of his being 'mortal'. But Ibn 'Arabī in this passage understands the word in terms of the verb *bāshara* (inf. *mubāsharah*) meaning 'to touch something directly with one's own hands'.

36. That is to say, in a non-material, non-anthropomorphic, sense.

37. Qoran, XXXVIII, 76.

38. They stand above the sphere of elements, though they are of the domain of Nature.

39. From *khullah*, meaning 'sincere friendship'.

40. *Fuṣ.*, pp. 71–72/80–81.

41. According to al-Qāshānī, this means the appearance of Abraham in the Form of the Absolute in such a way that the Absolute is his hearing, his sight, and all his other faculties – p. 72.

42. This means that the Absolute, by being 'determined' by the 'determination' of Abraham, becomes qualified by the attributes of Abraham and his form, so that all the attributes that are ascribed to Abraham are ascribed to the Absolute, too. The result of this process is that God does whatever He does through Abraham, hears by his hearing, and sees with his eyes – al-Qāshānī, p. 71.

43. Here Ibn 'Arabī takes up the second type of 'permeation' first.

44. This refers to the first type of 'permeation'.

45. Qāshānī, p. 72.

46. *Fuṣ.*, p. 73/81.

47. *Fuṣ.*, pp. 23–24/55.

48. 'because a vicegerent should know the will of the man who has appointed him as his representative, so that he might carry out his command. Thus if the vicegerent of God does not know Him with all His Attributes, he would not be able to carry out His Command' – al-Qāshānī, p. 23.

49. so that everything that exists in the world is reflected in Man by a corresponding element.

50. so that his inner form is modeled on the Name and Attributes of God. Thus he is 'hearing', 'seeing', 'knowing' etc., as God Himself is, i.e., he is qualified by all the Divine Attributes.

51. *Fuṣ.*, pp. 13–14/50.

52. 'The engraved seal is the Greatest of all the Divine Names, namely, the Divine Essence with all the Names. This seal is engraved on the 'heart' of the Perfect Man, which is symbolized here by the bezel of the royal seal. Thus the Perfect Man guards the treasury of the universe with all that is contained therein, and keeps them in the established order' – al-Qāshānī, p. 13.

53. Cf. Chapter IV

54. Cf. *Fuṣ.*, p. 53/71.

55. Chapter V, pp. 66–101. For a discussion of the historical relation between this Islamic *logos*-doctrine and the *logos*-Christology see Arthur Jeffery: *Ibn al-'Arabī's Shajarat al-Kawn* (Studia Islamica, X, Paris, 1959, pp. 45–62).

56. *Kantu nabiy wa-Ādam bayna al-mā' wa-al-ṭīn.*

57. Affifi, *Philosophy*, p. 69.

58. p. 266.

59. Reference to the Qoran, II, 31.

60. *Fuṣ.*, p. 267/214.

61. *Fuṣ.*, p. 275/220.

62. *Fuṣ.*, p. 26/56.

63. p. 26.

64. 'We shall show them Our signs on the horizons and in themselves'.

65. *Fuṣ.*, p. 19/53–54.

66. *Wa-antum al-a'lawna wa-Allāhu ma'a-kum*. Ibn 'Arabī's interpretation of this verse ('you are the highest and God, too, is the highest with you') is quite an original one. Contextually, the verse simply means: 'you, believers, will surely win (in your struggle with the disbelievers) for God is with you (i.e., on your side)'.

67. p. 62.

68. either in the sense of *makān*, i.e., physical place, or *makānah*, i.e., non-material place, position or rank.

69. *Fuṣ.*, pp. 82–83/85. The original is a part of a poem.

XV   The Perfect Man as an Individual

At the outset of the preceding chapter I pointed out that Man, in the thought of Ibn 'Arabī, is conceived on two different levels, cosmic and individual. The present chapter will be concerned with the second of these two levels.

Man on the first level, or – logically – Man as a species, is in the intermediary stage between the Absolute and the world, and, as an intermediary, occupies the highest position in the hierarchy of the created beings. As soon as we begin to consider Man on the individual level, however, we cannot help noticing the existence of many degrees (*marātib*). Otherwise expressed, on the cosmic level Man himself is the Perfect Man, but on the individual level not all men are 'perfect'; on the contrary, only a few deserve the title of the Perfect Man.

How is it possible that a such a fundamental difference should occur between the two levels? Any man, as long as he is a 'man', is expected to have the 'comprehensiveness' actualized in him, because the ontological 'comprehensiveness' belongs to the very nature of the human species. There can be no possible exception in this respect. Ontologically, there can be no difference in this respect between one individual and another. All this is certainly true. But individual differences arise in accordance with the degrees of lucidity in the mind of those who become conscious of this very fact. All men are naturally endowed with the same ontological 'comprehensiveness' but not all men are equally conscious of the 'comprehensiveness' in themselves. They are variously conscious of it, ranging from the highest degree of lucidity which comes very close to that of the Divine Consciousness of the Names and Attributes, down to the lowest which is practically the same as complete opaqueness. And only at the highest degree of lucidity can the human mind play the role of a 'polished mirror'. Only at the highest degree of lucidity can Man be the Perfect Man. This is the gist of the whole problem.

In a passage of the *Fuṣūṣ*, Ibn 'Arabī writes: 'God has brought to light their various degrees in him (i.e., Adam)'.[1] Here the pronoun 'their' refers to the sons of Adam. Thus the meaning of this short sentence may be paraphrased as: 'God has made clear the existence of various degrees among men within Adam, i.e., the same one species of Man'.

The cause which brings into being such degrees among individual men is explained by Ibn 'Arabī through the metaphor of colored glass, a metaphor which we have met in an earlier context. Just as one and the same light is variously colored as it passes through pieces of glass of various colors, the same Form of the Absolute is differently manifested in different men with different capacities.[2]

A man who has 'actualized in himself the Absolute' (*al-mutaḥaqqiq bi-al-ḥaqq*) is completely permeated by the Absolute, so much so that each of his bodily members is a self-manifestation of the Absolute. And yet, when such men – the people of God (*ahl Allāh*) – obtain knowledge by 'immediate tasting', one and the same knowledge becomes variously inflected according to the capacities of individual organs.

> Know that all mystical knowledges which, originating from the ontological level of the Name *Allāh*, are actualized in the people of God, differ from each other according to the differences in the cognitive faculties through which they are actualized, although all these knowledges are derived ultimately from one source. This last point is proved by the fact that God Himself declares (in a well-known Tradition): 'I am his hearing with which he hears, his sight with which he sees, his hand with which he seizes, his foot with which he walks', God declares in this way that His He-ness (*huwīyah*) is the very bodily members, which, in their turn, are the man himself. The He-ness is one, and the bodily members (of the man in whom the He-ness is actualized) are diverse. And each of his bodily members has a special knowledge by 'immediate tasting' which is peculiar to it and which is derived from the unique source (from which all the other bodily members obtain their peculiar knowledges). Thus (the same knowledge coming from one source) becomes differentiated by the different bodily members.[3]

In the passage just quoted, Ibn 'Arabī is speaking of the inflection of one and the same intuitive cognition in one and the same man through his different bodily members. He is not talking about differences in intuition among different 'men of God'. He describes here simply how one knowledge coming from one source becomes differently modulated in one man according to which of his faculties is used. But if in one and the same man the situation is like that, it is naturally to be expected that even greater differences should arise in different individuals. In his commentary on this passage, al-Qāshānī understands it in this sense and says:[4]

> Knowledges by 'immediate tasting' are differentiated by the differ-
> ence of natural capacities (lit. 'preparedness'), because the 'people of
> God' do not all stand on one level. And this causes a difference in
> their 'tasting' experiences and (the resulting) knowledges . . . just as
> one and the same person obtains different knowledges through dif-
> ferent faculties. Differences arise (in both cases) in spite of the fact
> that all these knowledges go back to one single source, which is the
> He-ness of the Absolute.

Ibn 'Arabī himself explains this phenomenon by comparing it to
water which may have different tastes despite the oneness of its
reality.

> This may be understood by the example of water. Water is every-
> where one single reality, but it has different tastes according to
> places. Here it is sweet, there it is salty and bitter. And yet water is
> water in all the states; its reality does not become different however
> different its tastes may be.[5]

The above explanation gives the ontological cause from which all
differences and degrees occur among men. In addition to this, Ibn
'Arabī gives another, theological cause for the same phenomenon:
the 'jealousy' (*ghayrah*) of God.

The idea of God being 'jealous' (*ghayūr*) goes back historically to
a very old Semitic conception of God. And it plays also a considerably important part in Sufism.

Now 'jealousy' in reference to God is capable of being understood in various meanings. God is 'jealous', for example, because
He does not like the secret between Him and His servants be
disclosed to others. Or God is 'jealous' in the sense that He forbids
that anything other than Himself be adored and worshipped. Ibn
'Arabī understands the idea of Divine 'jealousy' in terms of the
concept of 'self-manifestation' (*tajallī*).

The Absolute, he says, manifests itself endlessly; it freely discloses and reveals its inner mysteries. And yet the Absolute is,
paradoxically enough, 'jealous' of its mysteries, in the sense that it
conceals them from the eyes of ordinary men. From this particular
point of view, Ibn 'Arabī goes even to the extent of calling the
Divine self-manifestations *fawāḥish* (sg. *faḥishah* meaning literally
'shameful thing' 'something scandalous or disgraceful'). Here he is
looking at the whole matter from, so to speak, the subjective viewpoint of the Absolute itself. God's feeling, Ibn 'Arabī surmises,
would be that He should not have disclosed his secrets, that He
should rather have kept them forever hidden in Himself. On the
human level, it is always an act of shamelessness for man to disclose
to the eyes of the public what he should keep concealed.

Furthermore, Ibn 'Arabī exercises here again his favorite method of thinking by phonetic associations, and connects the word *ghayrah* (jealously) with *ghayr* ('other').

> God admits that He has the Attribute of 'jealousy' (*ghayrah*). It is out of 'jealousy' that He 'has forbidden the shameful things (*fawāḥish*)' (V, 33).
> But 'shameful' is only that which has been made openly manifest (while in truth it should have been kept concealed.) As to what is kept within, it is 'shameful' only to those who can see it.[6]

The last sentence would seem to need a few explanatory words. Here Ibn 'Arabī divides the 'shameful things', i.e., the self-manifestations of God, into two kinds. The first consists of those things that are openly manifest to our senses, in the world of concrete reality. The second refers to the 'inner' (*bāṭin*) self-manifestations of the Divine Essence in the form of the permanent archetypes. These are not manifest to the eyes of ordinary people, and in this respect they are not 'shameful'. And yet they are nonetheless manifested forms, and as such are clearly visible to those who have the proper eyes with which to perceive them. They are, to that extent, equally 'shameful'.[7]

> Thus God 'has forbidden the shameful things', that is, God has forbidden the reality to be known openly; namely, the fact that He is nothing other than the (created) things. So He has concealed the reality with the veil of 'jealousy' – 'other-ness' (*ghayrah*).[8] And (the 'other') is yourself (i.e., your ego which is conscious of being something independent and different from the Absolute). (This connection between 'jealousy' and 'other-ness' is natural) because *ghayrah* comes from *ghayr*.
> As a result of this, the 'other' judges that this (particular act of) hearing, for instance, is the hearing of such-and-such an individual person, while the 'knower' of the truth judges that the hearing (i.e., all particular acts of hearing) is the very (act of) the Absolute. And the same is true of all human faculties and bodily organs.
> Thus not everyone knows the Absolute (in the same degree). There are superior men and inferior men, and a number of ranks are clearly discernible among them.[9]

The highest rank, according to Ibn 'Arabī, belongs to a man who throws himself wholly into the act of 'remembrance' (*dhikr*) – that is, not only with his tongue and heart alone – and becomes internally unified with the Absolute.

It must be kept in mind that 'remembrance' (*dhikr*), for Ibn 'Arabī, does not simply mean the act of remembering God with one's tongue and heart; the word is rather synonymous with mystical 'self-annihilation' in God. The *dhikr* in this meaning is a spiritual state in which a mystic concentrates all his bodily and spiritual powers on God in such a way that his whole existence is united with

God completely, without any residue. When a mystic attains to this state, the distinction between the subject (who exercises the concentration of the mind) and the object (upon which his mind is concentrated) naturally disappears, and he experiences the immediate tasting' of the essential unity with the Absolute. The ordinary kind of *dhikr* which consists in merely 'remembering' the Absolute with tongue or mind without a total existential involvement of the person represents a lower degree of *dhikr*-experience.

When a *dhikr* of the highest rank actually occurs in a mystic, the natural perfection of Man is completely realized, and he occupies a position in the world higher than that of other creatures, including even angels. Of course all creatures manifest the glory of God each according to its degree of *dhikr*, but it is only in Man that this experience can be heightened to that of the essential unity with God.

> The real value of the human existence which is ours is known only to those who 'remember' God in the proper way of 'remembering'. For God is the intimate Companion (*jalīs*) of those who 'remember' Him, and those who 'remember' Him do witness the Companion. As long as a man who 'remembers' does not witness God who is his Companion, he is not 'remembering' (in the proper way).
>
> The 'remembrance' of God (when it is real) runs through all the parts of a man, unlike the case in which a man 'remembers' only with his tongue. For in the latter case, God happens to be only momentarily the Companion of the tongue exclusively, so that the tongue alone sees God while the man himself does not see Him by means of the sight by which he is properly supposed to see.
>
> You must understand (in the light of this explanation) the following mystery concerning the 'remembrance' of those who are not serious enough. Even in a man who is not serious enough, the (particular bodily organ) which happens to be 'remembering' Him is doubtless in the presence of God, and the object of 'remembrance' (i.e., God) is its Companion and it does witness Him. But the man himself, as long as he lacks seriousness, is not exercising 'remembrance' (as he should), and consequently God is not his Companion (in the real sense).
>
> All this comes from the fact that man is 'many' (i.e., composed of many parts); he is not one single (non-composite) reality. The Absolute, on the contrary, is One in its essential reality although it is Many in its Divine Names. But man is 'many' with his parts, so that, even if one of his parts is engaged in 'remembrance', it does not necessarily follow that other parts, too, are 'remembering'. The Absolute happens to be the Companion of that particular part of his which is actually engaged in 'remembrance', but his other parts are being negligent of 'remembrance'.[10]

Such being the case, it is naturally to be expected that there should arise many degrees among men regarding the capacity for knowing God and the mystery of Being. On the basis of this fact Ibn 'Arabī classifies men in several different ways, each classification having its peculiar standard. I have already introduced some of them. Here I shall give three typical classifications.

The first classification divides men into two categories: (1) those whose minds have an otherworldly structure and (2) those whose minds are of a worldly structure. The first category is represented by a man who, pure of mind and heart, free from all bodily desires, can see through things and grasp immediately the realities underlying them. A man like this knows God by 'unveiling' and 'immediate tasting', not by Reason. Of course, he, too, exercises his Reason within its proper domain, but never pushes it beyond its natural limits. Rather, he readily goes beyond the realm of Reason, and follows the judgments given by mystical intuition. Such a man is a 'knower' (*'ārif*) and a 'servant of the Lord' (*'abd rabb*).

The second category, on the contrary, is represented by a man whose mind is deeply involved in bodily attachments, who is completely under the sway of desires, and who, consequently, cannot see the reality of things. In trying to know God, such a man depends exclusively upon Reason. He cannot step over the boundaries of logical thinking. Even such a man may taste, on rare occasions, something of the experience of 'unveiling'. In such cases, his Reason recognizes the fact that he is experiencing something unusual. But this he knows only by Reason. So as soon as the experience ends, he falls into confusion, and ends up by submitting himself to the judgment of Reason. Such a man is not a 'servant of the Lord'; he is rather a 'servant of reasoning' (*'abd naẓar*).

It must be noticed that Ibn 'Arabī does not simply disparage and deprecate Reason. It has its own field in which to work properly. But it has its limitations. A real 'knower' is one who assigns to Reason a proper place and restrains it from overstepping its domain. The prophets and apostles are not people devoid of Reason. On the contrary, they are pre-eminently men of Reason. But they have a wider field at their command which lies beyond the reach of Reason.

> In fact, no one is more reasonable than the apostles. But (in addition to Reason) they are (endowed with another capacity by which) they bring informations directly from God.
> Thus the apostles admit the authority of Reason (within its proper domain), but add to it something which Reason cannot grasp by its own power, and which Reason rejects it at first; it is only in the Divine self-manifestation (i.e., during the time in which the mind happens to be actually experiencing it by 'unveiling') that it admits that it is true. However, as soon as the experience of the Divine self-manifestation leaves the mind, the latter falls into confusion concerning what it has

just seen. If the man in such a case happens to be a 'servant of the Lord', he immediately subjugates his Reason to Him, but if the man happens to be a 'servant of reasoning', he subjugates the truth to the judgment of Reason.

This state or affairs, however, occurs only as long as the man remains in the worldly dimension of existence, being veiled from the other worldly dimensions (which is realized) in the very midst of the present world.

Even the 'knowers' of the truth look in this world as if they were in a form peculiar to the present world because of the earthly properties appearing in them. In their 'interior', however, they have already been transported by God to the state of being which is peculiar to the Hereafter. There can be no doubt about it. So they are not recognizable outwardly except to those whose spiritual eyes have been opened by God to see through things. In reality, every true 'knower' of God, (who knows God) through the experience of (His direct) self-manifestation in himself, is actually living in a mode of being peculiar to the Hereafter. Such a man has, already in the present world, been resurrected from the dead and brought to life from his tomb. So he sees what others cannot see and witnesses what others cannot witness. This is a result of a special favor which God grants to some of His servants.[11]

The second classification which Ibn 'Arabī proposes consists in dividing men into three type : (1) 'knower' (*'ārif*), (2) 'non-knower' (*ghayr 'ārif*) and (3) 'ignorant' (*jāhil*).

He defines[12] the first type as 'a man who sees the Absolute from the Absolute, in the Absolute, and by the Absolute itself'. The second, the 'non-knower', is 'a man who sees the Absolute from the Absolute, in the Absolute, and by his own self'. The 'ignorant' is 'a man who sees the Absolute neither from the Absolute nor in the Absolute, and who expects to see the Absolute (in the Hereafter) by his own self'.

The 'knower' is a man who completely identifies himself with God in very possible respect and sees God with God's own eyes from the very viewpoint of God. Since he sees God with God's eyes, all the self-manifestations of God are within his sight. He actually witnesses the whole world of Being as it pulsates with Divine Life.

As to the 'non-knower', though he sees the Absolute in the Absolute and from the viewpoint of the Absolute, the eye with which he sees is his own. So the reality cannot but be deformed by his sight.

The 'ignorant' is by no means in a position to see the Absolute as it really is. His mind is naturally restricted in an extreme degree. Each 'ignorant' adores and worships God only in a form peculiar to a particular religion which he happens to hold, and denies all other forms of worshipping God.

Generally speaking each man (i.e., of the class of the 'ignorant') necessarily sticks to a particular religion ('*aqīdah*, i.e., religion as a system of dogmas) concerning his Lord. He always goes back to his Lord through his particular religious belief and seeks God therein. Such a man positively recognizes God only when He manifests Himself to him in the form recognized by his traditional religion. But when He manifests Himself in other religions, he flatly refuses to accept Him and runs away from Him. In so doing, he simply behaves in an improper way towards God, while imagining that he is practising good manners toward Him. Thus a man who sticks to the belief of his particular religion believes in a god according to what he has subjectively posited in his mind. God in all particular religions (*i'tiqādāt*) is dependent upon the subjective act of positing (*ja'l*) on the part of the believers. Thus a man of this kind sees (in the form of God) only his own self and what he has posited in his mind.[13]

The last paragraph of the passage just quoted discloses in a daring and outspoken way Ibn 'Arabī's fundamental position regarding the eternal Religion and various historical religions. As we have observed in an earlier context,[14] it is his unshakeable conviction that all religions are ultimately one because every religion worships the Absolute in a very particular and limited way. Whatever one worships as God, one is worshipping through that particular form the Absolute itself, nothing else, because there is nothing in the whole world but particular self-manifestations of the Absolute.

In this connection, Ibn 'Arabī draws our attention to a famous Tradition that depicts one of the occurrences of the day or Resurrection. It reads: 'On the day of Resurrection, God will appear to the creatures in a strange form and say, "I am your Lord, the Highest". The people will say, "No, we take refuge with God from thee!" Then He will make Himself manifest in a form familiar to them in their religions. Thereupon the people will cry out, "Glory be to Thee, o God"'. Ibn 'Arabī observes that this is not only a matter of the day of Resurrection, for exactly the same thing is actually happening in the present world. 'Behold how the degrees of men concerning their knowledge of God correspond exactly to their degrees concerning the seeing of God on the day of Resurrection'. And he closes the passage by giving us the following warning and advice:

Beware of being bound up by a particular religion and rejecting all others as unbelief! If you do that, you will fail to obtain a great benefit. Nay, you will fail to obtain the true knowledge of the reality. Try to make yourself a (kind of) Prime Matter for all forms of religious belief. God is wider and greater than to be confined to one particular religion to the exclusion of others. For He says: 'To whichever direction you turn, there surely is the Face of God' (II, 115). God does not specify (in this verse) a particular place in which the Face of God is to be found. He only said: '*There* is the Face of God.' The 'face' of a thing means its real essence. So God has admonished by this verse the hearts of the 'knowers' so that they might not be distracted by non-essential matters in the present world from being constantly conscious of this kind of thing. For no human being ever knows at which moment he will die. If a man happens to die at a moment when he is forgetful of this, his position will certainly be not equal to another who dies in the state of clear awareness.[15]

The third classification of men which Ibn 'Arabī proposes is also a tripartite division. According to this classification, the lowest degree is represented by a man who relies upon Reason and who, therefore, is content with understanding both God and the world by exercising his thinking power. The middle position is occupied by men of 'imagination' (*khayāl*), i.e., those who understand the Absolute according to the authentic imagery based on visions of prophets. And the highest degree is of those who know the reality of the things through the experience of 'unveiling' and 'immediate tasting'.

Let us begin with the lowest class, that is, men of Reason. These people blindly believe in Reason, do not recognize anything as truth unless it is acceptable to Reason, and refuse to admit anything which happens to be in conflict with Reason. They do not know that Reason, in matters concerning the Absolute, is utterly powerless, and that it can never go deep into the reality of Being. In various passages of the *Fuṣūṣ*, Ibn 'Arabī emphasizes the narrow limitations and the essential powerlessness of Reason in contrast to the 'unveiling' (*kashf*) which is for him the highest form of human cognition. He sees in the Theologians (*mutakallimūn*) a typical example of the men of Reason.

As an illustration, he adduces a Qoranic verse: 'thou (Muḥammad) wert not the one who threw when thou threwest, but God it was who really threw'[16] (VIII, 17). This verse, according to Ibn 'Arabī, is a most concise symbolic description of the essential relation between the Absolute and the world. The verse begins by negating that Muḥammad 'threw'. Then it affirms that he did throw – 'when thou threwest' – and finally Muḥammad's having thrown is again negated, and the verse ends by establishing that the real thrower was God Himself. All this is reducible to the proposition: 'the real thrower is God, but it is God in the phenomenal form of Muḥammad'. The verse, thus understood, expresses nothing other than the truth about the self-manifestation of the Absolute.

However, only a real 'knower' is capable of interpreting the verse in this sense. As for the Theologians, its true meaning is completely out of their reach. In confusion they interpret it arbitrarily according to the dictates of their Reason. As a result, their conclusion clashes with that of 'immediate tasting'. And in most cases they go to the extreme of declaring impossible and absurd what mystical intuition recognizes as true.

This and similar verses can be rightly understood only by those who are possessed of an infinitely flexible mind. On the basis of this single verse one can say, 'it was Muḥammad who threw', just as one can say, 'it was not Muḥammad who threw'. Likewise, one can say, 'it was God who threw', just as one can say, 'it was Muḥammad who threw, not God'. The verse, in this way, is liable to produce various statements that seemingly contradict each other. For, after all, the question is one of different relations and viewpoints. One and the same event can be looked at variously according to various possible viewpoints. And yet all this variation takes place within the infinitely wide Reality which comprises everything and every possible viewpoint. All are ultimately the activity of the Absolute. But Reason which by nature is one-sided, rigid, and inflexible, cannot accept such a view.

As another good example aptly illustrating the natural and essential deficiency of Reason, Ibn 'Arabī considers the problem of the relation between 'cause' and 'caused'. The Theologians and Philosophers, who try to understand everything in the light of what Reason tells them, often discuss the concept of 'cause' (*'illah*). The reality of 'cause', however, can never be revealed to their minds as long as they remain so utterly dependent upon logical thinking.

> As an illustration disclosing the natural weakness of Reason in its reasoning activity we may mention the judgment given by Reason concerning 'cause': that a 'cause' cannot be the 'caused' of that of which it is the 'cause'. This is evidently what Reason judges. But in the light of knowledge obtained by mystical illumination, we must assert precisely this proposition (which is rejected by Reason); namely, that a 'cause' does become the 'caused' of that of which it is the 'cause'.[17]
>
> The judgment given by Reason can be made (more) correct through theoretical elaboration within the boundaries of logical thinking. But, even so, the ultimate limit to which Reason can go, when it is actually faced with a state of affairs which contradicts the evidence furnished by logical proof, is to think that – admitting the essential unity of Reality through all the multifarious forms of things in the world – (this unique Reality), in so far as it actually and positively acts as a 'cause' in the form of some concrete thing (A, for example) and causes some other concrete thing (B), it can never be the 'caused' of that very thing (B) which it (A) has caused as long as it *is* the 'cause'. The truth of the matter, Reason will think, is rather that, as the Reality changes its form (from A to C, for example, and enters into a different relationship with B), its capacity may also change in such a

way that it (now in the form of *C*) could very well be the 'caused' of what (*B*) it has caused (in the capacity of *A*), so that, as a result, the 'caused' may become the 'cause' of its own 'cause'. This, I say, is the furthest limit to which Reason can go even when it perceives the reality (of Being, by perceiving one single Essence underlying all the things and events that stand in 'cause' – 'caused' relations), and steps beyond the proper domain of logical reasoning.[18]

The latter half of this passage may be explicated as follows. Properly speaking, Reason has a very narrowly limited domain of its own. As long as it remains within the strict limits of this domain, Reason cannot even see that everything is but a different self-manifestation of one single Reality, the Absolute. But if Reason does stretch itself forcibly to the furthest possible limit and goes beyond the domain of its natural capacity, it will be able to see that the Many in the possible world are ultimately so many different forms of one and the same Reality. Of course, such a cognition itself goes against the judgment of Reason in its normal activity. But at least this much may be conceded by it if it succeeds in extending its capacity in the way just described.

Reason, once it has admitted that the Many, i.e., all things and events in the world of concrete reality, are ultimately One and are but so many phenomenal forms assumed by one single Reality, must necessarily admit also that the distinction usually made between 'cause' and 'caused' is merely a relative matter, because both are two different forms assumed by one and the same thing. And in this particular sense, Reason will have to admit that a 'cause' can be a 'caused'.

However, even at this stage, Reason is limited by its own logic. It will still assert that so long as a certain concrete thing (*A*) actually *is* the 'cause' of another concrete thing (*B*), *A* remains a 'cause', and will never be a 'caused' of *B*. *A*, in the capacity of *B*'s 'cause', can never be a 'caused' of *B*. *A* can rightly be a 'caused' of *B* only when it is considered from a different angle in a different capacity, i.e., no longer exactly as *A* but rather as something different, *C*.

Thus it is the final judgment of Reason, even at its unusually extended limit, that a 'cause', unless it be considered in terms of a different relationship, cannot be caused by its own 'caused'. This is the self-evident and primary truth of reason which it can never abandon as long as Reason remains Reason.

However, if we look at the matter in the light of the intuition gained by the experience of 'immediate tasting', we find immediately that a 'cause' can possibly be a 'caused', just as a 'caused' can possibly be a 'cause'.

It is worthy of notice that the thought pattern that underlies this conception is very characteristic of Ibn 'Arabī; we have already met with it in the preceding in various forms. The idea, for example, that the creatures are 'food' of God, just as God is 'food' of the creatures, or the idea of the mutual *taskhīr* between God and the creatures, namely, that the creatures make God 'subservient' to themselves, just as God makes the creatures 'subservient' to Him – these and similar 'daring' ideas are structurally of the same category as that of the mutual causal relationship between God and the creatures.

How, then, can a 'caused' act positively upon its own 'cause' in such a way that it makes the latter its own 'caused'? The answer runs as follows. 'The 'cause-ness' (*'illīyah*) of a 'cause' (*'illah*) is inconceivable without the 'caused-ness' (*ma'lūlīyah*) of the 'caused' (*ma'lūl*), nor can the first actually exist without the latter. The 'cause-ness' completely depends upon the 'caused-ness' of the 'caused'. 'Cause', in this sense, contains in itself 'caused-ness', just as 'caused' contains 'cause-ness'. Moreover, all things, in Ibn 'Arabī's view, are but different phenomenal forms of one single Existence. So everything is in one aspect 'cause', and in another 'caused'.

Representing the people of 'immediate tasting', al-Qāshānī formulates the right answer in the following terms:[19]

The one single Reality appearing in two different forms (i.e., 'cause' and 'caused') is apt to receive the two qualifications according to (our subjective) points of view. That is to say, it has, when it is in the state of being a 'cause', the aptitude to be a 'caused', and when it is in the state of being a 'caused', it has the aptitude to be a 'cause'. For the one Reality comprehends in itself both 'cause-ness' and 'caused-ness' with all the properties peculiar to both. Thus one and the same thing is a 'cause' in its 'cause-ness', and a 'caused' in its 'caused-ness'. It has in itself all these and similar aspects (which it manifests) according to particular circumstances.

Exactly the same holds true of the phenomenon of the self-manifestation. For (such distinctions as) the 'self-manifester', the locus of self-manifestation, the act of self-manifestation, the being of the self-manifester a self-manifester and the being of the locus a locus, etc. (– all these are simply [reflections of our] subjective viewpoints.) In reality they are nothing other than the Absolute which is essentially One and which appears in these various capacities according to our subjective perspectives. These are all notions conceived by our discriminating Reason, the distinctions existing only in our Reason. They are all matters of relative forms, supposed relations secondarily derived from the one single Reality. This Reality is God, the One and the Unique. There is nothing in Being except God!

If we have gone into a considerably long digression on the problem of the 'cause' – 'caused' relationship, it is partly because of its intrinsic value as a theory of causality typical of Ibn 'Arabī. The main purpose, however, has been to give an illustration showing the natural incapability of Reason to reach any deep truth about the Absolute and the world of Being.

'He who knows himself (lit. 'his soul') knows his Lord' – this famous Tradition is one of Ibn 'Arabī's favorite adages. Here again he refers to it and declares that there has not been even a single person, among the Philosophers and Theologians, who has grasped his own 'self' (soul) in its real depth.

> Of all the men of knowledge no one has obtained a real insight into the 'soul' and its reality except the divinely inspired Apostles and great Sufis. As to the men of reasoning and logical thinking, whether the ancient Philosophers or the Theologians in Islam, not even one of them has hit upon the truth in their discussions on 'soul' and its quiddity. (This is but natural because) logical thinking can never arrive at the truth in this matter. Therefore, he who seeks the true knowledge of 'soul' by means of thinking is like a person who, looking at a man with a tumor, thinks him to be fat, or like a person who blows upon something which is not fuel.
>
> People of this kind are precisely 'those whose effort goes astray in the present world, being convinced that they are doing good work' (XVIII, 14). For he who seeks anything by a wrong method is sure to fail in achieving his aim.[20]

Between the real 'knowers' and the men of Reason are situated the people of Imagination (*khayāl*). These are men who try with sincerity to approach the Absolute by the aid of the images given by their Prophet and Apostle. Concerning the above-quoted Qoranic verse about the 'one who threw', for example, the men of this kind believe firmly that the true 'thrower' is God Himself, although the deep meaning of the verse escapes their understanding. They readily accept as true whatever their Prophet teaches them, and do not dare to be critical of anything which they think contradicts Reason. Ibn 'Arabī calls these men 'people of Belief (or Faith)' (*ahl al-īmān*).

> The 'people of Belief' are those who accept unquestioningly whatever the Prophets and Apostles convey from the Absolute. They should not be confused with those who accept unquestioningly the teaching of the (Philosophers and Theologians) who think by Reason and who are not content unless they interpret any message (i.e., Qoranic verse or prophetic Tradition) that is transmitted to them in the light of logical evidences.
>
> To these people (of Belief) refers the Qoranic expression: 'or he who lends his ear' (L, 37) to the Divine messages as they are conveyed through the tongues of the Prophets. And such a man, i.e., a man who lends his ear in this way, 'is a witness' (L, 37). God here refers to the ontological dimension of Imagination and the proper use of the faculty of Imagination. And this corresponds to the saying of the Prophet (Muḥammad) on the 'perfection of Belief'

(*iḥsān*): '[21] . . . that you worship God as if you saw Him'. God is always in the direction toward which man prays. This is why such a man is a witness.[22]

'Being a witness (*shahīd*)' in this passage means, in Ibn 'Arabī's interpretation, the spiritual state in which a man 'witnesses', i.e., is present by his heart to the ontological plane of Imagination. It is a state at which the heart of a 'knower' perceives in sensible imagery some of the things that properly belong to the world of the Unseen. The heart of a 'knower', when he reaches this stage, finds itself in the world of Imagination and begins to witness in images various states of affairs of the invisible world.

It is worthy of notice that toward the end of the passage just quoted, Ibn 'Arabī, referring to the famous Tradition about *iḥsān*, draws attention to the expression: '. . . that you worship Him as if you saw Him'. In Ibn 'Arabī's interpretation, this describes the lowest and weakest degree of the 'witnessing' here in question. It is the lowest degree of the mental presence in the ontological plane of Imagination, for it is said: 'as if you saw Him'. As the very wording of this phrase indicates, man is not as yet actually seeing God. There is as yet no actual vision. Man only acts *as if* he had a real vision.

But when the heart of the 'knower' becomes strengthened and mounts a step higher, the object of the 'witnessing' becomes visible to the internal, spiritual eye (*baṣīrah*), though as yet no vision occurs to his physical eye.[23]

As the 'knower' goes up to the next degree, the object becomes visible to both his physical eye and his spiritual eye. And if he still goes up and reaches finally the ultimate and highest stage, the one who 'witnesses' and the object 'witnessed' become completely unified. At this stage it is no longer the human heart that 'witnesses' its object; but it is the Absolute itself 'witnessing' itself in itself. And this is the stage of the 'saint' (*walīy*).

Thus when a man 'wakes up', and rises to the highest degree of 'saintship', he begins to witness an extraordinary phenomenon, for his spiritual eye is now open to the reality of what we have described earlier under the title of 'new creation'.

> In the eye of a real 'knower', the Absolute (in whatever form it may appear) remains always the 'recognized' one which is never denied.[24]
> The people who recognized the same Absolute under all phenomenal forms in the present world will do exactly the same in the Hereafter, too.
> This is why God (speaking of a man of this kind) says 'for whomever has a heart (*qalb*)' (L, 37). For (such a man) knows the constant changing of the Absolute in various forms; he knows this judging by

the fact that his 'heart' is constantly changing from one form to another.[25]

Thus such a man comes to know his own 'self' through (the knowledge of the constant transformation of) himself. (And from this he obtains the real knowledge about the Absolute, for) his own 'self' is nothing other than the He-ness of the Absolute, (and his knowledge thus obtained is easily extended to everything because) everything in the world of Being, whether present or future, is nothing other than the He-ness of the Absolute; indeed, everything is the He-ness itself.[26]

A real 'knower' who knows his 'heart' (*qalb*) sees with his own inner eye how it changes constantly and transforms itself (*qalb* or *taqallub*) at every moment in a myriad of modes and states. He knows at the same time that his 'heart' is but a self-manifestion of the Absolute, and that it is nothing other than the He-ness of the Absolute. Of course his 'heart' is the only thing in the whole world whose inner structure he can know through introspection. But he is well aware also that all other things must be exactly of the same structure as his 'heart'. Thus a man who knows his own 'heart' from inside knows also the Absolute as it goes on transforming itself moment after moment in all the possible forms of the world.

The category to which such a 'knower' belongs constitutes the highest degree on the scale of humanity. The subject of the next chapter will be this highest category of men.

Notes

1. *Fuṣ.*, p. 26/56.

2. *Fuṣ.*, p. 118/114. The whole passage has been given in translation in Chapter IV.

3. *Fuṣ.*, pp. 125–126/107.

4. p. 126.

5. *Fuṣ.*, p. 126/107.

6. *Fuṣ.*, p. 130/109-110.

7. Cf. Affifi, *Fuṣ.*, Com., p. 126.

8. As I have remarked above, the word *ghayrah* meaning 'jealousy' is, in the linguistic consciousness of Ibn 'Arabī, directly connected with *ghayr* meaning 'other'. So the sentence: 'God covered or concealed the reality with *ghayrah*' not only means that He concealed it with 'jealousy', but at the same time that He has concealed the reality by an infinite number of particular 'determinations', all of which are regarded as 'other' than God Himself, so that in this view everything appears as something

'other' than the rest of the things as well as 'other' than the Absolute. And the view of 'other-ness' covers the reality of Being and hinders it from being perceived by the eyes of ordinary people.

9. *Fuṣ.*, p. 130/110.

10. *Fuṣ.*, p. 211/168–169.

11. *Fuṣ.*, pp. 234–235/185–186.

12. *Fuṣ.*, pp. 135–136/113.

13. *ibid.*

14. Cf. Chapter V, where the same idea is dealt with in connection with a different problem, that of 'metaphysical perplexity'.

15. *Fuṣ.*, p. 136/113.

16. *Wa-mā ramayta idh ramayta wa-lākinna Allāha ramà.*

17. Suppose *A* is the 'cause' of *B*, for instance. *B* is of course the 'caused' of *A*. But there is also a certain respect in which *B* must be regarded as the 'cause' of *A*. In this latter respect, *A* would be the 'caused' of *B*.

18. *Fuṣ.*, p. 233/185.

19. p. 234.

20. *Fuṣ.*, p. 153/125.

21. On the exact meaning of the word *iḥsān* see my *The Concept of Belief in Islamic Theology,* Tokyo, 1965, pp. 58–60.

22. *Fuṣ.*, p. 149/123.

23. Qāshānī, p. 150.

24 The reference is to the Tradition, which has been quoted and explained earlier in the present chapter, concerning what will happen on the day of Resurrection.

25. By the 'etymological' way of thinking which, as we have observed several times, is so typical of Ibn 'Arabī, he brings together the 'heart' (*qalb*) and 'change' or 'transformation' (*qalb*).

26. *Fuṣ.*, p. 149/122.

XVI   Apostle, Prophet, and Saint

The preceding chapter has revealed that the moment we begin to consider Man on the individual level, we are faced with the existence of several degrees among men. We have seen also that the highest of all human degrees is 'saintship' (*walāyah*). The Saint (*waliy*) is the highest 'knower' of God, and consequently (in terms of the world-view of Ibn 'Arabī) of the essential structure of Being. Otherwise expressed, the Saint is the Perfect Man par excellence. The central topic of this chapter will be the concept of 'saintship'.[1]

We may begin by remarking that, in Ibn 'Arabī's understanding, the concept of Saint comprises both Prophet (*nabiy*) and Apostle (*rasūl*). Briefly stated, the Saint is the widest concept comprising Prophet and Apostle; next is the concept of Prophet which comprises that of Apostle; and the Apostle is the narrowest of all. As al-Qāshānī says, 'every Apostle is a Prophet, and every Prophet is a Saint', but not *vice versa*.

On the relation between the three concepts, there is a considerably long passage in the *Fuṣūṣ*[2] in which Ibn 'Arabī develops his thought. The argument is very entangled and somewhat confusing, but the gist of it may be clarified in the following way.

The first point to note concerning the concept of Saint is that *waliy* is properly a Divine Name. The fact that *waliy* is one of the Names of God implies that it is an aspect of the Absolute. In this respect, the Saint is radically different from the Prophet and the Apostle because the words *nabiy* and *rasūl* are not Divine Names; they are peculiar to human beings. '*Waliy* is a Name of God', as Ibn 'Arabī says, 'but God has neither called Himself *nabiy* nor *rasūl*, while He has named Himself *waliy* and has made it one of His own Names'.[3]

Thus *waliy* is a Divine Name. But even a man, when his knowledge of God attains to its highest point, becomes entitled to be called by the same name; he is a *waliy*. However, the human *waliy* himself, being so keenly conscious of his 'servant-ness' (*'ubūdiyah*) does not like to make the name publicly his own. For he knows that the word *waliy* properly belongs to God alone, and that when a human being becomes a *waliy* he is supposed to have transcended his position of 'servant-ness' and have put himself in the position of Lordship (*rubūbiyah*). But, whether he likes it or not, it does sometimes happen that a mystic transcends his position of 'servant-ness'. This occurs by a mystic being completely drowned in the Absolute and losing the consciousness of his own 'servant-ness'.[4]

It is to be remarked that, since *waliy* is a name common to God and Man, the *walāyah* never ceases to exist. As God exists everlastingly, the 'saintship' will exist forever. As long as there remains in the world even a single man of the highest spiritual power who attains to the rank of 'saintship' – and, in fact, such a man will certainly exist in every age – the 'saintship' itself will be kept intact.

In contrast to this, the prophethood and apostleship are historically conditioned, and can, therefore, be intermittent or even disappear completely.[5] As a matter of fact, we know that the chain of prophethood has historically come to an end at Muḥammad, the last of all authentic Prophets. After Muḥammad, there does not exist any longer a Prophet, who is at the same time a Law-giver (*musharri'*). After Muḥammad we have only what Ibn 'Arabī calls 'general prophethood' (*nubuwwah 'āmmah*), i.e., prophethood without institution of Law, which is nothing other than 'saintship'.

> Only this name (i.e., *waliy*) remains forever among mankind, not only in the present world but also in the Hereafter. As for the names which are peculiar to Man to the exclusion of God (i.e., Prophet and Apostle), they cease to exist with the cessation of prophethood and apostleship. God, however, has shown special mercy upon his servants and has allowed to subsist among them 'general prophethood' which is not accompanied by institution of Law.[6]

This passage makes it clear that, in the conception of Ibn 'Arabī, institution of Law (*tashrī'*) constitutes one of the characteristics of the Prophet. From this particular point of view, he divides the Prophets into two kinds: (1) those who institute Law (*nabiy musharri'*) and (2) those whose prophetic activity is done within a given Law (*nabiy musharra' la-hu*). The first category is represented by men like Moses, Jesus, and Muḥammad, each one of whom instituted a particular Law by a Divine Command. The second category is exemplified by those who, like the successive Prophets in Israel, live and fulfil their prophetic mission within the boundaries of a given Law instituted by Moses.

Since, as we have seen, the Saint is the widest concept in terms of extension and is the most basic one at that, there can be no Prophet, no Apostle unless the 'saintship' is first established. The Prophet is a

Saint who adds to his 'saintship' one more distinguishing mark; namely, a particular knowledge of things unknown and unseen. And the Apostle is a Saint who adds to his 'saintship' and 'prophethood' one more characteristic; namely being conscious of the mission and capacity of conveying Divine messages to the people who follow him.

From this we learn that the first requirement for a man to be a Perfect Man is to be in the rank of a *waliy*, and that *walāyah* is the most fundamental and most general attribute of all types of Perfect Man. What, then, does *walāyah* mean?

Walāyah implies, first and foremost, a perfect knowledge of the ultimate truth concerning the Absolute, the world, and the relation between the Absolute and the world.[7] A man who has attained to the rank of 'saintship' has a clear consciousness that he is a self-manifestation of the Absolute, and that, as such, he is essentially one with the Absolute, and, indeed, ultimately is the Absolute itself. He is also conscious of the fact that, on the analogy of the inner structure of himself, all the phenomenal Many are self-manifestations of the Absolute and are, in the sense, one with the Absolute. This precisely is the consciousness of the ultimate and essential 'oneness of Being' (*waḥdah al-wujūd*).

This consciousness of the 'oneness of Being' he obtains only by being 'annihilated' and completely immersed in the Absolute. Through the experience of 'self-annihilation' he transforms himself, so to speak, into the 'inside' of the Absolute, and from there sees the reality of all things by 'immediate tasting'. The concept of 'self-annihilation' (*fanā'*) in this sense plays an exceedingly important role in the theory of *walāyah*. The 'self-annihilation' is, in fact, the first item in the essential attributes of the Saint.

Ibn 'Arabī distinguishes three stages in 'self-annihilation'.[8] The first is the annihilation of the attributes. This stage is called by Ibn 'Arabī *takhalluq*. It means that the mystic has all his human attributes 'annihilated' and in their place 'assumes as his own' (*takhalluq*) the Divine Attributes. It is, as Bālī Efendi tersely describes it,[9] 'annihilating his attributes in the Attributes of the Absolute'. The second stage is called *taḥaqquq*. It means that the mystic has his essence (*dhāt*) 'annihilated' and realizes (*taḥaqquq*) in himself his being one with the Absolute. Bālī Efendi[10] describes it as 'annihilating his essence in the Essence of the Absolute'. The third and the last stage is called *ta'alluq*. The word *ta'alluq*, meaning literally 'firm adherence', indicates that the man in this state remains firmly attached to the essential property of *walāyah* so that he is never separated from it no matter what he may do in the world of empirical existence. The state of *ta'alluq* corresponds to what is more usually known as the state of 'self-subsistence' (*baqā'*) which comes after the state of *fanā'*. In this spiritual state, the mystic regains his self which he has once annihilated, but he regains it not in himself but in the very midst of the Divine Essence. In his fully illumined consciousness, there is no longer any trace of his old personal ego. He is only conscious that after having lost his life he now subsists in the Divine Essence, and that, therefore, it is, in reality, not he who exists but the Absolute itself. Whatever he does, it is not he but God who does it. Bālī Efendi describes it as 'annihilating his actions in the actions of the Absolute'.[11]

'Saintship' comes into existence only on the basis of the experience of 'self-annihilation' here depicted. And wide indeed is the consciousness of the Saint who has passed through such an experience. For he witnesses the astonishing scene of all things merging into the limitless ocean of Divine Life, and he is conscious that all this is actually taking place in himself. At the very height of this spiritual state, the consciousness of the Saint is identical with the Divine Consciousness which has not yet begun to become split into an infinity of 'determinations' (*ta'ayynnāt*).[12] Such a man *is* the highest 'knower'. And such a man naturally falls into deep silence (*sukūt*),[13] because the content of the deepest knowledge is ineffable.

Such is the existential ground on which stands 'saintship'. And on this basis stands 'prophethood' with an additional property, and on 'prophethood' stands 'apostleship' with a further addition. The Prophet and the Apostle are closely tied to the present world; their functions concern the life in this world, for institution of Law always aims at regulating the worldly life with a view to letting people obtain the everlasting happiness in the next world. 'Saintship', on the contrary, has no such essential relation to the present world.

Thus 'prophethood' and 'apostleship' can disappear from their subjects, but the quality or title of 'saintship' never leaves its subject. Those from whom the titles of 'prophethood' and 'apostleship' disappear become immediately Saints without any qualifications. And since, in the Hereafter, there can be no institution of Law, everybody who is in the present world a Prophet or Apostle will continue to exist in the next world in the rank of 'saintship'.[14]

As we have just remarked, the Prophet is a Saint with the addition of a different qualification (i.e., the rank of 'saintship' plus the rank of 'prophethood'), and the Apostle is a Prophet with the addition of a further qualification (i.e., the rank of 'saintship' plus the rank of 'prophethood' plus the rank of 'apostleship'). So the Prophet unites in one person two ranks, and the Apostle unites in himself three different ranks. There are thus three different ranks recognized: 'saintship', 'prophethood' and 'apostleship'. The question is naturally raised as to which of them is higher than which. With regard to this question, the most problematic point, according to Ibn 'Arabī, concerns the position of 'saintship'. Against those sufis who regard 'saintship' *qua* 'saintship' as higher than 'prophethood' and 'apostleship', he emphatically states that it is only when these two or three ranks co-exist in one person that we can rightly regard his 'saintship' as higher than his 'prophethood' and 'apostleship'.

> (When one and the same person unites in him these two or three qualifications) the man in the capacity of a 'knower' or Saint is more complete and more perfect than himself in the capacity of an Apostle or in that of a man who has instituted a Divine Law (i.e., Prophet). So whenever you hear a man belonging to the 'people of God' saying – or whenever such a saying is conveyed to you through somebody else – that 'saintship' is higher than 'prophethood', you must understand him to mean what I have just remarked.
>
> Likewise, when such a man declares that the Saint stands above the Prophet and the Apostle, he is simply talking about one and the same person. In fact, the Apostle *qua* Saint is more complete (and perfect) than himself *qua* Prophet and Apostle. It is not the case, however, that a Saint (i.e., a different person who happens to be a Saint) who follows (another person who happens to be a Prophet or Apostle in the community) is higher than the Prophet or Apostle.[15]

The last sentence of this passage points out the fact that in case the three qualifications (Saint, Prophet, and Apostle) do not concern one and the same person but three different persons, there is a respect in which the Saint must necessarily follow and be subordinate to the Prophet or Apostle. And this because the Apostle possesses a knowledge of the particular Law (i.e., 'exterior knowledge' *'ilm ẓāhir*) with which he has been sent to his community, while the Saint has no such knowledge. In what concerns the regulations of the Law, the latter must follow the Apostle of his age.

But there is also a certain respect in which the Saint is superior to the Apostle. For the Saint not only possesses a complete knowledge about God and the reality of things ('interior knowledge', *'ilm bāṭin*) but also is conscious of the fact that he has that knowledge. But neither the Apostle nor the Prophet is conscious of it, although they, too, do possess the same knowledge.

From the fact that 'apostleship' is based on three different constituents there naturally follows that there are differences among the Apostles regarding their degrees. This is the conception of the 'difference in degrees among the Apostles' (*tafāḍul al-rusul*).

All Apostles, in terms of their 'saintship', are equal and stand on the same level, but in actuality they must necessarily differ one from the other because of their intimate relations with the concrete situations of the age and country in which they live. And the same is true of the Prophet. The nature and rank of an Apostle is decisively affected by the conditions, material and spiritual, determining the situation of the nation of which he happens to be the Apostle. Likewise, the rank of a Prophet is gravely affected by the amount of knowledge he actually has.

> Know that the Apostles *qua* Apostles – not *qua* Saints or 'knowers' – stand in different degrees, each according to the state of his community. For the amount of his knowledge concerning his own apostolic mission is exactly measured to what his community needs, no more, no less. And since communities differ from each other in terms of relative superiority, the Apostles also are higher and lower in terms of the knowledge of their mission in exact accordance with the difference that exists among the nations. And to this refers the saying of God: 'Those Apostles, We have made some of them superior to others'. (II, 253)
>
> Likewise, (the Prophets) differ in rank among themselves in accordance with their individual capacities with regard to their personal knowledges and judgments. 'And to this refers the saying of God: And We have made some of the Prophets superior to others'. (XVII, 55)[16]

In the preceding chapter we have seen that the Perfect Man on the cosmic level is the 'vicegerent' of God. The same is true also of the Perfect Man on the individual level. Here on the level of individual persons, the idea of the Perfect Man is embodied by Saint, Prophet, and Apostle. These three are the 'vicegerents' (*khulafā'*) of God because they are the most perfect and most complete loci of theophany on the earth.[17] They are concrete manifestations of the 'Reality of Muḥammad' (*al-ḥaqīqah al-muḥammadīyah*) which we have discussed in the previous chapter.[18]

The term *khalīfah* meaning 'vicegerent' is a little ambiguous, because we ordinarily use it to designate the political head of the Muslim community, the Caliph.[19] In view of this fact, Ibn 'Arabī strictly distinguishes between two kinds of *khalīfah*: (1) the 'vicegerent of God' (*khalīfah Allāh*, or *khalīfah 'an Allāh*) and (2) the 'vicegerent (or successor) of the Apostle' (*khalīfah al-rasūl*, or *khalīfah 'an al-rasūl*). The 'vicegerent' in the sense of the Perfect Man (1) is totally different from the Caliph, the historical and political head of the Muslim community, who assumes the same name *khalīfah* (2).

> God has His 'vicegerents' on the earth; they are the Apostles. As for the Caliphs we know today, they are ('vicegerents' or 'successors') of the Apostles, not of God, because a Caliph governs (the community) strictly according to the dictates of the Law of an apostolic origin, and never goes beyond it.[20]

There are, however, exceptional cases in which a Caliph, i.e., a 'vicegerent' succeeding the Apostle, is in touch with the very source from which the latter has drawn his knowledge, and governs the community according to the inner Law which he receives direct from God. Such a man is outwardly a *khalīfah* of the Apostle, but inwardly is a *khalīfah* of God.

> Such a man is outwardly a follower (*muttabi'*, namely, of the Apostle) in the sense that he conforms himself (to the Law) in governing the community: Jesus, for example, when he will come down to the earth and govern the world.[21] Another example is the Prophet Muḥammad. And to this refers the saying of God: 'These are the men whom God has given guidance. So follow their guidance' (VI, 90). A man of this sort is, in virtue of the way in which he derives (his knowledge) and of which he is conscious, both 'specially privileged' (*mukhtaṣṣ*) and 'conforming' (*muwāfiq*).[22] In this respect he is somewhat in the same position as the Prophet (Muḥammad) who, confirming as he did the Law of the Apostles who had preceded him, confirmed it in his own name, so that we, his followers, actually follow him (accepting the Law) as *his* own, and not as a Law established by some of his predecessors. In like manner, the 'vicegerent of God' obtains (his knowledge) from exactly the same source as the Apostle.
>
> Such a man is called, in mystic terminology, 'the vicegerent of God', but, in ordinary (non-mystic) terminology, 'the vicegerent of the Apostle of God'.
>
> This is the reason why the Apostle of God (Muḥammad) died without explicitly designating anyone as his *khalīfah*. He acted in this way because he knew that among the believers there would appear someone who would receive 'vicegerency' directly from his Lord and thereby become a 'vicegerent of God', while conforming himself perfectly to the given Law (established by the Apostle).

One of the key-terms of Ibn 'Arabī's theory of *walāyah* is the 'Seal' (*khātam*), meaning the ultimate and final unit of a series. I should like to close this chapter by a brief consideration of this concept, although the problems it raises mostly go far beyond the scope of the present book which aims at elucidating the ontological structure of Ibn 'Arabī's world-view.

The term *khātam* appears in two phrases: (1) the Seal of the Prophets (*khātam al-anbiyā'*) or Seal of the Apostles (*khātam al-rusul*), and (2) the Seal of the Saints (*khātam al-awliyā'*). In conformity with the commonly-accepted usage in Islam, the first phrase 'Seal of the Prophets' designates the Prophet Muḥammad himself. The phrase in itself has nothing original about it; it is an expression often used in accordance with the common belief in Islam that the Prophet Muḥammad represents historically the last ring of a long chain of Prophets, there being absolutely no possibility of an authentic Prophet appearing after him.

By the second phrase: 'the seal of the Saints', which is naturally more problematic, Ibn 'Arabī means most probably himself, at least as long as the present world lasts,[23] although he does not say so explicitly in the *Fuṣūṣ*. As Affifi points out,[24] Ibn 'Arabī, besides hinting at the idea in many places of his writings by ambiguous expressions as, for example, 'the Seal of the Muḥammadan saintship (*walāyah muḥammadīyah*) is a man of noble Arab birth, living in our own time' etc., declares in one passage of the *Futuḥāt al-Makkiyyah*: 'I am the Seal of the saintship, no doubt, (the Seal of) the heritage of the Hāshimite (Muḥammad) and the Messiah'.

But whether or not Ibn 'Arabī really means by the Seal himself, the problem is merely of a peripheral significance to us. For the specific purposes of the present work, what is important is the concept of Seal itself.

The problem turns round the ultimate source of the highest knowledge peculiar to the class of the highest 'knowers'.

> This (highest) knowledge properly belongs only to the Seal of the Apostles and the Seal of the Saints. No one of the Prophets and Apostles obtains this knowledge except from the sacred niche of the Last Apostle,[25] and no one of the Saints obtains it except from the niche of the Last Saint.[26]

The last sentence might suggest the wrong idea that Ibn 'Arabī is speaking here of two different 'niches'. In truth, however, there is only one ultimate 'niche' from which all obtain the highest knowledge. For, as al-Qāshānī says,[27] if all the Apostles obtain it from the Seal of the Apostles, the latter obtains it from his own innermost 'niche', in the very capacity of the Seal of the Saints,[28] so that all the Apostles and the Saints ultimately obtain their Light from the Seal of the Saints.

As to the relative superiority between the Seal of the Apostles and the Seal of the Saints, Ibn 'Arabī gives his view as follows:[29]

> It is true that the Seal of the Saints follows externally what the Seal of the Apostles has established, namely, the Sacred Law. This, however, does not minimize in any way the spiritual rank of the Seal of the Saints. Nor does this contradict what I have said above (concerning all Apostles obtaining their esoteric knowledge from the 'niche' of the Seal of the Saints). For (it simply means that) the Seal of the Saints is in a certain respect lower in rank (than the Seal of the Apostles) but is higher in another respect.
>
> This interpretation is confirmed by what actually took place in our religion, namely, by the fact, (for instance) that 'Umar proved to be superior (to Muḥammad) in his decision about the right treatment of the prisoners of Badr and also regarding the fertilization of the date-palm. A 'perfect' man need not be superior to others in every

matter and in every respect. What the (spiritual persons) consider important is superiority in terms of knowledge about God. That only is the central point. As for worldly affairs, they are of no importance at all in the minds (of spiritual persons).

In connection with the problem of the relation between the Seal of the Saints and the Seal of the Apostles, Ibn 'Arabī refers to a famous Tradition in which Muḥammad compares himself to the one last brick that finishes and completes an entire wall. Then he correlates this Tradition with a vision he had at Mecca in the year 599 A.H.

In this vision Ibn 'Arabī saw the Ka'bah, the House of God. The Ka'bah was built of gold and silver brick ('silver brick' being a symbol of the Prophet, and 'gold brick' of the Saint). The wall of the Ka'bah as he saw it still lacked two final pieces of brick, one gold and another silver. Ibn 'Arabī, in the dream, keenly felt that the two missing bricks were no other than himself. And the construction of the Ka'bah was brought to completion when he filled the place of these two bricks.

> The Prophet (Muḥammad) once compared the 'prophethood' to a wall made of brick which was complete except in one place which was to be filled by a piece of brick. Muḥammad himself was that brick. The important point is that he saw, as he says (in this Tradition), only one single piece of brick still missing.
>
> As for the Seal of the Saints, he would surely have visions of a similar nature; he would surely see what the Prophet symbolized by a wall. (The only difference would, however, be that) he would see in the wall two bricks still missing, the entire wall being built of gold and silver bricks. And he would notice that the two bricks that were lacking in the wall were one gold and the other silver. Further, he would surely see in the vision himself just fit to be put into the place of these two bricks. Thus he would see that what was meant by the two bricks completing the wall was no other than the Seal of the Saints. The reason why he must necessarily see himself as two bricks is as follows. He is, externally, a follower of the Law established by the Seal of the Apostles. This fact was (symbolized in the vision by) the place for the silver brick. But this is only the 'external' side of the Seal of the Saints, concerning as it does only the legal regulations about which he simply follows the Seal of the Apostles. But, on the other hand, in his innermost heart, he obtains directly from God that very thing in which *externally* he is a simple follower (of the Seal of the Apostles).
>
> All this because he sees the state of affairs as it really is. So he cannot but see the matter in this way. And in this capacity he corresponds, internally, to the place for the gold brick, for he obtains his knowledge from the same source from which the angel (Gabriel) obtains that which he conveys to the Apostle.

If you have understood what I have here indicated metaphorically you have obtained an extremely valuable knowledge about everything. Thus every Prophet, (in the long historical chain of 'prophethood') beginning with Adam and ending with the last Prophet, invariably obtained his (prophetic Light) from the 'niche' of the Seal of the Prophets, although the corporeal existence of the latter was posterior to others. This because Muḥammad, in his Reality,[30] was existent (from eternity). To this refer his words (in a Tradition): 'I was a Prophet even while Adam was still between water and clay'.[31]

On the implication of this passage al-Qāshānī makes an interesting remark.[32] Ibn 'Arabī's description might be taken to imply the superiority of the Seal of the Saints to the Prophet Muḥammad, because the position of the latter is symbolized only by one brick, whereas that of the Seal of the Saints is symbolized by two bricks, one of silver as the sign of his 'external' subordination to Muḥammad, and the other of brilliant gold as the sign of his own Light. Against this understanding al-Qāshānī warns the reader and points out that, according to the Tradition in question, the Ka'bah had lacked one single piece of brick, and that when Muḥammad filled the place the building was completed. This means, he says, that Muḥammad was *de facto* the Seal of the Saints. Except that Muḥammad himself appeared only as a Prophet-Apostle, and did what he did only in that capacity, not in the capacity of a Saint. He did not, in other words, manifest the form of *walāyah*.

The vision which Ibn 'Arabī saw in Mecca was formed in the world of Imagination on the basis of this historical fact. Muḥammad was *de facto* the Seal of the Saints, but since he did not manifest himself as such, there still remained the necessity for another person to appear as a historical phenomenon in the capacity of the Seal of the Saints. Otherwise expressed, the 'saintships', with Muḥammad, remained to the last 'interior'. This 'interior', i.e., hidden, 'saintship' has come to light only with the appearance of the Seal of the Saints.

Regarding the difference between the Seal of the Saints and the rest of the Saints, Ibn 'Arabī remarks that in the former the 'saintship' is something essential while in the latter it is something that must be 'acquired' first. And this is the reason why (according to al-Qāshānī)[33] the 'saintship' of the former is called 'solar saintship' (*walāyah shamsīyah*) while that of the latter is called 'lunar saintship' (*walāyah qamarīyah*).

Notes

1. In this book I use provisionally the words 'saint' and 'saintship' as the English equivalents of *waliy* and *walāyah* respectively. Whether the meaning of the Arabic word *waliy* is covered by the English word 'saint' is another question.

2. *Fuṣ.*, pp. 160–169/135–136.

3. *Fuṣ.*, p. 168/135. See for example the Qoran (II, 257) where we read: 'God is the *waliy* (close, protecting Friend) of those who believe'.

4. *Fuṣ.*, p. 167/135.

5. Cf. also *Fuṣ.*, p. 34/62.

6. *Fuṣ.*, p. 167/135.

7. The concrete content of such a knowledge is precisely what we have analytically discussed throughout the preceding pages.

8. *Fuṣ.*, pp. 168–169/136.

9. p. 168.

10. *ibid.*

11. p. 169.

12. *Fuṣ.*, p. 89/88.

13. *Fuṣ.*, p. 34/62.

14. *Fuṣ.*, p. 169/136.

15. *Fuṣ.*, p. 168/135–136.

16. *Fuṣ.*, p. 162/132.

17. *Fuṣ.*, p.259/207.

18. Cf. Chapter XIV, (IV).

19. The English word Caliph is itself nothing but an Anglicized form of *khalīfah*.

20. *Fuṣ.*, p. 204/162–163.

21. The reference is to the eschatological figure of Jesus. According to the Muslim belief, Jesus will descend from Heaven once again at the end of the present world, and will govern the world by the Sacred Law of Islam. In that state, Jesus will be formally a 'vicegerent' of Muḥammad, while deriving his knowledge from the same source from which Muḥammad received his Law. Jesus will be, in that state, the Seal of the Saints.

22. 'Specially privileged', because he is conscious of the fact that he has received directly from God an inner Law by which he governs the community, but 'conforming', at the same time, because outwardly he owes his Law to his predecessors.

23. I say 'at least as long as the present world lasts' because, as we saw above (cf. note 21), at the very end of the present world, in the eschatological situation, Jesus will come down to the earth and assume the function of the Seal of the Saints. This latter is called the 'general saintship' (*walāyah 'āmmah*) as distinguished from the

'Muḥammadan saintship' (*walāyah muḥammadīyah*). Regarding this distinction, see the relevant passages quoted from the *Futūḥāt* by Dr Osman Yahya in his edition of *al-Tirmidhī: Khatm al-Awliyā*, Beyrouth, 1965, p. 161, Footnote 53.

24. *Philosophy*, pp. 100–101.

25. 'Niche' (*miskhāt*) symbolizes the Divine Light in the deepest core of the saintly heart; the Divine Light is nothing other than the 'Reality of Muḥammad'.

26. *Fuṣ.*, p. 34/62.

27. p. 34.

28. We have observed above that by the 'Seal of the Saints' Ibn 'Arabī means himself. But here al-Qāshānī seems to be saying that the Seal of the Apostles, i.e., Muḥammad, was also the Seal of the Saints. This, however, is not a contradiction. As we noticed before in discussing the 'Reality of Muḥammad', in the consciousness of Ibn 'Arabī, 'Muḥammad' is not only a historical individual person but a cosmic principle of creation, and the two aspects seem to be constantly present in his mind when he speaks about 'Muḥammad'.

29. *Fuṣ.*, pp. 34–35/62–63.

30. Reference to the above-mentioned 'Reality of Muḥammad'.

31. *Fuṣ.*, p. 35/63.

32. p. 36.

33. *ibid.*

XVII   The Magical Power of the Perfect Man

Ibn 'Arabī recognizes in the Perfect Man a particular kind of magical power. This is hardly to be wondered at, because the Perfect Man, as a 'knower' (*'ārif*), is by definition a man with an unusually developed spiritual power. His mind naturally shows an extraordinary activity.

This extraordinary power is known as *himmah*, meaning a concentrated spiritual energy. According to Ibn 'Arabī, a 'knower' can, if he likes, affect any object by merely concentrating all his spiritual energy upon it; he can even bring into existence a thing which is not actually existent. In brief, a 'knower' is able to subjugate anything to his will. He is endowed with the power of *taskhīr*.[1]

The word *taskhīr* reminds us of King Solomon. It is widely known and accepted in Islam that Solomon was in possession of a supernatural power by which he could dominate Nature and move it at will. He could, for instance, cause winds to blow in whatever direction he wished. He is said to have been able to control at will invisible beings.

According to Ibn 'Arabī, however, Solomon did not exercise his control over Nature by his *himmah*. In this respect, Solomon occupies a very special place. It was a special favor of God granted to him in a peculiar way. For, in order to work miracles, he did not have to have recourse to the particular concentration of mind known as *himmah*. He had only to 'command' (*amr*). Whatever was commanded by him to do anything, moved immediately as it was commanded. This kind of *taskhīr* is, in the judgment of Ibn 'Arabī, a degree higher than the *taskhīr* by *himmah*, because the former is a direct working upon the object.

> The *taskhīr* which was peculiar to Solomon, which made him superior to others, and which God had given him as (an essential) part of the kingship never to be given to anybody after him – this *taskhīr* was characterized by its being exercised by his 'command'. God says: 'Thus have We subjugated to him (i.e., Solomon) the wind so that it might blow by his command (XXI, 81) (That which is really

characteristic of Solomon's case) is not the simple fact that he could exercise *taskhīr*. For God says concerning all of us without any discrimination: 'And We have subjugated to you all that are in heaven and in earth' (XXXI, 20). Thus He speaks of having put under our control winds, stars, and others. But (in our case) the *taskhīr* occurs not by our command, but by the Command of God. So you will find by reflection that what was peculiar to Solomon was (not the *taskhīr* itself) but in fact that (the *taskhīr*) could be exercised by his own command. In order to do that, he did not need any mental concentration or *himmah*; all he had to do was to 'command'.

I mention this point specifically because we all know that the things of the world can be affected and influenced by a particular kind of mental force when the latter happens to be in a heightened state of concentration. I have witnessed this phenomenon in my own (mystical) life. Solomon, however, had only to pronounce the word of command to anything he wanted to control, without there being any need for *himmah* and concentration.[2]

What kind of thing, then, is this spiritual concentration called *himmah*? It may be most easily understood if we try to conceive it on the analogy of our ordinary experience of imagination. We can produce in imagination anything we like, even things that are not existent in the outside world. Such an imagined object exists only within our minds. In a somewhat similar way, a true 'knower' who has attained to the stage of *walāyah* is able to produce by his concentrated spiritual power things that are not actually there, with this difference, however, that he produces the object in the outer world of reality. This is obviously a kind of 'creation' (*khalq*). But it should not be identified or confused with the Divine act of creation.

Anybody can create within his mind by means of his faculty of imagination things that have no existence except in imagination itself. This is a matter of common experience. But the 'knower' creates by *himmah* things that do have existence outside the place of the *himmah* (i.e., outside the mind).

(However, the object thus created by *himmah* continues to exist) only as long as the *himmah* maintains it without being weakened by the keeping of what it has created. As soon as the concentration slackens and the mind of the 'knower' becomes distracted from the keeping of what it has created, the object created disappears. This, however, does not apply to those special cases in which a 'knower' has obtained a firm control over all the Presences (ontological levels of Being) so that his mind never loses sight of them all at the same time. In fact, the mind of such a man (even if it loses sight of the Presences, does not lose sight of all together); there surely remains at least one Presence present to his mind.[3]

We must recall at this juncture the five Presences of Being to which reference was made in the first chapter. The Presences are classified variously. One of the classifications, to give an example of classification which is a little different from the one explained in the first chapter, makes the whole world of Being consist of (1) the Presence of the senses (i.e., the plane of the sensible experience), (2) the Presence of Images-Exemplars, (3) the Presence of the Spirits (*arwāḥ*), (4) the Presence of the Intellects (*'uqūl*), and the Presence of the Essence. But the way in which the Presences are classified is not very important in the present context. What is of primary importance is to know that the world of Being is structured in terms of levels or planes and that these planes are related to each other in an organic way. This means that anything that exists in the plane of sensible experience, for instance, has a corresponding existence also in the higher planes in a particular form peculiar to each plane, so that ultimately it goes back to the very Essence of the Absolute as its ontological ground.

Because of this particular structure of Being, the 'knower' can, by concentrating his entire spiritual energy upon an object on one of the suprasensible levels, produce the object in a sensible form on the level of concrete reality. Also by maintaining spiritually the form of an object on a higher level he can maintain the forms of the same object on the lower levels of Being.

But this spiritual 'creation' is essentially different from the Divine Creation in one vital point. When, for example, the 'knower' has produced by *himmah* an object in a sensible form, the object thus 'created' on the level of sensible experience continues to subsist on that level only during the time in which he continues to maintain his spiritual concentration. The moment his attention becomes less keen by the effect of drowsiness or by a different idea occurring to his mind, the object ceases to exist on the level of the senses. However, Ibn 'Arabī adds, in the case of the highest 'knower', his spiritual power dominating all the basic five planes of Being, there is always at least one level on which the spiritual concentration is maintained even if his attention becomes less keen and less intense on other levels. In such a case, the object 'created' may be preserved for a long period of time.

By saying this, I have disclosed a secret which the people of God (i.e., mystics) have always jealously guarded themselves from revealing for fear that something might come to light which would contradict their claim to the effect that they *are* the Absolute. (Against this claim I have disclosed the fact that) the Absolute never becomes forgetful of anything, while man must necessarily be always forgetful of this particular thing or that.

Only as long as a man spiritually maintains what he has 'created', is he in a position to say, 'I am the Creator!' (*ana al-ḥaqq*). However, his maintaining the 'created' object is entirely different from God's maintaining. I have just explained the difference.

As long as he becomes forgetful of even one form and its ontological level, man is to be distinguished from the Absolute. He is naturally to be distinguished from the Absolute even if he maintains all the forms (of an object on different levels) by maintaining one of the forms on its proper level of which he happens to be unforgetful, because this is after all a kind of 'implicit' (*taḍammun*) maintaining. God's maintaining what He has created is not like this; He maintains every form 'explicitly' (i.e., He maintains all forms of the thing, each on its proper level individually).

This is a question which no one, as far as I know, has even written in any book, neither myself nor others. This is the only and the first book in which (the secret has been disclosed). The present work is in this sense a unique pearl of the age. Keep this well in mind!

The particular level of Being[4] to which the mind of the 'knower' is kept present, being concentrated on the form (of an object which he has created on that ontological level), may be compared to the 'Book' of which God says: 'We have not neglected anything in the Book (of Decrees)' (VI, 38), so that it comprehends both what has been actualized and what has not yet been actualized. But what I say here will never be understood except by those who are themselves the 'gathering' principle (*qur'ān*).[5]

Thus it has been clarified that a man who can gather his *himmah* in such a comprehensive way is able to do so because he 'gathers' together in his consciousness all the levels of Being into a comprehensive unity. Such a man stands closest to God, with the only difference which has just been explained. The difference, in short, results from the *furqān*. And precisely because of the *furqān* he is essentially distinguished from God.

The important point, however, is that this 'separating' is not an ordinary *furqān*. It is the highest *furqān* (*arfaʿ furqān*)[7] because it is a *furqān* after the 'gathering'. In the case of an ordinary man, the 'separating' which he exercises is a pre-*fanāʾ* phenomenon; he has not yet had any experience of 'self-annihilation', that is, he has not yet 'tasted' his essential oneness with the Absolute. The 'separating' he exercises in such a state is an absolute, unconditional 'separation'. He is absolutely and unconditionally 'separated' and distinguished' from the Absolute.

The 'knower', on the contrary, is a man who has already passed through the experience of 'self-annihilation' and, consequently, knows through personal experience his essential oneness with the Absolute. He knows it, and yet distinguishes in himself between the 'Divine aspect' (*lāhūt*) and the 'human aspect' (*nāsūt*), i.e., between the Absolute and the creature. This 'separating' is not a mere 'separating'; it is a 'separating' of a higher order. And this corresponds to what is generally known in Sufi terminology as 'self-subsistence' (*baqāʾ*).

Now, if we consider in the light of this conception the idea of *himmah*, we are led to the following understanding of it. The highest 'knower', while he is actually exercising his *himmah*, is in a certain sense a 'creator' (*khāliq*); all the traces of his 'servant-ness' disappear from his consciousness, and he feels 'Lordship' living and acting in himself. He feels himself to be a 'Lord', and has the clear consciousness that everything in the whole world is under his control. This is the stage of 'gathering' (*qur'ān*). However, this state is but a temporary and unstable one, because if his mind slackens and loses its highest intensity of concentration even for a moment, he becomes immediately conscious of his 'impotence' (*'ajz*) and is necessarily faced with his own 'servantness'. And this is the stage of 'separating' (*furqān*).[8]

We must observe also that *himmah* is, in its practical aspect, a free disposal of things (*taskhīr al-ashyā'*), while in its cognitive aspect it is an extraordinary power to penetrate the secret of Being which lies beyond the grasp of Reason. It is significant in this respect that Ibn 'Arabī in a passage of the *Fuṣūṣ*[9] declares that the true reality (*ḥaqīqah*) of Being can only be known by a 'servant endowed with *himmah*'. *Himmah* consists essentially in that a 'knower' concentrates all his spiritual powers upon one single point and projects his concentrated heart (*qalb*) toward a certain definite direction. This act works in two different, but closely related, ways: (1) producing something or some state of affairs in a place where such a thing or state of affairs does not sensibly exist, and (2) tearing apart the veil of Reason and bringing to light the reality lying behind it.

The supernatural power of *himmah* being as described, the next question that naturally arises is: Does the 'knower', i.e., the Perfect Man, work 'miracles' (*karāmāt*) as he likes?

According to the usual theory among Sufis, a 'knower' who has reached the stage of 'saintship' is in a position to perform 'things that go against the customs' (*khawāriq-al-'ādāt*), i.e., 'miracles'. Such a man is usually represented as a kind of superman who, projecting his spiritual power to anything and anybody, affects and changes the object at will.

Ibn 'Arabī does not accept this view. In the Qoran, he argues,[10] we find the Divine words: 'God is He who creates you of weakness' (XXX, 54). The very root of man's creation is 'weakness' (*ḍa'f*). Man is essentially and naturally 'weak' (*ḍa'īf*) and 'powerless' (*'ājiz*). He begins with the weakness of the infant and ends with the weakness of the old man. Of course, as the Qoran verse itself admits,[11] the child, as he grows into a man, acquires 'strength' (*quwwah*) and becomes conscious of his own strength. But this, after all, is a transitory state. Soon he grows old and falls into

decrepitude. Besides, the 'strength' which he obtains in the intermediary stage is but an 'accidental strength' (*quwwah 'araḍiyah*).
Moreover, this accidental strength is not something which he produces in himself, but is a result of God's 'putting'. In reality, he
shows strength only because he happens to be at that stage a locus of
theophany in which God manifests Himself under the Name
'Powerful' (*qawiy*).

What is by essence strong is the Absolute alone; man is strong
only by accident. Ordinary men do not know this. Only the true
'knower' knows that the strength (including *himmah*) which he feels
in himself is not his own but God's.

And since he is conscious of this, the 'knower' knows also that it is
not right for him to try to exercise at will the power of *himmah*. Thus
he confides its exercise to the real owner of that power, and puts
himself in the original state of the 'absolute powerlessness' (*'ajz
muṭlaq*).

> Someone may say: 'What prevents (the highest 'knower') from exer-
> cising his *himmah* that has a positive power to affect things? Since
> such a power does exist even in those mystics who merely follow the
> Apostles, the Apostles must be more appropriate to possess it'.
> To this I will answer: 'You are certainly right. But you do not know
> another important point. A true "knowledge" does not allow *him-
> mah* to be freely exercised. And the higher the knowledge, the less
> possibility there is for a free exercise of *himmah*'.
> And this for two reasons. One is that such a man fully realizes his
> state of 'servant-ness' and that he is always conscious of the original
> ground of his own creation (which is the above-mentioned 'weak-
> ness'). The other is the oneness of the subject who exercises *himmah*
> and the object upon which it is exercised (for both are essentially and
> ultimately the Absolute, nothing else), so that he does not know upon
> whom to project his *himmah*. This prevents him from exercising
> *himmah*.[12]

Then Ibn 'Arabī says[13] that another reason for which the 'knower'
refrains from working 'miracles' in the world is the knowledge
about the absolute determining power of the permanent
archetypes, which we have discussed in detail in an earlier chapter.

Suppose there is in the presence of the 'knower' a man who
disobeys the commands of the Apostle and thereby disobeys God.
Why does the 'knower' not exercise his *himmah* upon this man so
that he might be brought back to the right road? It is because
everything, every event in the world is in accordance with what has
been eternally determined in the form of an archetype or
archetypes. The 'knower' knows that this ontological determination
can never be changed. In the eyes of a man who has penetrated into
the depth of the structure of Being, everything follows the track

fixed by the very nature of Being, and nothing can deviate from it. In the light of this knowledge, even a man disobedient to God is walking along the God-determined way. And it is not in the power of an Apostle to bring such a man back to the 'right road', because the man is already on the 'right road'.

A certain Sufi of the highest rank once said to Master 'Abd al-Razzāq: Go and ask Master Abū Madyan, after salutations, 'O Abū Madyan, why is it that nothing is impossible to us, while everything is impossible to you? And yet here we are, aspiring to your spiritual stage, while you do not care for our spiritual stage. Why?'[14]

In fact, the situation was exactly like that (i.e., Abū Madyan really showed signs of 'powerlessness') in spite of the fact that Abū Madyan had, beside this state (i.e. the state of 'powerlessness'), the other state (i.e., that of free disposal of things by means of *himmah*).

We (i.e., Ibn 'Arabī himself) are even more complete as regards the state of 'weakness' and 'powerlessness'. But (even though Abū Madyan did not show so much of 'weakness' as we do) the afore-mentioned Sufi of the highest rank said to him what he said. (How much more should we be worthy of such a remark, if the same Sufi were to criticize us.) In any event, however, Abū Madyan's case clearly exemplifies that kind of thing (i.e., the showing of 'weakness' because of a deep knowledge of the truth).[15]

Ibn 'Arabī goes on to argue that even this state of 'weakness' or refraining from exercising *himmah* should not properly be taken as a willful act on the part of the 'knower'. The true 'knower' puts himself entirely in the hands of God; if He commands him to exercise his *himmah* he does, if He forbids him to do so he refrains from it, and if God Himself gives him a choice between the two he chooses refraining from the exercise of *himmah*.

Abu al-Su'ūd (Ibn al-Shibl) once said to his followers: Verily God gave me the power of the free disposal of things fifteen years ago. But I have refrained from exercising that power for the sake of courtesy (*tazarrufan*) toward God.

This saying implies too much bold familiarity (toward God). I myself do not refrain from exercising *himmah* for the sake of courtesy, because such an attitude would imply a willful choice on my part. No. I refrain from it because of the perfection of knowledge. The true knowledge of the matter does not require refraining from the exercise of *himmah* by way of willful choice. Whenever a 'knower' does exercise his *himmah* in this world, he does so in obedience to a Divine Command; that is to say, he does so because he is constrained to do so, not by way of willful choice.[16]

The position of an Apostle regarding this problem of 'refraining' is somewhat more delicate than that of a Saint.[17] Properly speaking the function itself of 'apostleship' requires his exercising *himmah* in order that his being an Apostle be made clear to the people. For only when he is accepted as such by the community, is he able to spread the true religion of God. The Saint *per se* has nothing to do with such a mission. And yet, even the Apostle (Muḥammad) did not try to show prophetic 'miracles' (*mu'jizāt*). For one thing, he refrained from exercising his *himmah* because of his compassion for the people. He did not go to extremes in manifesting the conclusive evidence of his 'apostleship' because it would have brought destruction to them. He spared them by not showing them too strong evidences of his 'apostleship'. Besides this, Muḥammad had another reason shared by all true Saints for refraining from working miracles; namely, his knowledge that a 'miracle' can never change the eternally fixed course of events. Whether a man becomes a Muslim or not is determined by his archetype; it is not something which can easily be changed by the Apostle accomplishing before his eyes a 'miracle'.

Thus even the most perfect of all Apostles (*akmal al-rusul*), Muḥammad, did not exercise *himmah*. There was actually a practical need for showing 'miracles', and he was unquestionably endowed with such a power. And yet he did not exercise his spiritual power in that way. For, being the highest 'knower', he knew better than anybody else that 'miracles' were, in truth, ineffective.

The most ideal state of the Perfect Man is a spiritual tranquility and quietude of an unfathomable depth. He is a quiet man content with a passivity in which he confides himself and every thing else to God's disposal. The Perfect Man is a man who, having in himself a tremendous spiritual power and being adorned with the highest knowledge of Being, gives the impression of a deep calm ocean. He is such because he is the most perfect image, in a concrete individual form, of the cosmic Perfect Man who comprehends and actualizes all the Names and Attributes of the Absolute.

Notes

1. *Taskhīr* literally means 'forcing somebody to compulsory service, controlling something at will'. In discussing the problem of the 'compulsory' force of the permanent archetypes we have already come across the word *taskhīr* in the form of a 'mutual *taskhīr*' between the Absolute and the world.

2. *Fuṣ.*, p. 199/158.

3. *Fuṣ.*, p. 90/88–89.

4. Again Ibn 'Arabī goes back to the case in which the 'knower' maintains spiritually all the forms of an object on all the levels of Being by actually concentrating on one of the levels.

5. *Fuṣ.*, p. 91/89–90.

6. On the difference between 'gathering' (*qur'ān*) and 'separating' (*furqān*) see above, Chapter II.

7. *Fuṣ.*, p. 91/90.

8. Cf. *Fuṣ.*, p. 92/90.

9. *Fuṣ.*, p. 148/121.

10. *Fuṣ.*, p. 156/127.

11. The verse reads: 'God is He who creates you of weakness, then puts (*ja'ala*) after weakness strength (*quwwah*), then again puts weakness after strength.'

12. *Fuṣ.*, p. 157/127–128.

13. *Fuṣ.*, pp. 157–158/128.

14. It means: We can freely accomplish 'miracles', but you apparently cannot. And yet we want to attain to your spiritual stage, while you do not show any sign of being desirous of attaining to our spiritual stage.

15. *Fuṣ.*, p. 158/129.

16. *Fuṣ.*, p. 159/129–130.

17. *ibid.*

Part II
Lao-Tzŭ & Chuang-Tzŭ

1 Lao-Tzŭ and Chuang-Tzŭ

The book called *Tao Tê Ching* is now world-famous, and is being widely read in the West in various translations as one of the most important basic texts of Oriental Wisdom. It is generally – or popularly, we should say – thought to be a philosophico-mystical treatise written by an ancient Chinese sage called Lao-tzŭ, a senior contemporary of Confucius. In more scholarly circles no one today takes such a view.

In fact, since the Ch'ing Dynasty when the question of the authorship of the book was first raised in China,[1] it has been discussed by so many people, it has provoked such an animated controversy not only in China but in Japan, and even in the West, and so divergent are the hypotheses which have been put forward, that we are left in utter darkness as to whether the *Tao Tê Ching* is a work of an individual thinker, or even whether a man called Lao-tzŭ ever existed in reality. We are no longer in a position to assign a proper chronological place to the book with full confidence.

For our particular purposes, the problem of authorship and the authenticity of the work is merely of peripheral importance. Whether or not there once existed as a historical person a sage called Lao-tzŭ in the state of Ch'u, who lived more than one hundred and sixty years,[2] whether or not this sage really wrote the *Tao Tê Ching* – these and similar questions, whether answered affirmatively or negatively, do not affect at all the main contention of the present work. What is of fundamental importance is the fact that the thought is there, and that it has a very peculiar inner structure which, if analyzed and understood in a proper way, will provide an exceedingly interesting Chinese counterpart to the 'Unity of Existence' (*waḥdah al-wujūd*) type of philosophy as represented by Ibn 'Arabī in Islam.

Lao-tzŭ is a legendary, or at the very most, semi-legendary figure, of whom it is an obvious understatement to say that nothing certain is known to us. For, even on the assumption that there *is* an historical core in his so-called biography, we must admit that the popular imagination has woven round it such a fantastic tapestry of impossible events and unbelievable incidents that no one can ever hope to disentangle the intricate web of legends, myths and facts.

Even the most sober and most dependable of all Chinese historians in ancient times, and the earliest to attempt a description of Lao-tzŭ's life and adventures in his *Book of History*,³ Ssŭ Ma Ch'ien of the Han Dynasty (the beginning of the 1st century B.C.), had to be content with giving a very inconsistent and unsystematic narrative made up of a number of stories stemming from heterogeneous origins.

According to one of those legends, Lao-tzŭ was a native of the state of Ch'u.⁴ He was an official of the royal Treasury of Chou, when Confucius came to visit him. After the interview, Confucius is related to have made the following remark to his disciples about Lao-tzŭ. 'Birds fly, fishes swim, and animals run – this much I know for certain. Moreover, the runner can be snared, the swimmer can be hooked, and the flyer can be shot down by the arrow. But what can we do with a dragon? We cannot even see how he mounts on winds and clouds and rises to heaven. That Lao-tzŭ whom I met to-day may probably be compared only to a dragon!'

The story makes Lao-tzŭ a senior contemporary of Confucius (551–479 B.C.). This would naturally mean that Lao-tzŭ was a man who lived in the 6th century B.C., which cannot possibly be a historical fact.

Many arguments have been brought forward against the historicity of the narrative which we have just quoted. One of them is of particular importance to us; it is concerned with examining this and similar narratives philologically and in terms of the historical development of philosophical thinking in ancient China. I shall give here a typical example of this kind of philological argument.

Sōkichi Tsuda in his well-known work, *The Thought of the Taoist School and its Development*,⁵ subjects to a careful philological examination the peculiar usage of some of the key technical terms in the *Tao Tê Ching*, and arrives at the conclusion that the book must be a product of a period after Mencius (372–289 B.C.). This would imply of course that Lao-tzŭ – supposing that he did exist as a historical person – was a man who came after Mencius.

Tsuda chooses as the yardstick of his judgment the expression *jĕn-i* which is found in Chap. XVIII of the *Tao Tê Ching*,⁶ and which is a compound of two words *jĕn* and *i*. These two words, *jĕn* ('humaneness' with particular emphasis on 'benevolence') and *i* ('righteousness'), properly speaking, do not belong to the vocabulary of Lao-tzŭ; they are key-terms of Confucianism. As representing two of the most basic human virtues, they play an exceedingly important rôle in the ethical thought of Confucius himself. But in the mouth of Confucius, they remain two independent words; they are not compounded into a semantic unit in the form of *jēn-i* corresponding almost to a single complex concept. The latter phenomenon is observed only in post-Confucian times. Tsuda points out that the thinker who first emphasized the concept of *jēn-i* is Mencius. This fact, together with the fact that in the above-mentioned passage Lao-tzŭ uses the terms *jēn* and *i* in this compound form, would seem to suggest that the *Tao Tê Ching*, is a product of a period in which the Confucian key-term *jēn-i* has already been firmly established, for the passage in question is most evidently intended to be a conscious criticism of Confucian ethics. Lao-tzŭ, in other words, could use the expression with such an intention only because he had before his eyes Mencius and his ethical theory.

Moreover, Tsuda goes on to remark, Mencius vehemently attacks and denounces everything incompatible with Confucianism, but nowhere does he show any conscious endeavour to criticize Lao-tzŭ or *Tao Tê Ching* in spite of the fact that the teaching of the latter is diametrically opposed to his own doctrine; he does not even mention the name Lao-Tzŭ. This is irrefutable evidence for the thesis that the *Tao Tê Ching* belongs to a period posterior to Mencius. Since, on the other hand, its doctrines are explicitly criticized by Hsün-tzŭ (c. 315–236 B.C.), it cannot be posterior to the latter. Thus, in conclusion, Tsuda assigns to the *Tao Tê Ching* a period between Mencius and Hsün-tzŭ.

Although there are some problematic points in Tsuda's argument, he is, I think, on the whole right. In fact, there are a number of passages in the *Tao Tê Ching* which cannot be properly understood unless we place them against the background of a Confucian philosophy standing already on a very firm basis. And this, indeed, is the crux of the whole problem, at least for those to whom the thought itself of Lao-tzŭ is the major concern. The very famous opening lines of the *Tao Tê Ching*, for instance, in which the real Way and the real Name are mentioned in sharp contrast to an ordinary 'way' and ordinary 'names',[7] do not yield their true meaning except when we realize that what is meant by this ordinary 'way' is nothing but the proper ethical way of living as understood and taught by the school of Confucius, and that what is referred to by these ordinary 'names' are but the Confucian 'names', i.e., the highest ethical categories stabilized by means of definite 'names', i.e., key-terms.

The *Tao Tê Ching* contains, furthermore, a number of words and phrases that are – seemingly at least – derived from various other sources, like Mo-tzŭ, Yang Chu, Shang Yang, and even Chuang-tzŭ, Shên Tao, and others. And there are some scholars who, basing themselves on this observation, go farther than Tsuda and assert that the *Tao Tê Ching* belongs to a period after Chuang-tzŭ and Shên Tao. Yang Jung Kuo, a contemporary scholar of Peking, to give one example, takes such a position in his *History of Thought in Ancient China.*[8]

Some of these alleged 'references' to thinkers who have traditionally been considered later than Lao-tzŭ may very well be explained as due to the influence exercised by the *Tao Tê Ching* itself upon those thinkers who, in writing their books, may have 'borrowed' ideas and expressions from this book. Besides, we have to remember that the text of this book as we have it to-day has evidently passed through a repeated process of editing, re-editing, and re-arranging in the Han Dynasty. Many of the 'references' may simply be later additions and interpolations.

Be this as it may, it has to be admitted that the *Tao Tê Ching* is a controversial work. And at least it is definitely certain that the formation of its thought presupposes the existence of the Confucian school of thought.

Turning now to another aspect of Lao-tzŭ, which is more important for the purposes of the present work than chronology, we may begin by observing that the Biography of Lao-tzŭ as given by Ssŭ Ma Ch'ien in his *Book of History* makes Lao-tzŭ a man of Ch'u.[9] Thus he writes in one passage, 'Lao-tzŭ was a native of the village Ch'ü Jên, in Li Hsiang, in the province of K'u, in the state of Ch'u'. In another passage he states that according to a different tradition, there was a man called Lao Lai Tzŭ in the time of Confucius; that he was a man of Ch'u, and produced fifteen books in which he talked about the Way. Ssŭ Ma Ch'ien adds that this man may have been the same as Lao-tzŭ.

All this may very well be a mere legend. And yet it is, in my view, highly significant that the 'legend' connects the author of the *Tao Tê Ching* with the state of Ch'u. This connection of Lao-tzŭ with the southern state of Ch'u cannot be a mere coincidence. For there is something of the spirit of Ch'u running through the entire book. By the 'spirit of Ch'u' I mean what may properly be called the shamanic tendency of the mind or shamanic mode of thinking. Ch'u was a large state lying on the southern periphery of the civilized Middle Kingdom, a land of wild marches, rivers, forests and mountains, rich in terms of nature but poor in terms of culture, inhabited by many people of a non-Chinese origin with variegated, strange customs. There all kinds of superstitious beliefs in supernatural beings and spirits were rampant, and shamanic practices thrived.

But this apparently primitive and 'uncivilized' atmosphere could provide an ideal fostering ground for an extraordinary visionary power of poetic imagination, as amply attested by the elegies written by the greatest shaman-poet the state of Ch'u has ever produced, Ch'ü Yüan.[10] The same atmosphere could also produce a very peculiar kind of metaphysical thinking. This is very probable because the shamanic experience of reality is of such a nature that it can be refined and elaborated into a high level of metaphysical experience. In any case, the metaphysical depth of Lao-tzŭ's thought can, I believe, be accounted for to a great extent by relating it to the shamanic mentality of the ancient Chinese which can be traced back to the oldest historic times and even beyond, and which has flourished particularly in the southern part of China throughout the long history of Chinese culture.

In this respect Henri Maspero[11] is, I think, basically right when he takes exception to the traditional view that Taoism abruptly started in the beginning of the fourth century B.C. as a mystical metaphysics with Lao-tzŭ, was very much developed philosophically by Chuang-tzŭ toward the end of that century and vulgarized to a considerable degree by Lieh-tzŭ and thenceforward went on the way of corruption and degeneration until in the Later Han Dynasty it was completely transformed into a jumble of superstition, animism, magic and sorcery. Against such a view, Maspero takes the position that Taoism was a 'personal' religion – as contrasted with the agricultural communal type of State religion which has nothing to do with personal salvation – going back to immemorial antiquity. The school of Lao-tzŭ and Chuang-tzŭ, he maintains, was a particular branch or section within this wide religious movement, a particular branch characterized by a marked mystical-philosophical tendency.

These observations would seem to lead us back once again to the problem of the authorship of *Tao Tê Ching* and the historicity of Lao-tzŭ. Is it at all imaginable that such a metaphysical refinement of crude mysticism should have been achieved as a result of a process of natural development, without active participation of an individual thinker endowed with an unusual philosophical genius? I do not think so. Primitive shamanism in ancient China would have remained in its original crudity as a phenomenon of popular religion characterized by ecstatic orgy and frantic 'possession', if it were not for a tremendous work of elaboration done in the course of its history by men of unusual genius. Thus, in order to produce the *Elegies of Ch'u* the primitive shamanic vision of the world had to pass through the mind of a Ch'ü Yüan. Likewise, the same shamanic world-vision could be elevated into the profound metaphysics of the Way only by an individual philosophical genius.

When we read the *Tao Tê Ching* with the preceding observation in mind, we cannot but feel the breath, so to speak, of an extraordinary man pervading the whole volume, the spirit of an unusual philosopher pulsating throughout the book. With all the possible later additions and interpolations, which I readily admit, I cannot agree with the view that the *Tao Tê Ching* is a work of compilation consisting of fragments of thought taken from various heterogeneous sources. For there is a certain fundamental unity which strikes us everywhere in the book. And the unity is a personal one. In fact, the *Tao Tê Ching* as a whole is a unique piece of work distinctly colored by the personality of one unusual man, a shaman-philosopher. Does he not give us a self-portrait in part XX of the book?

> The multitude of men are blithe and cheerful as though they were invited to a luxurious banquet, or as though they were going up a high tower to enjoy the spring scenery.
> I alone remain silent and still, showing no sign of activity. Like a new-born baby I am, that has not yet learnt to smile. Forlorn and aimless I look, as if I had no place to return.
> All men have more than enough. I alone seem to be vacant and blank. Mine indeed is the mind of a stupid man! Dull and confused it is! The vulgar people are all clever and bright, I alone am dark and obtuse. The vulgar people are all quick and alert, I alone am blunt and tardy. Like a deep ocean that undulates constantly I am, like a wind that blows never to rest.
> All others have some work to do, while I alone remain impractical and boorish. I alone am different from all others because I value being fed by the Mother.[12]

Similarly in another passage (LXVII), he says of himself:

> Everybody under Heaven says that I[13] am big, but look stupid. Yea, I look stupid because I am big. If I were clever I would have diminished long ago.

And again in LXX, we read:

> My words are very easy to understand and very easy to practise. Yet no one under Heaven understands them; no one puts them into practice.
> My words come out of a profound source, and my actions come out of a high principle. But people do not understand it. Therefore they do not understand me.
> Those who understand me are rare. That precisely is the proof that I am precious. The sage, indeed, wears clothes of coarse cloth, but carries within precious jade.

The passages just quoted give a picture of a very original mind, an image of a man who looks gloomy, stupid and clumsy, standing aloof from the 'clever' people who spend their time in the petty pleasures of life. He takes such an attitude because he is conscious of himself as utterly different from ordinary men. The important question we have to raise about this is: Whence does this difference come? The *Tao Tê Ching* itself and the *Chuang-tzŭ* seem to give a definite answer to this question. The man feels himself different from others because he is conscious that he alone knows the real meaning of existence. And this he knows due to his metaphysical insight which is based on what Chuang-tzŭ calls *tso wang* 'sitting in oblivion', that is, the experience of ecstatic union with the Absolute, the Way. The man who stands behind the utterances which we have quoted above is a philosopher-mystic, or a visionary shaman turned into a philosopher.

It is highly significant for our specific purpose to note that the spirit of a philosophically developed shamanism pervades the whole of the *Tao Tê Ching*. It is, so to speak, a living personal 'center' round which are co-ordinated all the basic ideas that we find in the book, whether the thought concerns the metaphysical structure of the universe, the nature of man, the art of governing people, or the practical ideal of life. And such an organic unity cannot be explained except on the assumption that the book, far from being a compilation made of fragmentary and disparate pieces of thought picked up at random from here and there, is in the main the work of a single author.

In studying a book like the *Tao Tê Ching* it is more important than anything else to grasp this personal unity underlying it as a whole, and to pinpoint it as the center of co-ordination for all its basic ideas. For, otherwise, we would not be in a position to penetrate the subtle structure of the symbolism of the *Tao Tê Ching* and analyze with precision the basic ideas of its metaphysics.

Turning from Lao-tzŭ to Chuang-tzŭ, we feel ourselves standing on a far more solid ground. For, although we are no better informed about his real life and identity, at least we know that we are dealing with an historical person, who did exist in about the middle of the fourth century B.C., as a contemporary of Mencius, the great shaman-poet Ch'ü Yüan of Ch'u to whom reference has been made, and the brilliant dialectician Hui Shih or Hui-tzŭ[14] with whom he himself was a good match in the mastery of the art of manipulating logical concepts.

According to the account given by Ssŭ Ma Ch'ien in the above-mentioned *Book of History*, Chuang-tzŭ or Chuang Chou[15] was a native of Mêng;[16] he was once an official at Ch'i-Yüan in Mêng; he had tremendous erudition, but his doctrine was essentially based on the teachings of Lao-tzŭ; and his writing, which counted more than 100,000 words, was for the most part symbolic or allegorical.

It is significant that Mêng, which is mentioned by Ssŭ Ma Ch'ien as Chuang-tzŭ's birthplace, is in present-day Ho Nan and was a place in the ancient state of Sung.[17] I regard this as significant because Sung was a country where the descendants of the ancient Yin[18] people were allowed to live after having been conquered by the Chou people.[19] There these descendants of the once-illustrious people, despised by the conquerors as the 'conquered' and constantly threatened and invaded by their neighbors, succeeded in preserving the religious beliefs and legends of their ancestors. The significance of this fact with regard to the thesis of the present study will at once be realized if one but remembers the animistic-shamanic spirit of Yin culture as manifested in its sacrificial ceremonies and rites of divination as well as in the myths connected with this dynasty. The people of Yin were traditionally famous for their cult of spirits and worship of the 'God-above'. From of old the distinction between Yin and Chou was made by such a dictum as: 'Yin worships spirits while Chou places the highest value on human culture.'[20]

Quite independently of the observation of this historical relation between the Yin Dynasty and the Sung people, Fung Yu Lang in his *History of Chinese Philosophy*[21] points out – quite rightly, to my mind – that the form of Chuang-tzŭ's thought is close to that of the Ch'u people. 'We should keep in mind', he writes, 'the fact that the state of Sung bordered Ch'u, making it quite possible that Chuang-tzŭ was influenced on the one hand by Ch'u, and at the same time was under the influence of the ideas of the Dialecticians. (Hui Shih, it will be remembered, was a native of Sung.) Thus by using the dialectics of the latter, he was able to put his soaring thoughts into order, and formulate a unified philosophical system.'

Of the 'spirit of Ch'u' we have talked in an earlier passage in connection with the basic structure of Lao-tzŭ's thought. Fung Yu Lang compares the *Elegies of Ch'u (Ch'u Tz'ŭ)*[22] with the *Chuang-tzŭ* and observes a remarkable resemblance between the two in the display of 'a richness of imagination and freeness of spirit'. But he neglects to trace this resemblance down to its shamanic origin, so that the 'richness of imagination and freeness of spirit' is left unexplained. However it may be, we shall refrain from going any further into the details of this problem at this point, for much more will be said in the following chapter.

The problem of the relationship between Lao-tzŭ and Chuang-tzŭ has been discussed at length by philologists. As we have already observed the major doctrines of Chuang-tzŭ have traditionally been regarded as being based upon the teachings of Lao-tzŭ. On this view, Lao-tzŭ of course was a predecessor of Chuang-tzŭ in Taoist philosophy; the main lines of thought had been laid down by the former, and the latter simply took them over from him and developed them in his own way into a grand-scale allegorical system according to the dictates of his philosophical and literary ability. This view seems to be a natural conclusion drawn from the observation of the following two facts: (1) the existence of an undeniable inner connection between the two in the very structure of their world-view and their mystical way of thinking; (2) Chuang-tzŭ himself often mentioning Lao-tzŭ as one of the earlier Taoist sages, and the expressions used being in some places almost the same.

The matter, however, is not as simple as it looks at the first glance. In fact serious questions have been raised in modern times about this problem. The *Tao Tê Ching* itself, to begin with, is nowhere referred to in the *Chuang-tzŭ*, although Lao-tzŭ, as a legendary figure, appears in its pages, and his ideas are mentioned. But this latter fact proves almost nothing conclusively, for we know that many of the persons who are made to play important rôles in the Chuang-tzŭ are simply fictitious. Similarities in language may easily be explained away as the result either of later interpolations in the *Tao Tê Ching* itself, or as going back to common sources.

Yang Jung Kuo, to whom reference has been made earlier, may be mentioned as a representative present-day scholar who not only doubts Lao-tzŭ's having been a predecessor of Chuang-tzŭ, but goes a step further and completely reverses the chronological order. In an interesting chapter of his above-mentioned book, *History of Thought in Ancient China*,[23] he decidedly takes the position that Chuang-tzŭ was not a disciple of Lao-tzŭ; that, on the contrary, the latter – or, to be more exact, the *Tao Tê Ching* – was nothing other than a continuation and further development of the *Chuang-tzŭ*. And the way he defends his position is strictly philological; he tries to prove his position through an examination of some of the key-concepts common to Lao-tzŭ and Chuang-tzŭ. And he concludes that the *Tao Tê Ching* presupposes the prior existence of the *Chuang-tzŭ*. For instance, the most important of all key-concepts of Taoism, *tao* (Wag) as the cosmic principle of natural growth, or Nature, is in the *Chuang-tzŭ* not yet fully developed in its inner structure. The concept is already there, he says, but it is as yet a mere beginning. The *Tao Tê Ching* takes over this concept at this precise point and elaborates it into an absolute principle, the absolutely unknowable Source, which is pre-eternal[24] and from which emanate all things.[25] And Yang Jung Kuo thinks that this historical relation between the two – Chuang-tzŭ being the initial point and Lao-tzŭ representing the culmination – is observable throughout the whole structure of Taoist philosophy.

This argument, highly interesting though it is, is not conclusive.

For the key-concepts in question allow of an equally justifiable explanation in terms of a process of development running from Lao-tzŭ to Chuang-tzŭ. As regards the metaphysics of *tao*, for instance, we have to keep in mind that Lao-tzŭ gives only the result, a definitely established monistic system of archetypal imagery whose center is constituted by the absolute Absolute, *tao*, which develops stage after stage by its own 'natural' creative activity down to the world of multiplicity. This ontology, as I have pointed out before, is understandable only on the assumption that it stands on the basis of an ecstatic or mystical experience of Existence. Lao-tzŭ, however, does not disclose this experiential aspect of his world-view except through vague, symbolic hints and suggestions. This is the reason why the *Tao Tê Ching* tends to produce an impression of being a philosophical elaboration of something which precedes it. That 'something which precedes it', however, may not necessarily be something taken over from others.

Chuang-tzŭ, on the other hand, is interested precisely in this experiential aspect of Taoist mysticism which Lao-tzŭ leaves untouched. He is not mainly concerned with constructing a metaphysics of a cosmic scale ranging from the ultimate Unknowable down to the concrete world of variegated colors and forms. His chief concern is with the peculiar kind of 'experience' itself by which one penetrates the mystery of Existence. He tries to depict in detail, sometimes allegorically, sometimes theoretically, the very psychological or spiritual process through which one becomes more and more 'illumined' and goes on approaching the real structure of reality hidden behind the veil of sensible experience.

His attitude is, in comparison with Lao-tzŭ, epistemological, rather than metaphysical. And this difference separates these two thinkers most fundamentally, although they share a common interest in the practical effects that come out of the supra-sensible experience of the Way. The same difference may also be formulated in terms of upward movement and downward movement. Lao-tzŭ tries to describe metaphysically how the absolute Absolute develops naturally into One, and how the One develops into Two, and the Two into Three, and the Three into 'ten thousand things'.[26] It is mainly a description of an ontological – or emanational – movement downward, though he emphasizes also the importance of the concept of Return, i.e., the returning process of all things back to their origin. Chuang-tzŭ is interested in describing epistemologically the rising movement of the human mind from the world of multiplicity and diversity up to the ontological plane where all distinctions become merged into One.

Because of this particular emphasis on the epistemological aspect of the experience of the *tao*, Chuang-tzŭ does not take the trouble of developing the concept itself of *tao* as a philosophical system. This is why his metaphysics of *tao* appears imperfect, or imperfectly developed. This, however, does not necessarily mean that he represents chronologically an earlier stage than Lao-tzŭ. For, as we have just seen, the difference between them may very well be only the difference of emphasis.

I shall now bring this chapter to a close by giving a brief explanation of the book itself known by the name *Chuang-tzŭ*.

The important *Bibliography* contained in the *Chronicle of the Han Dynasty*[27] notes that the *Chuang-tzŭ* consists of fifty-two chapters. But the basic text of the book which we actually have in our hands has only thirty-three chapters. This is the result of editorial work done by Kuo Hsiang.[28] In fact all the later editions of the *Chuang-tzŭ* ultimately go back to this Kuo Hsiang recension. This eminent thinker of the Taoist school critically examined the traditional text, left out a number of passages which he regarded as definitely spurious and worthless, and divided what survived this examination into three main groups. The first group is called *Interior Chapters* (*nei p'ien*) consisting of seven chapters. The second is called *Exterior Chapters* (*wai p'ien*) and consists of fifteen chapters. And the third is called *Miscellaneous Chapters* (*tza pi'en*) and contains eleven chapters.

Setting aside the problem of possible additions and interpolations we might say generally that the *Interior Chapters* represent Chuang-tzŭ's own thought and ideas, and are probably from his own pen. As to the two other groups, scholars are agreed to-day that they are mostly later developments, interpretations and elucidations added to the main text by followers of Chuang-tzŭ. Whether the *Interior Chapters* come from Chuang-tzŭ's own pen or not, it is definite that they represent the oldest layer of the book and are philosophically as well as literarily the most essential part, while the *Exterior* and *Miscellaneous Chapters* are of but secondary importance.

In the present study, I shall depend exclusively on the *Interior Chapters*. This I shall do for the reason just mentioned and also out of a desire to give consistency to my analytic description of Chuang-tzŭ's thought.[29]

Notes

1. Ts'ui Shu (崔述 in his「洙泗考信錄」I) may here be mentioned as one of the most eminent writers of the Ch'ing Dynasty who raised serious doubts about the reliability of the so-called biography of Lao-tzŭ. Of the *Tao Tê Ching* he says: 'As for the

five-thousand-words-about-the-Tao-and-Virtue, no one knows who wrote it. There is no doubt, in any case, that it is a forgery by some of the followers of Yang Chu.'

2. The name Lao-tzŭ, incidentally, simply means Old Master, the word 'old' in this context meaning almost the same as 'immortal'.

3. 司馬遷 : *Shih Chih*, 「史記」, LXIII, 「老莊申韓列傳」, III.

4. For my reason for translating 「周守藏室之史」, as 'an official of the royal Treasury of Chou', see Shigeta Koyanagi: *The Thought of Lao-tzŭ, Chuang-tzŭ and Taoism* 小柳司氣太「老莊思想と道教」, Tokyo, 1942, pp. 26–27.

5. 津田左右吉「道家の思想とその展開」, Complete Works of S. Tsuda, XIII, Tokyo, 1964. The work was published earlier in 1927 as a volume of the series of publications of Tôyô Bunko.

6. 「大道廢有仁義」, 'Only when the great Way declines, does the virtue of benevolence-righteousness arise.'

7. This passage will be translated and explained later.

8. 楊榮國「中國古代思想史」 Peking, 1954, 3rd ed. 1955, Chap. VII, 4, pp. 245–247. At the outset (p. 245), the author states: The Book of Lao-tzŭ is, in my opinion, a product of an age subsequent to the flourishing of the school of Chuang-tzŭ in the Warring States period.

9. 楚.

10. 屈原. We may note as quite a significant fact that this great poet of Ch'u was a contemporary of Chuang-tzŭ. According to a very detailed and excellent study done by Kuo Mo Jo (郭沫若「屈原研究」), Ch'ü Yüan was born in 340 B.C. and died in 278 B.C., at the age of sixty-two. As for Chuang-tzŭ, an equally excellent study by Ma Hsü Lun (馬叙倫「莊子年表」) has established that he lived c. 370 B.C.–300 B.C.

11. Henri Maspero: *Le Taoism* (*mélanges posthumes sur les religions et l'histoire de la Chine,* II) Paris, 1950, III.

12. 'Mother' here symbolizes the Way (*tao*). Just as a child in the womb feeds on the mother without its doing anything active on its part, the Taoist sage lives in the bosom of the Way, free and careless, away from all artificial activity on his part.

13. The text usually reads; 天下皆謂我道大 . . . . making 'my Way' the subject of the sentence.

14. 惠施 , 惠子, known as one of the representatives of the 'school of dialecticians (*pien chê*)', or 'sophists', in the Warring States period. The *Chuang-tzŭ* records several anecdotes in which Chuang-tzŭ is challenged by this logician, disputes with him, and scores a victory over him. The anecdotes may very well be fictitious – as almost all the anecdotes of the *Chuang-tzŭ* are – but they are very interesting in that they disclose the basic characteristics of the one as well as of the other.

15. 莊子, 莊周, *Chou* being his personal name.

16. 蒙.

17. 宋.

18. 殷.

19. 周.

20. 「商尚鬼周尚文」(Cf. 錢穆「莊老通辨」, Hong Kong, 1957, pp. 1–2).

21. Trans. by D. Bodde, 2 vols., Princeton, 1952–53; vol. I, pp. 221–222.

22. 「楚辭」, some of which are by the poet Ch'ü Yüan himself, *Li Sao*「離騷」being his representative work, while some others are by his followers. But, whether by Ch'ü Yüan or by others, all the *Elegies* are through and through shamanic. Some of them describe in a typical way the spiritual, visionary journeys of a shaman in an ecstatic state.

23. pp. 252–257.

24. 「道先天地」 lit. 'The Tao precedes Heaven and Earth'. The concept of *tao* in this respect may rightly be compared with the Islamic concept *qadîm*.

25. 「道生萬物」, lit. 'The Tao produces, or makes grow, the ten thousand things'.

26. See, *Tao Tê Ching*, XLII. The process of 'emanation' will be dealt with later in full detail.

27. 「漢書」藝文志 which was compiled in the 1st century B.C.

28. 郭象, a scholar of the 4th century A.D.

29. In quoting from the *Chuang-tzŭ* I shall give page numbers according to the Peking edition of *Chuang-tzŭ Chi Shih*「莊子集釋」, by Kuo Ch'ing Fan 郭慶藩, Peking, 1961, vol. 1. The editor was one of the outstanding philologists of the Ch'ing dynasty, and his edition is a very useful one, because it gives the commentary by Kuo Hsiang himself (「莊子注」) and two other equally famous glosses by Ch'êng Hsüang Ying 成玄英「莊子注疏」) and Lu Tê Ming 陸德明(「莊子音義」), supplemented by some of the results of modern scholarship. As for Lao-tzŭ, I shall quote from the edition of Kao Hêng: *Lao-tzŭ Chêng Ku*高享「老子正詁」, Shanghai, 1943, giving, as is usually done, chapter numbers instead of page numbers.

II From Mythopoiesis to Metaphysics

In the preceding chapter I indicated in a preliminary way the possibility of there being a very strong connection between Taoist philosophy and shamanism. I suggested that the thought or world-view of Lao-tzŭ and Chuang-tzŭ may perhaps be best studied against the background of the age-old tradition of the shamanic spirit in ancient China. The present chapter will be devoted to a more detailed discussion of this problem, namely, the shamanic background of Taoist philosophy as represented by the *Tao Tê Ching* and *Chuang-tzŭ*.

In fact, throughout the long history of Chinese thought there runs what might properly be called a 'shamanic mode of thinking'. We observe this specific mode of thinking manifesting itself in diverse forms and on various levels in accordance with the particular circumstances of time and place, sometimes in a popular, fantastic form, often going to the limit of superstition and obscenity, and sometimes in an intellectually refined and logically elaborated form. We observe also that this mode of thinking stands in sharp contrast to the realistic and rationalistic mode of thinking as represented by the austere ethical world-view of Confucius and his followers.

Briefly stated, I consider the Taoist world-view of Lao-tzŭ and Chuang-tzŭ as a philosophical elaboration or culmination of this shamanic mode of thinking; as, in other words, a particular form of philosophy which grew out of the personal existential experience peculiar to persons endowed with the capacity of seeing things on a supra-sensible plane of consciousness through an ecstatic encounter with the Absolute and through the archetypal images emerging out of it.

The Taoist philosophers who produced works like the *Tao Tê Ching* and *Chuang-tzŭ* were 'shamans' on the one hand, as far as concerns the experiential basis of their world-vision, but they were on the other, intellectual thinkers who, not content to remain on the primitive level of popular shamanism, exercised their intellect in order to elevate and elaborate their original vision into a system of metaphysical concepts designed to explain the very structure of Being.

Lao-tzŭ talks about *shêng-jên*[1] or the 'sacred man'. It is one of the key-concepts of his philosophical world-view, and as such plays an exceedingly important rôle in his thought. The 'sacred man' is a man who has attained to the highest stage of the intuition of the Way, to the extent of being completely unified with it, and who behaves accordingly in this world following the dictates of the Way that he feels active in himself. He is, in brief, a human embodiment of the Way. In exactly the same sense, Chuang-tzŭ speaks of *chên-jên*[2] or the 'true man', *chih-jên*[3] or the 'ultimate man', *shên-jên*[4] or the 'divine (or super-human) man'. The man designated by these various words is in reality nothing other than a philosophical shaman, or a shaman whose visionary intuition of the world has been refined and elaborated into a philosophical vision of Being.

That the underlying concept has historically a close connection with shamanism is revealed by the etymological meaning of the word *shêng* here translated as 'sacred'. The *Shuo Wên Chieh Tzŭ*, the oldest etymological dictionary (compiled in 100 A.D.), in its explanation of the etymological structure of this word states: '*Shêng* designates a man whose orifices of the ears are extraordinarily receptive'.[5] In other words, the term designates a man, endowed with an unusually keen ear, who is capable of hearing the voice of a super-natural being, god or spirit, and understands directly the will or intention of the latter. In the concrete historical circumstances of the ancient Yin Dynasty, such a man can be no other than a divine priest professionally engaged in divination.

It is interesting to remark in this connection that in the *Tao Tê Ching* the 'sacred man' is spoken of as the supreme ruler of a state, or 'king', and that this equation (Saint = King) is made as if it were a matter of common sense, something to be taken for granted. We must keep in mind that in the Yin Dynasty[6] shamanism was deeply related to politics. In that dynasty, the civil officials of the higher ranks who possessed and exercised a tremendous power over the administration of the state were all originally shamans. And in the earliest periods of the same dynasty, the Grand Shaman was the high priest-vizier, or even the king himself.[7]

This would seem to indicate that behind the 'sacred man' as the Taoist ideal of the Perfect Man there is hidden the image of a shaman, and that under the surface of the metaphysical world-view of Taoism there is perceivable a shamanic cosmology going back to the most ancient times of Chinese history.

For the immediate purposes of the present study, we do not have to go into a detailed theoretical discussion of the concept of shamanism.[8] We may be content with defining it in a provisional way by saying that it is a phenomenon in which an inspired seer in a state of ecstasy communes with supernatural beings, gods or spirits. As is well known, a man who has a natural capacity of this kind tends to serve in a primitive society as an intermediary between his tribesmen and the unseen world.

As one of the most typical features of the shamanic mentality we shall consider first of all the phenomenon of *mythopoiesis*. Shamans are by definition men who, in their ecstatic-archetypal visions perceive things which are totally different from what ordinary people see in their normal states through their sensible experiences, and this naturally tends to induce the shamans to interpret and structuralize the world itself quite differently from ordinary people. That which characterizes their reality experience in the most remarkable way is that things appear to their 'imaginal' consciousness in symbolic and mythical forms. The world which a shaman sees in the state of trance is a world of 'creative imagination', as Henry Corbin has aptly named it, however crude it may still be. On this level of consciousness, the things we perceive around us leave their natural, common-sense mode of existence and transform themselves into images and symbols. And those images, when they become systematized and ordered according to the patterns of development which are inherent in them, tend to produce a mythical cosmology.

The shamanic tradition in ancient China did produce such a cosmology. In the *Elegies of Ch'u* to which reference was made in the preceding chapter, we can trace almost step by step and in a very concrete form the actual process by which the shamanic experience of reality produces a peculiar, 'imaginal' cosmology. And by comparing, further, the *Elegies of Ch'u* with a book like *Huai Nan Tzŭ*,[9] we can observe the most intimate relationship that exists between the shamanic cosmology and Taoist metaphysics. There one sees *sur le vif* how the mythical world-view represented by the former develops and is transformed into the ontology of the Way.

Another fact which seems to confirm the existence of a close relationship, both essential and historical, between the Taoist metaphysics and the shamanic vision of the world is found in the history of Taoism after the Warring States period. In fact, the development of Taoism, after having reached its philosophical zenith with Lao-tzŭ and Chuang-tzŭ, goes on steadily describing a curve of 'degeneration' – as it is generally called – even under a strong influence of the *Tao Tê Ching* and *Chuang-tzŭ*, and returns to its original mythopoeic form, revealing thereby its shamanic basis, until it reaches in the Later Han Dynasty a stage at which Taoism becomes almost synonymous with superstition, magic and witchcraft. The outward structure of Taoist metaphysics itself discloses almost no palpable trace of its shamanic background, but in the philosophical description of the *tao* by Lao-tzŭ, for instance, there is undeniably something uncanny and uncouth that would seem to be indicative of its original connection with shamanism.

Lao-tzŭ depicts, as we shall see later in more detail, the Way (*tao*) as Something shadowy and dark, prior to the existence of Heaven and Earth, unknown and unknowable, impenetrable and intangible to the degree of only being properly described as Non-Being, and yet pregnant with forms, images and things, which lie latent in the midst of its primordial obscurity. The metaphysical Way thus depicted has an interesting counterpart in the popular mythopoeic imagination as represented by *Shan Hai Ching*,[10] in which it appears in a fantastic form.

> Three hundred and fifty miles further to the West there is a mountain called Heaven Mountain. The mountain produces much gold and jade. It produces also blue sulphide. And the River Ying takes its rise therefrom and wanders southwestward until it runs into the Valley of Boiling Water. Now in this mountain there lives a Divine Bird whose body is like a yellow sack, red as burning fire, who has six legs and four wings. It is strangely amorphous, having no face, no eyes, but it is very good at singing and dancing. In reality, this Bird is no other than the god Chiang.

In the passage here quoted, two things attract our attention. One is the fact that the monster-bird is described as being good at singing and dancing. The relevance of this point to the particular problem we are now discussing will immediately be understood if one remembers that 'singing and dancing', i.e., ritual dance, invariably accompanies the phenomenon of shamanism. Dancing in ancient China was a powerful means of seeking for the divine Will, of inducing the state of ecstasy in men, and of 'calling down' spirits from the invisible world. The above-mentioned dictionary, *Shuo Wên*, defines the word *wu* (shaman) as 'a woman who is naturally fit for serving the formless (i.e., invisible beings) and who, by means of dancing call down spirits'.[11] It is interesting that the same dictionary explains the character itself which represents this word, 巫, by saying that it pictures a woman dancing with two long sleeves hanging down on the right and the left. In the still earlier stage of its development,[12] it represents the figure of a shaman holding up jade with two hands in front of a spirit or god.

It is also significant that the monster is said to be a bird, which is most probably an indication that the shamanic dancing here in question was some kind of feather-dance in which the shaman was ritually ornamented with a feathered headdress.

The second point to be noticed in the above-given passage from the *Shan Hai Ching* – and this point is of far greater relevance to the

present study than the first – is the particular expression used in the
description of the monster's visage, *hun tun*,[13] which I have provisionally translated above as 'strangely amorphous'. It means a
chaotic state of things, an amorphous state where nothing is clearly
delineated, nothing is clearly distinguishable, but which is far from
being sheer non-being; it is, on the contrary, an extremely obscure
'presence' in which the existence of something – or some things, still
undifferentiated – is vaguely and dimly sensed.

The relation between this word as used in this passage and
Chuang-tzŭ's allegory of the divine Emperor *Hun Tun* has been
noticed long ago by philologists of the Ch'ing dynasty. The commentator of the *Shan Hai Ching*, Pi Yüan, for instance, explicitly
connects this description of the monster with the featureless face of
the Emperor Hun Tun.

The allegory given by Chuang-tzŭ reads as follows:[14]

> The Emperor of the South Sea was called Shu, the Emperor of the
> North Sea was called Hu,[15] and the Emperor of the central domain
> was called Hun Tun.[16] Once, Shu and Hu met in the domain of Hun
> Tun, who treated both of them very well. Thereupon, Shu and Hu
> deliberated together over the way in which they might possibly repay
> his goodness.
> 'All men', they said, 'are possessed of seven orifices for seeing,
> hearing, eating, and breathing. But this one (i.e., Hun Tun) alone
> does not possess any (orifice). Come, let us bore some for him.'
> They went on boring one orifice every day, until on the seventh day
> Hun Tun died.

This story describes in symbolic terms the destructive effect exercised by the essentialist type of philosophy on the Reality. It is a
merciless denunciation of this type of philosophy on behalf of a
peculiar form of existentialist philosophy which, as we shall see
later, Chuang-tzŭ was eager to uphold. Shu and Hu, symbolizing the
precariousness of human existence, met in the central domain of
Hun Tun; they were very kindly treated and they became happy for
a brief period of time as their names themselves indicate. This event
would seem to symbolize the human intellect stepping into the
domain of the supra-sensible world of 'un-differentiation', the
Absolute, and finding a momentary felicity there – the ecstasy of a
mystical intuition of Being, which, regrettably, lasts but for a short
time. Encouraged by this experience, the human intellect, or
Reason, tries to bore holes in the Absolute, that is to say, tries to
mark distinctions and bring out to actuality all the forms that have
remained latent in the original undifferentiation. The result of
'boring' is nothing but the philosophy of Names (*ming*) as represented by Confucius and his school, an essentialist philosophy,
where all things are clearly marked, delineated, and sharply disting-

uished from one another on the ontological level of essences. But the moment orifices were bored in Hun Tun's face, he died. This means that the Absolute can be brought into the grasp of Reason by 'essential' distinctions being made in the reality of the Absolute, and becomes thereby something understandable; but the moment it becomes understandable to Reason, the Absolute dies.

It is not time yet for us to go into the details of the existentialist position taken by Chuang-tzŭ. I simply wanted to show by this example how closely the shamanic mythopoeic imagination was originally related with the birth of Taoist philosophy, and yet, at the same time, how far removed the latter was in its philosophical import from the former.

This sense of distance between shamanism and philosophy may be alleviated to a considerable extent if we place between the two terms of the relation the cosmogonical story – a product of the same mythopoeic mentality – which purports to explain how Heaven and Earth came into being. It is not exactly a 'story'; it is a 'theory' and is meant to be one. It is a result of a serious attempt to describe and explain theoretically the very origin of the world of Being and the process by which all things in the world have come to acquire the forms with which we are now familiar. The cosmogony constitutes in this sense the middle term – structurally, if not historically – between the crude shamanic myth and the highly developed metaphysics of the Way.

Here we give in translation the cosmogony as formulated in the above-mentioned *Huai Nan Tzŭ*:[17]

Heaven and Earth had no form yet. It was a state of formless fluidity; nothing stable, nothing definite. This state is called the Great Beginning. The Great Beginning produced[18] a spotless void. The spotless void produced the Cosmos. The Cosmos produced (the all-pervading) vital energy.[19] The vital energy had in itself distinctions. That which was limpid and light went up hovering in thin layers to form Heaven, while that which was heavy and turbid coagulated and became Earth. The coming together of limpid and fine elements is naturally easy, while the coagulation of heavy and turbid elements is difficult to occur. For this reason, Heaven was the first to be formed, then Earth became established.

Heaven and Earth gathered together the finer elements of their vital energy to form the principles of Negative (*Yin*) and Positive (*Yang*), and the Negative and Positive gathered together the finer elements of their vital energy to constitute the four seasons. The four seasons scattered their vital energy to bring into being the ten thousand things. The caloric energy of the Positive principle, having been accumulated, gave birth to fire, and the essence of the energy of fire became the sun. The energy of coldness peculiar to the Negative principle, having been accumulated became water, and the essence of the energy of water became the moon. The overflow of the sun and the moon, having become refined, turned into stars and planets. Heaven received the sun, moon, stars, and planets. Earth received water, puddles, dust, and soil.

In the passage her quoted we encounter again that undifferentiated, featureless Something, the primordial Chaos, this time as a cosmogonic principle or the Great Beginning, representing the state of affairs before the creation of the world. The Great Beginning is certainly different from the mythical monster of the *Shan Hai Ching* and the metaphysical principle of the *Tao Tê Ching*. But it is evident at the same time that these three are but different 'phenomena' of one and the same thing.

Similarly in a different passage[20] in the same book we read:

> Long long ago, when Heaven and Earth were still non-existent, there were no definite figures, no definite forms. Mysteriously profound, opaque and dark: nothing was distinguishable, nothing was fathomable; limitlessly remote, vast and void; nobody would have discerned its gate.
> Then there were born together two divinities, and they began to rule Heaven and to govern Earth. Infinitely deep (was Heaven), and no one knew where it came to a limit. Vastly extensive (was Earth), and no one knew where it ceased.
> Thereupon (Being) divided itself into the Negative and the Positive, which, then, separated into the eight cardinal directions.
> The hard and the soft complemented each other, and as a result the ten thousand things acquired their definite forms. The gross and confused elements of the vital energy produced animals (including beasts, birds, reptiles and fish). The finer vital energy produced man. This is the reason why the spiritual properly belongs to Heaven, while the bodily belongs to Earth.

Historically speaking, this and similar cosmogonical theories seem to have been considerably influenced by Taoism and its metaphysics. Structurally, however, they furnish a connecting link between myth and philosophy, pertaining as they do to both of them and yet differing from them in spirit and structure. The cosmogony discloses to our eyes in this sense the mythopoeic background of the metaphysics of the Way as formulated by Lao-tzǔ and Chuang-tzǔ.

In a similar fashion, we can bring to light the subjective – i.e., epistemological – aspect of the relationship between shamanism and Taoist philosophy by comparing the above-mentioned *Elegies of Ch'u* and the books of Lao-tzǔ and Chuang-tzǔ. The possibility of obtaining an interesting result from a comparative study of Ch'ü Yüan, the great shaman-poet of the state of Ch'u, and the philosophers of Taoism was noted long ago by Henri Maspero,[21] although death prevented him from fully developing his idea.

In the *Li Sao*[22] and the *Yüan Yu*,[23] the shaman-poet describes in detail the process of visionary states through which a soul in an ecstatic state, helped and assisted by various gods and spirits, ascends to the heavenly city where the 'eternal beings' live. This is in reality nothing but a description of a shamanic *unio mystica*. And the shamanic ascension is paralleled by a visionary ascension of a similar structure in the *Chuang-tzŭ*, the only essential difference between the two being that in the latter case the experience of the spiritual journey is refined and elaborated into the form of a metaphysical contemplation. Just as the shaman-poet experiences in his ecstatic oblivion of the ego a kind of immortality and eternity, so the Taoist philosopher experiences immortality and 'long life' in the midst of the eternal Way, by being unified with it. It is interesting to notice in this respect that the poet says in the final stage of his spiritual experience that he 'transcends the Non-Doing,[24] reaches the primordial Purity, and stands side by side with the Great Beginning'.[25] In Taoist terminology, we would say that the poet at this stage 'stands side by side with the Way', that is, 'is completely unified with the Way', there being no discrepancy between them.

In the *Li Sao* the poet does not ascend to such a height. Standing on the basic assumption that both the *Li Sao* and *Yüan Yu* are authentic works of Ch'ü Yüan, Maspero remarks that the *Li Sao* represents an earlier stage in the spiritual development of the poet, at which he, as a shaman, has not yet attained to the final goal, whereas the *Yüan Yu* represents a later stage at which the poet 'has already reached the extremity of mysticism'.

Such an interpretation is of course untenable if we know for certain that the *Yüan Yu* is a work composed by a later poet and surreptitiously attributed to Ch'ü Yüan. In any case, the poem in its actual form is markedly Taoistic, and some of the ideas are undeniably borrowings from Lao-tzŭ and Chuang-tzŭ. Here again, however, the problem of authenticity is by no means a matter of primary importance to us. For even if we admit that the poem – or some parts of – it is a Han Dynasty forgery, it remains true that the very fact that Taoist metaphysics could be so naturally transformed – or brought back – into a shamanic world-vision is itself a proof of a real congeniality that existed between shamanism and Taoism.

A detailed analytic comparison between the *Elegies of Ch'u* and the books of Lao-tzŭ and Chuang-tzŭ is sure to make an extremely fruitful and rewarding work. But to do so will take us too far afield beyond the main topic of the present study. Besides, we are going to describe in detail in the first chapters of this book the philosophical version of the spiritual journey which has just been mentioned. And this must suffice us for our present purposes.

Let us now leave the problem of the shamanic origin of Taoism, and turn to the purely philosophical aspects of the latter. Our main concern will henceforward be exclusively with the actual structure of Taoist metaphysics and its key-concepts.

Notes

1. 聖人.

2. 眞人.

3. 至人, i.e., a man who has attained to the furthest limit (of perfection).

4. 神人. We may note that this and the preceding words all refer to one and the same concept which is the Taoist counterpart of the concept of *insân kâmil* or the Perfect Man, which we discussed in the first part of this study.

5. 「說文解字」: 「聖通也, 從耳王聲」.

6. Reference has been made in the preceding chapter to the possible historical connection between the Yin dynasty and the spirit of the state of Ch'u.

7. For more details about the problem of the shaman ((巫 wu) representing the highest administrative power in the non-secularized state in ancient China, see for example Liang Ch'i Ch'ao: *A History of Political Thought in the Periods Prior to the Ch'in Dynasty* 梁啓超 「先秦政治思想史」, 1923, Shanghai, Ch. II.

8. I would refer the reader to Mircea Eliade's basic work: *Shamanism, Archaic Techniques of Ecstasy*, English tr., London, 1964.

9. 「淮南子」, an eclectic work compiled by thinkers of various schools who were gathered by the king of Huai Nan, Liu An 劉安, at his court, in the second century B.C. The book is of an eclectic nature, but its basic thought is that of the Taoist school.

10. 「山海經」, one of the most important source-books for Chinese mythology, giving a detailed description of all kinds of mythological monsters living in mountains and seas. The following quotation is taken from a new edition of the book, 「山海經新校正」, (國學基本叢書), with a commentary by Pi Yüan of the Ch'ing dynasty, Tai Pei, 1945, p. 57.

11. 巫＝女能事無形以舞降神者也.

12. The character 巫 as it appears in the oracle-bones is: 爪 or 爪.

13. 渾敦. The word is written in the *Chuang-tzŭ* 渾沌.

14. Chapter VII entitled 'Fit to be Emperors and Kings', p. 309.

15. Both *shu* (儵) and *hu* (忽) literally mean a brief span of time, symbolizing in this allegory the precariousness of existence.

16. Important to note is the fact that *hun tun*, the 'undifferentiation' is placed in the center. It means that *hun tun* represents the true 'reality' of Being, bordering on both sides on 'precariousness'. The philosophical implication of all this will be elucidated in a later chapter.

17. 「淮南子」, III, *T'ien Wên* 天文訓.

18. The received text as it stands is apparently unintelligible. Following the emendation suggested by Wang Yin Chih (王引之) I read: 「故曰大昭道始于虛霩……」.

19. The 'all-pervading vital energy' is a clumsy translation of the Chinese word *ch'i* 氣, which plays an exceedingly important rôle in the history of Chinese thought. It is a 'reality', proto-material and formless, which cannot be grasped by the senses. It is a kind of vital force, a creative principle of all things; it pervades the whole world, and being immanent in everything, molds it and makes it grow into what it really is. Everything that has a 'form', whether animate or inanimate, has a share in the *ch'i*. The concept of *ch'i* has been studied by many scholars. As one of the most detailed analytic studies of it we may mention Teikichi Hiraoka: *A Study of Ch'i in Huai Nan Tzŭ*, 平岡禎吉「淮南子に現われた氣の研究」, Tokyo 1969.

20. *ibid.*, VII, 精神訓.

21. *ibid.*, III.

22. 「離騷」.

23. 「遠遊」. Many scholars entertain serious doubts – with reason, I think – as to the authenticity of this important and interesting work. Most probably it is a product of the Han Dynasty (see 胡濬源「楚辭新註求確」), composed in the very atmosphere of a fully developed philosophy of Taoism.

24. *wu-wei* 無爲, one of the key-terms of Taoist philosophy, which we shall analyze in a later passage. 'Non-Doing' means, in short, man's abandoning all artificial, unnatural effort to do something, and identifying himself completely with the activity of Nature which is nothing other than the spontaneous self-manifestation of the Way itself. Here the poet claims that at the final stage of his spiritual development he goes even beyond the level of 'non-activity' and of being one with Nature, and steps further into the very core of the Way. In his consciousness – or in his 'non-consciousness', we should rather say – his is no longer a human being; he is deified.

25. 「超無爲以至清兮，與泰初而爲隣」.

III Dream and Reality

In the foregoing chapter we talked about the myth of Chaos, the primordial undifferentiation which preceded the beginning of the cosmos. In its original shamanic form, the figure of Chaos as a featureless monster looks very bizarre, primitive and grotesque. Symbolically, however, it is of profound importance, for the philosophical idea symbolized by it directly touches the core of the reality of Being.

In the view of Lao-tzŭ and Chuang-tzŭ, the reality of Being *is* Chaos. And therein lies the very gist of their ontology. But this proposition does not mean that the world we live in is simply chaotic and disorderly as an empirical fact. For the empirical world, as we daily observe it, is far from being as 'featureless' and 'amorphous' as the face of the bird-monster of the *Shan Hai Ching*. On the contrary, it is a world where we observe many things that are clearly distinguishable from one another, each having its peculiar 'name', and each being definitely delineated and determined. Everything therein has its own place; the things are neatly ordered in a hierarchy. We live in such a world, and do perceive our world in such a light. According to the Taoist philosophers, that precisely is the malady of our Reason. And it is difficult for an ordinary mind not to see the distinctions in the world. The world, in brief, is *not* chaotic.

It will be the first task of a Chuang-tzŭ to shatter to pieces these seemingly watertight compartments of Being, allowing us to have a glimpse into the fathomless depth of primeval Chaos. But this is not in any way an easy task. Chuang-tzŭ actually tries many different approaches. Probably the easiest of them all for us to understand is his attempt at the 'chaotification' – if we are allowed to coin such a word – of 'dream' and 'reality'. By a seemingly very simple descriptive and narrative language, he tries to raise us immediately to an ontological level where 'dream' and 'reality' cease to be distinguishable from each other,[1] and merge together into something 'amorphous'.

The following is a very famous passage in the *Chuang-tzŭ*, in which the sage tries to give us a glimpse of the 'chaotification' of things:[2]

> Once, I, Chuang Chou,[3] dreamt that I was a butterfly. Flitting about at ease and to my heart's content, I *was* indeed a butterfly. Happy and cheerful, I had no consciousness of being Chou. All of a sudden I awoke, and lo, I was Chou. Did Chou dream that he was a butterfly? Or did the butterfly dream that it was Chou? How do I know? There *is*, however, undeniably a difference between Chou and a butterfly. This situation is what I would call the Transmutation of things.

The latter half of this passage touches upon the central theme of Chuang-tzŭ. In the kind of situation here described, he himself and the butterfly have become undistinguishable, each having lost his or its essential self-identity. And yet, he says, 'there is undeniably a difference between Chou and a butterfly'. This last statement refers to the situation of things in the phenomenal world, which man ordinarily calls 'reality'. On this level of existence, 'man' cannot be 'butterfly', and 'butterfly' cannot be 'man'. These two things which are thus definitely different and distinguishable from each other do lose their distinction on a certain level of human consciousness, and go into the state of undifferentiation – Chaos.

This ontological situation is called by Chuang-tzŭ the Transmutation of things, *wu hua*.[4] The *wu hua* is one of the most important key-terms of Chuang-tzŭ's philosophy. It will be dealt with in detail presently. Here I shall give in translation another passage in which the same concept is explained through similar images.[5]

> A man drinks wine in a dream, and weeps and wails in the morning (when he awakes). A man weeps in a (sad) dream, but in the morning he goes joyously hunting. While he is dreaming he is not aware that he is dreaming; he even tries (in his dream) to interpret his dream. Only after he awakes from sleep does he realize that it was a dream. Likewise, only when one experiences a Great Awakening does one realize that all this[6] is but a Big Dream. But the stupid imagine that they are actually awake. Deceived by their petty intelligence,[7] they consider themselves smart enough to differentiate between what is noble and what is ignoble. How deep-rooted and irremediable their stupidity is!
> In reality, however, both I and you are a dream. Nay, the very fact that I am telling you that you are dreaming is itself a dream!
> This kind of statement is liable to be labeled bizarre sophistry. (But it looks so precisely because it reveals the Truth), and a great sage capable of penetrating its mystery is barely to be expected to appear in the world in ten thousand years.

The same idea is repeated in the following passage:[8]

Suppose you dream that you are a bird. (In that state) you do soar up into the sky. Suppose you dream that you are a fish. You do go down deep into the pool. (While you are experiencing all this in your dream, what you experience *is* your 'reality'.) Judging by this, nobody can be sure whether we – you and I, who are actually engaged in conversation in this way – are awake or just dreaming.[9]

Such a view reduces the distinction between Me and Thee to a mere semblance, or at least it renders the distinction very doubtful and groundless.

Each one of us is convinced that 'this' *is* I (and consequently 'other than this' is You or He). On reflexion, however, how do I know for sure that this 'I' which I consider as 'I' is really my 'I'?[10]

Thus even my own 'ego' which I regard as the most solid and reliable core of existence, – and the only absolutely indubitable entity even when I doubt the existence of everything else, in the Cartesian sense – becomes transformed all of a sudden into something dreamlike and unreal.

Thus by what might seem 'bizarre sophistry' Chuang-tzŭ reduces everything to a Big Dream. This abrupt negation of 'reality' is but a first step into his philosophy, for his philosophy does have a positive side. But before disclosing the positive side – which our 'petty intelligence' can never hope to understand – he deals a mortal blow to this 'intelligence' and Reason by depriving them of the very ground on which they stand.

The world is a dream; that which we ordinarily consider solid 'reality' is a dream. Furthermore, the man who tells others that everything is a dream, and those who are listening to his teaching, are all part of a dream.

What does Chuang-tzŭ want to suggest by this? He wants to suggest that Reality in the real sense of the word is something totally different from what Reason regards as 'reality'. In order to grasp the true meaning of this, our normal consciousness must first lose its self-identity. And together with the 'ego', all the objects of its perception and intellection must also lose their self-identities and be brought into a state of confusion which we called above the primordial Chaos. This latter is an ontological level at which 'dream' and 'reality' lose the essential distinction between them, at which the significance itself of such distinctions is lost. On its subjective side, it is a state of consciousness in which nothing any longer remains 'itself', and anything can be anything else. It is an entirely new order of Being, where all beings, liberated from the shackles of their semantic determinations freely transform themselves into one another. This is what Chuang-tzŭ calls the Transmutation of things.

The Transmutation of things, as conceived by Chuang-tzŭ, must be understood in terms of two different points of reference. On the one hand, it designates a metaphysical situation in which all things are found to be 'transmutable' to one another, so much so that ultimately they become merged together into an absolute Unity. In this sense it transcends 'time'; it is a supra-temporal order of things. In the eye of one who has experienced the Great Awakening, all things are One; all things *are* the Reality itself. At the same time, however, this unique Reality discloses to his eye a kaleidoscopic view of infinitely various and variegated things which are 'essentially' different one from another, and the world of Being, in this aspect, is manifold and multiple. Those two aspects are to be reconciled with each other by our considering these 'things' as so many phenomenal forms of the absolute One. The 'unity of existence', thus understood, constitutes the very core of the philosophy of Lao-tzŭ and Chuang-tzŭ.

The same Transmutation can, on the other hand, be understood as a temporal process. And this is also actually done by Chuang-tzŭ. A thing, *a*, continues to subsist as *a* for some time; then, when the limit which has been naturally assigned to it comes,[11] it ceases to be *a* and becomes transmuted or transformed into another thing, *b*. From the viewpoint of supra-temporality, *a* and *b* are metaphysically one and the same thing, the difference between them being merely a matter of phenomenon. In this sense, even before *a* ceases to be *a* – that is, from the beginning – *a* is *b*, and *b* is *a*. There is, then, no question of *a* 'becoming' *b*, because *a*, by the very fact that it is *a*, is already *b*.

From the second viewpoint, however, *a* is *a* and nothing else. And this *a* 'becomes', in a temporal process, something else, *b*. The former 'changes' into the latter. But here again we run into the same metaphysical Unity, by, so to speak, a roundabout way. For *a*, by 'becoming' and 'changing into' *b*, refers itself back to its own origin and source. The whole process constitutes an ontological circle, because through the very act of becoming *b*, *a* simply 'becomes' itself – only in a different form.

Applied to the concepts of 'life' and 'death', such an idea naturally produces a peculiar Philosophy of Life, a basically optimistic view of human existence. It is 'optimisic' because it completely obliterates the very distinction between Life and Death. Viewed in this light, the so-called problem of Death turns out to be but a pseudo-problem.

Although it is thus a pseudo-problem from the point of view of those who have seen the Truth, Chuang-tzŭ often takes up this theme and develops his thought around it. Indeed, it is one of his most favorite topics. This is so because actually it *is* a problem, or *the* problem. Death, in particular, happens to be the most disquieting problem for the ordinary mind. And a man's having overcome the existential *angoisse* of being faced constantly and at every moment with the horror of his own annihilation is the sign of his being at the stage of a 'true man'. Besides, since it happens to be such a vital problem, its solution is sure to bring home to the mind the significance of the concept of Transmutation. Otherwise, everything else is exactly in the same ontological situation as Life and Death.

Now to go back to the point at which Chuang-tzŭ has reduced everything to a dreamlike mode of existence. Nothing in the world of Being is solidly self-subsistent. In scholastic terminology we might describe the situation by saying that nothing has – except in semblance and appearance – an unchangeable 'quiddity' or 'essence'. And in this fluid state of things, we are no longer sure of the self-identity of anything whatsoever. We never know whether *a* is really *a* itself.

And this essential dreamlike uncertainty of indetermination naturally holds true of Life and Death. The conceptual structure of this statement will easily be seen if one replaces the terms Life and Death by *a* and *b*, and tries to represent the whole situation in terms of the *a-b* pattern which has been given above.

Speaking of a 'true man' from the state of Lu, Chuang-tzŭ says:

> He does not care to know why he lives. Nor does he care to know why he dies. He does not even know which comes first and which comes last. (i.e., Life and Death are in his mind undifferentiated from each other, the distinction between them being insignificant). Following the natural course of Transmutation he has become a certain thing; now he is simply awaiting further Transmutation.
> Besides, when a man is undergoing Transmutation, how can he be sure that he is (in reality) not being transmuted? And when he is not undergoing Transmutation, how can he be sure that he has (in reality) not already been transmuted?[12]

In a similar passage concerned with the problem of Death and the proper attitude of 'true men' toward it, Chuang-tzŭ lets Confucius make the following statement.[13] Confucius here, needless to say, is a fictitious figure having nothing to do with the historical person, but there is of course a touch of irony in the very fact that Confucius is made to make such a remark.

> They (i.e., the 'true men') are those who freely wander beyond the boundaries (i.e., the ordinary norms of proper behavior), while men like myself are those who wander freely only within the boundaries. 'Beyond the boundaries' and 'within the boundaries' are poles asunder from one another.

They are those who, being completely unified with the Creator Himself, take delight in being in the realm of the original Unity of the vital energy[14] before it is divided into Heaven and Earth.
To their minds Life (or Birth) is just the growth of an excrescence, a wart, and Death is the breaking of a boil, the bursting of a tumor. Such being the case, how should we expect them to care about the question as to which is better and which is worse – Life or Death? They simply borrow different elements, and put them together in the common form of a body.[15] Hence they are conscious neither of their liver nor of their gall, and they leave aside their ears and eyes.[16] Abandoning themselves to infinitely recurrent waves of Ending and Beginning, they go on revolving in a circle, of which they know neither the beginning-point nor the ending-point.

For Chuang-tzŭ Death is nothing but one of the endlessly variegated phenomenal forms of one eternal Reality. To our mind's eye this metaphysical Reality actualizes itself and develops itself as a process evolving in time. But even when conceived in such a temporal form, the process depicts only an eternally revolving circle, of which no one knows the real beginning and the real end. Death is but a stage in this circle. When it occurs, one particular phenomenal form is effaced from the circle and disappears only to reappear as an entirely different phenomenal form. Nature continuously makes and unmakes. But the circle itself, that is, Reality itself is always there unchanged and unperturbed. Being one with Reality, the mind of a 'true man' never becomes perturbed.

A 'true man', Chuang-tzŭ related,[17] saw his own body hideously deformed in the last days of his life. He hobbled to a well, looked at his image reflected in the water and said, 'Alas! That the Creator has made me so crooked and deformed!' Thereupon a friend of his asked him, 'Do you resent your condition?' Here is the answer that the dying 'true man' gave to this question:

No, why should I resent it? It may be that the process of Transmutation will change my left arm into a rooster. I would, then, simply use it to crow to tell the coming of the morning. It may be that the process goes on and might change my right arm into a crossbow. I would, then, simply use it to shoot down a bird for roasting. It may be that the process will change my buttocks into a wheel and my spirit into a horse. I would, then, simply ride in the carriage. I would not have even to put another horse to it.
Whatever we obtain (i.e., being born into this world in a particular form) is due to the coming of the time. Whatever we lose (i.e., death) is also due to the arrival of the turn. We must be content with the 'time' and accept the 'turn'. Then neither sorrow nor joy will ever creep in. Such an attitude used to be called among the Ancients 'loosing the tie'.[18] If man cannot loose himself from the tie, it is because 'things' bind him fast.

Another 'true man' had a visit in his last moments from one of his friends, who was also a 'true man'. The conversation between them as related by Chuang-tzŭ[19] is interesting. The visitor seeing the wife and children who stood around the man on the deathbed weeping and wailing, said to them, 'Hush! Get away! Do not disturb him as he is passing through the process of Transmutation!'

Then turning to the dying man, he said:

> How great the Creator is! What is he going to make of you now? Whither is he going to take you? Is he going to make of you a rat's liver? Or is he going to make of you an insect's arm?'

To this the dying man replies:

> (No matter what the Creator makes of me, I accept the situation and follow his command.) Don't you see? In the relationship between a son and his parents, the son goes wherever they command him to go, east, west, south, or north. But the relation between the Yin-Yang (i.e., the Law regulating the cosmic process of Becoming) and a man is incomparably closer than the relation between him and his parents. Now they (the Yin and Yang) have brought me to the verge of death. Should I refuse to submit to them, it would simply be an act of obstinacy on my part . . .
> Suppose here is a great master smith, casting metal. If the metal should jump up and begin to shout, 'I must be made into a sword like Mo Yeh,[20] nothing else!' The smith would surely regard the metal as something very evil. (The same would be true of) a man who, on the ground that he has by chance assumed a human form, should insist and say: 'I want to be a man, only man! Nothing else!' The Creator would surely regard him as of a very evil nature.
> Just imagine the whole world as a big furnace, and the Creator as a master smith. Wherever we may go, everything will be all right. Calmly we will go to sleep (i.e., die), and suddenly we will find ourselves awake (in a new form of existence).

The concept of the Transmutation of things as conceived by Chuang-tzŭ might seem to resemble the doctrine of 'transmigration'. But the resemblance is only superficial. Chuang-tzŭ does not say that the soul goes on transmigrating from one body to another. The gist of his thought on this point is that everything is a phenomenal form of one unique Reality which goes on assuming successively different forms of self-manifestation. Besides, as we have seen before, this temporal process itself is but a phenomenon. Properly speaking, all this is something taking place on an eternal, a-temporal level of Being. All things *are* one eternally, beyond Time and Space.

Notes

1. We may do well to recall at this stage a chapter in the first part of the present study, where we took the undifferentiation or indistinction between 'dream' and 'reality' as our starting-point for going into the metaphysical world of Ibn 'Arabî. There Ibn 'Arabî speaks of the ontological level of 'images' and 'similitudes'. Chuang-tzǔ, as we shall see presently, uses a different set of concepts for interpreting his basic vision. But the visions themselves of these two thinkers are surprisingly similar to each other.

2. II, p. 112. The heading itself of this Chapter, *ch'i wu* 齊物, is quite significant in this respect, meaning as it does 'equalization of things'.

3. 莊周, the real name of Chuang-tzǔ.

4. 物化, meaning literally: 'things-transform'.

5. II., pp. 104–105.

6. i.e., everything that one experiences in this world of so-called 'reality'. 'Great Awakening': *ta chüeh* 大覺.

7. i.e., being unaware of the fact that 'life' itself, the 'reality' itself is but a dream.

8. VI., p. 275.

9. i.e., it may very well be that somebody – or something – is dreaming that he (or it) is a man, and thinks in the dream that he is talking with somebody else.

10. *ibid.*

11. This problem will be dealt with in detail in a later chapter which will be devoted to the problem of determinism and freedom in the world-view of Taoism.

12. The meaning of this sentence can, I think, be paraphrazed as follows. It may well be that 'being transmuted' (for example, from Life to Death, i.e., 'to die') *is* in reality 'not to be transmuted' (i.e., 'not to die'). Likewise nobody knows for sure whether by 'not being transmuted' (i.e., remaining alive without dying) he has already been transmuted (i.e., is already dead). The original sentence runs: 且方將化惡知不化哉. 方將不化惡知已化. Kuo Hsiang in his commentary – which happens to be the oldest commentary now in existence – explains it by saying: 已化而生, 焉知未生之時哉. 未化而死, 焉知已死之後哉, (p. 276), meaning; 'Once transmuted into a living being, how can a man know the state of affairs which preceded his birth? And while he is not yet transmuted and is not yet dead, how can he know the state of affairs that will come after death?' I mention this point because many people follow Kuo Hsiang's interpretation in understanding the present passage. (VI, p. 274).

13. VI, pp. 267–268.

14. i.e., the primordial cosmic energy which, as we saw in the last chapter, is thought to have existed before the creation of the world. It refers to the cosmogonic state in which neither Heaven and Earth nor the Negative and the Positive were yet divided. Philosophically it means the metaphysical One in its pure state of Unity.

15. According to their view, human existence is nothing but a provisional pheno-

menal form composed by different elements (i.e., four basic elements: earth, air, water and fire) which by chance have been united in the physical form of a body.

16. They do not pay any attention to their physical existence.

17. VI, pp. 259–260.

18. *Hsien chieh* 縣解, 'loosing the tie', i.e., an absolute freedom.

19. *ibid.*, p. 261–262.

20. A noted sword made in the state of Wu (吳) in the sixth century B.C.

IV Beyond This and That

We have seen in the last pages of the preceding chapter how Chuang-tzǔ obliterates the distinction or opposition between Life and Death and brings them back to the original state of 'undifferentiation'. We have spent some time on the subject because it is one of Chuang-tzǔ's favorite topics, and also because it discloses to our eyes an important aspect of his philosophy.

Properly speaking, however, and from an ontological point of view, Life and Death should not occupy such a privileged place. For all so-called 'opposites' are not, in Chuang-tzǔ's philosophy, really opposed to each other. In fact, nothing, in his view, is opposed to anything else, because nothing has a firmly established 'essence' in its ontological core. In the eye of a man who has ever experienced the 'chaotification' of things, everything loses its solid contour, being deprived of its 'essential' foundation. All ontological distinctions between things become dim, obscure, and confused, if not completely destroyed. The distinctions are certainly still there, but they are no longer significant, 'essential'. And 'opposites' are no longer 'opposites' except conceptually. 'Beautiful' and 'ugly', 'good' and 'bad', 'right' and 'wrong', 'pious' and 'impious' – all these and other conceptual pairs which are sharply distinguished, at the level of Reason, and which actually play a leading rôle in human life, are found to be far from being absolute.

This attitude of Chuang-tzǔ toward the 'opposites' and 'distinctions' which are generally accepted as cultural, esthetic, or ethical 'values', would appear to be neither more nor less than so-called relativism. The same is true of Lao-tzǔ's attitude. And, in fact, it *is* a relativist view of values. It is of the utmost importance, however, to keep in mind that it is not an ordinary sort of relativism as understood on the empirical or pragmatic level of social life. It is a peculiar kind of relativism based on a very peculiar kind of mystical intuition: a mystical intuition of the Unity and Multiplicity of existence. It is a philosophy of 'undifferentiation' which is a natural product of a metaphysical experience of Reality, an experience in which Reality is directly witnessed as it unfolds and diversifies itself into myriads of things and then goes back again to the original Unity.

This 'metaphysical' basis of Taoist relativism will be dealt with in detail in the following chapter. Here we shall confine ourselves to the 'relativist' side of this philosophy, and try to pursue Chuang-tzǔ and Lao-tzǔ as closely as possible as they go on developing their ideas on this particular aspect of the problem.

As I have just pointed out, the attitude of both Chuang-tzǔ and Lao-tzǔ toward the so-called cultural values would on its surface appear to be nothing other than 'relativism' in the commonly accepted sense of the term. Let us first examine this point by quoting a few appropriate passages from the two books. Even at this preliminary stage of analysis, we shall clearly observe that this relativism is directed against the 'essentialist' position of the school of Confucius. In the last sentence of the following passage[1] there is an explicit reference to the Confucian standpoint.

> If a human being sleeps in a damp place, he will begin to suffer from backache, and finally will become half paralyzed. But is this true of a mudfish? If (a human being) lives in a tree, he will have to be constantly trembling from fear and be frightened. But is this true of a monkey? Now which of these three (i.e., man, mudfish and monkey) knows the (absolutely) right place to live?[2]
>
> Men eat beef and pork; deer eat grass; centipedes find snakes delicious; kites and crows enjoy mice. Of these four which one knows the (absolutely) good taste?
>
> A monkey finds its mate in a monkey; a deer mates with a deer. And mudfishes enjoy living with other fishes. Mao Ch'iang and Li Chi[3] are regarded as ideally beautiful women by all men. And yet, if fish happen to see a beauty like them, they will dive deep in the water; birds will fly aloft; and deer will run away in all directions. Of these four, which one knows the (absolute) ideal of beauty?
>
> These considerations lead me to conclude that the boundaries between 'benevolence' (*jēn*) and 'righteousness' (*i*),[4] and the limits between 'right' and 'wrong' are (also) extremely uncertain and confused, so utterly and inextricably confused that we can never know how to discriminate (between what is absolutely right and what is absolutely wrong, etc.).

This kind of relativism is also found in the book of Lao-tzǔ. The underlying conception is exactly the same as in the book of Chuang-tzǔ; so also the reason for which he upholds such a view. As we shall see later, Lao-tzǔ, too, looks at the apparent distinctions, oppositions and contradictions from the point of view of the metaphysical One in which all things lose their sharp edges of conceptual discrimination and become blended and harmonized.

The only difference between Chuang-tzŭ and Lao-tzŭ in this respect is that the latter expresses himself in a very terse, concise, and apothegmatic form, while the former likes to develop his thought in exuberant imagery. Otherwise, the idea itself is common to both of them. In the first of the following quotations from the *Tao Tê Ching*, for instance, Lao-tzŭ implicitly criticizes the cultural essentialism of the Confucian school.[5]

> Cast off Learning,[6] and there will be no worries. How much in fact, difference is there between 'yes, sir' and 'hum!'? Between 'good' and 'bad' what distinction is there? 'Whatever others respect I also must respect', (they say).
> Oh, how far away I am from the common people (who adhere to such an idea). For (on such a principle) there will be absolutely no limit to the vast field (of petty distinctions).

People tend to imagine, Lao-tzŭ says, that things are essentially distinguishable from one another, and the Confucians have built up an elaborate system of moral values precisely on the notion that everything is marked off from others by its own 'essence'. They seem to be convinced that these 'distinctions' are all permanent and unalterable. In reality, however, they are simply being deceived by the external and phenomenal aspects of Being. A man whose eyes are not veiled by this kind of deception sees the world of Being as a vast and limitless space where things merge into one another. This ontological state of things is nothing other than what Chuang-tzŭ calls Chaos. On the cultural level, such a view naturally leads to relativism. Lao-tzŭ describes the latter in the following way:[7]

> By the very fact that everybody in the world recognizes 'beautiful' as 'beautiful', the idea of 'ugly' comes into being. By the very fact that all men recognize 'good' as 'good', the idea of 'bad' comes into being. Exactly in the same way 'existence' and 'non-existence' give birth to one another; 'difficult' and 'easy' complement one another; 'long' and 'short' appear in contrast to one another; 'high' and 'low' incline toward each other; 'tone' and 'voice' keep harmony with one another; 'before' and 'behind' follow one another.

Everything, in short, is relative; nothing is absolute. We live in a world of relative distinctions and relative antitheses. But the majority of men do not realize that these are relative. They tend to think that a thing which they – or social convention – regard as 'beautiful' *is* by essence 'beautiful', thus regarding all those things that do not conform to a certain norm as 'ugly' by essence. By taking such an attitude they simply ignore the fact that the distinction between the two is merely a matter of viewpoint.

As I remarked earlier, such equalization of opposites surely is 'relativism', but it is a relativism based on, or stemming from, a very remarkable intuition of the ontological structure of the world. The original intuition is common both to Lao-tzŭ and Chuang-tzŭ. But with the latter, it leads to the 'chaotic' view of things, the essential 'undifferentiation' of things, which in its dynamic aspect is conceived as the Transmutation of things. In the case of Lao-tzŭ, the same intuition leads, in its dynamic aspect, to an ontology of evolvement and in-volvement, the static aspect of which is the relativism we have just discussed.

As Transmutation (*hua*) is the key-word of Chuang-tzŭ in this section of his philosophy, Return (*fan*[8] or *fu*[9]) is the key-term which Lao-tzŭ chooses as an appropriate expression for his idea.

On the cosmic significance of the Return as understood by Lao-tzŭ we shall have occasion to talk in a later context. Here we shall confine ourselves to considering this concept in so far as it has direct relevance to the problem of relativism.

The Return is a dynamic concept. It refers, in other words, to the dynamic aspect of the above-mentioned relativism of Lao-tzŭ, or the dynamic ontological basis on which it stands. He explicates this concept in a terse form in the following passage, which may in fact be considered an epitome of the whole of his ontology.[10]

> Returning is how the Way moves, and being weak is how the Way works. The ten thousand things under heaven are born from Being, and Being is born from Non-Being.

It is to be remarked that there is in this passage a covert reference to two different meanings or aspects of 'returning' which Lao-tzŭ seems to recognize in the ontological structure of all things. The first meaning (or aspect) is suggested by the first sentence and the second meaning by the second sentence. The first sentence means that everything (*a*) that exists contains in itself a possibility or natural tendency to 'return', i.e., to be transformed into its opposite (*b*), which, of course, again contains the same possibility of 'returning' to its opposite, namely the original state from which it has come (*a*). Thus all things are constantly in the process of a circular movement, from *a* to *b*, and then from *b* to *a*. This is, Lao-tzŭ says, the rule of the ontological 'movement' (*tung*),[11] or the dynamic aspect of Reality. And he adds that 'weakness' is the way this movement is made by Reality.

The next sentence considers the dynamic structure of Reality as a vertical, metaphysical movement from the phenomenal Many to the pre-phenomenal One. Starting from the state of multiplicity in which all things are actualized and realized, it traces them back to their ultimate origin. The 'ten thousand things under heaven', i.e., all things in the world, come into actual being from the Way at its stage of 'existence'. But the stage of 'existence', which is nothing other than a stage in the process of self-manifestation of the Way, comes into being from the stage of 'non-existence', which is the abysmal depth of the absolutely unknown-unknowable Way itself. It is to be observed that this 'tracing-back' of the myriad things to 'existence' and then to 'non-existence' is not only a conceptual process; it is, for Lao-tzǔ, primarily a cosmic process. All things ontologically 'return' to their ultimate source, undergoing on their way 'circular' transformations among themselves such as have been suggested by the first sentence. This cosmic return of all things to the ultimate origin will be a subject of discussion in a later chapter. Here we are concerned with the 'horizontal' Return of things as referred to in the first sentence, i.e., the process of reciprocal 'returning' between *a* and *b*. Lao-tzǔ has a peculiar way of expressing this idea as exemplified by the two following passages.

> Misfortune is what good fortune rests upon and good fortune is what misfortune lurks in. (The two thus turn into one another indefinitely, so that) nobody knows the point where the process comes to an end. There seems to be no absolute norm. For what is (considered) just 're-turns' to unjust, and what is (considered) good 're-turns' to evil. Indeed man has long been in perplexity about this.[12]

> The nature of things is such that he who goes in front ends by falling behind, and he who follows others ultimately finds himself in front of others. He who blows upon a thing to make it warm ends by making it cold, and he who blows upon a thing to make it cold finally makes it warm. He who tries to become strong becomes weak, and he who wants to remain weak turns strong. He who is safe falls into danger, while he who is in danger ends by becoming safe.[13]

Thus in the view of both Chuang-tzǔ and Lao-tzǔ, everything in the world is relative; nothing is absolutely reliable or stable in this sense. As I have indicated before, this 'relativism', in the case of Lao-tzǔ and Chuang-tzǔ, must be understood in a peculiar sense, namely, in the sense that nothing has what is called 'essence' or 'quiddity'.

All things, on the deeper level of Reality, are 'essence-less'. The world itself is 'chaotic'. This is not only true of the external world in which we exist, but is equally true of the world within us, the internal world of concepts and judgments. This is not hard to understand, because whatever judgment we may make on whatever thing we choose to talk about in this 'chaotic' world, our judgment is bound to be relative, one-sided, ambiguous, and unreliable, for the object of the judgment is itself ontologically relative.

The argument which Chuang-tzǔ puts forward on this point is logically very interesting and important. The Warring States period witnessed a remarkable development of logico-semantical theories in China. In the days of Chuang-tzǔ, Confucians and Mohists[14] stood sharply opposed to each other, and these two schools were together opposed to the Dialecticians[15] (or Sophists) otherwise known as the school of Names[16]. Heated debates were being held among them about the foundation of human culture, its various phenomena, the basis of ethics, the logical structure of thought, etc., etc.. And it was a fashion to conduct discussions of this kind in a dialectical form. 'This is right' – 'this is wrong' or 'this is good' – 'this is bad', was the general formula by which these people discussed their problems.

Such a situation is simply ridiculous and all these discussions are futile from the point of view of a Chuang-tzǔ for whom Reality itself is 'chaotic'. The objects themselves about which these people exchange heated words are essentially unstable and ambiguous. The Dialecticians 'are talking about the distinction between "hard" and "white", for example, as if these could be hung on different pegs'.[17]

Not only that. Those who like to discuss in this way usually commit a fatal mistake by confusing 'having the best of an argument' with 'being objectively right', and 'being cornered in an argument' with 'being objectively wrong'. In reality, however, victory and defeat in a logical dispute in no way determines the 'right' and 'wrong' of an objective fact.

> Suppose you and I enter into discussion. And suppose you beat me, and I cannot beat you. Does this mean that you are 'right' and that I am 'wrong'?
> Suppose I beat you, instead, and you cannot beat me. Does this mean that I am 'right' and you are 'wrong'? Is it the case that when I am 'right' you are 'wrong', and when you are 'right' I am 'wrong'? Or are we both 'right' or both 'wrong'? It is not for me and you to decide. (What about asking some other person to judge?) But other people are in the same darkness. Whom shall we ask to give a fair judgment? Suppose we let someone who agrees with you judge. How could such a man give a fair judgment seeing that he shared from the beginning the same opinion with you? Suppose we let someone who agrees with me judge. How could he give a fair judgment, seeing that he shares from the beginning the same opinion with me?
> What if we let someone judge who differs from both you and me? But he is from the beginning at variance with both of us. How could such a man give a fair judgment? (He would simply give a third opinion.)
> What if we let someone judge who agrees with both of us? But from the beginning he shares the same opinion with both of us. How could such a man give a fair judgment? (He would simply say that I am 'right', but you also are 'right'.)
> From these considerations we must conclude that neither you nor I

nor the third person can know (where the truth lies). Shall we expect a fourth person to appear?[18]

How is this situation to be accounted for? Chuang-tzŭ answers that all this confusion originates in the natural tendency of the Reason to think everything in terms of the opposition of 'right' and 'wrong'. And this natural tendency of our Reason is based on, or a product of, an essentialist view of Being. The natural Reason is liable to think that a thing which is conventionally or subjectively 'right' is 'right' essentially, and that a thing which is 'wrong' is 'wrong' essentially. In truth, however, nothing is *essentially* 'right' or 'wrong'. So-called 'right' and 'wrong' are all relative matters.

In accordance with this non-essentialist position, Chuang-tzŭ asserts that the only justifiable attitude for us to take is to know, first of all, the relativity of 'right' and 'wrong', and then to transcend this relativism itself into the stage of the 'equalization' of all things, a stage at which all things are essentially undifferentiated from one another, although they are, at a lower stage of reality, *relatively* different and distinct from each other. Such an attitude which is peculiar to the 'true man' is called by Chuang-tzŭ *t'ien ni*[19] (Heavenly Levelling), *t'ien chün*[20] (Heavenly Equalization), or *man yen*[21] (No-Limits).

> 'Right' is not 'right', and 'so' is not 'so'. If (what someone considers) 'right' were (absolutely) 'right', it would be (absolutely) different from what is not 'right' and there could be no place for discussion. And if 'so' were (absolutely) 'so', it would be (absolutely) different from 'not-so' and there could be no place for discussion.
> Thus (in the endless chain of 'shifting theses'[22] (i.e., 'right' → 'not-right' → 'right' → 'not-right' . . .), (theses and antitheses) depend upon one another. And (since this dependence makes the whole chain of mutually opposing theses and antitheses relative), we might as well regard them as not mutually opposing each other.
> (In the presence of such a situation, the only attitude we can reasonably take) is to harmonize all these (theses and antitheses) in the Heavenly Levelling, and to bring (the endless oppositions among the existents) back to the state of No-Limits.[23]

'To bring back the myriad oppositions of things to the state of No-Limits' means to reduce all things that are 'essentially' distinguishable from each other to the original state of 'chaotic' Unity where there are no definite 'limits' or boundaries set among the things. On its subjective side, it is the position of abandoning all discriminatory judgments that one can make on the level of everyday Reason. Forgetting about passing judgments, whether implicit or explicit, on any thing, one should, Chuang-tzŭ emphasizes, put oneself in a mental state prior to all judgments, prior to all activity of Reason, in

which one would see things in their original – or 'Heavenly' as he
says – 'essence-less' state.

But to achieve this is by no means an easy task. It requires the
active functioning of a particular kind of metaphysical intuition,
which Chuang-tzǔ calls *ming*,[24] 'illumination'. And this kind of
illuminative intuition is not for everybody to enjoy. For just as there
are men who are physically blind and deaf, so there are also men
who are spiritually blind and deaf. And unfortunately, in the world
of Spirit the number of blind and deaf is far greater than that of
those who are capable of seeing and hearing.

> The blind cannot enjoy the sight of beautiful colors and patterns. The
> deaf cannot enjoy the sound of bells and drums. But do you think that
> blindness and deafness are confined to the bodily organs? No, they
> are found also in the domain of knowing.[25]

The structure of the *ming*, 'intuition', will be studied more closely in
due course. Before we proceed to this problem, we shall quote one
more passage in which Chuang-tzǔ develops his idea regarding the
relative and conventional nature of ontological 'distinctions'. The
passage will help to prepare the way for our discussion of the
'existentialist' position Chuang-tzǔ takes against the 'essentialist'
view of Being.[26]

> The nature of the things is such that nothing is unable to be 'that' (i.e.,
> everything can be 'that') and nothing is unable to be 'this' (i.e.,
> everything can be 'this').

We usually distinguish between 'this' and 'that' and think and talk
about the things around us in terms of this basic opposition. What is
'this' is not 'that', and what is 'that' is not 'this'. The relation is
basically that of 'I' and 'others', for the term 'this' refers to the
former and the term 'that' is used in reference to the latter.

From the viewpoint of 'I', 'I' am 'this', and everything other than
'I' is 'that'. But from the viewpoint of 'others', the 'others' are 'this',
and 'I' am 'that'. In this sense, everything can be said to be both
'this' and 'that'. Otherwise expressed, the distinction between 'this'
and 'that' is purely relative.

> From the standpoint of 'that' (alone) 'that' cannot appear (as 'that').
> It is only when I (i.e., 'this') know myself (as 'this') that it (i.e., 'that')
> comes to be known (as 'that').

'That' establishes itself as 'that' only when 'this' establishes itself
and looks upon the former as its object, or as something other than
'this'. Only when we realize the fundamental relativity of 'this' and
'that' can we hope to have a real understanding of the structure of
things.

Of course the most important point is that this relativity should be understood through 'illumination'. The understanding of this ontological relativity by Reason – which is by no means a difficult thing to achieve – is useless except as a preparatory stage for an 'illuminative' grasp of the matter. It will be made clear in the following chapter that 'relativity' does not exhaust the whole of the ontological structure of things. 'Relativity' is but one aspect of it. For, in the view of Chuang-tzǔ, the ontological structure of things in its reality is that 'chaotic undifferentiation' to which reference has often been made in the foregoing. The 'chaotic undifferentiation' is something which stands far beyond the grasp of Reason. If, in spite of that, Reason persists in trying to understand it in its own way, the 'undifferentiation' comes into its grasp only in the form of 'relativity'. The 'relativity' of things represents, in other words, the original ontological 'undifferentiation' as brought down to the level of logical thinking. In the present chapter we are still on that level.

> Hence it is held:[27] 'that' comes out of 'this', and 'this' depends upon 'that'. This doctrine is called the *Fang Shêng* theory,[28] the theory of 'mutual dependence'.
> However (this reciprocal relation between 'this' and 'that' must be understood as a basic principle applicable to all things). Thus, since there is 'birth' there is 'death', and since there is 'death' there is 'birth'. Likewise, since there is 'good' there is 'not-good', and since there is 'not-good' there is 'good'.

Chuang-tzǔ means to say that the real Reality is the One which comprehends all these opposites in itself; that the division of this original One into 'life' and 'death', 'good' and 'bad', or 'right' and 'wrong' etc., is due to various points of view taken by men. In truth, everything in the world is 'good' from the point of view of a man who takes such a position. And there is nothing that cannot be regarded as 'not-good' from the point of view of a man who chooses to take such a position. The real Reality is something prior to this and similar divisions. It is something which is 'good' *and* 'not-good', and which is neither 'good' *nor* 'not-good'.

> Thus it comes about that the 'sacred man'[29] does not base himself (upon any of these oppositions), but illuminates (everything) in the light of Heaven.[30]
> Certainly, this (attitude of the 'sacred man') is also an attitude of a man who bases himself upon (what he considers) 'right'. But (since it is not the kind of 'right' which is opposed to 'wrong', but is an absolute, transcendental Right which comprises in itself all oppositions and contradictions as they are), 'this' is here the same as 'that', and 'that' is the same as 'this'. (It is a position which comprehends and transcends both 'right' and 'wrong', so that here) 'that' unifies 'right' and 'wrong', but 'this' also unifies 'right' and 'wrong'.

(Viewed from such a standpoint) is there still a distinction between
'that' and 'this'? Or is there neither 'that' nor 'this' any longer?[31]
This stage at which each 'that' and 'this' has lost its companion to
stand opposed to – this stage is to be considered the Hinge of the
Way.
The hinge of a door can begin to function infinitely only when it is
fitted into the middle of the socket. (In the same way, the Hinge of the
Way can respond infinitely and freely to endlessly changing situations
of the phenomenal world only when it is placed properly in the
middle of the absolute One which transcends all phenomenal oppositions.) (In such a state) the 'right' is one uniform endlessness; the
'wrong' too is one uniform endlessness.
This is why I assert that nothing can be better than 'illumination'.

The absolute One is of course the Way which pervades the whole
world of Being; rather it *is* the whole world of Being. As such it
transcends all distinctions and oppositions. Thus from the point of
view of the Way, there can be no distinction between 'true' and
'false'. But can human language properly cope with such a situation? No, at least not as long as language is used in the way it is
actually used. 'Language', Chuang-tzǔ says, 'is different from the
blowing of wind, for he who speaks is supposed to have a meaning to
convey.'[32] However, language as it is actually used does not seem to
convey any real meaning, for those people, particularly the Dialecticians, who are engaged in discussing 'this' being right and 'that'
being wrong, or 'this' being good and 'that' being bad etc., are
'simply talking about objects which have no definitely fixed
contents'.

Are they really saying something (meaningful)? Are they rather
saying nothing?[33] They think that their speech is different from the
chirpings of fledglings. But is there any difference? Or is there not
any difference at all?
Where, indeed, is the Way hidden (for those people) that there
should be 'true' and 'false'? Where is Language (in the true sense)
hidden that there should be 'right' and 'wrong'? . . .
(The fact is that) the Way is concealed by petty virtues,[34] and Language is concealed by vainglories.[35] This is why we have the 'right' –
'wrong' discussions of the Confucians and the Mohists, the one party
regarding as 'right' what the other party regards as 'wrong', and the
one regarding as 'wrong' what the other regards as 'right'.
If we want to affirm (on a higher level) what both parties regard as
'wrong', and to deny what they regard as 'right', we have no better
means than 'illumination'.[36]

Thus we see ourselves brought back again to the problem of 'illumination'. The passages here quoted have made it already clear that
the 'illumination' represents an 'absolute' standpoint which transcends all 'relative' standpoints. It is a state of mind which is above

and beyond the distinctions between 'this' and 'that', 'I' and 'you'. But how can one attain to such a spiritual height, if in fact it really exists? What is the content and structure of this experience? These are the main problems that will occupy us in the following two chapters.

Notes

1. *Chuang-tzŭ*, II, p. 93.

2. i.e., there is no 'absolutely' proper place; for each being, the place in which it lives customarily *is* the right place, but the latter is 'right' only in a relative sense.

3. Two women famous for their supreme beauty.

4. That these concepts, 仁 *jên* and 義 *i*, represented two of the most typical moral values for Confucius and his school was pointed out in Chap. I.

5. *Tao Tê Ching*, XX.

6. By Learning (*hsüeh* 學) is meant the study of the meticulous rules of conduct and behavior – concerning, for instance, on what occasions and to whom one should use the formal and polite expression 'yes, sir' and when and to whom one should use the informal expression 'hum!' – the kind of learning which was so strongly advocated by the Confucian school under the name of Ceremonies (*li* 禮).

7. *op. cit.*, II.

8. 反.

9. 復 (歸) *fu(-kuei)*, lit. 'returning' – 'going-back'.

10. *op. cit.*, XL.

11. 勁.

12. *op. cit.*, LVIII.

13. *ibid.*, XXIX. This part of Chap. XXIX is regarded by Kao Hêng (*op. cit.*) as an independent chapter. He remarks in addition that the passage is typical of 'Lao-tzŭ's relativism' (老子之相對論也), p. 69. The last sentence of the passage quoted in its original form is 「或挫或隳」, which may be translated as 'a thing which one wants to crush (is not crushed), and a thing which one wants to destroy (is not destroyed).' But in the Ho Shang edition we find 載 instead of 挫 (河上註「載安也, 隳危也」), which, as Yü Yüeh (俞樾「諸子平議」) remarks, is probably the right reading.

14. The followers of Mo-tzŭ (墨子).

15. *pien chê* 辯者.

16. *ming chia* 名家.

17. *Chuang-tzŭ*, XII, p. 427, quote by Fung Yu Lang, *op. cit.*, I, p. 192. The reference is to the famous thesis put forward by the Dialectician Kung Sung Lung (公孫龍子), that a 'hard white stone' is in reality two things: a hard stone and a white stone, because 'hard' and 'white' are two entirely different attributes. The quoted sentence may also be translated: The distinction between 'hard' and 'white' is clearly visible as if they were hung on the celestial sphere.

18. II, p. 107.

19. 天倪. 倪, *ni*, means usually 'boundary', 'limit', 'division'. But here I follow the interpretation of Lu Shu Chih 陸樹芝 (「莊子雪: 天倪, 端倪之未露者, 猶天籟也」) and Pan Ku班固(quoted by Lu Tê Ming in 經典釋文) who makes it synonymous with天研.

20. 天鈞.

21. 曼衍. The lexical meaning of this expression is difficult to ascertain. In translating it as 'without limits' I am simply following an old commentator (司馬 quoted by 陸德明 in his「莊子音義」) who says「曼衍,無極也」, (p. 109). The same word is used in Bk. XXVII. And in Bk. XVII it appears in the form of反衍*fan yen* which obviously is the same as曼衍(a commentator spells it漫衍) because the passage reads: 'From the point of view of the Way, what should we consider "precious" and what should we consider "despicable"?'

22. 化聲 Cf. Kuo Hsiang's *Commentary* (p. 109):「是非之辯爲化聲，夫化聲之相待，俱不足以相正，故若不相待也」; and Chia Shih Fu (家世父):「言隨物而變，謂之化聲」.

23. *Chuang-tzŭ*, II, p. 108.

24. 明. The term literally means 'bright' or 'luminous'. We may compare it with the Islamic notion of *ma'rifah* 'gnosis' as opposed to, and technically distinguished from, *'ilm* '(rational) knowledge'.

25. I, p. 30.

26. The passage is taken from II, p. 66. I shall divide it into a number of smaller sections and quote them one by one, each followed by a brief examination.

27. by the Dialectician 惠施 Hui Shih.

28. 方生論, more exactly the 'theory of *fang shêng fang ssŭ*' (方生方死之說), held by Hui Shih, meaning literally: the theory of 'life' giving birth to 'death' and 'death' giving birth to 'life'. See *Chuang-tzŭ*, XXXIII. For this particular meaning of the word *fang* 方, see the *Shuo Wen* (說文): 「方, 併船也」 *'fang* means (originally) two ships placed side by side with each other'.

29. *shêng jên* 聖人, which is synonymous with 'true man' or 'divine man', i.e., the Perfect Man. The real meaning of the important word *shêng* has been elucidated earlier in its shamanic context; see Chapter II. The expression *shêng jen* is more often used by Lao-tzŭ than by Chuang-tzŭ.

30. *t'ien* 天, meaning the great Way of Nature, the absolute standpoint of Being itself, which is, so to speak, a viewpoint transcending all viewpoints.

31. This is a peculiar expression which Chuang-tzŭ uses very often when he wants to deny something emphatically.

32. 「夫言非吹也言者有言」, II, p. 63.

33. See above, Note (31).

34. The 'petty virtues' 小成 – or more literally, 'small acquirements' – refer to the five cardinal virtues of the Confucians – Ch'êng Hsüan Ying (成玄英「莊子注疏」).

35. i.e., the natural tendency of the human mind toward showing-off, which manifests itself typically in the form of discussions and debates.

36. *op. cit.*, II, p. 63.

V The Birth of a New Ego

We have seen in what precedes how futile and absurd, in the view of Chuang-tzǔ, is the ordinary pattern of thinking typified by the this-is-'right'-and-that-is-'wrong' kind of discussion. What is the source of all these futile verbalizations? Chuang-tzǔ thinks that it is to be found in the mistaken conviction of man about himself, namely, that he himself has (or is) an 'ego', a self-subsistent entity endowed with an absolute ontological independence. Man tends to forget that the 'ego' which he believes to be so independent and absolute is in reality something essentially relative and dependent. Relative to what? Relative to 'you' and 'them' and all other things that exist around himself. Dependent upon what? Dependent upon Something absolutely superior to himself, Something which Chuang-tzǔ calls the Creator, or more literally, the Maker-of-things.[1] Chuang-tzǔ describes this situation through a parable of 'Shadow and Penumbra'.[2]

> Penumbra[3] once said to Shadow: 'I notice you sometimes walking, but next moment you are standing still. Sometimes I notice you sitting, but next moment you are standing up. Why are you so fickle and unstable?
> Shadow replied: It seems to me that (in acting like this) I am simply dependent upon something (i.e., the body). But that upon which I depend seems to be acting as it does in dependency upon something else (i.e., the Creator). So all my activities in their dependency seem to be the same as the movements of the scales of a snake or the wings of a cicada.[4]
> How should I know, then, why I act in this way, and why I do not act in that way?

Chuang-tzǔ deprives the 'ego' at a stroke of its seeming self-subsistence and self-sufficiency. But such a view goes naturally against the everyday belief and conviction of man about himself. For according to the everyday view of things the 'ego' is the very basis and the core of man's existence, without which he would lose his personality, his personal unity, and be nothing. The 'ego' is the point of co-ordination, the point of synthesis, at which all the disparate elements of his personality, whether physical or mental, become united. The 'ego' thus understood is called by Chuang-tzŭ the 'mind'.⁵

I think it proper to introduce at this point a pair of key terms which seem to have played a decisive rôle in the formation of the main lines of thought of Chuang-tzŭ concerning the nature of the mind: *tso ch'ih*⁶ lit. 'sitting-galloping' and *tso wang*⁷ lit. 'sitting-forgetting'.

The first of them, *tso ch'ih*, refers to the situation in which the mind of an ordinary person finds itself, in constant movement, going this way at this moment and that way at the next, in response to myriad impressions coming from outside to attract its attention and to rouse its curiosity, never ceasing, to stop and rest for a moment, even when the body is quietly seated. The body may be sitting still but the mind is running around. It is the human mind in such a state that the word *hsin* (Mind) designates in this context. It is the exact opposite of the mind in a state of calm peaceful concentration.

It is easy to understand conceptually this opposition of the two states of the mind, one 'galloping around' and the other 'sitting still and void'. But it is extremely difficult for ordinary men to free themselves actually from the dominance of the former and to realize in themselves the latter. But in truth, Chuang-tzŭ teaches, man himself is responsible for allowing the Mind to exercise such a tyrannical sway over him, for the tyranny of the Mind is nothing else than the tyranny of the 'ego' – that false 'ego' which, as we have seen above, he creates for himself as the ontological center of his personality. Chuang-tzŭ uses a characteristic expression for this basic situation of man: *shih hsin* or 'making the Mind one's own teacher'.⁸

The 'ego', thus understood, is man's own creation. But man clings to it, as if it were something objective, even absolute. He can never imagine himself existing without it, and so he cannot abandon it for a moment; thus he makes out of his Mind his venerated 'teacher'.

This Mind, on a more intellectual level, appears as Reason, the faculty of discursive thinking and reasoning. Sometimes Chuang-tzŭ calls it *ch'êng hsin* or 'finished mind'.⁹ The 'finished mind' means the mind which has taken on a definitely fixed form, the mind in a state of coagulation, so to speak. It is the Reason by whose guidance – here again we come across the expression: 'making the Mind the teacher' – man discriminates between things and passes judgments on them, saying 'this is right' and 'that is wrong', etc., and goes on falling ever deeper into the limitless swamp of absurdities.

Everybody follows his own 'finished mind' and venerates it as his own teacher. In this respect we might say no one lacks a teacher. Those who know the reality of the unceasingly changing phenomena and accept (this cosmic law of Transmutation) as their standard (of judgment) are not the only people who have their teachers. (In the above-mentioned sense) even an idiot has his own teacher. It is impossible for a man to insist on the distinction between 'right' and 'wrong' without having a 'finished mind'. This is as impossible as a man departing (from a northern country) *to-day* and arriving in the country of Yüeh (in the southern limit of China) *yesterday!*[10]

Thus we see that all the pseudo-problems concerning the 'right' and 'wrong' or 'good' and 'bad', whose real nature was disclosed in the preceding chapter, arise from man's exercising his own 'finished mind'. The Mind, according to Chuang-tzŭ, is the source and origin of all human follies.

This idea of the Mind is shared by Lao-tzŭ, although his approach is a little different from Chuang-tzŭ's. That the idea itself is basically the same will immediately be perceived if one reads carefully, for example, Ch. XLIX of the *Tao Tê Ching*. Interestingly enough, Lao-tzŭ in this passage uses the term *ch'ang hsin*,[11] i.e., 'constant or unchangeable mind'. The term reminds us of Chaung-tzŭ's *ch'ēng hsin* 'finished mind'. By *ch'ang hsin* Lao-tzŭ designates a rigidly fixed state of mind deprived of all natural flexibility, or as he likes to say, the state of the mind that has lost the natural 'softness' of an infant. As the passage quoted shows, this unnatural rigidity of the mind is typically manifested in the distinguishing and discriminating activity of the mind which perceives everywhere 'good' and 'bad', 'right' and 'wrong' and regards these categories as something objective and absolute.

For Lao-tzŭ, it is not simply a matter of one's becoming partial, prejudiced, and bigoted. In his view the exercise of this function of the mind affects the very core of human existence. It is a question of the existential crisis of man. Man stands in a woeful predicament because he is – almost by nature, one would say – so made that he directs the activity of his mind toward distinguishing and discriminating things from one another.

> The 'sacred man' has no rigidly fixed mind of his own. He makes the minds of all people his mind.[12] (His principle is represented by the dictum): 'Those who are good I treat as good. But even those who are not good I also treat as good. (Such an attitude I take) because the original nature of man is goodness. Those who are faithful I treat as faithful. But even those who are not faithful I also treat as faithful. (Such an attitude I take) because the original nature of man is faithfulness.'
> Thus the 'sacred man', while he lives in this world, keeps his mind wide open and 'chaotifies'[13] his own mind toward all.
> The ordinary men strain their eyes and ears (in order to distinguish between things). The 'sacred man', on the contrary, keeps his eyes and ears (free) like an infant.[14]

Lao-tzŭ sometimes uses the word *chih*[15], 'knowing', to designate the discriminating activity of the mind here in question. But caution is needed in understanding this word, because for Lao-tzŭ it is not the act of 'knowing' itself that is blameful; its blamefulness is conditioned by the particular way in which 'knowing' is exercised and by the particular objects toward which it is directed.

The kind of 'knowing' which is wrong in the eyes of Lao-tzŭ is the same distinguishing and discriminating activity of intelligence as the one which we have seen is so bitterly denounced by Chuang-tzŭ.

Unlike Chuang-tzŭ, however, who develops this idea on a logical level as a problem of dialectics, taking his examples from the discussions on 'right' and 'wrong' as he observes them among the Dialecticians of his day, Lao-tzŭ is prone to consider the disastrous effects of this type of 'knowing' on a more practical level. He draws attention to the evaluational attitude which is the most immediate result of the 'distinguishing' activity of the mind. Here the this-is-'right'-and-that-is-'wrong' is not a logical problem. It is a matter of practical evaluation. And as such it is directly connected with the concrete facts of life. 'Knowing' understood in this sense, is denounced because it disturbs the minds of the people in an unnecessary and wrong way. And the disturbance of the mind by the perception of values, positive and negative, is regarded by Lao-tzŭ as wrong and detrimental to human existence because it tempts it away from its real nature, and ultimately from the Way itself. In the following passage,[16] the word *chih*, 'knowing', is evidently used in this sense.

> If (the ruler) does not hold the (so-called) wise men in high esteem, the people will (naturally) be kept away from vain emulation. If (the ruler) does not value goods that are hard to obtain, the people will be kept away from committing theft. If (the ruler) does not display things which are liable to excite desires, the minds of the people will be kept undisturbed.
> Therefore, the 'sacred man' in governing the people empties their minds,[17] while making their bellies full; weakens their ambitions[18] while rendering their bones strong.
> In this way, he keeps his people always in the state of no-knowledge[19] and no-desire, so that the so-called 'knowers'[20] might find no occasion to interfere.

The baneful influence of the discriminating activity of the Mind is so powerful that even a modicum of it is liable at any moment to make man deviate from the Way.

> If I happen to have even a modicum of 'knowing', I would be in grave danger of going astray even if I am actually walking on the main road (i.e., the Way). The main road is level and safe, but men tend to choose narrow by-ways.[21]

However, it is not 'knowing' itself that is so baneful; the quality of 'knowing' depends upon the particular objects on which it is exercised. The 'knowing', when its usual tendency of turning toward the outside and seeking after external objects is curbed and brought back toward the inside, transforms itself into the highest form of intuition, 'illumination' (*ming*).

> He who knows others (i.e., external objects) is a 'clever' man, but he who knows himself is an 'illumined' man.[22]

It is significant that here we come across exactly the same word, *ming* 'illumination', which we encountered in the *Chuang-tzŭ*. It is also very significant that in the passage just quoted the 'illumination' is directly connected with man's knowledge of himself.[23] It evidently refers to the immediate and intuitive knowledge of the Way. It is described as man's 'self-knowledge' or 'self-knowing', because the immediate intuitive grasp of the Way is only obtainable through man's 'turning into himself'.

Certainly, according to the view of Lao-tzŭ and Chuang-tzŭ, the Way is all pervading. It is everywhere in the world; the world itself *is* a self-manifestation of the Way. In this sense, even 'external' things are actually manifesting the Way, each in its own way and own form. But man alone in the whole world of Being is self-conscious. That is to say, man alone is in a position to grasp the Way from inside. He can be conscious of himself as a manifestation of the Way. He can feel and touch within himself the palpitating life of the Absolute as it is actively working there. He can *in*-tuit the Way. But he is unable to *in*-tuit it in external objects, because he cannot go into the 'inside' of the things and experience *their* manifestation of the Way as *his own* subjective state. At least the first subjective personal encounter with the Way must be made within himself.

For this purpose the centrifugal tendency of the mind must be checked and turned to the opposite direction; it must be made centripetal. This drastic turning of direction is described by Lao-tzŭ as 'closing' up all the openings and doors' of the body. By obstructing all the possible outlets for the centrifugal activity of the mind, man goes down deep into his own mind until he reaches the very existential core of himself.

This existential core of himself which he finds in the depth of his mind may not be the Way *per se*, because after all it is an individualized form of the Way. But, on the other hand, there is no real distinction or discrepancy between the two. Lao-tzŭ expresses this state of affairs symbolically by calling the Way *per se* the Mother, and the Way in its individualized form the Child. He who knows the Child, knows by that very knowledge the Mother herself.

In the passage which I am going to quote,[24] the importance of the 'closing up of all the openings and doors' is emphasized as the sole means by which man can come to know the Child, and through the Child, the Mother. And the ultimate state thus attained is referred to by the term 'illumination'. It may be pointed out that the Child (*tzŭ*)²⁵ which in this understanding represents an individualized duplicate of the Mother (*mu*),²⁶ is nothing other than what Lao-tzŭ calls elsewhere Virtue (*tê*) – or perhaps more strictly, an individual embodiment of the Way having as its existential core the creative and vital force, which is the Way itself as distributed among the 'ten thousand things'. As we shall see later, this creative and vital force of each individual, existent as an individual determination of the Way, is called by Lao-tzŭ 'Virtue'.²⁷

> All things under Heaven have a Beginning which is to be regarded as the Mother of all things.²⁸
> If you know the 'mother', you thereby know her 'child'. And if, after having known the 'child', you go back to the Mother and hold fast to Her, you will never fall into a mistake till the very end of your life.

> Block the openings, shut the doors (i.e., stop the normal functioning of the sense organs and the usual centrifugal activity of the Mind), and all through your life you (i.e., your spiritual energy) will not be exhausted.
> If, on the contrary, you keep the openings wide open, and go on increasing their activities till the end of your life, you will not be saved.
> To be able to perceive the minutest thing (i.e., the supra-sensible thing, which is the Child of the Way within yourself) is properly to be called Illumination. To hold on to what is soft and flexible (i.e., abandoning the rigidity of the Mind enslaved by the 'essential' distinctions among things and accepting 'softly' all things in their real state of mutual transformations) is properly to be called strength.
> If, using your external light, you go back to your internal Illumination, you will never bring misfortune upon yourself. Such an (ultimate) state is what is to be called 'stepping into the eternally real'.²⁹

The 'closing up all openings and doors' means, as I have indicated above, stopping the functioning of all the organs of sense perception in the first place, and then purifying the Mind of physical and material desires. This is made clear by our comparing the passage just quoted with XII which reads:

> The five colors (i.e., the primary colors: white, black, blue, red and yellow) make man's eyes blind. The five musical notes make man's ears deaf. The five flavors (i.e., sweet, salty, sour, pungent, bitter) make man's taste dull. (Games like) racing and hunting make man's mind run mad. Goods that are hard to obtain impede man's right conduct.
> Therefore the 'sacred man' concentrates on the belly (i.e., endeavors to develop his inner core of existence) and does not care for the eye

(i.e., does not follow the dictates of his senses). Verily he abandons
the latter and chooses the former.

The 'sacred man' cares for the belly and does not care for the eye,
because he is aware that the centrifugal activity of the Mind does
nothing other than lead him away from the Way. The Way is there in
his own 'inside' in the most concrete and palpable form. The further
one goes toward 'outside', the less he is in touch with the Absolute.
What one should try to do is to 'stay at home' and not to go
outdoors.

> Without going out of the door, one can know everything under
> Heaven (i.e., the reality of all things). Even without peeping out of
> the window, one can see the working of Heaven. The further one
> goes out, the less one knows.
> Therefore the 'sacred man' knows without going out. He has a clear
> view of everything[30] without looking. He accomplishes everything
> without acting.[31]

The passages which have now been quoted from the *Tao Tê Ching*
concern the epistemological aspect of the problem of the Way; the
problem, namely, of how and in what way man can 'intuit' the
Absolute. The answer given by Lao-tzŭ is, as we have seen, that the
only possible way for man to take in order to achieve this aim is to
obstruct totally the centrifugal tendency of his own mind and to
replace it by a centripetal activity leading ultimately to
'illumination'.

Lao-tzŭ, however, is not so much concerned with the epistemological process itself by which man cultivates such an 'inner
eye' as with the result and effect of this kind of intuition. Indeed, he
usually starts his argument precisely from the point at which such a
process reached completion. Two things are his main concern. One
is the practical and visible effect produced by the illuminative
intuition on the basic attitude and behavior of man. How does the
'sacred man' act in the ordinary situations of social life? That is one
of his primary problems. This problem will be dealt with in a later
chapter devoted to a discussion of the concept of the Perfect Man.

The second of Lao-tzŭ's main problems is the metaphysical structure of the world of Being, with the Way as the very source and basis
of all things. Here again the epistemological aspect of the problem is
either almost totally discarded or simply hinted at in an extremely
vague way. Lao-tzŭ is more interested to describe the ontological
process by which the Way as the absolutely Unknown-Unknowable
goes on making itself gradually visible and determined until finally it
reaches the stage of the infinite Multiplicity of the phenomenal
world. He also refers to the backward movement of all things, by
which they 'return' to the original state of absolute Unity.

What is remarkable about this is that all this description of the ontological process is made from the standpoint of a man who has already experienced 'illumination', with the eye of a man who knows perfectly the secret of Being. Chuang-tzŭ is different from Lao-tzŭ in this respect. He is vitally interested in the process which itself precedes the final stage of 'illumination' and by which the latter is reached. Chuang-tzŭ even tries to describe, or at least to indicate by means of symbolic descriptions, the experiential content of 'illumination' which he knows is by its very nature ineffable. The rest of the present chapter and the next will be concerned specifically with this aspect of the problem, which we might call the epistemological or subjective side of the Way-experience.

At the outset of this chapter, I drew attention to two cardinal concepts relating to the subjective side of the Way-experience, which stand diametrically opposed to each other: *tso ch'ih* 'sitting-galloping' and *tso wang* 'sitting-forgetting'. In the preceding pages we have been examining mainly the structure of the former concept. Now it is time we turned to the latter concept.

A man in the state of 'sitting-forgetting' looks so strange and so different from ordinary men that he is easily recognizable as such by an outsider-observer. In Bk II of his Book, Chuang-tzŭ gives a typical description of such a man. The man here described is Nan Kuo Tzŭ Ch'i, or Tzŭ Ch'i of the Southern Quarter. He is said to have been a great Sage of Ch'u,[32] living in hermitic seclusion in the 'southern quarter'. For Chuang-tzŭ he was surely a personification of the very concept of the Perfect Man.

> Once Tzŭ Ch'i of the Southern Quarter sat leaning against a tabouret. Gazing upward at the sky, he was breathing deeply and gently. Completely oblivious of his bodily existence, he seemed to have lost all consciousness of 'associates' (i.e., oppositions of 'I' and 'things', or 'ego' and the 'others').
> Yen Ch'eng Tzŭ Yu (one of his disciples), who was standing in his presence in attendance, asked him, 'What has happened to you, Master? Is it at all possible that the body should be made like a withered tree and the mind should be made like dead ashes? The Master who is now leaning against the tabouret is no longer the Master whom I used to see leaning against the tabouret in the past!'
> Tzŭ Ch'i replied, 'It is good indeed that you ask that question,[33] Yen! (I look different from what I have been) because I have now lost myself.[34] But are you able to understand (the real meaning of) this?

Following this introductory remark, the great Master goes on to describe for the bewildered disciple the state of 'having lost the ego', telling him what is actually experienced in that state. As a result, we have the very famous vision of the Cosmic Wind, one of the most beautiful and forceful passages in the whole book of *Chuang-tzŭ*. The passage will be given in translation in the following chapter. Here we have only to note that the Master's words: 'I have now lost myself', refer to nothing other than the state of 'sitting-forgetting' or 'sitting in oblivion' as opposed to the 'sitting-galloping'.

But what exactly is 'sitting in oblivion'? How can one experience it at all? This is something extremely difficult – or more properly we should say, almost absolutely impossible – to explain in words. Chuang-tzŭ, however, tries to do so.

In Bk VI he gives his own definition of 'sitting in oblivion'. The passage reads as follows.

> What is the meaning of 'sitting in oblivion'?
> It means that all the members of the body become dissolved, and the activities of the ears and eyes (i.e., the activities of all the sense organs) become abolished, so that the man makes himself free from both form and mind (i.e., both bodily and mental 'self-identity'), and becomes united and unified with the All-Pervader (i.e., the Way which 'pervades' all). This is what I call 'sitting in oblivion'.[35]

Externally, or physically, all the parts of the body become 'dissolved' and forgotten. That is to say, the consciousness of the bodily 'ego' is made to disappear. Internally, all mental activities are 'abolished'. That is to say, there no longer remains the consciousness of the inner 'ego' as the center and all-unifying principle of man's mental activity. The result of this total 'forgetting' of the inside and outside of the 'I' is called by Chuang-tzŭ *hsü*,[36] the Void, or a spiritual-metaphysical state in which there is nothing whatsoever to obstruct the all-pervading activity of the Way.

The word 'Void' must not be understood in this context in a purely negative sense. It does have a positive meaning. And in its positive aspect, the Void must be connected with the concept of the All-Pervader which appears in the passage just quoted.

I have translated the Chinese expression *ta t'ung*, lit. 'great pervasion', as the All-Pervader following the interpretation given by Ch'êng Hsüan Ying, who identifies *ta t'ung* with *ta tao*, the 'great Way', and says: '*ta t'ung* is the same as *ta tao*; since the Way pervades all things and enlivens them, it is in this sense entitled to be called All-Pervader'.[37] This interpretation seems to be right, but it must be supplemented by an understanding of another aspect of the matter, namely, that in the experience of the spiritual state here in question, all things in their infinite multiplicity interpenetrate each other freely, without any obstruction, and that the man who has lost his 'ego' rediscovers in this experience his 'ego' in a totally different form, reborn as what we might call the Universal, Cosmic, or Transcendental Ego which transforms itself freely into all things that are transforming themselves into each other.

Such must be the real implication of the use of the particular expression *ta t'ung* in place of the more usual word *tao*, the Way. The point is brought to light very clearly by Kuo Hsiang who explains this passage by saying: 'in the "inside" the man has no consciousness of his own bodily existence; in the "outside" he has no awareness of the existence of Heaven and Earth. It is only in such a state that he becomes completely identified with the (cosmic) process of Change (i.e., "transformations") itself without there being any obstruction at all. Once in such a state, there can be nothing he does not freely pervade.'[38]

Chuang-tzǔ himself expresses the same idea in a far more laconic way:

> Being unified, you have no liking. Being transmuted, you have no fixity.[39]

In the light of the explanation that has been given in the preceding, the meaning of this laconic expression can easily be clarified as follows. Being completely unified and identified with the Way itself, the man can have no likes and dislikes. The man in such a spiritual state transcends the ordinary distinctions between 'right' and 'wrong', 'good' and 'bad'. And since he is now identical with the Way, and since the Way is constantly manifesting itself in myriad forms of Being, the man himself is 'being transmuted' from one thing to another, without there being any obstruction, as if he were moving around in the great Void. He is not actually in the 'void', because there *are* things throbbing with all-pervading Life, appearing and disappearing in infinitely variegated forms. The point is, however, that in this metaphysical Void these things no longer present any obstacles to his absolute freedom. For he himself is, in this state, completely identical with every one of these things, participating from within in the cosmic flux of Transmutation; or rather he is the cosmic Transmutation itself. This is what is meant by the expression: 'you have no fixity'[40] 'No fixity' means boundless flexibility and absolute freedom.

It will be clear from what has preceded that the *hsü* is both the metaphysical Void and the spiritual Void. In truth, this very distinction between 'metaphysical' and 'spiritual' is in this context something artificial, because the state in question refers to a total and complete identification of man with the All-Pervader. Theoretically, however, there is some point in making such a distinction. For when the question is raised on a more practical level as to what concretely one should do in order to become so completely identified with the Way, we have to have recourse to the idea of making the mind 'void'. Only when one has succeeded in making

the mind completely 'void', does one find oneself in the very midst
of the metaphysical Void. This part of Chuang-tzǔ's teaching takes
on the form of practical instruction regarding the proper method by
which man can hope to attain to such a state. This method is called
by him 'fasting' or the purification of the Mind.

The purification of the Mind constitutes the pivotal point in the
development of man from the state of an 'ordinary' man to that of
the Perfect Man. An 'ordinary' man can never become a Perfect
Man unless he passes through this turning point. The significance of
this experience will be clear if one remembers what we have seen
above concerning Chuang-tzǔ's characteristic expression: 'making
the Mind one's own teacher'.⁴¹ Man naturally tends to cling to his
Mind – and Reason – and thinks and acts according to its dictates.
Whatever the Mind tells him to believe is absolutely true, and
whatever it commands him to do is absolutely good. In other words,
man venerates his own 'ego' as his 'teacher'.

In the light of this observation, the 'purification of the Mind'
means precisely that man should abolish this habit of the 'veneration' of the Mind, that he should cast away his own 'ego'. And that
will mark the first step toward his being transformed into a Perfect
Man.

In an imaginary conversation which Chuang-tzǔ fabricates with a
view to endorsing his thesis, Confucius – who is here ironically made
into a Taoist sage – teaches his disciple Yen Hui how to proceed in
order to succeed in purifying the Mind.

In this dialogue, Yen Hui is represented as a zealous disciple who
has desperately struggled to know the right way to become a Perfect
Man, but in vain. As the final resort, he turns to Confucius and
humbly asks for instruction. The following is the passage.⁴²

> Yen Hui: I cannot proceed any further. May I venture to ask
>   you to tell me the proper way?
> Confucius: Fast, first. Then I will teach you. Do you think it easy
>   (to see the Truth) while maintaining your Mind? If
>   anybody does think it easy, the vast and bright
>   Heaven will not approve of him.

The word translated here as 'fast', *chai*,⁴³ means the act of 'fasting'
which man practises in the period immediately preceding sacrificial
ceremonies in order to put himself into the state of religious 'purity'.
In the present context, Confucius uses the word not in this original
religious sense, but figuratively in the sense of the 'fasting of the
Mind', that is, the 'purification of the Mind'. Yen Hui, however,
does not understand this, and takes the word in its usual sense. He
imagines that Confucius means by the word the observance of the

ritual fasting which concerns eating and drinking. Hence the following ridiculous reply he gives to the Master:

Yen Hui: My family is poor, so much so that I have neither drunk liquor nor eaten garlic and onions for the past several months. Cannot this be considered fasting?

Confucius: What you are talking about is the fasting as a ritual proceeding. That is not the fasting of the Mind.

Yen Hui: May I ask what you mean by the fasting of the Mind?

Confucius: Bring all the activity of the Mind to a point of union. Do not listen with your ears, but listen with the Mind (thus concentrated).

(Then proceed further and) stop listening with the Mind; listen with the Spirit (*ch'i*).[44]

The ear (or more generally, sense perception) is confined to listening[45] (i.e., each sense grasps only its proper objects in a physical way).

The Mind is confined to (forming concepts) corresponding to their external objects.[46] The Spirit, however, is itself 'void' (having no definite proper objects of its own), and goes on transforming limitlessly in accordance with the (Transmutation of) things (as they come and go). The Way in its entirety comes only into the 'void' (i.e., the 'ego-less' Mind). Making the Mind 'void' (in this way) is what I mean by the 'fasting of the Mind'.

As I pointed out before, *hsü*, 'void', is a key term of the philosophy of Chuang-tzŭ. It represents in this context the subjective attitude of man corresponding to the very structure of the Way which is itself a Void. This latter point is very much emphasized by Lao-tzŭ, as we shall see in detail in a later chapter which will be devoted to a discussion of the metaphysics of the Way. Here we are still mainly concerned with the subjective aspect of the matter. The main idea is that when a man 'sits in oblivion' with his mind completely 'void', into this ego-less 'void' all things come exactly as they are, as they come and go in the cosmic process of Transmutation. In such a state, his mind is comparable to a clear mirror which reflects everything without the slightest distortion or disfigurement.

All this is of course a matter which must be directly experienced; a mere conceptual understanding is of little help. Yen Hui whose mind has already been fully ripened – in the anecdote we are now reading – for this kind of personal transformation, becomes suddenly 'illumined' by the teaching of his Master, and makes the following observation about himself.

Yen Hui: Before Hui (i.e., I) received this instruction, Hui was really nothing but Hui (i.e., 'I' have been my small 'ego', nothing else). However, now that I have

received this instruction, I have realized that from the
very beginning there never was (an 'ego' called) Hui.
Is this state worthy to be considered the 'void' (which
you have just spoken of)?

Confucius: So it is, indeed!

Then Confucius contrasts this state with the state of 'sitting-
galloping', and goes on to describe the former by comparing it to a
firmly closed empty room which mysteriously and calmly illumines
itself with a white light of its own.[47]

> Look into that closed room and see how its empty 'interior' produces
> bright whiteness. All blessings of the world come in to reside in that
> stillness.[48]
>
> If, on the contrary, (your Mind) does not stand still, you are in the
> state of what I would call 'sitting-galloping'.
>
> But if a man turns his ears and eyes toward the 'interior', and puts his
> Mind and Reason in the 'exterior' (i.e., nullifies the normal function-
> ing of the Mind and Reason), even gods and spirits come to reside
> freely (in his ego-less 'interior') not to speak of men. This is the
> Transmutation of ten thousand things.[49]

The last sentence represents one of the cardinal points of Chuang-
tzŭ's metaphysics. The peculiar meaning of the key term *hua* has
been explained above. What is important here to note is that in the
passage just quoted, the *hua*, Transmutation, is evidently described
as a subjective state of man, as something that occurs in his
'interior'. Rather, his 'interior' *is* the Transmutation of the ten
thousand things, that is, of all the phenomenal things and events of
the world. The man in the state of perfect 'sitting in oblivion' does
experience subjectively, as his personal experience, the Transmutation of all things.

The whole matter may be reformulated more theoretically in terms
of the process of the spiritual development of man toward
illumination.

    In ordinary human experience, the constant flux and reflux of
infinitely changing phenomena are in the position of the Lord. They
positively act upon man, influence him, push him around, and bind
him up. In such a situation man is a servant or slave. His mind
becomes torn asunder and runs in all directions in pursuit of
chameleonic forms of things and events.

    Once man frees himself from this bondage and transcends the
common pattern of experience, the scene before his eyes takes on a
completely different appearance. The kaleidoscopic view is still
there. The things and events still continue their changes and transformations as before. The only essential difference between the two

stages is that in the second all these things and events that go on appearing and disappearing are calmly reflected in the polished mirror of the man's 'interior'. The man himself is no longer involved in the hustle and bustle of incessantly changing phenomena.

The man at this stage is a calm observer of things, and his mind is like a polished mirror. He accepts everything as it comes into his 'interior', and sees it off, unperturbed, as it goes out of sight. There is for him nothing to be rejected, but there is nothing wilfully to be pursued either. He is, in short, beyond 'good' and 'bad', 'right' and 'wrong'.

A step further, and he reaches the stage of 'undifferentiation', where, as we saw earlier, all things become 'chaotified'. On this level there still *are* things. But these things show no limits and borderlines separating them 'essentially' from one another. This is the stage of the cosmic Transmutation. It goes without saying that in its subjective aspect, the Transmutation represents a spiritual stage of the man himself.

As a result of the 'fasting of the Mind', the man is now completely 'ego-less'. And since he is 'ego-less' he *is* one with the 'ten thousand things'; he *becomes* the 'ten thousand things'. And he himself goes on changing with the infinite change of all things. He is no longer a calm 'observer' of the changing things. He *is* the subject of the Transmutation. A complete and perfect harmony is here realized beween the 'interior' and the 'exterior'; there is no distinction between them.

Borrowing the terminology of Ibn 'Arabī we might say that the man on this high level of spiritual development is subjectively placed in the position of the Unity of Existence (*wahdah al-wujūd*), and personally experiences the whole world of Being in that position. The situation is described by Chuang-tzŭ in the following way:[51]

> Dying and being alive, being subsistent and perishing, getting into a predicament and being in the ascendant, being poor and being rich, being clever and being incompetent, being disgraced and being honored, being hungry and thirsty, suffering from cold and heat – all these are but constant changes of (phenomenal) things, and results of the incessant working of Fate.
>
> All these things go on replacing one another before our own eyes, but no one by his Intellect can trace them back to their real origin.
>
> However, these changes are not powerful enough to disturb (the man who 'sits in oblivion' because he is completely one with the Transmutation itself), nor can they intrude into the 'innermost treasury'[52] (of such a man).
>
> On the contrary, he maintains (his 'innermost treasury') in a peaceful harmony with (all these changes) so that he becomes one with them without obstruction, and never loses his spiritual delight.

Day and night, without ceasing, he enjoys being in spring-tide with all things. Mingling with (the infinitely changing things on a supra-sensible level of existence) he goes on producing within his 'interior' the 'time'[53] (of the world).
Such a state I would call the perfection (i.e., perfect actualization) of the human potentiality.[54]

When a man attains to this height of spiritual development, he fully deserves the title of Perfect Man. This, however, is not the last and ultimate stage of 'sitting in oblivion'. There is a still higher stage beyond. That is the stage of 'no more Death, no more Life'. Chuang-tzŭ sometimes calls it the 'extreme limit (*chih*)'[55] of knowledge (*chih*).[56] At this last stage, the man is completely unified not with the ever changing 'ten thousand things' – as was the case when he was in the previous stage – but with the 'Mystery of Mysteries',[57] the ultimate metaphysical state of the Absolute, at which the latter has not yet come down to the sphere of universal Transmutation. The man is here so completely one with the Way that he has not even the consciousness of being one with the Way. The Way at this stage is not present *as* the Way in the consciousness of the man. And this is the case because there is no 'consciousness' at all anywhere, not even a trace of it. The 'oblivion' is complete. And the actualization of such a perfect 'oblivion' is to be accounted for in reference to the metaphysical fact that the ultimate Absolute, the Way, is in its absolute absoluteness Something which one cannot call even 'something'. Hence the usual custom in oriental philosophies of referring to the Absolute as *Nothing*.

The stages of the above-described spiritual development of 'sitting in oblivion' are variously discussed by Chuang-tzŭ in several places of his book. Sometimes he takes an ascending course, and some-times a descending course. The former corresponds to the real process by which the mind of a man gradually proceeds toward spiritual perfection. A typical example of this type of description is found in a passage[58] which claims to reproduce a conversation between a certain Nan Po Tzŭ K'uei and a Perfect Man (or Woman?) called Nü Yü. In this passage, Chuang-tzŭ gives a description of the stages which are traversed by a man who is born with a special potentiality to be a Perfect Man until he really reaches the last stage. The description is very interesting when it is considered as a Taoist counterpart to the Islamic *fanā'* or self-annihilation'.

The conversation starts from Nan Po Tzŭ K'uei's astonishment at the complexion of old Nü Yü, which, as he observes, is like that of a child.

Nan Po Tzŭ K'uei:	You are old in years, Master, and yet your complexion is like that of a child. Why?
Nü Yü:	(This is because) I have come to know the Way.
Nan Po:	Is it possible for me to learn the Way?
Nü Yü:	No. How could it be possible? You are not the right kind of man to do so.

> You know Pu Liang I. He had (from the beginning) the natural potentiality to be a 'sacred man', but he had not yet acquired the Way, whereas I had the Way but lacked the 'potentiality'.[59] I wanted to give him guidance to see if, by any chance, he could become a 'sacred man'. Even if I should fail to achieve my goal, it was, (I thought), easy for a man in possession of the Way to communicate it to a man in possession of the potentiality of a 'sacred man'.
>
> Thus I persistently taught him. After three days, he learnt how to put the world outside his Mind.

The 'putting the world outside the Mind' i.e., forgetting the existence of the world, marks the first stage. The 'world' being something objective – and therefore relatively far from the Mind – is the easiest thing for man to erase from his consciousness.

> After he had put the world outside himself, I continued persistently to instruct him. And in seven days he learnt how to put the things outside his Mind.

The 'putting the things outside the Mind' represents the second stage. Forgetting the existence of the world was not so difficult, but 'things' which are more intimately related with man resist being erased from the consciousness. As Kuo Hsiang remarks: 'The things are needed in daily life. So they are extremely close to the ego. This is why they are so difficult to put outside the Mind'.[60] And Ch'êng Hsüan Ying:[61] 'The states of the whole world are foreign and far removed from us; so it is easy for us to forget them. The things and utensils that actually serve us in our everyday life are familiar to us; so it is difficult for us to forget them'.

By forgetting the familiar things that surround us and are connected with us in various ways in daily life, the external world completely disappears from our consciousness.

> After he had put things outside his Mind, I still continued to instruct him. And in nine days he learnt how to put Life outside the Mind.

This is the third stage. It consists in the man's forgetting Life, that is to say, erasing from his consciousness the fact of his own Life, i.e., his own personal existence. This is the stage of dropping the 'ego'. As a result, the world, both in its external and internal aspects, disappears from the consciousness. This stage is immediately followed by the next which is the sudden coming of the dawn of 'illumination'.

> After he had put Life outside his Mind, (his inner eye
> was opened just as) the first light of dawn breaks
> through (the darkness of night).

Once this 'illumination' is achieved, there are no more stages to come. Or should we say, there are stages to come, but they do not come successively; all of them become actualized simultaneously. If they are to be considered 'stages', they must be described as horizontal stages which occur at once and all together the moment the inner eye is opened by the penetrating ray of spiritual daybreak. The first of such stages is 'perceiving the absolute Oneness'.

> The moment the day dawned, he saw the Oneness.

This is the moment when all things and 'I' become absolutely one. There is no more opposition of subject and object – the subject that 'sees' and the object 'seen' being completely unified – nor is there any distinction between 'this' and 'that', 'existence' and 'non-existence'. 'I' and the world are brought back to their absolute original unity.

> And after having seen the Oneness, there was (in his
> consciousness) neither past nor present.

At the stage of the absolute Oneness, there is no more consciousness of the distinction between 'past' and 'present'. There is no more consciousness of 'time'. We may describe this situation in a different way by saying that the man is now in the Eternal Now. And since there is no more consciousness of ever-flowing 'time', the man is in the state of 'no Death and no Life'.

> After having nullified past and present, he was able to
> enter the state of 'no Death and no Life'.

The state of 'no Death and no Life' can be nothing other than the state of the Absolute itself. The man at this stage is situated in the very midst of the Way, being identified and unified with it. He is beyond Life and Death, because the Way with which he is one is beyond Life and Death.

The state of the Way or the Absolute, however, is not simply being beyond Life and Death. As is clearly shown by the very epistemological process by which man finally attains to it, this state is not sheer 'nothing-ness' in the purely negative sense. It is rather the ultimate metaphysical state, the absolute Unity, to which the dispersion of the ontological Multiplicity is brought back. It is a

Unity formed by the unification of 'ten thousand things', a Unity in which all the things are existent, reduced to the state of Nothing-ness.
There is 'no Death and no Life' here. That is to say, it is a state of complete Tranquillity and Stillness. There is no more even a trace of the noise and fuss of the world of sensible existence. And yet the Stillness is not the stillness of Death. There is no more movement observable. But it is not a state of non-movement in a purely negative sense. It is rather a dynamic non-movement, full of internal ontological tensions, and concealing within itself infinite possibilities of movement and action.

Thus it is, in both of the aspects just mentioned, a *coincidentia oppositorum*. The Absolute, in this view, is Something which goes on realizing and actualizing 'ten thousand things' in their myriad forms and transforming them in a limitless process of Transmutation, and yet at the same time keeping all these things in their supra-temporal and supra-spatial Unity. It is a Unity which is itself a Multiplicity. It is Stillness which is itself Ebullition.

In the end of the passage Chuang-tzŭ refers to this aspect of the Way in the following words.

> That which kills Life does not die.⁶² That which brings to Life everything that lives does not live.⁶³ By its very nature it sends off everything, and welcomes everything. There is nothing that it does not destroy. There is nothing that it does not perfect. It is, in this aspect, called Commotion-Tranquillity.⁶⁴ The name Commotion-Tranquillity refers to the fact that it (i.e., the Way) sets (all things) in turmoil and agitation and then leads them to Tranquillity.

We must keep in mind that at this highest stage of spirituality, the man is completely unified and identified with the Way. Since, however, the Way is nothing other than Commotion-Tranquillity, the man who is in complete union with the Way, goes through this cosmic process of the absolute Unity being diversified in turmoil and agitation into 'ten thousand things', and the latter going back again to the original state of Tranquillity. The ontology of Taoism is an ontology which is based upon such an experience. It would be natural for us to imagine that the view of Being in the spiritual eyes of a Taoist sage will be of an essentially different nature and structure from that of an Aristotle, for example, who founds his philosophical edifice upon the ordinary ontological experience of an average man looking at the world around him at the level of sound and solid common sense. The most natural standpoint of philosophers of the latter kind is essentialism. In ancient China, the essentialist standpoint is represented by Confucius and his school. Both Lao-tzŭ and Chuang-tzŭ take a determined position against it.

The next chapter will be devoted to an elucidation of this particular point.

Notes

1. *tsao wu chê* 造物者 (see VII, p. 280). The name designates the Way in its 'personal' aspect. This aspect of the Way is referred to also by the name Great Lord, *ta shih* 大師. The word Heaven, *t'ien* 天 is also sometimes used with the same meaning. More details will be given later when we discuss the concept of 'determinism' (Chap. IX).

2. II, pp. 110–111.

3. 罔兩 is explained by Kuo Hsiang as「景外之微陰也」, 'faint darkness surrounding the shadow'.

4. The scales of a snake and the wings of a cicada have no independence in their movements. On the contrary all their movements are dictated by the snake and the cicada respectively.

5. *hsin* 心.

6. 坐馳. The word appears in an important passage (IV, p. 150) which will be given in translation presently.

7. 坐忘.

8. 師心, IV, p. 145.

9. 成心, II, p. 56. My interpretation of this word is based on that given by Kuo Hsiang and Ch'êng Hsüan Ying. The latter says: 夫域情滯著，執一家之偏見者，謂之成心。夫随順封執之心，師之以爲準的世皆如此，故誰獨無師乎, (p. 61). Some commentators (like Lin Hsi I 林希逸, for instance, in his famous 莊子口義) interpret the word in the opposite sense, as the inborn, naturally given mind, which is the mind in its celestial purity. But this latter interpretation does not, I think, do justice to the basic thought of Chuang-tzŭ on this problem.

10. *ibid.*

11. 常心. The word *ch'ang* is an ambiguous term in the *Tao Tê Ching*, because Lao-tzŭ uses it in two diametrically opposed meanings. Sometimes – as is the case with the usage of the word in this passage – it means 'unflexible', 'rigidly fixed', which is the worst possible state of things in the philosophy of Lao-tzŭ. Sometimes – particularly in many of the passages of primary importance, as we shall see later – it is used in the sense of 'never-changing', 'eternal', and 'absolute'.

12. Having no 'fixed mind' of his own, he accepts everything, whether 'good' or 'bad'; rather, he does not distinguish between 'good' and 'bad'.

13. *hun* 渾, a characteristic word, whose meaning has been explained in an earlier passage in connection with Chuang-tzŭ's concept of the 'chaotification' of things.

14. XLIX.

15. 知.

16. *Tao Tê Ching*, III.

17. *hsin* 心, the discriminating activity of the intellect, the natural tendency of the Mind toward gaining 'knowledge'.

18. *chih* 志, that aspect of the Mind, which manifests itself in insatiably desiring more and more.

19. *wu chih* 無知.

20. *chih chê,* 知者 lit. 'knowing men', those men who claim to know the reality of things; who, therefore, are convinced that they are capable of giving the best advice on every important matter of human life.

21. LIII.

22. XXXIII.

23. We are reminded of the Islamic adage: *Man 'arafa nafsa-hu 'arafa rabba-hu* 'He who knows himself knows his Lord', which, as we saw in the first Part of this study, plays an important rôle in the philosophy of Ibn 'Arabî.

24. LII.

25. 子.

26. 母.

27. That the word *tê* 德, here translated as Virtue, is one of the most important of all the key terms of Lao-tzǔ, will be seen from the very fact that the Book itself is known by the title *Tao Tê Ching*, i.e., the 'Canonical Book of the Way and the Virtue'.

28. 'All things under Heaven' represent the Multiplicity of the phenomenal world, while the Beginning is the Unity as their ultimate ontological origin and source.

29. *hsi ch'ang*襲常. For the meaning of the word *ch'ang* 常, see above, note (11). The word *hsi* means 'step into', 'enter', here in the mystical sense of the 'inner' grasp of a thing, *in*-tuition. The word is used in XXVII in a very characteristic combination: *hsi ming,* 襲明, 'stepping into illumination'.

30. 名. The word is here the same as 明– both having the same pronunciation. As quoted by *Han Fei Tsǔ* (喻老篇) we see 明 actually used in this passage (不見而明).

31. XLVII.

32. 楚 . On the relevance of his being a man of Ch'u to the whole topic of the present study, see above, Chap. I.

33. i.e., I am glad that you are keen enough to notice the difference.

34. i.e., I have lost my 'ego' and have stepped into the state in which there is no more distinction between 'ego' and 'things'. Lin Hsi I (林希逸) says in his commentary: As

long as there is 'ego' there are 'things'. But when I lose my 'ego', there is no 'I'. And since there is no 'I', there are no 'objects'. (莊子口義 *ad loc.*)

35. VI, p. 284.

36. 盧; cf. Ch'êng Hsüan Ying:「旣悟一身非有，萬境皆空」, p. 285.

37.「大通猶大道也．道能通生萬物，故謂道爲大道也」, p. 285.

38.「內不覺其一身，外不識有天地，然後曠然與變化爲體而無不通也」, p. 285.

39. *ibid.*

40. The word used here for 'fixity' is *ch'ang* 常, whose double meaning has been explained above; see notes 11 and 29.

41. See above, Chap. IV.

42. IV, pp. 146–148.

43. 齋.

44. 氣. The word has already been explained before, Ch. II, Note 19. It is a proto-material and formless cosmic 'reality' which pervades the whole world of Being and which constitutes the ontological core of every single thing, whether animate or in-animate. Man is, of course, no exception to this. Thus man, on the level of the *ch'i* is homogeneous with all things as well as with the universe itself. Man cannot 'listen with the *ch'i*,,' unless he has been completely unified with the universe. The 'ego' which listens, i.e., perceives, with the *ch'i* is no longer an ordinary epistemological 'subject'; it is the Cosmic Ego.

45. The text reads:「聽止於耳」, 'listening stops with the ears', which gives but a poor meaning. Following Yü Yüeh (兪樾) I read 「耳止於聽 (cf.王先謙「莊子集解」, *ad loc.*).

46. i.e., the Mind is confined to elaborating the images received from the sense organs and fabricating out of them concepts that correspond to external objects which are fixed once for all in terms of 'essences'. It cannot identify itself, with infinite flexibility, with each of the infinitely varying phenomenal forms of 'reality'.

47. IV, p. 150.

48. The repetition of the word 止 in「吉祥止止」is a little difficult to account for. Yü Yüeh simply disposes of the second as a scribal error on the ground that the sentence as quoted in other books does not have it. (兪樾「止止連文，於義無取。『淮南子』一 俶眞篇一作 ·『虛室生白，吉祥止也』。疑 此文下止亦也字之誤。唐盧重元注『列子』一天瑞篇一曰『虛室 生白，吉祥止耳』亦可證止連文之誤)。However, the second 止 can very well be understood also in the sense of 'stillness' or 'no-motion' as I have done following Ch'eng Hsüan Ying who says:「止者，凝靜之智。言吉祥善福止在凝靜之心」, p. 151.

49.「萬有之化」, 'The *hua* of ten thousand things'.

50. In doing this, I shall strictly follow Chuang-tzŭ's own description which he gives in Bk. II, p. 74. The passage itself will be given in translation at the outset of the following chapter.

51. V, p. 212.

52. *ling fu*, 靈府 the most secret part of the heart which is the central locus of all spiritual activity.

53. i.e. he goes on experiencing within himself, without being perturbed, the alternation of the four seasons, which is the 'time' of all phenomenal things. That is to say he is completely one with all things which are in the incessant process of transformation.

54. *ts'ai ch'üan* 才全, one of the key terms of Chuang-tzŭ. It means the natural human ability brought to the highest degree of perfection.

55. 至.

56. 知 II, p. 74,「其知所有至」.

57. *Hsüan chih yu hsüan*「玄之又玄」, the expression is from the *Tao Tê Ching*. It denotes the Way, but with a peculiar connotation which will be explained in the chapter concerning the concept of Way.

58. VI, pp. 252–253.

59. i.e., I had not the 'ability' or 'potentiality' to become a Perfect Man; I had 'actually' the Way from the very beginning.

60.「物者, 朝夕所須, 切己難忘」, p. 253.

61.「天下萬境疏遠, 所以易忘, 資身之物親近, 所以難遺」, p. 254.

62. The Way brings everything existent to naught. But if it brings everything to naught and death, it must itself be something beyond Death.

63. Since the Way brings into existence everything that exists, it must itself be something that transcends Life, i.e., Becoming.

64. *Ying ning* 攖寧. It is one of the key terms of Chuang-tzŭ. According to Ch'êng Hsüan Ying, *ying* means 'commotion', 'agitation', and *ning* 'tranquillity', 'stillness' (「攖擾動也, 寧寂靜也」, p. 255).

VI   Against Essentialism

Toward the end of the preceding chapter I pointed out the fact that in the *Chuang-tzŭ*, the stages of the 'sitting in oblivion' are traced in two opposite directions: ascending and descending. The first consists in starting from the lowest stage and going up stage by stage toward the ultimate and highest one. A typical example of this kind of description has just been given.

The second, the descending course, is the reverse of the first. It starts from the highest stage and comes down to the lowest. As a proper introduction to the main topic of the present chapter, we shall begin by giving in translation a passage[1] from the *Chuang-tzŭ* in which the stages are described in this way. In this passage, Chuang-tzŭ, instead of speaking of 'sitting in oblivion', divides human knowledge of Reality into four classes which constitute among themselves a chain of successive degrees. These degrees are the epistemological stages corresponding to the ontological stages which Lao-tzŭ in his *Tao Tê Ching* distinguishes in the process by which all things in the world of Being issue forth continuously from the absolute Unity of the Way.

> What is the ultimate limit of Knowledge? It is the stage represented by the view that nothing has ever existed from the very beginning. This is the furthest limit (of Knowledge), to which nothing more can be added.

As we saw in the previous chapter, this is the ultimate stage to which man attains at the end of 'sitting in oblivion'. Here the man is so completely unified with the Way and so perfectly identified with the absolute Reality, that the Way or the Reality is not even felt to be such. This is the stage of Void and Nothing-ness in the sense that has been explained above.

About this stage Kuo Hsiang says:[2] 'The man at this stage has completely forgotten Heaven and Earth, has put all existent things out of his mind. In the outside, he does not perceive the existence of the whole universe; in the inside, he has lost all consciousness of his own existence. Being limitlessly "void", he is obstructed by nothing.

He goes on changing as the things themselves go on changing, and there is nothing to which he does not correspond.'

Next is the stage at which there is the consciousness of 'things' being existent. But (in this consciousness) 'boundaries' between them have never existed from the very beginning.

At this second stage, the man becomes conscious of the Way which contains all things in a state of pure potentiality. The Way will diversify itself at the following stage into 'ten thousand things'. But here there are no 'boundaries' yet between them. The 'things' are still an undivided Whole composed of a limitless number of potentially heterogeneous elements. They are still an even plane, a Chaos, where things have not yet received 'essential' distinctions.

Next (i.e., the third) is the stage at which 'boundaries' are recognized (among the things). However, there is as yet absolutely no distinction made between 'right' and 'wrong'.

Here the Chaos begins to disclose the definite forms of the things which it contains within itself. All things show their own demarcations, and each thing clearly marks its own 'boundary' by which it distinguishes itself from others. This is the stage of pure 'essences'. The original Unity divides itself, and is diversified into Multiplicity, and the Absolute manifests itself as numberless 'relative' existents. As a result, the Reality which has previously been beyond the ken of human cognition comes for the first time into the limits of its grasp.

And yet, even at this stage, the distinction is not made between 'right' and 'wrong'. This indicates that at this third stage we are still in touch with the Way in its original integrity, although, to be sure, the contact with the Way is already indirect, because it is made through the veil of the 'essences'. We may recall the myth of the Emperor Chaos (Hun Tun), which we read in Chapter II, who died as soon as his friends bored holes in his 'featureless' visage. In the light of the present passage, there is in this myth an oversimplification. For Chaos does not 'die' simply by 'holes' (i.e., 'essential' distinctions) being made in it. The true death of the Chaos occurs at the next stage.

As soon as, however, 'right' and 'wrong' make their clear appearance, the Way becomes damaged. And as soon as the Way is thus damaged, Love is born.

With the appearance of 'right' and 'wrong', Chaos loses its natural vitality and becomes fossilized as 'essential forms' stiff and inflexible as corpses. As Wang Hsien Ch'ien says: 'When "right" and "wrong" are recognized, the "chaotic" integrity of the Way is immediately injured'.[3]

And no sooner this happens than Love is born. The birth of Love symbolizes the activity of such human emotions as love and hate, like and dislike. This is the last and lowest stage of Knowledge.

Of course there is another aspect to the problem. The Way is here said to die with the appearance of human emotions like love and hate. But this is so only when one considers the situation in refence to the original 'chaotic' integrity, i.e., the original 'undifferentiation' of the Absolute. Otherwise, everything is a particular manifestation of the Way itself. And as such even a fossilized 'essence' is nothing other than a 'self-determination' of the Absolute. This aspect of the matter, however, is irrelevant to our present topic.

As I remarked before several times – and it is particularly important to recall it once again for the right understanding of the philosophical position Chuang-tzǔ takes against 'essentialism' – the description just given of the four stages is not an abstract theory; it is a description of an experiential fact. It is a phenomenological description of the experience of *ekstasis*. In the passage which has just been quoted, the process of *ekstasis* is described in a descending order. That is to say, Chuang-tzǔ describes the 'return' of consciousness. He starts from the highest stage of contemplation at which the 'oblivion' has been completed, and goes down step by step until he reaches the stage of normal consciousness.

What is to be kept in mind in connection with this problem is that the whole process of *ekstasis*, whether considered in a descending or ascending order, is composed of two aspects which exactly correspond to each other. One is the subjective aspect, which we might call 'epistemological', and the other is the objective, or 'metaphysical' aspect.

Take, for example, the highest stage. On its subjective side, it is, as I have just said, a stage at which the contemplative in actual contemplation has consummated the *ekstasis*. He is now in complete 'oblivion' of everything, the world and himself included. This would naturally mean that he is in the state of Nothing-ness, because he is conscious of nothing, because there is no 'consciousness'. And this subjective Nothing-ness corresponds to the objective Nothing-ness of the Way. For the Way, too, is in its original absolute purity Nothing-ness, a state 'where nothing has ever existed from the very beginning', that is, a metaphysical state where nothing whatsoever is distinguishable as an existent.

From such a state of perfect Void, subjective and objective, the contemplative starts coming back toward the daily state of mind. There begins to stir something in himself. Consciousness awakes in him to find 'things' existent. The consciousness, however, is still at this stage a dim and subdued light. It is not yet the glaring brilliance of full daylight. It is the crepuscule of consciousness, a twilight in which all things are only indistinctly and confusedly observable. Such a description of the situation might strike one as a negative evaluation. The state of consciousness at this stage is described as being a dim light merely because the description is made from the point of view of the 'normal' consciousness of an ordinary mind. For the latter, the light of the ecstatic consciousness looks dim and indistinct because it does not distinguish and discriminate things from each other. In reality, however, such indistinctiveness *is*, for a Chuang-tzŭ, Reality as it really is.

And since the real state of Reality is itself 'dim' and 'indistinct', the consciousness must of necessity be correspondingly 'dim', and 'indistinct'. Only with such a dim light can Reality in its integrity be illumined. The glaring and dazzling light of normal consciousness does cast a strong spotlight on this or that particular object. But by concentrating the light on the particular object, it makes all the rest of the world sink into darkness. Referring to this point Chuang-tzŭ remarks:[4]

> Therefore, the diffused and indistinct Light is what is aimed at by the 'sacred man'. He does not, however, use this Light (in order to illumine particular things), but lends it to all things universally. This is what is called 'illumination'.

The phrase here translated as 'diffused and indistinct Light'[5] means a kind of light of which one cannot be certain as to whether it exists or not; a light which, instead of being concentrated upon this or that particular object, is 'diffused' and pervades all. It is not a glaring, dazzling light. It is a dim, indistinct light, neither bright nor dark. In reality, however, it is the Universal Light which illumines everything as it really is.

Chuang-tzŭ calls this kind of spiritual Light also the 'shaded Light' (*pao kuang*).[6] The word *pao* means 'to cover', 'to conceal within'. As Ch'êng Hsüan Ying explains: '(The mind of the "sacred man") forgets (to distinguish between things) and yet illumines all. And as it illumines them, it forgets them. That is why it shades and obscures its light, yet becomes ever more brilliant.'

The corresponding 'objective' side of this stage is ontologically the most important of all stages for Chuang-tzŭ. For this precisely is the stage of 'chaotification'. In the subdued and diffused Light of the consciousness of the contemplative, the 'ten thousand things' loom up as if through the mist. They appear dim and indistinct because there are no 'boundaries', i.e., definite 'essences' or 'quiddities', to differentiate them one from the other.

I say that this is ontologically the most important stage for

Chuang-tzǔ, because the higher stage, that of the Absolute in its absoluteness, is properly speaking beyond all thinking and reasoning,[7] while the lower one is the stage of 'essences' or 'quiddities', where all things appear to the consciousness distinctly separated from each other through their 'boundaries'. And Chuang-tzǔ fights against the view that this latter stage does represent Reality as it really is.

Thus we see that the stage of 'chaotification', at which all things are observed in their original 'undifferentiation', that is, beyond and apart from their 'essences', constitutes the pivotal point of Chuang-tzǔ's metaphysics. We might call this metaphysics 'existentialism', taking the word 'existence' (*existentia*) in the same sense as *wujūd* in the metaphysical system of Ibn 'Arabī.

From the very outset I have been emphasizing implicitly as well as explicitly the 'existentialist' attitude of Chuang-tzǔ. I think I have made it sufficiently clear by now that its real meaning becomes understandable only when we relate it to the second stage (from above) of the 'sitting in oblivion'. It is a philosophical position based on the vision of Chaos. In this respect it stands opposed to the position taken by 'essentialism' which is based on a vision of Reality peculiar to, and typical of the epistemological-ontological stage where the 'ten thousand things' appear, each with a clearly marked 'boundary' of its own. In terms of the process of 'sitting in oblivion' – the Return process from the complete *ekstasis* back toward the 'normal' world of common sense – the 'essentialist' position belongs to the third stage explained above.

Thus in the framework of such an experience, 'existentialism' represents a vision of Reality which is a stage higher than 'essentialism'. It is important to note that the latter is regarded as the third stage in the Return process of the ecstatic contemplation only as long as it is considered within this particular framework. In reality, however, the contemplative, when he comes down to this stage and becomes conscious of the things with clear 'boundaries', he is actually already on a par with any ordinary man who knows nothing about the experience of *ekstasis*. His view of Being at this particular level is nothing unusual from the standpoint of common sense. On the contrary, it is a view of Being common to, and shared by, all men who are at all endowed with a 'sound' and 'normal' mind. 'Essentialism', in other words, is the typical ontology of common sense.

This statement, however, should not be understood as implying that, for a Chuang-tzǔ or a Lao-tzǔ, 'essentialism' is a wrong and mistaken view of Being, and that it distorts and disfigures the real structure of things. For 'essentialism' does represent and correspond to a certain definite stage in the evolving process of the

Absolute itself. Besides, on its subjective side, 'essentialism' constitutes, as we have just seen, the third stage of the 'sitting in oblivion' in the Return process of the contemplation. And as such, there is nothing wrong about it.

The serious problem arises only when the common sense refuses to see any difference in terms of ontological 'levels' between 'existentialism' and 'essentialism' and begins to assert that the latter is *the* right view of Being. It is only then that a Chuang-tzǔ rises in an open revolt against 'essentialism'. Since, however, it is of the very nature of common sense to view the things in an 'essentialist' way, Chuang-tzǔ and Lao-tzǔ constantly find themselves forced to manifest the attitude of revolt against such a view. Their philosophy, in this respect, may properly be characterized as a revolt against the 'tyranny' of Reason.

Chuang-tzǔ sees a typical exemplification of the 'essentialist' position in the moral philosophy of Confucius. Confucian philosophy is, in Chuang-tzǔ's view, nothing but an ethical elaboration of ontological 'essentialism'. The so-called cardinal virtues of Confucius like 'humaneness', 'justice', etc., are but so many products of the normal activity of the Mind which naturally tends to see everywhere things rigidly determined by their own 'essences'. The Reality in its absoluteness has no such 'boundaries'. But a Confucius establishes distinctions where there are none, and fabricates out of them rigid, inflexible ethical categories by which he intends to regulate human behavior.

> Stop! Stop approaching men with (your teaching of) virtues! Dangerous, dangerous, indeed, is (what you are doing), marking off the ground and running within the boundaries![8]

Ontological 'essentialism' is dangerous because as soon as we take up such an attitude, we are doomed to lose our natural flexibility of mind and consequently lose sight of the absolute 'undifferentiation' which is the real source and basis of all existent things. 'Essentialism' will not remain in the sphere of ontology; it naturally grows into a categorization of values which, once established, begins to dominate our entire behavioral system.

Chuang-tzǔ in the following passage[9] gives with keen sarcasm a symbolic picture of those people who are vainly engaged in animated discussions over the 'values' of things, considering them as something absolute, something unalterably determined.

> The spring has dried up, and the fish are all on the ground. (In the agonies of death) they are spewing each other with moist breath and trying to moisten each other with froth and foam. It would be far better for them if they could forget each other in a wide river or sea. Likewide, the people praise a 'great man' and condemn a 'bad man'.

But it would be much better if they could forget both ('good' and 'bad') together and be freely 'transmuted' with the Way itself.

'Essentialism' would seem to be a philosophical position which is most suitable to the human mind. At any rate the Reason and the common sense which is but a vulgarized form of Reason naturally tend to take an 'essentialist' position. And the latter is that upon which our ordinary thinking depends.

The gist of the 'essentialist' view may be concisely presented as a thesis that all things are endowed with 'essences' or 'quiddities', each thing being clearly marked off by its 'essence' from all others. A table is a table, for example, and it can never be a chair. The book which is upon the table is 'essentially' a book, and it is 'essentially' different from, or other than the table. There are 'ten thousand', i.e., innumerable, things in the world. But there is no confusion among them, for they are separated from one another by clear-cut lines of demarcation or 'boundaries' which are supplied by their 'essences'.

As I have said before, this 'essentialist' ontology in itself is nothing to be rejected. It gives a true picture of things, if it is put in the right place, that is to say, as long as one understands it to be the picture of things at a certain ontological level. Chuang-tzŭ takes no exception to this. The point he wants to make is that 'essentialism' should not be regarded as the one and ultimate view of things. And he does rise in revolt against it the moment one begins to make such a claim. For he is convinced that it is *not* the ultimate view of things.

From the standpoint of a man who has seen things in a different light in his ecstatic vision, there is ontologically a stage at which the 'essences' become annihilated. This would simply mean for a Chuang-tzŭ that there are 'from the very beginning' – as he says – no such things as 'essences' in the sense of hard and solid ontological cores of things. In any event, the so-called 'essences' lose, in this view, their solidity, and become liquefied. 'Dream' and 'reality' become confused in the vast, limitless world of 'undifferentiation'. There is no longer here any marked distinction to be drawn between a table and a chair, between a table and a book. Everything is itself, and yet, at the same time, all other things. There being no 'essences', all things interpenetrate each other and transform themselves into one another endlessly. All things are 'one' – in a dynamic way. We might properly compare this view with Ibn 'Arabī's concept of the Unity of Existence, *waḥdah al-wujūd*. And we know already that this is what Chuang-tzŭ calls Chaos.

Ibn 'Arabī could speak of the Unity of Existence because he looked at the world of Multiplicity, the illimitable existents, as so many self-determinations or self-manifestations of the Absolute which is itself the absolute Unity. In a similar way, Chuang-tzŭ came to the idea of the 'chaotification' of things because he looked at them from the point of view of the Way, which is also the absolute metaphysical Unity.

In contemporary Western philosophy, special emphasis has often been laid upon the 'tyrannical' power of language, the great formative influence exercised by linguistic patterns on the molding of our thought. The influence of language is particularly visible in the formation of the 'essentialist' view of things.

From the point of view of an absolute 'existentialism', there are no watertight compartments in the world of Being. Man, however, 'articulates', that is, cuts up – arbitrarily, in most cases – this originally undivided whole into a number of segments. Then he gives a particular name to each of these segments. A segment of Reality, thus given a name, becomes crystallized into a 'thing'. The name gives it an 'essential' fixity, and thus ensures it from disintegration. For better or for worse, such is in fact the power of language. Language, in other words, positively supports 'essentialism'.

Once a 'thing' is established with a definite name, man is easily led into thinking that the thing is *essentially* that and nothing else. If a thing is named A, it acquires A-ness, that is, the 'essence' of being A. And since it is A 'by essence', it can never be other than A. One could hardly imagine under such conditions the thing's being B, C or D. The thing thus becomes something unalterably fixed and determined.

This fundamental relation between 'essentialism' and language is noticed by Chuang-tzŭ. He notices it because he looks at the matter from the point of view of the absolute Way in which, as we have repeatedly pointed out, there is not even a trace of 'essential' determinations.

> The Way has absolutely no 'boundaries'. Nor has language (which produces and expresses such 'boundaries') absolutely any permanency.[10]
> But (when the correspondence becomes established between the two) there arise real (essential) 'boundaries'.[11]

Referring to the sophistic logic of the school of Kung Sun Lung, Chuang-tzŭ points out that this kind of logic is a product of linguistic 'essentialism'.[12]

> Rather than trying to prove by means of 'finger' that a 'finger' is not a 'finger', why not prove by means of 'non-finger' that a 'finger' is not a 'finger'?

The meaning of this passage will become clear only when we understand it against the background of the sophistic logic which was prevalent in Chuang-tzŭ's time. The argument of the Sophists of the school of Kung Sun Lung may be summarized as follows. The concept of 'finger' comprises within itself the concepts of the thumb, the index, the middle, the third, and the little fingers. Actually there is no 'finger' other than these five. That is to say, the 'finger' must necessarily be one of these five. And yet, if we take up any one of them, the 'index finger' for example, we find it negating and excluding all the rest, because the 'index finger' is *not* any of the other four fingers. Thus it comes about that the 'index finger' which *is* a real 'finger', is *not* a 'finger', because its concept applies exclusively to itself, not to the others.

Against this Chuang-tzŭ remarks that such an argument is simply a shallow and superficial piece of sophistry. We do not gain anything even if we prove in this manner that a 'finger' is not a 'finger'. However, there is a certain respect in which a 'finger' is properly to be considered a 'non-finger'. And this latter view – although superficially it gives the same conclusion; namely, that a 'finger' is not a 'finger' – is not a piece of sophistry. It is a view standing on the 'chaotification' of things, and it goes to the very heart of the structure of Reality.

The term 'non-finger' which appears in the second half of the above-quoted statement is not intended to be the logical contradictory of 'finger'. It means something like a 'super-finger', or an ontological state in which a 'finger' is no longer a 'finger'. 'Why not prove by means of "non-finger"?', Chuang-tzŭ asks. He means to say: instead of wasting time in trying to prove by logical tricks – as Kung Sun Lung and his followers are doing – that 'a finger is not a finger' on the very level of 'a finger is a finger', we had better transcend at a stroke the ontological level of 'essential' distinctions and see with the eye of 'illumination' the reality of the situation. For, in fact, on the level of 'chaotification', a 'finger' is no longer necessarily a 'finger', it is no longer so solidly fixed that it can never be anything other than itself. All things are one, and we have no reason to stick obstinately to the idea that since *A* is *A*, it cannot be anything other than *A*. Thus the statement: 'a "finger" is not a "finger" ' is found to be true; but, this time, on a higher level than the one on which the Sophists are trying hard to establish the same statement.

Chuang-tzŭ gives one more example, that of a 'horse' not being a 'horse', which was also a notorious topic of the Sophists of his time.

> Rather than trying to prove by means of 'horse' that a 'horse' is not a 'horse', why not prove by means of 'non-horse' that a 'horse' is not a 'horse'?

The structure of the argument is exactly the same as the previous one. The Sophists claim that a 'horse' is not a 'horse' on the basis of the following observation. The concept of 'horse', they say, must be applicable to horses of different colors like 'white horse', 'yellow horse', 'black horse' etc., and no 'horse' which is actually existent is colorless. Every actually existent horse is either white, or black, or yellow, etc. And there can be no exception. Let us take a 'white horse' as an example. The 'white horse', being white, naturally excludes all horses of other colors. The concept cannot apply to a 'black horse', for instance, or a 'yellow horse'. And the same is true of any horse of any color. Since, however, the concept of 'horse' must be such that it applies to all horses of all colors, we must conclude that no actually existent horse is a 'horse'.

The Sophists in this way establish, or claim to establish, that a 'horse' is not a 'horse'. Against this, Chuang-tzŭ takes the position that, even admitting that they are right in this argument, the conclusion which they reach thereby is devoid of real significance. As in the case of the preceding argument about 'finger', Chuang-tzŭ points out that there is a respect in which exactly the same conclusion can be maintained, but with an entirely new meaning. Here again the term 'non-horse' refers to the metaphysical level at which all 'essential' distinctions are eliminated through 'chaotification'.

Once we put ourselves on such a level, we perceive that a 'finger' *is* a 'finger' and yet, at the same time, is *not* a 'finger', that a 'horse' *is* a 'horse' and yet is *not* a 'horse'. And the same holds true of everything else. We can even go to the extreme of asserting that the whole world is a 'finger', and the whole world is a 'horse'.

> Heaven and Earth (i.e., the whole universe) are a 'finger'. All things are a 'horse'.

Heaven and Earth with 'ten thousand things' that exist therein are but an 'undifferentiated' whole, in which all things ontologically interpenetrate one another. In such a state, a 'horse' is not unalterably a 'horse'; it can be anything else. Looking at this particular situation from the reverse side we could say that all things are entitled to be regarded as a 'horse' or 'finger', or indeed, anything else.

From such a standpoint, Chuang-tzŭ goes on to criticize the 'essentialist' position in the following manner.[13]

> (Instead of looking at the matter from the viewpoint of 'non-finger' and 'non-horse', people divide up the originally undifferentiated whole of Being into various categories which, again, they classify into 'right' and 'not-right') and insist on the 'right' being unalterably 'right' and the 'not-right' being unalterably 'not-right'. (The distinction, however, between 'right' and 'not-right', far from being

something 'essential', i.e., something based on the very nature of Being, is but a matter of custom and habit, just as) a road is formed (where there was none before) merely by people walking constantly upon it. Likewise, the 'things' are formed by their being designated by this or that particular name (simply by virtue of a social custom or convention).[14]

(And once the 'things' are thus crystallized, they are considered as either 'right' or 'not-right', 'so' or 'not-so'). On what ground does man judge a thing to be 'so?' He judges to be 'so' whatever (other people or 'society' by custom) judge to be 'so'. On what ground does man judge a thing to be 'not-so'? He is merely judging it to be 'not-so' because (other people) judge it (by custom) to be 'not-so'.

(However, from the viewpoint of 'illumination', the reality of things can only be grasped when one puts oneself on a higher level of non-discriminating acceptance which transcends all such relative distinctions. And viewed from such a place) there is a certain respect in which everything without exception is to be regarded as being 'so' (i.e., affirmable and acceptable), and everything without exception is to be regarded as 'right'. There is nothing that is not 'so'. There is nothing that is not 'right'. Whether a stalk of grain or a great pillar, whether a leper or a (beautiful lady like) Hsi Shih, however strange , bizarre, ugly and grotesque things may be, the Way makes them all one.

The Reality perceived on such a level is called by Chuang-tzǔ Heavenly-Equalization,[15] or Walking-Two-Ways (at the same time).[16] The former term means a 'natural' metaphysical state in which all things, without being disturbed by the distinctions between 'good' and 'bad', 'right' and 'wrong', etc., repose in their original harmony or equality. And since, as Ch'êng Hsüan Ying observes, the 'sacred man' always sees things in such a state of Equality, his mind too reposes in an eternal peace, being never disturbed by the distinctions and differences among things. The second term, literally meaning 'going both ways', refers to the same metaphysical state in which 'good' and 'bad', or 'right' and 'wrong', are both equally acceptable; a state, in other words, in which all opposites and contradictories become acceptable in the ultimate Unity of *coincidentia oppositorum*.

It is highly significant that the second chapter of the *Chuang-tzǔ* is entitled *Ch'i Wu Lun*,[17] i.e., 'Discourse on Equalizing (All) Things'. The chapter is so entitled because it is mainly concerned with the view according to which all things are 'equal', that is, ultimately One. And since, according to this view, such 'equalization' of things is justifiable only at the level of 'existence', not at that of 'essences', I consider this theory rightly comparable with Ibn 'Arabī's Unity of Existence.

'Essentialism', if it is to be a philosophical view of existents, must be able to explain the whole of the world of Being. And it does intend – and does claim, implicitly at least – to be comprehensive enough to cover all things. But how, in actual fact, could it be so when its very nature consists in isolating single ontological units, making them 'essentially' independent of one another? If one makes such an approach to things, and yet wants to comprehend all of them, one is forced to have recourse to the method of enumeration and addition. But, however far one may go in this direction, one will never reach the ultimate end. For no matter how many independent units one may pile up one upon another, one will be left with an infinite number of things still untouched and uncomprehended.

Thus 'essentialism' is by its very nature utterly incapable of grasping the reality of the world of Being in its infinite complexity and in its limitless development and transformation. In order to comprehend the whole of the world of Being as it really is and as it really works, we must, Chuang-tzŭ maintains, abandon the level of 'essential' distinctions, and, by unifying ourselves with 'existence' itself which pervades all things, look at all things in their original state of 'chaotification' and 'undifferentiation'. Instead of formulating this thesis in such a theoretical form, Chuang-tzŭ explains his point through the concrete example of Chao Wên, a famous lute player.

> That a thing can become 'perfect' and 'defective' (at the same time) may aptly be exemplified by what happens when Chao Wên plays the lute. That a thing can remain 'not-perfect' and 'not-defective' may aptly be exemplified by what happens when Chao Wên does not play the lute.[18]

The meaning of the passage may be explicated as follows. Chao Wên is a musician of genius. When he plays the lute, the particular piece of music which he plays becomes actualized in a perfect form. This is what is referred to by the expression: 'that a thing can become perfect'.

However, by the very fact that Chao Wên plays a particular piece of music and actualizes it in a perfect form, the infinite number of other pieces which are left behind become darkened and nullified. This is what is meant by the thing being 'defective' at the same time. Thus a perfect actualization of one single piece of music is at the same time the negation and nullification of all other possibilities. Only when Chao Wên does not actually play, are we in a position to enjoy all the pieces of music which he is capable of actualizing. And only in such a form is his music 'perfect' in an absolute sense, that is, in a sense in which it transcends the very distinction between 'perfection' and 'imperfection' (or 'defectiveness').

The 'equalization' of all things thus brings us into the very core of the reality of Being. If, however, one sticks to this idea and discards completely the phenomenal aspect of things, one falls into an equally inexcusable error. For, after all, the infinitely various and variegated phenomena *are* also an aspect of Reality. Certainly, the music of Chao Wên is 'perfect' in an absolute sense, only when he does not play his lute. But it is also true that the possibilities that lie hidden in his ability are destined to be 'perfected' in a relative sense and will never cease to work up their way from possibility to actuality even to the detriment of one another. Both forms of 'perfection', absolute and relative, fundamental and phenomenal, are essential to the reality of his music.

Likewise, in the ontological structure of things, both the original 'undifferentiation' and the phenomenal 'differentiation', or Unity and Multiplicity, are real. If Chuang-tzŭ emphasizes so much the former aspect, it is chiefly because at the common sense level of human experience the phenomenal aspect is so prominent and so dominant that it is commonly considered *the* reality.

The root of Being is absolutely one. But it does not repose forever in its original Unity. On the contrary, it belongs to the very nature of Being that it never ceases to manifest itself in infinite forms. It goes on diversifying itself into 'ten thousand things' which, again, go on endlessly transforming themselves into one another. This is the phenomenal aspect of Being. But by going through this very process of ontological 'diversification' and 'differentiation' all things are returning to their ultimate metaphysical source. The process of 'descent' and the process of 'ascent' are paradoxically one and the same thing. The relation between Unity and Multiplicity must be understood in this way. Just as Unity is not a static 'oneness' of death and rigidity, but is a never-ceasing dynamic process of a *coincidentia oppositorum*, Multiplicity is not a static 'differentia-tion' of things that are rigidly fixed once for all, but is a constant life process which contains within itself the ontological tension of Unity in Multiplicity.

> If looked at from the viewpoint of 'differentiation', (nothing is the same as anything else), and even liver and gall (a typical example of two things closely resembling each other), are as different and as far apart as the country of Ch'u and the country of Yüeh.
> However, looked at from the viewpoint of 'sameness', all things are one and the same.[19]

Unfortunately, the eyes of ordinary men are dazzled by the pheno-menal scintillations of Multiplicity and cannot perceive the pro-found Unity that underlies the whole. They cannot, as Chuang-tzŭ says, 'unify the objects of their knowledge'.[20]

The only right attitude we can take in such a situation is to 'let our minds be at ease in the harmony of spiritual perfection'.[21] The word 'harmony' (*ho*) here refers, as Ch'êng Hsüan Ying remarks, to the fact that when we 'unify the objects of our knowledge' and 'chaotify' all things, our mind enjoys a perfect peace, being no longer disturbed by 'what our ears and eyes approve'; it refers also to the fact that all things at this level are peacefully together, there being no 'essential' oppositions between them. We must not be blind to the phenomenal aspect of Being, Chuang-tzǔ says; but it is wrong for us to remain confined in the same phenomenal world and observe the Multiplicity of things exclusively from the phenomenal point of view. We must transcend such a stage, go up to a higher level, and looking down from that height observe the kaleidoscope of the ever-shifting Multiplicity of things. Only when we do this, are we in a position to know the reality of Being.

The dynamic relation between the original absolute Unity and the phenomenal Multiplicity, that is to say, the process by which the Absolute, stepping out of its metaphysical darkness, diversifies itself into a myriad of things of the phenomenal world is something which, as I have repeatedly pointed out discloses its reality only to a mind in the state of *ekstasis*, or as Chuang-tzǔ calls it, 'sitting in oblivion'. Particularly difficult to understand for a non-ecstatic mind is the ontological status of 'essences'.

As the Absolute divides itself through a process of ontological evolvement into 'ten thousand things', each one of the latter does seem to acquire a particular 'essence'. For, after all, what is the meaning of talking about 'ten thousand things', if they are not distinguishable from each other? How could they be distinguishable from each other if they were devoid of 'essences'? When we recognize *A* as being different and distinguishable from *B*, are we not at the same time recognizing *A* as being endowed with an 'essence' which is different from that of *B*?

From the viewpoint of Chuang-tzǔ, however, the things being endowed with 'essences' and their being 'essentially' distinguishable from one another is simply a matter of appearance. Each of the 'ten thousand things' appears to have its own 'essence' unalterably fixed once for all. In fact, it merely *appears* or *seems* to have such an 'essence'.

But our picture inevitably becomes complicated by the fact that those *seeming* 'essences' are not sheer nothing, either. They are not mere products of hallucination. They do have an ontological status peculiar to them. They are not ontologically groundless. The absolute all-pervading 'existence' can take on an infinite variety of forms because there is a kind of ontological basis for them. We cannot certainly say that the 'essences' *exist* in the ordinary sense of the world. But we cannot say either that they are absolutely non-existent.

It is at this point that Ibn 'Arabī, as we remember, introduced the concept of 'permanent archetypes' (*a'yān thābitah*) into his metaphysical system. And the concept did work admirably well. For Ibn 'Arabī succeeded thereby in philosophically settling the difficulty raised by this paradoxical situation. The 'permanent archetypes' are those metaphysical principles which can 'be said neither to exist nor not to exist', and through which the all-pervading divine Existence becomes inflected into a myriad of 'things'. But for him, too, it was not basically a philosophical question; it was rather a matter of an ecstatic vision.

Chuang-tzǔ has no such philosophical device. Instead, he resorts directly, as he often does, to a symbolic presentation of the content of his metaphysical vision. As a result, we now have what is unanimously acknowledged to be one of the most masterly descriptions of Wind in Chinese literature. It is not, of course, a mere literary piece of work. It is a philosophical symbol which Chuang-tzǔ uses for the purpose of expressing verbally what is verbally inexpressible. Furthermore, the whole passage is philosophically of supreme importance, because, as we shall see immediately, it constitutes what we might call a Taoist 'proof of the existence of God'.

The beginning part of the passage is purely symbolic. Its real philosophical meaning may best be understood if, in reading it, one keeps in mind that the Cosmic Wind symbolizes 'existence', or the Absolute in its all-pervading *actus*, and that the hollow 'openings' of the trees symbolize 'essences'.

> The Great Earth eructates; and the eructation is called Wind.[22] As long as the eructation does not actually occur, nothing is observable. But once it does occur, all the hollows of the trees raise ringing shouts.
> Listen! Do you not hear the trailing sound of the wind as it comes blowing from afar? The trees in the mountain forests begin to rustle, stir, and sway, and then all the hollows and holes of huge trees measuring a hundred arms' lengths around begin to give forth different sounds.
> There are holes like noses, like mouths, like ears; some are (square) like crosspieces upon pillars; some are (round) as cups, some are like mortars. Some are like deep ponds; some are like shallow basins. (The sounds they emit are accordingly various): some roar like torrents dashing against the rocks; some hiss like flying arrows; some growl, some gasp, some shout, some moan. Some sounds are deep and muffled, some sounds are sad and mournful.
> As the first wind goes away with the light trailing sound, there comes the following one with a deep rumbling sound. To a gentle wind the

hollows answer with faint sounds. To a stormy wind they answer with loud sounds.

However, once the raging gale has passed on, all these hollows and holes are empty and soundless. You see only the boughs swaying silently, and the tender twigs gently moving.[23]

As I said before, this is not intended to be a mere literary description of wind. Chuang-tzŭ's real intention is disclosed by what follows this passage. The philosophical intention of Chuang-tzŭ may be formulated in the following way. The 'hollows' and 'holes' of the trees *imagine* that they are independently existent, that *they* emit these sounds. They fail to notice that they emit these sounds only by the active working of the Wind upon them. It is, in reality, the Wind that makes the 'hollows' resound.

Not that the 'hollows' do not exist at all. They are surely there. But they are actualized only by the positive activity of the Wind. As is evident, this is a very apt description of the ontological status of 'essences', which was mentioned earlier.

It is also evident that the Wind here is not an ordinary physical wind. It is the Cosmic Wind corresponding exactly to Ibn 'Arabī's concept of *sarayān al-wujūd*, lit. the 'spreading of Existence'. It is interesting and, indeed, extremely significant, that both Ibn 'Arabī and Chuang-tzŭ conceive of 'existence' as something moving – 'blowing', 'flowing', or 'spreading'. For both of them, 'existence' is *actus*.

> (One and the same Wind) blows on ten thousand things in different ways, and makes each hollow produce its own peculiar sound, so that each imagines that its own self produces that particular sound. But who, in reality, is the one who makes (the hollows) produce various sounds?[24]

Who is it? In order to give *the* right answer to this crucial question, we must remark first of all that the Cosmic Wind has no sound of its own. The 'sound of Heaven' (*t'ien lai*) is soundless. What is audible to our physical ears are only the ten thousand sounds produced by the hollows of the trees. They are not the sound of Heaven; they are but the 'sound of Earth' (*ti lai*). But, Chuang-tzŭ insists, we must hear the soundless sound of Heaven behind each of the ten thousand sounds of Earth. Rather, we must realize that in hearing the sound of Earth we are really hearing nothing other than the sound of Heaven. The infinitely various sounds which the hollows emit are no other than the one, absolute sound of Heaven.

It is to be remarked that exactly the same question: 'Who is it?' can and must be asked of what actually is observable in the 'interior' region of our own being. Just as the 'hollows' of the trees emit all kinds of sounds as the Wind blows upon them, the 'interior' of man is in a state of constant turmoil. Who causes all this commotion? That is the central question. Are the minds of men themselves responsible for it? Or are the stimuli coming from external things its causes? No, Chuang-tzŭ answers. But let us first see how he describes the inner 'hollows' interminably producing noises and sounds.

> Even while asleep, the souls of men are (tormented) by coming into touch with various things (in dreams). When they wake up, the bodily functions begin to be active; they get entangled with external things, and all kinds of thoughts and emotions are aroused in them. And this induces them to use their mind every day in quarreling with others. Some minds are idle and vacant. Some minds are abstruse. Some are scrupulous. Those who have petty fears are nervous; those who are assailed by great fears are simply stupefied.
>
> The way they argue about the rightness and wrongness of matters reminds us of those who shoot arrows and missiles (i.e., they are extremely quick and active). They endeavor to secure a victory (in disputes) as if they had sworn before the gods. The way they go on consuming (their mental energy) day by day reminds us of (the leaves of trees) fading away in autumn and winter.
>
> They have gone so far into delusion and perlexity that it is no longer possible for them to be brought back. The way they fall deeper and deeper into infatuation as they grow older reminds us of minds firmly sealed with seals (of cupidity). Thus, when their minds draw near to death, there is no means of bringing them back to youthful brightness.
>
> Indeed (the movements of human minds are infinitely various as are the sounds produced by the hollows of the trees): joy, anger, sadness, and delight! Sometimes they worry about the future; sometimes they vainly bewail the irretrievable past. Sometimes fickle, sometimes obstinate. Sometimes flattering, sometimes self-conceited. Sometimes candid, sometimes affected.
>
> They remind us of all kinds of sounds emerging from the empty holes (of a flute), or mushrooms coming up out of warm dampness. Day and night, these changes never cease to replace one another before our eyes.
>
> Where do these (incessant changes) sprout from? No one knows their origin. It is impossible to know, absolutely impossible! It is an undeniable fact, however, that morning and evening these things are actually happening (in ourselves). Yea, precisely the fact that they are happening (in ourselves) means that we are alive![25]

After describing in this way the endless psychological events which are actually taking place in our minds day and night, Chuang-tzŭ proceeds to an interpretation of this bewildering phenomenon. What is the real and ultimate cause of all this? He asks himself whether the ultimate cause of this psychological turmoil is our 'ego'.

To say that the 'ego' is the cause of all this is nothing other than recognizing – indirectly – that the stimuli coming from the external world are the causes of our psychological movement. He describes this relation between the external stimuli and the changing states of our minds in terms of a relation between 'that' (i.e., the objects) and 'ego'.

> Without 'that', there would be no 'ego'. Without 'ego', 'that' would have nothing to lay hold of. (Thus our 'ego', i.e., the whole of our psychological phenomena, would seem to owe its existence to external stimuli). This view appears to come close to the truth. And yet it still leaves the question unanswered as to what really does make (our minds) move as they do.[26]

Chuang-tzŭ admits that external stimuli do excite commotions in our minds. Such a view, however, does not reach the very core of the matter. Those who imagine that this view is capable of fully accounting for the psychological changes that are taking place in ourselves are comparable to the 'holes' and 'hollows' of the trees that naively imagine that they themselves are producing the sounds they produce, without paying attention to the activity of the Wind.

Beyond the stimuli coming from the external objects, there is Something which is the ultimate cause, Something which induces external objects to act upon our minds and thereby cause the latter to become agitated. Beyond and behind all these phenomena there seems to be a real Agent who moves and controls all movements and all events in our minds, just as there is a Wind behind all the sounds produced by the 'holes'. However, just as the Wind is invisible and impalpable, so is this Agent unknowable and unseen. But just as we can feel the existence of the Wind – although it is invisible – through its activity, we can feel the existence of the Agent through His *actus*.

> It would seem that there is some real Ruler.[27] It is impossible for us to see Him in a concrete form. He is acting – there can be no doubt about it; but we cannot see His form. He does show His activity, but He has no sensible form.[28]

It is philosophically very important that Chuang-tzŭ asserts that the Absolute in its personal aspect, i.e., as the absolute Agent, is only accessible to our understanding as *actus*. The Absolute in this aspect is *actus*; it is not a 'thing'. Without having any sensible form, that is, without being a 'thing', it never ceases to manifest its activity. We can only follow its trace, everywhere, in everything. But we can never see its form because it has no form and because it is not a 'thing'. However, the human mind is by its own nature an 'essentialist'. It finds it extremely difficult, if not absolutely impossible to represent anything except in the form of a 'thing'. It cannot, except in very rare cases, conceive of anything as Nothing. The conception of the Absolute as Something which is *Nothing* is to an ordinary mind simply an intolerable paradox, if not sheer nonsense.

In order to render this metaphysical paradox a bit more acceptable, Chuang-tzŭ compares the situation with the complicated functioning of the members and organs of the body, the whole mechanism of which is governed and controlled by an invisible 'something': the soul.

> One hundred joints, nine openings, six entrails – these constitute a human body. Now of all these, which one should we respect most (i.e., which should we regard as the Ruler of the body)? Do you say that you respect (as the Rulers) all of them equally? (No, that is impossible). Then, do you favor one of them as particularly your own? (No, that again is impossible). But, if not (i.e., if neither all of them nor any particular one of them is in a position to rule over the body), is it the case that all of them are mere servants and maids? (However, if they were all servants and maids), how could the country (i.e., the body) be kept in order? Or is it the case that they rule and are ruled, occupying the positions of the Ruler and the subjects by turns?
>
> No, there does exist a real Ruler (who governs them all). And whether or not man knows the concrete form of this Ruler, his reality is never affected thereby; it neither increases nor decreases thereby.[29]

The true Ruler in this case is the soul whose concrete form is known to nobody. But of course this is here put forward as an image which would clarify the relation between the Absolute and all events and all phenomena in the world of Being. Just as the bodily organs and members are under the domination of the invisible soul, all that exists and happens in the world is under the dominion of the unknown-unknowable Ruler.

As I pointed out earlier, it is highly significant that Chuang-tzŭ here presents the 'true Ruler' of the world as *actus*. No one can see the Absolute itself as 'something' existent, but no one can deny, either, the presence of its *actus*. And that *actus* is philosophically nothing other than Existence.

We have to notice also that the *actus* of the Absolute which, in the earlier passage, was described as the Cosmic Wind, i.e., a cosmic force, is here presented as something personal – God. In the world-view of Chuang-tzŭ, the Absolute or the Way has two different aspects, cosmic and personal. In its cosmic aspect the Absolute is Nature, a vital energy of Being which pervades all and makes them exist, grow, decay, and ultimately brings them back to the original source, while in its personal aspect it is God, the Creator of Heaven and Earth, the Lord of all things and events. As conceptions and representations, the two are totally different from one another, but in reality both point to exactly one and the same thing. The difference between Nature and God is merely a matter of points of view, or the ways in which the human mind conceives of the Absolute which is in itself wholly unknown and unknowable. To this ultimate metaphysical mystery we shall try to come closer in the following chapter.

Notes

1. II, p. 74.

2. *ibid.*, p. 75: 「此忘天地, 遺萬物, 外不察乎宇宙, 內不覺其一身, 故能曠然無累, 與物俱, 往, 而無所不應也」.

3. 王先謙,「見是非, 則道之渾然者傷矣」.

4. II, p. 75.

5. 「滑疑之耀」.

6. 葆光, II, p. 83 成玄英:「葆蔽也. 至忘而照, 卽照而忘, 故能韜蔽其光, 其光彌朗」, II, p. 89.

7. Lao-tzǔ, however, does think and talk about this 'ineffable' Something. We shall come to this point in the following chapter.

8. *Chuang-tzǔ* IV, p. 183.

9. VI, p. 242.

10. i.e., the words which correspond to these 'boundaries' have no unalterable semantic fixity.

11. II, p. 83.

12. II, p. 66.

13. II, pp. 69–70.

14. Note again how Chuang-tzǔ attributes 'essence'-forming power to language. A thing which in its original state, is 'nameless', turns into something rigidly fixed and unchangeable, once it is given a definite name.

15. *t'ien chün* 天鈞, p. 70. Ch'êng Hsüan Ying:「天均(＝鈞) 者自然均平之理也. 夫達道, 聖人, 虛懷不執, 故能和是於無是,同非於無非,所以息智乎均平之鄉, 休心乎自然之境也」, p. 74.

16. *liang hang* 兩行, p. 70.

17. 齊物論. This can also be understood as meaning 'Equalization of Various Views on Being', i.e., the nullification of the opposition among various views on Being on the level of absolute transcendence.

18. II, p. 74.

19. V, p. 190.

20. V, p. 193. 「一知之所知」, lit. 'to unify what is known by the knowledge'.

21. V, p. 191 「遊心乎德之和」. Commenting upon this phrase Ch'êng Hsüan Ying says: 「既而混同萬物, 不知耳目之宜, 故能遊道德之鄉, 故乎至道之境者也」, p. 192.

22. The issuing forth of the phenomenal things from the absolute One is here compared to the great Earth belching forth the Wind. Note the remarkable similarity of this mythopoeic image to that used by Ibn 'Arabî when the latter tries to describe the ontological inner tension of the Divine Names within the Absolute, which is so acute that it cannot but be relieved by the Names 'bursting out'; see Part I, pp. 125–126.

23. pp. 45–46.

24. II, p. 50.

25. II, p. 51.

26. II, p. 55.

27. *chên tsai*, 眞宰.

28. II, p. 55.

29. II, pp. 55–56.

VII   The Way

Up to this point we have been following the footprints of Chuang-tzŭ as he tries to describe analytically the process by which a vision of the Absolute is revealed to the Taoist Perfect Man, opening up in his mind a new vista of the whole world of Being which is totally different from, and radically opposed to, that shared by ordinary men on the level of common sense. In so doing we have discarded Lao-tzŭ except in a few places. Nor have we analyzed in a systematic manner the philosophical thought expressed in the *Tao Tê Ching.* We have adopted this course for several reasons, the most important of them being that Chuang-tzŭ, as I have pointed out a number of times, is vitally interested in describing the epistemological aspect of the problem of the Tao, while Lao-tzŭ is almost exclusively interested in giving the result of the experience of the Absolute, i.e., what comes after, and out of, that experience.

We have seen in the preceding chapter how Chuang-tzŭ submits to an elaborate theoretical analysis the process of the gradual development of the human mind toward a Taoist perfection. He attempts to give an accurate description of the Taoist variety of metaphysical or spiritual experience by which man 'ascends' toward the Absolute until he becomes completely unified with it. Certainly, Chuang-tzŭ is equally interested in the 'descending' movement of the mind, from the state of *ekstasis* back to the level of daily consciousness, that is, from the stage of the absolute Unity back to that of 'essential' Multiplicity. But even then, his description of the Descent is epistemological as well as ontological. That is to say, his description is made so that to each objective stage of Being there corresponds a subjective stage of spiritual experience, so that the ontological system, in the case of Chuang-tzŭ, is at the same time a complete epistemological system, and *vice versa.* Moreover, it is typical of Chuang-tzŭ that these two aspects are so completely fused together that it is at times difficult for us to decide whether a given passage is intended to be a description of the subjective side of the matter or of the objective, ontological structure of things. The 'sitting in oblivion' is an example in point.

Lao-tzŭ, on the contrary, does not seem to be very much interested in the experiential stages which precede the ultimate vision of the Absolute. He does not take the trouble to explain *how* and by what process we can obtain the vision of the Absolute. He seems to be more interested in the questions: (1) What is the Absolute, i.e., the Way?; and (2) How is the 'sacred man' expected to behave in ordinary circumstances of social life on the basis of his vision of the Way?

From the very outset he utters his words in the name of the Absolute, as a representative of those who have already attained to the highest stage of Taoist perfection. Behind the pages of the *Tao Tê Ching* we feel the presence of a man who has experienced the most intimate union with the Absolute, who, consequently knows what the Absolute is.

Quite abruptly Lao-tzŭ sets out to talk about the Way. He tries to impart to us his personal knowledge of the Absolute, and his strange – so it seems to common sense understanding – vision of the world. If it were not for Chuang-tzŭ, we would hardly be able to know for sure what kind of experiential background this extraordinary vision of the world has as its unstated 'prehistory'. This is why we have up till now intentionally refrained from turning systematically toward an analysis of Lao-tzŭ's thought, and confined ourselves to the task of clarifying this 'prehistory' in the light of what Chuang-tzŭ says about it.

But the particular situation which we have just mentioned concerning Lao-tzŭ's basic attitude would seem to suggest that the *Tao Tê Ching* is the best possible thing for us to have recourse to, if we want to obtain a clear understanding of the Taoist conception of the Absolute, its reality and its working. As we shall realize immediately, the Absolute as conceived by Lao-tzŭ and Chuang-tzŭ is by its very nature beyond all verbal description. Despite that, Lao-tzŭ does endeavor to describe, at least symbolically, this ineffable Something. And he succeeds marvellously. In point of fact, the *Tao Tê Ching* is a remarkable work in that it attempts to delineate to the utmost limit of possibility the Absolute which is essentially indescribable. This is why we shall be greatly dependent in the present chapter upon this book for elucidating the metaphysical structure of the Absolute.

We must remark, however, that here again, Lao-tzŭ does not explain how and why it is ineffable, and indescribable. He simply states that the Way is 'nameless', 'formless', 'imageless', 'invisible', 'inaudible', etc., that it is 'nothing' (*wu wu*)[1] or Nothing (*wu*)[2]. As to the psychological or logical process by which one reaches this conclusion, he says nothing positive. This process is clarified in an interesting way by Chuang-tzŭ in a passage which bears ample witness to his being an excellent dialectician. Let us begin by reading the passage in question as an illuminating theoretical introduction to Lao-tzǔ's conception of the Absolute.

Chuang-tzǔ is keenly conscious of the fact that the Way, or the Absolute in its absoluteness, defies all verbalization and reasoning; that, if brought down to the level of language, the Way will immediately and inevitably turn into a concept. As a concept, even the Absolute is exactly in the same rank as any other concept. He makes this observation the starting-point of his argument. People, he says, distinguish between 'right' and 'wrong' in all matters and thus take the position of there being a fundamental distinction between 'right' and 'wrong'. Chuang-tzǔ, on his part, puts forward the thesis that there is no distinction between 'right' and 'wrong'.[3] Ordinary people and Chuang-tzǔ are in this respect diametrically opposed to each other. And yet, he goes on to say, as a logical proposition, 'there-is-no-distinction-between-right-and-wrong' is no less a logos[4] than the opposite proposition: 'there-is-a-distinction-between-right-and-wrong'. In this respect, both belong to one and the same category.[5]

In reality, the two propositions refer to two completely different levels of discourse. The difference, as we already know, comes out only when one realizes that the positive statement is a statement typical of the empirical level of discourse, while the negative one is orginally intended to represent the ontological 'chaotification' which is experienced by the Perfect Man in the moments of his ecstatic union with the Absolute. As an expression of this original experience, the statement is not a logical proposition except in its outward form. But as long as it does have a logical form, it is a logical proposition; and as such, it does not properly represent the unique experience of 'chaotification', being as it is nothing but the contradictory of the proposition: 'there-is-a-distinction-between-right-and-wrong'. If such is the case, could there be any other attitude for us to take than maintaining a complete silence? 'Despite this', he says, 'I would dare to discuss the problem (on the logical or conceptual level).' With these preliminary remarks, he sets out to develop an extremely interesting argument in the following way. The argument, in brief, establishes that the Absolute in its original absoluteness is *conceptually* the negation-of-negation-of-negation, that is, the negation of the Absolute's being Nothing which, again, is the negation of Being. And that is the furthest limit to which our logical thinking can go in its venturesome attempt at grasping the Absolute on the level of concepts.

We have seen in the preceding chapter how Chuang-tzǔ, in describing the stages of the spiritual development of 'sitting in oblivion', mentions as the ultimate limit of ecstatic cognition the view that 'nothing has ever existed from the very beginning'.

> What is the ultimate limit of Knowledge? It is the stage represented by the view that nothing has ever existed from the very beginning. This is the furthest limit (of Knowledge), to which nothing more can be added.[6]

'Nothing has ever existed from the very beginning' appearing in this quotation is the key-phrase for the right understanding of the passage we are going to read.[7] It is important to keep in mind, however, that in this latter passage we are no longer concerned with the epistemological question of the utmost limit of human cognition. Our problem here is essentially of a metaphysical nature. For it concerns the ultimate origin of Being, or of the Universe. The 'beginning' here in question means the beginning point of the world of Being. Whenever we think logically of the formation of the world of Being, we have to posit a 'beginning'. Our Reason cannot conceive of the world of Being without imagining a point at which it 'began' to exist.

> So we posit Beginning. (But the moment we posit Beginning, our Reason cannot help going further back and) admit the idea of there having been no Beginning. (Thus the concept of No-Beginning is necessarily established. But the moment we posit No-Beginning, our logical thinking goes further back by negating the very idea which it has just established, and) admits the idea of there having been no 'there-having-been-no-Beginning'. (The concept of 'No-No-Beginning' is thus established.)

The concept of Beginning, i.e., the initial point of the whole world of Being, is but a relative concept. It can be conceptually pushed further and further back. But no matter how far we may push it back, this conceptual process does not reach an end. In order to put a definite end to this process we have to transcend it at one stroke by negating the Beginning itself. As a result, the concept of No-Beginning is obtained.

However, the concept of No-Beginning is, again, a relative one, being as it is a concept that subsists only by being opposed to that of Beginning. In order to remove this relativity and attain to the *absolute* No-Beginning, we have to transcend the No-Beginning itself by negating it and establishing No-No-Beginning. The No-No-Beginning – which must be articulated as No-[No-Beginning] – is, however, a concept whose real significance is disclosed only to those who are able to understand it as signifying a metaphysical state of affairs which is to be grasped by a kind of metaphysical intuition. And this would seem to indicate that

No-No-Beginning, although it is something that has been posited by Reason, lies beyond the grasp of all logical reasoning.

> In the same manner, (we begin by taking notice of the fact that) there is Being. (But the moment we recognize Being, our Reason goes further back and admits that) there is Non-Being (or Nothing). (But the moment we posit Non-Being we cannot but go further back and admit that) there has not been from the very beginning Non-Being. (The concept of No-[Non-Being] once established in this way, the Reason goes further back and admits that) there has been no 'there-having-been-no-Non-Being' (i.e., the negation of the negation of Non-Being, or No-[No Non-Being]).

This concept of No-[No Non-Being] or No-No-Nothing represents the ultimate logical stage which is reached by our negating – i.e., transcending – the negation itself of the opposition of Being and Non-Being. This is the logical and conceptual counterpart of the Way or the metaphysical Nothing which is not a simple 'nothing', but a transcendent Nothing that lies beyond both 'being' and 'non-being' as ordinarily understood.

We have thus seemingly succeeded in conceptualizing the Way as an absolutely transcendent Nothing. However, does the Absolute thus conceptualized mirror faithfully the reality of the Absolute? To this question, we can say neither Yes nor No. As in the case of the concept of No-No-Beginning, we must remark that the concept of No-No-Nothing does justice to the reality of the Absolute only when we transcend, in understanding it, the sphere of logical thinking itself into that of ecstatic or mystic intuition. But when we do so, the concept of No-No-Nothing will immediately cease to be a concept. And we shall end up by realizing that all the logical reasoning that has preceded has in reality been futile and of no use. If, on the contrary, we refuse to transcend the level of reasoning, the concept of No-No-Nothing will remain for ever an empty concept devoid of all positive meaning and, therefore, in no position to do justice to the reality of the Absolute. Thus, either way, the conceptualizing activity of the mind proves powerless in grasping the Absolute as it really is.

> (When Reason begins to be active), all of a sudden we find ourselves confronted with 'being' and 'non-being'. (Since, however, these are relative concepts in the sense that 'being' at this stage turns into 'non-being' at the next stage, and so on and so forth), we can never know for sure which is really 'being' and which is really 'non-being'. Now I have just established something (that looks) meaningful, (i.e., I have established the Absolute as No-No-Nothing). But I do not know whether I have truly established something meaningful or whether what I have established is, after all, nothing meaningful.

At this point, Chuang-tzŭ suddenly changes the direction of his thinking and tries another approach. This time he turns to the aspect of Unity which, as we have seen earlier, is one of the most salient features of the Absolute. But before discussing the problem on the level of logical reasoning, he reminds us by way of caution of what is to be understood by the statement that the Absolute is 'one'. The Absolute, he says, is 'one' as a *coincidentia oppositorum*. We have already examined in Chapter IV Chuang-tzŭ's position concerning this problem. The key-term is 'equalization' of all things in the Absolute.

The Way or the Absolute, according to Chuang-tzŭ, is the metaphysical state of Heavenly Equalization, that is, the absolute One which 'equalizes' all oppositions and contradictions. At this stage, the smallest is at the same time the biggest, and a moment is eternity.

> (The state of Heavenly Equalization defies common sense and reason, for we admit at this stage that) there is in the world nothing bigger than the tip of a hair of an animal in autumn, while Mount T'ai (which is usually mentioned as an example of a very big thing) is considered extremely small. No one lives longer than a child who dies before coming of age, while P'êng Tsu (who is related to have lived 800 years) is considered to have died young. Heaven and Earth endure for the same length of time as I do (i.e., the eternal duration of Heaven and Earth is equivalent to the momentary duration of my individual existence in this world). And the ten thousand things are exactly the same as my own self.

Thus, from the viewpoint of Heavenly Equalization, all things become reduced to a single unity in terms of both time and space. How does logical reasoning grasp such an absolute Oneness? That is the question we are faced with now.

> All things (at this stage) are absolutely 'one'. But if so, how is it possible for us to say something? (i.e., Since all things are *absolutely* 'one', there is no longer anything whatsoever opposed to anything else whatsoever. And since there is no opposition, it is meaningless even to say: 'one').
> (But in order to *reason*, I have to posit something). So I have said: 'one'. But how could I judge that (it is, or they are) 'one' without explicitly positing the term (i.e., word or concept: 'one')? However, (the moment I posit the term 'one'), the (original) 'one' (i.e., the absolute One which is a *coincidentia oppositorum*) and the term (or concept of) 'one' necessarily make 'two'. (This would mean that the least amount of reasoning makes the original One split itself into Two and thus produces dualism.)
> Then, these 'two' (i.e., the two-term judgment: 'The Way is One') together with the 'one' (i.e., the absolute One which is prior to any judgment) make 'three'.

And from this point on the process extends endlessly, so much so that even a talented mathematician will not be able to count out the number, much less ordinary people.
If, in this way, moving from Non-Being to Being leads us inevitably to (at least) 'three', where shall we get if we move from Being to Being (i.e., if, instead of starting from the absolute One, we take a relativist point of view and begin to pursue the individual things which go on being endlessly diversified)? Better not to make any move (i.e., better not to exercise reasoning concerning the Absolute and the things). Let us content ourselves with abiding by the (great) Yes (which transcends all oppositions and contradictions, and leaves everything as it is)!

Thus after developing an elaborate reasoning on the nature of the Absolute, Chuang-tzŭ, ironically enough, ends by asserting the futility of reasoning. He advises us to abandon all logical thinking about the Absolute and to remain immersed ecstatically in the absolute intuitive Knowledge. For only by doing so can we hope to be in direct contact with the absolute One.

Thus the highest stage of Knowledge is remaining motionless in what cannot absolutely be known (by reasoning). Is there anyone who knows the Word which is no longer a 'word'? Is there anyone who knows the Way which is not even a 'way'? If there is a man who knows such a thing, he deserves to be named the 'Treasury of Heaven' (i.e., he who is in possession of the key to the limitless treasure house of Being. Nay, he is the same as the 'treasury' itself). (The Treasury of Heaven with which such a man is completely identical and unified is like an unbounded ocean); no matter how much you pour water into it, it will never become full; and no matter how much you dip up water therefrom, it will never run dry. And nobody knows how and from where all these (limitless) things come into being.
It is the Knowledge of such a man that is properly to be called the 'shaded Light'.

Thus by following step by step Chuang-tzŭ's argument we have been led to the conclusion that the Way or the Absolute in its ultimate reality transcends all reasoning and conceptualization. This conclusion forms the starting-point for the metaphysical thinking of Lao-tzŭ. As I remarked at the outset of this chapter, Lao-tzŭ does not take the trouble of explaining the logical or epistemological process which underlies his metaphysical system. But we are now in a position to understand the background against which this metaphysics must be set.

Quite naturally, the metaphysics of Lao-tzŭ begins by mentioning negative attributes of the Way. The Way, to begin with, is 'nameless'.[8]

The Way in its absolute reality (*ch'ang*) has no name.[9]

Interminably continuous like a thread, no name can be given to it.[10]

The Way is hidden and nameless.[11]

That the Way is 'nameless' implies that the very name 'Way' (*tao*) is nothing other than a makeshift. Lao-tzŭ forcibly calls it 'Way' because without naming it he cannot even refer to it. This fact is clearly indicated by the very famous opening sentence of the *Tao Tê Ching*.

> The 'way' which can be designated by the word 'way' is not the real[12] Way.
> The 'name' which can be designated by the word 'name' is not the real[12] Name.[13]

It is interesting and important to remark that this passage, besides being a clear statement to the effect that the Absolute is 'nameless', is designed to be an implicit criticism of Confucian realism. The 'way' which is here said to be not the real Way is the human (or ethical) 'way' as understood in the Confucian school. And the 'name' which is said to be not the real Name refers to the so-called 'names' of the Confucianists, such as 'benevolence', 'righteousness', 'wisdom', etc., which the Confucianists consider cardinal virtues.

As to the meaning of the word 'way' (*tao*) as it was originally used by Confucius himself and his circle, authentic information is furnished by the *Lun Yü* ('The Analects'). Entering into the fine details of the problem would lead us too far beyond the scope of the present study. Here I shall confine myself to giving a few examples just to clarify the most essential characteristics of the Confucian concept of *tao*.

> Master Yu (one of the disciples of Confucius) once remarked: Those who are by nature filial and fraternal (i.e., those who behave with an inborn goodwill toward their parents and elder brothers) at home are seldom inclined (in public life) toward comporting themselves against the will of their superiors. And (of those who do not comport themselves against the will of their superiors) none, indeed, has ever wanted to stir up confusion (in society).
> (The observation of this fact makes us realize that) the 'princely man' should strive (to establish) the root, for the root once established, the 'way' (*tao*) will naturally grow up. The right attitude toward parents and elder brothers may, in this respect, be considered the root of 'benevolence' (or 'human love').[14]

It is contextually clear that the 'way' in this passage means the proper ethical attitude of man toward his brethren in society. The argument is typical of Confucianists. It recognizes man's inborn goodwill toward those closest in blood as the 'root' or 'origin' of human morals. This inborn goodwill, when expanded into a universal goodwill toward all fellow-members of society, turns into the highest principle of ethical conduct, the 'way', as exemplified by the virtue of 'benevolence'.

Clearly, the conceptual structure of the argument is based on the terms 'filial piety', 'fraternal respect', and 'benevolence'. The word 'way' is mentioned almost in a casual way. It is not even a key term in the real sense of the word.

> The Master (Confucius) said: O Shên,[15] my 'way' is a unity running through (all forms of my behavior). Master Tsêng respectfully replied: Yes!
> When the Master left the place, the other disciples asked (Master Tsêng) saying: What did he mean?
> Master Tsêng said: Our Master's 'way' consists in 'loyalty' (i.e., being loyal or faithful to one's own conscience) and, 'kindness' (i.e., being thoughtful for others, as if their problems were one's own).[16]

In this passage, the 'way' means again the leading principle of ethical conduct. By the statement: 'my way is a unity running through' Confucius means to say that although his behavior appears concretely in various forms, there underlies them all a unique ethical principle. The 'way', in other words, is here the unifying principle of all forms of moral conduct.

> The Master said: In case the 'way' prevails in a state, you may be daring in both speech and action. But in case the 'way' does not prevail, you may be daring in action, but you should be reserved in speech.[17]

Confucius often speaks of the 'way' prevailing in a state – or more literally 'a state's possessing the way'.[18] What is meant by the word in such contexts is too clear to need elucidation.

> The Master said: The 'way' of the 'princely man' is (manifested) in three (forms). But I myself am equal to none of them. He who is really virtuous does not worry. He who is really wise is never perplexed. He who is really bold does not fear.
> Master K'ung (one of the disciples of Confucius) said: Master, these precisely are your own 'way'![19]

The interpretation of the word *tao* may vary more or less in accordance with contexts, but the fundamental meaning is observable in all the uses of the word. It means the right or proper 'way' of acting in social life. The 'way' for Confucius is the highest principle of ethical conduct.

It would be going too far to assert that this Confucian concept of the 'way' is exclusively human. For, although it *is* essentially human and ethical in its concrete manifestation, the concept would seem to have in the moral consciousness of Confucius something cosmic as its metaphysical core. The 'way' in its original metaphysical form is the all-pervading supreme law of Being. The supreme law governing the working of the universe in general, and governing man as a part of the whole universe in particular, is called 'way' when it is comprehended by, or reflected in, the consciousness of man. The highest principle of ethical conduct is, in this sense, nothing other than a particular manifestation of the universal law of Being in the form of the supreme law governing the right forms of human life. The principle of ethical conduct is, for Confucius, by no means a man-made rule, or set of rules, regulating from outside the behavior of man. It is a reflection in the human consciousness of the highest law of the universe. And as such, it is the 'internalized' cosmic law regulating human behavior from within.

Thus to know the 'way' does not consist merely in learning the formal rules of good manners and correct behavior. It consists in man's coming into contact with the all-pervading metaphysical law of the Cosmos through becoming conscious of it. The following very forceful and passionate statement would sound absurd or even ridiculous if the Confucian 'way' were merely a matter of etiquette and correct behavior.

> The Master said: If a man hears (i.e., understands the profound meaning of) the 'way' in the morning, he may die contented in the evening.[20]

In this 'cosmic' aspect, the Confucian conception of the 'way' might be said to have something in common with the Taoist counterpart. The difference between the two, however, is far more conspicuous and essential than the point of contact, as we shall see presently. There is, in any case, a conscious attitude noticeable on the part of Lao-tzŭ and Chuang-tzŭ to reject the 'way' as understood by Confucius and his followers. The 'way', Lao-tzŭ says, which can be recognized as the 'way' by ordinary people – Confucius and his followers being their representatives – is not the real Way. The real Way, or the Absolute in its absoluteness, is not something which an ordinary mind can become conscious of. How could one 'know' it? How could one 'hear' it? It is by nature something unknown, unknowable and inaudible.

Being essentially unknown and unkowable, the Way is 'nameless'. Here agin we encounter Lao-tzŭ consciously taking up a position against the Confucian attitude toward the 'names'. Certainly, Lao-tzŭ too speaks of 'names'. The 'nameless' Way, he says, goes on assuming various 'names' in its process of self-determinations.

> The Way in its absolute reality has no 'name'. It is (comparable to) uncarved wood.[21] . . . Only when it is cut out are there 'names'.[22]

But there is a basic difference between Lao-tzŭ and Confucius with regard to 'names' in that Lao-tzŭ does not regard these 'names' as absolutely established. As we have learnt from the explanation given by Chuang-tzŭ of 'chaotification' as well as from Lao-tzŭ's thesis that everything in this world is 'relative', all 'names' – and ultimately the 'things' designated by the 'names' – are but of a relative nature. Confucian 'realism' on the contrary, takes the position that behind every 'name' there is a corresponding objective and permanent reality. And to the highest Names there correspond the highest realities. These Names represent the cardinal virtues: 'benevolence', 'righteousness', 'decorum', 'wisdom', 'truthfulness'. Against this, Lao-tzŭ puts forward the view that these 'names which may be mentioned as names' are not real 'names'. In his mind, the Names, or the cardinal virtues, which are so highly valued by the Confucians are but so many symptoms of degeneration and corruption, that is, symptoms of men's having alienated themselves from the Absolute.

> Only when the great Way declines, do 'benevolence' and 'righteousness' arise. Only when cleverness and sagacity make their appearance do wiles and intrigues arise. Only when the six basic kinship relations (i.e., the relationships between father and son, elder and younger brothers, husband and wife) are out of harmony do filial sons make their appearance. Only when the state falls into confusion and disorder, do loyal subjects make their appearance.[23]

> It is only after Virtue is lost that 'benevolence' becomes prominent. It is only after 'benevolence' is lost that 'righteousness' becomes prominent. And it is only after 'righteousness' is lost that 'decorum' becomes prominent.
> Indeed, 'decorum' emerges in an age in which 'loyalty' and 'faithfulness' have become scarce. It marks the beginning of disorder (in society).[24]

Far from being real values as the Confucians assert, all these so-called Names are but signs of man's alienation from Reality. In the very establishment of these Names as absolute and permanent values there is an unmistakable indication that the Absolute has been lost sight of. Speaking more generally, no 'name' is absolute. For, as Lao-tzŭ says, a 'name which can be designated by the word "name" ' is not the real Name. The only 'real Name' (*ch'ang ming*) which is absolute is the Name assumed by the Absolute. However, that absolute Name is, paradoxically, 'Nameless', or as we shall see presently, the 'Mystery of Mysteries', the 'Gate of all Wonders'.

I have just used the phrase: 'the Name assumed by the Absolute'. And in fact, as Lao-tzŭ himself explicitly admits, the 'nameless' Way does assume a more positive 'name' at its very first stage of

self-manifestation or self-determination. That first 'name' assumed
by the Absolute in its creative activity is Existence (*yu*).[25] Lao-tzŭ,
making a concession to popular parlance, sometimes calls the latter
Heaven and Earth (*t'ien ti*).[26] Strictly speaking, the Way at this stage
is not yet actually Heaven and Earth. It is Heaven and Earth only *in
potentia*. It is that face of the Absolute by which it turns, so to speak,
toward the world of Being which is to appear therefrom. It refers to
the Absolute as the principle of eternal and endless creativity.

> The Nameless is the beginning of Heaven and Earth. The Named is
> the Mother of the ten thousand things.[27]

But before we go into the details of the problem of the Named, we
must pursue further the 'nameless' aspect of the Way.

With a view to making a fresh start in the consideration of this
aspect of the Way, we may conveniently begin by recalling the
opening words of the *Tao Tê Ching*, which has been quoted above[28]
and which has led us into a sort of long digression on the fundamental difference between Confucianism and Taoism regarding the
understanding of 'way' (*tao*) and 'name' (*ming*). The passage reads:
The 'way' which can be designated by the word 'way' is not the real
Way. The 'name' which can be designated by the word 'name' is not
the real Name.

The same conception of the Way is expressed by Chuang-tzŭ in a
somewhat different way as follows.

> If the Way is made clear, it is no longer the Way.[29]

He means to say by this that a thing which can be pointed to as the
Way is not the real Way. And again,

> Is there anyone who knows the Way which is not a 'way'?[30]

This, of course, means that the real Way has no visible form by
which one could designate it by the word 'way'.

To say that the Way or the Absolute in its absoluteness is 'nameless', that it refuses to be designated by any 'name' whatsoever, is to
say that it transcends all linguistic comprehension. And this is the
same as to say that the Way is beyond the grasp of both thought and
sense perception. The Way is of such a nature that Reason cannot
conceive of it nor the senses perceive it. The Way, in other words, is
an absolute Transcendent.

> Even if we try to see it, it cannot be seen. In this respect it is called
> 'figureless'.[31]
> Even if we try to hear it, it cannot be heard. In this respect it is called
> 'inaudibly faint'.
> Even if we try to grasp it, it cannot be touched. In this respect it is
> called 'extremely minute'.

In these three aspects, it is totally unfathomable. They merge into One.[32]
(Ordinarily, the upper part of a thing is brightly visible, while the lower part is dark and obscure. But this is not the case with the Way.)
Upward, it is not bright. Downward, it is not dark.
It continues interminably like a thread, but no name can be given to it. And (this interminable creative activity) ultimately returns to the original Nothingness.
Shall we describe it as a shapeless Shape, or imageless Image? Shall we describe it as something vague and undeterminable? Standing in front of it, we do not see its head. Following behind it, we do not see its rear.[33]

Thus the 'namelessness' of the Way is the same as its being Non-Being. For whatever is absolutely imperceptible and inconceivable, whatever has no 'image' at all, is, for man, the same as 'non-existent'. It is 'Nothing' (*wu*).[34]

It is important to notice that the Way appears as 'Nothing' only when looked at from *our* point of view. It is Nothing for us because it transcends human cognition. It is, as Islamic philosophers would say, a matter of *i'tibār* or (human) 'viewpoint'. Otherwise, the Way in itself is – far from being 'nothing' – Existence in the fullest sense of the term. For it is the ultimate origin and source of all Being.

For ordinary human consciousness the Way *is* Nothing. But it is not 'nothing' in a purely negative sense. It is not a *passive* 'nothing'. It is a *positive* Nothing in the sense that it is Non-Being pregnant with Existence.

It goes without saying that this positive aspect of the Way is far more difficult to explain than its negative side. Properly speaking it is absolutely impossible to explain it verbally. As we have just seen, the reality of the Way is indescribable and ineffable. And yet Lao-tzŭ does try to describe it, or at least to give some hints as to how we should 'feel' its presence in the midst of the world of Being. Quite naturally, the hints are extremely dim and obscure. They are of necessity of a symbolic nature.

The Way in its reality is utterly vague, utterly indistinct.[35]
Utterly indistinct, utterly vague, yet there is within it an Image.
Utterly vague, utterly indistinct, yet there is within it Something.
Utterly profound, utterly dark, yet there is within it the purest Essence.
The purest Essence is extremely real.
(Eternally and unchangingly its creativeness is at work, so that) from of old till now its Name[36] has never left it. Through this Name it governs the principles of all things.
How do we know that it is so with the principles of all things? From what I have just said.[37]

Thus the Way in its purely negative aspect which is absolutely beyond human cognition is Nothing and Non-Being. In this aspect the Way has no 'name' whatsoever. Even the word 'way' (*tao*) is properly inapplicable to it. It is 'nameless'.

This absolutely intangible and impenetrable Mystery steps out of its own darkness and comes a stage closer to having a 'name'. It is, at this stage of self-manifestation, a faint and shadowy 'Image'. In the Image we feel vaguely the presence of Something awful and mysterious. But we do not yet know what it is. It is felt as Something but it has still no 'name'.

In the first part of the present study we saw how, in the metaphysical system of Ibn 'Arabī, the Absolute in its absoluteness is 'nameless'. We saw how the Absolute in such a state is even beyond the stage at which it is properly to be designated by the name *Allāh*. Likewise in Lao-tzŭ, this Something is made to be antecedent even to God (lit. the heavenly Emperor).

> Unfathomably deep it is like the ancestor of the ten thousand things
> . . .
> Like a deep mass of water it is (and nothing is visible on the surface),
> yet Something seems to be there.
> I know not whose son it is.[38]
> It would seem to be antecedent even to the Emperor (i.e., God.[39]

This 'nameless' Something, in its positive aspect, i.e., in its eternal and everlasting creativeness, may be 'named' provisionally the 'way'. Lao-tzŭ himself admits that it is a provisional 'name'. But of all the possible provisional 'names', the 'way' is the representative one. Actually, Lao-tzŭ proposes several other 'names' for the Way, and points out several typical 'attributes', each one of which refers to this or that particular aspect of the Way.[40]

> There is Something, formless but complete,[41] born before Heaven and Earth.
> Silent and void, it stands alone,[42] never changing. It goes round everywhere, never stopping.[43] It may be considered the Mother of the whole world.[44]
> I know not its 'name'. Forging a pseudonym, I call it the 'Way'.
> Being forced to name it (further), I call it 'Great'.
> Being 'Great' would imply 'Moving-forward'.[45] 'Moving-forward' would imply 'Going-far'.[46] And 'Going-far' would imply 'Turning-back'.[47]

In the passage just quoted Lao-tzŭ suggests the possibility of the Absolute being named in various ways. At the same time, however, he makes it clear that all these 'Names' or 'attributes' are provisional, relative, and partial. For instance, he proposes to call the Absolute the 'Great'. He is justified in doing so because the Absolute or the Way *is* 'great'. But it is, we have to remember, 'great' only in a certain sense, from a particular standpoint. To look upon the Way as something 'great' represents but one particular point of view which we human beings take with regard to the Absolute. This naturally implies that there is also a certain respect in which the Way should be called 'small'. It can be considered 'great'; it can be considered 'small'. Both 'names' are right, but neither of them can do full justice to its reality.

In this respect, the Way is comparable to a water plant adrift, turning this way or that. It has no fixity. Having no fixity, it accepts any 'name', but no 'name' can represent it perfectly.

> The great Way is like a thing drifting on the water. It goes every-where, left and right.
> The ten thousand things owe their existence to it. And yet it does not boast (of its own creative activity). It accomplishes its work, yet makes no claim. It clothes and nourishes the ten thousand things, yet never domineers over them. Being absolutely free of desire, it may be called 'Small'.
> The ten thousand things go back to it, yet it makes no claim to being their Master. In this respect, it may also be called 'Great'.[48]

This difficulty which we inevitably encounter in attempting to give a proper 'name' to the Absolute is due not only to the fact that it is essentially 'nameless' but also to the fact that the Absolute is *not* a 'thing' in the sense in which we usually understand the term 'thing'. The descriptive power of human language is tragically limited. The moment we linguistically designate a state of affairs, whether metaphysical or empirical, by a noun, it becomes reified, that is, it turns into a 'substance' in our representation. We have earlier referred to the Absolute as Something; but 'Something' is in our imagination *some substance*, however mysterious it may be. And exactly the same is true of such 'names' as 'Mother', 'Way', etc., or even 'Nothing'.

The Absolute which we designate by these 'names', however, is not a 'substance'. And it should not be understood as a 'substance'. This is the reason – or at least one of the main reasons – why Lao-tzŭ emphasizes so much that all the 'names' he proposes are nothing but makeshifts. Whatever 'name' he may use in referring to the Absolute, we should try not to 'reify' it in understanding what he says about it. For as a 'thing' in the sense of a 'substance', the Absolute is 'nothing'. How can a thing be a 'substance' when it is absolutely 'formless', 'invisible', 'inaudible', 'intangible', and 'taste-less'?[49] The Absolute is 'Something' only in the sense of an Act, or the act of Existence itself. Scholastically we may express the concep-tion by saying that the Absolute is *Actus Purus*. It is *Actus Purus* in

the sense that it is pre-eminently 'actual', and also in the sense that it
exists as the very act of existing and making 'things' exist. The
following words of Lao-tzŭ and Chuang-tzŭ makes this point clear.
Lao-tzŭ says:

> He who goes through the world, holding in hand the great Image,[50]
> wherever he may go will meet with no harm.[51] Safe, tranquil and calm
> he will always remain.
> Beautiful music and delicious food will make wayfarers stop. The
> Way, on the contrary, uttered in words is insipid and flavorless.
> One looks at it, and finds it unworthy to be seen.
> One listens to it, and finds it unworthy to be heard.
> Yet when one uses it, one finds it inexhaustible.[52]
>
> The loudest sound is hardly audible.
> The greatest Image has no form.
> The Way is hidden and has no name. And yet it is the Way alone that
> really excels in bestowing help and bringing things to completion.[53]

And Chuang-tzŭ:

> The Way does have a reality and its evidence.[54] But (this does not
> imply that it) does something intentionally. Nor does it possess any
> (tangible) form. So it may be transmitted (from heart to heart among
> the 'true men'), but cannot be received (as in the case of a thing
> having an external form). It may be intuited, but cannot be seen.
> It is self-sufficient. It has its own root in itself.
> It existed even before Heaven and Earth existed. It has unmistakably
> existed from ancient times.[55]
> It is the thing that confers spirituality upon the Spirits. And it is the
> thing that makes the Heavenly Emperor (i.e., God) divine.
> It produces Heaven. It produces Earth.
> It exists even above the highest point of the sky. And yet it is not
> 'high'.[56] It exists even beneath the six directions.[57] And yet it is not
> 'deep'.
> It was born before Heaven and Earth. And yet it is not 'ancient'. It is
> older than the oldest (historical) time. And yet it is not 'old'.[58]

Thus Lao-tzŭ and Chuang-tzŭ agree with each other in asserting
that the Way is *actus*. It goes without saying that *actus* exists. But it
does not exist as a 'substance'. It should not be 'reified'. In order not
to reify it, we have to intuit it. For we cannot possibly imagine,
represent, or conceive the Absolute without turning it into a kind of
'substance'. Metaphysical or ecstatic intuition is the only possible
means by which we can approach it without doing serious harm to its
image. But an intuition of this sort is open only to those who have
experienced to the utmost limit what Chuang-tzŭ calls 'sitting in
oblivion'.

However this may be, the preceding explanation has at least made it clear that the Way has two opposite aspects, one positive and the other negative. The negative side is comparable with the metaphysical Darkness of Ibn 'Arabī. In the world-view of the latter too, the Absolute (*ḥaqq*) in itself, i.e., in its absoluteness, is absolutely invisible, inaudible and ungraspable as any 'form' whatsoever. It is an absolute Transcendent, and as such it is 'Nothing' in relation to human cognition. But, as we remember, the Absolute in the metaphysical intuition of the Arab sage is 'Nothing', not because it is 'nothing' in the purely negative sense, but rather because it is too fully existent – rather, it is Existence itself. Likewise, it is Darkness not because it is deprived of light, but rather because it is too full of light, too luminous – rather, it is the Light itself.

Exactly the same holds true of the Way as Lao-tzŭ intuits it. The Way is not dark, but it *seems* dark because it is too luminous and bright. He says:

> A 'way' which is (too) bright seems dark.[59]

The Way in itself, that is, from the point of view of the Way itself, is bright. But since 'it is too profound to be known by man'[60] it is, from the point of view of man, dark. The Way is 'Nothing' in this sense.

This negative aspect, however, does not exhaust the reality of the Absolute. If it did, there would be no world, no creatures. In the thought of Ibn 'Arabī, the Absolute by its own unfathomable Will comes down from the stage of abysmal Darkness or 'nothingness' to that of self-manifestation. The Absolute, although it is in itself a Mystery having nothing to do with any other thing, and a completely self-sufficient Reality – has another, positive aspect in which it is turned toward the world. And in this positive aspect, the Absolute contains all things in the form of Names and Attributes. In the same way, the Way of Lao-tzŭ too, although it is in itself Something 'nameless', a Darkness which transcends all things, is the 'Named' and the 'Mother of the ten thousand things'. Far from being Non-Being, it is, in this respect, Being in the fullest sense.

> The Nameless is the beginning of Heaven and Earth. The Named is the Mother of ten thousand things.[61]

This passage can be translated also as follows:

> The term 'Non-Being' could be applied to the beginning of Heaven and Earth. The term 'Being' could be applied to the Mother of ten thousand things.

Whichever translation we may choose, the result comes to exactly the same thing. For in the metaphysical system of Lao-tzŭ, the

'Nameless' is, as we have already seen, synonymous with 'Non-Being', while the 'Named' is the same as 'Being'.

What is more important to notice is that metaphysically the Nameless or Non-Being represents a higher – or more fundamental – stage than the Named or Being within the structure of the Absolute itself. Just as in Ibn 'Arabī even the highest 'self-manifestion' (*tajallī*) is a stage lower than the absolute Essence (*dhāt*) of the Absolute, so in Lao-tzŭ Being represents a secondary metaphysical stage with regard to the absoluteness of the Absolute.

> The ten thousand things under Heaven are born out of Being (*yu*), and Being is born out of Non-Being (*wu*).[62]

If we put these two passages side by side with each other, we understand that in Lao-tzŭ's conception the Absolute in its ultimate metaphysical stage is the Nameless and Non-Being, while at the first stage of the emergence of the world it becomes the Named and Being. The expression: 'the beginning of Heaven and Earth', which Lao-tzŭ uses in reference to the Nameless, would seem to suggest that he is here considering the Absolute in terms of a temporal order. And we must admit that only from such a point of view can we properly talk about the 'creation' or 'production' of the world. The temporal expression, however, does not do full justice to the reality of the matter. For, as in the case of the successive stages of Divine self-manifestation in Ibn 'Arabī's metaphysics, the 'beginning' here in question is not properly speaking a temporal concept. It simply refers to that aspect of the Absolute in which it embraces in itself 'the myriad things under Heaven' in the state of *potentia*. Otherwise expressed, the Absolute *qua* the myriad things in the state of metaphysical concealment is the Beginning. The Beginning in this sense is the same as Non-Being. We would make the meaning of the word 'Beginning' more understandable if we translate it as the 'first principle' or the *Urgrund* of Being.

The concept of 'production', or 'coming-into-being' of all existent things, is also non-temporal. In our temporal representation, the 'coming-into-being' is a *process*, the initial stage of which is Non-Being and the last stage of which is Being. Metaphysically, however, there can be no temporal development in the Absolute. The Absolute, for Lao-tzŭ, is both Non-Being and Being, the Nameless and the Named at the same time.

Lao-tzŭ describes the relationship between Non-Being and Being in the following way.

> In its state of eternal (or absolute) Non-Being one would see the mysterious reality of the Way. In its state of eternal Being one would see the determinations of the Way.
> These two are ultimately one and the same. But once externalized,

they assume different names (i.e., 'Non-Being' and 'Being'). In (the original state of) 'sameness', (the Way) is called the Mystery. The Mystery of Mysteries it really is! And it is the Gateway of myriad Wonders.[63]

The Non-Being (or Nameless) in which the mysterious Reality (*miao*)[64] is to be observed would correspond to the state of the Absolute (*ḥaqq*), in the conception of Ibn 'Arabī, before it actually begins to work in a creative way. And the Being (or Named) in which the Way manifests itself in infinite 'determinations' (*chiao*)[65] would find its counterpart, in Ibn 'Arabī's thought, in the state of the Absolute when its creative activity spreads itself, as the Breath of the Merciful, being 'determined' in an infinite number of things.

It is remarkable that in this passage Lao-tzŭ goes beyond even the distinction between Being and Non-Being. Non-Being is surely the ultimate metaphysical principle, the most fundamental source of Being. It *is* the Way, just as Being also *is* the Way. And yet, since it is here conceptually opposed to 'Being', it cannot be the last thing. The basic opposition itself must be transcended. And Lao-tzŭ sees beyond the opposition of Being and Non-Being Something absolutely ineffable which he symbolically calls *hsüan*.[66] The word originally means 'black' with a mixture of redness, a very appropriate term for something absolutely 'invisible', an unfathomable Mystery ('black'), but revealing itself, at a certain stage, as being pregnant with the ten thousand things ('red') in their state of potentiality. In this Mystery of Mysteries Lao-tzŭ sees the Absolute in a state in which even Being and Non-Being are not yet distinguished from each other, an ultimate metaphysical state in which 'these two are one and the same thing'.

The Absolute or the Way, in so far as it is the Mystery of Mysteries, would seem to have nothing to do with the phenomenal world. But, as we have just observed, in the utter darkness of this great Mystery ('black'), we already notice a faint foreboding ('red') of the appearance of phenomenal things. And the Mystery of Mysteries is at the same time said to be the 'Gateway of myriad Wonders'. In the following chapter we shall be concerned with the process by which the ten thousand things stream forth out of this Gateway.

Notes

1. 無物, XIV.

2. 無, XL.

3. See Chapter IV.

4. *yen*, 言.

5. *lei*, 類.

6. See above, Chapter VI.

7. II, p. 79.

8. 「道常無名」.

9. *Tao Tê Ching*, XXXII. The word *ch'ang* here is synonymous with 眞 (*chên*) meaning 'true' or 'real'. For a similar use of the word, see XVI, XXVIII, LII, LV. The original meaning of the word *ch'ang* is 'constant' or '(eternally) unalterable'. Han Fei Tzŭ (韓非子) in his chapter on the *Interpretation of Lao-tzŭ* (解老篇) says: 'Those things that flourish first but later decay cannot be called *ch'ang*. Those things only deserve to be called *ch'ang* which came into being together with the separation of Heaven and Earth and which will neither die nor decay even when Heaven and Earth will be dispersed into nothing. That which is really *ch'ang* never changes.' The *ch'ang* is, in brief, the true reality which remains for ever unalterable.

10. XIV.

11. XLI.

12. Note again the use of the word *ch'ang* in the sense of 'real', 'eternal', 'unalterable' or 'absolute'.

13. I.

14. *Confucian Analects*, I, 2.

15. Confucius addresses himself to his disciple Master Tsêng.

16. *Analects*, IV, 15.

17. *ibid.*, XIV, 4.

18. See VIII, 13; XIV, 1.

19. *ibid.*, XIV, 30.

20. *ibid.*, IV, 8.

21. *p'u* 樸, meaning 'uncarved block'. The uncarved block from which all kinds of vessels are made is still 'nameless'. Only when it is carved into vessels does it acquire various 'names'.

22. *Tao Tê Ching*, XXXII. 'Being cut out' (*chih* 制) is a symbolic expression for the 'nameless' Way becoming 'determined' into myriad things.

23. *ibid.*, XVIII.

24. *ibid.*, XXXVIII.

25. 有.

26. 天地.

27. *op. cit.*, I.

28. See p. 99.

29. *Chuang-tzŭ*, II, p. 83.

30. *ibid.*, II, p. 83.

31. 夷 (=幾) meaning 'dim and figureless'.

32. The three aspects represent sense perception in general. The Way is beyond the reach of sense perception so that at the ultimate limit of the latter the Way only appears as an unfathomable and imperceptible One. Everything supposedly perceptible is 'merged into' it; that is to say, it has absolutely no articulation.

33. *Tao Tê Ching*, XIV.

34. *ibid.*, XL.

35. i.e., a metaphysical state in which Being and Non-Being are indistinguishable from each other.

36. In this passage Lao-tzŭ is trying to describe the absolute One which is both Non-Being and Being at the same time. The two aspects are in fact indistinguishable from one another. But if we concentrate our attention upon the positive side, the Way appears first as a vague and obscure Image of Something, then as a pure Reality which is eternally creative. In this aspect and at this stage the Way has an eternal Name: *yu* or Existence.

37. *op. cit.*, XXI.

38. 'Nobody knows who is the father of the Absolute.' That is to say, the Way has no 'cause' for its existence; it is its own cause.

39. *op. cit.*, IV.

40. *op. cit.*, XXV.

41. *hun ch'êng* 混成.

42. *tu li* 獨立, 'standing alone', that is 'self-sufficient', an expression corresponding to the Arabic term *ghanî*.

43. *tai* 殆 (=佁). See 羅運賢「老子餘義」, 1927, *ad loc*.:「殆佁同聲通用. 司馬相如傳『佁儽』, 張揖訓爲『不前』, 不前疑止之意也. 故『不殆』猶不止, 與『周行』義相成」.

44. 天下, 'all-under-Heaven'. Ma Hsü Lun (馬叙倫「老子覈詁」) proposes to read: 天地, 'Heaven and Earth', which is most probably right. The reading is based on an old edition (范應元「老子道德經古本集註」) of the Sung Dynasty. It accords with the expression: 'born before Heaven and Earth' which is found in the first sentence of the present passage.

45. 'Moving-forward' means that the working of the 'Great' permeates Heaven and Earth without being obstructed.

46. i.e., the working of the 'forward-mover' goes to the extremity of the world of Being.

47. 'Turning-back' means returning to the original point of departure, so that the metaphysical movement of the Way forms a big universal circle. And being circular, it never comes to an end.

48. *op. cit.*, XXXIV.

49. *ibid.*, XXXV.

50. *ta hsiang* 大象 (「象」=「像」). For the expression *ta hsiang* in the sense of 'great Image', see the next quotation from the *Tao Tê Ching*. Compare also XXI which has been quoted above (p. 106), where Lao-tzŭ uses the word *hsiang* '(a faint and shadowy) Image (of Something beyond)' in reference to the first self-manifestation of the Absolute.

51. See *Chuang-tzŭ*, I, pp. 30–31: 'Nothing can harm this man. Even if flood waters reach the sky, he will never be drowned. Even if in a burning heat metals and stones begin to flow and the earth and mountains are burned down, he alone will never feel hot.'

52. *Tao Tê Ching*, XXXV.

53. *ibid.*, XLI.

54. 「夫道有情有信」, The Way possesses a reality as *actus*, and it presents unmistakable evidence of its existence in the effects it produces.

55. We have already seen above how Chuang-tzŭ solves the problem of the Beginning of the Way. The statement: 'It has unmistakably existed from ancient times' should not tempt us into imagining that Chuang-tzŭ recognizes a 'beginning-point' in 'ancient times' or 'eternity'. It is merely a figure of speech. It is significant in this connection that Chuang-tzŭ, a few paragraphs down in the same chapter, calls the Way *i shih* (疑始) meaning literally 'likening to a beginning'. The Way is so called because it is something to be 'likened to a thing having a beginning', or more exactly, something which looks as if it had a beginning, though in reality it has none.

56. 'High' is, as we have seen, a relative concept which cannot be applied to the Absolute.

57. The 'six directions' means the whole universe.

58. *Chuang-tzŭ*, VI, p. 247.

59. *Tao Tê Ching*, XLI.

60. *ibid.*, XV.

61. *ibid.*, I.

62. *ibid.*, XL. See also XLI quoted above, which reads: The Way in its absolute reality has no 'name'. It is (comparable to) uncarved wood. Only when it is cut out are there 'names'.

63. *ibid.*, I.

64. 妙, meaning something unfathomably profound and mysterious.

65. 徼, literally meaning a 'fortress in a frontier district'; and by extension a 'border' or 'limit'.

66. 玄.

VIII The Gateway of Myriad Wonders

We have learnt in the preceding chapter that the name 'Way' is, after all, but a makeshift, a forced expression for what is properly not to be named. The word 'Way' is a symbol conveniently chosen for referring to Something which is, strictly speaking, beyond even symbolic indication. With this basic understanding, however, we may use – as Lao-tzŭ himself does – the term in describing the metaphysical world-view of Lao-tzŭ and Chuang-tzŭ.

It will be clear that, of the three primary aspects of the Absolute, which Lao-tzŭ distinguishes: the Mystery (*hsüan*), Non-Being (*wu*), and Being (*yu*), the first alone is the one to which the word 'Way' properly and directly applies. The rest, that is, Non-Being, Being, and even the 'ten thousand things' that effuse from the latter, are, all of them without exception, the Way, but not primarily. They are the Way in the sense that they represent various stages of the Mystery of Mysteries as it goes on determining itself. In other words, each one of them is the Way in a secondary, derivative, and limited sense, although in the case of Non-Being, which is nothing but pure Negativity, 'limitation' or 'determination' is so weak and slight that it is almost the same as 'non-limitation'.

It is true, however, that even the stage of Non-Being is not the ultimate and absolute stage of the Way, as long as the concept of 'Non-Being' is understood in opposition to, and in contradistinction from, that of 'Being'. In order to reach the ultimate and absolute stage of the Way in this direction, we have to negate, as Chuang-tzŭ does, the concept itself of Non-Being and the very distinction between Non-Being and Being, and conceptually posit No-[Non-Being], more exactly, No-[No Non-Being]. This we have learnt in the first part of the preceding chapter.

In the present chapter we shall no longer be primarily concerned with this absolute aspect of the Way, but rather with that aspect in which it turns toward the empirical or phenomenal world. Our major concern will be with the problem of the creative activity of the Way. This being the case, our description here will begin with the stage which stands slightly lower, so to speak, than that of the Mystery of Mysteries.

I have just used the phrase: 'the stage which stands slightly lower than that of the Mystery of Mysteries'. But it *is* the last and ultimate stage which we can hope to reach if we, starting from the world of phenomenal things, go up stage after stage in search of the Absolute. For, as we have seen above, the Mystery *per se* has nothing to do with the phenomenal world. And this makes us understand immediately that when Lao-tzŭ says:

The Way is the Granary[1] of the ten thousand things,[2]

he refers by the word Way to the 'stage which is slightly lower' than the Mystery of Mysteries. It is precisely at this stage that the Way is to be considered the Granary of the ten thousand things. It is at this stage that it begins to manifest its creativity. The word 'granary' clearly gives the image of the Absolute as the very ontological source of all things in the sense that all things are contained therein in the state of potentiality. Lao-tzŭ refers to this aspect of the Absolute as 'the eternal (or absolute) Non-Being' or the 'Nameless'. It is to be noted that the 'Nameless' is said to be the 'Beginning of Heaven and Earth'.[3] The Absolute at the stage of 'Nameless' or 'Non-Being' is actually not yet Heaven and Earth. But it is destined to be Heaven and Earth. That is to say, it is potentially already Heaven and Earth. And the expression: 'Heaven and Earth' is here clearly synonymous with the more philosophical term, 'Being'.

At this juncture, Lao-tzŭ introduces into his system another important term, 'One'. In the first part of the present study we saw how the concept of 'one' in the forms of *aḥadīyah* and *wāḥidīyah* plays a decisive rôle in the thought of Ibn 'Arabī concerning the 'self-manifestations' (*tajallīyāt*) of the Absolute. No less an important rôle does the concept of 'one' play in the thought of Lao-tzŭ.

For Lao-tzŭ, the One is something closest to the Way; it is almost the Way in the sense of the Mystery of Mysteries. But it is not exactly the Way as the Mystery. Rather, it is an aspect of the latter. It represents the stage at which the Way has already begun to move positively toward Being.

A very interesting explanation of the whole situation is found in a passage of the *Chuang-tzŭ*, in a chapter entitled 'On Heaven and Earth'. The chapter is one of the 'Exterior Chapters' (*wai p'ien*),[4] and may not be from the pen of Chuang-tzŭ himself. But this does not detract from the importance of the idea itself expressed in the passage. It reads as follows:

Before the creation of the world,[5] there is only No-[Non-Being][6]

(Then) there appears the Nameless. The latter is that from which the
One arises.

Now the One is there, but there is no form yet (i.e., none of the
existential forms is manifest at this stage). But each (of the ten
thousand things) comes into existence by acquiring it (i.e., the One,
by participation). In this particular respect, the One is called Virtue.[7]

Thus (the One at the stage of being itself) does not manifest any form
whatsoever. And yet it contains already (the potentiality of) being
divided (into the ten thousand things).

Notwithstanding that, (since it is not yet actually divided) it has no
break. This (potentiality of being divided and diversified into myriad
things) is called the Command.[8]

This important passage makes it definitely clear that the One is not
exactly the same as the Way *qua* the Mystery. For in the former
there is observable a sort of existential potentiality, whereas the
latter allows of no potentiality, not even a shadow of possibility. It is
the *absolute* Absolute.

At the stage of One, the Way is found to be already somehow
'determined', though it is not yet fully 'determined' or 'limited'. It is,
according to the explanation given by Chuang-tzŭ, a metaphysical
stage that comes after the Nameless (or Non-Being) which, again,
comes after the original No-[Non-Being]. And as such, it is a halfway stage between pure Non-Being and pure Being. It stands at the
end of Non-Being and at the initial point of Being.

The One is, thus, not yet *actually* Being, but it is potentially
Being. It is a metaphysically homogeneous single plane which is not
yet externally articulated; it is a unity which is going to diversify
itself, and in which the creative activity of the Way will be fully
manifested.

The whole process by which this creative activity of the Way is
manifested in the production of the world and the ten thousand
things is described by Lao-tzŭ in the following way.

The Way begets 'one'; 'one' begets 'two'; 'two' begets 'three'; and
'three' begets the ten thousand things.

The ten thousand things carry on their backs the Yin energy[9] and
embrace in their arms the Yang energy[10] and the two (i.e., Yin and
Yang) are kept in harmonious unity by the (third) energy emerging
out of (the blending and interaction of) them.[11]

From the Way as the metaphysical Absolute – or more strictly, from
the metaphysical Absolute at the stage of Non-Being – there
emerges the One. The One is, as we have just seen, the metaphysical
Unity of all things, the primordial Unity in which all things lie
hidden in a state of 'chaos' without being as yet actualized as the ten
thousand things.

From this Unity there emerges 'two', that is, the cosmic duality of

Heaven and Earth. The former symbolizes the principle of Yang, the latter that of Yin. At this stage, the Way manifests itself as Being and the Named. The Named, as we have learnt from a passage quoted earlier,[12] 'is the Mother of the ten thousand things'. Before the 'two' can begin to work as the 'Mother of ten thousand things', however, they have to beget the third principle, the 'vital force of harmony' formed by the interaction and mixture of the Yin and the Yang energy. The expression: 'two begets three' refers to this phase of the creation of the world.

The combination of these three principles results in the production of the ten thousand things. Thus it comes about that everything existent, without exception, has three constituent elements: (1) the Yin which it 'carries on its back' – a symbolic expression for the Yin being negative, passive 'shadowy' and 'dark' – (2) the Yang which it 'embraces in its arms' – a symbolic expression for the Yang being positive, bright and 'sunny' – and (3) the vital force which harmonizes these two elements into an existential unity.

It is to be remarked that Heaven and Earth, that is, the Way at the stage of Being, or the Named, is considered the 'Mother of the ten thousand things'. There is a firm natural tie between the 'Mother' and her 'children'. This would seem to suggest that the 'ten thousand things' are most intimately related with Heaven and Earth. The former as the 'children' of the latter provide the most exact image of the Way *quâ* the Named.

> All things under Heaven have a Beginning, which is to be regarded as the Mother of all things.
> If one knows the 'mother', one knows the 'child'. And if, after having known the 'child' one goes back to the 'mother' and holds fast to her, one will never fall into a mistake until the very end of one's life.[13]

These words describe in a symbolic way the intimate ontological relationship between the Way at the stage of the Named, or Being, and the phenomenal world. The phenomenal things are to be regarded as the 'children' of the Named. That is to say, they are not to be regarded as mere objective products of the latter; they are its own flesh and blood. There is a relationship of consanguinity between them.

And since the Named, or 'Heaven and Earth', is nothing else than a stage in the self-evolvement of the Way itself, the same relationship must be said to hold between the Way and the phenomenal things. After all, the phenomenal things themselves are also a stage in the self-evolvement of the Way.

I have just used the expression: 'the self-evolvement of the Way'. But we know only too well that any movement on the part of the Way toward the world of phenomena begins at the stage of the One.

The One represents the initial point of the self-evolvement of the Way. All things in the phenomenal world partake of the One. By being partaken of in this way, the One forms the ontological core of everything. The Way *per se*, that is, *qua* the Mystery, is beyond that stage. Thus Lao-tzǔ often mentions the One when he speaks about the phenomenal things partaking of the Way. In a looser sense, the word 'Way' may also be used in that sense, and Lao-tzǔ does use it in reference to that particular aspect of the Way. But in the most rigorous usage, the 'One' is the most appropriate term in contexts of this sort.

> Heaven, by acquiring the One, is serene.
> Earth, by acquiring the One, is solid.
> The Spirit, by acquiring the One, exercise mysterious powers.
> The valleys, by acquiring the One, are full.
> The ten thousand things, by acquiring the One, are alive.
> The lords and kings, by acquiring the One, are the standard of the world.
> It is the One that makes these things what they are.
>
> If Heaven were not serene by the One, it would break apart.
> If Earth were not solid by the One, it would collapse.[14]
> If the Spirits were not able to exercise mysterious powers by the One, they would cease to be active.[15]
> If the valleys were not full by the One, they would run dry.
> If the ten thousand things were not kept alive by the One, they would perish.
> If the lords and kings were not noble and lofty by the One, they would be overthrown.[16]

The first half of the passage expresses the idea that everything in the world is what it is by virtue of the One which 'it acquires', i.e., partakes of. Viewed from the side of the phenomenal things, what actually happens is the 'acquisition' of the One, while from the side of the Way, it is the creative activity of the Way as the One.

The second half of the passage develops this idea and emphasizes the actual presence of the Way in the form of the One in each of the things that exist in the world, ranging from the highest to the lowest. The One is present in everything as its ontological ground. It acts in everything as its ontological energy. It develops its activity in everything in accordance with the latter's particular ontological structure; thus, the sky is limpid and clear, the earth solidly settled, the valley full of water, etc. If it were not for this activity of the One, nothing in the world would keep its existence as it should.

The Way in this sense is an indwelling principle of all things. It pervades the whole phenomenal world and its ontological activity affects everything. Nothing lies outside the reach of this universal immanence of the Way.

> The Net of Heaven has only wide meshes. They are wide, yet nothing slips through them.[17]

The 'immanence' of the Way in the phenomenal world must not be taken in the sense that something completely alien comes from outside into the phenomenal world and alights on the things. To put it in a different way, the phenomenal things are not moved by force by something which is not of their own. On the contrary, the Way is 'immanent' in the sense that the things of the phenomenal world are so many different forms assumed by the Way itself. And this must be what Lao-tzǔ really means when he says that the Way is the 'Mother of the ten thousand things'. There is, in this respect, no ontological discrepancy between the Way and the things that exist in the world.

Thus, to say that the phenomenal things are as they actually are by virtue of the activity of the Way is to say that they are what they are by virtue of their own natures. Lao-tzǔ speaks in this sense of 'the natures – or Nature – of the ten thousand things'.[18] It is significant that the original word here translated as 'nature', *tzǔ jan*,[19] means literally 'of-itself it-is-so'. Nothing is forced by anything to be what it is. Everything 'is-so of-itself'. And this is possible only because there is, as I have just said, no ontological discrepancy between the immanent Way and the things of which it is the vital principle. The very driving force by which a thing is born, grows up, flourishes, and then goes back to its own origin – this existential force which everything possesses as its own 'nature' – is in reality nothing other than the Way as it actualizes itself in a limited way in everything.

The Way, in acting in this manner, does not force anything. This is the very basis on which stands the celebrated Taoist principle of 'Non-Doing' (*wu wei*)[20]. And since it does not force anything, each of the ten thousand things 'is-so of-itself'. Accordingly the 'sacred man' who, as we shall see later, is the most perfect image of the Way, does not force anything.

> Thus the 'sacred man' . . . only helps the 'being-so-of-itself' (i.e., spontaneous being) of the ten thousand things. He refrains from interfering with it by his own action.[21]

> To be calm and soundless – that is the 'natural' (or 'being-so-of-itself'). This is why a hurricane does not last all morning, and a rainstorm does not last all day. Who is it that causes wind and rain? Heaven and Earth. Thus, if even Heaven and Earth cannot perpetuate (excessive states of affairs), much less can man (hope to succeed in maintaining an 'unnatural' state)![22]

This idea of the 'nature' or 'being-so-of-itself' of the existent things leads us immediately to another major concept: Virtue (*tê*).[23] In fact the *tê* is nothing other than the 'nature' of a thing viewed as something the thing has 'acquired'. The *tê* is the Way as it 'naturally' acts in a thing in the form of its immanent ontological core. Thus a Virtue is exactly the same as Nature, the only difference between them being that in the case of the former concept, the Way is considered as an 'acquisition' of the thing, whereas in the case of the latter the Way is considered in terms of its being a vital force which makes the thing 'be-so of-itself'.

Everything, as we saw above, partakes of the Way (at the stage of the One). And by partaking of the Way, it 'acquires' its own existential core. As Wang Pi says;[24] 'The Way is the ultimate source of all things, whereas the Virtue is what all things acquire (of the Way)'. And whatever a thing is, whatever a thing becomes, is due to the 'natural' activity of its own Virtue.

It is characteristic of the metaphysical system of Lao-tzŭ that what is here considered the 'natural' activity or Virtue of a thing is nothing other than the very activity of the Way. The Way exercises its creative activity within the thing in the capacity of the latter's *own* existential principle, so that the activity of the Way is in itself the activity of the thing. We encounter here something comparable with Ibn 'Arabī's concept of the 'Breath or the Merciful' (*al-nafas al-raḥmānī*), or more generally, the concept of Divine Mercy (*raḥmah*),[25] which, issuing forth from the unfathomable depth of the Absolute, spreads itself over the whole extent of possible Being and brings into actual existence all the phenomenal things of the world. It is interesting to note in this connection that in the Book of *Kuan-tzŭ* – spuriously attributed to Kuan Chung, the famous statesman of the 7th century B.C. – we find this significant statement: 'Virtue (*tê*) is the Way's act of giving in charity',[26] that is, Virtue is the act of Mercy manifested by the Way toward all things. And this act of Mercy is concretely observable, as Kuo Mo Jo says, in the form of the 'bringing up, or fostering, the ten thousand things'.

This conception completely squares with what Lao-tzŭ remarks about the activity of Virtue in the following passage.

> The Way gives birth to (the ten thousand things), the Virtue fosters them, things furnish them with definite forms,[27] and the natural impetus completes their development.
> This is why none of the ten thousand things does not venerate the Way and honor the Virtue. The Way is venerated and its Virtue honored not because this is commanded by somebody, but they are naturally so.[28]
> Thus the Way gives them birth. The Virtue fosters them, makes them

grow, feeds them, perfects them, solidifies[29] them, stabilizes them,[30] rears them, and shelters them.
In this way, the Way gives birth (to the ten thousand things), and claims no possession. It does great things, yet does not boast of it.
It makes (things) grow, and yet exercises no authority upon them.
This is what I would call the Mysterious Virtue.[31]

We saw earlier how Lao-tzŭ 'provisionally' and 'by force' gives 'names' to the Way, that is, describes it by various attributes. In a similar way, he distinguishes in Virtue several attributes or qualities. And, accordingly, he refers to Virtue by different 'names', as if he recognized the existence of various kinds of Virtue. The 'Mysterious Virtue' (*hsüan tê*) which we have just come across is one of them. Other 'names' are found in the following passage.

The 'high' Virtue (*shang tê*) looks like a valley,[32] as the purest white seems spoiled.
The 'wide' Virtue (*kuang tê*) looks insufficient.
The 'firm' Virtue (*chien tê*) looks feeble.
The 'simple' Virtue (*chih tê*)[33] looks deteriorated.

All these 'names', however, do not designate different 'kinds' of Virtue, no less than the different 'names' of the Way indicate the existence of different kinds of Way. They simply refer to different 'aspects' which we can 'forcibly' distinguish in that which is properly and in itself indeterminable. In this sense, and only in this sense, is Virtue 'high', 'wide', 'firmly-established', 'simple', etc.

There is one point, however, which deserves special mention. That is the distinction made in the *Tao Tê Ching* between 'high' Virtue and 'low' Virtue. The distinction arises from the fact that Virtue, representing as it does concrete forms assumed by the Way as it actualizes itself in the phenomenal world, is liable to be affected by 'unnatural', i.e., intentional, activity on the part of phenomenal beings. Quite ironically, Man, who is by nature so made as to be able to become the most perfect embodiment of Virtue – and hence of the Way – is the sole creature that is capable of obstructing the full activity of Virtue. For nothing other than Man acts 'with intention'. Things are naturally as they are, and each of them works in accordance with its own 'nature'. Whatever they do is done without the slightest intention on their part to do it. Man, on the contrary, may 'lower' his naturally given Virtue by his very intention to be a perfect embodiment of the Way and to make his Virtue 'high'.[35]

A man of 'high' Virtue is not conscious of his Virtue.
That is why he has Virtue.
A man of 'low' Virtue tries hard not to lose his Virtue.
That is why he is deprived of Virtue.[36]

The 'high' Virtue consists in Virtue being actualized completely and perfectly in man when the latter is not even conscious of his Virtue. Consciousness obstructs the natural actualization of the Way. And in such a case, Virtue, which is nothing but the concrete actualization of the Way, becomes imperfect and 'low'. For when a man is conscious of Virtue, he naturally strives hard 'never to abandon' it. And this very conscious effort hinders the free self-manifestation of the Way in the form of Virtue.

Virtue in such a case is considered 'low', i.e., degenerate and imperfect, because, instead of being perfectly united with the Way as it should, it is somehow kept away from the Way, so that there is observable a kind of discrepancy between the two.

> A man of Great Virtue in his behavior follows exclusively (the Command) of the Way.[37]

The 'low' Virtue, following as it does the command of human intention as well as the Command of the Way, and not exclusively the latter, is no longer Virtue as the most direct actualization of the Way.

The foregoing discussion most naturally leads us to the problem of Non-Doing (*wu wei*).

The Way is eternally active. Its activity consists in creating the ten thousand things and then – in the particular form of Virtue – in fostering them and bringing them up to the limit of their inner possibility. This creative activity of the Way is really great. However, the Way does not achieve this great work with the 'intention' of doing it.

> Heaven is long lasting and Earth is long enduring. The reason why Heaven and Earth are long lasting and long enduring is that they do not strive to go on living. Therefore they are able to be everlasting.[38]

In his passage the Way is referred to as 'Heaven and Earth', that is, the Way at the stage of Heaven and Earth. We already know the metaphysical implication of this expression. The expression is here in the proper place because it is precisely at this stage that the creative activity of the Way is manifested. In the following passage, Lao-tzŭ refers 'Heaven and Earth' back to their ultimate metaphysical origin.

> The Valley-Spirit is immortal. It is called the Mysterious Female.[39] The gateway of the Mysterious Female is called the Root of Heaven and Earth. (The Way in these various forms) is barely visible, yet it never ceases to exist. Unceasingly it works, yet never becomes exhausted.[40]

The Mysterious Female, Lao-tzŭ says, is unceasingly creative, yet it never becomes exhausted because it 'does not do anything', i.e., consciously or intentionally. When we try hard to do something with the definite intention of doing it, we may achieve that very thing which we expect to achieve, but nothing else. The field of human action is, therefore, always limited and determined in varying degrees by consciousness and intention. The activity of the Way is of a totally different nature from human action. For the Way acts only by 'not acting'.

> The Way is permanently inactive, yet it leaves nothing undone.[41]

Since, thus, the Way is not conscious of its own creative activity, it is not conscious of the results of its activity either. The concept of the Mysterious Virtue, to which reference was made a few pages back, is based on this very idea. The Way, in this particular aspect, is infinitely gracious to all things. Its activity is extremely beneficial to them. And yet it does not count the benefits and favors which it never ceases to confer upon the things. Everything is done so 'naturally' – that is, without any intention on the part of the Way of doing good to the things – that what is received by the things as benefits and favors does not in any way constitute, from the point of view of the Way itself, benefits and favors.

> (The Way) gives birth (to the ten thousand things) and brings them up.
> It gives them birth, and yet does not claim them to be its own possession.
> It works, yet does not boast of it. It makes (things) grow, and yet exercises no authority upon them. This is what I would call the Mysterious Virtue.[42]

The principle of Non-Doing – the principle of leaving everything to its 'nature', and of doing nothing consciously and intentionally – assumes special importance in the world-view of Lao-tzŭ in connection with the problem of the ideal way of life in this world. We shall come back to this concept in a later chapter. Here I shall be content with quoting one more passage from the *Tao Tê Ching*, in which Lao-tzŭ talks about Non-Doing in reference to both the Way and the 'sacred man' at one and the same time. In this particular passage the 'sacred man' is represented as having made himself so completely identical with the Way that whatever applies to the latter applies to the former.

> Therefore the 'sacred man' keeps to the principle of Non-Doing, and practises the teaching of No-Words.
> The ten thousand things arise (through its, or his, activity), and yet he (or it) does not talk about it boastfully. He (or it) gives life (to the

things), and yet he (or it) does not claim them to be his (or its) own.
He (or it) works, and yet he (or it) does not boast of his (or its)
own work. He (or it) accomplishes his (or its) task, and yet he (or it)
does not stick to his (or its) own merit. He (or it) does not stick to his
(or its) own merit; therefore it never deserts him (or it).[43]

Thus the Way never makes a boast of its own activity. Whatever it
does, it does 'naturally', without the slightest intention of 'doing' it.
One may express the same idea by saying that the Way is totally
indifferent to both its creative activity and the concrete results it
produces. The Way does not care about the world it has created. In
one sense this might be understood as the Way giving complete
freedom to all things. But in another we might also say that the Way
lacks affection for its own creatures. They are simply left uncared-
for and neglected.

With a touch of sarcasm Lao-tzŭ speaks of the Way having no
'benevolence' (or 'humaneness', *jên*). The *jên*, as I have pointed out
earlier, was for Confucius and his disciples the highest of all for
ethical values.

> Heaven and Earth lack 'benevolence'. They treat ten thousand things
> as straw dogs.[44]
> Likewise, the 'sacred man' lacks 'benevolence'. He treats the people
> as straw dogs.[45]

What Lao-tzŭ wants to assert by this paradoxical expression is that
the Great Way, because it is great, does not resort, as Confucians
do, to the virtue of *jên* in its activity. For the *jên*, in his eye, implies
an artificial, unnatural effort on the part of the agent. The Way does
not interfere with the natural course of things. Nor does it need to
interfere with it, because the natural course of things *is* the activity
of the Way itself. Lao-tzŭ would seem to be suggesting here that the
Confucian *jên* is not the real *jên*; and that the real *jên* consists rather
in the agent's being seemingly ruthless and *jên*-less.

There is another important point which Lao-tzŭ emphasizes very
much in describing the creative activity of the Way. That is the
'emptiness' or 'voidness' of the Way.

We have often referred to the conception of the Way as
'Nothing'. There 'Nothing' meant the absolute transcendence of the
Way. The Way is considered 'Nothing' because it is beyond human
cognition. Just as a light far too brilliant for human eyes is the same
as darkness or lack of light, the Way is 'Nothing' or 'Non-Being'
precisely because it is plenitude of Being. The concept of 'Nothing'
which is in question in the present context is of a different nature. It
concerns the 'infinite' creativity of the Way. The Way, Lao-tzŭ says,
can be infinitely and endlessly creative because it contains within

itself nothing substantial. It can produce all things because it has nothing definite and determined inside it. The *Kuan-tzŭ* clearly reflects this idea when it says: 'Empty and formless – that is what is called the Way',[46] and 'The Heavenly Way is empty and formless'.[47] For this idea Lao-tzŭ finds in the daily experience of the people several interesting symbols. An empty vessel, for example:

> The Way is an empty vessel.[48] No matter how often you may use it, you can never[49] fill it up.[50]

It is a sort of magical vessel which, being forever empty, can never be filled up, and which, therefore, can contain an infinity of things. Looked at from the opposite side, this would mean that the 'vessel' is infinitely full because it is apparently empty. Thus we come back exactly to the same situation which we encountered above in the first of the two meanings of 'Nothing' with regard to the nature of the Way. The Way, we saw there, is Nothing because it is too full of Being – rather, it is Being itself – and because, as such, it is absolutely beyond the reach of human cognition. Here again we find ourselves in the presence of something which looks 'empty' because it is too full. The Way, in other words, is 'empty'; but it is not empty in the ordinary sense of a thing being purely negatively and passively void. It is a positive metaphysical emptiness which is plenitude itself.

> Great fullness seems empty. But (its being, in reality, fullness is proved by the fact that) when actually used, it will never be exhausted.[51]

The Way, in this particular aspect, is also compared to a bellows. It is a great Cosmic Bellows whose productive activity is never exhausted.

> The space between Heaven and Earth is indeed like a bellows. It is empty, but it is inexhaustible. The more it works the more comes out.[52]

Lao-tzŭ in the following passage has recourse to more concrete and homely illustrations to show the supreme productivity of 'emptiness'.

> (Take for example the structure of a wheel). Thirty spokes share one hub (i.e., thirty spokes are joined together round the center of the wheel). But precisely in the empty space (in the axle-hole) is the utility of the wheel.
> One kneads clay to make a vessel. But precisely in the empty space within is the utility of the vessel.
> One cuts out doors and windows to make a room. But precisely in the empty space within is the utility of the house. Thus it is clear that if Being benefits us, it is due to the working of Non-Being.[53]

It is, I think, for this reason that the symbol of 'valley' plays such a prominent part in the *Tao Tê Ching*. The valley is by nature hollow and empty. And precisely because it is hollow and empty, can it be full. Add to this the fact that the valley always occupies a 'low' place – another important trait of anything which is really high, whether human or non-human. The valley is thus an appropriate symbol for the Way understood as the absolute principle of eternal creativeness, which is the plenitude of Being because it is 'empty', or 'Nothing'.

We have already quoted two passages in which Lao-tzŭ uses this symbol in talking about the inexhaustible creative activity of the Way.

> The Valley-Spirit is immortal.[54]

> The 'high' Virtue looks like a valley.[55]

The underlying idea is made more explicitly clear in another place where Lao-tzŭ discusses the problem of anything being capable of becoming truly perfect because it is (apparently) imperfect.

> It is what is hollow that is (really) full.[56]

Being 'hollow' and 'low' suggests the idea of 'female'. This idea too has already been met with in the foregoing pages. In fact, the emphasis on the feminine element in the creative aspect of the Way may be pointed out as one of the characteristic features of Lao-tzŭ. It goes without saying that, in addition to the idea of 'hollowness' and 'lowliness', the 'female' is the most appropriate symbol of fecundity.

The Way, for instance, is the *Mother* of the ten thousand things.

> The Nameless is the beginning of Heaven and Earth. The Named is the Mother of the ten thousand things.[57]

> All things under heaven have a Beginning which is to be regarded as the Mother of the world.
> If one knows the 'mother', one thereby knows the 'child'. If, after having known the 'child', one holds fast to the 'mother', one will escape error, even to the end of one's life.[58]

The metaphysical implication of the Way being the Mother of all things and the things being her 'children' has been elucidated earlier in the present chapter.

We have also quoted in this chapter in connection with another problem a passage where mention is made of the 'Mysterious Female'.

> The Valley-Spirit is immortal. It is called the Mysterious Female. The gateway of the Mysterious Female is called the Root of Heaven and Earth.[59]

In the expression: Mysterious Female (*hsüan p'in*), we encounter again the word *hsüan*[60] which, as we sae above, is used by Lao-tzǔ in reference to the Way as the unknown-unknowable metaphysical Absolute, that is, the Way as it lies even beyond Being and Non-Being.

> The Mystery of Mysteries it really is! And it is the Gateway of myriad Wonders.[61]

It is remarkable, further, that in both passages the endless and inexhaustible creativeness of the Way is symbolized by the 'gateway' (*mên*).[62] And this clearly indicates that the 'gateway of the Mysterious Female' is exactly the same thing as the 'gateway of myriad Wonders'. The Absolute in its active aspect is symbolically imaged as having a 'gateway', or an opening, from which the ten thousand things are sent out to the world of Being. The image of the 'female' animal makes the symbol the more appropriate to the idea because of its natural suggestion of fecundity and motherhood.

As I pointed out earlier, the image of the 'female' in the world-view of Lao-tzǔ is suggestive, furthermore, of weakness, humble-ness, meekness, stillness, and the like. But, by the paradoxical way of thinking which is peculiar to Lao-tzǔ, to say that the 'female' is weak, meek, low, etc. is precisely another way of saying that she is infinitely strong, powerful, and superior.

> The female always overcomes the male by being quiet. Being quiet, she (always) takes the lower position. (And by taking the lower position, she ends by obtaining the higher position)[63]

As is clear from these words, the weakness of the 'female' here spoken of is not the purely negative weakness of a weakling. It is a very peculiar kind of weakness which is obtained only by overcom-ing powerfulness. It is a weakness which contains in itself an infinite possibility of power and strength. This point is brought into the focus of our attention by what Lao-tzǔ says in the following passage, in which he talks about the basic attitude of the 'sacred man'. Since, as we know, the 'sacred man' is for Lao-tzǔ the perfect per-sonification of the Way itself, what is said of the former is wholly applicable to the latter. It is to be noticed that here again the image of the 'female' is directly associated with that of the 'valley'.

> He who knows the 'male', yet keeps to the rôle of the 'female', will become the 'valley' of the whole world.
> Once he has become the 'valley' of the whole world, the eternal Virtue[64] will never desert him[65]

And it is evidently in this sense that the following statement is to be understood:

'Being weak' is how the Way works.[66]

We have been in what precedes trying to describe the ontological process – as conceived by Lao-tzŭ – of the ten thousand things coming out of the 'gateway' of the 'Absolute. 'The Way begets One; One begets Two; Two begets Three. And Three begets the ten thousand things'.[67] The ten thousand things, that is, the world and all the things that exist therein, represent the extreme limit of the ontological evolution of the Way. Phenomenal things, in other words, make their appearance at the last stage of the Descent of the Way. From the point of view of phenomenal things, their very emergence is the perfection of their own individual natures. For it is here that the Way manifests itself – in the original sense of the Greek verb *phainesthai* – in the most concrete forms.

This, however, is not the end of the ontological process of Being. As in the case of the world-view of Ibn 'Arabī, the Descent is followed by the reversal of the creative movement, that is, Ascent. The ten thousand things, upon reaching the last stage of the descending course, flourish for a while in an exuberance of colors and forms, and then begin to take an ascending course back toward their original pre-phenomenal form, that is, the formless Form of the One, and thence further to 'Nothing', and finally they disappear into the darkness of the Mystery of Mysteries. Lao-tzŭ expresses this idea by the key term: *fu*[68] or Return.

> The ten thousand things all arise together. But as I watch them, they 'return' again (to their Origin).
> All things[69] grow up exuberantly, but (when the time comes) every one of them 'returns' to its 'root'.
> The Return to the Root is what is called Stillness. It means returning to the (Heavenly) Command (or the original ontological allotment of each).[70]
> The Return to the Heavenly Command is what is called the Unchanging.[71]
> And to know the Unchanging is what is called Illumination.[72]

The plants grow in spring and summer in full exuberance and luxuriance. This is due to the fact that the vital energy that lies in *potentia* in their roots becomes activated, goes upward through the stems, and at the stage of perfection becomes completely actualized in the form of leaves, flowers, and fruits. But with the advent of the cold season, the same vital energy goes down toward the roots and ends by hiding itself in its origin.[73]

Lao-tzŭ calls this final state Stillness[74] or Tranquillity. We have noticed above that 'stillness' is one of his favorite concepts. And it is easy to see that this concept in its structure conforms to the general pattern of thinking which is typical of Lao-tzŭ. For the 'stillness' as understood in terms of the present context is not the stillness of death or complete lifelessness. The vital energy hidden in the darkness of the root is actually motionless, but the root is by no means dead. It is, rather, a stillness pregnant with infinite vitality. Externally no movement is perceptible, yet internally the incessant movement of eternal Life is carried on in preparation for the coming spring.

Thus the creative activity of the Way forms a cyclic process. And being a cyclic process, it has no end. It is an eternal activity having neither an initial point nor a final point.

We have also to keep in mind in understanding this idea another typical pattern of Lao-tzǔ's thinking, which we have encountered several times. I am referring to the fact that Lao-tzǔ often describes a metaphysical truth in a temporal form. That is to say, his description of a metaphysical truth in terms of time (and space) does not necessarily indicate that it is, in his view, a temporal process.

The emanation of the ten thousand things out of the womb of the Way and their Return to their original source is described in the *Tao Tê Ching* in a temporal form. And what is thus described *is* in fact a temporal process.

> Returning is how the Way moves.
> Being weak is how the Way works.
> The ten thousand things under Heaven are born out of Being. And Being is born out of Non-Being.[75]

But in giving a description of the process in such a form, Lao-tzǔ is trying to describe at the same time an eternal, supra-temporal fact that lies over and above the temporal process. And looked at from this second point of view, the Return of the phenomenal things back to their origin is not something that happens in time and space. Lao-tzǔ is making a metaphysical statement, referring simply to the 'immanence' of the Way. All the phenomenal things, from this point of view, are but so many forms in which the Way manifests itself concretely – *phainesthai*. The things are literally *phainomena*. And since it is the Way itself that 'uncovers itself' or 'reveals itself' in these things, it is 'immanent' in each of them as its metaphysical ground. And each of the things contains in itself its own source of existence. This is the metaphysical meaning of the Return. As we have seen above, the Way in this particular form is called by Lao-tzǔ *tê* or Virtue.

Notes

1. *ao* 奥 (See 廣雅釋詁「奥，藏也」河上公注「奥，藏也. 道爲萬物之藏，無所不容也」).

2. *Tao Tê Ching*, LXII.

3. *ibid.*, I, quoted and explained toward the end of the preceding chapter.

4. For the significance of this classification, see Chapter I.

5. Here again Chuang-tzǔ describes the situation in chronological order, in the form of historical development. But what he really intends to describe thereby is clearly a metaphysical fact having nothing to do with the 'history' of things. The situation referred to by the expression: 'before the creation of the world', accordingly, does not belong to the past; it directly concerns the present, as it did concern the past and as it will continue to concern the future forever.

6. In interpreting this opening sentence of the passage I follow Lin Yün Ming 林雲銘 (of the Ch'ing Dynasty,「莊子因」, *ad loc.*:「泰初,「泰初, 造化之始初也. 無無者, 連無之字… 無名者, 卽老子所謂無名天地之始也」) who punctuates it:「泰初有無無, 有無名, 一之所起」. The ordinary reading represented by Kuo Hsiang articulates the sentence in a different way:「泰初有無, 無有,無名」etc. which may be translated as: 'Before the creation of the world there was Non-Being. There was (then) no Being, no Name'.

7. *tê*, 德. This is, as we shall see, one of the key terms of Lao-tzǔ. The word *tê* literally means 'acquisition' or 'what is acquired', that is, the One as 'acquired' by each of the existent things. This part of the semantic structure of the word is admirably clarified by the explanation which Chuang-tzǔ has just given in this passage.

8. ming, 命, 'command' or 'order'; to be compared with the Islamic concept of *amr* '(Divine) Command'. The corresponding concept in Chinese is often expressed by the compound *t'ien ming*, meaning 'Heavenly Command'. The underlying idea is that everything in the world of Being is what it actually is in accordance with the Command of the One. All things participate in the One and 'acquire it', but each of them 'acquires it in its own peculiar way. And this is the reason why nothing is exactly the same in the whole world, although all uniformly owe their existence to the One. All this would naturally lead to the problem of 'predestination', which will be elucidated in a later context.

9. i.e., the Cosmic element which is 'shadowy', dark, negative, and passive.

10. i.e., the 'sunny', light, positive element.

11. *Tao Tê Ching*, XLII.

12. *Tao Tê Ching*, I.

13. *ibid.*, LII.

14. 發, which is the same as 廢 (劉師培:「發讀爲廢. 說文: 廢, 屋頓也」).

15. 歇, which, according to the *Shuo Wên*, means to 'take a rest' (「歇, 息也」).

16. *Tao tê Ching*, XXXIX.

17. *op. cit.*, LXXIII.

18. *ibid.*, LXIV.

19. 自然.

20. 無爲. The concept will be explained in more detail presently.

21. *op. cit.*, LXIV.

22. *ibid.*, XXIII.

23. See above, note 7.

24. 王弼 (3rd. century A.D.); *ad* LI: 「道者物之所由也. 德者物之所得也」. See also his words: 「德者得也. 常得而無喪利而無害. 故以德爲名焉」, *ad* XXXVIII.

25. See Part One, Chapter IX.

26. 「德者道之舍」(管子, 心術篇, 上). For the interpretation of the last word, 舍 (*shê*), see Kuo Mo Jo's remark in the Peking edition of the *Kuan-tzǔ* (管子集校), 1965, vol. I, pp. 642–644. He says: 「舍字當爲施舍之舍. 下文云『道也者, 動不見其形, 施不見其德』('The Way acts, but its figure is invisible. It gives in charity, but its Virtue is invisible') 可證……故知舍與施同義. 施舍亦卽化有萬物之意」.

27. i.e., being fostered by Virtue, they grow up and become 'things' each having a definite form.

28. 自然.

29. 亭, 亭＝凝結(傅奕) or 亭＝停(「釋名」), meaning to 'crystallize' into a definite form.

30. 毒, 毒＝安(according to「廣雅」).

31. *op. cit.*, LI.

32. 'Valley' (谷) is a favorite symbol of Lao-tzǔ, which he uses in describing the nature of the Way and the nature of the 'sacred man'.

33. The standard Wang Pi edition reads:「質眞若渝」. Following Liu Shih P'ei 劉師培 who argues:「案上文言『廣德若不足, 建德若偸』 此與並文, 疑眞亦作德. 蓋德字正文作悳與眞相似也」, I read:「質德若渝」.

34. *op. cit.*, XLI.

35. The idea here described is comparable with what Ibn 'Arabī observes about Man being situated in a certain sense on the lowest level on the scale of Being. Inanimate things have no 'ego'. That makes them obedient to God's commandments unconditionally; that is to say, they are exposed naked to God's activity upon them, there being no hindrance between them. The second position is given to the plants, and the third to the animals. Man, because of his Reason, occupies in this respect the lowest place in the whole hierarchy of Being.

36. *op. cit.*, XXXVIII.

37. *ibid.*, XXI.

38. *ibid.*, VII.

39. The symbol, meaning of the 'Valley' and 'Female' will be elucidated presently.

40. *op. cit.*, VI.

41. *op. cit.*, XXXVII.

42. *ibid.*, X. The same sentences are found as part of LI which I have already quoted.

43. *ibid.*, II.

44. Straw dogs specially prepared as offerings at religious ceremonies. Before the ceremonies, they were treated with utmost reverence. But once the occasion was over, they were thrown away as waste material and trampled upon by the passers-by.

45. *op. cit.*, V.

46. 「虛而無形 , 謂之道」. The second word of this sentence according to the commonly accepted reading is 無 (「虛無無形」etc.). That this is wrong has been established by the editors of the Peking edition (See above, Note, 26), vol. II, pp. 635–636.

47. *ibid.*

48. 道沖. As Yü Yüeh rightly observes, the character 沖 stands for 盅 which, according to the *Shuo Wên*, means the emptiness of a vessel. (俞樾「諸子平議」VIII:「說文 皿部, 盅, 器虛也.   老子曰: 『道盅而用之』盅訓虛,   與盈正相對,   作沖者假字也……第四十五章 , 『大 盈若沖』沖亦當作盅」).

49. 或 must be emended to 久 – meaning 'for an extremely long time', i.e., 'forever' – on the basis of the reading of a T'ang inscription (唐景龍碑:「久不盈」); see again Yü Yüeh, *ibid.*

50. *op. cit.*, IV.

51. *ibid.*, XLV,「大盈若沖」. Concerning the character 沖, see above, Note 49.

52. *ibid.*, V.

53. *ibid.*, XI.

54. *op. cit.*, VI.

55. *ibid.*, XLI.

56. *ibid.*, XXII.

57. *ibid.*, I, quoted above.

58. *ibid.*, LII, quoted above.

59. *ibid.*, VI.

60. 玄.

61. *op. cit.*, I. See above, p. 113.

62. 門.

63. *op. cit.*, LXI.

64. 常德. Note again the use of the word *ch'ang* whose meaning in this context has been explained earlier; see Chapter VII, Note 9. The *ch'ang tê*, in accordance with what we have established above is synonymous with 'high' Virtue. See in particular *Tao Tê Ching*, XLI, in which the 'high' Virtue is associated with the image of a 'valley': 'The high Virtue looks like a valley'.

65. *op. cit.*, XXVIII.

66. *ibid.*, XL.

67. *ibid.*, XLII.

68. 復.

69. Here the ten thousand things that grow up with an amazing vitality are compared to plants that vie with one another in manifesting their vital energy in spring and summer.

70. *ming*, 命 (= 天命). For a provisional explanation of *t'ien ming* (Heavenly Command), see above, Note 8.

71. *ch'ang*, 常.

72. *ming* 明. The epistemological structure of the experience of Illumination has been fully elucidated in Chapters VI and V in accordance with what is said concerning it in the Book of *Chuang-tzŭ*. The passage here quoted is from the *Tao Tê Ching*, XVI.

73. This part of my explanation is an almost literal translation of the comment upon the passage by Wu Ch'êng 吳澄 (of the Yüan Dynasty, 道德眞經註): 「藝藝, 生長而 勁之貌. 凡植物春夏則生氣自根而上達干枝葉, 是曰動, 秋冬則生氣自上反還, 而下藏干根 · 是曰靜 · 天以此氣. 生而爲物者曰命. 復干其初生之處, 故曰復命」.

74. *ching*, 靜.

75. *op. cit.*, XL.

IX Determinism and Freedom

In the previous chapter we came across the concept of the Heavenly Command (*t'ien ming*). The concept is philosophically of basic importance because it leads directly to the idea of determinism which, in Western thought, is known as the problem of 'predestination', and in the intellectual tradition of Islam as that of *qaḍā'* and *qadar*.[1]

The most interesting part of the whole problem is admittedly its profound theological implication within the context of monotheistic religions like Christianity and Islam. The problem as a theological one might, at first sight, seem to be quite foreign to the world-view of Lao-tzŭ and Chuang-tzŭ. That such is not the case, however, will become clear if we but remember that Taoism too has its own theological aspect.

In the foregoing chapters the Way or the Absolute has been approached almost exclusively from the metaphysical point of view. We have been, in other words, trying to analyze the metaphysical aspect of the Way. And with reason. For that, after all, is the most fundamental theme upon which is based the whole system of Taoist philosophy.

But the Way as conceived by the Taoist philosophers is not simply and exclusively the metaphysical Ground of all beings. It is also God – the Creator (lit. the Maker-of-things, *tsao wu chê*), Heaven (*t'ien*), or the Heavenly Emperor (*t'ien ti*), as He is traditionally called in Chinese. The 'personal' image of the Absolute in ancient China had a long history prior to the rise of the philosophical branch of Taoism which we are considering in this book. It was quite a vigorous living tradition, and exercised a tremendous influence on the historical molding of Chinese culture and Chinese mentality. And we would make a fatal mistake if we imagined that the Way as conceived – or 'encountered', we should rather say – by the Taoist sages were a purely metaphysical Absolute. For them too the Way was a metaphysical Absolute as well as a personal God. The image of the Maker-of-things must not be taken as a metaphorical or figurative expression for the metaphysical Principle. The *Chuang-tzŭ* has a chapter entitled 'The Great Lordly Master'.[2] The title refers to this 'personal' aspect of the Way.

If we are to analyze this 'personal' concept of the Absolute in terms of the metaphysical structure of the Way, we should perhaps say that it corresponds to the stage of 'Being' at which the creative activity of the Way becomes fully manifested. For, strictly speaking, the Way at the stage of the Mystery, or even at the stage of Nothing, is absolutely beyond common human cognition. Just as in the world-view of Ibn 'Arabī the word 'Lord' (*rabb*) refers to the ontological stage at which the Absolute manifests itself through some definite Name – like Producer, for instance – and not to the absolute Essence which transcends all determinations and relations, so is the Taoist concept of 'Maker-of-things' properly to be taken as referring to the self-manifesting, or creative, aspect of the Way, and not to its self-concealing aspect. All this, however, is but a theoretical implication of the metaphysical doctrine of Lao-tzǔ and Chuang-tzǔ. They themselves do not elaborate this point in this particular form. Besides, the concept of the Absolute as the highest Lord of Heaven belongs to a particular domain of religious experience which is of quite a different nature from that of the ecstatic intuition of the Absolute as the One, then as 'Nothing', then as the Mystery of Mysteries, although it is also true that the two types of religious experience seem to have greatly influenced each other in the historical process of the formation of Taoist philosophy, so much so that the Taoist concept of the Absolute as it actually stands can justifiably be said to contain two different aspects: metaphysical and personal.

However this may be, the description given by Chuang-tzǔ of the activity of the Great Lordly Master in the administration of the affairs of the creaturely world is exactly the same as what he and Lao-tzǔ say about the working of Nature or the Absolute. The following is one of a number of passages which could be cited as evidence in support of this statement.

> Oh my Master, my (sole) Master – He cuts the ten thousand things into minute pieces.[3] And yet He has no consciousness of doing 'justice'. His bounty extends to the ten thousand generations. And yet He has no consciousness of doing any particular act of 'benevolence'.[4] He is older than the oldest time (of history). And yet he has no consciousness of being aged. He covers Heaven (which covers everything) and sustains Earth (which sustains everything). He carves and models all kinds of forms. And yet he has no consciousness of being skilful.[5]

The point I am making will become clear if one compares this passage with the words of Lao-tzǔ about the activity of the Way in the form of Virtue, which were quoted in the previous chapter.

The Way gives birth (to the ten thousand things), yet claims no possession. It does great things, yet does not boast of it. It makes things grow, yet exercises no authority upon them. This is what I would call the Mysterious Virtue.[6]

With this general theological background in mind we may rightly approach the problem of necessity or 'predestination' in Taoism. In discussing this idea, we shall be mainly dependent upon Chuang-tzŭ, because he seems to have been particularly interested in the problem of Necessity and human Freedom within the particular context of Taoist philosophy.

We have pointed out earlier in this book the central importance observed of the concept of Chaos in the philosophical system of Chuang-tzŭ. We have observed there that, according to Chuang-tzŭ, Being which surrounds us from all sides and in which we live as part of it, reveals itself as a Chaos when we intuit its reality in the experience of 'sitting-in-oblivion'. In the ecstatic vision peculiar to this experience, all things appear 'chaotified'. Nothing remains solid and stable. We witness the amazing scene of all things being freely and unobstructedly transmuted into one another.

This image of Being must not mislead us into thinking only that Reality is literally chaotic and nothing but chaotic. Chaos *is* a metaphysical reality. But it represents only one aspect of Reality. In the very midst of this seeming disorder and confusion, there is observable a supreme order governing all things and events in the phenomenal world. In spite of their apparent utter confusion, all things that exist and all events that occur in the world exist and occur in accordance with the natural articulations of Reality. In this respect, the world we live in is a world determined by a rigorous Necessity. And how could it be otherwise? For the ten thousand things are nothing but forms in which the Absolute appears as it goes on determining itself; they are so many forms of the self-revelation of God.

This concept of the ontological Necessity is expressed by Chuang-tzŭ by various terms, such as *t'ien* (Heaven), *t'ien li* (the natural course of things determined by Heaven), *ming* (Command), and *pu tê i* ('that which cannot be evaded').

Chuang-tzŭ regards 'living in accordance with the *t'ien li*' as the ideal way of living in this world for the 'true man'. The expression means 'to accept whatever is given by nature and not to struggle against it'. It suggests that there is for everybody and everything a natural course to take, which has been determined from the very beginning by Heaven. The world of Being, in this view, is naturally articulated, and nothing can happen against or outside of the fixed course. All things, whether inanimate or living, seem to exist or live in docile obedience to their own destinies. They seem to be happy and contented with existing in absolute conformity with the inevitable Law of Nature. They are, in this respect, naturally 'living in accordance with the *t'ien li*'.

Only Man, of all existents, can and does revolt against the *t'ien li*. And that because of his self-consciousness. It is extremely difficult for him to remain resigned to his destiny. He tends to struggle hard to evade it or to change it. And he thereby brings discordance into the universal harmony of Being. But of course all his violent struggles are vain and useless, for everything is determined eternally. Herein lies the very source of the tragedy of human existence.

Is there, then, absolutely no freedom for man? Should he acquiesce without murmuring in his naturally given situation however miserable it may be? Does Chuang-tzǔ uphold the principle of negative passivity or nihilism? Not in the least. But how could he, then, reconcile the concept of Necessity with that of human freedom? This is the question which will occupy us in the following pages.

The first step one has to take in attempting to solve this question consists in one's gaining a lucid and deep consciousness that whatever occurs in this world occurs through the activity of Heaven – Heaven here being understood in a 'personal' sense. Chuang-tzǔ gives a number of examples in the form of anecdotes. Here is one of them.

A certain man saw a man who had one foot amputated as a punishment for some crime.

> Greatly surprised at seeing the deformity of the man, he cried out: 'What a man! How has he come to have his foot cut off? Is it due to Heaven? Or is it due to man?'
> The man replied: 'It is Heaven, not man! At the very moment when Heaven gave me life, it destined me to become one-footed. (Normally) the human form is provided with a pair,[7] (i.e., normally man is born with two feet). From this I know that my being one-footed is due to Heaven. It cannot be ascribed to man!'[8]

Not only this and similar individual cases of misery and misfortune – and also happiness and good fortune – but the very beginning and end of human existence, Life and Death, are due to the Heavenly Command. In Chapter III we discussed the basic attitude of Chuang-tzǔ on the question of Life and Death, but from an entirely different angle. There we discussed it in terms of the concept of Transmutation. The same problem comes up in the present context in connection with the problem of destiny or Heaven.

When Lao-tzŭ died, (one of his close friends) Ch'in Shih went to the
ceremony of mourning for his death. (Quite perfunctorily) he wailed
over the dead three times, and came out of the room.
Thereupon the disciples (of Lao-tzŭ) (reproved him for his conduct)
saying, 'Were you not a freind of our Master?'
'Yes, indeed,' he replied.
'Well, then, is it permissible that you should mourn over his death in
such a (perfunctory) way?'
'Yes. (This is about what he deserves.) Formerly I used to think that
he was a ('true') man. But now I have realized that he was not. (The
reason for this change of my opinion upon him is as follows.) Just now
I went in to mourn him; I saw there old people weeping for him as if
they were weeping for their own child, and young folk weeping for
him as if they were weeping for their own mother. Judging by the fact
that he could arouse the sympathy of his people in such a form, he
must have (during his lifetime) cunningly induced them somehow to
utter words (of sorrow and sadness) for his death, without explicitly
asking them to do so, and to weep for him, without explicitly asking
them to do so.[9]
This,[10] however, is nothing but 'escaping Heaven' (i.e., escaping the
natural course of things as determined by Heaven), and going against
the reality of human nature. These people have completely forgotten
(from where) they received what they received (i.e., the fact that they
have received their life and existence from Heaven, by the Heavenly
Command). In days of old, people who behaved thus were considered liable for punishment for (the crime of) 'escaping Heaven'.
Your Master came (i.e., was born into this world) quite naturally,
because it was his (destined) time (to come). Now he has (departed)
quite naturally, because it was his turn (to go).
If we remain content with the 'time' and accept the 'turn', neither
sorrow nor joy can ever creep in. Such an attitude used to be called
among the Ancients 'loosing the tie of the (Heavenly) Emperor'.[11]

The last paragraph of this passage is found almost *verbatim* in
another passage which was quoted earlier in Chapter III,[12] where
the particular expression: 'loosing the tie' appears with the same
meaning; namely, that of complete freedom. And this idea would
seem to indicate in which direction one should turn in order to solve
the problem of the conflict between Necessity and human freedom
on the basis of a lucid consciousness that everything is due to the
Will of Heaven.

The next step one should take consists, according to what
Chuang-tzŭ observes about 'loosing the tie of the Heavenly
Emperor', in one's becoming indifferent to, or transcending, the
effects caused by the turns of fortune. In the latter half of the
anecdote about the one-footed man, the man himself describes the
kind of freedom he enjoys by wholly submitting himself to whatever
has been destined for him by Heaven. Other people – so the man

observes – might imagine that, being one-footed, he must find his life unbearable. But, he says, such is not actually the case. And he explains his situation by the image of a swamp pheasant.

> Look at the pheasant living in the swamp. (In order to feed itself) the bird has to bear the trouble of walking ten paces for one peck, and walking a hundred paces for one drink. (The onlookers might think that the pheasant must find such a life miserable.) However it will never desire to be kept and fed in a cage. For (in a cage the bird would be able to eat and drink to satiety and) it would be full of vitality, and yet it would not find itself happy.[13]

To be deprived of one foot is to be deprived of one's so-called 'freedom'. The one-footed man has to endure inconvenience in daily life like the swamp pheasant which has to walk so many paces just for the sake of one peck and one drink. A man of normal bodily structure is 'free' to walk with his two feet. But the 'freedom' here spoken of is a physical, external freedom. What really matters is whether or not the man has a spiritual, inner freedom. If the man with two feet does not happen to have inner freedom, his situation will be similar to that of a pheasant in a cage; he can eat and drink without having to put up with any physical inconvenience, but, in spite of that, he cannot enjoy being in the world. The real misery of such a man lies in the fact that he struggles helplessly to change what can never be changed, that he has to fret away his life.

Chuang-tzŭ's thought, however, does not stop at this stage. The inner 'freedom' which is based on a *passive* acceptance of whatever is given, or the tranquillity of the mind based on mere resignation in the presence of Necessity, does not for him represent the final stage of human freedom. In order to reach the last and ultimate stage of inner freedom, man must go a step further and obliterate the very distinction – or opposition – between his own existence and Necessity. But how can this be achieved?

Chuang-tzŭ often speaks of 'what cannot be evaded' or 'that which cannot be made otherwise'. Everything is necessarily fixed and determined by a kind of Cosmic Will which is called the Command or Heaven. As long as there is even the minutest discrepancy in the consciousness of a man between this Cosmic Will and his own personal will, Necessity is felt to be something forced upon him, something which he has to accept even against his will. If, under such conditions, through resignation he gains 'freedom' to some extent, it cannot be a complete freedom. Complete freedom is obtained only when man identifies himself with Necessity itself, that is, the natural course of things and events, and goes on transforming himself as the natural course of things turns this way or that.

> Go with things wherever they go, and let your mind wander about (in the realm of absolute freedom). Leave yourself wholly to 'that which cannot be made otherwise', and nourish and foster the (unperturbed) balance of the mind.[14] That, surely, is the highest mode of human existence.[15]

To take such an attitude toward the inexorable Necessity of Being is, needless to say, possible only for the 'true man'. But even the ordinary man, Chuang-tzŭ says, should not abandon all hope of coming closer to this highest ideal. And for this purpose, all that ordinary people are asked to do is positively accept their destiny instead of committing themselves passively and sullenly to fatalistic resignation. Chuang-tzŭ offers them an easily understandable reason why they should take the attitude of positive and willing acceptance. Quite naturally Necessity is represented at this level by the concrete fact of Life and Death.

> Life and Death are a matter of the (Heavenly) Command. (They succeed one another) just as Night and Day regularly go on alternating with each other. This strict regularity is due to Heaven. There are things in this world (like Life and Death, Night and Day, and countless others) which stand beyond the reach of human intervention. This is due to the natural structure of things.
> Man usually respects his own father as if the latter were Heaven itself,[16] and loves him (i.e., his father) with sincere devotion. If such is the case, how much more should he (respect and love) the (Father) who is far greater than his own!
> Man usually regards the ruler whom he serves as superior to himself. He is willing to die for him. If such is the case, how much more should he (regard as superior to himself) the true (Ruler)![17]

The expression 'what cannot be evaded' (*pu tê i*) is liable to suggest the idea of man's being under unnatural constraint. Such an impression is produced only because our attention is focused – usually – on individual particular things and events. If, instead, we direct our attention to the whole of 'that which cannot be evaded', which is no other than the Way itself as it manifests its creative activity in the forms of the world of Being, we are sure to receive quite a different impression of the matter. And if, further, we identify ourselves with the working of the Way itself and become completely united and unified with it,[18] what has been an inexorable Necessity and 'non-freedom' will immediately turn into an absolute freedom. This *is* Freedom, because, such a spiritual state once achieved, man suffers nothing from outside. Everything is experienced as something coming from inside, as his own. The kaleidoscopic changes that characterize the phenomenal world are his own changes. As Kuo Hsiang says: 'Having forgotten (the distinction between) Good and Evil, and having left aside Life and Death, he is now completely one with the universal Transmutation. Without encountering any obstruction, he goes wherever he goes'.[19]

And since everything is his own – or we should say, since everything is himself as he goes on transforming himself with the cosmic Transmutation – he accepts willingly and lovingly whatever happens to him or whatever he observes. As Lao-tzǔ says:

> The 'sacred man' has no rigidly fixed mind of his own.[20] He makes the minds of all people his mind.
> 'Those who are good, (he says), I treat as good. But even those who are not good also I treat as good. (Such an attitude I take) because the original nature of man is goodness.
> Those who are faithful I treat as faithful. But even those who are not faithful I treat as faithful. (Such an attitude I take) because the original nature of man is faithfulness.
> Thus the 'sacred man', while he lives in the world, keeps his mind wide open. He 'chaotifies' his own mind toward all. Ordinary men strain their eyes and ears (in order to distinguish between things). The 'sacred man', on the contrary, keeps his eyes and ears (free) like an infant.[21]

Here the attitude of the 'sacred man' toward things is sharply contrasted with that of ordinary people. The former is characterized by not-having-a-rigidly-fixed-mind, that is, by an endless flexibility of the mind. This flexibility is the result of his having completely unified himself with the Transmutation of the ten thousand things.

The 'sacred man' is also said to have 'chaotified' his mind. This simply means that his mind is beyond and above all relative distinctions – between 'good' and 'bad', 'right' and 'wrong', 'truthful' and 'untruthful', etc. Being one with the Way as it manifests itself, how could he make such distinctions? Is everything not a particular form of Virtue which is itself the activity of the Way? And is it not also the case that every particular form of Virtue is his own form?

Chuang-tzǔ sees in such a situation the manifestation of the absolute freedom of man.

> The great clod (i.e., the earth – Heaven and Earth, or Nature) has placed me in a definite form (i.e., has furnished me with a definite bodily form). It has placed upon me the burden of life. It will make my life easier by making me old. And (finally) it will make me restful by letting me die. (All these four stages are nothing but four different forms of my own existence, which, again, are four of the infinitely variegated forms of Nature.) If I am glad to have my Life, I must be glad also to obtain my Death.

What Chuang-tzǔ is concerned with in this particular context is not the problem of transcending Life and Death. The question at issue is that of Necessity, of which Life and Death are but two concrete conspicuous examples. The gist of his argument is that the Necessity of Being will no longer be 'necessity' when man becomes completely one with Necessity itself. Wherever he may go, and into whatever form he may be changed, he will always be with the Necessity which has ceased to be 'necessity'. If, on the contrary, the union is not complete, and if there is even one part of the whole left alien to himself, that particular part may at any moment damage his freedom.

> (A fisherman) hides his boat in the ravine, and hides his fishing-net[22] in the swamp, thinking that the boat and net are thereby ensured (against thieves). In the middle of the night, however, a powerful man (i.e., a thief) may (come and) carry them off on his back, without the stupid (fisherman) noticing it.
>
> Hiding, in this way, a small thing in a large place will certainly serve your purpose to some extent. But (that will guarantee no absolute security, for) there will still be ample possibility (for the small thing) to escape and disappear.
>
> If, on the contrary, you hide the whole world in the whole world itself,[23] nothing will find any place through which it might escape. This is the greatest truth common to all things.
>
> It is quite by chance that you have acquired the form of a man. Even such a thing is enough to make you glad. But (remember that) a thing like the human form is nothing but one of the infinitely variegated (phenomenal) forms of the universal Transmutation. (If only one phenomenal form is sufficient to make you so glad) incalculable indeed will be your joy (if you could experience with the Way all the transformations it manifests). Therefore the 'sacred man' wanders to his heart's content in the realm of 'that from which there is no escape and in which all things have their existence'. And (being in such a spiritual state) he finds everything good – early death is good, old age is good, the beginning is good, the end is good. (The 'sacred man' is, after all, a human being). And yet he serves as a model for the people in this respect. All the more so, then, should (the Way itself be taken as the model for all men – the Way) upon which depend the ten thousand things and which is the very ground of the universal Transmutation.[24]

In Chapter III we read a story of a 'sacred man' whose body was made hideously deformed by some serious illness and who made the following remark upon his own situation.[25]

> Whatever we obtain (i.e., Life) is due to the coming of the time. Whatever we lose (i.e., Death) is also due to the arrival of the turn. We must be content with the 'time' and accept the 'turn'. Then neither sorrow nor joy will creep in. Such an attitude used to be called among the Ancients 'loosing the tie (of Heaven)'. If man cannot loose himself from the tie, it is because 'things' bind him fast.

And to this he adds:

From of old, nothing has ever won against Heaven. How could I resent (what has happened to me)?

Instead of 'loosing the tie of Heaven', people ordinarily remain bound up by all things. This is to say, instead of 'hiding the whole world in the world', they are simply trying to 'hide smaller things in larger things'. In the minds of such people, there can be no room for real freedom. They are, at every moment of their existence, made conscious of the absolute Necessity of the Will of Heaven or – which is the same thing – the Law of Nature, oppressing them, constraining them against their will, and making them feel that they are in a narrow cage. This understanding of the Will of Heaven is by no means mistaken. For, ontologically, the course of things is absolutely and 'necessarily' fixed by the very activity of the Way, and no one can ever escape from it. And 'nothing has ever won against Heaven'. On the other hand, however, there is spiritually a certain point at which this ontological Necessity becomes metamorphosed into an absolute Freedom. When this crucial turning point is actually experienced by a man, he *is* a 'sacred man' or Perfect Man as understood in Taoist philosophy. In the following chapters we shall be concerned with the structure of the concept of the Perfect Man in Taoism.

Notes

1. In the first Part of the present book Ibn 'Arabī's interpretation of the *qadâ'* and *qadar* has been given in detail.

2. 大宗師 (王先謙「莊子集解」:「本篇云, 人猶效之. 效之言師也. 又云, 吾師乎, 吾師乎, 以 道爲師也. 宗者主也」). *shih* means a teacher or leader who is obediently followed by his followers. Here the Absolute or God who 'instructs' all existent things as to how they should exist is compared to an aged venerable Master instructing his students in the Truth. The idea is comparable with the Western concept of 'Lord' as applied to God.

3. 螯. The word here is usually interpreted as meaning 'to crush'. Ch'êng Hsüan Ying (成玄英「莊子疏」p. 282), for example explicates the sentence 「螯萬物」 as follows: (This may be visualized by the fact that) when autumn comes, frost falls and crushes the ten thousand things (and destroys them). Frost does not cut them down and crush them with any special intention to do so. How could it have the feeling of administering 'justice'? (「螯碎也. 至如素秋霜降, 碎落萬物, 豈有情斷割而爲義哉」). Ch'êng Hsüan Ying's idea is that the 'justice' of the Way corresponds to the relentless destructive activity of the cold season, while the aspect of 'benevolence' corresponds to the 'fostering' activity of spring. Concerning this latter aspect he says: 'The mild warmth of spring fosters the ten thousand things. But how is it imaginable that spring should have the emotion of love and affection and thereby do the work of 'benevolence'? It would seem, however, better to understand the word 'cutting to pieces' as referring to the fact that the creative activity brings into actual existence an infinite number of individual things.

4. Note again the sarcastic tone in which the Confucian virtue is spoken of.

5. VI, 281.

6. *Tao tê Ching*. LI.

7. 有與. Kuo Hsiang says: 'Having a pair here means man's walking (usually) with two feet. Nobody would ever doubt that the human form being provided with two feet is due to the Heavenly Command (or destiny)'. (「兩足共行曰有與. 有與之貌, 未有疑 其非我也」). To this Ch'êng Hsüan Ying adds: Since being biped is due to the Heavenly Command, it is evident that being one-footed also is not due to man. (「以有與者命也，故知獨 者亦非我也」).

8. *Chuang-tzŭ*, III, p. 124.

9. Since he himself was not a 'true man', he could not teach his people how to behave properly.

10. 'This' refers to the behavior of the people who were weeping so bitterly for him.

11. *op. cit.*, III, pp. 127v–128.

12. *ibid.*, VI, p. 260.

13. *ibid.*, III, p. 126.

14. *chung* 中 (王先謙：「中，吾心不動之中」).

15. *op. cit.*, IV, p. 160.

16. Reading「以父爲天」instead of「以天爲父」.

17. *op. cit.*, VI, p. 241.

18. To express the idea Chuang-tzŭ uses the phrase:「化其道」meaning 'to be transmuted into the Way' (Cf. VI, p. 242).

19. 「忘善惡，遺死生，與變化爲一，脗然無不適矣」, VI, p. 243.

20. 常心. In this combination, the word *ch'ang* (常) – whose original meaning is, as we saw earlier, 'eternal', 'unalterable' – means 'stiff' and 'inflexible'.

21. *Tao Tê Ching*, XLIX.

22. The text has「藏山於澤」which is meaningless. Following the suggestion by Yü Yüeh 俞樾 (「諸子平議」：「山非可藏於澤， 且亦非有力者所能負之而走， 其義難通， 山疑當讀爲汕」) I read 汕 instead of 山.

23. This refers to the spiritual stage of complete unification with the Way which comprises everything. 'Hiding the whole world in the whole world' is contrasted to hiding, as we usually do, smaller things in larger things. In the latter case, there are always possibilities for the smaller things to go somewhere else, while in the former, there is absolutely no such possibility. Thus 'hiding the whole world in the whole world' is paradoxically tantamount to 'hiding nothing' or 'leaving everything as it naturally is'.

24. *Chuang-tzŭ*, VI, pp. 243–244.

25. *ibid*., VI, p. 260.

X Absolute Reversal of Values

Throughout the *Tao Tê Ching* the term *shêng jên* ('sacred man')[1] is consistently used in such a way that it might justifiably be considered the closest equivalent for the Islamic *insān kāmil* ('perfect man').
This word seems to go back to remote antiquity. In any case, judging by the way it is used by Confucius in the *Analects*, the word must have been widely prevalent in his age.

> The Master said: A 'sacred man' is not for me to meet. I would be quite satisfied if I could ever meet a man of princely virtue.[2]

> The Master said: How dare I claim for myself being a 'sacred man' or even a man of (perfect) 'benevolence'?[3]

It is not philologically easy to determine the precise meaning attached by Confucius to this word. But from the general contexts in which it is actually used as well as from the dominant features of his teaching, we can, I think, judge fairly safely that he meant by the term *shêng jên* a man with a sort of superhuman ethical perfection. Confucius did not dare even to hope to meet in his life a man of this kind, not to speak of claiming that he himself was one.

This, however, is not the problem at which we must labor in the present context. The point I would like to make here is the fact that the word *shêng jên* itself represented a concept which was apparently quite understandable to the intellectuals of the age of Confucius, and that Lao-tzŭ wrought a drastic change in the connotation of this word. This semantic change was effected by Lao-tzŭ through his metaphysical standpoint, which was of a shamanic origin.

We have already seen in the first chapters of this book how Lao-tzŭ – and Chuang-tzŭ – came out of a shamanic milieu. The Perfect Man for Lao-tzŭ was originally a 'perfect' shaman. This fact is concealed from our eyes by the fact that his world-view is not nakedly shamanic, but is presented with an extremely sophisticated metaphysical elaboration. But the shamanic origin of the Taoist concept of the 'sacred man' will be disclosed if we correlate the following passage, for example, from the *Tao Tê Ching* with what Chuang-tzŭ remarks concerning the ecstatic experience of 'sitting in oblivion'.

> Block all your openings (i.e., eyes, ears, mouth, etc.), and shut all your doors (i.e., the activity of Reason), and all your life you (i.e., your spiritual energy) will not be exhausted.
>
> If, on the contrary, you keep your openings wide open, and go on increasing their activities, you will never be saved till the end.
>
> To be able to perceive the minutest thing[4] is properly to be called Illumination (*ming*).
>
> To hold on to what is soft and flexible[5] is properly to be called strength.
>
> If, using your external light, you go back to your internal illumination, you will never bring misfortune upon yourself. Such an (ultimate) state is what is to be called 'stepping into'[6] the eternally real'.[7]

The 'eternal real' (*ch'ang*), as we have often noticed, refers to the Way as the eternally changeless Reality. Thus the concept of the 'sacred man' as we understand it from this passage, namely, the concept of the man who 'has returned to Illumination' and has thereby 'stepped into', that is, unified himself with, the Way, is exactly the same as that of the man who is completely one with 'that which cannot be made otherwise', which we have discussed in the previous chapter in connection with the problem of Necessity and Freedom.

The 'sacred man', for both Lao-tzŭ and Chuang-tzŭ, is a man whose mind is 'wandering about in the realm of absolute Freedom', away from the bustle of the common people. It is quite natural, then, that such a man, when judged by the yardstick of common sense, should appear as outrageously 'abnormal'. If worldly-minded people represent the 'normal', the 'sacred man' is surely to be considered a strange, bizarre creature.

> An 'abnormal'[8] man – what kind of man is he, if I may ask?
>
> The answer: An 'abnormal' man is one who is totally different from other men, while being in perfect conformity with Heaven. Hence the saying: a petty man from the viewpoint of Heaven is, from the viewpoint of ordinary men, a man of princely virtue;[9] while a man of princely virtue from the viewpoint of Heaven is, from the viewpoint of ordinary men, a petty man.

Thus the Perfect Man, by the very fact that he is in perfect conformity with Heaven, is in every respect in discordance with ordinary men. His behavior pattern is so totally different from the commonly accepted one that it excludes him from 'normal' human society. The latter necessarily regards him as 'abnormal'. He is 'abnormal' because the Way itself with which he is in perfect conformity is, from the standpoint of the common people, something strange and 'abnormal', so 'abnormal' indeed that they treat it as funny and ridiculous. As Lao-tsŭ says:

> When a man of low grade hears about the Way, he bursts into laughter.
> If it is not laughed at, it would not be worthy to be the Way.[10]

If the Way is of such a nature that it looks not only strange and obscure but even funny and ridiculous, it is but natural that the Perfect Man who is a living image of the Way should also look ridiculous or sometimes vexatious and unbearably irritating. Chuang-tsŭ often describes in his Book the 'strange' behavior of the 'abnormal'.

Once a disciple of Confucius – this is of course a fictitious story – saw two 'abnormal' men merrily and playfully singing in unison in the presence of the corpse of their friend, another 'abnormal' man, instead of duly performing the funeral service. Vexed and indignant, he hastened back and reported to his Master what he had just seen. 'What sort of men are they?' he asked Confucius.

> 'What sort of men are they? They do not observe the rules of proper behavior. They do not care at all about external forms. In the presence of the corpse they sing a song, without even changing their countenances. Their conduct (is so abnormal that) I am completely at a loss to characterize them. What kind of men are they?'

Quite ironically, Chuang-tzŭ makes Confucius perspicacious enough to understand the real situation in terms of Taoist philosophy and explain the nature of their conduct to his perplexed disciple. Here is what Confucius says about it.

> They are those who freely wander beyond the boundaries (i.e., the ordinary norms of proper behavior), while men like myself are those who wander freely only within the boundaries. 'Beyond the boundaries' and 'within the boundaries' are poles asunder from one another. . . .
> They are those who, being completely unified with the Creator Himself, take delight in the realm (i.e., spiritual state) of the original Unity of the vital energy before it is divided into Heaven and Earth. To their minds Life is just the growth of an excrescence, a wart, and Death is the breaking of a boil, the bursting of a tumor. . . . They simply borrow different elements, and put them together in the common form of body (i.e., in their view a human being is a composite made of different elements which by chance are placed together into a bodily unit). Hence they are conscious neither of their liver nor of their gall, and they leave aside their ears and eyes. Abandoning themselves to infinitely recurrent waves of Ending and Beginning, they go on revolving in a circle, of which they know neither the beginning-point nor the ending-point.

Thus, without being conscious (of their personal existence), they roam beyond the realm of dust and dirt, and enjoy wandering to their heart's content in the work of Non-Doing.

How should such men bother themselves with meticulously observing the rules of conduct peculiar to the vulgar world, so that they might attract (i.e., satisfy) the ears and eyes of the common people?[11]

Thus the behavior pattern of these men necessarily brings about a complete overturn of the commonly accepted order of values. Of course it is not their *intention* to turn upside down the ordinary system of values. But as these men live and behave in this world, their conduct naturally reflects a very peculiar standard of values, which could never square with that accepted by common sense and Reason.

Chuang-tzŭ expresses this idea in a number of ways. As one of the most interesting expressions he uses for this purpose we may mention the paradoxical-sounding phrase: 'deforming, or crippling the virtues'.[12] After relating how a man of hideous deformity – Shu the Crippled – because of his deformity, completes his term of life safely and pleasantly, Chuang-tzŭ makes the following observation:

If even a man with such a crippled body was able to support himself and complete the span of life that had been assigned to him by Heaven, how much more should this be the case with those who have 'crippled the virtues'![13]

To 'cripple' or 'deform' the virtues is a forceful expression meaning: to damage and overturn the common hierarchy of values. And since the system of values on which is based the mode of living or principle of existence peculiar to these 'cripples' is thus radically opposed to that of the common people, their real greatness cannot be recognized by the latter. Even the most sophisticated man of Reason – Reason being, after all, an elaboration of common sense – fails to understand the significance of the 'abnormal' way of living, although he may at least vaguely sense that he is in the presence of something great.

Hui Shih (Hui-tzŭ), a famous dialectician of Chuang-tzŭ's time, of whom mention was made earlier,[14] criticizes Chuang-tzŭ – in one of the anecdotes about this 'sophist' recorded in the Book of *Chuang-tzŭ* – and remarks that Chuang-tzŭ's thought is certainly 'big', but it is too big to be of any use in the world of reality. It is 'big but crippled'. Against this Chuang-tzŭ points out that the eyes of those who are tied down to a stereotyped and fossilized system of traditional values cannot see the greatness of the really great. Besides, he says, things that are 'useful' in the real sense of the term are those things that transcend the common notion of 'usefulness'.

The 'usefulness' of the 'useless', the greatness of the 'abnormal', in
short, an absolute reversal of the order of values – this is what
characterizes the world-view of the Perfect Man.

Let us, first, see how Hui-tzŭ describes the 'uselessness' of things
that are 'abnormally big'.

> The king of Wei once gave me the seeds of a huge gourd. I sowed
> them, and finally they bore fruit. Each gourd was big enough to
> contain as much as five piculs. I used one of them to contain water and
> other liquids; but I found that it was so heavy that I could not lift it by
> myself. So I cut it into two pieces and tried to use them as ladles. But
> they were too flat and shallow to hold any liquid.
> Not that it was not big enough. Big it surely was, to the degree of
> monstrosity! But it was utterly useless. So I ended up by smashing
> them all to pieces.[15]

It is interesting to notice that Hui-tzŭ does recognize the gourds as
big, very big indeed. But their excessive bigness renders them
unsuitable for any practical use. Through this symbol he wants to
indicate that the spiritual size of the Perfect Man may be very large,
but that when his spiritual size exceeds a certain limit, it turns him
practically into a stupid fellow. This, however, only provokes a
sharp retort from Chuang-tzŭ, who points out that Hui-tzŭ has
found the gourd to be of no use 'simply because he does not know
how to use big things properly'. And he adds:

> Now that you had a gourd big enough to contain as much as five
> piculs, why did it not occur to you that you might use it as a large
> barrel? You could have enjoyed floating over rivers and lakes,
> instead of worrying about its being too big and shallow to contain any
> liquid! Evidently, my dear friend, you still have a mind overgrown
> with weeds![16]

Exactly the same kind of situation is found in another anecdote
which immediately follows the preceding one.

> Hui-tzŭ once said to Chuang-tzŭ: 'I have (in my garden) a big tree,
> which is popularly called *shu* (useless, stinking tree). Its main stem is
> gnarled as with tumors, and nobody can apply a measuring line to it.
> Its branches are so curled and bent that no one can use upon them
> compass and square. Even if I should make it stand by the thorough-
> fare (in order to sell it), no carpenter would even cast a glance at it.
> Now your words, too, are extremely big, but of no use. That is why
> people desert them and nobody wants to listen to you'.
> Chuang-tzŭ said: 'You must have observed a weasel, how it hides
> itself crouching down, and watches for carelessly sauntering things
> (i.e., chickens, rats, etc.) to pass by. Sometimes, again, it nimbly leaps
> about east and west, jumping up and jumping down without any
> hesitation. But finally it falls into a trap or dies in a net.

Now look at that black ox. It is as big as an enormous cloud hanging in the sky. It *is* big, indeed! And it does not know how to catch a rat. (It is useless in this sense, but it does not die in a trap or a net.) You say you have a big tree, and you are worried because it is useless. Well, then, why do you not plant it in the Village of There-Is-Absolutely-Nothing,[17] or in the Wilderness of the Limitlessly-Wide,[18] idly spend your days by its side without doing anything, and lie down under it for an untroubled sleep? The tree, then, will never suffer a premature death by being cut down by an axe. Nor will there be anything there to harm it. If it happens to be of no use, why should it cause you to fret and worry?'[19]

The passage just quoted, in which Chuang-tzŭ clarifies his attitude against the kind of rationalism and utilitarianism represented by Hui-tzŭ is of great importance for our purposes, containing as it does in a symbolic form some of the basic ideas of Chuang-tzŭ. These ideas are so closely interrelated with each other that it is difficult to deal with them separately. Besides, some of them have already been discussed in detail in connection with other problems, and others are directly or indirectly related with those that have been touched upon in the foregoing. Here for convenience I will classify them under four heads, and discuss them briefly one by one from the particular viewpoint of the present chapter. These four are: (1) The image of a strange, fantastic region which is designated by such expressions as the Village of There-Is-Absolutely-Nothing and the Wilderness of the Limitlessly-Wide; (2) the idea of idling away one's time; (3) 'abnormal bigness'; and (4) the idea of free wandering.

(1) The two expressions: the Village of There-Is-Absolutely-Nothing and the Wilderness of the Limitlessly-Wide, are very characteristic of the philosophical anthropology of Chuang-tzŭ. They describe symbolically the spiritual state in which the Perfect Man finds his absolute tranquillity and freedom. In another passage Chuang-tzŭ gives us a hint – symbolically, again – through the mouth of a fictitious Perfect Man[20] as to what he means by these terms.

> I am going to unify myself with the Creator Himself. But when I become bored with that, immediately I will mount on the Bird-of-Pure-Emptiness and travel beyond the limits of the six directions (i.e., the Universe).
> There I shall wander to my heart's content in the Village of There-Is-Absolutely-Nothing and live alone in the Wilderness of the Limitlessly-Wide.[21]

In the light of what we already know about the major ideas of Chuang-tzŭ, the 'Village of There-Is-Absolutely-Nothing' or the

'Wilderness of the Limitlessly-Wide' evidently refer to the spiritual
state of Nothingness or Void in which the perfect Man finds himself
in the moments of his ecstatic experience. At the highest stage of
'sitting in oblivion' the mind of the Perfect Man is in a peculiar kind
of blankness. All traces of phenomenal things have been erased
from his consciousness; even consciousness itself has been erased.
There is here no distinction between 'subject' and 'object'. For both
mind and things have completely disappeared. He is now an
inhabitant of a strange metaphysical region which is 'limitlessly
wide' and where 'there is absolutely nothing'.

This, however, is but the first half of his being an inhabitant of the
Village of There-Is-Absolutely-Nothing or the Wilderness of the
Limitlessly-Wide. In the second half of this experience, the reality
of the phenomenal world begins to be disclosed to his spiritually
transformed eyes. All the things that have once been wiped out
from his consciousness – including his own consciousness – come
back to him in an entirely new form. Being reborn at a new level of
existence, he is now in a position to command an extensive and
unobstructed view of the whole world of Being as it pulsates with
eternal life, in which infinitely variegated things come and go,
appear and disappear at every moment. We know already that this
aspect of the Perfect Man, namely, his being an inhabitant of the
region of Nothingness and Limitlessness, is discussed by Chuang-
tzŭ in a more philosophical way as the problem of the Transmutation of all things.

> Being perfectly familiar with that which has no falsehood (i.e., the
> true Reality, the Way), he does not shift about driven by the shifting
> things.[22] He regards the universal Transmutation of things as (the
> direct manifestation of) the Heavenly Command, and holds fast to
> (i.e., keeps his inner gaze inalterably focused upon) their Great
> Source.[23]

(2) The Idea of idling away one's time is closely related to the idea of
living in the region of Nothingness and Limitlessness. For the Perfect Man cannot be an inhabitant of such a country unless he is idling
away his time, doing nothing and enjoying from time to time an
untroubled sleep. 'To be idle' is a symbolic way of expressing the
basic idea of Non-Doing. The principle of Non-Doing which, as we
saw earlier, represents, for Lao-tzŭ and Chuang-tzŭ, the highest
mode of human existence in this world, demands of the Perfect Man
'being natural' and leaving everything in its natural state and to its
natural course. He does not meddle with the fate of anything. This is
the 'indifference' of the Perfect Man to the ten thousand things, of
which mention was made earlier.

But 'indifference' in this case does not imply ignorance or lack of cognition. On the contrary, all things, as they come and go, are faithfully reflected in the 'void' of the mind of the Perfect Man. His mind in this respect is comparable to a spotless mirror. A well-polished mirror reflects every object, as long as the latter stands in front of it. But if the object goes away, the mirror does not show any effort to detain it; nor does it particularly welcome a new object when it makes its appearance. Thus the mind of the Perfect Man obtains the most lucid images of all things, but is not perturbed thereby.

(The Perfect Man)[24] does not become the sole possessor of fame, (but lets each thing possess its own fame). He does not become the treasury of plans (but lets each thing make a plan for itself). He does not undertake the responsibility for all things, (but lets each thing undertake the responsibility for itself). He does not become the sole possessor of wisdom, (but lets each thing exercise its own wisdom). He embodies completely what is inexhaustible (i.e., the 'limitless' activity of the Way), and wanders to his heart's content in the Land-of-No-Trace (i.e., the region of Nothingness).

He employs to the utmost what he has received from Heaven, and yet he is not conscious of having acquired something. He is 'empty' – that is what he is.

The 'ultimate man' makes his mind work as a (spotless) mirror. It detains nothing. It welcomes nothing. It simply responds to, and reflects, (whatever comes to it). But it stores nothing. This is why he can exercise mastery over all things, and is not hurt by anything.[25]

I have heard that if a mirror is well-polished, dust cannot settle upon its surface; (that is to say) if dust settles upon a mirror, (we can be sure that) the mirror is not well-polished.[26]

The image of the perfectly polished mirror as a symbol for the state of the mind of the Perfect Man is found also in the *Tao Tê Ching*.

Purifying your Mysterious Mirror, can you make it spotless?[27]

Thus the Perfect Man does not *do* anything – that is, with the intention of doing something. The moment a man *does* something, his very consciousness of doing it renders his action 'unnatural'. Instead, the Perfect Man leaves all things, himself and all other things, to their own natures. This is the meaning of the term Non-Doing (*wu wei*). And since he does not *do* anything, he leaves nothing undone. By virtue of his Non-Doing, he ultimately does everything. For in that state, his being is identical with Nature. And Nature accomplishes everything without forcing anything.

(3) The 'abnormal bigness' of the Perfect Man has produced a number of remarkable symbols in the Book of *Chuang-tzǔ*. We have already seen some of them: the huge gourd which is too big to

be of any use, the big useless *shu*-tree in the garden of Hui-tzŭ, the black ox, lying in the meadow, doing nothing, being unable to catch even a rat. These, however, are relatively homely symbols; they are things of a moderate size compared with others which we find in the same Book. As an example of such fantastic symbols, we may mention the famous story of a huge mythical Bird, which we encounter on the very first page of the *Chuang-tzŭ*.

> In the dark mysterious ocean of the north (i.e., the northern limit of the world) there lives a Fish whose name is K'un. Its size is so huge that nobody knows how many thousand miles it is.
> (When at last the time of Transmutation comes) the Fish is transmuted into a Bird known as P'êng. The back of the P'êng is so large that nobody knows how many thousand miles it is.
> Now the Bird suddenly pulls itself together and flies off. Lo, its wings are like huge clouds hanging in the sky. And as the ocean begins to be turbulent (with raging storms of wind) the Bird intends to journey towards the dark mysterious ocean of the south. The southern ocean is the lake of Heaven.
> In fact, in the Book entitled *Ch'i Hsieh*[28] which records strange events and things, we find the following description (of this Bird). 'When the P'êng sets off for the dark mysterious ocean of the south, it begins by beating with its wings the surface of the water for three thousand miles. Then up it goes on a whirlwind to the height of ninety thousand miles. Then it continues to fly for six months before it rests'.[29]

This is immediately followed by a masterly description of the impression which the Bird is supposed to receive when it looks down upon our earth from the height of ninety thousand miles. The Bird is already wandering in a region which is far above the 'worldly' world where all kinds of material interests and inordinate desires are bubbling and foaming in an endless turmoil. It is not that the Bird does not see the 'dirty' world of vulgarity. The 'dirty' world is still there, under the Bird. The only difference is that the world looked down from this vertiginous height strikes the Bird's eyes as something beautiful, infinitely beautiful – another symbolic expression for the way the mind of the Perfect Man mirrors everything on its spotless surface.

> (Look at the world we live in. You will see there) ground vapor stirring; dust and dirt flying about; the living things blowing (fetid) breaths upon each other!
> The sky above, on the contrary, is an immense expanse of deep blue. Is this azure the real color of the sky? Or does it look (so beautifully blue) because it is at such a distance from us? (However this may be), the Bird now, looking down from its height, will surely be perceiving nothing but a similar thing, (i.e., our 'dirty' world must appear to the eyes of the Bird as a beautiful blue expanse).[30]

Chuang-tzŭ brings this description of the Bird's journey to an end by going back again to the idea of the 'bigness' of the Bird and the corresponding 'bigness' of its situation. By the force of his pen, the Bird is now alive in our imagination as an apt symbol for the Perfect Man who, transcending the pettiness and triviality of human existence is freely wandering in the 'void' of Infinity and Nothingness.

> (Why does the Bird soar up to such a height?) If the accumulation of water is not thick enough, it will not have the strength to bear a big ship. If you pour a cup of water into a hollow on the ground, tiny atoms of dust will easily float on it as if they were ships. If, however, you place a cup there, it will stick fast to the ground, because the water is too shallow while the 'ship' is too large.
> (Likewise) if the accumulation of wind is not thick enough, it will not have the strength to support huge wings. But at the height of ninety thousand miles, the (thick accumulation of) wind is under the Bird. Only under such conditions can it mount on the back of the wind, and carry the blue sky on its back, without there being anything to obstruct its flight. And now it is in a position to journey toward the south.[31]

Here the Perfect Man is pictured as a colossal Bird, soaring along far above the world of common sense. The Bird is 'big', and the whole situation in which it moves is correspondingly 'big'. But this excessive 'bigness' of the Perfect Man makes him utterly incomprehensible, or even ridiculous, in the eyes of the common people who have no other standard of judgment than common sense. We have already seen above how Lao-tzŭ, in reference to the 'abnormality' of the Way, makes the paradoxical remark that the Way, if it is not laughed at by 'men of low grade', would not be worthy to be considered the Way. In fact, the Bird P'êng is 'abnormally big'. Chuang-tzŭ symbolizes the 'men of low grade' who laugh at the 'bigness' of the Perfect Man by a cicada and a little dove.

> A cicada and a little dove laugh scornfully at the Bird and say, 'When we pluck up all our energies to fly, we can reach an elm or sapanwood tree. But (even in such flights) we sometimes do not succeed, and are thrown down on the ground. (Of small scale it may be, but our flight *is* also a flight.) Why is it at all necessary that (the Bird) should rise ninety thousand miles in order to journey towards the south?'
> A man who goes on a picnic to a near-by field, will go out carrying food sufficient only for three meals; and he will come back (in the evening) with his stomach still full. But he who makes a journey to a distance of one hundred miles, will grind his grain in preparation the night before. And he who travels a thousand miles, will begin to gather provisions three months in advance.
> What do these two creatures (i.e., the cicada and the dove) know about (the real situation of the Bird)? Those who possess but petty

wisdom are not able to understand the mind of those who possess Great Wisdom.[32]

This description of the imaginery flight of the Bird P'êng across the world is a very famous one. It is significant that the passage is placed at the very outset of the whole Book of *Chuang-tzŭ*. The uninitiated reader who approaches the Book for the first time will simply be shocked by the uncouth symbols that constitute the story, and will be driven into bewilderment not knowing how to interpret the whole thing. But by this very bewilderment, he will be directly led into the strange mythopoeic atmosphere which is typical of what we might call the shamanic mode of thinking. Unlike the ordinary kind of shamanic visions, however, there reigns over this image of the Bird's journey an unusual air of serenity, purity, and tranquillity. And this is a reflection of the inner state of the Perfect Man who is no longer a mere 'shaman', but rather a great 'philosopher' in the original Greek sense of the word.

Be this as it may, the forceful, dynamic style of Chuang-tzŭ and his creative imagination has succeeded in producing an amazing symbol for the spiritual 'greatness' of the Perfect Man.

(4) As regards the idea of free wandering, there remains little to say. For the foregoing description of the flight of the Bird is itself an excellent description of the 'free wandering' as well as of the 'bigness' of the Perfect Man.

The 'free wandering' is a symbolic expression for the absolute freedom which the Perfect Man enjoys at every moment of his existence. What is meant by 'absolute freedom' must be, by now, too clear to need any further explanation. The Perfect Man is absolutely free, because he is not dependent upon anything. And he is not dependent upon anything because he is completely unified with the Way, there being no discrepancy between what he does and what Heaven-and-Earth does. In the following passage, Chuang-tzŭ, from the viewpoint of 'dependence' and 'independence', divides men into four major categories. The first is the man of 'petty wisdom'; the second is the man of middle wisdom, represented by Sung Jung-tzŭ;[33] the third is the man of 'great wisdom' who is still somewhat defective in his spiritual perfection, represented by the famous Taoist sage Lieh-tzŭ; and the fourth and the last is the man of ultimate perfection, who is the real Perfect Man.

> Here is a man whose wisdom is good enough to make him suitable for occupying with success an official post, whose conduct is good enough to produce harmony in one district, whose virtue is good enough to please one sovereign, and whose ability is good enough to make him conspicuous in the politics of one state. Such a man looks

upon himself with self-conceit just like (the above-mentioned small creatures).[34]

Sung Jung-tzŭ would surely laugh at such a man. Sung is the kind of man who, even if the whole world should praise him, would not be stimulated thereby to increase his usual (moral) exertion, and even if the whole world should blame him, would not be affected thereby and become disheartened.

This is due to the fact that he draws a clear line of demarcation between the internal and the external.[35] He is, thus, clearly conscious of the boundaries of real glory and real disgrace. This makes him rather indifferent to petty interests in this world. However, he is not yet firmly established (i.e., completely self-sufficient and independent).

Next comes Lieh-tzŭ.[36] He rides on the wind and goes wandering about with amazing skilfulness. He usually comes back to earth after fifteen days (of continuous flight). He is not at all interested in obtaining happiness. Besides, (his ability to fly) saves him the trouble of walking. And yet, he has still to be dependent upon something (i.e., the wind).

As for the man (of absolute freedom and independence) who mounts on the natural course of Heaven and Earth, controls at will the six elemental forms of Nature, and freely wanders through the realm of the Limitlessness – on what should he be dependent?

Therefore it is said: The Ultimate Man has no ego, (and having no ego, he adapts himself to everything and every event with limitless flexibility). The Divine Man has no merit (because he does nothing intentionally). The Sacred Man has no fame (because he transcends all worldly values).[37]

The last of the four classes of men here described is the Perfect Man. And the 'free wandering' is nothing other than a symbolic expression for the absolute spiritual independence which characterizes his mode of existence in this world. It refers to his absolute Freedom, his not being retained in one place, and his not being tied to any particular thing. The expression is also interesting in that it is evocative of the original form of the Taoist Perfect Man as a shaman who, in his ecstatic state, used to make a mythopoeic journey around the limitless universe freely, without being obstructed by the shackles of his material body. The first chapter of the Book of *Chuang-tzŭ* is entitled 'Free Wandering'. It is not, I think, a mere coincidence that one of the masterpieces of shamanic poetry, *Yüan Yu* ('Traveling Afar'), which is found in the *Elegies of Ch'u*, presents striking similarities to the mythopoeic part of the world-view of Taoism. Both the Taoist Perfect Man and the great Shaman of Ch'u 'mount on the clouds, ride a flying dragon, and wander far beyond the four seas'.[38]

Notes

1. 聖人.

2. *Analects*, VII, 25.

3. *ibid.*, VII, 33.

4. The 'minutest thing' here means the Way as it manifests itself within the mind of man. The shaman-mystic, by closing up all the apertures of the senses and the intelligence, turns back into the depth of himself, where he perceives the Way working as a very 'small thing'.

5. For the idea that the 'sacred man' constantly maintains the flexibility of the mind of an infant, see above, Chapter IX, p. 144. The point will be further elaborated in the following chapter.

6. 襲常. For an explanation of the meaning of this expression, see above, Chapter V. Note 29.

7. *Tao Tê Ching*, LII.

8. *Chi jên* 畸人.

9. The ordinary text reads:「人之君子，天之小人也」which, as Wang Hsien Ch'ien remarks, does nothing but repeat exactly the same thing as the first half of the sentence in a reversed order:「天之小人，人之君子」. Following his suggestion I read the second half:「天之君子，人之小人」(王先謙:「莊子集解」); *Chuang-tzŭ*, VI, p. 273.

10. *Tao Tê Ching*, XLI.

11. *Chuang-tzŭ*, VI, pp. 267–268.

12. *Chih li tê*, 支離德.

13. *op. cit.*, IV, p. 180.

14. See Chapter I, Note 15.

15. *op. cit.*, I, p. 36.

16. *ibid.*, p. 37.

17. 無何有之鄉.

18. 廣莫之野.

19. *op. cit.*, I, pp. 39–40.

20. It is interesting that the name of that Perfect Man is 'Nameless-Man'.

21. *op. cit.*, VII, p. 293. See also VII, p. 296:「立乎不測，而遊於無有者也」.

22. This does not simply mean that the Perfect Man remains rigidly fixed and devoid of flexibility. On the contrary, he goes on shifting himself in accordance with the

universal Transmutation of all things. Since he is in this way completely unified with ever-changing Nature, all the 'shifts' he makes ultimately amount to his being changeless.

23. *op. cit.*, V, p. 189.

24. In this passage, the Perfect Man is designated by the term *chi jên* 至人, 'ultimate man', one of the several terms which Chuang-tzŭ uses to express the concept of the Perfect Man.

25. *op. cit.*, VII, p. 307.

26. *ibid.*, V, p. 197.

27. *Tao Tê Ching*, X.

28. 齊諧, 'Equalizing Harmony' or the '(Cosmic) Harmony in which all things are equalized', a title very typical of Chuang-tzŭ's ontology (see Chapter III, Chapter IV). Some scholars are of the opinion that this is not the title of the book, but the name of its author. In any case, it is apparently an invention of Chuang-tzŭ's imagination. He simply wants to imitate jokingly and sarcastically the habit of the thinkers of his age who substantiate their assertions by making references to ancient authorities.

29. *Chuang-tzŭ*, I, pp. 2–4.

30. *ibid.*, I, p. 4.

31. *ibid.*, I, p. 7.

32. *ibid.*, I, pp. 9–11.

33. Sung Jung-tzŭ 宋榮子 (= Sung Chien 宋鈃), a man who was famous for his teaching of pacifism and non-resistance. His thought is expounded in the last chapter (XXXIII) of the *Chuang-tzŭ*. His name is mentioned also by Mencius, Hsün-tzŭ, and Han Fei-tzŭ.

34. Like the cicada and the little dove who scornfully laugh at the 'big' project of the big Bird.

35. He knows that what is really important is the inner judgment of himself, and therefore, does not care about how other people judge him from outside.

36. Traditionally, Lieh-tzŭ is considered to have been a Perfect Man who, together with Chuang-tzŭ, represented the school of Taoist philosophy that had been inaugurated by Lao-tzŭ. He is made to stand chronologically between Lao-tzŭ and Chuang-tzŭ.

37. *op. cit.*, I, pp. 16–17.

38. *ibid.*, I, p. 28.

XI The Perfect Man

Most of the characteristic features of the Perfect Man have already
been mentioned explicitly or implicitly in the foregoing chapters.
Some of them have been fully discussed, while others have been
touched upon in a cursory manner. Besides, we have repeatedly
pointed out that the Perfect Man as understood by Lao-tzŭ and
Chuang-tzŭ is nothing else than the personification of the Way
itself. The Perfect Man is 'perfect' because he is an exact personal
imago of the Way. In this sense, by describing the nature and the
activity of the latter we can be said to have been describing the
former. Thus in a certain respect, all the preceding chapters may be
regarded as a description of the characterizing properties of the
Perfect Man. We are already quite familiar with the Taoist concept
of the Perfect Man. And the present chapter will necessarily take
the form of a mere systematic recapitulation of what has been
discussed in the course of this book concerning the Perfect Man.

Let us begin by repeating the most basic observation about the
concept of the Perfect Man, namely, that he is a man who is
completely unified and united with the Way. When a man in the
course of his spiritual discipline reaches the ultimate stage of
Illumination, a stage at which there remains no trace of his 'ego',
and therefore no discrepancy between 'himself' and the Way – that
marks the birth of a Perfect Man. Lao-tzŭ calls this stage 'embracing
the One'.[1]

> The 'sacred man' embraces the One, and thereby becomes the
> exemplar for all things under Heaven.[2]

> Controlling his vacillating soul, (the Perfect Man) embraces the One
> in his arms and is never separated therefrom.[3]

The opening clause[4] of this second quotation is interesting because
of its shamanic reminiscence. In ancient China, what corresponds to
the English 'soul' (Greek *psyche*) was held to consist of two separate
substances, one of them being *hun*,[5] and the other *p'o*.[6] Or we could
say that man was believed to possess two souls. The former was the

superior or spiritual soul, the principle of mental and spiritual functions. The latter was the inferior or physical (or animal) soul, charged with bodily and material functions. When a man died, the *hun* was believed to ascend to Heaven, while the *p'o* was to go down into Earth.[7] As for the phrase *ying p'o*, here translated as 'the vacillating (physical) soul', it is significant that exactly the same combination is found in the famous shamanic poem 'Traveling Afar' (*Yüan Yu*) of the *Elegies of Ch'u*:

> Controlling my vacillating soul, I ascend to a misty height,
> And riding on the floating clouds, I go up and ever higher.[8]

But of course the Perfect Man knows how to put under control his fretful and unstable soul by 'sitting-in-oblivion', so that he might ascend to the height of Unity and embrace the One, never to quit it.

The Perfect Man is no longer harassed by the fretfulness of his soul. On the contrary, he always maintains his soul unperturbed.

> What do I mean by the 'true man'? (I am thinking of) the 'true men' of ancient times. They did not revolt against scarcity (i.e., adverse fortune). They did not become haughty in favorable conditions. They did not make positive plans with the intention of accomplishing things.
> Such a person does not repent though he might commit an error; he does not fall into self-complacency though he might meet with success.
> Such a man does not become frightened even if he ascend to the highest place. He does not get wet even if he enters the water. He is not burnt even if he enters the fire.
> All this is the result of the (true) Wisdom having attained to the ultimate point of perfection in (being unified with) the Way.[9]

The Taoist principle of 'unperturbedness' is best illustrated by the attitude taken by the Perfect Man toward his own Life and Death. The problem has been fully discussed in earlier contexts. Here we shall be content with giving one more passage in translation, which would seem to provide a good summary of the whole argument concerning this idea.

> The 'true men' of ancient times knew nothing of loving Life and disliking Death. They came out (into this world) without any particular delight. They went in (i.e., died) without any resistance. Calmly they came, calmly they went. They did not forget how they had begun to exist (i.e., that the beginning of their Life was due to the natural working of the Way). Nor did they worry about the end of their existence.
> They simply received (Life) and they were happy (to live that Life). But (when Death came) they simply gave (their Life) back and forgot it.

This is what I would call: not revolting against the working of the Way
by the use of Reason, and not interfering with what Heaven does by
straining (petty) human (efforts).
Such is the 'true man'.[10]

Such an inner state cannot but produce its effect on the physical
conditions of the Perfect Man. His calm unperturbed mind is
reflected by the very peculiar way in which his bodily functions are
performed. The Perfect Man is different from the common people
not only in his spiritual state, but also in his physical constitution.

The 'true men' of ancient times did not dream when they slept. They
felt no anxiety when they were awake. They did not particularly
enjoy food when they ate.
Their breathing was calm and deep. They used to breathe with their
heels.[11] The common people, on the contrary, breathe with their
throats (i.e., their respiration is shallow). You know those who are
cornered in argument – how desperately they try to vomit out the
words sticking in their throats. (Compared with the breathing of the
Perfect Man, the breathing of ordinary people is just like that.) (This
is due to the fact that, unlike the Perfect Man who has no desire, the
common people) are deep in their desires, and shallow in their
natural spiritual equipment.[12]

The common people are here characterized as being 'deep in their
desires' and 'shallow in their natural equipment'. In this respect
they represent exactly the opposite of what Lao-tzŭ emphasizes as
the ideal of the Taoist mode of human existence: 'no-wisdom and
no-desire' (*wu-chih wu-yu*)[13]. 'Wisdom' here means the exercise of
Reason.
   We know already that purifying the Mind of physical and material
desires by 'closing up all openings and doors' is the first necessary
step toward the actualization of the idea of the Perfect Man.

The five colors make man's eyes blind. The five musical notes make
man's ears deaf. The five flavors make man's taste dull. (Games like)
racing and hunting make man's mind run mad. Goods that are hard to
obtain impede man's right conduct.
Therefore the 'sacred man' concentrates on the belly (i.e., endeavors
to develop his inner core of existence) and does not care for the eye
(i.e., does not follow the dictates of his senses). Thus he abandons the
latter and chooses the former.[14]

We have already seen above how, in the view of Lao-tzŭ and
Chuang-tzŭ, Reason obstructs the free activity of Nature. Reason in
its lowest form is the 'sound' or 'normal' common sense. The mode
of living of the common people goes against the natural course of
things because they are at the mercy of Reason and common sense.
   Boundless desire and the argumentative Reason constitute the

core of the 'ego'. And the 'ego', once formed goes on growing ever stronger until it dominates the whole existence of a man; all his actions are dictated by it, and all his feelings, emotions, and thinking are subjugated to its supreme command. This is why it is extremely difficult for an ordinary man to 'nullify his own self'.[15]

Reason makes man 'stiff' and 'inflexible'. Desire induces him forcibly to fight against the naturally given conditions and to 'intend' to obtain the objects of desire. This is the exact opposite of the Taoist ideal of conforming to the natural course of things, without reasoning and without desiring anything, and thus becoming completely unified with Nature. Lao-tzǔ finds in the 'infant' an apt symbol for his ideal.

> He who possesses within himself the plenitude of Virtue may be compared to an infant.
>
> Poisonous insects dare not sting it. Ferocious animals dare not pounce upon it. Birds of prey dare not strike it.
>
> Its bones are frail and its sinews tender, yet its grip is firm. It does not know yet of the union of male and female, yet the whole body is full of energy.[16] This is because its vitality is at its height.
>
> It howls and cries all day long, yet does not become hoarse. This is because the natural harmony in it is at its height.
>
> To know the natural harmony is to be (one with) the eternal Reality (*ch'ang*). And to know the eternal Reality is to be illumined (*ming*).[17]

Thus the infant is 'naturally' at the stage of Illumination, because it is 'naturally' one with the Way. And the 'weakness' or 'softness' of the infant is a living image of the creative activity of the Way, which is eternally supple, soft and lissom. It is a symbol of real Life.

> Man, at his birth, is tender and weak, but, when dead, he is hard and stiff.
>
> The ten thousand things, grass and trees, are tender and fragile while alive, but once dead, they are dry and stiff.
>
> Thus the hard and stiff are companions of Death, while the tender and weak are companions of Life.
>
> Thus an army which is too powerful is liable to lose the battle, and a tree that is too rigid is breakable.
>
> The powerful and mighty end by being cast down, whereas the soft and weak end by occupying higher places.[18]

The following passage is remarkable in that it gathers together the majority of Lao-tzǔ's favorite symbols for 'flexibility', 'softness', 'being low', 'being simple', in short, the virtue of Negativity.

> He who knows the 'male', yet keeps to the rôle of the 'female', will become the 'ravine' of the whole world.
>
> And once he has become the 'ravine' of the whole world, then the eternal Virtue will never desert him. And he will again return to the state of 'infancy'.

He who knows the 'white', yet keeps to the rôle of the 'black', will become the model for all under Heaven.
And once he has become the model for all under Heaven, then the eternal Virtue will never fail him. And he will again return to the Limitless.
He who knows the 'glorious', yet keeps to the rôle of the 'ignoble' will become the 'valley' of all under Heaven.
And once he has become the 'valley' of all under Heaven, then the eternal Virtue will be complete. And he will again return to the state of 'uncarved wood'.
'Uncarved wood' (in its 'simplicity' contains potentially all kinds of vessels); when it is cut out, it becomes various vessels. Likewise, the 'sacred man', by using it (i.e., the virtue of 'uncarved wood'), becomes the Lord over all officials. The greatest carving is non-carving.

The highest key term in the particular semantic field of Negativity is the *wu wei*, Non-Doing, which we have met several times in the foregoing. As we have noticed, the most basic meaning of Non-Doing is the negation of all 'intention', all artificial (or 'unnatural') effort on the part of man. And the Perfect Man is able to maintain this principle constantly and consistently because he has no 'ego', because he has 'nullified himself'. But the 'nullification' of the 'ego' as the subject of all desires and all intentional actions implies at the same time the establishment of a new Ego – the Cosmic Ego – which is completely at one with the Way in its creative activity.

Heaven is long lasting and Earth is long enduring. The reason why Heaven and Earth are long lasting and long enduring is that they do not strive to go on living. Therefore they are able to be everlasting. In accordance with this, the 'sacred man' puts himself in the rear, and (precisely because he puts himself in the rear) he comes (naturally) to the fore. He remains outside, and because of that he is always there. Is it not because he possesses no 'self' (i.e., the small ego) that he can thus establish his Self?[20]

Thus the Perfect Man is in every respect a Perfect image of Heaven and Earth, i.e., the Way as it manifests itself as the world of Being. The Perfect Man exists by the very same principle by which Heaven and Earth exist. And that principle common both to the Perfect Man and the activity of the Way is the principle of Non-Doing or 'being-so of-itself'. The conscious effort on the part of man to live or to procure his purpose violates this supreme principle and ends by bringing about a result which is just the contrary of what he intended to achieve.

He who stands on tiptoe cannot stand firm.
He who strides cannot walk far.
He who displays himself does not shine.

He who considers himself right cannot be illustrious.
He who praises himself cannot achieve real success.
He who places too great confidence in himself cannot endure.
From the point of view of the Way, such attitudes are to be called
'superfluous food and useless tumors'. They are detested by all.
Therefore, he who possesses (i.e., is unified with) the Way never
takes such an attitude.[21]

Therefore, the 'sacred man' keeps to the principle of Non-Doing, and
practises the teaching of No-Words.[22]

If one pursues knowledge, knowledge goes on increasing day by day.
If one pursues the Way, (what one obtains) goes on decreasing day by
day.
Decreasing, and ever more decreasing, one finally reaches the state
of Non-Doing. And when one practises Non-Doing, nothing is left
undone. Therefore even an empire is sure to be gained by practising
(the principle of) There-Is-Nothing-To-Do. If one adheres to (the
principle of) There-Is-Something-To-Do, one can never gain an
empire.[23]

Without going out of the door, one can know everything under
Heaven.
Without peeping out of the window, one can see the working of
Heaven.
The further one goes out, the less one knows.
Therefore the 'sacred man' knows (everything) without going out.
He has a clear view of everything without looking. He accomplishes
everything without 'doing'.[24]

What I have translated here as the 'working of Heaven' is in the
original *t'ien tao* meaning literally the 'way of Heaven'. It means the
natural activity of Heaven. And 'Heaven' here means the Way as it
manifests itself in the form of Nature, or the 'being-so of-itself' of
everything. Heaven, in this sense, is constantly active; it works
without a moment's intermission; it 'does' innumerable things. Its
'doing', however, is essentially different from the intentional 'doing'
of man. Heaven 'does' everything without the slightest intention on
its part to 'do' something. Its 'doing' consists in the ten thousand
things being or becoming what they are 'of themselves'. Heaven, in
other words, exemplifies in the most perfect form the principle of
Non-Doing.

Commenting upon Chuang-tzŭ's statement:

He who knows what Heaven does (i.e., the 'way of Heaven') . . . is at
the highest limit (of human Wisdom). For he who knows what
Heaven does lives in accordance with (the same principle as)
Heaven,[25]

Kuo Hsiang makes the following interesting and important remark:

'Heaven' in this passage means Nature ('being-so of-itself'). He who
'does doing' (i.e., does something with the intention or consciousness
of doing it) cannot 'do' anything (in the real sense of the word).
(Real) 'doing' is that the thing 'does itself' (i.e., it is done 'of itself',
according to its own nature). Likewise, he who 'does knowing' (i.e.,
tries to know something intentionally and consciously) cannot 'know'
anything (in the real sense of the word). (Real) 'knowing' consists in
(the thing) coming to 'be known of itself'. The thing 'becomes known
of itself', I say. So (real 'knowing' is, in truth), 'non-knowing'. It is
'non-knowing', I say. So the ultimate source of 'knowing' is 'non-
knowing'.
In the same way, 'doing' consists in the thing 'being done of itself'. So
(real 'doing', in truth,) is 'non-doing'. It is 'non-doing', I say. So the
ultimate source of 'doing', is 'non-doing'.
Thus, 'non-doing' must be considered the principle of 'doing'. Likewise, 'knowing' originates in 'non-knowing', so that 'non-knowing
must be considered the basis of 'knowing'.
Therefore, the 'true man' leaves aside 'knowing', and thereby
'knows'. He 'does not do', and thereby 'does'. Everything comes into
being 'of itself', (and that is the meaning of the 'doing' of the 'true
man'). He simply sits, oblivious of everything, and thereby obtains
everything.
Thus (with regard to the 'true man') the word 'knowing' loses its
applicability, and the term 'doing' disappears completely.[26]

This is, indeed, an excellent explanation of the key term 'Non-
Doing' as understood by Lao-tzŭ and Chuang-tzŭ, so much so that it
makes all further efforts to clarify the concept superfluous.

There is, however, one more thing which must be mentioned here
not in order to clarify the concept of Non-Doing, but rather in order
to clarify a peculiarity of Lao-tzŭ's way of thinking. I have
repeatedly pointed out as something typical of Lao-tzŭ the 'symbolic' way in which he develops his thinking. In the majority of
cases, particularly in dealing with problems which he considers of
crucial importance, he develops and elaborates his thought by
means of imagery. 'Water' is one of his favorite symbols. He uses it
in reference to the supreme power of Non-Doing. The empirical
observation of the activity of water provides at once conclusive
evidence for his theory of Non-Doing and a picturesque presentation of the way in which Non-Doing produces its effect.

The softest of all things in the world (i.e., water) dominates over the
hardest of all things in the world (like stones and rocks). Having no
definite form of its own, it penetrates even into that which has no
crevices.
By this I realize the value of Non-Doing.
However, the teaching through No-Words (i.e., the word-less teaching given by the Perfect Man, himself remaining silent but his per-

sonal influence affecting 'naturally' all about him) and the effect of Non-Doing – few in the whole world can understand them.[27]

In this passage no explicit mention is made of water. But that Lao-tzŭ means water by 'the softest of all things' is made clear by the following passage.

> There is under Heaven nothing softer and weaker than water. And yet in attacking things hard and strong, nothing can surpass it. For there is nothing that can destroy it.[28]
> The weak overcomes the strong, and the soft overcomes the hard. This everybody in the world knows, yet no one is able to put this (knowledge) into practice.[29]

The 'positive passivity' or the 'powerful weakness' of water is for Lao-tzŭ one of the most appropriate images of the Way and, therefore, of the Perfect Man.

> The highest goodness is like water. Water benefits the ten thousand things, yet it never contends with anything. It stays in (low) places loathed by all men. But precisely because of this, it is closest to the Way (and the 'sacred man').[30]

'Never-contending-with-anybody' which is suggested by the nature of water is another highest principle that governs the conduct of the Perfect Man.

> An excellent warrior does not use violence. An excellent fighter does not lose himself in anger. He who excels in defeating does not treat his enemy as an enemy. He who excels in employing men humbles himself before them.
> This I would call the Virtue of 'non-contending'. This may also be called making the best use of the ability of others.
> And such a man may rightly be regarded as being in perfect conformity with the Supreme Principle of Heaven.[31]

> The 'sacred man' . . . never contends with anybody. This is why nobody under Heaven contends with him.[32]

Thus the Perfect Man does not contend with anybody or anything. Like a good fighter he does not allow himself to be roused and excited. In this respect, he may be said to lack ordinary human emotions and feeling. In fact, he is not a 'man', if one understands by this word an ordinary human being. He is, in reality, an infinitely large cosmic being. Concerning this problem Chuang-tzŭ has left an interesting record of a discussion between himself and the Dialectician Hui-tzŭ to whom reference was made earlier. We do not know for sure whether the dialogue is fictitious or real. But, whether fictitious or real, it is a valuable document for us in that it elucidates one important aspect of the connotation of the Perfect Man.

The discussion starts when Chuang-tzŭ makes the following statement:

> The 'sacred man' has the physical form of a man, but no emotion of a man. Since he has the form of a man, he lives among other human beings as one of them. But since he has no emotion of a man, 'right' and 'wrong' (or likes and dislikes) cannot have access to him. Ah how insignificant and small he is, in so far as he belongs to common humanity! But infinitely great is he, in so far as he stands unique (in the world) in perfecting Heaven in himself![33]

Against this statement, Hui-tzŭ raises a serious question. And the question provokes a theoretic discussion over the theme between Chuang-tzŭ and Hui-tzŭ.

Hui-tzŭ:	Is it at all possible that a man should be without emotions?
Chuang-tzŭ:	Yes, it is.
Hui-tzŭ:	But if a man lacks emotions, how could he be called a 'man'?
Chuang-tzŭ:	The Way has given him human features. And Heaven has given him a bodily form. How, then, should we not call him a 'man'?
Hui-tzŭ:	But since you call him a 'man', it is inconceivable that he should be without emotions.
Chuang-tzŭ:	What you mean by 'emotions' is different from what I mean by the same word. When I say 'he is without emotions', I mean that the man does not let his inner self be hurt (i.e., perturbed) by likes and dislikes, and that he conforms to the 'being-so of-itself' of everything, never trying to increase his vital energy.
Hui-tzŭ:	If he does not try to increase his vital energy (i.e., by eating nutritious food, clothing himself, etc.),[34] how could he preserve his body alive?
Chuang-tzŭ:	The Way has given him human features. And Heaven has given him a bodily form. (And as a result, he has come into existence as a 'man'.) This being the case, all he has to do is not to let his inner self be hurt by likes and dislikes. (This is what I mean by 'not trying to increase life'.) You 'externalize' your spirit (i.e., you constantly send out your spirit toward the external objects in the world) and wear out your mental energy, sometimes leaning against a tree, moaning, and sometimes leaning on your desk with your eyes closed. Heaven itself has selected for you a bodily form. But you (instead of conforming to the Will of Heaven, waste your time in) making a fuss about '(a stone) being hard and white'.[35]

Thus it is clear that 'the Perfect Man having no emotions' means nothing other than his being absolutely unperturbed whatever may happen to him and whatever may occur before his eyes. And there is a deep metaphysical reason for this. He can maintain this fundamental attitude under all conditions because he is 'one' with all things which are themselves ultimately 'one'. Since, as we saw earlier, all things are metaphysically 'one', the attitude of the Perfect Man toward them cannot also but be 'one'.

The concept of the Perfect Man 'having no emotions' is, in this way, ultimately reducible to the more fundamental idea which is by now fully familiar to us; namely, that the Perfect Man has no 'ego' of his own. Having no 'ego' of his own, he makes no distinction between things. He is, in other terms, constantly 'one'. And his being personally 'one' – which is precisely what is meant by the expression: 'having no emotions' – is based on the objective fact that Reality is 'one'. This, however, does not necessarily mean that the Perfect Man does not know in any sense the distinction between the infinitely variegated things of the phenomenal world. Rather, his 'making no distinction between the things' means only that, being fully conscious of all these things as *different* things, he is possessed of a spiritual eye with which he intuits behind the kaleidoscope of the changing forms the metaphysical 'One', of which they are but various manifestations. And when he looks at these seemingly different things from such a particular point of view, they disclose themselves to his eyes as so many repetitions of one and the *same* thing 'piled up one upon the other', all being equally 'good'.

> (The true man') is 'one', whether he (seemingly) likes something or dislikes something. He is also 'one', whether he regards all things as being 'one' or as not being 'one'.
> When he takes the position of (everything being) 'one' he is acting as a companion of Heaven; (i.e., he is taking the position of Heavenly Equalization).[36] When he takes the position of (all things) not being 'one', he is acting as a companion of Man; (i.e., he is looking at the phenomenal world of Multiplicity as it appears to the human eye). Thus in him Heaven and Man do not defeat each other (i.e., he unites in himself harmoniously and without contradiction both the 'absolute' viewpoint of Heaven and the 'relative' viewpoint of Man). Such indeed is the nature of the 'true man'.[37]

'Being without emotions' should not be taken to mean that the Perfect Man does not actually experience anger, delight, sadness, gladness. He does experience all these and other human emotions. The only difference between him and ordinary people in this matter consists in the fact that in the case of the former, there always remains something unperturbed and unperturbable at the innermost core of his heart, even while he is experiencing strong emotions, something which is not affected by them, which is not touched by them. The emotions come and go in his inner world as naturally as the four seasons of the year come and go in the outer world.

> His mind is content with being in whatever situation it happens to be.[38] His outward appearance is still and calm. His forehead is broad and looks carefree.
>
> Sometimes he is coldly relentless like autumn; sometimes he is warmly amiable like spring. Joy and anger come and go as naturally as the four seasons do in Nature. Keeping perfect harmony with all things (which endlessly go on being 'transmuted' one into another) he does not know any limit.[39]

Such being his basic spiritual state, the Perfect Man perceives in the whole world nothing to disturb his cosmic balance of mind, although he does notice accurately all things that happen to him and to others. He does participate in the activities of the world together with all other men, yet at the same time, at the very core of his heart, he remains detached from the clamor and bustle of the world. Calmness and tranquillity are the most salient features that characterize both the inside and outside of the Perfect Man.

> Attaining to the utmost limit of (inner) 'emptiness', I firmly maintain myself in Stillness.[40]

> (The 'sacred man'), by being limpid and serene, becomes the norm of all under Heaven.[41]

Chuang-tzŭ, as usual, is less laconic in describing the virtues of 'calmness' and 'tranquillity':

> Of all level things, the most perfect is the surface of water at rest. Because of this (perfect levelness), it can be used as a standard in levelling. And (the perfect levelness of still water) is due to the fact that (water at rest) maintains in its inside (profound calmness) and shows no agitation outside.
>
> Likewise, Virtue is a (spiritual) state which is attained when a man has perfected the calmness (of the mind). (In such a case) Virtue does not come out in a visible form, (i.e., since the inside of such a man is perfectly calm, no agitation comes out to the surface). But things, on their part, (are spontaneously attracted by his invisible Virtue and) cannot separate themselves therefrom.[42]

Notes

1. *pao i*, 抱一.

2. *Tao Tê Ching*, XXII.

3. *ibid.*, X.

4. 「載營魄」.

5. 魂.

6. 魄.

7. *Li Chi, Chiao Tê Shêng* (禮記「郊特牲」): 「魂氣歸于天, 形魄歸于也」. Concerning the *p'o* we find in the *Tso Ch'uan* (左傳, 昭公七年) the following statement: 'When a man is born, (we see) in his first bodily function what is called the *p'o*'.

8. 「載營魄而登霞兮, 掩浮雲而上征」. This interpretation of the word *ying* (營) is corroborated by another verse in the same poem, in which the shaman-poet describes the instability and fretfulness of his soul – this time the word *hun* is used instead of *p'o* – which keeps him awake all through the night: 夜耿耿子寐兮, 魂營營而至曙.

9. *Chuang-tzŭ*, IV, p. 226.

10. *ibid.*, IV, 229.

11. The expression: 'they breathed with their heels' indicates the incomparable depth and tranquillity of their respiration. The vital energy contained in the inhaled air is made to circulate all through the body, in such a way that one is left with the impression that the breathing naturally welled up from the heels.

12. *op. cit.*, VI, p. 228.

13. 「無知無欲」, *Tao Tê Ching*, III.

14. *Tao Tê Ching*, XII.

15. *ibid.*, XIII.

16. 「全作」. Yü Yüeh (俞樾「諸子平議」VIII) thinks that the word 全 is a mistake for 舍 meaning 'hidden place', i.e., the genitals. The sentence would then mean: 'yet its male member is full of force'. In some other editions we find 㕙 and 朘 used instead of 全.

17. *op. cit.*, LV.

18. *ibid.*, LXXVI.

19. *ibid.*, XXVIII.

20. *ibid.*, VII.

21. *ibid.*, XXIV.

22. *ibid.*, II.

23. *ibid.*, XLVIII.

24. *ibid.*, XLVII.

25. *Chuang-tzŭ*, VI, p. 224.

26. 郭象：「天者自然之謂也. 夫爲爲者不能爲，而爲自爲耳..爲知者不能知，而知自知耳. 自知耳，不知也. 不知也，則知出於不知矣. 自爲耳，不爲也. 不爲也，則爲出於不爲矣，爲出於不爲. 故 以不爲爲主，知出於不知. 故以不知爲宗，是故眞人遺知而知，不爲而爲. 自然而生. 坐忘而得. 故知 稱絶，而爲名去也」. p. 224.

27. *Tao Tê Ching*, XLIII.

28. 「易之」 The character 易 here stands for 夷 meaning 'conquering the barbarians'. The idea evidently is that even the sharpest sword cannot cut water and 'kill' it.

29. *op. cit.*, LXXVIII.

30. *ibid.*, VIII.

31. *ibid.*, LXVIII.

32. *ibid.*, XXII.

33. *Chuang-tzŭ*, V, p. 217.

34. Here again, Hui-tzŭ misunderstands what Chuang-tzŭ means by 'not trying to increase life'.

35. *op. cit.*, V, pp. 220–222. 'A stone being hard and white' is a reference to the famous sophistic thesis that a 'hard and white stone' is really two things, not one, because 'hard' and 'white' are two entirely different attributes; see above, Chapter IV. Note 18.

36. See above, Chapter VI, Note 17.

37. *ibid.*, VI, pp. 234–235.

38. 「其心志」 The last word 志 is explained by Kuo Hsiang as 'being contented with whatever place it happens to be in' (「所居而安，爲志」). See *Shuo Wên*: 「志，心之所之也」. There are many scholars who think that it is a mistake for 忘 (See, for example, Hsüan Ying 宣穎 「南華經解」: 「志，當作忘，無思」), meaning 'forgetful' or 'oblivious' (of the essential distinctions between the ten thousand things).

39. *op. cit.*, VI, pp. 230–231.

40. *Tao Tê Ching*, XVI.

41. *ibid.*, XLV.

42. *Chuang-tzŭ*, V, pp. 214–215.

XII *Homo Politicus*

Throughout the preceding chapters we have been describing the Taoist Perfect Man as a man of absolute transcendence. He wholly transcends the world of ordinary men and ordinary things in the sense that he is 'oblivious' of all distinctions between them, that nothing perturbs his mind, and that, consequently, he sits alone in the midst of the profound 'tranquillity' of being one with the One. He is 'without – or above – human emotions', accepting the good as 'good' and also the non-good as 'good'. He holds fast to the principle of Non-Doing, and does not meddle with the natural course of things. Instead, he leaves the ten thousand things alone as they come into being, grow, and then disappear in accordance with the 'times' and 'turns' of each of them. He is 'indifferent' just as Heaven and Earth are 'indifferent' to the ten thousand things, treating them all as if they were 'straw dogs'.

The Perfect Man in this respect is a man of absolute Negativity. And all these and still other 'negative' properties belong to him because he is completely unified with the 'way' (i.e., natural, spontaneous working) of Heaven, and ultimately with the Way itself. In comporting himself in this manner, the Perfect Man embodies the Way.

But it is very important to remember that pure negativity or passivity does not exhaust the activity of the Way. In fact, the passivity of the Way is not 'passivity' as ordinarily understood. It is a 'passivity' backed with 'positivity'. Or perhaps we should say that the Way is – or looks – 'passive' precisely because it is too positive to be just 'positive' in the generally accepted sense. Non-Doing, for example, is certainly a passive and negative principle, but it is in reality a positive force in that it 'leaves nothing undone'. This fact is an exact counterpart of the Way being described as 'Nothing' not because it is purely negatively and passively 'nothing', but because it is over-plenitude of Being.

The Perfect Man, as a perfect embodiment and personification of the Way, must necessarily reflect this 'positive' – or 'supra-positive' – aspect of it, too. Just as the Way itself is positively – and more than positively – engaged in the administration of the created world and governs, through the very principle of Non-Doing, the whole process of Nature to the minutest details of individual events, so is the Perfect Man positively interested in governing the world, again through the principle of Non-Doing.

Besides, it is, more generally speaking, very characteristic of philosophical thinking in ancient China that it is vitally concerned with the problem of governing the people. *Homo Politicus* has, in fact, always been a central theme of all the major schools of Chinese thought. Lao-tzŭ and Chuang-tzŭ are no exception to this general rule. It is extremely interesting to notice in this respect that a man like Lao-tzŭ who develops, on the one hand, a sophisticated metaphysics of the Way and describes the ideal man as an absolutely unworldly-minded man living high above the noise and fuss of everyday life, shows himself so keenly interested in the art of ruling an empire. For Lao-tzŭ, the Perfect Man cannot be really 'perfect', unless he stands at the head of an empire as the supreme Ruler of its people. The Perfect Man is at once a philosopher and a politician.

This, of course, does not mean that the Perfect Man must positively strive to gain political power or to conquer the world. He does not even try to make himself conspicuous.

> He does not display himself. Therefore he is conspicuous.
> He does not justify himself. Therefore he is illustrious.
> He does not praise himself. Therefore his merit is recognized.[1]

He does not try to make himself conspicuous. But due to that 'negative' attitude toward himself – and more basically, because he is 'perfect' – he 'naturally' becomes conspicuous. He does not do anything on his part to attract attention, but the people spontaneously gather around him. He keeps himself in the rear, but the people spontaneously, and even without being conscious of it, push him to the fore. The *Tao Tê Ching* is filled with expressions referring to this peculiarity of the Perfect Man. The most famous and most typical of them all is probably 'softening the glare and falling into line with the dust (of the common people)'.

> (The 'sacred man') blunts his sharpness, unfastens his knots, softens his glare, and falls into line with the dust. Such I would call the state of Mysterious Indistinction.
> Such a man cannot be approached too intimately. Nor can one remain too remote from him. One cannot bestow benefit upon him, nor can one harm him. One cannot ennoble him, nor can one humiliate him.
> Thus he becomes the noblest of all beings under Heaven.[2]

The 'Mysterious Indiscrimination' (*hsüan t'ung*)[3] is a very significant expression. The Perfect Man, as a human being, lives among ordinary people as a member of society. He exists there in the midst of everyday life, quietly and calmly, behind and beneath other men. He 'levels' himself with the common people, without 'discriminating' himself from other men. Outwardly he seems to be exactly the same as ordinary people. But this is, in reality, a very peculiar 'sameness', for in his spiritual structure, he is soaring like the Bird P'êng in the azure of absolute freedom and independence.

And it is through the spontaneous activity of such a man that the Virtue of the Way materializes in the form of a perfect political rule. According to the pattern of thought peculiar to Lao-tzŭ and Chuang-tzŭ, the Perfect Man, because of his spiritual 'perfection', spontaneously occupies the highest place in the spiritual world; and because he occupies the highest place in the spiritual world he must necessarily occupy the highest place in the world of reality. He must be the 'lord over the officials'.[4]

Thus here again we come across the paradoxical way of thinking which characterizes the Taoist sages. For according to them, the Perfect Man is a man who 'freely roams beyond the realm of dust and dirt, and enjoys wandering to his heart's content in the Village of There-Is-Absolutely-Nothing'. But exactly because he exists permanently beyond the world of dust and dirt, he can actually keep himself in the very midst of the dust and dirt of the real, material world. By remaining absolutely 'indifferent' to petty interests in the world, he *is* interested in the great problems of the actual world. Surely, he is not a man 'whose ability is good enough to make him conspicuous in the politics of *one* state.'[5] But he is good enough to be the absolute ruler of an empire, or even of 'all under Heaven'.

What, then, are the politics of the Perfect Man? From the point of view of common sense, Chuang-tzŭ says, the most ideal form of the management of political affairs consists in that 'the ruler should devise all the rules and regulations for his own self, and thereby govern his people, for, in such a case, who would dare to disobey him and not to be "transformed" by his virtue?'.[6]

Chuang-tzŭ declares that such a thing is nothing other than a 'deceptive virtue'.[7] 'To govern the world by means of such a principle is like trying to wade through the ocean, to dig a large river with one's own hands, or to let a mosquito carry on its back a mountain!'[8]

The Perfect Man does not govern the world by means of man-made laws, which are but external matters designed to control only the external aspects of human life. He governs the world by 'governing himself', that is, by perfecting his inner Virtue.

> When the 'sacred man' is in the position of the ruler, how could he
> conceivably be interested in governing the external life of the people?

What he is interested in is that he should rectify his 'inside', (i.e., bring his inner Virtue to perfection) and then govern (his people). He is exclusively interested in firmly establishing his own affair. (Thus he leaves all other things in charge of their own natures.) Just think of a bird flying high in the sky, escaping thereby the danger of being shot down by a stringed arrow; or of a little mouse living in a deep hole under the sacred hill, avoiding thereby being dug out or smoked out. (Every living being has its own natural wisdom by which it knows instinctively how to live safely.) Do human beings possess less knowledge than these two little creatures?[9]

What Chuang-tzǔ means by 'rectifying one's inside' is explained by himself in more concrete terms as follows:

Let your mind wander freely in (the field of) Simplicity (where there is not even a trace of desires), unify your vital energy with the limitless Tranquillity, and follow the natural course (lit. 'being-so of-itself') of all things without letting your 'ego' interfere with it. Then the whole world will be governed (spontaneously).[10]

Briefly stated, this means that when the Perfect Man in the real sense of the word is actualized, the world becomes governed 'of itself'. Not that the Perfect Man positively governs the world by instituting severe laws and enforcing them. The right ordering of the world is spontaneously actualized as the Perfect Man, on his part, 'rectifies his inner state'. It is clear that this is nothing but putting into practice the fundamental principle of Non-Doing. And that is, for Lao-tzǔ, and Chuang-tzǔ, the highest and most ideal form of politics.

Lao-tzǔ describes the situation in the following terms:

A state may well be governed by 'rectitude'.[11] A war may well be won by tactics. The empire, however, can be obtained only by Non-Action.[12]
How do I know that it is so? By the following observation.
The more restrictions and prohibitions there are in the world, the poorer the people.
The more civilized instruments the people possess, the more confused the land.
The more skills and crafts the people have, the more bizarre (useless) objects will be produced.
The more laws and regulations are promulgated, the more thieves and robbers there will be.
Therefore the 'sacred man' says: I remain in Non-Doing, and the people are (morally) transformed of themselves. I enjoy quietude, and the people become righteous of themselves. I do not meddle with anything, and the people become prosperous of themselves. I remain free from desires, and the people of themselves become like the 'uncarved block of wood'[13]

As I have repeatedly emphasized, this supreme ability of the Perfect Man as a statesman is due to the fact that in practising Non-Doing, he is a perfect copy of the Way itself.

> The Way in its absolute reality is inactive (i.e., 'non-doing'), yet it leaves nothing undone.
> If lords and kings abide by this principle, the ten thousand things will grow up and develop of their own accord.
> But if in the process of growth, desire (to act positively, against Nature) should arise (on the part of some of the ten thousand things), I would calm it down by the weight of the 'nameless' (simplicity of) 'uncarved wood'.[14] The 'nameless' (simplicity of) 'uncarved wood' will take things back to the (original) state of desirelessness.
> And if (the people) become 'desireless' and, consequently, 'tranquil', the whole world will of itself become peaceful.[15]

> The Way in its absolute reality is 'nameless'. (It is in this respect like 'uncarved wood').[16] The 'uncarved wood' may look insignificant, but nothing under Heaven is able to subjugate it.
> If lords and kings abide by the principle (of 'uncarved wood'), the ten thousand things will of themselves come to pay homage to them.
> Heaven and Earth will join their forces to send down sweet dew, and the people will of themselves become peacefully governed, even if no decrees and ordinances are published.[17]

Thus the Perfect Man in the capacity of a statesman exercises his rule in accordance with the principle of Non-Doing. 'He does nothing other than doing-nothing.'[18] But by 'doing-nothing' he is in truth doing a great thing. For 'doing-nothing' means in his case to do nothing against the natural course of all things. Therefore his 'doing-nothing' is tantamount to 'assisting' the natural and spontaneous development of all things.

> The 'sacred man' desires to be desireless. He learns not to learn.[19]
> He thereby turns back constantly to (the Ultimate Source) which is passed by unnoticed by the common people.
> He assists the spontaneous being of the ten thousand things. He refrains from interfering with it by his own action.[20]

Many other passages could be adduced from the *Tao Tê Ching*, in which the idea of Non-Doing is extolled as the supreme principle of Taoist politics. But for our particular purposes what has been given is quite sufficient.

There is, however, one more point to make in connection with Non-Doing as a political idea. In the foregoing we have been concerned mainly with the attitude of the Perfect Man in governing the empire in accordance with the principle of Non-Doing. We have not yet dealt with the problem of the inner state or attitude of those who are governed, the common people as the subjects over whom the Perfect Man rules.

Already in some of the above-quoted passages it has been suggested that the ideal rule of the Perfect Man encounters hindrance if
his subjects happen to have 'desire' and 'knowledge'. The Perfect
Man himself may be absolutely above all human 'desires' – because
he is 'without emotions' – and above petty 'knowledge' to be
acquired by the exercise of the rational faculty of the mind – because
he has completely 'chaotified' his mind. But however Perfect he
may be in this respect, he is not in a position to realize the ideal of
ruling by the principle of Non-Doing unless the people, on their
part, be also perfectly prepared for accepting his rule. And they are
perfectly prepared for accepting his rule only when they are purified
of 'desire' and 'knowledge'. Thus the act of purifying the people of
these obstacles constitutes part of the politics of Non-Doing.

> If (the ruler) does not hold the (so-called) wise men in high esteem,
> the people will be kept away from contending with one another.
> If he does not value goods that are hard to obtain, the people will be
> kept away from committing thefts.
> If he does not display things that are liable to excite desires, the minds
> of the people will be kept undisturbed.
> Therefore, the 'sacred man' in governing the people empties their
> minds,[21] while making their bellies full; weakens their wills[22] while
> rendering their bones strong.
> In this way, he keeps his people always in the state of no-knowledge
> and no-desire, so that the so-called 'knowers' might find no occasion
> to interfere (and influence the people).
> If he thus practises Non-Doing, the world cannot but be governed
> well.[23]

> From of old those who excel in the practice of the Way do not try to
> make the people wise and clever. Rather they try to keep the people
> in the (simple) state of knowledgelessness. If the people are difficult
> to rule it is because they have too much 'knowledge'.
> He who rules a state by (giving the people) 'knowledge' damages the
> country. He who rules a state by depriving (the people) of 'know-
> ledge' brings prosperity to the country.
> To know (the difference between) these two (forms of government)
> belongs to the standard measure (of the ruler). And to know the
> standard measure in every matter is what I would call the Mysterious
> Virtue. How profound and far-reaching the Mysterious Virtue is! (Its
> profundity is shown by the fact that) it works contrariwise to the
> nature of things, yet ultimately turns back to the Great Conformity;[24]
> (i.e., at first sight the working of the Mysterious Virtue looks as if it
> were against the natural order of things, but in reality it is in confor-
> mity with the very working of the Great Way).[25]

The Great Conformity which is to be achieved by the practice of
Non-Doing represents the highest degree of perfection among the
various possible forms of governing the state. It is the art of gov-

ernment peculiar to the Perfect Man. And judged by this standard, all the remaining political forms are found to be imperfect in varying degrees.

> The highest of all types of the ruler is such that the people under him are only aware of his presence.
> The next is the ruler to whom they feel attached and whom they praise.
> The next is the ruler whom they fear.
> The next is the ruler whom they despise. If (the ruler) is not trusted enough, it is because he is not truthful enough.
> If (on the contrary) the ruler is cautious and weighs the words he utters, then his task will be accomplished, his work done, and the people will all say: 'All this we have done naturally, by ourselves.'[26]

The people feel this way because the Perfect Man rules over them by the principle of Non-Doing. They are vaguely conscious of his presence over them, but they do not notice that things run so smoothly because of his being their ruler.

It is very interesting to observe that the second of the types of the ruler enumerated in this passage, namely, the case in which the people feel attached to the ruler and greatly praise him, evidently refers to the Confucian ideal of governing the people with 'benevolence'. We would do well to recall in this connection the words of Lao-tzŭ which we have quoted earlier.[27] 'Only when the great Way declines, do "benevolence" and "righteousness" arise.' The implication is that the highest ideal of politics from the point of view of Confucius and his school is, from the point of view of Lao-tzŭ, not only the second-best, but something indicative of the decline of the great Way.

> Only when the great Way declines, do 'benevolence' and 'righteousness' arise.
> Only when cleverness and sagacity emerge in the world, do wiles and intrigues arise.
> Only when the six basic kinship relations are out of harmony do filial sons make their appearance.
> Only when the state is in confusion and disorder, do loyal subjects make their appearance.[28]

> If the ruler abolishes 'cleverness' and abandons 'intelligence', the benefit received by the people will increase a hundredfold.
> If he abolishes 'benevolence' and abandons 'righteousness', the people will (spontaneously) return to 'filial piety' and 'paternal love'.[29]
> If he abolishes artifice and abandons (the pursuit of) profit, there will be no more thieves and robbers.
> If with these three (principles) alone one should think adornments are too scanty, let there be, then, something additional. Show outwardly the plainness of undyed silk and embrace inwardly the simplicity of uncarved wood. Reduce selfishness and lessen desires.[30]

In one of the passages quoted above, we saw how in Lao-tzŭ's view the highest type of government is represented by the ruler who governs the country so 'naturally' that the 'people' are conscious only of there being a ruler over them', without attributing to him any particular virtue or merit. Chuang-tzŭ unreservedly agrees with Lao-tzŭ on this point. It goes without saying that, according to both Lao-tzŭ and Chuang-tzŭ, in such a form of ideal government not only do the people not notice the merit of the ruler, but the ruler himself is not conscious of his own merit.

Lao-tzŭ:

> The 'sacred man' is such that he does great things, yet does not boast of his own achievement; he accomplishes his task, yet does not stick to his own merit. Is this not because he does not wish to display his superiority over others?[31]

And Chuang-tzŭ:

> When an 'illumined king' reigns over the world, his merit covers all under Heaven. But he is not conscious of the merit as something proceeding from himself.
> His transforming power affects the ten thousand things. But the people do not feel dependent upon him.
> There *is* 'something' occurring (in the world, because of his presence as the ruler), but no one could definitely name it. (The existence of that 'something' is clearly shown only by the fact that) it actually renders all things spontaneously happy and contented.
> He himself stands in (the spiritual state of) the Unfathomable, and wanders to his heart's content in the There-Is-Nothing,[32]

I shall bring this chapter to a close by quoting from the *Tao Tê Ching* a passage in which Lao-tzŭ pictures in an idyllic tone an imaginary state which is governed by a 'sacred man' – a state based on the principle of Non-Doing, in which the highest ideal of Taoist politics is actualized in a concrete form. It is by no means a grand-scale ideal state like the Republic of Plato. It is almost a village. Yet, who knows? The people of this small country may possibly be even happier and more contented than the inhabitants of the Platonic state.

> A small country, with small population. There are (in this country) various tools of war, but the people are not tempted to use them. The people (are so happy and contented that) they regard death as no slight matter (i.e., they are reluctant to die because life is so enjoyable). Nor do they want to move to distant places. Though there are ships and carts, there is no place to go with them. Though there are armor and weapons, there arises no occasion to display them.
> The people are taught to go back to (the Simplicity of immemorial antiquity) using knotted cords (instead of the complicated system of writing).

They find relish in their food, and beauty in their clothes. Happy and contented with their own homes, they find delight in their old customs.
The neighbouring country is just there, within sight. The people of this country can hear even the cocks crowing and dogs barking in that country. And yet, the inhabitants of the two countries grow old and die without ever visiting one another.[33]

Notes

1. *Tao Tê Ching*, XXII.

2. *ibid.*, LVI; see also IV.

3. 玄同. It may be translated also as 'Mysterious Levelling'.

4. *op. cit.*, XXVIII.

5. *Chuang-tzǔ*, I, p. 16.

6. *ibid.*, VII, p. 290.

7. 欺德, *ch'i tê.*

8. *ibid.*, VII, p. 291.

9. *ibid.*, VII, p. 291.

10. *ibid.*, VII, p. 294.

11. This is an ironical reference to the Confucian idea of the ideal politics. A man once asked Confucius about the art of ruling the state. Confucius replied: 'Ruling' (*chêng* 政) means 'rectitude' (*chêng* 正). If you (govern the people) by 'rectifying' yourself in the first place, no one would venture to act against 'rectitude' – *Analects*, XII, 17.

12. 無事, *wu shih*, synonymous with *wu wei*. *Shih* is defined by Hsün-tzǔ as 'doing something in expectation of getting a profit' (正利而爲謂之事), 荀子, 正名篇 XXII.

13. *Tao Tê Ching*, LVII.

14. i.e., I, the ruler, would calm down the desire of the people, not by supressing it by laws and edicts, but by disclosing myself to them as a living embodiment of the Way in its aspect of absolute 'simplicity', that is, the state of being completely purified of all desires and passions.

15. *op. cit.*, XXXVII.

16. Because it is not yet carved into various vessels, each of which is distinguished from others by a special 'name'.

17. *op. cit.*, XXXII.

18. 爲無爲,   (*ibid.*, LXIV).

19. Ordinary men try hard to study and learn in order to increase their knowledge. The Perfect Man, on the contrary, learns to be without learning, so that at the ultimate stage of the decrease of knowledge he might be unified with the 'simplicity' of the 'uncarved wood'.

20. *op. cit.*, LXIV.

21. It is the 'mind' that insatiably seeks for 'knowledge'.

22. The 'will' drives man toward gratifying his limitless desires.

23. *op. cit.*, III.

24. 大順.

25. *ibid.*, LXV.

26. *ibid.*, XVII.

27. See Chap. I, Note 6.

28. *op. cit.*, XVIII.

29. This may be thought to contradict what we have read in the preceding passage. In reality, however, there is no contradiction. For there, the point at issue was 'filial piety' and 'paternal love' being *verbally emphasized*. Here Lao-tzŭ is simply talking about the natural state of 'filial piety' and 'paternal love' which is actualized in the minds of the people, without there being anybody who 'emphasizes' the importance of these virtues.

30. *op. cit.*, XIX.

31 *Tao Tê Ching*, LXXVII.

32. *Chuang-tzŭ*, VII, p. 296.

33. *Tao Tê Ching*, LXXX.

Part III
CONCLUSION
– A Comparative Reflection –

I Methodological Preliminaries

As stated in the Introduction to Part One of this work, I started this study prompted by the conviction that what Professor Henry Corbin calls 'un dialogue dans la métahistoire' is something urgently needed in the present world situation. For at no time in the history of humanity has the need for mutual understanding among the nations of the world been more keenly felt than in our days. 'Mutual understanding' may be realizable – or at least conceivable – at a number of different levels of life. The philosophical level is one of the most important of them. And it is characteristic of the philosophical level that, unlike other levels of human interest which are more or less closely connected with the current situations and actual conditions of the world, it provides or prepares a suitable locus in which the 'mutual understanding' here in question could be actualized in the form of a meta-historical dialogue. And meta-historical dialogues, conducted methodically, will, I believe, eventually be crystallised into a *philosophia perennis* in the fullest sense of the term. For the philosophical drive of the human Mind is, regardless of ages, places and nations, ultimately and fundamentally one.

I readily admit that the present work is far from even coming close to this ideal. But at least such was the motive from which I undertook this study. In the first Part, an attempt was made to lay bare the fundamental philosophical structure of the world-view of Ibn 'Arabī, one of the greatest mystic-philosophers. The analytic work was done quite independently of any comparative considerations. I simply tried to isolate and analyze as rigorously as possible the major concepts that constitute the basis of Ibn 'Arabī's philosophical world-view in such a way that it might form a completely independent study.

The second Part dealing with Lao-tzŭ and Chaung-tzŭ is of a slightly different nature. Of course it is in itself an equally independent study of Taoist philosophy, which could very well be read as such. But it is slightly different from the first Part in one point, namely, that in isolating key-concepts and presenting them in a systematic way, I already began preparations for the work of co-ordination and comparison. By this I am not simply referring to the fact that in the course of this work mention was made from time to time of this or that part of Ibn 'Arabī's thought. I am referring to something more fundamental and of a more methodological nature.

I have just spoken of the 'preparatory work for co-ordination and comparison'. Concretely, this refers to the fact that I consciously arranged and presented the whole matter in such a way that the very analysis of the key-concepts of Taoism might bring to light the common philosophical ground upon which the meta-historical dialogue could become possible. Let this not be taken to mean that I modified the given material with a view to facilitating comparison, let alone distorted the given facts, or forced something upon Lao-tzŭ and Chuang-tzŭ for such a purpose. The fact is rather that an objective analysis of Taoist key-terms naturally led me to the discovery of a central idea which might work as the most basic connecting link between the two systems of thought. The only arbitrary thing I did – if 'arbitrary' it was – consisted in my having given a philosophical 'name' to the central idea. The name is 'existence'. And the name once established, I could characterize the guiding spirit of the philosophical world-view of Lao-tzŭ and Chuang-tzŭ as 'existentialist' as opposed to the 'essentialist' tendency of the Confucian school.

I think I have made it abundantly clear in the course of the second Part that by understanding the philosophy of Lao-tzŭ and Chuang-tzŭ in terms of 'existence', I have not arbitrarily forced upon them anything alien to their thought. The only point is that the Taoist sages themselves do not propose any definite 'name' for this particular idea, whereas Ibn 'Arabī has the word *wujūd* which is, historically as well as structurally, the exact Arabic expression for the same idea. Certainly, Lao-tzŭ and Chuang-tzŭ do use the word *yu* meaning 'being' or 'existence' in contradistinction from *wu* 'non-being' or 'non-existence'. But, as we have seen, *yu* in their system plays a very special rôle which is different from that of 'existence' here in question. The *yu* refers to a particular aspect or stage of the creative activity of the Absolute, the stage at which the absolutely 'nameless' Absolute definitely turns into the 'named' and begins to be diversified into myriads of things.

Far better than *yu* in this respect is the word *tao*, the Way, which is primarily an exact Taoist counterpart of the Islamic *ḥaqq*, the Truth or Reality. But *tao*, to begin with, is a word having an extremely complex connotative structure. It covers an extensive semantic field, ranging from the Mystery of Mysteries to the 'being-so-of-itself' of all existents. Its meaning is, so to speak, tinged with variegated nuances and charged with many associations. Certainly it does cover to a great extent the meaning of 'existence'. But if used as an equivalent of 'existence' it would inevitably add many elements to the basic meaning of 'existence'. The use of the term 'taoism', for example, instead of 'existentialism' in those contexts where we want to bring out the radical contrast between the fundamental position of Taoism and 'essentialism' – which by the way, is an English equivalent chosen for the Confucian conception of 'names' (*ming*) – would make the whole situation more obscure and confusing. In order to refer to the particular aspect of the *tao* in which it is conceived as the *actus purus*, it is absolutely necessary that we should have a far less 'colorful' word than *tao*. And 'existence' is just the word for its purpose.

These considerations would seem to lead us to a very important methodological problem regarding the possibility of meta-historical dialogues. The problem concerns the need of a common linguistic system. This is only natural because the very concept of 'dialogue' presupposes the existence of a common language between two interlocutors.

When our intention happens to be to establish a philosophical dialogue between two thinkers belonging to one and the same cultural and historical background, Plato and Aristotle, for instance, or Thomas Aquinas and Duns Scotus, Kant and Hegel, etc., the problem of the necessity of a common language does not of course arise. The problem begins to make itself felt when we pick up within a cultural tradition two thinkers separated one from the other by a number of factors, like Aristotle and Kant, for example. Each of them philosophized in a language which is different from that of the other. There is, in this sense, no common language between them. But in a broad sense, we can still say that there is a common philosophical language between the two, because of the strong tie of a common philosophical tradition that bind them together inseparably. It is, in fact, hardly imaginable that any key-term of primary importance in Greek should not find its equivalent in German.

The linguistic distance naturally becomes more conspicuous when we want to establish a dialogue between two thinkers belonging to two different cultural traditions, Avicenna and Thomas Aquinas, for example. But even here we are still justified in recognizing the existence of a common philosophical language in view of the fact that in the last analysis they represent but two varieties of scholastic philosophy, both of which ultimately go back to one and the same Greek source. The concept of 'existence', for instance – in the linguistic form of *wujūd* in Arabic and in that of *existentia* in Latin – appears with the same basic connotation in both the Eastern and Western scholastic traditions. Thus the problem of a common language does not arise in a very acute form.

The problem does arise with real acuity where there is no historical connection in any sense whatsoever between the two thinkers. And this is precisely the case with Ibn 'Arabī and Lao-tzǔ or Chuang-tzǔ. In such a case, if there happens to be a central concept active in both systems, but having its linguistic counterpart only in one of the systems, we have to pinpoint the concept in the system in which it is in a state of non-linguistic fluidity or amorphousness, and then stabilize it with a definite 'name'. The 'name' may be borrowed from the other system, if the term actually in use in it happens to be a really appropriate one. Or some other word may be chosen for the purpose. In our particular case, Ibn 'Arabī offers the word *wujūd*, which, in its translated form, 'existence' serves exactly our purpose, because it does express the concept to be expressed in as simple a manner as possible, that is, without 'coloring' it with special connotations. The word remains connotatively colorless mainly due to the fact that Ibn 'Arabī uses by preference a variety of other terms, like *tajallī*, *fayḍ*, *raḥmah*, *nafas*, etc., in order to describe the same concept with special connotations.

That we are not doing any injustice to the reality of the world-view of the Taoist sages by applying the word 'existence' to the central idea of their thought will be clear if one takes the trouble of re-examining Chuang-tzǔ's description of the Cosmic Wind together with the analytic interpretation of it which has been given in Chapter VI.

However this may be, with the establishment of 'existence' as the central concept of both systems, we are now in possession of a common philosophical ground on which to establish a meta-historical dialogue between Ibn 'Arabī on the one hand and Lao-tzǔ and Chuang-tzǔ on the other. With this in mind, let us review the main points of the two philosophical systems which we have already analyzed in detail in the preceding pages.

I would like to point out at the outset that the philosophical structure of both systems as a whole is dominated by the concept of the Unity of Existence. This concept is expressed in Arabic by *waḥdah al-wujūd*, literally the 'one-ness of existence'. For expressing the same basic concept, Chuang-tzǔ, uses words like *t'ien ni* 'Heavenly Levelling' and *t'ien chün* 'Heavenly Equalization'.

The very words 'levelling' and equalization' clearly suggest that the 'unity' in question is not a simple 'unity', but a 'unity' formed by many different things. The idea, in brief, is this. There are actually different things, but they are 'equalized' with each other, or 'levelled down' to the state of 'unity', losing all their ontological distinctions in the midst of the original metaphysical Chaos. More briefly stated, the 'unity' in question is a 'unity' of 'multiplicity'. The same is true of the '*waḥdah*' of Ibn 'Arabī.

In both these systems, the whole world of Being is represented as a kind of ontological tension between Unity and Multiplicity. Unity in the world-view of Ibn 'Arabī is represented by *ḥaqq*, 'Truth' or 'Reality' while in that of Taoism it is represented by the *tao*, 'Way'. And Multiplicity is for Ibn 'Arabī the *mumkināt* 'possible beings', and for Lao-tzŭ and Chuang-tzŭ the *wan wu*, 'ten thousand things'.

$$
\begin{array}{c}
tajall\bar{\imath} \\
\d{h}aqq \xrightarrow{\hspace{2cm}} mumkin\bar{a}t \\
sh\hat{e}ng^1 \\
tao \xrightarrow{\hspace{2cm}} wan\ wu
\end{array}
$$

And the relation between the two terms of the ontological tension is that of Unity. It is a Unity because all the things that constitute Multiplicity are, after all, so many different phenomenal forms assumed by the Absolute (the Truth and the Way respectively). The phenomenal process by which the original One diversifies itself into Many is considered by Ibn 'Arabī as the *tajallī*, 'self-manifestation' of the One, and by Lao-tzŭ and Chuang-tzŭ as *shēng* 'producing'. And Chuang-tzŭ, in particular, further elaborates this idea into that of the universal Transmutation, *wu hua*, lit. 'things-transforming'.

Such is the broad conceptual framework which is shared by the world-views of Ibn 'Arabī and the Taoist sages. The framework is in its entirety constructed on the most basic concept of 'existence'. In what follows we shall examine in terms of this framework and in terms of this basic concept the major points of emphasis which characterize the two philosophical systems.

Note

1. 生, *shêng*: 'produces' or 'brings into existence'.

II The Inner Transformation of Man

The philosophical world-view of the 'Unity of Multiplicity', whether in the form of the 'Unity of Existence' or in the form of 'Heavenly Equalization', is an unusual – to say the least – world-view. It is an extraordinary world-view because it is a product of an extraordinary vision of Existence as experienced by an extraordinary man. The most characteristic point about this type of philosophy is that philosophizing act starts from an immediate intuitive grasp of Existence at its metaphysical depth, at the level of its being the 'absolute' Absolute.

Existence – which has always and everywhere been the central theme for innumerable philosophers – can be approached and grasped at a number of different levels. The Aristotelian attitude represents in this respect the exact opposite of the position taken by the philosophers of Taoism and Sufism. For an Aristotle, Existence means primarily the existence of individual 'things' on the concrete level of phenomenal 'reality'. And his philosophizing starts from the ordinary experience of Existence shared by all men on the level of common sense. For an Ibn 'Arabī or Chuang-tzŭ, however, these 'things' as experienced by an ordinary mind on the physical level are nothing but a dream, or of a dreamlike nature. From their point of view, the 'things' grasped on that level – although ultimately they are but so many phenomenal forms of the Absolute, and are, as such, no other than Existence – do not reveal the real metaphysical depth of Existence. And an ontology based on such an experience touches only shallowly the surface of the 'things'; it is not in a position to account for the structure of the 'things' in terms of the very ground of their Existence. A philosopher of this type is a man standing on the level of the 'worldly mode of being' (*nash'ah dunyawīyah*), in the terminology of Ibn Arabī. Such a man lacks the 'spiritual eyesight' (*'ayn al-baṣīrah*) – or 'illuminating light' (*ming*) as Chuang-tzŭ calls it – which is absolutely necessary for a deeper penetration into the mystery of Existence. In order to obtain such an eyesight, man must experience a spiritual rebirth and be transferred from the 'worldly mode of being' to the 'otherworldly mode of being' (*nash'ah ukhrawīyah*).

Since the former is the way the majority of men naturally are, men of the 'otherwordly mode of being' must necessarily appear as 'abnormal' men. The world-view of Taoism and Sufism represents in this sense a vision of Existence peculiar to 'abnormal' men.

It is significant that the process by which this spiritual transformation occurs in man is described by Ibn 'Arabī and Chuang-tzŭ, in such a way that it discloses in both cases exactly the same basic structure. Ibn 'Arabī describes it in terms of 'self-annihilation' (*fanā'*), and Chuang-tzŭ in terms of 'sitting in oblivion' (*tso wang*). The very words used: 'annihilation' and 'forgetting', clearly point to one and the same conception. And the same underlying conception is the 'purification of the Mind', or as Chuang-tzŭ calls it, the spiritual 'fasting'.

As to what actually occurs in the process of 'purification', details have been given in the first and second Parts of this book. And it would be pointless to repeat the description here. The 'purification' in both Taoism and Sufism consists, in brief, the man's purifying himself of all desires as well as of the activity of Reason. It consists, in other words, in a complete nullification of the 'ego' as the empirical subject of all activities of Reason and desires. The nullification of the empirical ego results in the actualization of a new Ego, the Cosmic Ego, which, in the case of Taoism, is considered to be completely at one with the Absolute in its creative activity, and, in the case of Ibn 'Arabī, is said to be unified with the Absolute to the utmost limit of possibility.

Perhaps the most interesting point concerning this topic from the viewpoint of comparison is the problem of the 'stages' of the 'purification.' A comparative consideration is here the more interesting because both Ibn 'Arabī and Chuang-tzŭ distinguish in the process three basic stages. The two systems differ from each other in details, but agree with each other in the main.

Let us begin by recapitulating the thesis put forward by Chuang-tzŭ. The first stage, according to him, consists in 'putting the world outside the Mind', that is to say, forgetting the existence of the objective world. The world as something 'objective' being by nature relatively far from the Mind from the very beginning, it is relatively easy for man to erase it from his consciousness through contemplation.

The second stage consists in 'putting the things outside the Mind', that is, erasing from consciousness the familiar things that surround man in his daily life. At this stage, the external world completely disappears from his consciousness.

The third stage is said to consist in man's forgetting Life, that is, his own life or his personal existence. The 'ego' is thereby completely destroyed, and the world, both external and internal, disappears from the consciousness. And as the 'ego' is nullified, the inner eye of the man is opened and the light of 'illumination' suddenly breaks through the darkness of spiritual night. This marks the birth of a new Ego in man. He now finds himself in the Eternal Now, beyond all limitation of time and space. He is also 'beyond Life and Death', that is, he is 'one' with all things, and all things are unified into 'one' in his 'no-consciousness'. In this spiritual state, an unusual Tranquillity or Calmness reigns over everything. And in this cosmic Tranquillity, away from the turmoil and agitation of the sensible world, man enjoys being unified and identified with the very process of the universal Transmutation of the ten thousand things.

Ibn 'Arabī who, as I have just said, also divides the process into three stages, provides a markedly Islamic version of spiritual 'purification'. The first stage is the 'annihilation of the attributes'. At this stage man has all his 'human' attributes nullified, and in their place he assumes as his own the Divine Attributes.

The second stage consists in that man has his own personal 'essence' nullified and realizes in himself his being one with the Divine Essence. This is the completion of the phenomenon of 'self-annihilation' in the proper sense of the word. This stage corresponds to the first half of the third stage of Chuang-tzŭ, in which the man is said to abandon his old 'ego'.

The third stage, according to Ibn 'Arabī, is the stage at which man regains his 'self' which he has 'annihilated' at the previous stage. Only he does not regain his 'self' under the same conditions as before, but rather in the very midst of the Divine Essence. This is evidently but another way of saying that having abandoned his old 'ego' he has obtained a new Ego. Having lost his life, he has found a new Life in being unified with the Divine Reality. In the technical terminology of the Sufism, this is known as 'self-subsistence' (*baqā'*).

This third stage corresponds to the latter half of the third stage according to Chuang-tzŭ's division of the process. Now man witnesses all phenomenal things mingling with each other and merging into the boundless ocean of Divine Life. His consciousness – or, to be more exact, supra-consciousness – is in the utmost propinquity to the Divine Consciousness in an ontological stage previous to its actual splitting into an infinity of determinations and particular forms. Naturally he falls into profound Silence, and an extraordinary Tranquillity reigns over his concentrated Mind.

There is another important point to be mentioned in connection with the problem of the 'purification' of the Mind. It concerns the centripetal direction of the 'purification'. The process of 'self-annihilation' or 'self-purification', if it is to succeed, must definitely

be turned and directed toward the innermost core of human existence. This direction clearly goes against the ordinary movements of
the Mind. The activity of the mind is usually characterized by its
centrifugal tendency. The Mind has a very marked natural tendency
to 'go out' toward the external world, attracted by, and in pursuit of,
external objects. For the sake of 'purification', this natural tendency
must be curbed and turned to the opposite direction. The 'purification' is realizable only by man's 'turning into himself'. This is
expressed by Ibn 'Arabī through the famous Tradition: 'He who
knows himself knows his Lord.' To this corresponds on the side of
Taoism the dictum of Lao-tzŭ: 'He who knows others (i.e., external
objects) is a "clever" man, but he who knows himself is an
"illumined" man.' In reference to the same situation, Lao-tzŭ also
speaks of 'closing up all the openings and doors'. 'Closing up all the
openings and doors' means obstructing all the possible outlets for
the centrifugal activity of the mind. What is aimed at thereby is
man's going down deep into his own mind until he comes into direct
touch with the existential core of himself.

The reason why this point must be mentioned as being of special
importance is that such a thesis would appear at first sight to
contradict the more fundamental thesis of the Unity of Existence.
For in the world-view of both Ibn 'Arabī and the Taoist sages, not
only ourselves but all things in the world, without a single exception,
are phenomenal forms of the Absolute. And as such, there can be
no basic difference between them. All existents equally manifest,
each in its particular way and particular form, the Absolute. Why,
then, are the external things to be considered detrimental to the
subjective actualization of the Unity of Existence?

The answer is not far to seek. Although external things are so
many forms of the Absolute, and although we know this intellectually, we cannot penetrate into them and experience from the
inside the palpitating Life of the Absolute as it is actively working
within them. All we are able to do is look at them from the outside.
Only in the case of our own selves, can each of us go into his 'inside'
and *in*-tuit the Absolute as something constantly at work within
himself. Only in this way can we subjectively participate in the
Mystery of Existence.

Besides, the centrifugal tendency of the mind is directly connected with the discriminating activity of Reason. And Reason
cannot subsist without taking an 'essentialist' position. For where
there are no conceptual boundaries neatly established Reason is
utterly powerless. In the view of Reason, 'reality' consists of various
'things' and 'qualities', each having what is called 'essence' by which
it is distinguished from the rest. These 'things' and 'qualities' are in
truth nothing but so many forms in which the Absolute manifests

itself. But in so far as they are self-subsistent entities, they conceal the Absolute behind their solid 'essential' veils. They intervene between our sight and the Absolute, and make our direct view of Reality impossible. The majority of men are those whose eyesight is obstructed in this way by the thick curtain of 'things'. They have their counterpart in Taoism in those people who, unable to 'chaotify' the 'things', cannot interpret reality except in terms of 'this'-or-'that', 'good'-or-'bad', 'right'-or-'wrong', etc.

When the 'purification' of the Mind is completed, and when man has turned into a metaphysical Void, forgetting both the inside and the outside of himself, he is allowed to experience what the Taoist sages call 'illumination' (*ming*) and what Ibn 'Arabī calls 'unveiling' (*kashf*) or 'immediate tasting' (*dhawq*). It is characteristic of both 'illumination' and 'unveiling' (or 'tasting') that this ultimate stage once fully actualized, the 'things' that have been eliminated in the process of 'purification' from the consciousness all come back once again, totally transformed, to his Mind which is now a well-polished spotless mirror – the Mysterious Mirror,[1] as Lao-tzŭ calls it. Thus it comes about that the highest stage of metaphysical intuition is not that of those who witness only the Absolute, wholly oblivious of its phenomenal aspect. The highest 'unveiling', according to Ibn 'Arabī, is of those who witness both the creatures and the Absolute as two aspects of one Reality, or rather, who witness the whole as one Reality diversifying itself constantly and incessantly according to various aspects and relations, being 'one' in Essence, and 'all' with regard to the Names.

Likewise, the Perfect Man of Taoism does perceive infinitely variegated things on the phenomenal level of Existence, and the spotless surface of his Mysterious Mirror reflects all of them as they appear and disappear. But this kaleidoscope of ever shifting forms does not perturb the cosmic Tranquillity of the Mind, because behind these variegated veils of the phenomenal world, he intuits the metaphysical 'One'. He himself is one with the constant flux of Transmutation, and being one therewith, he is one with the 'One'.

The philosophical world-view of an Ibn 'Arabī, a Lao-tzŭ and a Chuang-tzŭ is a product of such an 'abnormal' spiritual state. It *is* an ontology, because it is a philosophized vision of Existence. But it is an extraordinary ontology, because the underlying vision of Existence is far from being an ordinary one.

Note

1. 玄覧, *Hsüan lan*, X.

III The Multistratified Structure of Reality

In terms of historical origin there is obviously no connection at all between Sufism and Taoism. Historically speaking, the former goes back to a particular form of Semitic monotheism, while the latter – if the hypothesis which I have put forward at the outset of this study is correct – is a philosophical elaboration of the Far Eastern type of shamanism.

It is highly significant that, in spite of this wide historico-cultural distance that separates the two, they share, on the philosophical level, the same ground. They agree with each other, to begin with, in that both base their philosophical thinking on a very peculiar conception of Existence which is fundamentally identical, though differing from one another in details and on secondary matters.

They further agree with one another in that philosophizing in both cases has its ultimate origin not in *reasoning* about Existence but in *experiencing* Existence. Furthermore, 'experiencing' Existence in this particular case consists in experiencing it not on the ordinary level of sense perception, but on the level (or levels) of supra-sensible intuition.

Existence or Reality as 'experienced' on supra-sensible levels reveals itself as of a multistratified structure. The Reality which one observes in this kind of metaphysical intuition is not of a uni-stratum structure. And the vision of Reality thus obtained is totally different from the ordinary view of 'reality' which is shared by the common people.

It is extremely interesting that both Ibn 'Arabī and Chuang-tzǔ begin by giving a rude shock to common sense by flatly refusing to admit any reality to so-called 'reality', saying that the latter is nothing but a dream. Quoting the famous Tradition: 'All men are asleep; only when they die, do they wake up', Ibn 'Arabī says: 'The world is an illusion; it has no real existence. . . . Know that you yourself are an imagination. And everything that you perceive and say to yourself, "this is not me", is also an imagination.' In an exactly similar way Chuang-tzǔ remarks: 'Suppose you dream that you are a bird. (In that state) you soar up into the sky. Suppose you dream that you are a fish; you go down deep into the pool. (While you are experiencing all this in your dream, what you experience *is* your "reality".) Judging by this, nobody can be sure whether we – you and I, who are actually engaged in conversation in this way – are awake of just dreaming.' Thus we see so-called 'reality' being all of a sudden transformed and reduced to something dreamlike and unreal.

Far more remarkable, however, is the fact that for both Ibn 'Arabī and Chuang-tzǔ the dictum: 'All is a dream' has a very positive metaphysical meaning. It is not in any way an emotive statement to the effect, for instance, that the world we live in is like a dream, that everything in this world is tragically ephemeral and transient. It is, on the contrary, a definite ontological statement recognizing the existence of a higher ontological level where all things are deprived of their seemingly solid essential boundaries and disclose their natural amorphousness. And paradoxically enough, this 'dreamlike' level of Existence is, in the view of both Ibn 'Arabī and Chuang-tzǔ, far more 'real' than so-called 'reality'.

This dreamlike level of Existence is in the ontological system of Ibn 'Arabī what he calls the 'world of similitudes and Imagination', while in that of Chuang-tzǔ it is the Chaos.

Thus the basic proposition that all is a dream does not mean that so-called 'reality' is a vain and groundless thing. Instead of meaning simply that the physical world is a sheer illusion, the proposition indicates that the world which we experience on the sensible level is not a self-subsistent reality, but is a Symbol – an *āyah* (pl. *āyāt*), or 'indicator' as Ibn 'Arabī calls it, using the Quranic term – vaguely and indistinctively pointing to 'Something beyond'. The sensible things, thus interpreted, are phenomenal forms of the Absolute itself, and as such, they *are* 'real' in a particular way.

However, this again is a matter of immediate intuitive experience. The metaphysical fact that behind and beyond so-called 'reality', which is apparently a colorful fabric of fantasy and imagination, there lies hidden the 'real' Reality, does not become clear except to those who have learnt how to 'interpret' rightly – as Ibn 'Arabī says – the infinitely variegated forms and properties as so many manifestations of Reality. This is what is meant by Ibn 'Arabī when he says that one has to 'die and wake up'. 'The only "reality" (in the true sense of the term) is the Absolute revealing itself as it really is in the sensible forms which are nothing but the loci of its self-manifestation. This point becomes understandable only when one wakes up from the present life – which is a sleep of forgetfulness – after one dies to this world through self-annihilation in God.' Chuang-tzǔ, likewise, speaks of the need of experiencing a Great

Awakening. 'Only when one experiences a Great Awakening does one realize that "reality" is but a Big Dream. But the stupid imagine that they are actually awake. . . . How deep-rooted and irremediable their stupidity is!'

In the eye of those who have experienced this spiritual Awakening, all things, each in its own form and on its own level, manifest the presence of 'Something beyond'. And that 'Something beyond' is ultimately the *haqq* of Ibn 'Arabī and the *tao* of Lao-tzŭ and Chuang-tzŭ – the Absolute. Both Ibn 'Arabī and the Taoist sages distinguish in the process of the self-revealing evolvement of the Absolute several degrees or stages. Ontologically speaking this would mean that Existence is of a multistratified structure.

The strata, according to Ibn 'Arabī, are:

(1)   The stage of the Essence (the absolute Mystery, abysmal Darkness);
(2)   The stage of the Divine Attributes and Names (the stage of Divinity);
(3)   The stage of the Divine Actions (the stage of Lordship);
(4)   The stage of Images and Similitudes;
(5)   The sensible world.

And according to Lao-tzŭ:

(1)   Mystery of Mysteries;
(2)   Non-Being (Nothing, or Nameless);
(3)   One;
(4)   Being (Heaven and Earth);
(5)   The ten thousand things.

The two systems agree with each other in that (I) they regard the first stage as an absolute Mystery, that is, something absolutely unknown-unknowable, transcending all distinctions and all limitations, even the limitation of 'not being limited'; and that (2) they regard the four remaining stages as so many various forms assumed by this absolute Mystery in the process of its ontological evolvement, so that all are, in this sense, 'one'. This latter point, namely, the problem of Unity, will be further discussed in the following chapter.

IV Essence and Existence

As we have seen above, both Chuang-tzǔ's 'Heavenly Levelling' and Ibn 'Arabī's 'Unity of Existence' are based on the idea that all things are ultimately reducible to the original Unity of the Absolute in its absoluteness, that is, the 'Essence at the level of Unity (*ahadīyah*)'.

It is to be remarked that the *Essence* in the Unity of its unconditional simplicity is, in Ibn 'Arabī's view, nothing other than pure *Existence*, there being here not even the slightest discrepancy between 'essence' (i.e., 'quiddity') and 'existence'. In other words, the Absolute is *actus purus*, the act itself of 'existing'. The Absolute is not a 'thing' in the sense of a 'substance'.

As Qāshānī says: 'The Reality called the "Essence at the level of Unity" in its true nature is nothing other than Existence pure and simple in so far as it is Existence. It is conditioned neither by non-determination nor by determination, for in itself it is too sacred to be qualified by any property and any name. It has no quality, no delimitation; there is not even a shadow of Multiplicity in it. It is not a substance . . . , for a substance must have an 'essence' other than "existence", a "quiddity" by which it is a substance as differentiated from all others.'

The conception of the Absolute being conditioned neither by determination nor by non-determination is more tersely expressed by Lao-tzǔ through single words like 'Nothing' and 'Nameless', and by Chuang-tzǔ through the expression No-[No Non-Being]. The last expression, No-[No Non-Being], indicates analytically the stages in the logical process by which one arrives at the realization of the Absolute transcending all determinations. First, the idea that the Absolute is *Being*, i.e., 'existence' as ordinarily understood, is negated. The concept of *Non-Being* is thus posited. Then, this concept of Non-Being is eliminated, because, being a simple negation of Being, it is but a relative Non-Being. Thus the concept of *No-Non-Being* is obtained. This concept stands on the negation of both Being and Non-Being, and as such it still keeps in itself a trace or reflection of the opposition which exists between the contradictories. In order to eliminate even this faint trace of relativity, one has to negate the No-Non-Being itself. Thus finally the concept of No-[No Non-Being] is established, as 'Nothing' in its absolutely unconditional transcendence.

And Chuang-tzŭ clarifies through the admirable symbol of the Cosmic Wind that this transcendent Nothing is not a purely negative 'nothing' in the usual sense of the word; that, on the contrary, it is a supra-plenitude of Existence as the ultimate ontological ground of everything, as Something that lies at the very source of all existents and makes them exist. 'It would seem', Chuang-tzŭ says, 'that there is some real Ruler. It is impossible for us to see Him in a concrete form. He is *acting* – there can be no doubt about it; but we cannot see His form. He does show His *activity*, but He has no sensible form.' This simply means that the No-[No Non-Being] – or theologically, the real Ruler of the world – is *actus*, creative energy, not a substance. The Cosmic Wind in itself is invisible and impalpable – because it is not a substance – but we know its presence through its ontological activity, through the ten thousand 'holes' and 'hollows' producing each its peculiar sound as the Wind blows upon them.

The basic idea underlying the use of the symbol of the Wind is comparable with Ibn 'Arabī's favorite image of the 'flowing' of Existence (*sarayān al-wujūd*). 'The secret of Life (i.e., Existence) lies in the act of flowing peculiar to water.' The 'water' of Existence is eternally flowing through all things. It 'spreads'' throughout the universe, permeating and pervading everything. It is significant that both Chuang-tzŭ and Ibn 'Abrabī represent Existence as something moving: 'blowing', 'flowing', 'spreading', 'permeating', etc. This is a definite proof that Existence as they have come to know it through 'immediate tasting' is in reality *actus,* nothing else.

Existence which is *actus*, thus spreading itself out far and wide, goes on producing the ten thousand things. The latter, as I have repeatedly pointed out, are various forms in which Existence (or the Absolute) manifests itself. And in this sense, all are Existence, nothing but Existence. And there is nothing but Existence. Viewed from this angle, the whole world of Being is one.

On the other hand, however, it is also an undeniable fact that we actually see with our own eyes an infinity of infinitely variegated 'things' which are different from one another. 'It is evident', Ibn 'Arabī says, 'that *this* is different from *that* . . . And in the Divine world, however wide it is, nothing repeats itself. This is a truly fundamental fact.' From this point of view, there is not a single thing that is the same as any other thing. Even 'one and the same thing' is in reality not exactly the same in two successive moments.

These individually different things, on a more universal level of Existence, still retain their mutual differences and distinctions, not 'individually' this time, but in terms of 'essences'. And these ontological differences and distinctions which the 'things' manifest on this level are far more solid and unalterable because they are based on, and fixed by, their 'essences'. The latter provide the 'things' with an 'essential' fixity which ensures them from disintegration. A 'horse' is a 'horse' by its 'essence'; it can never be a 'dog'. A 'dog' is 'essentially' a 'dog', nothing else. It goes without saying that this is the very basis on which stands the 'essentialist' type of ontology.

How could we account for the apparent contradiction between the above-mentioned absolute Unity of Existence, Unity of all things, and the undeniable Multiplicity of the ten thousand things which are not reducible to each other, let alone to a unique and single thing? Surely, if one puts these two points of view side by side with each other, one's mind cannot help being thrown into bewildering confusion. To see the One in the Many and the Many in the One, or rather to see the Many as One and the One as Many – this naturally causes what Ibn 'Arabī calls (metaphysical) 'perplexity' (*ḥayrah*).

Faced with this problem, Chuang-tzŭ takes a thoroughgoing anti-essentialist position. The view of things, each being distinguished from the rest by a solid 'boundary' of 'essence', he maintains, does not give a true picture of these things themselves. The 'essential' distinctions which common sense and Reason recognize between things are, according to him, devoid of reality. The 'things' ordinarily look as if they were distinct from each other in terms of 'essences', simply because ordinary men are not 'awake'. If they were, they would 'chaotify' the things and see them in their original 'undifferentiation'.

The things being 'chaotified', however, is not the same as their being sheer nothing. The very concept of 'chaotification' would be meaningless if there were no plurality at all in the world of Being. It is, as Ibn 'Arabī maintains, a truly fundamental fact that many 'different' things do exist, no matter how 'unreal' they may be in themselves and from the viewpoint of the higher metaphysical level of Existence. The differences and distinctions that are observable in the world may reveal themselves as 'unreal' when observed with the 'spiritual eyesight' of an ecstatic philosopher, but in so far as things are *factually* different and distinct from each other, there must be some ontological ground for that, too. And the ontological ground cannot be anything other than 'essences'.

The 'essences' are symbolically designated by Chuang-tzŭ through the image of the 'hollows' in the trees, which emit all kinds of sounds as the Wind blows upon them. Chuang-tzǔ does not assert that the 'hollows' do not exist in any sense whatsoever. They are surely there. The only point is that they do not produce any sound by themselves. It is the Wind, not the 'hollows', that really produces the sounds. '(One and the same Wind) blows on the ten thousand things in different ways, and makes each "hollow" produce its own peculiar sound, so that each imagines that its own self produces that particular sound. But who, in reality, is the one who makes (the "hollows") produce various sounds?'

All this would seem to be tantamount to saying – although Chuang-tzǔ himself does not talk in terms of these concepts – that the 'essences' are not sheer nothing, that they are potentially exist-ent. The 'essences' do exist, but only *in potentia*, not *in actu*; they are not actual or real in the fullest sense of the word. What is really 'real' is Existence, nothing else. And the 'essences' look as if they were 'real' only by dint of the actualizing activity of Existence.

The position of the 'hollows' in the ontology of Chuang-tzǔ corresponds to that of the 'permanent archetypes' in the ontology of Ibn 'Arabī. The main difference between the two lies in the fact that in the former the relation between Essence and Existence is merely symbolically suggested, whereas Ibn 'Arabī consciously takes up the problem as an ontological theme and elaborates it far more theoretically.

Details have been given in Chapter XII of the first Part regarding the conceptual structure of the 'permanent archetypes'. Suffice it here to note that the 'permanent archetypes' are the 'essences' of the things, and that they are described as 'neither existent nor non-existent' – which would exactly apply to the 'hollows' of Chuang-tzǔ. It is remarkable, however, that the 'permanent archetypes' are also described by Ibn 'Arabī as 'realities (*ḥaqā'iq*) eternally subsistent in the world of the Unseen'. That is to say, the 'permanent archetypes', although they are 'non-existent' in terms of 'external existence', do exist *in actu* within the Divine Conscious-ness. The ontology of Ibn 'Arabī is, in this respect, Platonic; it is more 'essentialist' than that of Chuang-tzǔ who does not concede anything more than sheer potentiality to the 'essences'.

V The Self-Evolvement of Existence

The absolute and ultimate ground of Existence is in both Sufism and Taoism the Mystery of Mysteries. The latter is, as Ibn 'Arabī says, the *ankar al-nakirāt* 'the most indeterminate of all indeterminates'; that is to say, it is Something that transcends all qualifications and relations that are humanly conceivable. And since it is transcendent to such a degree, it remains for ever unknown and unknowable. Existence *per se* is thus absolutely inconceivable and inapproachable. Ibn 'Arabī refers to this aspect of Existence by the word *'ghayb*, 'concealment' or 'invisibility'. In the Taoist system, it is *hsüan* or Mystery that is the most proper word for referring to this absolutely transcendent stage of Existence.

The Taoist sages have also a set of negative words like *wu*, Non-Being, *wu-wu*, No-thing or 'Nothing', *wu-ming*, Nameless, etc. These terms are properly to be considered as functioning still within the domain of the original transcendence. Conceptually, however, there is already observable a distinction between these negative terms and the 'Mystery', because their very 'negative-ness' indicates their opposition to something 'positive', i.e., the following stage of *yu* or Being, at which the 'boundaries' of the things-to-be are adumbrated. This is the reason why Chuang-tzŭ proposes to use the complex expression, No-[No Non-Being] or No-No-Nothing in order to refer to the ultimate stage of Existence (i.e., the Mystery of Mysteries) without leaving the level of negativity. However, this distinction between the Mystery and these negative terms is exclusively conceptual. Otherwise, 'Non-Being', 'Nothing', and 'Nameless' denote exactly the same thing as the 'Mystery'. They all denote the Absolute in its absoluteness, or Existence at its ultimate stage, *qua* Something unknown-unknowable, transcending all qualifications, determinations, and relations.

It is important to note that Ibn 'Arabī calls this ontological level the 'level of Unity (*aḥadīyah*)'. The Absolute at this stage is 'One' in the sense that it refuses to accept any qualification whatsoever. Thus, being one here means nothing other than absolute transcendence.

The Taoist sages, too, speak of the Way as 'One'. As I have tried to show earlier, the 'One' in the Taoist system is conceptually to be placed between the stage of Non-Being and that of Being. It is not exactly the same as the Way *qua* Mystery, because it is considered as something which the ten thousand things 'acquire', i.e., partake of. The One, in other words, is the principle of immanence. The Way is 'immanent' in everything existent as its existential core, or as its Virtue, as Lao-tzŭ calls it. But whether regarded as 'immanent' or 'transcendent', the Way is the Way. What is immanent in everything is exactly the same thing as that which transcends everything. And this situation corresponds to the conceptual distinction between *tanzīh* and *tashbīh* and the factual identity of the two in the system of Ibn 'Arabī.

Thus the Taoist concept of One, in so far as it refers to the Absolute itself, is an exact counterpart of Ibn 'Arabī's *aḥad*, the 'absolute One', but in so far as it is 'One' comprising within itself the possibility of Multiplicity, it is a counterpart of *wāḥid*, i.e., the 'One at the level of the Names and Attributes', or the Unity of the Many. In short, the Taoist One comprises both the *aḥad* and the *wāḥid* of Sufism.

These considerations make us realize that the first and ultimate stage of Existence itself can naturally be considered from two different angles: (1) as the Absolute *per se*, and (2) as the Absolute as the very origin and starting-point of the process of self-evolvement. In the first of these two aspects, the Absolute is Mystery and Darkness. In the second aspect, on the contrary, a faint foreboding of light is already perceivable in the very midst of utter darkness. As Ibn 'Arabī says: 'Everything is contained in the bosom of the Breath, just as the bright light of day in the very darkness of dawn'.

It is quite significant in this respect that the word used by the Taoist sages to denote the Mystery, *hsüan*, originally means 'black' with a mixture of redness. Lao-tzŭ, as we have noticed, likes us to use in this sense also the word *p'u* meaning originally 'uncarved wood'. Existence, at this stage of absolute simplicity, is like 'uncarved wood'. In so far as it still remains 'uncarved', there is nothing observable but 'wood'. But in so far as it contains the possibility of producing all kinds of vessels and utensils, it is more than sheer 'wood'. Actually it is still 'Nothing', but potentially it is all things. There is at least a vague and indistinct feeling that something is about to happen. And that is the 'positive' aspect of the Mystery, the face of the Absolute turned toward the world of creation. Ibn 'Arabī conveys the same idea by the expression: 'hidden Treasure', which he has taken from a Tradition. And it is of the very nature of the 'hidden Treasure' that it 'loves to be known'.

It is, however, at the stage of the Divine Names and Attributes – in terms of Ibn 'Arabī's world-view – that this 'love of being known', i.e., the inner ontological drive of Existence, becomes actualized. At the stage of the absolute Unity, the Absolute *qua* Absolute is characterized by a perfect 'independence', and does not require by itself and for itself any creative activity. If 'creation' is at all conceivable at this stage, it is simply in the form of a faint foreboding. In the System of Taoism the concept of Non-Being or Nothing refers precisely to this delicate situation. 'Deep and Bottomless', Lao-tzŭ says, 'it is like the origin and principle of the ten thousand things. . . . There is *nothing*, and yet there seems to be something. I know not whose son it is. It would seem to be antecedent even to the Heavenly Emperor.' 'The Way in its reality is utterly vague, utterly indistinct. Utterly indistinct, utterly vague, and yet there is in the midst of it an Image. Utterly vague, utterly indistinct, and yet there is in the midst of it Something.'

The 'hidden Treasure loves to be known'. The Treasure lies 'hidden', and yet it is, so to speak, pressed from inside by the 'desire to be known'. Speaking less symbolically, the infinite things that are contained in the Absolute in the state of pure *potentia* forcefully seek for an outlet. This naturally causes an ontological tension within the Absolute. And the internal ontological compression, growing ever stronger finally relieves itself by bursting forth. It is highly interesting to notice that both Ibn 'Arabī and Chuang-tzŭ resort to the same kind of imagery in trying to describe this situation. Chuang-tzŭ talks about 'eructation'. He says: 'The Great Earth eructates; and the eructation is called Wind. As long as the eructation does not actually occur, nothing is observable. But once it does occur, all the hollows of the trees raise ringing shouts.' The issuing forth of the ten thousand things from the Absolute is here compared to the Great Earth belching forth the Wind.

No less bold and picturesque is the mythopoeic image of 'breathing out' by which Ibn 'Arabī tries to depict the matter. The ontological state of extreme tension which precedes the 'bursting out' and which has been caused by an excessive amount of things accumulated inside is compared to the state in which a man finds himself when he holds his breath compressed within himself. The tension reaches the last limit, and the air compressed in the breast explodes and gushes forth with a violent outburst. In a similar way, the creative drive of Existence gushes forth out of the depth of Absolute. This is the phenomenon which Ibn 'Arabī calls the 'breath of the Merciful'. In the theological language peculiar to Ibn 'Arabī, the same phenomenon can also be described as the Divine

Names, at the extreme limit of inner compression, suddenly bursting out from the bosom of the Absolute. 'The Names, previous to
their existence in the outer world (in the form of phenomenal
things) exist hidden in the Essence of the Absolute (i.e., the Mystery
of Mysteries), all of them seeking an outlet toward the world of
external existence. The situation is comparable to the case in which
a man holds his breath within himself. The breath, held within,
seeks an outlet toward the outside, and this causes in the man a
painful sensation of extreme compression. Only when he breathes
out does this compression cease to make itself felt. Just as the man is
tormented by the compression if he does not breathe out, so the
Absolute would feel the pain of (ontological) compression if it did
not bring into existence the world in response to the demand of the
Names.' This may also be compared with the image of a great
Cosmic Bellows by which Lao-tzŭ symbolically describes the inexhaustible creative activity of the Way. 'The space between Heaven
and Earth is comparable to a bellows. It is empty (i.e., the Absolute
qua the Mystery of Mysteries is "Nothing"), but its activity is
inexhaustible. The more it works the more it produces.'

Thus Existence, in compliance with its own necessary and natural
internal demand, goes on inexhaustibly determining itself into an
infinity of concrete things. And the 'breath of the Merciful' or the
ontological Mercy pervades all of them, constituting the very existential core of each one of them. And the existential core thus
acquired by each phenomenal thing is what The Taoist sages call *tê*
or Virtue.

It is worth remarking that the *rahmah* or Mercy as understood by
Ibn 'Arabī is primarily an ontological fact. It refers to the *actus* of
Existence, namely, the act of making things exist. It does not
primarily denote the emotive attitude of compassion and benevolence. But Mercy as *bestowal* of existence of course carries an
emotive and subjective overtone. And this squares well with the
ethical understanding of God in Islam. The creative activity of
Existence is represented in Taoism in a form which is diametrically
opposed to such a conception. For in Taoism the Way is said to be
'non-humane' (*pu jēn*). 'Heaven and Earth', Lao-tzŭ says, 'lack
"benevolence" (i.e., lack mercy).' They treat the ten thousand
things as if the latter were straw dogs.' The difference between the
two systems, however, is only superficial. For whether described in
terms of Mercy (in Sufism) or non-Mercy (in Taoism), the basic fact
described remains exactly the same. This because the ontological
Mercy, in the conception of Ibn 'Arabī, is absolutely gratuitous.
What is meant by both Mercy and non-Mercy is nothing other than
the all-pervading creative activity of Existence. Ibn 'Arabī himself

warns us against understanding the word *raḥmah* with its usual associations. 'There does not come into its activity any consideration of attaining an aim, or of a thing's being or not being suitable for a purpose. Whether suitable or unsuitable the Divine Mercy covers everything and anything with existence.'

This explanation of Mercy by Ibn 'Arabī is so congenial to the spirit of Taoism that it will pass *verbatim* for an explanation by a Lao-tzŭ of the Taoist concept of non-Mercy which is as equally impartial and indiscriminating as Ibn 'Arabī's Mercy in bestowing the gift of 'existence' upon everything and everybody. In the view of Lao-tzŭ, the creative activity of the Absolute is extended over the ten thousand things without a single exception precisely because it stands on the principle of non-Mercy. If even a trifling amount of human emotion were involved therein, the Absolute would not be acting with such an absolute impartiality. In the view of Ibn 'Arabī, on the contrary, the Absolute bestows 'existence' to all things without excluding anything precisely because it is the *actus* of Mercy. The Divine Mercy being by nature limitlessly wide, it covers the whole world. As is obvious, the underlying idea is in both cases one and the same.

The structure itself of this concept of Mercy or non-Mercy is directly connected with another important idea: that of the Absolute being 'beyond good and evil'. The creative activity of the Absolute, which consists in the bestowal of 'existence' *qua* 'existence' upon everything involves no moral judgment. From the point of view of the Absolute, it does not matter at all whether a given object be good or bad. Rather, there is absolutely no such distinction among the objects. The latter assume these and other evaluational properties only after having been given 'existence' by the indiscriminating act of the Absolute; and that from the particular points of view of the creatures. Otherwise, all existents are on the 'straight way' – as Ibn 'Arabī says – or all existents are 'so-of-themselves' – as the Taoist sages say. There is no distinction at this stage between good and evil.

This idea is formulated by Lao-tzŭ and Chuang-tzŭ in terms of a 'relativist' view of all values. Ordinary men distinguish between 'good' and 'bad', 'beautiful' and 'ugly', 'noble' and 'ignoble', etc., and construct their life social as well as personal, on these distinctions as if they were objective categories that have been fixed in an unalterable way by the very nature of the things. In truth, however, these and other seemingly solid objective categories, far from being 'objective', are but products of 'subjective' and 'relative' points of view. A 'beautiful' lady from the human point of view, Chuang-tzŭ argues, is 'ugly' and 'terrifying' enough, from the point of view of other animals, to make them run away as fast as their legs or wings can carry them. The distinctions are a sheer matter of relative viewpoints, a matter of likes and dislikes. As Ibn 'Arabī says: 'The bad is nothing other than what one dislikes, while the good is nothing other than what one likes.'

Thus in both Sufism and Taoism the basic proposition holds true that everything is primarily, that is, *qua* 'existence', neither good nor evil. However there is a certain respect – again both in Sufism and Taoism – in which everything is to be considered fundamentally 'good'. This because everything *qua* 'existence' is a particular self-manifestation of the Absolute itself. And looked at from such a viewpoint, all things in the world are 'one'. As Chuang-tzŭ says: '(However different they may look from each other) they are, in reality no other than so many things that are "affirmable" piled up one upon the other.' They are at one with each other in being fundamentally 'affirmable', i.e., good. The Perfect Man 'is "one"', whether he (seemingly) likes something or dislikes something'. And Lao-tzŭ: 'Those who are good I treat as good. But those who are not good also I treat as good. For the original nature of man is goodness. Those who are faithful I treat as faithful. But even those who are not faithful I treat as faithful. For the original nature of man is faithfulness.' Such an attitude would immediately be approved by Ibn 'Arabī, who says: 'What is bad is bad simply because of (the subjective impression caused by) the taste; but the same thing will be found to be essentially good, if considered apart from the (subjective attitude on the part of man) of liking or disliking.'

These considerations make it clear that for both Ibn 'Arabī and the Taoist sages there is the closest and most intimate relationship between the Absolute and the things of the phenomenal world. Although the latter are apparently far removed from the Absolute, they are after all so many different forms which the Absolute assumes in making itself manifest at various stages and in various places. This intimate ontological relationship between the two terms of the creative process is in Taoism symbolically expressed by the image of the Mother-Child relationship. The Way at the stage of the 'Being' or 'Named' is considered by Lao-tzŭ the 'Mother of the ten thousand things'. The symbolic implication of this statement is that all things in the phenomenal world are the very flesh and blood of the Absolute. And the Taoist ideal consists in man's 'knowing the Children by knowing the Mother, and in his knowing the Children and yet holding fast to the Mother'.

On the side of Ibn 'Arabī, the same ontological relationship between the Absolute and phenomenal things is compared to the inseparable relationship between 'shadow' and its source, i.e., the man or object that projects it upon the earth. 'Do you not see', Ibn

'Arabī asks, 'how in your ordinary sensible experience shadow is so closely tied up with the person who projects it that it is absolutely impossible for it to liberate itself from this tie? This is impossible because it is impossible for anything to be separated from itself.' The world is the 'shadow' of the Absolute, and, as such, it is connected with the latter with the closest relationship which is never to be cut off. Every single part of the world is a particular aspect of the Absolute, and is the Absolute in a delimited form.

Ibn 'Arabī describes the same relationship by referring to the Divine Name: 'Subtle' (*laṭīf*). The 'subtleness' in this context means the quality of an immaterial thing which, because of its immateriality, permeates and pervades the substances of all other things, diffusing itself in the latter and freely mixing with them. 'It is the effect of God's "subtleness" that He exists in every particular thing, designated by a particular name, as the very essence of that particular thing. He is immanent in every particular thing in such a way that He is, in each case, referred to by the conventional and customary meaning of the particular name of that thing. Thus we say: "This is Heaven", "This is the earth", "This is a tree", etc. But the essence itself that exists in every one of these things is just one.'

We shall do well to recall that in a passage of his commentary upon the *Fuṣūṣ* Qāshānī also uses the Mother image. 'The ultimate ground of everything is called the Mother (*umm*) because the mother is the (stem) from which all branches go out.'

It is worth noticing, further, that both Ibn 'Arabī and the Taoist sages picture the process of creation as a perpetual and constant flow. Their world-view in this respect is of a markedly dynamic nature. Nothing remains static. The world in its entirety is in fervent movement. 'As water running in a river, which forever goes on being renewed continuously' (Ibn 'Arabī), the world transforms itself kaleidoscopically from moment to moment. The Cosmic Bellows of Lao-tzŭ is an appropriate symbol for this incessant process of creation. 'The space between Heaven and Earth is comparable to a bellows. It is empty, but its activity is inexhaustible. The more it works, the more it produces.'

The thesis of the universal Transmutation of things which Chuang-tzŭ puts forward also refers to this aspect of Reality. All things in the phenomenal world are constantly changing from one form to another. Everything is ontologically involved in the cosmic process of Transmutation. 'Dying and being alive, being subsistent and perishing, getting into a predicament and being in the ascendant, being poor and being rich, being clever and being incompetent, being disgraced and being honored . . . all these are but the constant changes of things, and the results of the incessant working of Fate. All these thing go on replacing one another before our own eyes, but no one by his Intellect can trace them back to their real origin.' These changes 'remind us of all kinds of sounds emerging from the empty holes (of a flute), or mushrooms coming out of warm dampness. Day and night, these changes never cease to replace one another before our eyes.'

Ibn 'Arabī pursues this perpetual flux of things down to a single moment. The result is his theory of 'new creation', that is, the thesis that the world goes on being created anew at every single moment. At every moment, countless things and properties are produced, and at the very next moment they are annihilated to be replaced by another infinity of things and properties. And this ontological process goes on repeating itself indefinitely and endlessly.

It is remarkable that neither in Sufism nor in Taoism is the ontological Descent – from the Mystery of Mysteries down to the stage of phenomenal things – made to represent the final completion of the activity of Existence. The Descent is followed by its reversal, that is, Ascent. The ten thousand things flourish exuberantly at the last stage of the descending course, and then take an ascending course toward their ultimate source until they disappear in the original Darkness and find their resting place in the cosmic pre-phenomenal Stillness. Thus the whole process of creation forms a huge ontological circle in which there is in reality neither an initial point nor a final point. The movement from one stage to another, considered in itself, is surely a temporal phenomenon. But the whole circle, having neither an initial point nor a final point, is a trans-temporal or a-temporal phenomenon. It is, in other words, a metaphysical process. Everything is an occurrence in an Eternal Now.